Using a World Wide Web Browser (NCSA Mosaic)

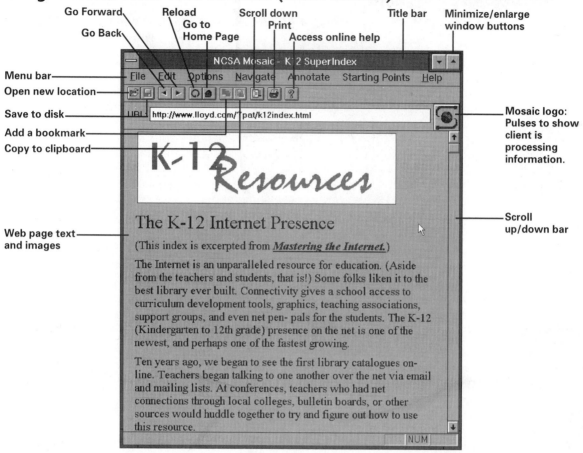

Go Forward

Go Back

Reload

Go to Home Page

Scroll down

Print

Access online help

Title bar

Minimize/enlarge window buttons

Menu bar

Open new location

Save to disk

Add a bookmark

Copy to clipboard

Web page text and images

Mosaic logo: Pulses to show client is processing information.

Scroll up/down bar

NCSA Mosaic - K 2 SuperIndex

File   Edit   Options   Navigate   Annotate   Starting Points   Help

URL: http://www.lloyd.com/~pat/k12index.html

K-12 Resources

The K-12 Internet Presence

(This index is excerpted from *Mastering the Internet*.)

The Internet is an unparalleled resource for education. (Aside from the teachers and students, that is!) Some folks liken it to the best library ever built. Connectivity gives a school access to curriculum development tools, graphics, teaching associations, support groups, and even net pen- pals for the students. The K-12 (Kindergarten to 12th grade) presence on the net is one of the newest, and perhaps one of the fastest growing.

Ten years ago, we began to see the first library catalogues on-line. Teachers began talking to one another over the net via email and mailing lists. At conferences, teachers who had net connections through local colleges, bulletin boards, or other sources would huddle together to try and figure out how to use this resource.

NUM

Important Starting Points for Successful Internet Exploration

John December's list of Internet Resources:

http://www.rpi.edu/Internet/Guides/decemj/text.html

University of Illinois at Urbana-Champaign Index to Web Pages:

http://www.cen.uiuc.edu/~jj9544/index.html

The InterNIC (Network Information Center):

http://www.internic.net/infoguide.html

The Virtual Reference Desk from UC Irvine:

gopher://peg.cwis.uci.edu:7000/11/gopher.welcome/peg/VIRTUAL%20REFERENCE%20DESK

Scott Yanoff's list of Internet Resources:

http://slacvx.slac.stanford.edu:80/misc/internet-services.html

NCSA Mosaic World Wide Web Starting Points Document:

http://www.ncsa.uiuc.edu/SDG/Software/Mosaic/StartingPoints/NetworkStartingPoints.html

The CERN World Wide Web Overview:

http://info.cern.ch/hypertext/WWW/Provider/Style/Overview.html

FOR EVERY COMPUTER QUESTION,
THERE IS A SYBEX BOOK THAT HAS THE ANSWER

Each computer user learns in a different way. Some need thorough, methodical explanations, while others are too busy for details. At Sybex we bring nearly 20 years of experience to developing the book that's right for you. Whatever your needs, we can help you get the most from your software and hardware, at a pace that's comfortable for you.

We start beginners out right. You will learn by seeing and doing with our **Quick & Easy** series: friendly, colorful guidebooks with screen-by-screen illustrations. For hardware novices, the **Your First** series offers valuable purchasing advice and installation support.

Often recognized for excellence in national book reviews, our **Mastering** titles are designed for the intermediate to advanced user, without leaving the beginner behind. A **Mastering** book provides the most detailed reference available. Add our pocket-sized **Instant Reference** titles for a complete guidance system. Programmers will find that the new **Developer's Handbook** series provides a more advanced perspective on developing innovative and original code.

With the breathtaking advances common in computing today comes an ever increasing demand to remain technologically up-to-date. In many of our books, we provide the added value of software, on disks or CDs. Sybex remains your source for information on software development, operating systems, networking, and every kind of desktop application. We even have books for kids. Sybex can help smooth your travels on the **Internet** and provide **Strategies and Secrets** to your favorite computer games.

As you read this book, take note of its quality. Sybex publishes books written by experts—authors chosen for their extensive topical knowledge. In fact, many are professionals working in the computer software field. In addition, each manuscript is thoroughly reviewed by our technical, editorial, and production personnel for accuracy and ease-of-use before you ever see it—our guarantee that you'll buy a quality Sybex book every time.

To manage your hardware headaches and optimize your software potential, ask for a Sybex book.

FOR MORE INFORMATION, PLEASE CONTACT:

Sybex Inc.
2021 Challenger Drive
Alameda, CA 94501
Tel: (510) 523-8233 • (800) 227-2346
Fax: (510) 523-2373

Mastering the
Internet

Mastering the
Internet

Glee Harrah Cady

Pat McGregor

San Francisco ▲ Paris ▼ Düsseldorf ▲ Soest

SYBEX®

Acquisitions Editor: Kristine Plachy
Developmental Editors: Steve Lipson, Brenda Kienan
Editor: James A. Compton
Technical Editor: Kevin Savetz
Book Designer: Suzanne Albertson
Technical Art: Cuong Le, John Corrigan
Screen Graphics: Aldo Bermudez
Typesetter: Dina F. Quan
Production Coordinator: Sarah Lemas
Indexer: Nancy Guenther
Cover Designer: Design Site

Screen reproductions produced with Collage Plus

Collage Plus is a trademark of Inner Media Inc.

"Hobbes' Internet Timeline" copyright © 1993–94 by Robert H. Zakon. Reproduced by permission.
"Internet Standards for Business Users" and "Dern's Selected Internet Service Providers" copyright © 1994 by Daniel P. Dern. Reproduced by permission.
Brevard County (Florida) School District "Acceptable Use Policy" reproduced by permission.
"Bill of Rights and Responsibilities for the Electronic Community of Learners" reproduced by permission of EDUCOM.
"Policy: Proper Use of Information Resources, Information Technology, and Networks at the University of Michigan" reproduced by permission of the University of Michigan.
"Netcom On-Line Communication Services, Inc. Terms and Conditions for Most Dial-Up Services" reproduced by permission of Netcom On-Line Communication Services, Inc.
"The Net: User Guidelines and Netiquette" reproduced by permission of Arlene H. Rinaldi.
"General Hints for the New Online User" reproduced by permission of Hilary Gardner.
"K–12 Internetworking Guidelines" reproduced by permission of the Internet Engineering Task Force.

NetCruiser software ©1994-1995 Netcom.

Chameleon Sampler software ©1994-1995 NetManage.

► *Warranty*

On the enclosed Disk 1 is a licensed copy of NetCruiser, from Netcom On-Line Communication Services, Inc. Support for this software is available from Netcom at (408) 983-5970.

On the enclosed Disk 2 is a licensed copy of Chameleon Sampler, from NetManage, Inc. Support for this software is available from Net-Manage at (408) 973-7171.

SYBEX warrants the enclosed disks to be free of *physical* defects for a period of ninety (90) days after purchase. If you discover a defect in the disks during this warranty period, you can obtain a replacement disk(s) at no charge by sending the defective disk(s), postage prepaid, with proof of purchase to:

> SYBEX Inc.
> Customer Service Department
> 2021 Challenger Drive
> Alameda, CA 94501
> (800)227-2346
> Fax: (510) 523-2373

After the 90-day period, you can obtain a replacement disk(s) by sending us the defective disk(s), proof of purchase, and a check or money order for $10, payable to SYBEX.

► *Disclaimer*

SYBEX makes no warranty or representation, either express or implied, with respect to this software, its quality, performance, merchantability, or fitness for a particular purpose. In no event will SYBEX, their distributors, or dealers be liable for direct, indirect, special, incidental, or consequential damages arising out of the use of or inability to use the software even if advised of the possibility of such damage.

The exclusion of implied warranties is not permitted by some states. Therefore, the above exclusion may not apply to you. This warranty provides you with specific legal rights; there may be other rights that you may have that vary from state to state.

▶ *Copy Protection*

None of the programs on the disk is copy-protected. However, in all cases, reselling or making copies of these programs without authorization is expressly forbidden.

▶▶ Acknowledgments

Jennie Brown, a novice Internet user, read all the chapters in the hope that if she was able to understand and learn something from them, others could, too. (Besides, if your mother writes a book, you'd best read it, eh?)

Brian and *Kevin Cady* put up with a mother who spent every waking hour on the keyboard for what seemed like forever. When your mother is writing a book you have to eat strange dinners at strange times even when you come home from college just for the food.

Jim Compton, our editor at Sybex, helped us make things clearer for you to understand, and asked critical questions at the right points. *Vivian Perry* reminded us that those of you reading this book probably don't know what we know, and need more information to understand it.

Steve Lipson, our first developmental editor at Sybex, helped us figure out what was going on in time to do it. *Brenda Kienan* then stepped in to fill Steve's shoes at the end of the project.

Sue Davidsen of the University of Michigan's Harlan Hatcher Library and technical manager for the University's M-Link program was an invaluable research assistant for the book.

Daniel Dern and *David Peal* provided inspiration, insight, and impetus. Without them this book would likely never have happened.

Dusty Deryck and *Carl Duncan* of Duncan Computing in Placerville, CA, came up with hardware and software on demand, quickly enough that we could make the deadlines for the book.

Jean Marie Diaz, also known as AMBAR, helped develop the material on MUDs and MOOs. *Cameron Lloyd,* an up-and-coming Internet hacker, play-tested many of the MUDs and other resources. *Robert Hodkinson*, of Bradford University (famous for curry and rain) in the UK, was of great help with last-minute details about the nature of various MUD varieties.

Susan and *David Fiedler* of InfoPro Systems provided experienced advice and brainstorming on the process of writing books. Susan also endured dozens of early morning Donut discussions on the practical aspects of book authoring.

Joe Gelinas, postmaster general for the Information Technology Division at the University of Michigan, was invaluable as a research assistant, critical reader, and provider of key bits of information, particularly on troubleshooting Net connections and tricks of the trade. He researched and wrote the chapter on communications software.

Brendan Kehoe (whom one might have expected to be annoyed when his officemate became a competitor) helped think things through, answered e-mail questions like "What's the URL for the thing with the charts?" at odd hours, and gave us navigation advice for the big scary world of publishing.

Jeff Marraccini researched and wrote the chapter on Internet Relay Chat. A long-time professional lurker of the Internet (and a talented electronic musician), Jeff is the System Administrator of the popular OAK Repository and software archive, `oak.oakland.edu`, managed by Oakland University's Academic Computing Services.

Shannon McElyea lent Glee a portable PC so that she could spend her erstwhile vacation writing.

Glenn McGregor, VP of Engineering at Lloyd Internetworking, spent hours making sure that all the applications we needed to make the screen shots for this book were installed and working on the various machines, UNIX and otherwise, that we used. He also read many chapters and drew many diagrams on napkins to help keep us on track.

Duncan McGregor went to daycare throughout his entire summer vacation to stay out from underfoot while Mom slaved over a hot computer.

Jeffrey Osier of Cygnus coped and still loved us when his only helper in the doc department decamped all summer to write the book. Thanks to him and to the folks at Cygnus Support for giving Pat a leave of absence.

Jon Rami of Ramifications spent many hours discussing and reacting to ideas and assertions, in general providing that very valuable other point of view.

Jennifer Tifft, of Sybase, Inc., and *Richard Smiley* of the Sacramento Public Schools, newcomers to the Net, kept us focused on the needs of real people instead of network nerds.

Much of the modem, SLIP, and PPP troubleshooting sections of this book come from the collective wisdom of the network consultants and systems administrators at MichNet, the University of Michigan,

NetManage, CICNet, Cygnus Support, Lloyd Internetworking, and NETCOM. We are particularly grateful to *Bob Williams, Pritish Shah, Laura Bollettino, Mark Davis-Craig, Christine Wendt, Howard Chu, Sarah Stapleton Gray, Brian Smith, Kathy Madison,* and *Rhana Jacot* for the collection and distillation of this wisdom, and for permission to use some of their consulting tip sheets in pulling all this information together.

Other valuable tidbits, insights, and work which we could build on come from members of various Internet Engineering Task Force Working Groups, especially the User Services Area of the Internet Engineering Task Force (IETF).

The Technical Support and System Administration folks at Netcom all helped. Particular mention goes to *Jeff Rizzo* and *Brian Thomas* for answering "stupid networking questions," to *Greg Andrews* for more time than anyone could possibly spend answering modem questions, and to the people reporting to Glee who suffered through lots during this period: *Steve Covington, Bryant Durrell, Brad Grantham, John Mooney, Steve Lee, Kael Loftus, Trevor Placker, Sheri Shipe, Alan Stewart, Gretchen Shanrock, Bill Stivers,* and *John Wu.*

The software development folks at Netcom helped by providing fresh views as well as the working software to try a lot of this stuff out on: *Rick Francis, Jie Fu, Andrew Hao,* and *Roger Lian.* Special mention goes to *Peter Kaminski* who provided thoughtful and considered answers to grand philosophical questions as well as an FTP client that worked so we could move the materials back and forth.

Ed Vielmetti of MSEN, Inc., and *Brian Lloyd* and *Connie Fleenor* of Lloyd Internetworking provided invaluable information and insight into how businesses get started using the Internet and how to solve their problems. Lloyd Internetworking also provided insight into K–12 networking solutions, as well as the Internet connections and host accounts that let us exchange chapters in the book.

Michael Gross and *Erik Ingenito* wrote the instructions for installing and using the software on the companion disks.

Contents at a Glance

Table of Contents

Chapter 6   Communication Software   **201**

Chapter 18   Rules, Policies, and Other Mutual Agreements   597

Chapter 19   Building the Resource   623

Chapter 23   Resources for Kids   **757**

▶▶ Introduction

communicate (verb transitive) **1. a.** To convey information about; make known; impart: *communicated the new data to our office* **b.** To reveal clearly; manifest: *"Music…can name the unnamable and communicate the unknowable"* (Leonard Bernstein) **2.** To spread (a disease, for example) to others; transmit: *a carrier who communicated typhus.* (verb intransitive) **1.** To have an interchange, as of ideas **2.** To express oneself in such a way that one is readily and clearly understood: *"That ability to communicate was strange in a man given to long, awkward silences"* (Anthony Lewis). **3.** To receive Communion **4.** To be connected: *apartments that communicate.*

▶▶ *The Internet as Communication Medium*

These definitions come from *The American Heritage Dictionary of the English Language*, 3rd edition. Except for the religious sense (and there are those who would no doubt feel it applies, too), all of the definitions can be applied to using and enjoying the global Internet, whether as information consumers or as information providers.

Most of us are both consumers and providers at different times. Sometimes we take both roles simultaneously. This book will help you function effectively in both capacities.

 ▶ ▶**W A R N I N G**

Like the ocean, the Internet is vast and ever-changing. No one is truly its master; no one has plumbed its depths *in toto;* no one knows everything about it, because it changes on a daily basis. But, like master navigators, you can learn to chart the familiar seas and figure out how to safely travel the unfamiliar ones, bringing back treasure and new information with every trip.

▶▶ *Who Is This Book For?*

If you have never used the Internet before, this book will help you get started. Both of us were beginners once, and we've gotten feedback from other Net neophytes on ways to improve our text to make sure newcomers won't get lost. All we expect is that you know how to turn your computer on, load software onto it, and run at least one application in your operating system or environment, whether that's DOS, Windows, the Mac, or UNIX. We don't, for example, show Windows or Mac users how to work with the Clipboard. If you've never used a computer before, or are just beginning, we encourage you to develop the basic skills before you begin using this book to explore the Net.

But if you do have the basic computer skills, you're ready to begin. When you finish reading the book, you'll be netsurfing like a pro: you'll be able to converse fluently with e-mail and the instantaneous communication services such as IRC and Talk, read and reply to Usenet news, and explore the world of vast resources using Gopher and the World Wide Web.

If you've been using the Net for a while and know how to use your modem to connect to a network, then you're probably familiar with basic Internet services such as e-mail, Gopher, and FTP, and you are probably not afraid to explore and try things out. This book can help you learn to use the Internet more efficiently and more enjoyably. For experienced users, we've included plenty of hints and tips for shortcuts and troubleshooting. We hope you'll use this book as a well-thumbed reference to services, providers, and troubleshooting tips.

If you're thinking about putting your company, organization, or school online, we offer special sections about becoming an Internet presence, from how to assess your needs to strategies for developing good employee use policies. We will equip you to understand the new world you're entering into, and help you assess how best to proceed.

If you're interested in publishing information on the Net using some of the remarkable new network services, such as the World Wide Web and Gopher, we provide step-by-step instructions and valuable insights for building those resources.

If you're a systems administrator, network protocol programmer, or professional network consultant, you probably know most of the facts in this book. We think you might enjoy some of our insights and learn a tip or two.

▶▶ *What's in This Book?*

Because we've designed this book to serve the broadest possible range of Internet users, we don't expect that all of you will want to read every chapter or appendix in order. Here's a quick guide to help you find the parts of the book that best meet your needs, current and future.

▶ *Part I: Becoming an Effective Internet User*

This first section of the book builds your knowledge from the ground up: What is a network? How did the Internet get started? What can I do with it? These chapters will help you build skills to navigate the Net and help you understand the strengths and limitations of the various network services and applications.

- In **Chapter 1** we introduce basic networking and data communication concepts. You'll learn about various kinds of networks, how they interconnect, and what the underlying principles of the Internet are.

- How you think about a thing as immense as the Internet helps you understand it. The best way to understand the Internet is not by its technology, but by its potential for communication. In **Chapter 2** we describe the various Internet services and applications in light of how they help you communicate.

- How do you find things on the Internet? How are the names of computers chosen, and what do they mean? Is there a difference in how computers find each other, and how people locate resources on the Net? **Chapter 3** answers all these questions and more.

- Getting on the Internet is not as simple as ordering phone or cable service—at least not yet. In **Chapter 4** we discuss the ways you can get connected, from a simple phone line and modem for home use to a high-speed dedicated link for your business or organization. Included in this chapter are tips on assessing your needs for network connectivity and a comparison of the major multistate network providers and the services they offer.

- **Chapter 5** shows what to do once the basic connection from the Internet into your home or office is made and outlines your options for software and services for your desktop computer: what you can use at home, how you can turn your desktop computer into an Internet host, and what you can with a traditional host-dial account.

- **Chapter 6** gives you information on some of the more popular communications software packages available for desktop computers, what the packages will and won't do for you, and how to get the software in the first place.

- Where do I park? What's the speed limit? Where do I find the rule book? Do I need a license? Just as in learning to drive, you need to know the rules of the road. On the Information Superhighway, the rules aren't always written down online, so we've put them in **Chapter 7**.

- **Chapter 8** covers electronic mail, or e-mail—one of the most popular services on the Internet. Friends, coworkers, even heads of state use e-mail to communicate. How can you get started? What's the best way to make sure your message gets through? Here we discuss both the basics and the advanced skills for using e-mail, including ways to diagnose bounced messages and get them back on track.

- Once you've mastered e-mail, you need to know how to get to other resources and bring your treasures home with you. FTP, or File Transfer Protocol, lets you bring files across the Net to your own desktop. In **Chapter 9** we teach you how to move one or many files in the fastest, most efficient way. Telnet is the Internet way to create an interaction encounter with other hosts on the network. This chapter also shows how to establish your connection correctly and make sure you can work efficiently once you're there.

- Not even Columbus really knew when he was in the right spot when he set off to discover India and stumbled into the New World instead. How can an Internet navigator feel confident of finding cool things to do (and being able to get back to them whenever she wants)? **Chapter 10** tells you the best way to find and keep track of people as well as resources.

- **Chapter 11** covers Gopher and the World Wide Web. These are the hottest, fastest-growing services on the Internet, simply because they are so easy to use. These two major services use the principle of discovery by serendipity, but you shouldn't have to discover them by chance.

- Usenet News is one of the biggest sources of conversation, information, and entertainment on the Internet, yet without some guidance you can get lost in this world, either by information overload or by falling prey to a rude individual. In **Chapter 12** we discuss how to read and reply to News, how to filter the flood of information to get what you want, and what the courtesies and expectations of your fellow News readers are.

- How do I set up my modem to talk to CompuServe? Where can I get information on special education for disabled children? Hundreds of questions are asked and answered each day on the Internet. The system of Frequently Asked Questions records these answers so you can get them (and not feel foolish for asking something that has been asked a hundred times before). **Chapter 13** tells you what FAQs are, where to get them, and how to contribute to them.

- Some conversations on the Internet are immediate and personal. IRC (Internet Relay Chat) and Talk are two ways to communicate right now, without the delay of e-mail, with folks around the world. **Chapter 14** talks about how to use these tools, what the rules are, and what the bonuses of instantaneous communication are.

- Once solely the province of hackers and role-playing gamers, Multiple User Dungeons (and their various cousins) are moving into the corporate world as a place to hold meetings between scattered employees, stimulate creativity, and generate team spirit. **Chapter 15** explains how MUDs work, how to get into them and move around in them, and what the attraction is.

▶ *Part II: Becoming an Information Provider*

Once you've mastered the Internet basics, you will want to become a provider of information as well as a consumer. In Part II, we'll show how to use the basic tools to build an Internet presence for your organization, be it a commercial corporate entity, school, or nonprofit organization. We also will discuss management and planning issues that you should consider: that is, what connection options exist, how to develop your own appropriate usage policies, and how to incorporate appropriate system security right from the start.

- How do you put your business or organization on the Net? What can you do with a network connection, and how do you make sure you come up with appropriate policies for employee use of your connection? **Chapter 16** is for business people, administrators, and anyone who wants to get their organization connected without encountering potholes on the Information Highway.

- The Internet has been called one of the greatest boons to education since the library, but how do you make use of that resource? Why should you get your school connected? In **Chapter 17** we talk about getting the money for a connection, share case histories of schools that are successfully using the Net, and share strategies for effective use of the Internet in the lives of our schoolchildren.

- Even a vast resource like the Internet has limits. Acceptable use policies help guide us all to courteous, legal, ethical use of the resources, and help define what is and isn't appropriate on the Net. In **Chapter 18** we discuss what constitutes a good policy, how to integrate your network policies with other organizational policies, and how to get compliance without being a network cop.

- Once you're connected and everything is working smoothly, you'll want to use the network to distribute information: one of the reasons you got on the Internet in the first place. In **Chapter 19** you'll learn how to build a "gopher hole," "spin" a Web page, and set up an FTP site. Step-by-step instructions, as well as notes on the philosophical and legal considerations, make the job easier.

▸ *Part III: Internet Resources*

Whether you're exploring the Net for business, education, or pleasure, you'll want to know where to find the most interesting, useful, or just plain fun resources that are now available. The four chapters in Part III present some of our favorites.

- **Chapter 20** is an annotated list of cool general resources we want to share with you. Here we have the best of the best. We list libraries, indexes, newsgroups, Web pages, and on and on. Every user of the Net should know and use these basic resources.

- More and more specialized resources are appearing on the Net. **Chapter 21** covers the information resources provided by governments and businesses, including state and federal agencies, storehouses of important documents, and commercial resources.

- **Chapter 22** shows where teachers and students can turn to find curriculum modules, teaching guidelines, support groups and pen-pals, projects to join or observe, or research resources.

- Playing on the Net can be fun and educational. What time is it in Tanzania? Will they close the schools because of snow tomorrow? Who won the National Hockey league finals in 1987? Where's the best collection of computer games on the Net? **Chapter 23** offers cool resources for kids (of all ages).

▶ Part IV: Glossary

The Internet has generated a whole new language. In the Glossary we have collected hundreds of network terms (including those aggravating acronyms) and defined them for you in clear, concise language.

▶ Appendices

As appendices, we've collected several documents, written or compiled by authorities in various aspects of the Internet, that shed light on topics raised earlier in the book.

- What were the scientific and social developments that contributed to the Internet? When did the first connections get made? **Appendix A** presents Hobbes' Timeline, which helps you understand how a wide array of influences shaped the Net as we know it, and continue to shape the Net our children will use.

- **Appendix B** presents the standard netiquette document you will encounter as part of your network education, and sometimes as part of the Appropriate Use Policy at network sites you use. In addition, we include guidelines for "Safe and Smart" computing, particularly directed at preserving your privacy in a computer-filled world.

- When you plan your network, you'll be swamped with new terms, new concepts, and new technologies. **Appendix C** is a guide to Internet protocols and technology, specifically designed with the business user in mind, that will help you better understand what the technical issues are surrounding your new network installation.

- **Appendix D** presents Doran's MUD List, *the* guide to MUDs and other shared environments on the network. This tells you what the topic or theme of the game is, what software it uses, and how to get to it.

- **Appendix E** presents an exceptional paper, titled "Internetworking Guidelines for K–12," that describes everything you need to know to get your school online, from technology to policies.

- In **Appendix F**, one of the nation's top university computing policy-makers discusses the administrative and personal dilemmas faced by college and university administrators when faced with tough issues such as pornography, harassment, and inappropriate materials on the Internet.

- **Appendix G** presents an extensive selected listing of FTP sites that helps you pinpoint where to get shareware software, historical documents, song lyrics—anything you might want to retrieve off the network.

- **Appendix H** shows how to install, configure, and use the two software packages included on this book's accompanying disks. Net-Cruiser is an easy-to-use interface for anyone connected to the Internet via the service provider Netcom; the Chameleon Sampler is for users with a SLIP/PPP connection (through any Internet service provider that offers one).

Also included in this book are several types of notes that serves as tools in exploring the Internet: Master Words, Warnings, and other notes. Master Words give definitions, anecdotes, or pointers to more information. Warnings, obviously, point out potential pitfalls.

Becoming an Effective Internet User

PART ONE

1

What Is
the Internet?

▶ ▶ **W**hat is the Internet? There is no single, generally agreed-upon answer to this question because the Internet is different for each of us:

- *It is a set of computers talking over fiber optics, phone lines, satellite links, and other media.*

- *It is a place where you can talk to your friends and family around the world.*

- *It is a place to get neato game demos.*

- *It is an ocean of resources waiting to be mined.*

- *It is a place to do research for your thesis or a business presentation.*

- *It is a place where "crackers" and other shady characters lurk, waiting to wreak havoc.*

- *It is unlimited commercial opportunity.*

- *It is a world-wide support group for any problem or need.*

- *It is a gold mine of professionals in all fields sharing information about their work.*

- *It is hundreds of libraries and archives that will open to your fingertips.*

- *It is the ultimate time waster.*

- *It is the technology of the future which will help make our lives, and those of our children, brighter.*

All these answers are right; none of them is complete. Today the Internet is much more than it was in the 1980s, and in five more years it will have grown so far that the cool toys we use today will be the ancient grandparents of the tools in use then. But there are some ways to talk about the Internet on which we can all agree.

GROWTH OF THE INTERNET

In 1989, fewer than 12 million packets (or pieces) of information passed through the Internet. By December 1992, 6 *billion* packets per year were being transferred, and by May 1994, information was flowing across the fiber and computer links of the network at the rate of 21 billion packets per year. Here's a quick look at the growth in several of the Internet's most widely used services since December 1992 (you'll learn about these services in various chapters throughout this book.):

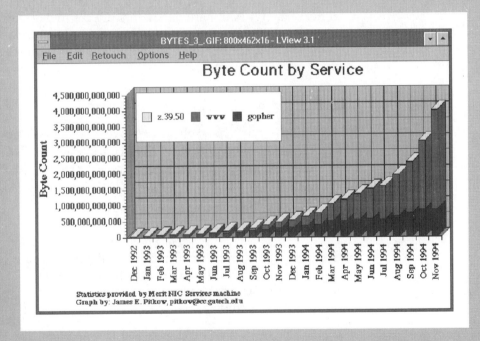

One technically correct way to talk about the Internet is to say that it is "the network formed by the cooperative interconnection of computing networks." In fact, the word "Internet" was coined from the words "interconnection" and "network." What this jargon means is that hundreds of connecting networks, usually made up of differing kinds of computers and different technologies, are put together so smoothly that the individual parts appear to be one network. These connected networks usually use the *TCP/IP (transmission control protocol/internet protocol) communications suite.*

Protocols (the word comes out of diplomatic language, and is used to mean the rules under which official transactions take place) are the rules that the networks all use to understand each other. The various protocols are sets of technical specifications that let computers exchange information, no matter what kind of computers they are, or what kind of technology hooks them together. Vendors of software and hardware want their products to be useful on the Internet, and so they make sure those products understand and operate with the Internet protocols. The term *interoperability* has been coined to describe this ability of disparate types of hardware and software to work together under a common set of rules. Interoperability is a hot market commodity today, and so you'll see the term in advertising and product reviews for all kinds of computer products.

▶ ▶ **M A S T E R   W O R D S**

TCP/IP and the various protocols that are used on the Internet are important underlying concepts for the Net. Unless you need to configure TCP/IP software on a computer, you need to only know they exist: the specifics aren't important to you.

Some people say "It's on the Internet" to describe where some information is located. In that sense, the word *Internet* is used to describe the services that can be reached using the interconnected networks. Some of those services include:

- library catalogs
- Usenet news groups and electronic mailing lists—forums in which you can discuss any of thousands of topics with people who share your interests
- archives of free or shareware software
- customer service information for commercial companies

- free information on not-for-profit and political organizations

- text of books, papers, and historical documents

and much, much more.

The Internet is also the community of people who work together to use the networks. The Internet is a cooperative effort of many people and organizations, all working to enhance the Net by their participation. It's important to realize that people don't just use the information on the network—by contributing to electronic mailing lists, by building information services and archives of various kinds, all the users of the Internet are information providers. You will be, too.

▶ ▶ *Who Owns It?*

No one owns the Internet.

It was not funded by any single person, service, corporation, university, or government. Every person who makes a connection, every group whose Local Area Network (LAN) becomes connected, owns a slice of the Internet.

Because we have grown used to the model of centralized, cooperating utilities, such as the phone companies and the electric companies, we can comfortably compare the Internet to a utility. For example, there is phone service in almost every part of the United States. With a phone company, each person who wants telephone service contacts a local area service provider. The service provider provides a "hook-up" from the residence or business to the service network. The person wanting service actually provides the telephone instrument and the connections within the residence or business.

As long as you want to place calls to other telephones only within your local area, you don't need anything else. However, if you want to place a call to someone in another area, you need to purchase services from a long distance service provider. The local area provider supplies the connection from the local network into the long distance network. This arrangement allows you to connect to telephones almost anywhere in the world. Moving among networks of computers works much the same way (which is not surprising since the telephone networks—that is, the physical cables—are being used to connect the computers).

▶ *No One Owns the Internet*

But lots of people care about it. Later in this chapter you'll learn about the organizations that set standards for the Internet. In addition, all the people who use it to just send a note to someone on some other network that is gatewayed into the Internet care about it. Each computer connected is owned by someone or some enterprise. The owner of the connected equipment therefore "owns" a piece of the Internet. The telephone companies "own" the pieces that carry the packets. The service providers "own" the packet routing equipment. So, while no one person or entity owns the Internet, all who use it or supply materials for it play a part in its existence.

▶▶ *What Is a Network, Anyway?*

The formal definition of a network is: "a data communications system that interconnects computer systems at various sites. A network may be composed of any combination of LANs (Local Area Networks), MANs (Municipal Area Networks), or WANs (Wide Area Networks)." But what does that mean to the user?

At its simplest, a network consists of two computers or devices with a length of wire between them, letting them communicate. At its most complex, as in the Internet, a network is a globe-spanning, heterogeneous mix of technologies and operating systems. Figure 1.1 illustrates several kinds of networks.

▶ *"A Network of Networks"*

The Internet mostly connects networks of computers. Think of a corporate-wide network: each department has a LAN that allows it to share files and maybe a printer or two. Several departments, working together, interconnect their networks so that information may be shared more easily among the departments. These "regional" networks are interconnections based on geography (same city, same state, same group of states) or function (accounts-receivable grouped with accounts-payable into an accounting network, for example).

Then the regional networks are connected together onto a corporate network, sometimes called a *backbone*. So, there is a user connected to

FIGURE 1.1

What is a network?

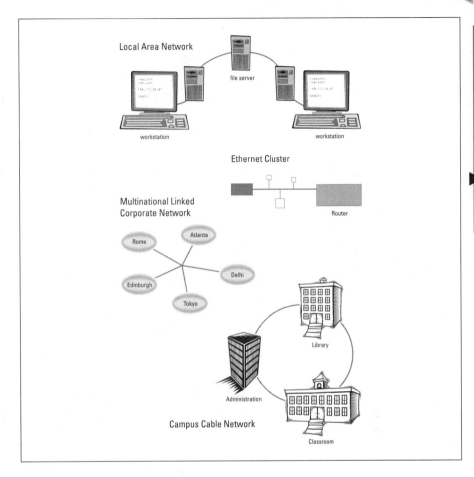

a local net; a local net connected into a regional net; and regional nets connected to a backbone.

This is actually the way the modern Internet grew: the collection of organizations of various kinds shown in Figure 1.2, with backbones connected to each other at gateways, illustrates the global Internet. We say "global" because networks from most countries with some sort of telephone service infrastructure are connected to it. Practically, this means people can use their computers on their local networks to send messages or exchange files with people using computers in another company or in another state, in another region, in another country: anywhere, in fact, that is connected.

FIGURE 1.2 ▶

A network of networks.

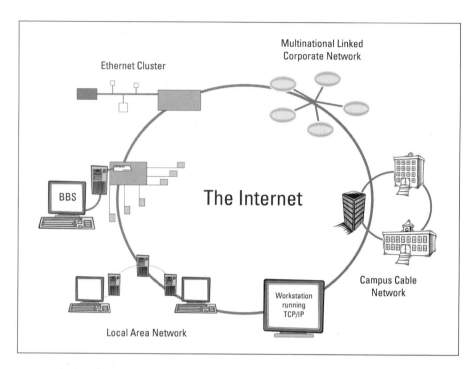

MASTER WORDS

For several years now, the hottest controversy on the Internet has been whether businesses could use the Net to do business: to solicit customers, to support those customers, to advertise, to communicate with their remote offices. For a long time, the major backbone of the Internet was supported with tax dollars, by way of grants from the United States National Science Foundation. In the past few years, commercial Internet providers have sprung up, opening the potential and resources of the Internet to businesses of all sorts and their customers. Probably you are one of those customers: if you're not connected to a university or other educational organization, you probably got your Internet connection through a commercial provider.

▶▶ *How Is the Internet Administered?*

To many people's surprise, there really is no central administration to the Internet.

The Internet has been described as cooperative anarchy: each individual network has its own rules and its own organization chart. But communication between networks can't happen without cooperation, and so there are committees and working groups hard at work all the time to make sure the Beast hangs together.

There is a formal administration chart for the Internet. It shows the Network Information Center (NIC) that is sponsored by the United States National Science Foundation (NSF) to register the domains, names, and addresses of new computers being added to the network. Internet service providers are encouraged to provide registration service and assistance for each new connected network.

Each individually connected network maintains its own user policies and procedures—who can be connected, what kind of traffic the network will carry, and so on. Each manages its own network—engineering the network, choosing to provide particular services or not. And each network cooperatively carries the traffic from its connected networks to gateways and from gateways to its connected networks.

The technical rules (protocols) are agreed upon after proposal, trial, and discussion in the networking community. No one person can "lay down the law" to the rest of the community, because there is no law and there is no one person.

▶ ## SEEN ON THE OFFICIAL INTERNET ENGINEERING TASK FORCE T-SHIRT FOR FALL 1993

We reject kings, presidents, and voting.

We believe in rough consensus and running code.

Dave Clark (1992)
(Internet wizard)

►► ►**W A R N I N G**

When you read this formal description, you might imagine calm committee meetings full of men and women in business attire, discussing and passing rules for the Internet. Not a chance: the 500–600 folks who help plan and administer the Internet would be horrified to think they'd turned into a bunch of "suits." At the Internet Engineering Task Force (IETF) meetings, held three times a year, T-shirts and flannels, chinos and jeans are the uniform of the day, and beards and balding domes compete with acne and skater cuts. The meetings are frequently loud and argumentative, and standing around in the hallways debating the fate of the Internet is a time-honored tradition. It's true that most attendees at the IETF are traditional male programmer types, but women (and suits) are coming up fast in the halls of Internet power. Catering an IETF meeting requires good relations with the local Coca-Cola distributor and a direct line to the local cookie factory. IETF participants can go through about three times as many catered goodies as an equivalent number of, say, accountants.

►► *How Does the Internet Work?*

At the simplest level, there is one user sitting in front of one computer on a network. Let's say that this person is in Durham, England. Let's also say that this person wants to get information to another person in Seattle, Washington. Now, if these people are in the same company, using some corporate-wide e-mail system, the first person just enters in the name of the second person as it is known to the corporate e-mail system—usually, a user name. This serves as an address for the electronic message, and the Send command has the e-mail system deliver the message to the second person.

If our English networker is called Hilary, his address on the company system might be simply `hilary`. His coworker in Seattle, Sue, would likely just be `sue`.

Again, let's compare this to a telephone system. Within the same local company and exchange, some telephone systems allow you to dial a digit or two to reach someone else also connected to the same local system. If the two people are not on the same exchange, then (within the United States, anyway) you will need to dial the full seven digits and perhaps a three-digit area code.

If the two people are *not* on the same e-mail system, whether or not it is corporate-wide, the message needs to have some extension that serves the same function as the full seven digits plus the area code in the phone number. This address extension is found following the @ sign in an Internet e-mail address. For example, `totn@npr.org` is the complete Internet address for the staff of the National Public Radio show Talk of the Nation. This type of address is spoken of as the *fully qualified* address—this means that it has all the parts to let it be delivered from anywhere on the network.

Let's look at Hilary and Sue again. Hilary's full address might be: `hilary@durham.org`. Sue's full address is: `sue@seattle.org`. (These are fictitious addresses used for example only.)

Once a message has an address on it, the interconnected Internet systems take over. The e-mail handling system on the sender's computer packages the message and prepares it for "shipping." The message is broken up into small pieces called "packets." The packets are all addressed to the final destination. The path from Durham, England, to Seattle, Washington, may have many different networks in it. In fact, the packets that contain the message may not all travel the same path.

MASTER WORDS

Packets are one of the basic units of measurement on the Internet. Packets have different sizes, depending on what application "packed" them. You can think of them as envelopes or suitcases full of information.

Along the possible paths are special-purpose computers called *routers*. These computers do nothing but look at network addresses and figure out from the address what is the current best route to the destination address. Once the packets reach their destination, they are reassembled into the original message.

Routers make their decisions based on information that is constantly reaching them from all over the Net. They hear from other routers about links that are down, about others that may be congested and slow, or about routers that are no longer accepting packets for certain destinations. Each packet's destination and proposed route is evaluated individually, in the blink of an eye, and sent off along the best route for that particular packet at that particular moment. Figure 1.3 shows how Hilary's message to Sue might look as it is being routed.

The same sort of decision-making is made for all packets that traverse the Internet. Each time a packet reaches a router, its address is examined and the packet is forwarded either to another router nearer its ultimate destination or to that destination if the router is the final router on the path. The destination computer is the one that unpacks the

FIGURE 1.3 ►

Packets don't all take the same route

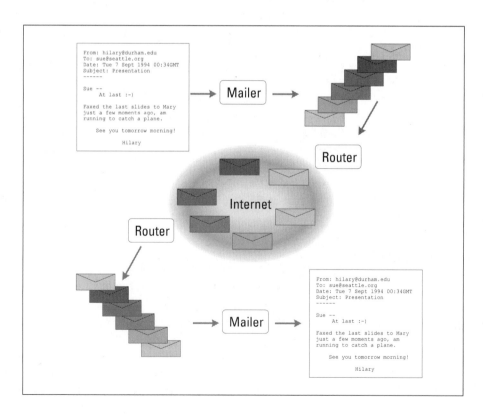

What Is the
Internet?

packets, throws away the "envelopes," and hands off the e-mail message (or the Gopher menu instruction, or the file transfer request to the
appropriate program on the destination machine).

▶ ▶**M A S T E R   W O R D S**

**The concept of packets flying off from your
workstation and being reassembled correctly at the
other end, no matter what route the individual pieces
take to get there, is the basic idea underlying Internet
technology. Once you get a few more terms and ideas
under your belt, you'll be ready to move out into
Internet exploration.**

▶ ▶

ch.

1

▶ *Being Connected as a Node vs. Connecting to a Host*

Being *connected* to the Internet means that your computer system or
network is actually a *node* on the Internet. It has an individually assigned Internet address, and client programs running on the computer
system can take full advantage of the computer's capabilities. Your
workstation is a peer of every other computer on the Net, be it another
personal computer dialed in with a modem, or a large UNIX installation with a hundred users currently signed onto it. Your workstation,
depending on the software, can do many of the most useful functions
of the Internet: *e-mail, Gopher, WWW, FTP.* You can *communicate, and
all on your own.* Figure 1.4 shows several kinds of nodes on a network.

FIGURE 1.4

*A node can be any de-
vice on the network.*

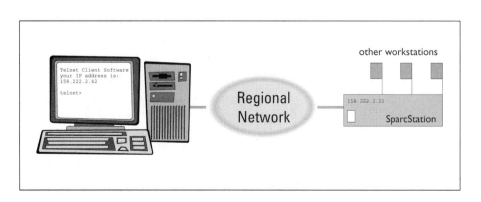

▶ ▶**M A S T E R W O R D S**

A *node* is any "addressable device" attached to a computer network. This means it has a separate, distinct Internet address and can be reached by other computers and devices on the Net. Printers, file servers, workstations, and packet routing devices are all nodes. Your computer, when you link it to the Net with TCP/IP software, also becomes a node. You can reach other devices, and they can reach you.

In contrast, if you connect to and log into a *host,* and then use *its* functions to reach out onto the Internet, you are using *your* computer as a terminal to reach another computer. Usually host connections are designed to use very simple text-based interactions—not the sophisticated Graphic User Interfaces we'll see in later chapters of the book—because those interactions are possible on the slowest and oldest equipment that potential users are likely to have. This is how you will interact with computers to which you *Telnet.* (Services such as CompuServe, America Online, and Netcom, however, offer custom software that lets you work with a Graphic User Interface even though your connection is through a host. You'll find Netcom's package, called NetCruiser, on this book's Companion Disk 1.)

 ▶ ▶**M A S T E R W O R D S**

Telnet is a major Internet application. Telnet is the tool that delivers you to the front door of other networks, other services, and other resources. You use Telnet to connect from your workstation or node to another node. You can think of Telnet, in the Internet Information Highway metaphor, as the car that gets you places. A version of Telnet is included in the Chameleon Sampler on this book's Companion Disk 2.

If you are using your computer as a terminal to someone else's computer, you are restricted to the interactions possible between that other computer and your computer. Those interactions are governed by the host computer. Even if your workstation is capable of other interactions, you won't be able to use them from the host computer. To use those functions, you'll need to use the *client/server* software on your own machine. We cover how these two kinds of connections work, and the advantages and disadvantages, in Chapter 5.

▶ *Are You Being Served?—Clients and Servers*

The concept of *client/server* computing has particular importance on the Internet because so many popular programs are built using this design. A *server* is a program that "serves" (or delivers) something, usually information, to a client program. A server usually runs on a computer that is connected to a network. The size of that network is not important to the client/server concept—it could be a small local area network or the global Internet. The server is designed to interact with a client program or client programs so that people using the system can determine whether the information they want is there, and if so, have it sent. You don't have to take care of most of the underlying operations necessary to get the information: the server and client programs do that for you.

 ▶▶ **M A S T E R   W O R D S**

Popular client/server software includes Eudora e-mail software, WinGopher, Mosaic World-Wide-Web software, Fetch (a Macintosh file transfer program), and Novell NetWare File server software.

A client program is designed for a particular computing platform (for example, Windows, Macintosh, UNIX) to take advantage of the strengths of the platform. The client software is designed to make you comfortable: it uses environmental elements just like the ones you use to do word processing or a spreadsheet, or even to play a game.

Your *environment* is the *user interface* you see: the menu bars at the top of the screen, whether you click on icons or type in the names of programs you want to use, whether there are buttons or pull-down screens to give you choices and so on. Internet applications programmers try to write client software that looks just like those interfaces. The ultimate goal is that eventually, you won't need to know whether what you are doing happens on your computer or on one a hundred miles away: the client/server software will look just like everything else, and the transaction will take place just as quickly as everything else you run.

Using your familiar computer environment, the client may help you locate servers of interest, send a query, process the query results, and display them using the tools familiar to you. For example, if you use the Macintosh Fetch program, the screens and push buttons look like other programs you use on the Macintosh. Similarly, if you use a Windows program like WFTP (shown in Figure 1.5), you'll see a version of the familiar Windows interface.

The advantage of this type of design is that a server with multiple client programs only has to store the information in one format: the various client programs can present it to different users in different places who are using different computers. The client program creates the data presentation. This ensures that the information looks familiar to the person making the request. It also spreads the cost of presenting the information: computing resources used in developing the presentation are consumed by the person who made the request.

▶▶ *Anyone Can Play and Pay*

An important part of the cooperative nature of the Internet is the provision of information that is "free" via the network. "Free" information means that you may use the information (within the bounds of copyright law, of course) without paying a fee. However, the Internet itself *is*

FIGURE 1.5 ▶

A Windows-based FTP client.

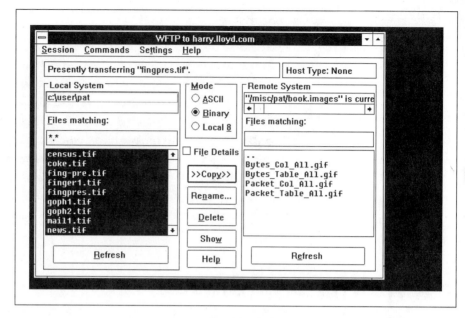

not free. Someone, somewhere is paying for the part of the network each of us uses.

Sometimes the fees are direct and we are aware of them, like those charged by the Internet access providers like Netcom or PSI. Direct provider fees range from all-inclusive monthly fees to itemized connect time, basic service, e-mail, or per-attachment costs.

Sometimes the fees are direct, but you are not aware you are paying for Internet access with them. For example, if you are a college student and you are charged a "computing services" fee, some part of that money pays for your Internet usage.

Sometimes the fees are paid by the enterprise that you work for, when your company is connected. Sometimes the fee is paid indirectly, when you use a service sponsored by a government. The government may have received money from you in the form of taxes which are in turn being used to provide the service.

With all of these different models of payment and provision, it's no wonder we say that "Anyone can pay... and play."

MASTER WORDS

Because so much of the Internet was originally funded by governments grants—by tax dollars—the issue of commercial use, and particularly of advertising, is a hot one. We are beginning to see the advent of junk mail, unsolicited offers, and other intrusive commercial materials. A subtler form of commercial advertising on the Net is the rise in World Wide Web pages with descriptions of services available, product reviews, and so on. The issue of commercial advertising on the Net will continue to be hotly contested before it is resolved.

▶▶ *A Brief and Biased Historical Review*

Here's a short history for those of you who would like a brief review of how the Internet got to where it is now. Other books address this topic in greater detail, and we refer you to them if you would like more information. Robert Hobbes Zakon has collected a timeline which is included as Appendix A for further reference.

▶ *ARPANET*

While the interest in science and technology was fueled by the competition that began with the Sputnik satellite, from the networking point of view, it all started with the ARPANET and a few resourceful computer scientists who wanted to share files among people working on the same or similar projects. ARPA is the acronym for Advanced Research Projects Agency of the United States' Department of Defense. In order to share information and experiment results, and to more easily collaborate on papers, scientific colleagues and the people who worked to support their efforts connected together computers at initially a very few research universities and research laboratories.

From the few connected institutions, word spread about the value and ease of collaborative work and, over time, more and more people connected their research institutions to each other. They also began to connect the manufacturers of equipment, computers, and software used to support the scientific and research mission. For over twenty years, the network served the research community well, and it grew each year as more people moved out from the larger, earlier-connected institutions to smaller institutions.

The trend toward connection followed the general trend of more-affordable technology, as technology itself became more available to the general populace. As part of the continuing expansion and enhancement of the ARPANET, the TCP/IP protocols came to replace the older, less powerful protocols. The idea behind TCP/IP was to connect unlike things together in a way that made using the equipment more transparent, so that users didn't have to understand the inner workings of each particular computer and its native operating system. The official change to TCP/IP happened in 1983. In the same year, the ARPANET split into the MILNET (for military network), which served the defense community, and the ARPANET, which served the research and education community.

MASTER WORDS

Today you can send e-mail to folks on MILNET, and access information in other limited ways from their hosts, but it is still essentially an independent network. For security reasons, the MILNET administrators have built an e-mail-only gateway, and backup security structures to protect the US defense information from attack by folks with malicious or destructive intent. If any of the automatic triggers sends a message that MILNET is under attack, the "firewall" slams down, severing all contact with the rest of the network. Modern companies have taken this concept to their own security installations. Many corporate networks now have firewalls and "bastion" hosts to protect their systems and data. (A "bastion" is a curtain wall or other defensive structure on a castle.)

▶ *Supercomputing Centers*

In the mid-1980s, the National Science Foundation looked to form a shared resource of supercomputing centers that could be used by researchers at multiple institutions. At that time, a supercomputer was a very rare and expensive thing: not every institution, even among the research universities, could afford to buy these very costly things, nor could they necessarily afford to maintain the environment and the support staff necessary to run a supercomputer center. However, many institutions and their research scientists needed access to such computing power. The National Science Foundation (NSF), an agency of the United States Federal government, conceived of and funded a small number of supercomputer centers, strategically located geographically throughout the United States, which could be used by many researchers.

The supercomputer centers ranged from the San Diego Supercomputer Center (SDSC) in San Diego, California to the Cornell Theory Center at Cornell University in Ithaca, New York. Each center was to furnish computing power and staff resources to a group of institutions that were organized either along geographic lines or by common research interests.

The original plan called for scientists to prepare their computing problems on their home computers and then travel to the regional supercomputer centers. However, it became apparent that traveling to the supercomputer centers was less desirable for researchers than staying at their home institution with their research staffs and familiar tools (not to mention being able to fulfill their numerous other responsibilities). So NSF thought to provide a high-speed connection among the supercomputer centers and then from home institutions to the centers. In 1987, high-speed was considered a 56 Kbps (56,000 bits per second) connection. But it soon became obvious that even that speed was inadequate for the demand.

▶ *NSFNET*

The NSFNET was the first step along that path of increased demand. As more and more researchers exchanged data and collaborated on papers using data from the supercomputer centers, more people wanted to get involved. Scientists told scientists in other disciplines. Scientists

WHAT'S A SUPERCOMPUTER?

A supercomputer is a computer that can process a great deal of information, or make involved and extensive calculations, very, very quickly. Supercomputers can resolve complex mathematical equations in just a few hours that would take lifetimes for a person using a pencil and paper, or years using a hand calculator. Scientists using supercomputers calculated the flight path of the comet that recently struck Jupiter, in just a few weeks after its discovery; without the supercomputer, we might not have been able to determine the orbit of the comet before it struck the planet.

Supercomputers are also used to create fantastic computer animation, like that seen in the recent Disney movies *The Lion King* and *Beauty and the Beast,* or in the weekly TV show *Babylon 5.* Creating the wildebeest stampede in *The Lion King,* which lasted less than a minute on screen, would take over two weeks using a top-of-the-line Macintosh computer; using a supercomputer, the sequence took less than five hours to compile and run.

Many supercomputers are cooled by liquid nitrogen: the extreme cold helps make the electrical currents within the computer even faster.

If you ever see a Cray supercomputer, you might not recognize it: many Cray computers have their main computational units and coolant recirculators made to look like large lobby benches or other furniture.

told their colleagues in medicine. Scientists told their colleagues in the arts and the humanities.

Soon many, many people were devising very useful things to be done with a network. Demand began to grow rapidly. The NSFNET backbone needed to be replaced with something faster. In 1990–91, the initial backbone was replaced with the very fast T-1 NSFNET. This

▶

RELATIVE LINE SPEEDS

Connection speeds have changed in the past 10 years at, well, blinding speed. In 1987, whole colleges and universities shared a 56 Kbps line, and many felt too much of the capability of the line (its *bandwidth*), was going to waste. Today many Internet users believe that 56Kbps is just the right speed for connecting a personal workstation to the Net in order to view color graphics. (If pressed, we might graciously share the connection with another workstation or two.)

As an example of the difference that line speeds can make, consider the Oxford English Dictionary (OED), whose most recent edition is estimated to have 41.5 million words in it. Here's how long it would take to transfer the OED at various common Internet line speeds:

Rate	Transfer Time
9600 bps	9.6 hours
14,400 bps	6.4 hours
56,000 bps	1.6 hours
T1 (1.544 million bps)	3.6 minutes
T3 (45 million bps)	0.92 seconds

created a new problem, in that not every scientist was located at an institution that could connect to the NSFNET backbone that connected the supercomputer centers. But the NSF proposed and funded intermediaries that would help with this problem.

Figure 1.6 shows graphically the amount of data flowing across the NSFNET backbone and to each of the supercomputer centers. It was created using actual data for each router on the Net and then superimposing the resulting figure over a map of the United States.

FIGURE 1.6

Internet traffic superimposed over the US map.

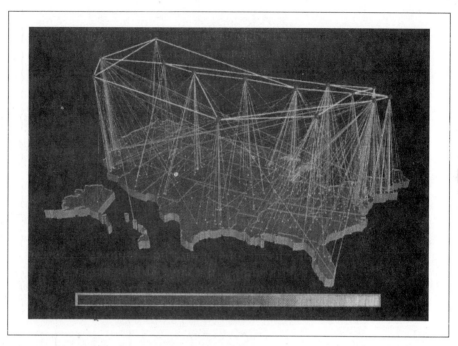

▶ *Midlevel Regional Networks*

The NSF conceived of the *Midlevel Regional Networks*, which were networks that served regions by connecting the institutions both with each other and with the NSFNET backbone. Now, instead of a researcher at Colorado State University in Fort Collins dialing into a modem at the University of Illinois in Urbana-Champaign, the researcher would connect from Fort Collins to his regional network (Westnet), and Westnet would connect to the NSFNET backbone, and the packets would be carried on the network to Urbana-Champaign.

Some of the original Midlevel Regional Networks were

CERFNet	(Southern California)
NorthWestNet	(Pacific Northwest)
NYSERNet	(New York State)
NEARNET	(New England)
SURANet	(Southern Seaboard)
MichNet	(Michigan)

| BARRNet | (Northern California) |
| SesquiNet | (Texas) |

Most likely, the original connections would have been from a communications processor added to a college campus academic computing system. Most campuses did not think about global networking when they designed their campus computing resources: most were based around a mainframe academic computing system. The sudden growth in popularity of networked communications caught most universities unprepared.

The basic academic computing system at most colleges and universities would have supported some sort of electronic mail system and some method of moving files to departmental computing systems, if such systems existed. Sometimes, it was the scientific community's departmental systems that carried the networking burden for the research community because the larger academic system might not have been able to connect to the network. Physics and Electrical Engineering/Computer Science departments frequently led the way to Internet connectivity on their campuses.

▶ *Local/Campus/Enterprise Nets*

The increasing demand for connections, the availability of more powerful desktop computers, and the advances in networking technology led to the continued growth of local and campus networks, and also the growing number of companies with their own networks. These became third-level networks connected into the Internet. Now the network really was *interconnected*. The campus researcher AND the corporate administrative support person AND the home-office entrepreneur were connected into first-level networks based on departments in companies or universities, or based on geographical proximity, or based on organizational function within larger organizations.

Originally, the goal was for a person sitting at home to have her home computer connected directly to a larger computer, emulating a terminal. This became common in many workplaces. Because of the growth of networking technology, our worker can now connect directly to her machine in her office or to a computer across the globe. Her local network is connected to her campus or enterprise network, which is connected to a midlevel network or commercial service provider. This intermediate network can deliver packets to other networks connected through it or can transfer packets to the tertiary-level backbones like the NSFNET.

► *Commercial Service Providers*

The most recent development in the Internet's history, and the one that may have brought you into the picture, is the rise of commercial service providers.

With the impetus provided by influential people within the United States Federal Government networking community and within the human network of interested people, the value of networked information has become more obvious to the general populace. People who were not affiliated with institutions of higher education wanted to send messages and exchange files. People who worked for connected enterprises wanted to be able to exchange messages with other enterprises who were not connected.

But the NSF and other operators of government-sponsored network backbones continued to be concerned about the appropriateness of carrying commercial or non-mission-oriented traffic on their networks. A less restrictive alternative was needed.

Several companies not affiliated with the US government were started to provide access to these newly interested customers. Some of the commercial providers grew out of organizations that provided networking expertise to the research and education community. Some of the companies grew out of organizations whose networking expertise came from other types of networks. Some of the companies grew out of smaller providers of host computing systems. All these types of companies worked together to form the Commercial Internet eXchange (CIX).

►► *IAB/IETF—Standards and Agreements*

All of the Internet works because of the standards and agreements forged by the Internet Engineering Task Force (IETF). The IETF creates the "prototypes" of the "design by prototype" engineering model.

In the Internet environment, new ideas in networking technology go through these steps:

- conceive and design a useful thing
- share it with a few colleagues to refine the design
- design and implement a trial to prove the concept
- improve the design based on feedback from the trial
- disperse the implementation details widely so that other people can test it
- after everyone agrees that it works, document the refined design as a standard

The IETF is a part of the Internet Architecture Board (IAB) upon which sit some of the guiding lights of internetworking (those jeans-and-T-shirt-clad men and women we talked about before). The IETF is charged with designing, implementing, and deploying the Internet itself. Another part of the IAB is the IRTF, the Internet Research Task Force, which is charged with looking into the future of Internetworking.

The IETF meets in person three times each year, but much of the important activity happens in the working groups which "meet" in mailing lists and Usenet news groups to discuss (well, argue about, really) the whole scope of Internet architecture and support:

- the fine points of routing protocols
- the definitions of words to put into a glossary for users
- security issues
- technical details for end-to-end connectivity

and the many other issues that keep the Internet functioning behind the scenes. People representing the network services providers; the computing and networking equipment manufacturers; the fiber optic cable manufacturers; and the user services people who try to answer user's questions and provide training all meet to solve the current and future problems. It is an extremely cooperative effort.

▶▶ *And What the Internet Isn't— Other Nets and Services*

You will find references to many other kinds of services as you cruise the Net: you'll see e-mail addresses from other places and read conversations where people talk about other services. These services are not part of the Internet, even though they may be linked to it, because they do not run the same protocols as the Net. Many times they simply have a gateway between their service and the greater Internet. We will probably see more integration of these services into the Internet as their customers begin to demand better access to Internet resources.

▶ *FidoNet and BBSs*

Bulletin Board Systems (BBSs) have long been used to connect small, local conferencing and e-mail systems to one another using "store-and-forward" technology. As the name implies, store-and-forward systems allow you to send a message at any time, without worrying about whether the recipient will be ready to retrieve it at exactly that moment— they can pick it up at their convenience. You don't establish a direct connection. By contrast, in client/server networking you need to make such a connection, in "real time." This type of network can work on either a small scale or a very large scale. Frequently these systems are run by volunteer systems operators (sysops). More and more, these BBSs have either gateways to the Internet or actual network connections to it. FidoNet is a network of bulletin board systems.

 ▶ ▶**W A R N I N G**

Small BBS operators have been hit recently for storing pornography and other materials on their systems. In a recent explosively controversial case, a BBS in Milpitas, California, was offering erotic material for users to download to their home systems. A prosecutor in Tennessee, who was able to download this material into a computer in Tennessee, tried and convicted the BBS operators under Tennessee pornography laws. Small

system operators are easy targets for enforcement officials because they frequently don't have the resources to hire expensive lawyers, and they also believe that because they are small they won't be noticed. If you use a BBS that has erotic or other material which may skirt the edge of legality, beware: If this system is ever captured by law enforcement, information about you, who you correspond with, and whatever material you have been storing onthe BBS will also be captured. No matter whether the information you are storing is acceptable under your own community standards, if people can access it through the Net, it can be judged by the standards of the community in which *they* live. Whatever you put out there may be illegal somewhere.

► Usenet/Net News

Usenet is a community of bulletin board systems that is a separate system, although it is closely allied with the Internet and the Internet community. It grew out of the loosely interconnected network of UNIX sites, where the software to run "Usenet News" was developed.

You'll find more in Chapter 12 about Net News and newsgroups and you can connect to Usenet with the NetCruiser software on Companion Disk 1. The important thing to know is that by copying files from one bulletin board to another, many, many thousands of people can contribute their thoughts to the thousands of Usenet news forums. No one specific method is used to transmit each and every contribution. The contributions are accepted at the millions of Usenet sites around the world and passed on and back to the other sites. It is a cooperative effort of each and every site that is connected to and by the Usenet.

► BITNET and CSNET

BITNET and CSNET were parallel and complementary efforts to the ARPANET. BITNET (or Because It's Time Network) connected a number of the larger computers used for academic and administrative computing among universities throughout the world. Originally, BITNET operated between IBM mainframes, although software modifications to allow BITNET technology to work on other mainframe operating systems were written.

BITNET originally transferred information in a format which mimicked computer punch cards: the punch-card images were reassembled at the remote end and turned back into files. BITNET's logical organization remains today, long after much of the traffic on the network is actually made into packets and transported on the Internet.

CSNET stood for the Computer + Science Network. It remained an important part of the networking community until the end of the 1980s when the network itself was dismantled and the organization was merged with the administration of BITNET to form CREN (Corporation for Research and Educational Networking).

▶ *MCIMail, AT&TMail, and SprintMail*

MCIMail and AT&TMail are e-mail and conferencing services provided by some of the same companies that provide long distance telephone services. MCIMail was a relatively early entry into the electronic mail provider market, and its addresses are interestingly constructed to resemble telephone numbers.

These services usually offer a method of exchanging e-mail with the Internet. They aren't really networks themselves, but information services that grew out of efforts of the telephone carrier companies to provide added value and attract a different type of client.

▶ ▶ M A S T E R   W O R D S

> **SprintMail has a gateway to the Internet, operated by Merit Network, Inc., who also operate the Michigan midlevel network. But CompuServe users cannot take advantage of this gateway: SprintNet, because of its competition with CompuServe, rejects any CompuServe mail that passes through the gateway.**

▶ CompuServe, AOL, Prodigy, and Genie

These commercial, for-fee services are the consumer information service providers. Specializing in discussion forums, airline reservation systems, encyclopedias, and the like, these services deployed private networks throughout the US and Canada to provide services to individual consumers.

With the rise in popularity of the Internet, more cross-connections have sprung up—otherwise, these providers would have lost customers. It is now possible to send electronic mail from and to each of these three services from the Internet. Subscribers to these services usually pay surcharges for their electronic mail and may pay surcharges to receive mail from or send mail to the Internet.

CompuServe has long been the home of discussion forums for some vendors of computing and telecommunications equipment. It is an excellent service for business people and is particularly strong in its collection of databases.

 ▶ ▶ **WARNING**

> **CompuServe charges for receiving and sending Internet-originated e-mail are extremely high, and there are also strict message length limits. It may not be possible to successfully subscribe to electronic mailing lists that originate on the Internet (you'll learn about these mailing lists in Chapter 12) without spending a large amount of money.**

America Online (AOL) has recently been specializing in newspapers and discussions focused on current news. It is a middle-ground between the business orientation of CompuServe and the home orientation of Prodigy. Prodigy has professional hosts for some of their forums and provides contributions from professionals in many fields to add to the value of the discussions. Each service is designed to serve a specific information market and the offerings of the services will change with time as the wishes of the marketplace dictate. All these services now provide access to and from the Internet (via e-mail, Gopher, and newsgroups).

► ►MASTER WORDS

As this book went to press, America Online had just bought one of the largest commercial providers, ANS. This may change their provision of services dramatically in 1995. Also note that America Online has strong restrictions in their appropriate-use policies about what kinds of material can pass through their machines. If you are considering getting an account with them, be sure and check out what you are agreeing to before you sign it.

GEnie had a relatively early separate user interface that worked with some of the more graphically oriented small computers like the Atari.

In general, though, the basic difference between these commercial services and the Internet is that they are coherent environments. Someone selects and presents the information. The Internet is not a coherent environment, and until additional ways of indexing are invented and deployed, discovering the information available takes much hard work.

Luckily for users, the tools for accessing information over the Internet are improving constantly. If you learn to use the tools we present in the book, your search for information will be much easier and even a lot of fun.

► *Dialog, Dow Jones News/Retrieval, Lexis and Nexus*

Dialog and Dow Jones News/Retrieval are two of the information providers whose databases are available via Internet doorways. In these cases, the Internet does indeed serve as an Information Highway, but it only delivers you to the front door of these services, which have long provided dial-up access to their databases.

Dialog and Dow Jones are expensive, fee-based services. You must have arranged for an account in advance; you are charged either for time spent on the service, for materials retrieved, or a combination. It is possible to spend quite a bit of money searching these services for information if you do not know how to properly frame the search.

Dialog users pay fees based on a combination of connect time and records retrieved. Dialog provides a large number of databases and their indexes, for searching by experienced professional researchers. In general, Dialog's services are best employed by trained searchers who can design "search arguments" to best find the information you seek.

While some of the material indexed by Dialog is also present in the Dow Jones News/Retrieval system, Dow Jones specializes in information for businesses: articles from the business press and stock information are the specialties of this group. Like Dialog, this service was originally available through a private network and a combination of other connection options. Dow Jones expanded into using the Internet when they became aware how many of their academic customers were already connected to the Internet.

Lexus and Nexus are, respectively, Legal and Journalism archives, operated by Mead Data Central. Both have gateways from the Internet; like Dialog and Dow Jones, these are specialized, fee-based services.

▶▶ *The Game of Life*

Watching the Internet grow has been a little like a popular time-eater on many mainframes in the 70s and 80s: The Game of Life. In Life you develop figures on a grid, set the game running, and see whether your figures will grow into a stable configuration, grow and expand, or eventually eat each other and die.

The Internet's phenomenal growth in just the past few years has been much like that game: from a few groups doing really exciting projects in isolation; to a point where *Newsweek* has had at least two cover stories in 1994 exploring the phenomenon of the Internet. Now the Net is growing explosively, new services are springing up all around us, and there appear to be plenty of rich resources to keep it growing. As more and more people discover that the Internet can be theirs to use—to communicate better, to get better information for their work and play— the Net can only continue to grow.

For beginners, netsurfing (a common metaphor for exploring the Net) has never been easier. With the advent or the World Wide Web, Gopher searching tools, and graphical interfaces which let you use familiar tools to do your work, communicating, finding and distributing information, and sharing really cool resources on the Net is much simpler than it was even five years ago. School kids and grandparents are surfing the Net and coming up with treasures to make life more interesting and easier.

For those who have been watching the development of the Net through the popular media, or even swimming in the shallows, there are exciting things on the horizon: the development of audio and visual conferencing; more countries getting better connections; more schools, small businesses, and non-profit organizations getting linked in so they can talk to each other, and provisions in many broad, sweeping bills in the US Congress to include a data infrastructure along with the social or economic advantages of the legislation.

There have been some scary moments for all of us: the Morris worm, when the newspapers and radio waves were full of reports about how the worm was going to bring down the entire network (and did, in fact, bring down large chunks of it); and the security scares of sniffers, when lots of folks discovered that even having a password wasn't good enough, because someone might steal it. But we have also learned how to protect ourselves and our data better. We learned we didn't live in a small town anymore: we'd better lock our doors and our cars and take the keys with us.

We're out of the infancy of the Internet, and into the toddlerhood. It's an exciting time of growth and learning, and occasionally we may fall and bump our nose. But the opportunities, and the adventure, are there for everyone.

## CHAPTER 2

Picking a Model of the Internet

▶ ▶ **L**ike anything else, the Internet is easier to learn about if you can develop a model that helps you think about it.

When we study the theory of any subject, we first learn to develop maps that enable us to return to the same departure point and then perhaps start off in another direction, mapping new areas as we travel. Each time we review our knowledge, we add enhancements to our notes, and while we don't necessarily end up with something as valuable as *The Journals of Lewis and Clark*, we do add to our own body of knowledge and to our own understanding. Sometimes we are able to borrow from one discipline to help our understanding of another, and all of us borrow from the ideas of other individuals we know.

For the authors of this book the value of the Internet lies in the way people communicate with each other. When we were planning this book, we talked about why we wanted to share our knowledge of the Internet with you. For both of us, the important element is not the resources you can use, the things you can get, or the limitless commercial opportunities available on the Internet. It's the ability to communicate quickly—to get information to one or many people efficiently and effectively.

Communication is the key.

Communication happens between people, not between machines. Machines, fiber optics, modems, and software are not the heart of this resource. *People*, and the ways they communicate, are what intrigues us.

▶ ▶ *Getting Personal over the Net*

For you to understand why the authors are so excited about the Internet, it's important that you understand a little about how we use it.

When we first met, Pat was a consultant for MichNet (the regional Internet for Michigan) and Glee came to the NSFNET Information Services group at Merit. It became apparent to us that we were alike in some fundamental ways. The most important of them was that we are *people* people, and that good communication between people was one of the cornerstones of all our relationships.

We are both readers (perhaps a dying breed: recent studies show people who read regularly make up less than 20 percent of the population of the United States), as well as parents, writers, and journalists. Our training and inclination lead us to use every tool at our disposal to communicate. And so we came to use the networks.

Glee's first use of networks was as part of a problem-solving effort in the larger community of her work life. She used networking tools—file sharing, e-mail, talk functions—as simply one option to improve communication and solve problems.

Glee is one of the people who helped start the process of getting library card catalogues on-line; first, for just the use of folks within the library walls, and then for the world to access. She's helped develop not only the technology to share information about acquisitions and circulation, but the policies to keep that information flowing within the comfort zones of the folks who have to baby-sit it.

As her career expanded, and as networking technology evolved, communications via the network became one of the easiest and cheapest ways to keep in touch. It's a lot easier in the middle of a hectic working day to dash off a note to a collaborator at another university via e-mail than it is to type it up, put it in an envelope, find a stamp, and remember to stick it in the mailbox. And Glee's work has always put her in contact with folks all over the world: when Pat met her she was corresponding regularly and fluently over the bewildering array of e-mail networks with folks Pat had only heard of by name or seen mentioned in footnotes or resource lists.

Glee introduced Pat to the world of interest-based mailing lists: lists about mystery writers, journalism, and parent resources. Pat used to think Glee knew everything; now Pat realizes that she simply knows who to ask, over the expanding net of people on-line.

▸ *Electronic Lifelines*

This wide network of correspondents and friends became a lifeline when Glee's husband Frank was diagnosed with cancer. Glee turned to her friends and contacts, and found medical information, support groups, people to help with financial planning and legal matters. And she found a way to be surrounded by loving friends who were accessible without regard to time zones, work schedules, or physical location.

(No, electronic communities can't take the place of people being there to help with cooking and visits. Virtual hugs can't replace strong arms and shoulders. But they can go a long way, especially when the networks let you link up with so *many* people and keep you in touch with people you haven't seen in years.)

Frank was able to keep working for a long time after his illness became acute, because he could use a computer that connected him to the exceptional University of Michigan campus network right from his bedside in the UM Hospital. And we could talk to him daily, keep him involved with the details of life around him, and be reassured about him the same way.

After Frank's death, Glee's network of people on the Net was one of her best support groups. And when she decided to go back to California from Michigan, they helped with everything from moving arrangements to school registration, arranging lunches, and welcoming parties. After she left, she and Pat still talked. It seemed to Pat that their friendship was kept strong, like those of the ladies in the Victorian epistolary societies, by the letters they exchanged via e-mail.

▸ *Teething on Data Communication*

For Pat computer networks started as a way to stay home and do college homework on icy Massachusetts winter evenings. She used a 300 bps modem to dial into the Massachusetts State College system infant network and type programs (and term papers!) into the Dec20 mainframe. Her fellow students left messages in files, where they traded notes on eighteenth-century literature and programming algorithms.

When Pat went to work for the Michigan State University College of Agriculture, she discovered on-line information systems and e-mail. She could talk to all of the state's 80 counties at once, with one message, or talk to individual staff members about their computing problems. Pat was giddy with the power of easily accessible information. Her group set up an exchange listing for farmers who wanted to either sell or buy hay in Michigan's severe drought, creating on-line newsletters, system notices, and a database of all the Cooperative Extension Service bulletins.

From there it was a tiny step to staff conferencing, electronic postmastering, anonymous FTP, and all the other tools we had at hand at MichNet. Pat is not sure which was more fulfilling: teaching folks at other universities about the ease and utility of communicating via the network, or doing it. She watched as more and more colleges and universities came on-line via Merit, and then we saw the NSFNET Information team not only teaching about the ocean of resources available on the Net but building some of those resources.

Now Pat, too, is living in California. (She got her current job answering an on-line job announcement in the MSEN Gopher server. She faxed a copy of her resume, sent an e-mail letter of introduction, and had a phone interview less than 4 hours later.) Pat has used e-mail to talk to her teenager living with her father back in Michigan, she touches bases with her husband using UNIX *talk* at least twice a day (their offices are 200 miles apart), and Glee and Pat have planned this book together over e-mail.

▶ *Not Consumers, but Communicators*

As we explore the Internet in the next few years, as some of the wild expansion starts to slow down and the bewildering flurry of TLAs (three letter acronyms) and competing technologies shake out, people will begin to see that the point is not being *consumers* of resources, but *communicators*.

Teachers in schools linked to the Internet find that kids who previously had no interest in verbal communication are learning to read and write. Why? Because they are communicating with their peers over e-mail and conferencing systems, and they have to be able to effectively communicate using written language to get the respect of the people who matter to them. We've struggled to encourage literacy in our children: perhaps computers, and the ability to communicate, will be the best incentive.

PC Magazine's Jim Seymour has written about the death of David Alsberg. Alsberg was a friend he had come to know only over the Net, but his tragic shooting death affected hundreds, perhaps thousands who knew his integrity, his involvement with humanity, and his passionate beliefs only from his on-line participation. Seymour talks about the community of friends and colleagues on the Net, and how the virtual involvement of these people with one another had created real feeling links between them.

Finally, we saw the power of network-mediated communications when Pat's friend and co-worker at Cygnus Support, Brendan Kehoe, had a terrible car accident the morning of December 31, 1993. He was hospitalized, in a coma, and initial reports said that the injury was in the part of the brain that controls language functions. It was thought this talented programmer and writer (author of *Zen and the Art of the Internet*) might not be able to speak again. E-mail bulletins began to go out. Electronic mailing lists were formed.

Jeffrey Osier, another co-worker, went from California to Pennsylvania to help Brendan and his family, and almost immediately someone volunteered a network connection to help him stay in touch. Cygnus put up public information files and mail reflectors so people could get automatic updates, like the one shown in Figure 2.1, pulled from Jeffrey's messages back to Cygnus. Brendan not only recovered but, as you can see from this note in his .plan file, is back to work and doing well.

Pat handled mail from hundreds of people sending good wishes to Brendan, and much of it was from people who, like him, had suffered closed-head trauma. Some of them had found that the Internet was a godsend: they could communicate effectively even when they had lost the power to speak. We discovered, once again, what we had always known: The most important use of the network is to communicate. To make the connection between people, and let them share information, feelings, and concern for one another.

Everything else is just technology.

FIGURE 2.1

An update on Brendan via Finger.

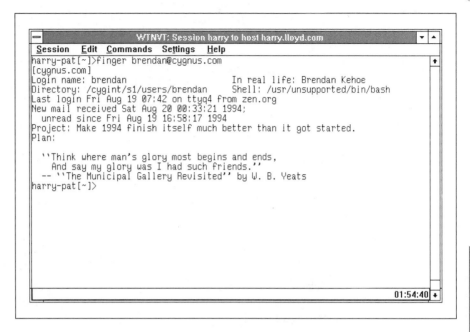

►► *Communication Is the Key*

The Internet, in some ways a model of the way people interact in real space, can be described using several kinds of theories. Computer scientists have a variety of technical models of the Internet: They largely describe the mechanisms which facilitate communication, but don't aid in understanding how and why communication happens on the Internet. For us, the theories about *communication* prove most useful in understanding the tools and interactions in cyberspace.

Communication theories talk about how information is disseminated, who is providing it, and how trustworthy that information is. This is precisely what we need to know about information we get via the Internet.

Elementary communication theory describes the methods of communication as falling into a very few categories: one provider to one recipient, one provider to many recipients, and many providers to many recipients. Rob Raisch of the Internet Company (raisch@internet.com) developed an applied taxonomy for Internet tools that defined the types of on-line communication outlined below.

Communication Method	Tools	Type
One to one	E-mail, talk	Individual communication
One to many	Gopher, WAIS, WWW, mailing lists	Distributed communication
Many to many	Usenet news, IRC	Collaborative communication

As part of his Raisch's taxonomy, he placed the various Internet tools in the appropriate categories. Daniel P. Dern (ddern@world.std.com) developed a slightly different matrix when he described the tools in terms of communication activities instead of communication types, as shown here.

Communication Method	Tools	Activities
One to one	e-mail, anonymous FTP	Narrowcasting: explicit delivery/Respond to requests
One to many	Gopher WWW, anonymous FTP, Usenet news	Broadcasting/ Publishing

Both of these groupings are helpful in seeing possibilities, but two-dimensional matrices (even with three columns!) are not really adequate to describe communication via the Internet, particularly the important additional concepts of temporality, public versus private communication, and the authoritativeness (trustworthiness) of the information received. We've made our own attempt in Table 2.1.

▶ **TABLE 2.1:** *Internet Communication Modes*

TYPE	COMMUNICATION	NON-SIMULTANEOUS	INTERACTIVE/ SIMULTANEOUS
Type I	Private; individual to individual recipient; may be authoritative	e-mail including prepared e-mail auto-responses; individual files placed for ftp; files displayed by finger	talk
Type II	Public; many contributors to many recipients; non-authoritative	Unmoderated mailing lists; unmoderated Usenet newsgroups	IRC; MUDs and MUSEs
Type III	Public; many contributors to many recipients; may be authoritative	Moderated mailing lists; moderated Usenet newsgroups	CU-SeeMe and Maven
Type IV	Public; published contributions to many recipients; authoritative	Web pages; gopher servers; corporate/ organizational files placed for ftp and finger; searchable databases	Broadcast messages on systems and networks

▶▶ *Looking over the Tools*

As with any kind of framework, there are cases where the frame cannot be bent to fit. In the case of Internet tools, there is one glaring omission from the tools so nicely placed in the box above: Telnet. Figure 2.2 shows a sample Telnet session.

▶ ▶ **M A S T E R   W O R D S**

> **Remember that we talked about telnet in the last chapter. If the Internet is the Information Highway, telnet is the automobile or vehicle we use to get us to the various resources on the Net.**

FIGURE 2.2 ▶

*A simple Telnet session
to the Merit/Michnet
Gateway.*

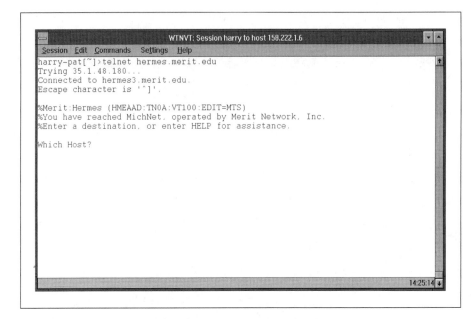

```
WTNVT: Session harry to host 158.222.1.6
Session  Edit  Commands  Settings  Help
harry-pat[~]>telnet hermes.merit.edu
Trying 35.1.48.180...
Connected to hermes3.merit.edu.
Escape character is '^]'.

%Merit:Hermes (HMEAAD:TN0A:VT100:EDIT=MTS)
%You have reached MichNet, operated by Merit Network, Inc.
%Enter a destination, or enter HELP for assistance.

Which Host?
                                                                    14:25:14
```

Telnet is an anomalous case because rather than searching, retrieving, indexing, or displaying data or information, it simply allows you to transport your point of view. Telnet logs you in to another computer system as if your computer system were a terminal.

There is also no tool that easily fits into the Interactive/Simultaneous, Public category. The developing use of the MBONE (Multicast Backbone) system for audio broadcasts over the Net begins to fit this box when it is used to broadcast conference proceedings and meetings. An early start at conferencing systems for relatively inexpensive desktop systems is the program CU-SeeMe developed at Cornell University. Used effectively by the Global Schoolhouse Project (http://k12.cnidr.org/gshwelcome.html), CU-SeeMe has been used to link classrooms in shared activities quite successfully using Macintosh and Windows machines in the schoolroom, connected via the Internet. Early use of the video software demonstrated that audio was necessary, too. George H. Brett of CNIDR (The Clearinghouse for Networked Information Discovery and Retrieval) tells how the kids began writing signs and holding them up to the cameras so they could "talk" to their connected colleagues. Charley Kline of the University of Illinois contribued Maven, an audio tool for the Macintosh, that has been incorporated into later versions of CU-SeeMe for that computer. VAT and nv, audio and video conferencing tools, provide similar function on UNIX workstation computers.

The matrix is useful in discussing how and why people want to use the Internet, because it describes the number of respondents, the validity of the information in communication, whether the communication is public, and whether it is interactive—all the things you need to know about communicating on a network.

▶▶ *"Can We Talk?": Type I Internet Communications*

E-mail, e-mail auto-responses, FTP, files displayed by Finger, and Talk are all Type I Internet communications.

▶ *E-Mail*

The most common of the communication methods used by people on the Internet is the private letter, written by one individual to another individual recipient (on any subject and in any language), and sent between any two connected Internet sites or through an Internet e-mail gateway to or from a service which provides an Internet gateway. Figure 2.3 shows a typical e-mail message.

You can exchange e-mail using either NetCruiser, on Companion Disk 1, or the Chameleon Sampler, on Companion Disk 2. E-mail is the subject of Chapter 8.

As a *recipient* you need to evaluate the information in the message by the same criteria you would use to judge the value of a similar communication received in a letter, phone call, or fax. It *may* be valid, or it may be rumor. Since (generally) e-mail is unmonitored, only you can judge. Remember, the only difference between e-mail and these other methods of communication is that it is occasionally easier to send e-mail than it is to make a telephone call, and sometimes it is less expensive.

FIGURE 2.3 ▸

A typical e-mail message.

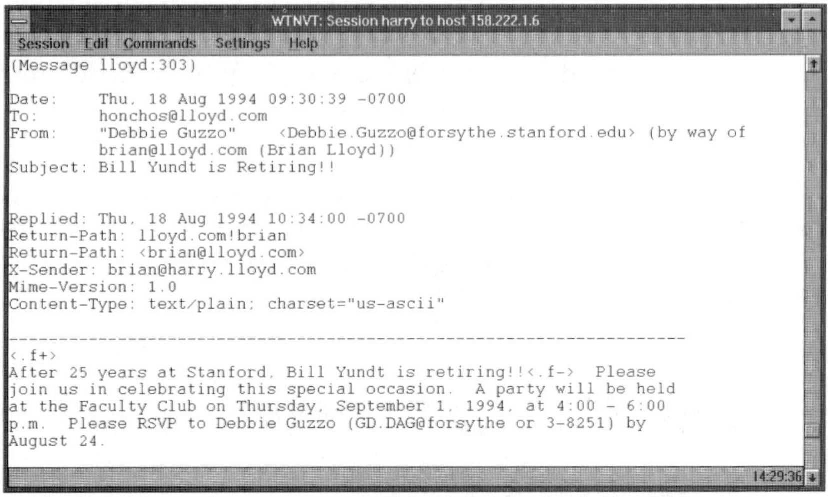

```
┌─────────────────────────────────────────────────────────────────┐
│ ▄                  WTNVT: Session harry to host 158.222.1.6    ▾ ▲│
│ Session  Edit  Commands   Settings  Help                         │
│ (Message lloyd:303)                                            ↑  │
│                                                                  │
│ Date:      Thu, 18 Aug 1994 09:30:39 -0700                       │
│ To:        honchos@lloyd.com                                     │
│ From:      "Debbie Guzzo"    <Debbie.Guzzo@forsythe.stanford.edu> (by way of│
│            brian@lloyd.com (Brian Lloyd))                        │
│ Subject: Bill Yundt is Retiring!!                                │
│                                                                  │
│                                                                  │
│ Replied: Thu, 18 Aug 1994 10:34:00 -0700                         │
│ Return-Path: lloyd.com!brian                                     │
│ Return-Path: <brian@lloyd.com>                                   │
│ X-Sender: brian@harry.lloyd.com                                  │
│ Mime-Version: 1.0                                                │
│ Content-Type: text/plain; charset="us-ascii"                     │
│ ─────────────────────────────────────────────────────────────── │
│ <.f+>                                                            │
│ After 25 years at Stanford, Bill Yundt is retiring!!<.f->  Please│
│ join us in celebrating this special occasion.  A party will be held│
│ at the Faculty Club on Thursday, September 1, 1994, at 4:00 - 6:00│
│ p.m.  Please RSVP to Debbie Guzzo (GD.DAG@forsythe or 3-8251) by  │
│ August 24.                                                       │
│                                                       14:29:36 ↓  │
└─────────────────────────────────────────────────────────────────┘
```

MASTER WORDS

Not all e-mail stays confidential. Some systems administrators monitor e-mail via automated programs to look for key words which indicate that illicit or commercially damaging e-mail is being sent. If you don't know whether your e-mail is being monitored, find out. Also, if there is a problem with your e-mail, it may bounce, text and all, to the mailbox of a postmaster on your system or another system. Remember: *Never send anything via e-mail you wouldn't want to see posted on the cafeteria bulletin board!*

Trustworthy or Not?

How should you evaluate the validity of the contents of an e-mail message? Ask yourself the following kinds of questions:

- Who was the sender?
- Was this person someone you know?

- Was it someone you can believe wholeheartedly?

- Was it someone who is an expert in the field being discussed?

- Is this letter in response to something you sent? If yes, is the response appropriate for the type of query?

If none of these things are true, and the sender is not known to you, is the message in response to something you "said" somewhere on the Net? If yes, is the message an appropriate response?

You can *sort* your e-mail using much the same criteria that you use with your postal mail. Some gets answered immediately, some gets put by until more information or time is available to answer it, some is saved for reference, and some gets deleted immediately.

Contact with Strangers

There are several reasons you may receive more e-mail than paper mail from people you do not know. E-mail is private and easy to send; you may not receive the e-mail immediately and be able to respond; and the sender need not actually be in the room with you or talk with you *in person*.

For example, Bill Gates, founder of Microsoft, once had his e-mail address published in an article which appeared in the national press. His mailbox was inundated. We're betting that he had that e-mail address changed almost immediately.

During the first debates about gays in the military, CompuServe reported that the CompuServe e-mail address of President Bill Clinton, which was set up during the campaign but was not set up to handle mass quantities of e-mail, was receiving over 400 e-mail messages *per hour*. The mailbox soon ran out of disk space, and more had to be hastily allotted. Because the White House wasn't set up to handle e-mail yet, each of these messages had to be printed out to be sorted and dealt with.

Other e-mail users may send you mail because they associate your e-mail address with a product or idea that they believe you know about. You may be a published expert in some field. If your e-mail address becomes known, you may receive inquiries asking your opinions about ideas in your field, or from people seeking advice. In the Internet community, such inquiries are common and people generally reply. If you do not wish to reply, you need not. Or you may just reply that you prefer not to answer unsolicited mail.

Safety at a Distance

We have systems set up to handle problems with annoying or obscene paper letters or phone calls, but some people don't know what to do if they get e-mail that they find inappropriate. E-mail may contain messages that are rude or suggestive because the sender knows that it is relatively safe to act without consideration for the recipient. You may be nothing more than just a few characters on the screen to the sender.

If you receive offensive e-mail, respond promptly with a request that you not receive further e-mail from this person. If the sender continues to send e-mail you do not wish to receive, contact the postmaster at the site from which the mail is sent. Just as with paper mail or phone calls, there are policies in place at almost every e-mail provider to prevent people from sending you e-mail you do not want. The electronic postmaster, whose tasks are actually much like his or her paper mail colleagues, is there to assist you.

Is It Really Confidential?

Finally, e-mail, while private between individuals, should not necessarily be considered privileged. If you really need to say something that must remain absolutely confidential, you probably shouldn't say it in e-mail. Some e-mail systems automatically file copies of all e-mail you send. Sometimes e-mail *bounces* (is undeliverable for any number of reasons) and your e-mail will end up in the mailbox of a postmaster along the route. Sometimes your recipient will print your message and the printed copy will lay near the printer for others to read. Your recipient may forward it on to someone else, without thinking about your privacy or your concerns. All sorts of things that you didn't intend to happen, can happen.

▶ E-Mail Auto-Responses

The e-mail equivalent of the direct response postal card is the prepared e-mail auto-response. The message is a composed one, especially prepared as an automatic answer to any e-mail that gets sent to that address.

There are two common uses for this type of message. The first is to notify the sender that the receiver may not answer the e-mail for some time—like when you are away from your e-mail system. If you (and your correspondents) are lucky, the automated program that sends these messages will only send a response once per week to each individual e-mail address that it receives messages from.

The other use is to distribute messages about products or services of a particular organization. When you send messages to an address like info@clue.org, you will most likely receive an individual piece of e-mail delivered to your mailbox that will explain the types of clues that you can obtain from this organization, perhaps where to get them and how much you would be charged if you wanted to purchase one. The message will usually contain something that will tell you where to get more information.

Sometimes people get creative with automatic e-mail responses. At Cygnus Support in Mountain View, California, folks who sent e-mail to xmastree@cygnus.com got the response shown in Figure 2.4.

FIGURE 2.4 ▶

Cygnus Christmas tree viewed by Finger.

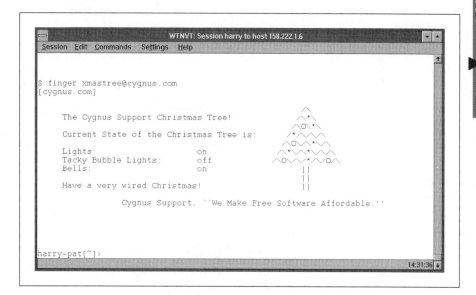

► FTP

FTP is an Internet tool that copies a file from one Internet site to another. FTP stands for both *file transfer protocol* and *file transfer program*, the specific program that implements the transfer. With the Internet address or domain name of a site, you can use FTP to connect to a specific location on that site (specific directory path and file name) and copy a file containing information to or from your computer for your own use. This activity is individual and private, although many FTP sights log (or register) file copy transactions for either market research or as security precautions. In the case of individuals sharing information, the file was prepared and stored specifically for you by the person distributing the information.

FTP is one of the ways the authors shared our work in writing this book—a splendid example of individual communication. One of us would prepare a file for transmission and then send e-mail to the other which contained the name of the file and its location. We used a special kind of security to make sure that no one could access this information without our permission, by using a special form of FTP program which requires a password before allowing access to the FTP directory. Figure 2.5 shows how we copied files from one workstation to the computer we used as a host.

FIGURE 2.5 ►

FTPing files for this book.

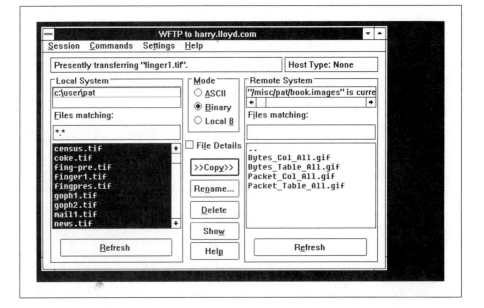

FTP does not require that both individuals be logged into connected networks during the file transmission. This makes FTP an *asynchronous* or non-simultaneous activity. When Pat prepared files for Glee to receive, she would sometimes place them in the wee hours of the morning, and Glee would grab them off the FTP machine in mid-morning or late afternoon. Their computers didn't have to both be logged in at the same time.

MASTER WORDS

While FTP does not need sender and recipient to be logged into their respective computers at the same time, it does require that both sites be connected at the same time. If either host goes down (stops working or *crashes*), the FTP transaction will halt. One of the best times to use FTP is overnight. Start the transfer just before you go to bed, and let it work overnight while you sleep.

Please note: FTP can also be used for mass distribution. We will discuss how it functions in that capacity in Chapters 9 and 16. You can try FTP using either NetCruiser, on Companion Disk 1, or the Chameleon Sampler, on Companion Disk 2.

▶ Files Displayed by Finger

The Finger command displays the contents of a file associated with a particular user ID at a particular Internet site. Not all sites support access to information files via the Finger command. Some sites don't support Finger because they wish to preserve the privacy of their user community. Some sites don't support access via the Finger command for security reasons. And some sites don't support it because the operating system they use makes it difficult to support this type of access. For sites that do support such access, sending

```
finger skywalker@tatooine.org
```

will usually return information about whether that user ID is being used at that moment, and whether the user has mail waiting to be read. Lastly, it will display the contents of a .plan file. This file can contain any information that the file owner wishes. Some people use this file to convey information about sports scores or climatic conditions or earthquake activity. Both Internet sites need to be on the network to support the transaction, but the user being fingered need not be connected to the network to have information conveyed to the requester. Figure 2.6 shows a typical .plan file.

▶ ▶ M A S T E R   W O R D S

EDUCOM, the association of educators using computers, recommended in mid-1994 that Finger be disabled on all network-linked computers, because of the security and privacy hole it created. See Chapter 7, "Observing the Rules of the Road," for more detailed information on Finger and what can be learned from it.

FIGURE 2.6 ▶

Using Finger to find out how to send e-mail to someone.

```
┌─────────────────────────────────────────────────────────────────────┐
│ ═     WTNVT: Session harry to host harry.lloyd.com        ▼ ▲ │
│  Session  Edit  Commands  Settings  Help                              │
│ harry-pat[~]>finger jeffrey@zen.org                                ↑ │
│ [zen.org]                                                             │
│ Login name: jeffrey                    In real life: Jeffrey Osier   │
│ Directory: /home/jeffrey               Shell: /bin/bash              │
│ Last login Fri Aug 19 18:49 on console                               │
│ New mail received Fri Aug 19 22:19:02 1994;                          │
│   unread since Fri Aug 19 17:35:49 1994                              │
│ Project: Life, in general.                                           │
│ Plan:                                                                │
│                                                                      │
│ Hey, thanks for the finger!  All mine are still in working order, but│
│ you never know when you might need an extra digit.                   │
│                                                                      │
│ Current plans:                                                       │
│         on vacation until August 1                                   │
│         working on a hypertext book (ask me about it!)               │
│         trying to figure out what life's really about                │
│                                                                      │
│ harry-pat[~]>                                                        │
│                                                                      │
│                                                                      │
│                                                                      │
│                                                                      │
│                                                         01:53:24 ↓ │
└─────────────────────────────────────────────────────────────────────┘
```

▶ *Talk*

E-mail, FTP, and Finger are *asynchronous*. That is, the two communicating parties need not be connected to the Internet at the same time in order to exchange information. E-mail-delivery systems, for example, store your messages until you connect and ask to see them. The *synchronous* or *interactive* equivalent to e-mail is *Talk*, discussed in Chapter 14.

Talk is also private communication between two individuals. The individuals can be connected through any two Internet sites and the content of the messages is not monitored. Talk is simultaneous: it does require that both parties be connected at the same time. Figure 2.7 shows a typical Talk session. Conversations, or *Talk sessions*, may be initiated by any party with a request. The recipient of the request may accept the invitation and begin a conversation. If you don't want to talk, simply don't respond to the invitation. In the "Sex in Cyberspace" stories, there seem to be hints of lots of unwanted approaches to talk across the Internet. Since there is no way to monitor content, it is unclear how many uses of Talk are the sort of *private* that should stay private. Talk can be very useful, however, for the sort of quick check needed between housemates as to who is going home to feed the cats or who is dropping by the store to pick up the milk. In other words,

Picking a Model of the Internet

▶ ▶

ch.
2

FIGURE 2.7 ▶

Beginning a Talk session.

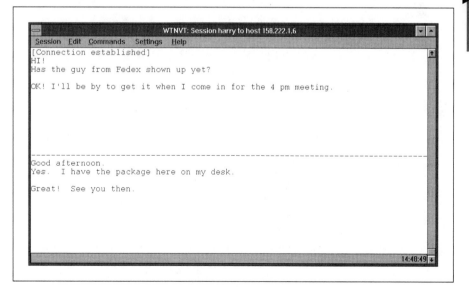

Talk is appropriate for ephemeral conversations—those just for fun—or for quick communications among co-workers and colleagues. Talk is for the sort of communication that doesn't need to be recorded for posterity.

►► *"Citizens' Band (CB) Internet": Type II Internet Communications*

Perhaps the most talked about aspect of Internet communications is the very public communications that take place on unmoderated mailing lists or within unmoderated newsgroups. These communications come from many contributors and are distributed to many recipients. While the information contained in them may be very useful, in general the information is non-authoritative. That means that, while the person giving the information may have the best of intentions, the information may not be true. Much of the discussion will be subjective: one person's opinion versus another's. Again you will need learn to filter the information and find out what is useful and trustworthy.

► *Unmoderated Mailing Lists*

A mailing list is a list of e-mail addresses. A message sent to a mailing list is re-sent to each e-mail address on the list. Many of the mailing lists (groups of people who wish to receive the same information) are unmoderated and open. This means that you are welcome to join (or subscribe to) a list and to post your contributions to the list. You may also unsubscribe at will. Therefore, the people who read the list will vary widely from time to time.

There will probably be a charter or statement of purpose and some general statements about what topics are acceptable to the mailing list and what topics are not. In general, while you may make contributions that are *off topic*, if you persist, others on the list will attempt to enforce the "rules" via peer pressure—e-mail to you personally and to the list suggesting that you keep to the topic. It is best to find a list that is discussing the topic in which you are interested.

Mailing lists are simply an extension of e-mail—easily copying a single mail message to many potentially interested persons, using e-mail as the transmission medium. As such, this type of communication is non-simultaneous.

▶ *Unmoderated Usenet Newsgroups*

A newsgroup is similar to a BBS or bulletin board system but one that has been copied to hundreds of computers throughout the world. People read a newsgroup on some local site and post their contributions to that local site. The contributions are then copied to the other sites which carry that particular newsgroup. Like unmoderated mailing lists, unmoderated newsgroups may be read and contributed to by anyone who can receive the newsgroup. You may *subscribe* to the newsgroup and post your own contributions. Also, as with mailing lists, it is possible to contribute to a newsgroup without actually following the newsgroup (reading the group consistently to understand the tenor of the discussion), but this is considered rude and you may well receive e-mail stating that opinion with varying degrees of vigor. Figure 2.8 shows a typical news item.

FIGURE 2.8 ▶

A typical news item on an unmoderated group.

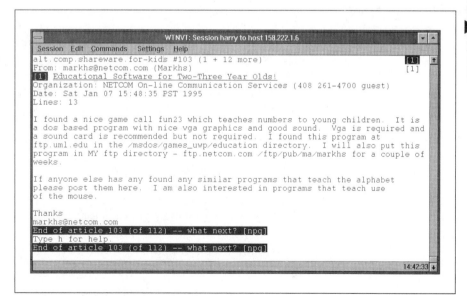

Each newsgroup has a charter that states the topic for discussion and the type of contributions that the newsgroup entertains. Again, a single off-topic posting usually will be tolerated as long as it does not continue. If the posting is clearly off-topic, particularly if the posting is construed as a commercial posting, complaints will be sent to the postmaster at your site. Depending on the policies of your site, you will probably be warned that you are not observing the charter of the group and you will be asked to stop. Some sites will take away your privileges if you persist in inappropriate postings.

Newsgroups are transmitted automatically. The messages are copied to each computer that runs news servers and that accepts and transmits postings for particular groups. Net News is co-operative and no site is required to accept the news feed for each and every newsgroup. Because each message is copied individually as part of a batch of messages, the communication is not simultaneous. Postings may take several days to reach all the sites that carry a particular group.

Usenet is the subject at Chapter 12, and you can connect to it using either NetCruiser, on Companion Disk 1, or the Chameleon Sampler, on Companion Disk 2.

▶ IRC

IRC stands for Internet Relay Chat and it can best be compared to CB (Citizen's Band) Radio. From an IRC server, you elect to *join* a *channel*. In IRC, each participant's contributions are displayed on the screens of all the others taking part in a conversation. Physically, this can be quite disconcerting until you are experienced enough not to be bothered by entering data into an environment where you can't really see what you have written until you press the Enter key.

In IRC, you can join an existing conversation or try to start one of your own. The topics being discussed will be as varied as the people participating. When you join, your name (or nickname) will be announced to others on that channel. Therefore, while you can be anonymous (by using a nickname that will hide your real identity) you cannot *lurk* as you can in mailing lists and newsgroups. Others will know that another person is there watching and listening.

IRC is definitely individual and simultaneous. There can be few or many participants at any given time.

IRC is discussed in Chapter 14, and you can try it out using Net-Cruiser, on Companion Disk 2.

▶ ▶ MASTER WORDS

One of the most fascinating uses of IRC came during the Gulf War when participants in Tel Aviv, inside their plastic-sealed living rooms and bedrooms, kept the rest of the world informed about the progress of the Iraqi attack on their city. IRC participants could "hear" first-hand accounts of sirens, bomb impacts, and the spectacular Patriot-SCUD explosions over the city. They also learned how teens and older people felt, living in danger of poison gas, huddled in their homes for what little protection they offered. The humanity of the people in the war became personal for a generation removed from the realities of Vietnam or the radio broadcasts from the London Blitz.

▶ MUDs and MUSEs

MUDs (Multi-User Dungeons) and MUSEs (Multi-User Simulation Environments) are contributions from the gaming community. When you participate in these shared worlds, you communicate with others who are simultaneously taking part.

The difference between MUDs and MUSEs and IRC is not in the number and type of participants, nor in the general technology used. It's that MUDs and MUSEs postulate rules and environments that are shared. The environments may be imaginary or not. You may participate as yourself or as a character you construct (by your own rules or by the rules of the world you wish to share). In these shared worlds, the characters you construct walk around and converse with other characters created by other participants. Most of the shared worlds are intended for recreational use, but some are educational. Some corporations and think tanks are beginning to use this technology to have multi-level discussions not bounded by physical location or time zones. And some of the shared environments have been running for years (although not with exactly the same participants, of course).

Picking a Model
of the Internet

▶ ▶

ch.
2

MUDs are the subject of Chapter 15.

▶▶ *"Tower of Babel": Type III Internet Communications*

Some mailing lists and newsgroups are moderated. Moderation is not intended to make the postings more or less authoritative, but to make sure the postings stick to the topic. The moderator may be the person who started the mailing list or newsgroup, or it may be someone selected later. The duties of the moderator vary according to the available software and according to the nature of the group. Since only mailing lists and newsgroups are moderated, this type of communication, like all unmoderated mailing lists and newsgroups, is non-simultaneous.

▶ *Moderated Mailing Lists*

On a moderated mailing list all messages sent to it go directly to a moderator. The moderator then determines if the message should be sent on to the list. The moderator will forward the message or return it with a message explaining that it was inappropriate.

Participants in a moderated mailing list will never receive a request to subscribe accidentally posted to the entire list. This is the easiest of decisions that a moderator makes, and the easiest for mailing list participants to understand. In a large mailing list, one with several hundred participants, mis-sent subscription requests can clutter network bandwidth with useless transmissions.

Difficult decisions for moderators are those that involve deciding not to forward a posting that contains a request for information about something not quite *on topic*. Many moderators will let a discussion that is *off topic* continue for several days and then intervene by sending a message to the list reminding the participants of the purpose of the list. This way, a list intended to discuss murder mysteries does not end up being dominated by discussions of the names of the participants' cats and dogs for longer than a day or two.

> ## UNDERSTANDING BANDWIDTH
>
> *Bandwidth* is a technical term that describes the capacity of the physical network to carry traffic. It comes from radio technology, where it described how wide a radio channel or *band* was—how much information could be transmitted on it.
>
> Today networkers use bandwidth to describe not only the amount of data that can be transmitted over a network link (remember the OED table in Chapter 1?), but the amount of information available in a message. You may well see messages that talk about "emotional bandwidth" in e-mail messages or other on-line information sources. This describes how difficult it is to tell the speaker's emotions from the letters on the screen.
>
> Experienced networkers are very jealous of their bandwidth, and some can get pretty rude if they think you're wasting time, resources, or money.

▶ Moderated Usenet Newsgroups

Similar decisions are made by the moderators of newsgroups. Moderators are found particularly in the `*.announce` newsgroups. Because these groups are intended for announcements, an effort is made to make certain that the postings are appropriate for the newsgroup. Participants reading the group `ba.announce` (Bay Area Announce) want to be certain that posted announcements are for events in the next week or so and in the geographical location of the San Francisco Bay Area. The moderators reject postings that are not timely or not taking place in the Bay Area. This activity makes the postings authoritative, that is trustworthy.

▶ MBONE

MBONE (Multicast BackbONE) is an emerging technology that may very shortly fill the empty block in the chart we created above. MBONE is audio and video transmission over the Net. The group of engineers, scientists, and user services folks who are working on the structure of the Internet itself are experimenting with broadcasts of their conferences over MBONE. Speeches, news conferences, and other informational events have also been broadcast. Listeners all over the world could hear the conference proceedings right at their workstations.

When listening to an MBONE conference , you can hear many people discussing their views *in real time,* and hundreds of other listeners are hearing it, too. (It does indeed sometimes resemble the cacophony of the Tower of Babel.)

Because MBONE requires special routing hardware and software right now, it's not interactive, nor is it available to everyone. But within the next few years MBONE promises to become truly interactive, allowing video conferencing among multiple participants from their workstations anywhere on the Internet.

▶ *CU-SeeMe, Maven, and VAT*

CU-SeeMe, a video client/server program, and its companion audio program, Maven (for the Macintosh), come closer to the dream of a "picture telephone" over the Internet. CU-SeeMe was originally developed for the Macintosh and later also made available for Windows. CU-SeeMe can be used point to point (one machine connected to just one machine) or by using one of the reflector servers, you can get one-to-many or many-to-many conferences. With the CU-SeeMe client program, you can connect to a server and communicate! CU-SeeMe client programs can be senders or receivers or both. Receiving is simpler, of course, requiring only the client software and an Internet connection. Sending requires more equipment: a video board, a camera, and software to capture and transmit the video information.

Maven audio capabilities are built in to the later versions of the CU-SeeMe client programs for the Macintosh (Version 0.7 and later). More information and the programs themselves can be found at `ftp://ftp.gated.cornell.edu/pub/video`. Maven information can be found at

`http://pipkin.lut.ac.uk/WWWdocs/LUTCHI/misc/maven.html`

The program itself can be found at `ftp://k12.cnidr.org/pub/Mac`. Other programs of interest to people using Macintosh computers in the classroom will also be found there.

▶▶N O T E

> **Integrated audio and video requires a connection at 56 Kbps or higher or the video transmissions will be jerky and the audio will drop significant amounts of information. This means that you can run the programs at slower speeds, but the audio will not be intelligible. An alternative is to use CU-SeeMe to transmit the video and use a direct telephone connection between two points or an audio conference call between multiple points. With speaker telephones, this method will sometimes be quite effective.**

CU-SeeMe reflectors are run on UNIX systems that are enabled for Multicast transmission. This requires the cooperation of your network administrator and your network provider. Not all network providers offer multicast service.

Another available audio conferencing tool is VAT, available for some UNIX workstations (Some Sun Sparcstations, some Silicon Graphics workstations, some DECstations, and others). VAT supports both point-to-point and broadcast of audio using either multicast or unicast IP.

VAT is available from `ftp://cs.ucl.ac.uk/mice/videoconference/vat`. There is a Web page with a little information about VAT available at

`http://www.cs.ucl.ac.uk/mice/mice-nsc/s-vat.html`

Nv is a similar concept in video conference tools for UNIX workstations. It is availabe for Sun workstations with videopix and parallax framegrabbers, Silicon Graphics workstations with Indigo framegrabbers, and Decstations with Jvideo framegrabbers. More information is available from Ron Frederick (`frederic@parc.xerox.com`). The nv program is briefly described at `http://www.cs.ucl.ac.uk/mice/mice-nsc/s-nv.html` and is available itself from `ftp://cs.ucl.ac.uk/mice/video-conference/nv`.

It is possible for people running VAT to participate in audio conferences with people running Maven. The CU-SeeMe to VAT connections are being investigated.

▶▶ *"The Internet Daily Planet": Type IV Internet Communications*

The final type of communications that can be found on the Internet are the public, published contributions of individuals and companies that can be received by many recipients, and that may be thought of as authoritative. In effect, rather like a book, a directory, a magazine, or a radio or television broadcast.

Some authority has exercised editorial control over the content of this type of communication. The content represents an official statement, information about a product or a service, editorial or procedural matters, art work, catalogs, calendars for schools, colleges or universities. In short, these are published works intended for general or specific consumption, using the tools of the Internet for the communication medium.

▶ *Broadcast Messages*

There is only one type of communication in this category that is truly simultaneous: the broadcast message that is used by a system or network operator to communicate about the state of the network or system itself with everyone currently using it. Broadcast messages are sent from an operator to every person using a system at that time.

Broadcast messages are usually warnings about unusual activities such as system instabilities or outages. They are transmitted this way to reach the maximum number of affected people as quickly as possible.

▶ *World Wide Web Pages*

The World Wide Web, discussed in Chapter 11, is a distributed, hypertext collection of clients and servers that link a *page* to other *pages* throughout the global Internet. A page is simply a title, a collection of information, and pointers (hyperlinks) to other information. You view it using a client program which connects you to a server. Depending on the client you have, you can see color representations of lighthouses, art work, hear audio clips from recorded music, see movie clips, or fill out survey forms. For example, Figure 2.9 shows a picture from the Le WebLouvre Collection, which contains many of the pictures housed in the Louvre museum. Page designers publish their pages, leaving you to decide whether or not to view them at some subsequent time.

World Wide Web pages have become the glossy catalogs and magazines of the Internet community. Some pages are published by colleges and universities and serve as interactive catalogs representing their institutions. Other pages are catalogs of jewelry or shoes. And some pages are published materials that describe the person who designed and built the page. Pages representing institutions and enterprises are authoritative, that is they are authorized by the company or enterprise and can be trusted.

FIGURE 2.9 ▶

One of the images available through the Le WebLouvre page.

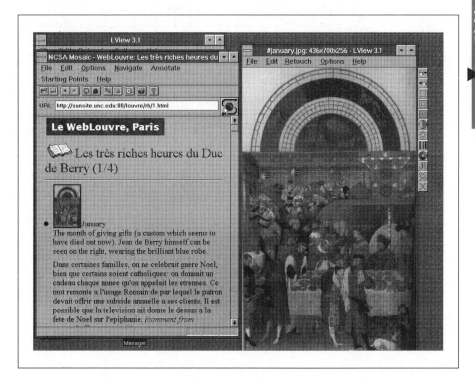

▶ ▶**TRY IT OUT!**

NetCruiser, on Companion Disk 1, includes a Web browser, and both Pat and Glee have Web pages you can look at. Look at Glee's pages by using a WWW client to find the Uniform Resource Locator (URL) http://www.netcom.com. **Pat can be reached by going to** http://www.lloyd.com/ **and clicking on the menu item with her name on it.**

▶ Gopher Servers

Gopher, also discussed in Chapter 11 and included in the NetCruiser software on Companion Disk 1, is another quickly spreading method of publishing material on the Internet. Gopher is a menu-driven client/server program that allows you to connect to and display files on your own system, or to transmit image files encoded for other clients, such as .gif or .tif image files. Gopher lets you link to and display menus and files from other Gopher servers throughout "gopherspace," making it unnecessary to gather all the information needed and place it on a single server. Figure 2.10 shows the U.S. government's Gopher server at the National Archives.

Since access to Gopher clients is provided by almost any site that has Internet access, it is easy to find. Using Gopher usually means entering the word **gopher** and pressing the Enter key, and then pressing Enter for each menu choice. It is one of the easiest of the Internet tools to use.

Most Gopher clients support a bookmark function, making it easy to return to a useful server without traversing a complicated menu tree. Gopher's ease of use and near ubiquity make it a popular platform for delivering information that can be structured into directories of files with menu pointers. Gopher can also link other servers and services, making serendipitous discovery very likely and interconnected travels easy.

FIGURE 2.10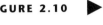

The National Archives Gopher server.

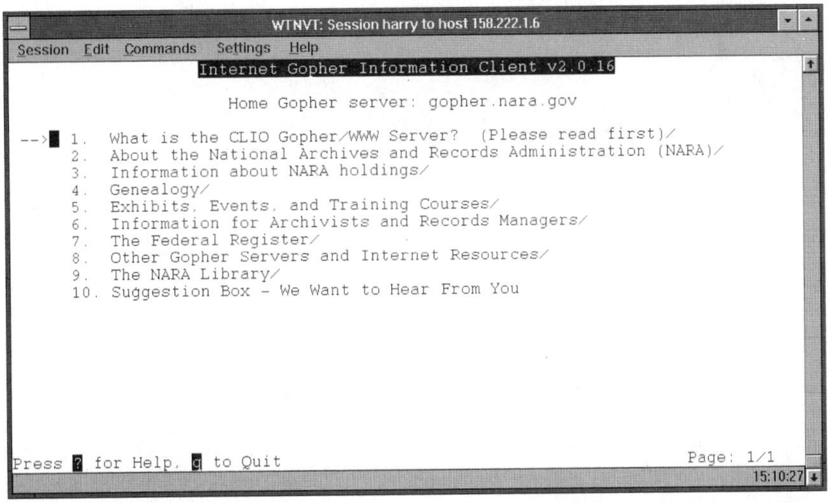

```
WTNVT: Session harry to host 158.222.1.6
Session  Edit  Commands   Settings   Help
            Internet Gopher Information Client v2.0.16

              Home Gopher server: gopher.nara.gov

--> 1.  What is the CLIO Gopher/WWW Server?  (Please read first)/
    2.  About the National Archives and Records Administration (NARA)/
    3.  Information about NARA holdings/
    4.  Genealogy/
    5.  Exhibits, Events, and Training Courses/
    6.  Information for Archivists and Records Managers/
    7.  The Federal Register/
    8.  Other Gopher Servers and Internet Resources/
    9.  The NARA Library/
   10.  Suggestion Box - We Want to Hear From You




Press ? for Help, q to Quit                              Page: 1/1
                                                           15:10:27
```

 T R Y   I T   O U T !

If you have an account on a Internet host, type gopher
**at the main prompt. If you have a specific Gopher
client which runs on your home or office workstation,
such as WinGopher or TurboGopher, click the icon to
launch the application. If you don't specify a particular
server, these clients will take you to the Mother Gopher
in Minnesota. From the first menu, you will see the
possibilities for traveling via Gopher all over the Internet.**

▶ Files Placed for FTP

Remember the automatic response e-mail communication? An organization's automatic response message frequently includes instructions
for how to obtain more information about an organization and its services. Those instructions may well tell you how to receive a type of non-
simultaneous, published communication: information files placed for
anonymous FTP. These files, like those in Web pages and in gopherspace, are prepared specifically for the convenience of others. The requester explicitly asks for it, so there is no question that it was wanted.

**Picking a Model
of the Internet**

ch.
2

USING ANONYMOUS FTP

Anonymous FTP lets you get information off a host without having to have an account on that host. To use an anonymous FTP service, the transaction generally goes like this:

```
ftp ftp.anyhost.com
Connected to ftp.anyhost.com. Enter password: anonymous
Anonymous identity accepted, enter full e-mail address as
password: yourname@yourhost.edu
ftp>
```

and you're in!

Anonymous FTP users do not have full run of the system, and are usually granted only limited access to files on that system. The use of the e-mail address helps with security and marketing research.

The biggest problem with anonymous FTP can be learning to spell *anonymous.*

No one asks for information they don't want to receive. Figure 2.11 gives an example of how to start an anonymous FTP session.

► *Information Displayed by Finger*

Above we listed how information can be displayed as the result of a Finger command. If you so choose, you can set up specific user IDs that will enable you to publish information about services and status, for example. The only difference between public and private publishing with Finger is whether the published information represents an entity rather than a person. Figure 2.12 shows a fun use of Finger—checking the status of the Coke machine at Carnegie Mellon University.

► *Searchable Databases*

A more specific kind of published information can be provided with databases and search engines. Many databases on the Internet, including library catalogs, archives of articles, and books on line, have their own

FIGURE 2.11 ▶

*Starting an anony-
mous FTP session to
the Electronic Freedom
Foundation (eff.org).*

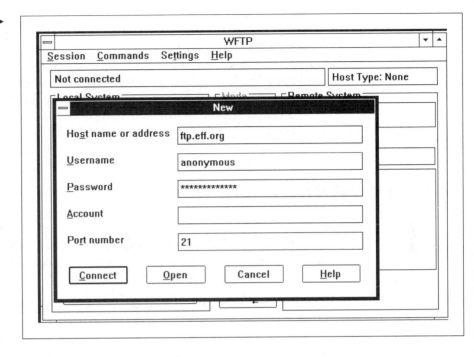

FIGURE 2.12 ▶

*Fingering the Coke
machine at CMU.*

```
                        WTNVT: Session harry to host 158.222.1.6
 Session  Edit  Commands  Settings  Help
harry-pat[~]>finger coke@g.gp.cs.cmu.edu
[G.GP.CS.CMU.EDU]
Login name: coke                        In real life: Drink Coke
Directory: /usrg1/coke                  Shell: /usr/cs/bin/csh
Last login Tue Nov 15 13:50 on ttyv8 from PTERO.SOAR.CS.CMU.EDU
Mail is forwarded to coke@L.GP.CS.CMU.EDU
Plan:
Thu Sep 29 17:33:39 1994
M&M validity: 0     Coke validity: 0  (e.g. da interface is down, sorry!)
Exact change required for coke machine.
    M & M                     Buttons
  /-----\              C: CCCCCCCCCCCC............
 |       |        C: CCCCCC......    D: CCCCCC......
 |  **   |        C: CCCCCC......    D: CCCCCC......
 | ***** |        C: CCCCCC......    D: CCCCCC......
 | ***** |                          C: CCCCCC......
  \-----/                           S: CCCCCC......
     |           Key:
     |              0 = warm;  9 = 90% cold;  C = cold;  . = empty
     |              Leftmost soda/pop will be dispensed next
 ___^___
harry-pat[~]>

                                                              14:45:06
```

specific interface. Database interfaces, or search programs, are called *search engines*.

Using one of the other Internet tools (such as Gopher or WWW) or using a specific client tailored for that database, you can publish information that users specifically request. Database publishing allows the user to access indexes to materials, making sure that the user gets what he or she wants more quickly, with fewer false starts.

▶▶ *Expanding the Matrix*

Many resources exist only to tell you how to take advantage of what the Internet has to offer. Most of them take the viewpoint that you are primarily a consumer of information; that you are mostly interested in what you can get from the Net.

And you can get a lot—one of the great boons of an Internet connection is the ability to quickly access information and data in usable chunks without having to physically go anywhere to get it. While working on a chapter for this book one morning, the authors were able to simultaneously receive copies of documents we wanted to reference, technical information we needed to abstract and describe, and letters of permission to reprint many things included in this book. Research and data gathering over the Internet is changing the scope of many projects, including the education of our children. We think this is a very good thing.

But for us, and we hope for you, too, *getting* things is only part of the Internet's value. Being able to communicate effectively, to share your views and hear the views of others, to receive information from others and to distribute information you want others to have, brings the richness of the Internet's potential to life.

## CHAPTER 3

Locations in Cyberspace: Domains and Addresses

▶ ▶ **S**hortly after you begin working on the Internet, you're likely to run into the term *cyberspace*. *Cyber* comes from the 50s term *cybernetics*, which was used to describe electronic control systems and the human systems they replaced. *Space* hearkens back to the 60s terms *inner space*, *head space*, and so on. Cyberspace is a term coined by either computer hackers or science fiction writers (both claim credit) to describe the place you are when you are traversing the virtual geography of the Internet.

Just as in our physical lives we need some way to tell other people where things are, in the Internet's cyberspace we have to have a way to tell people how to find us or how to locate the interesting resources we have found. There are two kinds of addresses in the Internet: *Domain Names* and *IP Addresses*.

Once you figure out how to find the computer, host, or service in cyberspace, you can move on to e-mail addresses and other services which depend on knowing the address.

 ▶ ▶ M A S T E R   W O R D S

> **With the advent of Gopher, WWW, and other servers which give you menu-driven access to services, you will find yourself using domain addresses less as you explore the network. More and more often you will need to know *only* a URL (Uniform Resource Locator) if you have to know *anything at all*. Most URLs have a domain name embedded in them, and you'll need to know that name. Many Internet clients (the software that helps you do things) have *bookmark* functions which remember the URL for you. However, if your eventual goal is to become an *Internet Information Provider*, you should understand the Domain and IP address systems which underlie the user clients.**

▶▶ *The Domain Name System (DNS)*

Humans like using names that mean something to them, an idea they can remember easily or which looks like it might have something to do with the language they speak. So when the people in the IETF who designed the addressing system were planning the way people would interact with each other, they used a system using what look like words. These words roughly map to a parallel system of addresses called *Internet Protocol (IP) Addresses,* which we describe below. Every computer on the Internet has both a domain name and an IP address, and when you use a domain name, the computers translate that name to the corresponding IP address.

The names of the *domains* describe organizational or geographic realities. They indicate what country the network connection is in, what kind of organization owns it, and, in some cases, the names are defined in even more detail.

Since the folks who designed this system were computer programmers, and their way of thinking ran along programmer lines, the Domain Name System organizes names into hierarchies, as shown in Figure 3.1, similar to the directory structures in a computer file system.

FIGURE 3.1 ▶

Domain name hierarchies.

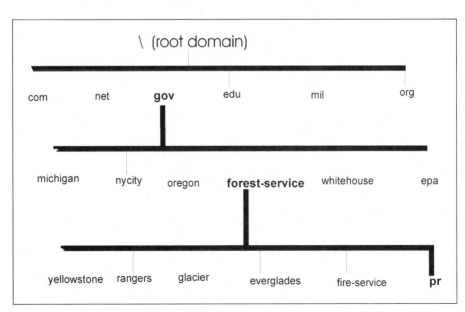

▶ ▶

ch.
3

► Non-Geographic Domains

There are six common domain types that are non-geographical:

- .com for commercial organizations, such as netcom.com, apple.com, sun.com, etc.

- .net for network organizations, such as internic.net

- .gov for parts of governments within the United States, such as nasa.gov, oklahoma.gov, etc.

- .edu for organizations of higher education, such as sjsu.edu, ucsc.edu, mit.edu, etc.

- .mil for nonclassified military networks, such as army.mil, etc. (The classified networks are not connected to the wider Internet.)

- .org for organizations that do not otherwise fit the commercial or educational designations, such as eff.org, farnet.org, etc.

Each domain has a number of hosts, as shown in Table 3.1.

► **TABLE 3.1:** *Host Distribution by Top-Level Domain Name (see Table 3.2 for country codes).*

NUMBER OF HOSTS	DOMAIN
856234	edu
774735	com
169248	gov
155706	uk
149193	de
130176	mil
127516	ca
127514	au
72409	jp
71899	fr
66459	org

TABLE 3.1: *Host Distribution by Top-Level Domain Name (see Table 3.2 for country codes). (continued)*

NUMBER OF HOSTS	DOMAIN
59729	nl
53294	se
49598	fi
47401	ch
38759	no
30993	net
23616	it
21147	es
20130	at
16556	us
15595	za
14830	nz
12109	kr
12107	dk
12107	be
10314	tw
9141	hk
8464	il
7392	pl
5896	br
5639	cz
5390	hu
5164	mx
4518	pt
4014	sg

► **TABLE 3.1:** *Host Distribution by Top-Level Domain Name (see Table 3.2 for country codes).* *(continued)*

NUMBER OF HOSTS	DOMAIN
3703	cl
3308	ie
3268	is
3145	su
2958	gr
1869	cs
1322	my
1204	tr
1197	th
868	sk
838	hr
659	ee
574	si
544	cr
453	ro
420	lu
399	ve
339	ua
325	cn
322	ru
316	in
315	int
297	kw
256	ec
248	ar

▶ **TABLE 3.1:** *Host Distribution by Top-Level Domain Name (see Table 3.2 for country codes). (continued)*

NUMBER OF HOSTS	DOMAIN
180	lv
144	co
101	uy
79	bg
75	pr
65	ph
54	id
53	lt
52	eg
46	tn
42	pe
38	cy
27	li
24	pa
23	ni
12	mo
7	dz
5	fj
4	ir
4	aq
2	md
1	sa

Because domain names are political rather than simply geographical, machines which are owned by the same organization but which are located far apart can be named similarly. For example, `tweedle-dum.cygnus.com` is a machine owned by Cygnus Support, as is `canth.cygnus.com`. But `tweedledum` lives in Boston, with a physical wire connection to the New England regional network NEARNET, and `canth` is in Mountain View, California, and is physically connected to a network cooperative called *The Little Garden*. Never assume location from the domain name of the computer!

MASTER WORDS

Domain addresses can be easy to mis-hear when you are telling your address to someone. Remember that the period is called a *dot*, and that you should let your listener know whether there are spaces or other punctuation in the name. Thus, `vienna.hh.lib.umich.edu` **would be read aloud as *"vienna dot hh dot libe dot u-mish dot edu."***

▶ Geographic Domains

The geographically based top-level domains use two-letter country designations specified by the International Standards Organization in ISO document 3166. For example, `.us` is used for the United States, `.ca` for Canada (not California), `.uk` or `.gb` for the United Kingdom or Great Britain, and `.il` for Israel.

Table 3.2 shows a complete list of the geographically based top-level domain names.

▶ **TABLE 3.2:** *International Standards Organization country codes*

COUNTRY NAME	ABBREVIATION	COUNTRY NUMBER
Afghanistan	AF	004
Albania	AL	008
Algeria	DZ	012

▶ **TABLE 3.2:** *International Standards Organization country codes (continued)*

COUNTRY NAME	ABBREVIATION	COUNTRY NUMBER
American Samoa	AS	016
Andorra	AD	020
Angola	AO	024
Anguilla	AI	660
Antarctica	AQ	010
Antigua & Barbuda	AG	028
Argentina	AR	032
Armenia	AM	051
Aruba	AW	533
Australia	AU	036
Austria	AT	040
Azerbaijan	AZ	031
Bahamas	BS	044
Bahrain	BH	048
Bangladesh	BD	050
Barbados	BB	052
Belarus	BY	112
Belgium	BE	056
Belize	BZ	084
Benin	BJ	204
Bermuda	BM	060
Bhutan	BT	064
Bolivia	BO	068
Bosnia & Herzegowina	BA	070
Botswana	BW	072

▶ **TABLE 3.2:** *International Standards Organization country codes (continued)*

COUNTRY NAME	ABBREVIATION	COUNTRY NUMBER
Bouvet Island	BV	074
Brazil	BR	076
British Indian Ocean Territory	IO	086
Brunei Darussalam	BN	096
Bulgaria	BG	100
Burkina Faso	BF	854
Burundi	BI	108
Cambodia	KH	116
Cameroon	CM	120
Canada	CA	124
Cape Verde	CV	132
Cayman Islands	KY	136
Central African Republic	CF	140
Chad	TD	148
Chile	CL	152
China	CN	156
Christmas Island	CX	162
Cocos (Keeling) Islands	CC	166
Colombia	CO	170
Comoros	KM	174
Congo	CG	178
Cook Islands	CK	184
Costa Rica	CR	188
Cote D'ivoire	CI	384
Croatia (Local Name: Hrvatska)	HR	191

▶ **TABLE 3.2:** *International Standards Organization country codes (continued)*

COUNTRY NAME	ABBREVIATION	COUNTRY NUMBER
Cuba	CU	192
Cyprus	CY	196
Czech Republic	CZ	203
Denmark	DK	208
Djibouti	DJ	262
Dominica	DM	212
Dominican Republic	DO	214
East Timor	TP	626
Ecuador	EC	218
Egypt	EG	818
El Salvador	SV	222
Equatorial Guinea	GQ	226
Eritrea	ER	232
Estonia	EE	233
Ethiopia	ET	231
Falkland Islands (Malvinas)	FK	238
Faroe Islands	FO	234
Fiji	FJ	242
Finland	FI	246
France	FR	250
France, Metropolitan	FX	249
French Guiana	GF	254
French Polynesia	PF	258
French Southern Territories	TF	260
Gabon	GA	266

Locations in Cyberspace

ch. **3**

▶ **TABLE 3.2:** *International Standards Organization country codes (continued)*

COUNTRY NAME	ABBREVIATION	COUNTRY NUMBER
Gambia	GM	270
Georgia	GE	268
Germany	DE	276
Ghana	GH	288
Gibraltar	GI	292
Greece	GR	300
Greenland	GL	304
Grenada	GD	308
Guadeloupe	GP	312
Guam	GU	316
Guatemala	GT	320
Guinea	GN	324
Guinea-Bissau	GW	624
Guyana	GY	328
Haiti	HT	332
Heard & Mcdonald Islands	HM	334
Honduras	HN	340
Hong Kong	HK	344
Hungary	HU	348
Iceland	IS	352
India	IN	356
Indonesia	ID	360
Iran (Islamic Republic of)	IR	364
Iraq	IQ	368
Ireland	IE	372

▶ **TABLE 3.2:** *International Standards Organization country codes (continued)*

COUNTRY NAME	ABBREVIATION	COUNTRY NUMBER
Israel	IL	376
Italy	IT	380
Jamaica	JM	388
Japan	JP	392
Jordan	JO	400
Kazakhstan	KZ	398
Kenya	KE	404
Kiribati	KI	296
Korea, Democratic People's Republic of	KP	408
Korea, Republic of	KR	410
Kuwait	KW	414
Kyrgyzstan	KG	417
Lao People's Democratic Republic	LA	418
Latvia	LV	428
Lebanon	LB	422
Lesotho	LS	426
Liberia	LR	430
Libyan Arab Jamahiriya	LY	434
Liechtenstein	LI	438
Lithuania	LT	440
Luxembourg	LU	442
Macau	MO	446
Macedonia, the Former Yugoslav Republic of	MK	807

▶ **TABLE 3.2:** *International Standards Organization country codes (continued)*

COUNTRY NAME	ABBREVIATION	COUNTRY NUMBER
Madagascar	MG	450
Malawi	MW	454
Malaysia	MY	458
Maldives	MV	462
Mali	ML	466
Malta	MT	470
Marshall Islands	MH	584
Martinique	MQ	474
Mauritania	MR	478
Mauritius	MU	480
Mayotte	YT	175
Mexico	MX	484
Micronesia, Federated States of	FM	583
Moldova, Republic of	MD	498
Monaco	MC	492
Mongolia	MN	496
Montserrat	MS	500
Morocco	MA	504
Mozambique	MZ	508
Myanmar	MM	104
Namibia	NA	516
Nauru	NR	520
Nepal	NP	524
Netherlands	NL	528
Netherlands Antilles	AN	530

▶ **TABLE 3.2:** *International Standards Organization country codes (continued)*

COUNTRY NAME	ABBREVIATION	COUNTRY NUMBER
New Caledonia	NC	540
New Zealand	NZ	554
Nicaragua	NI	558
Niger	NE	562
Nigeria	NG	566
Niue	NU	570
Norfolk Island	NF	574
Northern Mariana Islands	MP	580
Norway	NO	578
Oman	OM	512
Pakistan	PK	586
Palau	PW	585
Panama	PA	591
Papua New Guinea	PG	598
Paraguay	PY	600
Peru	PE	604
Philippines	PH	608
Pitcairn	PN	612
Poland	PL	616
Portugal	PT	620
Puerto Rico	PR	630
Qatar	QA	634
Reunion	RE	638
Romania	RO	642
Russian Federation	RU	643

▶ **TABLE 3.2:** *International Standards Organization country codes (continued)*

COUNTRY NAME	ABBREVIATION	COUNTRY NUMBER
Rwanda	RW	646
Saint Kitts & Nevis	KN	659
Saint Lucia	LC	662
Saint Vincent & the Grenadines	VC	670
Samoa	WS	882
San Marino	SM	674
Sao Tome & Principe	ST	678
Saudi Arabia	SA	682
Senegal	SN	686
Seychelles	SC	690
Sierra Leone	SL	694
Singapore	SG	702
Slovakia (Slovak Republic)	SK	703
Slovenia	SI	705
Solomon Islands	SB	090
Somalia	SO	706
South Africa	ZA	710
South Georgia & the South Sandwich Islands	GS	239
Spain	ES	724
Sri Lanka	LK	144
St. Helena	SH	654
St. Pierre & Miquelon	PM	666
Sudan	SD	736
Suriname	SR	740
Svalbard & Jan Mayen Islands	SJ	744

▶ **TABLE 3.2:** *International Standards Organization country codes (continued)*

COUNTRY NAME	ABBREVIATION	COUNTRY NUMBER
Swaziland	SZ	748
Sweden	SE	752
Switzerland	CH	756
Syrian Arab Republic	SY	760
Taiwan, Province of China	TW	158
Tajikistan	TJ	762
Tanzania, United Republic of	TZ	834
Thailand	TH	764
Togo	TG	768
Tokelau	TK	772
Tonga	TO	776
Trinidad & Tobago	TT	780
Tunisia	TN	788
Turkey	TR	792
Turkmenistan	TM	795
Turks & Caicos Islands	TC	796
Tuvalu	TV	798
Uganda	UG	800
Ukraine	UA	804
United Arab Emirates	AE	784
United Kingdom	GB	826
United States	US	840
United States Minor Outlying Islands	UM	581
Uruguay	UY	858
Uzbekistan	UZ	860

▶ **TABLE 3.2:** *International Standards Organization country codes (continued)*

COUNTRY NAME	ABBREVIATION	COUNTRY NUMBER
Vanuatu	VU	548
Vatican City State (Holy See)	VA	336
Venezuela	VE	862
Viet Nam	VN	704
Virgin Islands (British)	VG	092
Virgin Islands (U.S.)	VI	850
Wallis & Futuna Islands	WF	876
Western Sahara	EH	732
Yemen	YE	887
Yugoslavia	YU	891
Zaire	ZR	180
Zambia	ZM	894
Zimbabwe	ZW	716

Updated by the RIPE Network Coordination Centre, in coordination with the ISO 3166 Maintenance Agency at DIN Berlin. Latest change: Thu Feb 10 10:20:28 MET 1994 Source: `gopher://ns.ripe.net/00/iso/codes`

▶ *Solving the Name Puzzle*

In a complete domain name (called *fully qualified* in the design documents for the Internet), the part furthest to the right is the top level domain, representing either a type of organization or a country. As you read in from the right, the name gets more specific until you reach the name of the individual host computer. For instance:

`rubens.anu.edu.au`

is the name of a computer. It is in Australia (the geographically based domain is au), in the educational area (edu), at the Australian National University (anu), and the host computer is named rubens.

The best planned names describe where in the organizational structure of the company or organization the owner of the machine can be found. For example:

```
doc.cis.myuniversity.edu
```

would show that this host or server is in the documentation department of the Computer Information Services Division at My University, which is an educational organization.

Some organizations let the person who uses the computer most name the machine something distinctive. So, you might see a server or host name that says something about the person's interests, such as:

```
terminator.itd.umich.edu
```

and

```
predator.itd.umich.edu
```

(These guys are Arnold fans!) or

```
taliesin.sybase.com
```

(this person studies Welsh poetry?) or

```
bach.juliard.edu
```

for the music lovers among us.

While it is possible to have very long domain names for machines (such as `birth12.maternity.womens.chicago.org`, and no, this doesn't really exist), such names would eliminate the usefulness of having names that are easy to remember and type. Most systems can be planned with simpler and easier names for the computers and local networks in the organization.

Four times a year, SRI sends out a list of the most popular names for computers used on the Internet. Some names reflect the fact that many large computing labs have many machines of the same type (mac01, mac02, sun01, sun10, etc.), but some folks claim the name trends show something about the culture or mindset of the folks who are naming the machines. Table 3.3 shows an example of the list.

▶ **TABLE 3.3:** *Top 50 Host Names*

NUMBER OF HOSTS	NAME
1284	ns
1178	venus
1099	pc1
1078	pluto
1015	mars
946	zeus
933	jupiter
919	pc2
888	saturn
845	mac1
840	mercury
802	cisco
796	iris
784	pc3
765	ftp
751	router
751	orion
751	gw
738	mac2
682	pc4
681	charon
679	eagle
664	alpha
661	neptune
644	newton
627	pc01

▶ **TABLE 3.3:** *Top 50 Host Names (continued)*

NUMBER OF HOSTS	NAME
622	pc10
621	mac3
621	hermes
614	apollo
608	mail
607	pc11
603	mac10
602	pc5
602	pc02
596	gateway
594	www
589	gopher
588	pc03
584	pc04
571	thor
562	pc12
562	merlin
554	mac4
551	pc6
546	gauss
544	athena
543	mac11
541	mac12
540	titan

Locations in
Cyberspace

ch.
3

▶▶ *IP Addresses*

Connected nodes on the Internet have names and addresses that obey
certain conventions. We've already talked about the Domain Name System, designed to be easy for humans to read and remember. In a wider
sense, every node on the Net, every end point (which might be a computer or a dial-in modem), has a unique identifying address. These
unique identifiers are called *Internet Protocol (IP) Addresses.*

The computer or server is known as a *host,* and the IP address, its physical network connection, is known as the *host address.* The IP address
can be difficult to remember, is easy to enter incorrectly, and will not
necessarily remain the same if someone needs to reorganize his or her
network. The difficulty with these addresses is what led to the creation
of DNS names, which map IP addresses to a set of more easily remembered words.

The IP address is a set of numbers that expresses the exact physical
connection between a computer and the network on the Internet. In
some senses you can think of them in the same way you think about
telephone numbers: a phone number uniquely describes your connection to the telephone network.

▶ What Do All Those Numbers Mean?

IP addresses contain four sets of numbers separated by periods or dots. These combined parts are unique on the network and allow it to know specifically which computer is to receive which electronic packet as well as from which specific computer the electronic packet came.

IP addresses look like this:

35.1.1.42

or

154.154.34.245

Unlike domain names, these addresses are now primarily read and managed by computers. IP addresses are organized from left to right, with the left-hand octet describing the largest network organization, and the rightmost octet describing the actual network connection.

To make this easier, let's go back to the telephone number analogy:

+1 415 555 1212

When we look at this number, we decipher where it is and what it means starting at the left. The +1 tells me I am accessing the United States long-distance service. The 415 says I am looking for a number in California, specifically in the Bay area. 555 is a number owned by the local phone service, and 1212 is specifically the directory information service.

IP addresses work somewhat similarly but are more complex than phone numbers because there are literally millions of network connections possible and because IP addresses are intended for use by computers rather than people. Given an IP address that looks like this:

154.135.186.235

we can untangle it similarly. First, though, some explanations. Each of the parts of this address—the numbers between the periods—is called an *octet*. Octet is a word that comes out of computer science, and each octet has a value of 8 bits within the computer. When the four octets of the address are added together, the total address has a value of 32 bits. Using the various combinations of these octets, several million unique identifiers can be assigned. (You don't need to know much more about the computer math if you are not going to be doing network programming. But you'll hear the term from people who do know the jargon, and it's nice to know what they're talking about.)

Locations in
Cyberspace

ch.
3

▶ Classes of Networks

Just as with our phone number, we can look at the leftmost octet and determine something about the network. Network addresses are divided into classes, which are assigned depending on the size of the physical network. The class of address determines the number of network connections that can be linked to the physical network. The value of the first octet tells us what class the network is in, and how large the physical network that underlies the numbers is. The first octet is sometimes called the *network address* or *net number.* Figure 3.2 gives an snapshot of the number of hosts and domains.

Class A: Over 16 Million Served

Class A network addresses are assigned to major service providers—the big regional or national nets. NEARNET, Sprint, ANSnet, Merit, and AT&T are examples of organizations with Class A network numbers. Class A numbers have a first octet with a value of 1–126. There can only be 126 Class A nets, but each can have up to 16,777,214 hosts. Following are some sample Class A addresses.

FIGURE 3.2

Estimate of hosts and domains as of July 1994.

```
┌───────────────────────────────────────────────────────────────────────┐
│ ═  WTNVT: Session harry to host harry.lloyd.com               ▼ ▲       │
│  Session   Edit   Commands   Settings   Help                           │
│   Number of Hosts, Domains, and Nets Advertised in the Domain Name System  ▲
│                                                                         │
│               July 94    Apr 94    Jan 94    Oct 93    Jul 93  Change (year) │
│   ===================================================================== │
│   Hosts:     3,212,000     N/A   2,217,000 2,056,000 1,776,000    81%   │
│                                                                         │
│   Domains:      46,000             30,000    28,000    26,000     77%   │
│                                                                         │
│   PingReply:   707,000*           576,000#     N/A    464,000#    52%   │
│   %ofHosts:         22%               26%                 26%           │
│   [* = estimated by pinging a random sample of 1% of all hosts]         │
│   [# = estimated by pinging a random sample of 5% of all hosts]         │
│                                                                         │
│   Nets:                                                                 │
│    Class A:         89     N/A         74        69        67     33%   │
│    Class B:       4493               4043      3849      3728     21%   │
│    Class C:      20628              16422     12615      9972    107%   │
│    Total:        25210              20539     16533     13767     83%   │
│                                                                         │
│              Number of 2nd-Level Domains:  20,295                       │
│         Number of 2nd-Level Domains under selected Top-Level Domains    │
│            12687 com     1388 org     1292 edu      545 net    202 gov  │
│                                                                         │
│                                                            17:49:13  ▼  │
└───────────────────────────────────────────────────────────────────────┘
```

IP Address	Who Is It?
54.0.0.0	Merck Pharmaceuticals
36.0.0.0	SU-Net
12.0.0.0	AT&T

Class B: Larger Nets

Class B addresses go to organizations with larger nets, such as universities or large businesses. They have a first octet value between 128 and 191. The first two octets in a Class B address describe the network itself, and the second two identify the host. There are 16,382 possible network identifiers, and each has a potential of 65,534 connections. Some Class B addresses are shown below:

IP Address	Who Is It?
128.29.154.1	Mitre
128.54.16.1	University of California at San Diego
147.174.1.5	Southeastern Louisiana University
132.162.32.243	Oberlin
129.34.129.4	IBM Watson Research
140.147.2.12	Library of Congress
148.129.129.10	Census Bureau

Running Out of Room: the Class B and C Crisis

Class C addresses have first octet values of 192–223. The first three octets are used for the network numbers and the last octet is the host number. Since smaller networks are likely to be the most numerous, this class is where most networks will be assigned. There are over 2 million potential network numbers in Class C, but each can support only 254 hosts. Originally, Class C addresses were intended for small company networks, K-12 schools, and single machines which weren't connected to other, larger nets.

In the past few years, however, the original *address space* (the blocks of addresses originally allotted) has gotten cramped. Although the original designers had assumed that there would never be more than 126 Class A nets, and 16,382 Class B nets, we're quickly running out of address room. Some larger companies are getting multiple Class C addresses, and a new method of doing routing and other services for those addresses has been devised. This new routing protocol is called CIDR (Classless Internet Domain Routing).

The list below shows a few of the many Class C addresses.

IP Address	Who Is It?
192.216.246.0	Stanford Federal Credit Union
198.200.160.0	Berkeley Unified School District
192.195.245.3	University Microfilms
198.137.240.10	Whitehouse.gov
199.0.132.66	National Public Radio

Class D addresses, with a first octet value of 224–239, are reserved for *multicasting,* which is a way of grouping addresses so that you can send messages to them all at once. It's something like a mailing list for host addresses.

Class E addresses, 240–247, are reserved for future use.

▶ *Unsnarling the Tangles*

So, let's go back to our sample address:

154.135.186.235

We now know that this is a Class B address (remember, the first octet is 154, between 128 and 191). Looking at the very last octet, 235, we know that this is the physical point on the network where this host or service is connected. Just as with the phone number, the address 154.135.186.235 *pinpoints a specific, unique address.*

There are two problems with human beings using these numeric IP addresses to reach hosts and services. First, they're hard to remember and easy to type incorrectly. Second, if a specific computer gets moved to some other physical connection point (say, if the machine gets moved to a new office down the hall, or even across the country!), its network IP address will change. This is why the DNS addresses are mapped onto the IP addresses. The only thing you need to know is how to reach a translator machine for this mapping. Sometimes you put a numeric address into the software on your workstation so it can reach a DNS translator directly; sometimes the modem pool or other network hardware is connected to a computer that knows how to do this translation.

 ▶ ▶ **W A R N I N G**

> **If you get a message from your systems administrator notifying you of an impending IP address change for a DNS server, don't ignore it! If you don't know what it means or what you need to do about it, ask. Otherwise, you could suddenly find yourself cut off from the network.**

▶ *What Do I Need to Know?*

As a general user, you'll usually never have to know anything about IP addresses. You'll only need to know about IP numbers if you do any of the following:

- Set up your office or home workstation to use IP communications software.

- Call back into your home workstation or a computer service you use regularly from an unfamiliar server (see the tip below).

- Help plan for your local area network.

- Set up your own information services.

 ▶ ▶ **M A S T E R   W O R D S**

> **Make sure you know the IP address of the machine, gateway, or service you want to use when you're traveling, particularly if you are going to be at a conference or other location where courtesy e-mail services have been set up. Sometimes these courtesy labs don't use a DNS server which knows your machine name, and if you know the IP address, you can simply Telnet to** 154.135.186.235 **rather than having to find someone who knows how to get you connected.**

▶ ▶

ch.

3

► ► ► **CHAPTER** **4**

Options for Connecting

►► **T**his chapter is for those of you who don't have current access to the Internet. You should also read it if you have current access through your work or organization and want to obtain access at home to further your personal interests, or if you already have a personal account and want to learn more about how to connect your business, school, or organization.

 ► ►**N O T E**

> **You may actually have access without knowing it. It may be that your organization has an Internet connection, but the connection hasn't been made available to your department; or a connection is available but the word hasn't spread yet; or someone's been working on it and the installation isn't yet complete and therefore hasn't been announced. So if you are part of a larger enterprise, you might go and check with the systems people and see what they can make available to you. After investigation, if the answer is still "my organization is not connected," then you'll want to read this chapter.**

Whatever your motivation, there are a few criteria that will make your search for the appropriate type of connection easier.

►► *What Do You Want to Do?*

If a simple e-mail connection is your primary need, your options are wider than if you plan to offer audio files on an Internet server.

▶▶ *Where Are You Geographically Located?*

In general, Internet service providers serve some geographic areas and not others. Some service providers, of course, offer services throughout the United States. You will need to contact still other providers if you are outside of the United States.

▶▶ *Determining Which Provider Is for You*

Choosing a provider of network services involves the same process as with any other type of service provider.

First determine what services you want to purchase—just what type of access do you need and what type of equipment do you have? Are you trying to connect only one computer, or a LAN? Are there files your organization wants to make available to the public?

Then, determine who among the providers can deliver those services in a manner you consider effective.

When you have the potential providers located, you need to consider the level of service you wish to purchase and the costs for those services. For Internet services costs, mostly you pay for the connection itself, not for what you do with that connection (although like everything else on the Internet, that too may change).

With the information you have gathered, you can determine which provider is best for you.

To help you start your search, we have provided a list of network providers who sell connections to large regions or across the entire United States. Some provide international access.

▶▶ *What Equipment Do You Have (or Plan to Obtain)?*

If you want to connect your department's Local Area Network (LAN) to the Internet, you will need different software and hardware than if you want to have dialup access through your personal computer and modem at home.

▶▶ *How Much Are You Willing to Budget for Your Internet Access?*

Rate structures vary widely from "free" and fixed-cost, terminal-emulating accounts to high-speed connections to very large servers. If you haven't much experience with the Internet, you might want to start out with a lower cost account and learn how to use the Internet effectively for your organization before you invest in a lot of equipment.

▶

BUT ISN'T IT FREE?

There is no such thing as a free connection to the Internet. Someone, somewhere is paying the bills for the equipment, the software, the routing, the network engineers, the telephone lines, and so on.

You will hear that universities in the United States have "free" connections. This is just not true. All the universities run their own networks. They have significant investments in equipment and management to connect smaller networks (for example, departmental networks) into something like a campus-wide network backbone (or larger bandwidth network) that can carry more traffic. Some universities have been working for years to connect their major academic departments to their networks. Many universities are working to build network connections into the residence halls for their students. Some fund extensive computing laboratories where students without personal computers can go to use the equipment and the Internet. The physical network is expensive to install and maintain. The software to route packets must be written (by employees) or purchased from a vendor. The computers that are used to route the packets must be purchased. The employees who install the connections or watch the network to make sure it continues to function must be paid their salary and benefits. Someone must have paid for the computers that are used for access and the software licenses for that access. And we haven't even routed a packet off the campus yet!

Most universities belong to a regional research and education network. The fees for these vary, but they are typically thousands of dollars per year. Each regional network needs to maintain its physical and logical network and therefore needs to pay for equipment, physical infrastructure and people costs, too. These networks are membership organizations and, while some of the costs for the regional networks were originally met by the National Science Foundation (as were some of the universities' expenses, for that matter), the members are paying at least part of the expense. Some of the regional networks are, in turn, paying gateway fees to the owners of the larger national network backbones. These networks also have personnel and equipment expenses that must be met.

So how can anyone say all this is free? Well, if you are an individual user on one of these campuses, you are possibly not being billed directly for your access. It might be included in your student computing fees, for example, or your student registration fees, or, if you are an employee, as part of the general expense of running the department for which you work. Many universities like to think of access to networks and computing as an academic overhead expense similar to the costs incurred in maintaining an academic library. These costs are shared across the organizations, but the individual user may not see them.

▶▶ *Dialup Connections*

If you have a computer, some communications software, a telephone line, and a modem, you can connect to the Internet. The types of connections listed here are in order of least complicated and expensive to most complicated and expensive. The major ways that you can link to the Net using dialup are:

- Host/Terminal Connection (Shell Accounts)
- Individual Computer TCP/IP Link
- Dialup or On-Demand TCP/IP Link through Your LAN

Each of these has variations, of course, and we discuss them individually below.

▶ MODEMS

In order for your computer to communicate over telephone lines with another computer, it is necessary to convert the information you wish to send or receive into electrical impulses that can be sent over the connection. The device that makes that happen is a *modem* (*mo*dulator/*dem*odulator). The higher the number of bits per second the modem will transmit, the faster you will receive the information. But, because the modem is translating your signals into a carrier language, it is necessary to have a translator that "speaks the same language" on the other end. Therefore, you need to select a modem that speaks to your service provider, or select a service provider that can speak to your modem.

Some modems provide the extra service of data compression. If your modem compresses in a way not understood by your service provider, you will not be able to take advantage of the compression. There are standards for these compression algorithms and many manufacturers build modems to these standards. There are also proprietary protocols that will make effective transmissions even faster. The disadvantage of these proprietary protocols is that both ends of the transmission must have the same type of modem. If you use standard transmission protocols, you will be able to transmit data to and from most of the service providers.

A good rule of thumb is to purchase the fastest modem that you can reasonably afford (and that is not speaking a proprietary language). Modem technology is changing rapidly and there are now (in late 1994) 14.4 Kbps modems using compression protocols readily available for less than $100. Just two years ago, those same modems cost around $400. This means that many people can afford to buy 1.4 Kbps modems that will run at 19.2 Kpbs, which makes using graphical interfaces quite a bit more enjoyable.

▶ Host/Terminal Connection (Shell Accounts)

In a host/terminal connection, your computer acts as if it were a terminal directly connected to some Internet host. You use a terminal emulation program that can make your computer act like a VT100 terminal. (A VT100 terminal is the lowest common denominator of emulation: the simplest to implement, and a terminal that can display visual information.) The program signals your modem to dial and handles the transfer of characters from your computer to the host computer and back. Your connection is at one remove: that is, the host computer is the one that is "on the Internet." This means that when you transfer files using FTP (discussed in Chapter 9), for example, the files are transferred to the host. You will then need to download the file to your computer using your communications program.

What Types of Users Is This Best For?

Host dial connections are best for people on limited budgets, for pe/ ple who don't need constant connectivity, for people who don't wa manage systems and network connections themselves, and for pe/ who may need to connect from many different locations and w/

have access to a network system that supports dynamic TCP/IP addressing. (*Dynamic addressing* supplies you with a different TCP/IP address depending on where you are connected from. Some software and security systems cannot handle these differing addresses.) If you have access to the Internet from your work location and you want to have a personal Internet account, a host dial connection works well, too. This is because you can use Telnet to connect to your personal account from your work site. Host dial connections are appropriate for entry-level users because they allow inexpensive access while you learn what your future needs will be.

What You Can Do with It

This depends directly on the features offered on the host computer. If the host offers a Gopher client, you will be able to use it. If the host offers a World Wide Web client, you will be able to use it. You will read and send your electronic mail to and from the host computer. Some host accounts will support your use of programming-language compilers. Some host accounts will allow you to store files on their disk drives or make available information via anonymous FTP from their host. Typical service providers offer e-mail, access to newsgroups, Gopher, WWW, Telnet, FTP, Finger, Netfind, and Internet Relay Chat. Some providers offer a menu interface to these applications to make them easier for the new user to operate. For example, NetManage offers the Chameleon suite of programs; you can find the Chameleon Sampler on the accompanying Disk 2.

What You Cannot Do with It

Most host/terminal connection accounts do not offer graphical interfaces; you interact with the host by typing commands rather than by clicking on icons. You will, however, be able to download graphics to your computer, where you can use your own graphical viewing programs to see the images. A host/terminal connection does not allow you to "serve" information that is on your computer. You will need to move the information from your computer to an Internet-attached host. With a terminal connection, you will not be able to take advantage of any multitasking features of your computer: a terminal connection is a one-thing-at-a-time operation, so you cannot (for example) download a file and also be connected to a library catalog for searching at the same time.

What Will It Cost?

Host dial accounts are the least expensive of the possible types of Internet connections. Restricted host accounts (e-mail only, for example) may be quite inexpensive. You might be able to find them for less than $10 per month. Some services will offer unlimited connect-time (the amount of time you are connected to their network and host) for a flat fee of less than $20 per month. Others will offer a lower account fee and charge for connect time.

What Do I Need to Know to Use It?

You'll need to understand how to connect your computer to your modem and how to run your terminal software. You'll need a basic understanding of the features offered on the host computer. The most difficult part for many newcomers is learning how to give the host computer the correct command to accomplish what you want to do. In this book you'll find that information for all of the most important Internet services. And in many cases, the user interfaces for the host computers have been (or are being) improved so that it is less necessary to know all the ins and outs of the UNIX operating system, which is used on many Internet hosts. As with many things we do, practice does indeed make us more effective, if not perfect.

Types of Host Dial Connections

Local Dial The local number host dial connection is the least expensive type available. (Unfortunately, this kind of connection is not available in all areas.) With an access point that is a local telephone call from your geographical location, a telephone connection that does not incur measured time costs, and a flat rate Internet service, you may stay connected to your provider's system for long periods without incurring extra charges.

Long Distance Dial, Connection Services, or Public Data Networks
If you are not located where you can reach a service provider with a local call, you will need to consider whether a long distance call, a connection service, or a public data network is best for your connection. These are not really Internet service provider accounts but other way of establishing your connection. Some nationwide service provider fer 1-800 or 1-900 service and essentially pass through their cost

you. This can be more expensive than simple long distance. A connection service is one that offers local or 800/900 access and then, once you are connected, lets you use Telnet to connect from the terminal server to your Internet service. This type of connection may be flat-rate, too. Investigate the speed at which you are allowed to connect. If the speed is very low, it might be less expensive to connect via long distance using a faster transmission speed because you will be connected for less time.

Another connection method is that of a public data network like CompuServe's Packet Network or SprintNet. These services offer connections to local access points that may be more convenient for you. Be sure and investigate how fast these connections are because they might not offer the type of service that will serve your needs.

 ▶ ▶ M A S T E R   W O R D S

> **When investigating providers, be sure to request a complete list of local access points. Because of the structure of regulated telephone tariffs, it may be less expensive for you to dial an out-of-state point than to connect to the geographically nearest point. For example, if you happen to be located in Lake Tahoe, California, on the California/Nevada border, the nearest local access point for many service providers is Sacramento, California. The day rate (8 AM to 5 PM) for connections from Lake Tahoe to Sacramento is 40 cents per minute. However, if you call Las Vegas, Nevada, or Phoenix, Arizona, or Denver, Colorado, or even Raleigh, North Carolina, the day rate from one long distance carrier is around 27 cents per minute. This is a significant savings.**

Telnet from Another Internet Site Sometimes you may want a personal account on a commercial provider, but you do not have a modem at home. Or, say, your commercial provider does not have a local phone access number but you can reach it from other Internet sites using Telnet (further explained in Chapter 9). Or, suppose your local campus or regional network offers local dialup from which you can make an Internet connection to another host. These are all ways to use the Internet itself to facilitate reaching your host service provider.

This is the same as a local call from the expense point of view. You need to be connected to some system that offers Telnet. It may be from a connection provider or from another Internet site (some people maintain accounts with more than one Internet service provider because of features that are offered on one and not on the other). Again, these connections may be a local call for you. Or you might not call at all. For example, you could Telnet in from your work site. In this case, you are most likely using the connections provided for your work, such as a LAN or an enterprise TCP/IP network, to your own advantage.

Restricted Access Accounts If you are seeking only e-mail access, or perhaps a combination of e-mail with a few Usenet newsgroups (discussed in Chapter 12), a restricted-access account may be the best choice. These are offered by some freenets (community access host systems), for example, whose equipment budgets aren't large so they offer fewer newsgroups. Or by public-access UNIX sites or bulletin boards, whose general purpose is for some other special interest: a local government bulletin board, or one devoted to providing information about health care. These sites may offer inexpensive e-mail access.

Yet another variation of this type of account is the gateway from an information provider. America Online offers its own services (chat rooms, files, and so on) as well as access to newsgroups and e-mail to Internet users. Prodigy offers an Internet e-mail gateway, as does CompuServe. These services may be charged at a premium rate over the regular service. The premium may well be less than the cost of a connection to an Internet service provider, however, if you need or want the information service anyway.

▶ *Individual Computer TCP/IP Link*

An individual computer TCP/IP link allows your computer to function as an Internet host. It's your host running whatever software you elect to run, providing only the service you've chosen to provide. These links are called either SLIP (for serial link Internet protocol) or PPP (for point-to-point protocol) links. Both types of links will handle dialup. Both can take advantage of new software techniques that condense or "compress" the data being transmitted so that transferring information takes less time. The Chameleon Sampler, on Companion Disk 2, is a TCP/IP software package that includes both SLIP and PPP.

Although you might feel nervous at first about setting up and running your own Internet host, it's not rocket science. And most TCP/IP-based software for desktop computers is designed to work just like the other software you use on that machine. For example, Windows-based applications have the same kind of pull-down menus, dialogue boxes, and error messages as your other applications. The same holds true for Macintosh or X-terminal applications.

What Types of Users Is This Best For?

People who want the benefits of working in a computing environment with which they are familiar and being connected to the Internet at the same time are candidates for this type of connection. People who want to use a graphical WWW browser, direct file transfer, or PC-based mail services that depend upon direct Internet connectivity need to use this type of service.

What You Can Do with It

With an individual link, using dial IP access, you have the benefits of direct e-mail (with multiple login-accounts if your e-mail software supports that), some sort of newsgroup access, and, again depending on the software you are running, the full suite of Internet tools—Telnet for connecting to other machines, FTP for transferring files directly to your machine, Finger for looking up information on people and organizations, and usually, an Internet browser or two for Gopher and WWW (text and image-viewing services). With this link you can run one of the graphical World Wide Web browsers like NCSA's Mosaic or Cornell Law School's Cello.

With your computer directly connected, you can transfer files directly to your personal computer, rather than to an intermediate host owned by an access provider. In contrast, if you have a host-based account, you must transfer the file from the source to your host, and then download it to your personal machine.

What You Cannot Do with It

There are only a few limitations on what you can do with an IP-based link.

The disk space available for you to use is limited to that on your local computer, unless you also have an account with a public access site. If you have a slower link (14.4 Kbps or less) you probably won't want to have people accessing your host via FTP, Telnet, Gopher, or WWW, even if your software and link will support that access, because their access will slow down your own use of the link. And for you real programmer types, you won't have access to UNIX compilers this way, unless you are already running UNIX on your local computer. You'll need to have an account with some public access site.

What Will It Cost?

Dialup IP connections for individuals can run less than $20 per month (although most providers charge somewhat more than this). Some service providers charge a flat fee. Others charge a fee that includes a certain number of connect hours in the monthly fee and charge extra if you use more than that number of hours. Still others charge a monthly fee and charge a per-hour usage fee.

The best way to compare costs is to make a chart of the various options, and then talk to other folks using the services about how they use the service. Depending on what you want to do, differing charging structures may make more sense for you. For example, if you want to be online for long periods of time (if you want to participate in online forums, interactive communications, or spend a lot of time looking at resources at other sites), a flat-rate service is best for you. If, on the other hand, you want to upload and download files, including e-mail, and then get off the connection to process those files, a per-hour fee or minimum-use fee structure would suit you best.

What Do I Need to Know to Use It

As of this writing, it is still not simple to install an individual SLIP or PPP connection. You will need to understand the basics of TCP/IP, like what is a default gateway and what is an IP address. Fortunately, this book and others like it are available to help you. Furthermore, vendors like Spry are offering "Internet in a box" products, designed to make the installation and connection process easier for nontechnical folk. (One of the most convenient such packages is *Access the Internet!*. This book/disk combination from Sybex fully describes the use of Net-Cruiser, Netcom's Windows interface to Internet. NetCruiser software

A TIP FOR TRAVELERS

If you travel frequently and want to have your portable computer directly connected to the Internet, you will need to investigate services and software that provide dynamically assigned IP addresses. If you have an IP address that is assigned permanently to your connection, you will need to call that specific access point to connect. For example, if you are usually connected through Washington, DC, and you travel to Las Vegas for a meeting, you will need to dial Washington if you have a static IP address. A service that provides dynamic IP addressing, however, may provide you access in Las Vegas. Another way around this is to have a combination account. Some service providers will provide a host dial account that can access their network at various points as part of their SLIP or PPP connection accounts. Then you use the SLIP or PPP connection when you are at your home site and your host dial connection when you are traveling.

is included with *Access the Internet!*, as it is with this book.) At a minimum, you should be familiar with the terminology used in these types of connections, or you will not be able to take advantage of the materials provided to help you install your software and bring up your connection.

▶ Dialup or On-Demand TCP/IP Link through Your LAN

A dialup link from your LAN is the intermediate step between individual dialup and a dedicated high-speed link. It is therefore somewhat like dialup and somewhat like having a direct link.

The main difference between this type of connection and one to your individual computer is that the TCP/IP software runs on the LAN server, and your connection is to the server. A LAN for purposes of this discussion includes PC and Mac-based networks, such as Banyan, Novell, or AppleTalk, or a UNIX-based server with Ethernet links. A TCP/IP connection through a LAN, either on a dialup connection or a direct connection, is the most common type of IP connection, much more common than a personal dialup IP connection. (We talk about dedicated links in the next section.)

With a dialup or on-demand connection to your LAN, software in your server dials up your service provider when you tell the server you want to make a network connection. It may also dial into the network on a regular schedule to exchange e-mail.

What Types of Users Is This Best For?

A dialup or on-demand connection is best for users who would like to exchange e-mail with the Internet from the e-mail system running on the LAN, but who do not have a lot of Internet traffic. Or for the user who only wants to occasionally use an Internet service. For example, a small law office might want only occasional access to a server than contains court decisions or governmental data. Other than that, the users would like to exchange e-mail with other lawyers and perhaps belong to a mailing list dealing with legal issues. These uses are similar to individual uses, and dialup connections would be a reasonable choice. Dial connections are intermittent. They must be initiated by someone or by some program. They can meet busy signals from the provider's system. But they can be much less expensive than a dedicated link.

What You Can Do with It

A dialup link to your server will allow you (if your network has an e-mail gateway) to exchange e-mail with Internet users, using your regular LAN-based mail software.

The client software you choose and the LAN server TCP/IP software you choose will dictate which Internet functions you can use. There are LAN clients for many of the Internet tools like Telnet, Gopher, FTP, and so on. A particular advantage of an FTP client on a LAN server is that files transferred there are available to all users of the LAN, just like any other shared file. Because the file space available on a shared server is usually larger than on the individual computers hooked into the LAN, you may be able to transfer larger files than you would be able to transfer to your individual machine.

Your LAN server may allow more than one person on the LAN to connect to the Internet at the same time. This is, of course, one of the many benefits of shared resources.

What You Cannot Do with It

The limitations of this type of connection are the same as for individual TCP/IP connections. The speed of the connection may limit your activity. There may not be clients for all the Internet functions for your particular type of LAN. (Check your applications menu or icons, or ask your systems administrator which network applications are available to you.) In addition, unless you have a very fast line and very fast server software, you will experience delays and congestion if several people try and use the Internet services at the same time.

What Will It Cost?

Costs for this type of connection vary widely. For you, the individual end user, a connection through a workplace based LAN may not be charged to you directly. Students and faculty at schools and universities may have to pay some sort of technology fee in order to use the computer resources at your site, even if they are not connected to the Internet. If you are the business owner or the person who pays the bills for that workplace LAN, you will need to evaluate your costs carefully. Some providers base their fees on the number of connections within your LAN. Some providers base their fees on a flat rate. Some providers see no difference between this type of connection and one that is on an individual computer. Careful investigation of the providers available to you will be necessary to determine the actual costs for what you have in mind. (We have included a list of regional and national providers at the end of this chapter. You may have other, local providers available in your area.)

What Do I Need to Know to Use It?

For this type of connection, you will need a knowledgeable network administrator who can configure the TCP/IP software for your particular LAN and train people how to use the connection.

▶▶ *Dedicated Link Connections*

A *dedicated link* is a permanent connection over a telephone line between a modem and a modem or a router and a router. A *router* is a specialized computer that reads the addresses of each TCP/IP packet and sends the packet to its destination. At lower transmission speeds (up to 28.8 Kbps), modems are used. At higher speeds (56 Kbps and above), routers are used. With a dedicated link, your personal computer or LAN is connected to the Internet at all times.

 ▶ ▶ M A S T E R   W O R D S

> **How many people and workstations are connected to the net? Let's look at the numbers: there are a reputed 20,000,000 Internet users world-wide. The largest commercial provider in the US has slightly over 40,000 users, including both dialup and direct links. Estimates based on domain names and IP number assignments indicate that there are close to 2 million dedicated workstations.**

What Types of Users Is This Best For?

A full, dedicated, high-speed network connection is best for organizations that want to provide information to the Internet and who desire a 24-hour, 7-day connection. In general, this type of connection is best for a larger organization that is serving many internal as well as external customers. Smaller organizations may do better by obtaining individual accounts with a service provider and using the services of an information publishing organization.

What You Can Do

With a permanent connection, you have all the basic Internet applications available to you. Once you have installed the software on your end of the link, the basic Internet tools and resources are always at your fingertips. However, with this type of connection it is relatively easy to become an information provider yourself. (Becoming an information provider is discussed in Part II.) You could set up your computer or your network server to be accessible to anyone connected to the Internet 24 hours a day, 7 days a week. This makes it easier for your customers to obtain information or support, or for information about your organization or school to be made available. (Remember that to make information available, or to access information over the Net, still requires that you install and run Internet tools on your end of the connection. Some of these are more difficult than others: particularly those tools that allow others to get to your information, such as servers for file transfer, Gopher, and World Wide Web access.)

What You Cannot Do with It

This connection is what is described as a "full" connection. There are no features available to the Internet that you cannot use. You may choose not to use some of them for security, privacy, or policy reasons, but there is nothing you *cannot* do.

What Will It Cost?

Full connection costs have four components:

1. the network connection charge
2. the local loop (sometimes called tail circuit) charge (this is the charge for the physical line to your site)
3. the necessary one-time hardware and software and setup charges
4. recurring maintenance costs.

Network connection fees vary based on speed of the connection. A 14.4 Kbps connection can cost less than $150 per month. (Note, however, that many providers are moving away from direct connections at this speed, because of the popularity and availability of dialup modems that handle these speeds.) A T-1 (or 1.5 Mbps) connection can run more than $1000 per month. A T-3 (45 Mbps) connection can cost even more than that. (See the provider chart at the end of this section for more specific cost information.)

The local loop charges also vary with the speed of the connection and with distance from your Internet access provider's network access point. (These are sometimes called *points of presence* or *POPs*.) Local line charges are usually based on cost per mile or cost per foot from the point of presence. In general, however, because local rate and line charges are "tariffed" (or set by Public Utilities Commissions), there will not be much difference among providers.

Some of you will have several choices of provider in your geographical area: some only one. It largely depends on the competition for data services in your area, the remoteness of your location, and other local

HOW MANY STAFFERS WILL IT TAKE TO MAINTAIN YOUR RESOURCE?

In general, your support staff varies based on what you are doing and how many people you are supporting.

For an office of 1–10 workstations, expect one part-time systems administrator (sysadmin) and one person who knows what to do in a pinch (someone who knows where the manuals are and knows the appropriate systems passwords).

For 10–20 workstations, plan on two part-time systems administrators or one full-time and one part-time admininistator (and if you are providing online resources for customers, one full-time person to handle those resources).

For 20–50 workstations, you need two full-time administrators (and a vacation or emergency backup), and at least one part-time internal customer support person. If you also support external clients or have online resources, you need at least one full-time person to handle that support (preferably, one person to handle maintenance of the resource and another to answer customer questions).

Once you get beyond 50 workstations, you will need a network administration department, and the manager you hire for that job will be best able to determine how many staff are necessary to keep you up and running smoothly.

and regional regulations. Be sure and call several providers to determine if there is more than one provider in your area.

One-time hardware and software costs vary widely depending on what's available from your provider, what you already have, what discounts you can get from vendors, and so on. Your best bet is to get several estimates and compare carefully. If you do not feel comfortable making the determination of the best deal for you, consider hiring a network consulting firm. Ask your provider candidates who they work with, or ask other businesses who they used or were happy with. In calculating recurring costs, you should not neglect to consider personnel training, salaries, and benefit costs for the people it will take to maintain your server and network connection. People with the requisite technical knowledge are in high demand and can command high salaries. If you choose to train someone already on your staff to troubleshoot and maintain your connection, you must consider the lead time for the person to learn the necessary skills, the training costs, and the costs incurred in reassigning some of that person's tasks to another staff member. It is important for you to consider all your recurring costs when contemplating a network connection.

What Do I Need to Know to Use It?

Using your own network connection well requires several kinds of skills. You need people who know how to design and present information using the Internet tool kits (such as Gopher, WWW, and FTP archive software). You need people who know how to build and maintain networks themselves and are able to work with the network engineers of your service provider to find and repair problems. And, finally, you need to have people who understand how to use the Internet tools to find information that will be needed by your organization.

▶ *Information Publishers (Dialup)*

Information publishing is one of the newer ways to make your organization's information available without requiring the initial outlay of resources (time as well as money) that comes with obtaining a full Internet connection. Essentially, having your information published is "out-sourcing" the development, presentation, and maintenance of the information server to a company that takes your materials and works with you to design an appropriate presentation of your material on the Internet.

Besides designing the presentation, an information publisher can also publish your information on the Internet. For example, Internet Distribution Services of Palo Alto, California, will design and build a series of pages for the World Wide Web for you (the Web is discussed in Chapter 11). You can then contract with IDS to publish the pages on their server or present them on your own server. If they publish the pages, there is no need for your company to manage its own network connection. This option is particularly attractive to organizations that are not ready to maintain their own connections, or don't want to do so. With an information publisher, you can use lower-bandwidth, lower-cost connections for your personnel and yet still reap the benefits of maintaining a presence on the Internet.

What Types of Users Is This Best For?

Organizations that want an Internet presence and aren't ready (or don't want) to manage their own connections can benefit from this service. So, too, can small or geographically distant organizations for whom the cost of a full connection would be prohibitive.

What You Can Do with It

Information publishers generally support access through Gopher and/or WWW. Some will also provide access to FTP libraries, so that you can store material for your clients/customers to download. Finally, an information publisher may file domain registration forms for you and manage the publishing system as if it were in your network domain. This means that to the user, the computer system managed at the publisher's location would carry a domain address that identified it as part of your organization's domain. For example, if SmallCo, Inc., wanted to have a Web server but didn't want to maintain their own machine, they would contract with NetPublishers, Inc., to handle the Web server and information. The Web server would be running on NetPublisher's machine, `clients.netpub.com`. However, SmallCo could advertise to their customers that they had a Web server running at `www.smallco.com`.

What You Cannot Do with It

Usually information publishers will have secure systems, so you will not be able to give accounts on that machine for your customers to log in to, for example. You may be able to leave materials on the system (perhaps by anonymous FTP, for example) for the publisher to convert into Web or other server information.

What Will It Cost?

As you'll see in the list that follows, costs can vary widely. They will include both development costs and recurring management costs. You can compare the recurring management costs to those you would incur if you wished to manage your own server and network connections.

What Do I Need to Know to Use It?

You need only be able to select a publisher that meets your needs.

► A List of Information Publishers

This is a partial list of companies providing various information publishing services. We make no recommendations of any of these services by providing this list. In choosing which services to include, we have selected those who have high-speed links, offer a wide variety of services, or who are addressing a specialty market.

Comments and service descriptions are provided by the companies themselves, or taken from their marketing literature. We make no guarantees of accuracy. Prices are subject to change. Many of the companies offer services beyond the Web information-publishing services listed here; contact them for further information.

A complete list of providers is maintained by Mary E. S. Morris of Finesse Liveware (`marym@finesse.com`). You can obtain a copy of her list using:

- Anonymous FTP: `ftp://ftp.einet.net`. Then choose /pub/INET-MARKETING/www-svc-providers.

- E-mail: `wwwproviders@finesse.com`—no message needed.

- NetNews: Routine posts to : `alt.internet.services` and `comp.infosystems.www.providers`.

A+ Marketing

Contact Info: `Sully@digimark.net` for WWW services; `bbrca@aol.com` for mailserv's

Link Speed: To the Internet: 56 Kbps.

URL: `http://www.digimark.net/A+/`

WWW Services Provided: Home/basic Web page serving, HTML authoring/Web application development.

Setup Cost: $50 for Regular service

Monthly Cost: $150

Atlantic Computing Technology Corporation

Contact Info: Rick Romkey (`pokey@atlantic.com`)

Link Speed: 56 Kbps

URL: `http://www.atlantic.com/`

WWW Services Provided: Home/basic Web page serving, CGI script processing, WAIS or other search utilities, HTML authoring/Web application development, pre-built applications, Other— Any type of Internet publishing or business solutions.

Setup Cost: Starting at around $1450 for WWW, $200 for Gopher/FTP.

Monthly Cost: Starting at around $75 for WWW, $50 for Gopher/FTP

Baynet Co.

Contact Info: Joe Mizrahi, 408-720-8892

Link Speed: ISDN (128 Kbps)

WWW Services Provided: Home/basic Web page serving, CGI script processing, WAIS or other search utilities, HTML authoring/Web application development.

Cost: Pricing is different for the different vertical markets we are focusing on. Example: For a real estate agent to advertise one home listing it costs $35 1st mo./$25 following months. That includes a "standard" listing and one photo. However, there are quite different service and pricing schemes for mail-order catalogs or newspapers. For these customers only, we offer the electronic newsletter service bundled with the complete service package. For non-profits, we even offer free Web services as long as they do most of the editing.

BEDROCK Information Solutions, Inc.

8000 Towers Crescent Drive, #1350
Vienna, VA 22182

Voice: 703-760-7898

Contact Info: Barry Jackson (barry@end2.bedrock.com)

Link Speed: T-1

URL: http://www.bedrock.com/

WWW Services Provided: Home/basic Web page serving, CGI script processing, training on Internet tools usage and WWW server setup.

Setup Cost: Approximately $50–$7000+ varies based on desired options and services.

Monthly Cost: Approximately $50–$1250+ varies based on desired options and services.

Branch Information Services

Contact Info: Jon Zeeff (jon@b-tech.ann-arbor.mi.us)

Link Speed: T-1

URL: http://branch.com

WWW Services Provided: Home/basic Web page serving, CGI script processing, WAIS or other search utilities, HTML authoring/Web application development, pre-built applications, Other—Order-to-FAX processing.

Setup Cost: $480

Monthly Cost: $40

Catalog.Com Internet Services (by Network Wizards)

Contact Info: info@catalog.com

Link Speed: T-1

URL: http://www.catalog.com

WWW Services Provided: Home/basic Web page serving.

Setup Cost: $50 setup gives 3 months basic service

Monthly Cost: $10 includes 5Mb disk and 100Mb transmission per month additional at .20/Mb (disk) and .10/Mb (transmission). DNS consulting/services are available for an additional fee. Additional info on http://www.catalog.com.

The Computing Support Team, Inc.

URL: http://www.gems.com/

800-493-GEMS or +1.315.453.2035

staff@gems.com

Contact Info: George Boyce (george@csteam.com)

Link Speed: T-1

WWW Services Provided: Home/basic Web page serving, CGI script processing, WAIS or other search utilities, HTML authoring/Web application development, Other—Easy-to-use catalog services.

Setup Cost: $50

Monthly Cost: None. First document is $150 per year, additional documents are $20 per year. Production services are $50 per hour.

Comments: Our own Web service is called Global Electronic Marketing Service and is at http://www.gems.com/. We are a full-service software design and development firm. We have a federal contract to develop a 2nd generation Web service for the Department of Education. We have special focus areas for real estate and general marketing. Our net is connected to the NYSERNet (New York State) backbone at the NYSERNet corporate office which is located across the hall.

CyberBeach Publishing/CyberGate

Link Speed: T-1

Contact Info: Dirk Herr-Hoyman (hoymand @gate.net)

1-800-NET-GATE

Geographic Area Served: Much of Florida, 305, 407, 813, 904 area codes

URL: http://www.gate.net/

WWW Services Provided: Home/basic Web page serving, CGI script processing, WAIS or other search utilities, HTML authoring/Web application development, pre-built applications, database-to-HTML conversions.

Cyberspace Development, Inc.

(owners and operators of The Internet Information Mall™)

Contact Info: Andrew Currie, President or Karyn German, Accounts Manager (kgerman@marketplace.com) (303) 759-1289

URL: http://marketplace.com

Link Speed: T-1 (1.544 Mbps)

Options for Connecting

▶▶

ch.
4

WWW Services Provided: Home/basic Web page serving, WAIS or other search utilities, HTML authoring/Web application development.

Setup Cost: Please see prices@marketplace.com.

Monthly Cost: Please see prices@marketplace.com.

Demon Internet Ltd

Phone: 44 181-349 0063

FAX: 44 181-349 0309

Contact Info: Grahame Davies (grahame@demon.co.uk)

Link Speed: We have 256K to the States and offer up to 64K links

URL: http://www.demon.co.uk/

WWW Services Provided: Home/basic Web page serving, CGI script processing, WAIS or other search utilities, HTML authoring/Web application development.

Setup Cost: For Web: #50 (pounds sterling)

Monthly Cost: For Web: From #25 per month (5Mb).

Digital Marketing, Inc. (DigiMark)—An Internet Services Company

Contact Info: Gary Goldberg (og@digimark.net)

Link Speed: T-1

URL: http://www.digimark.net/

WWW Services Provided: Home/basic Web page serving, CGI script processing, HTML authoring/Web application development, Other—mailing list services, on-site server hosting.

Monthly Cost: $25 for 25MB, $1/MB additional on personal business plans, content preparation, consulting available.

Downtown Anywhere Inc.

Phone: 617-522-8102

FAX: 617-522-5734

32 Woodland Road
Boston, MA 02130

URL: http://www.awa.com/

Contact Info: Sandy Bendremer (sandy@awa.com)

Link Speed: Frac T-1

WWW Services Provided: Home/basic Web page serving, CGI script processing, WAIS or other search utilities, HTML authoring/Web application development, pre-built applications, Other—Secure order and credit card processing.

Setup Cost: $0 and up

Monthly Cost: $0 and up

Comments: Downtown Anywhere provides for both a rent and commission model for payment. Although we can provide prime virtual real estate at competitive flat monthly rates, we are prepared to accept commissions on sales in lieu of up-front payments. Downtown Anywhere is also unique in that it attracts visitors by providing free and friendly access to valuable resources.

Electric Press, Inc.

URL: http://www.elpress.com

Contact Info: Robert Main (703) 742-3308 (Rob_Main@notes.elpress.com)

Link Speed: T-1

WWW Services Provided: Home/basic Web page serving, CGI script processing, WAIS or other search utilities, HTML authoring/Web application development, pre-built applications, Other—Complete turnkey systems including requirements, analysis, design layout, marketing, and public relations.

Options for
Connecting

ch.
4

Setup Cost: $6950 (including separate machine and design and layout of up to 25 pages) + $6000 for conversion and load of large product catalog.

Monthly Cost: $1125

Global OnLine (part of CityScape Internet Services Ltd)

Phone: (UK) 0223 566950

Contact Info: Tony Jewell (tony@cityscape.co.uk)

Link Speed: 128K

WWW Services Provided: Home/basic Web page serving, CGI script processing, WAIS or other search utilities, HTML authoring/Web application development, pre-built applications, single-user dialup WWW access in the UK.

Setup Cost: From 400 GBP per day.

Monthly Cost: From 100 GBP per month per meg.

IDS World Network Internet Access Services

3 Franklin Rd
East Greenwich, RI 02818

Phone: (800)IDS-1680

Contact Info: Customer Services, info@ids.net

Link Speed: Dialup: 28.8k baud. To the Internet: T1 and 56k

URL: http://www.ids.net

WWW Services Provided: Home/basic Web page serving, CGI script processing, WAIS or other search utilities, HTML authoring/ Web application development, pre-built applications, photograph digitizing (scanning), newsprint to HTML conversions, electronic newspapers.

Setup Cost: For standard dialup accounts–none.

Monthly Cost: For standard dialup accounts–$15 to $17/month.

InfoMatch Communications Inc.

Phone: Vancouver BC 604-421-3230

Contact Info: John Chapman (john@infomatch.com)

URL: http://infomatch.com

Link Speed: 56K–T2

WWW Services Provided: Home/basic Web page serving, CGI script processing, WAIS or other search utilities, HTML authoring/Web application development, pre-built applications.

Setup Cost: None for first-time clients.

Monthly Cost: $40 per meg or portion.

The Innovation Group/Metro.net

Contact Info: Mike Greenhalgh or Mike Kovatch (Postmaster@igdell.mk.slip)

Link Speed: up to 10 million bits per second!

WWW Services Provided: Home/basic Web page serving, CGI script processing, WAIS or other search utilities, HTML authoring/Web application development, pre-built applications.

Setup Cost: $250

Monthly Cost: $50

Interlink On-Line Services

Contact Info: Dave Allen (allen@freenet.victoria.bc.ca)

Link Speed: 56 K

URL: http://www.interlink.bc.ca/

WWW Services Provided: Home/basic Web page serving, CGI script processing, HTML authoring/Web application development.

Setup Cost: Home Page: $100.00CDN No setup for subsequent pages changes to pages after setup $25.00 + hourly rate

Monthly Cost: $45.00–$720.00 (Varies by term of service and volume). There is a 10% discount for prepayment of account. All amounts are Canadian Dollars which means approximately a 45% discount to US Businesses.

Internet Distribution Services, Inc.

Contact Info: Marc Fleischmann 415-856-8265 (marcf@netcom.com)

Link Speed: Multiple links, 56Kb–T1

URL: http://www.service.com/

WWW Services Provided: Home/basic Web page serving, CGI script processing, WAIS or other search utilities, HTML authoring/Web application development, pre-built applications. Other: IDS provides complete packages containing market analysis, promotion development, graphic design, implementation, and Internet hostings.

Setup Cost: Generally running from $5,000 to $15,000

Monthly Cost: Generally running from $500 to $2500

The Internet Group

245 Lehigh Avenue, Pittsburgh, PA 15232

Phone: 412-661-4247

FAX: 412-661-6927

E-mail: bauer@tig.com

Contact Info: Michael Bauer, President

URL: http://www.tig.com/

Link Speed: T-1

WWW Services Provided: Home/basic Web page serving, CGI script processing, WAIS or other search utilities, HTML authoring/Web application development, Other—We specialize in installing Direct Internet, Marketing Channels for companies. Our clients include Black Box and Fisher Scientific.

Other Services Provided: FTP, E-mail, Auto Response E-mail, Gopher servers

Setup Cost: $325

Monthly Cost: $85

Internet Information Services, Inc.

Home of the IIS Internet Business Center

Contact Info: Chris Clark (`cjc@iis.com`)

Voice: 1 800 NET SVC1 (638 7821)

Auto Reply Info: `info@iis.com`

URL: `http://www.iis.com`

Link Speed: T1

Geographic Area Served: 301, 410 and 703 area codes. There is also 800 number access.

WWW Services Provided: Home/basic Web page serving, CGI script processing, WAIS and other database search utilities, HTML authoring/Web application development, pre-built applications, scanning, graphic design and duplication, customized announcements on the Internet, and other on-line services.

Setup Cost: $75/hour for setup virtual domain, $5,000 setup for dedicated domain.

Monthly Cost: $125/month for virtual domain, $1,000/month for dedicated domain.

Comments: Try `http://www.iis.com`, `http://www.iis.com/iis/prices.html`

Internet Marketing Inc.

Contact Info: 312-248-8649 or info@mcs.net

Link Speed: T-1

URL: http://cybersight.com/cgi-bin/imi/s?main.gmmland or http://cybersight.com/cgi-bin/cs/s?main.gmml

WWW Services Provided: Home/basic Web page serving, CGI script processing, WAIS or other search utilities, HTML authoring/Web application development, Other—Links to on-line publications: CyberSight (targeting "Generation X readers"), BusinessWeb.

Setup Cost: $100/hour; varies.

Monthly Cost: Links: $200/month; storage: varies.

Internet Media Services

Contact Info: John Celestian/Andrew Conru (conru@cdr.stanford.edu), 415-328-4638

Link Speed: T-1

WWW Services Provided: Home/basic Web page serving, CGI script processing, WAIS or other search utilities, HTML authoring/Web application development, pre-built applications.

Setup Cost: depends ($200-20,000)

Monthly Cost: depends ($20-300+)

Internet Presence & Publishing, Inc.

1700 World Trade Center
Norfolk, Virginia 23510

Phone: 804-446-9060

FAX: 804-446-9061

Contact Info: Keith Basil (keith@tcp.ip.net)

Link Speed: T-1

URL: http://www.shopkeeper.com/shops.html

WWW Services Provided: Home/basic Web page serving, CGI script processing, WAIS or other search utilities, HTML authoring/Web application development, pre-built applications, Other— Internet Business Reply(™) forms.

Setup Cost: Varies depending on service.

Monthly Cost: Varies depending on service.

InterNex Information Services, Inc.

Robert J. Berger—President
1050 Chestnut Street Suite 202, Menlo Park, CA 94025

Voice: 415-473-3060

FAX: 415-473-3062

E-mail: rberger@internex.net

Contact Info: Bill Selmeir

Link Speed: T-1

URL: http://www.internex.net/

WWW Services Provided: Home/basic Web page serving, CGI script processing, WAIS or other search utilities, HTML authoring/Web application development.

Setup Cost: Varies.

Monthly Cost: Varies.

Internex Online

Contact Info: Marc Fournier, scrappy@io.org

Link Speed: 14.4K dialup

Options for Connecting

ch.
4

Geographic Area Served: Metro Toronto calling area (all of 416, some of 905). Basically anyone with a postal code starting with M.

URL: http://www.io.org/

WWW Services Provided: Home/basic Web page serving, CGI script processing, pre-built applications.

Mainsail Marketing Information, Inc.

Contact Info: Mark White (mmi@mainsail.com)

Link Speed: 28,800

URL: http://mainsail.com/

WWW Services Provided: We are creating an electronic directory of the direct marketing industry. Up until now the industry relies on a very large, 2000 page, print directory. Companies will list their services and we will include detailed information on thousands of mailing lists that are offered for 'rent' to direct marketers. It will also include an on-line booklet about direct marketing, a job center for jobs wanted and jobs offered postings and a 'magazine section' that will be comprised of submissions from directory users about anything of interest to the industry. Unlike the expensive print directory, this information will be freely available to everyone on the Internet.

Setup Cost: $50.00 account set up

Monthly Cost: $18.00 per month for company listing and full page ad

NetAxis

65 High Ridge Rd, Suite 363
Stamford, CT 06902

Phone: 203-969-0618

FAX: 203-921-1544

Contact: Luis Hernandez, sales—luis@netaxis.com

Link Speed: T1

Web Page Pointer: www.netaxis.com

WWW Services Provided: Home/basic Web page serving, CGI script processing

Local calling area: Connecticut

Setup Cost: From $60

Monthly Cost: From $25

Comments: Home of The Online Advertiser, providing regional and national advertising space via WWW.

The New York Web

URL: http://nyweb.com/

Contact Info: Stephan Moskovic (mosco@mailhost.nyweb.com)

Link Speed: T-1

WWW Services Provided: Home/basic Web page serving, CGI script processing, WAIS or other search utilities, HTML authoring/Web application development, pre-built applications, Other—custom databases and custom multimedia, including video and audio.

Setup Cost: negotiable

Monthly Cost: negotiable

NSTN Inc.

Voice: 902-481-4505

FAX: 902-468-3679

E-mail: heath@nstn.ca

URL: http://www.nstn.ca or gopher.nstn.ca:70/

Contact Info: Steven Heath (HEATH@hawk.nstn.ca)

Link Speed: T1, member of the CA*net

Geographic Area Served: 902, 506, 613, 813 area codes

URL: http://www.nstn.ca/

WWW Services Provided: Home/basic Web page serving, CGI script processing, WAIS or other search utilities, HTML authoring/Web application development, pre-built applications, Other— SecureWeb, a method to restrict access to pages, HTTP forms.

Setup Cost: Custom quote, based on the role of NSTN and the requirements.

Monthly Cost: $75 per month and up; we will quote a flat rate upon receipt of requirements

Comments: NSTN Inc. has being running the CyberMall for over a year. The CyberMall is a location for business to pool together to share costs and leads. NSTN Inc. is also the largest Internet provider in Canada.

Oslonett, Inc.

Contact Info: Tore Karlsen (tore@oslonett.no)

Link Speed: 128K and 64K full synchronous, dialup up to 28,800 (V.fast)

WWW Services Provided: Home/basic Web page serving, CGI script processing, WAIS or other search utilities, HTML authoring/Web application development, pre-built applications, Other—see info on URL http://www.oslonett.no.

Charges: Yearly charge for a dialup user is 550 NOK (about $80). Connection charges depending on time-of-day, full info on e-mail auto responder info@oslonett.no.

Yearly account fee 550 NOK US$ 80.88

Low volume Web page/yr 3,800 NOK US$ 558.82

High volume Web page/yr34,000 NOK US$ 5000.00

Company profile: http://www.oslonett.no/html/adv/ON/ON.html/

Primenet

Contact Info: Jim Lippard (602) 870-1010 ext. 108 (lippard@primenet.com)

Link Speed: Internet Connection: T-1 Dialup lines: 28.8 and 56K Frame relay

URL: http://www.primenet.com/

WWW Services Provided: Home/basic Web page serving, CGI script processing, HTML authoring/Web application development, pre-built applications.

Setup Cost: Varies with amount and type of material (e.g., extra costs for scanning images and OCR scanning).

Monthly Cost: $50 for up to 10 Mb. $10 for each additional 10Mb.

Quadralay Corporation

Phone: 512-346-9199

FAX: 512-346-8990

FTP Address: ftp.quadralay.com

WWW Server: www.quadralay.com

Contact Info: Brian Combs (combs@quadralay.com)

Link Speed: T-1

URL: http://www.quadralay.com/home.html/

WWW Services Provided: Home/basic Web page serving, CGI script processing, WAIS or other search utilities, HTML authoring/Web application development, pre-built applications.

Setup Cost: Variable. There is no installation charge for Web space *per se*, but HTML authoring is billed.

Monthly Cost: Highly variable depending upon what the customer wants. The basic rate is $550/month which buys the customer up to 50K worth of text and 200K worth of graphics. Send for price sheet.

Quantum Networking Solutions

Contact Info: Patrick A. Linstruth (patrick@ukelele.GCR.COM)

Link Speed: T-1

URL: http://www.gcr.com/mall/

WWW Services Provided: Home/basic Web page serving, CGI script processing, HTML authoring/Web application development, Other—merchant services, order processing, on-line catalogs (an Internet Shopping Mall).

Setup Cost: $400 for basic WWW merchant storefront setup.

Monthly Cost: $350 for basic storefront.

RTD Systems & Networking, Inc.

4003 E Speedway Blvd, Ste 123, Tucson AZ 85712

E-Mail: rawn@rtd.com

Phone: 602-318-0696

FAX: 602-322-9755

Contact Info: Rawn Shah

Link Speed: T-1

URL: http://www.rtd.com/

Geographic Area Served: 602 Area Code LATA: 668, Tucson.

WWW Services Provided: Home/basic Web page serving, CGI script processing, HTML authoring/Web application development, pre-built applications.

Setup Cost: File Processing/Conversion: $50/hr File Editing: $50/hr

Monthly Cost: File Storage: $1 per 100 KB of data. Maintenance: $50. Advertising: $100

Sell-it on the WWW

Contact Info: Brian Knight (dknight@powergrid.elec-triciti.com)

Link Speed: WWW server runs on a T1 connection

URL: http://www.electriciti.com/www-ads/index.htm/

WWW Services Provided: Home/basic Web page serving, HTML authoring/Web application development. Other: E-mail forms—send e-mail to an Internet address directly from WWW page.

Setup Cost: None

Monthly Cost: $5 plus storage charge if HTML documents are already written and will be maintained/updated (if necessary) by the owner. $10 plus storage charge if Sell-it writes and updates HTML documents. Storage charge: $0.25 per 10K (per month) of data and additional features (sounds, graphics, movies, etc.) used for the WWW pages.

The Sphere Information Services

Contact Info: Dan Pritchett (dlp@netcom.com)

Phone: 408-369-9105

Link Speed: 56 Kbps

URL: http://www.thesphere.com/

WWW Services Provided: Home/basic Web page serving, CGI script processing, HTML authoring/Web application development.

Setup Cost: Hourly cost for web authoring: $50, No setup cost for pre-authored pages.

Monthly Cost: $50/month—first 5 pages; $10/page/month—next 5 pages; $5/page/month—pages beyond first 10. Page is 50 lines of text. Graphics counts as 20 lines.

SSNet, Inc.

Contact Info: Russ Sarbora (russ@marlin.ssnet.com)

Link Speed: 56K

URL: http://ssnet.com:8010/ssnet/ssnhome.html/

WWW Services Provided: Home/basic Web page serving, CGI script processing, WAIS or other search utilities, HTML authoring/Web application development, pre-built applications.

Setup Cost: $25

Monthly Cost: $25 (These prices are for our most basic service. More advanced projects are more expensive.)

Stelcom, Inc.

661A East Broadway
Long Beach, NY 11561

Phone: 516-897-8168

FAX: 516-897-3793

Contact Info: David Staschover (davids@webscope.com)

Link Speed: Frac T1

URL: http://www.webscope.com/

WWW Services Provided: Home/basic Web page serving, CGI script processing, HTML authoring/Web application development.

Setup Cost: $600

Monthly Cost: $350 Our monthly cost provides 5 pages + a form page.

TeleVisions Inc.

Boston Area Internet Marketing Company

Contact Info: Ralph Folz (folz@tvisions.com)

Phone: 508-263-0430

FAX: 508-263-5604

E-mail: info@tvisions.com

URL: http://www.tvisions.com/

Link Speed: T1

WWW Services Provided: Home/basic Web page serving, HTML authoring/Web application development, Complete Internet marketing solutions, establishment of web servers, tools for creating and maintaining electronic documents, mechanisms for tracking and billing customers, development of novel customer interaction features, video digitization including MPEG, M-JPEG, AVI, and QuickTime.

Setup Cost: On-Line Quote Service.

Monthly Cost: On-Line Quote Service.

WorldWide Access

Computing Engineers, Inc.

Home of WorldWide Access (SM)

Data: 312-282-8605 or 708-367-1871

Voice: 708-367-1870

Info: info@wwa.com

Support: support@wwa.com

Link Speed: 56K

Geographic Area Served: 312 and 708 calling areas

URL: http://www.wwa.com/

WWW Services Provided: Home/basic Web page serving, CGI script processing, WAIS or other search utilities, HTML authoring/Web application development, pre-built applications

Monthly Cost: $50/month with 25M of disk space.

XOR Network Engineering/The Internet Plaza

Contact Info: plaza@plaza.xor.com

Link Speed: Full T-1

Phone: 303-440-6093

URL: http://plaza.xor.com/

Gopher: plaza.xor.com

WWW Services Provided: Home/basic Web page serving, CGI script processing, WAIS or other search utilities, HTML authoring/Web application development, Other—Hyperlinks to existing servers.

Costs: Premium Package (both a Gopher and a World Wide Web server): $150/document (up to 4 images per page, additional images $50 each); $250 Startup Fee; $275/month rental fee. For companies that take online orders, there is a transaction fee of 10% of each order.

Basic Package (Gopher server): $50/document(1); $75 setup fee; $100/month rental fee (3 month minimum).

Hyperlink Package (A Plaza link to an already existing Gopher/WWW server): $45 annual fee.

▶▶ How Big a Connection Do I Need?

To answer that question, you first need to understand what "big" means in terms of data transfer capabilities.

▶ Measurements

Data transfer speeds are usually expressed in bits per second. Sometimes you may see faster speeds expressed in bytes (or thousands of bytes) per second. A byte is roughly the equivalent of a single character. (There are 8 bits in a byte. A single bit is represented by either a 1 or a 0. These digits are our visual representation of the on/off impulses that are carried on the network.)

Note that we said *network*, not *wire*. Many times a network is not a wire. The medium may be copper wire in some places. It may also be a fiber optic link, a microwave link, a radio transmission; in short, any method that can be used to carry the impulses. The network providers and the telephone companies continually strive to improve the transmission media and the rules by which the data are carried. As an example, in the late 1980s, when the NSFNET was implemented, the ultra-high speed connection that was estimated to be appropriate (considering availability, current technology, and costs) was a 56 Kbps connection. At that time, the connection was considered "state-of-the-art."

Almost before the connections were completed, the demand exceeded the ability of the network to carry the traffic. So the T-1 NSFNET was proposed. T-1 transfers data at the rate of 1.544 Mbps (1.5+ million bits per second). This was *so* fast and could carry so much more data that some people believed the expense in implementation and recurring costs would not be practical—the network, they believed, would be underutilized. Instead, what happened is that new applications were developed and more and more new users were connected; and the T-1 network, too, became saturated.

The T-3 NSFNET was begun. The T-3 rate is 45 Mbps. The network designers had, however, learned well. Before the T-3 NSFNET backbone was fully operational, designers and researchers had begun work on additional technologies to meet the needs of as-yet-unanticipated applications.

▶ **BITS AND BYTES: A QUICK SUMMARY**

Files are measured in bytes:

   KB = kilobytes=thousand bytes

   MB=megabytes=million bytes

   GB=gigabytes=trillion bytes

Transfer speeds are measured as bits:

   byte=8 bits

When we start talking about how much traffic can go over a network connection, you will begin to hear people talk about *bandwidth*. This term comes out of radio and television, where it defines the range of a frequency, or band, that signals can be carried on. Carried over into data networking, bandwidth describes the amount of information that can be carried on a specific connection. Extremely fast connections have a lot of bandwidth: a great deal of information can be carried on those links. Applications that require high bandwidth include audio, video, and graphic-intensive applications such as World Wide Web.

► Estimating Bandwidth: How Wide a Band Do I Need?

The answer to this question depends entirely on what information you want to move. There are enormous differences in file size for different kinds of information:

Type of Information	Typical File Size
e-mail message	2.2 KB
longer document (20 pgs)	44 KB
Graphic image	330 KB
1 minute of audio	475 KB
1 minute video	2400 KB

Network connections are sometimes call *pipelines*. This helps us visualize how we transfer data. You can think of the data as a liquid you are pouring into a pipe. Data to be transferred is contained; that is, it is of fixed size: the user or even the user's application may not report what the exact size of the data is, but the transfer protocols themselves use the size information to make sure that the transfer is complete and correct. Because the amount of data is known and the size of the pipeline can be known, it is possible to estimate how long it will take to move your data through a pipe of a specific size.

▶ ▶ **M A S T E R W O R D S**

Some service providers offer what they call "bitpipe" service. This means that they simply provide a wire over which bits can be pushed. You provide all the maintenance and programming expertise.

Now, think about the kind of information you want to move. Let's say we have an e-mail message of approximately 2.2 KB. Remember, we need to multiply by 8 to count the number of bits: 2.2 KB × 8 bits/byte = 17,600 bits. If we divide that by 2400 bps (a common _slow_ modem in 1994) we arrive at 17600/2400 or a little less than 7.5 seconds. At 2400 bps, it doesn't really matter if we round off this way, because the speed is relatively slow and it's hard to optimize sufficiently well so that the "extra" seconds used are really noticeable.

However, if we take that same message and send it at 9600 bps (a typical faster modem rate), it will take only 1.83 seconds. Table 4.1 summarizes the difference in transfer rates.

▶ **TABLE 4.1:** _Relative Speeds of an E-Mail Message of 2.2 KB_

RATE	TRANSFER TIME	IMPROVEMENT
2400 bps	7.3 seconds	(base)
9600 bps	1.83 seconds	3.98 times faster
19200bps	0.916 seconds	7.96 times faster
56 Kbps	0.314 seconds	23.24 times faster
1.5 Mbps	0.0113 seconds	646.01 times faster
45 Mbps	0.00039 seconds	1871.79 times faster

MASTER WORDS

The strength of a TCP/IP connection is that each packet can be routed through any open point in the connected networks. This allows transmission, even if some point in the connected network becomes unavailable during the transmission itself. The weakness of packet routing is that since no particular packet is guaranteed to traverse any particular network route, no one can guarantee that your packets will have the same bandwidth available to them from the beginning to the end of their route. This means that if you want to move data from point A to point B, you need to consider the bandwidth of the networks between those two points. If you are considering purchasing a T-1 connection, but the network to which you wish to deliver information has a 56 Kbps connection, the network can only deliver information to the destination effectively at 56 Kbps. The data will queue on the network and will take longer to deliver than if there were a T-1 connection all the way through.

Diagnosing Congestion and Bandwidth Problems

Once you begin to gain expertise in file transfers and other network information transfers, you will begin to care even more about the bandwidth between you and your target. Particularly if you want to get information from a host that's behind a slow link, or if you find yourself on a very congested connection, you'll want to know how to connect to and use more efficient connections. You may not care during the early days of your Internet exploration (although we know you will be frustrated if you get stuck on a really slow resource).

If you care about estimating bandwidth and about understanding bottlenecks and congestion, these next paragraphs are for you.

In packet routing, you may not know all the points in the network between the starting and ending points. But you can ask in general about the bandwidth of your network provider, about the bandwidth of their connection into the larger Internet, or their connection into parallel networks.

The easiest method for figuring bandwidth is for you and the other party to be served by the same provider and know the bandwidth of all the network connections between your two points. Then you just need to look at three factors: your connection to the network provider, the provider's network bandwidth, and the connection to the target destination. The smallest number will be the effective throughput rate. If you are not connected through the same service provider, the exercise remains the same, but finding out all the possible bottlenecks becomes more difficult.

Here's a simple exercise in determining bandwidth:

SmallCo is connected to the Net at 56Kbps. This means that their link is capable of handling 56,000 bits per second of information. If the whole pathway was running at this speed, it would take 2.3 minutes to transfer 1 megabyte of data, about the same as a full 3.5″ high-density diskette.

Their network provider has a backbone speed of T-1 (1.5 million bits per second). If the whole pathway was running at T-1, it would take .08 minutes to transfer the data.

SmallCo wants to transfer this file to MyCustomer, who has an account on HappyBBS, which has a 14,400 bps link to the same network provider.

The data leaves SmallCo's machine at 56,000 per second. When it gets to the network backbone, it speeds up to T-1 speeds. But when it gets to the link at HappyBBS, it has to slow down to 14,400 bps.

The most important thing to remember here, despite all the numbers, is that the data can't be transferred faster than the slowest link. Thus, it takes 9 minutes to transfer the data from SmallCo to MyCustomer's account space on HappyBBS.

Choosing a Provider of Dialup Internet Services

Finding Who the Providers Are The easiest way to do this is to ask someone you know who is already connected about their provider. Find out if you need to be a member of some organization or if anyone can join. Ask them if they like the service provided. Would they recommend that service or some other one instead? If you ask them nicely, maybe you can get this person to obtain information for you on the Internet itself. One of the first places to look is at the InterNIC, the Internet Network Information Center, which is funded to help with questions like this. The InterNIC maintains information that points to lists like Peter Kaminski's PDIAL list of public access providers or the Nix-Pub list of Public access UNIX sites. This information is also readily available throughout the Internet via Gopher servers and WWW pages from the providers themselves. (For example, you can use `gopher.psi.com`, `www.merit.edu`, or `www.ans.net`.)

Most of the providers also have automated e-mail replies in response to an e-mail message to the address `info@provider.com`. If e-mail is sent to that address, an e-mail reply will be sent describing the offered services. The InterNIC can be found at

`http://is.internic.net`

or at

`Gopher://is.internic.net`

or by anonymous FTP to

`is.internic.net`

To get the current PDIAL list, use anonymous FTP to

`FTP.netcom.com cd pub/info-deli-server get pdial`

or by e-mail to

`info-deli-server@netcom.com`

with the message `Send Pdial`.

To get the nixpub list, send e-mail to `nixpub@digex.com`, no message needed.

Both of these lists are regularly published in the `alt.internet.access.wanted` and `news.answers` newsgroups (among others).

Of course, since you're looking for a provider, you may not yet have any way to use these online contact methods. The list of providers at the end of this section includes telephone and FAX contact info as well.

Criteria to Consider

Here are some questions you might consider in choosing a dialup service provider:

- What type of account is it? IP dial or host-based/shell?
- What is the setup fee for the account?
- What is the fixed monthly charge?
- How many connect hours are included?
- What is the charge for the extra connect hours?
- What is the telephone charge to connect to the provider's network?
- What other costs are there?
- What is the availability of my connection? (That is, are there time restrictions? Are there dialup numbers in a wide variety of locations? Do they have enough dialup ports that I will not have many busy signals?)
- What kind of assistance is available when things go wrong?

Choosing a Provider of Dedicated Internet Services

Finding Who the Providers Are The process for finding a provider of a dedicated Internet connection is the same as for finding one for a dialup account; you just look in slightly different places.

Remember to consider the costs of the dedicated service carefully: a glance at our provider's list and their various charges will help you understand more fully how expensive a dedicated line can be.

Again, asking your acquaintances and people in similar organizations who have Internet connections for the name of their providers is a good idea.

The equivalent to Peter Kaminski's PDial list for access providers is the D-list. You'll find it on the Internet by sending e-mail to `dlist@ora.com`. This list was developed by Susan Estrada for her book, *Connecting to the Internet*, which covers the same topics as this chapter, although in much greater detail.

Criteria to Consider

Here are some questions you should ask in choosing a service provider for a dedicated connection:

- What is the speed of the connection proposed?
- What is the installation charge?
- What is the monthly recurring connection fee?
- What is the monthly local loop charge?
- What is the separate cost of the required equipment?
- What other costs are there?
- What is the availability of my connection?
- What kind of assistance is available when things go wrong?
- Is training offered?
- How secure is the connection? Does it provide what I need?
- Can I get a service guarantee? If so, what is it?
- What are the long-term prospects for the viability of the provider? Will they be in business next year?

With the answers to these questions and an up-to-date list of network service providers, you should be well-equipped to pick a provider that is appropriate for you. The following list (Copyright © 1994 Daniel Dern) was current as of September, 1994. (Daniel Dern is available at `ddern@world.std.com`.)

▶▶ *Dern's Selected Internet Service Providers*

The following is a sampling of Internet service providers.

Prices reflect monthly/installation costs as of 9/94 for one (1) full-time leased-line connection (port) between customer site and Internet service provider point of presence (POP). Prices exclude (in most cases) line, hardware, software, and support costs. Obviously, prices and availability are subject to change. Call the provider for a consultation or quotation.

► Notes

1. Other types/levels of service offerings may be available besides those listed.

2. Prices do not reflect volume discount (i.e., for multiple connections).

3. Providers were selected based on providing service to multistate/ national North America coverage (single-state providers were not listed); services listed may not necessarily be available at every provider site or at the prices stated.

► AlterNet

Area: US and International

Voice: 1-800-4UUNET3

E-mail: alternet-info@uunet.uu.net

Comments: AlterNet also has package deals available combining hardware and six months' connections.

Service	$/Month	$/Install	Notes
14.4Kbps	250	750	
56Kbps	795	795	
T1	1,250	5,000	(averaging below 128Kbps)
T1	2,000	5,000	(full)
10Mbps	1,500–3,000	1,500	
Frame Relay	695	N/A	

▶ *ANS (Advanced Network & Services)*

Area: US

Voice: 800-456-8267

E-mail: info@ans.net

FAX: 703-758-7717

Comments: ANS only sells connections on an annual basis. Prices given in monthly figures for comparison purposes.

Service	$/Month	$/Install	Notes
56Kbps	1,150		Includes installation, hardware, maintenance
T1	2,750		
T3	Call for pricing		

▶ *AT&T Data Communications*

Area: US (inc Alaska, Hawaii)

Voice: 1-800-248-3632

E-mail: not available at this time

FAX: 1-800-532-3487

Service	$/Month	$/Install	Notes
32Kbps Frame Relay	550	1,000	
56Kbps Frame Relay	650	1,000	
T1 Frame Relay	2,000	1,500	

▶ *CERFnet*

Area: Western US and International

Voice: 800-876-2373, 619-455-3900

E-mail: sales@cerf.net

FAX: 619-455-3990

Service	$/Month	$/Install	Notes
56Kbps	750	2,500	
56Kbps Fr.Relay	750	2,500	
1.2Mbps SMDS	1,150	3,000	(also called T1 SMDS)
T1	1,500	4,000	
T3	(call)		

▶ *CICnet*

Area: Midwest US (MN, WI, IA, IN, IL, MI, OH)

Voice: 800-947-4754 or 313-998-6703

E-mail: info@cic.net

FAX: 313-998-6105

Comments: "Bitpipe" service also available; prices do not include monthly InterLATA circuit fees.

Service	$/Month	$/Install	Notes
56Kbps	1,000	5,995	Includes line, router
T1	2,000	9,995	

▶ *Digital Express Group*

Area(s): Greater DC/Baltimore, Southern Ca, NYC, NJ

Voice: 1-800-969-9090

E-mail: info@digex.com

FAX: 301-345-6017

Service	$/Month	$/Install	Notes
56Kbps	500	1,000	
T1	2,000	4,000	
T1/fT1 Frame Relay	Call		

▶ *NEARNET*

Area(s): Northeastern US (CT MA ME NH NJ NY RI VT)

Voice: 800-NEARNET; 617-873-8730

E-mail: nearnet-join@near.net

FAX: 617-873-5620

Comments: Commercial routing charges will be added where applicable.

Service	$/Month	$/Install	Notes
19.2Kbps	630	3,950	
56Kbps	900	3,950	
256Kbps	1,200	3,950	
T1	2,290	3,950	
T3	(call)		

▶ *NETCOM*

Area: 15 states inc. CA, NY, Northwest US, MA, NC, TX

Voice: 1-800-353-6600

E-mail: info@netcom.com

Comments: Packages including hardware and line fees are available.

Service	$/Month	$/Install	Notes
14.4Kbps	160	750	
56Kbps	400	1,200	
56/Frame Relay	400	500	
T1	1,000	3,000	
T1/Frame Relay	1,000	1,200	

▶ *PSI Inc.*

Area: US and International

Voice: 800-82PSI82 or 703-620-6651

E-mail: info@psi.com

FAX: 703-620-2430

Comments: PSI provides "basic" reduced cost Service for those able and willing to do their own DNS and other technical support. Also offers a 5% discount for yearly contracts.

Service	$/Month	$/Install	Notes
64Kbps ISDN	400	500	1 B channel
56Kbps	760	1,000	
256Kbps	1,500	2,400	
T1	3,000	2,400	

▶ *SprintLink*

Area: US and International

Voice: 800-817 7755

E-mail: info@sprintlink.net

FAX: 703-904-2680

Service	$/Month	$/Install	Notes
9.6Kbps	550	660	
56Kbps	1,000	750	
T1	2,700	1,000	

▶ *SURAnet*

Area(s): Southeastern US (WV, VA, SC, NC, TN, KY, LA, MS, AL GA, FL, DC, MD, DE), S.America, Puerto Rico

Voice: 1-800-SURANET or (301) 982-4600

E-mail: kdonalds@sura.net

FAX: 301-982-4605

Service	$/Month	$/Install	Notes
			Annual costs available only
9.6Kbps	460	1,600	
56Kbps	750	1,600	
T1	1,250	3,500	
T3	Call for availability		

► *Uunorth*

Area: 416 area code area (Canada)

Voice: 1-800-INET-CAN (within Canada) or 416-225-8649

E-mail: not available at this time

Service	$/Month	$/Install	Notes
19.2Kbps	600 C$	300 C$	Canadian dollars
56Kbps	1,000 C$	1,250 C$	

▶ ▶ CHAPTER **5**

Once You're Connected: Working with Direct and Dialup Links

►► *In* the last chapter we discussed the criteria you need to consider in choosing how you want to be connected to the Internet. You learned that there are basically two ways to make a network connection: the *direct* (or *dedicated*) *link* and the *dialup link*. As the names imply, a *direct link* has a continuous connection from your workstation to the computer or network, and a *dialup link* is one you initiate by dialing into a modem over a phone line.

In general, you are more likely to have a direct connection to a router or LAN (Local Area Network), and a dialup connection to a modem pool that lets you access either a LAN, a BBS, or a general access launching point from a network service provider. Because of cost, most direct connections are at offices, dormitories, or workstation clusters, and most home systems use some variety of dialup.

The good news about direct and dial-up connections is that, in most cases, you can use similar communications software no matter how you are connected. You will need to configure the software to know whether to wake up a modem or a direct connection, but the basic settings remain the same.

In this chapter we talk about the basic characteristics of direct and dialup connections, and some simple troubleshooting tips.

►► *What You Need to Know First (Datacom 101)*

The following section is a review of basic data communications terms and theory. If you're pretty familiar with these concepts, feel free to go on to the next section, Plugged In: Using a Direct Link.

▶ ▶ M A S T E R   W O R D S

Many of these concepts apply whether you have a direct connection or a dialup link, or host-dial or TCP/IP-based software. Because of differences in technology between host-dial and TCP/IP-based software, some of these concepts apply more to one technology than the other.

▶ *Host-Dial versus TCP/IP Connections*

When we discuss *direct* versus *dialup* connections, we're talking about a difference in the physical wire connection to the Internet. Another fundamental distinction between types of connection has to do with the protocols used to govern the connection. *Host-dial* communications have been in use for over 35 years, successfully connecting users to their computers and to their network providers. Host-dial connections allow you to become a terminal on your provider's network, usually connected to a host or terminal server. You can have a session where you use Internet tools such as Telnet or FTP, but the actual work of using those tools is handled by the server or host you are signed on to.

There are several names for host-dial type connections. You may see them called:

- dumb terminal
- shell account
- terminal or TTY
- host connection
- asynchronous, or asynch

The other variety of connection is *TCP/IP-based*, in which software running in your workstation allows you to act as a Internet host, using the standard set of TCP/IP tools such as Gopher, Telnet, FTP, World Wide Web, and so on.

You can have either of these two varieties of connections with either sort of physical connection. Table 5.1 shows how the four possible combinations are generally used.

▶ **TABLE 5.1:** *Host-Dial vs. TCP/IP Software*

	DIRECT LINK	DIALUP CONNECTION
HOST-DIAL	Traditional mainframe link, as well as some LANs; passing away	CompuServe, AOL, etc., as well as many older dialup providers
TCP/IP BASED	Most common LAN and WAN links	Home users, those dialing onto LANs at work, most commercial consumer providers

Host-Dial Connections

Host-dial users generally have no "smarts" in their terminals beyond the simple visual session management, and some don't have even that much control. Their high powered workstation acts just like an old-fashioned printing terminal. For this reason, this kind of access is also called "dumb terminal" access.

Most host-dial dial-up users have a limited range of Internet services available *end-to-end;* that is, they must Telnet or connect to a host that handles the Internet services for them. Most have some method of file transfer (such as Kermit or screen capture), but usually they cannot FTP a file from a distant service directly to their machine. They must, instead, FTP it to their host, and then download from the host to their local workstations.

The most common host-dial connection these days is into a bulletin board system or other host on which you can do work such as read mail or use a client such as Gopher or World Wide Web (WWW). Many network providers, however, are now using some sort of network access server, which allows users to dial into the network, but which has no particular services itself. Many network access servers that accept host-dial connections (not all of them do) will let you use Telnet, WWW, or Gopher to reach other services, but you don't have access to file space, FTP, or e-mail services from the server itself. Figure 5.1 illustrates both types of host-dial sessions.

FIGURE 5.1 ▶

Host-dial sessions.

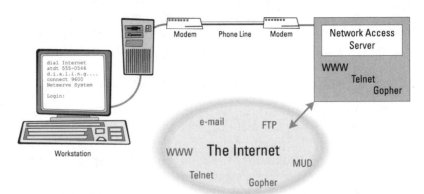

Host-Dial Connection

User logs into a network access server, on which network clients such as Telnet, WWW, and Gopher run.

Usually there is no file space for FTP or download; the user generally Telnets to a BBS or host for e-mail and FTP services.

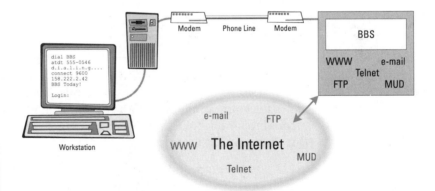

User logs into a bulletin board or other host. Internet clients such as Telnet, FTP, e-mail, and network news run on the host.

Users usually have file space; downloading of files or pop mail services is available.

TCP/IP-Based Connections

The user with TCP/IP software on her computer is leveraging all the computing power of her own machine, turning it into a true Internet host in the process. With the right client software, you can use Telnet, FTP, WWW, and so on, without an intervening host. Most folks particularly like the ability to use their computer to get their electronic mail, using e-mail client software.

In a TCP/IP connection, you make a connection to the network (either by a direct link or dialup). The network access server (the name for the computer which handles your physical connection to the network; sometimes the same kind of computer that host-dial users connect to, but not always) "authenticates" you (establishes your identity) and "authorizes" you (checks to see which services you are allowed to use). Then, that computer drops into the background, and your own computer takes over the client side of the services you want to access. The network access server is still working silently in the background, handling routing requests, some DNS requests, and sometimes the flow control for your session, but in general your workstation is in charge of it all. Figure 5.2 illustrates a typical TCP/IP session.

▶ SLIP and PPP: True Network Interactions

SLIP (Serial Line Internet Protocols) and PPP (Point-to-Point Protocols) are software tools that turn your connection from "dumb terminal access" to full-fledged Internet node. This software negotiates the rules for your connection with the Internet access point you're connected to, and it takes care of packaging your data so that it meets the Internet standards.

SLIP has been around for many years, but it was painful and unpleasant to work with over slow lines (under 9600 bps). Once inexpensive 9600 and 14400 baud modems came on the market, along with data compression protocols (which eliminate the "wasted" space in a packet and make smaller packets which can be transmitted more rapidly), SLIP has metamorphosed from something that more or less worked to a powerful method of real-time data interaction.

PPP is a more modern protocol that is slowly replacing SLIP. PPP software is easier for the user to configure, since PPP can automatically determine the network address assigned to it. The user does not need to

FIGURE 5.2 ▶

Using a TCP/IP-based software package.

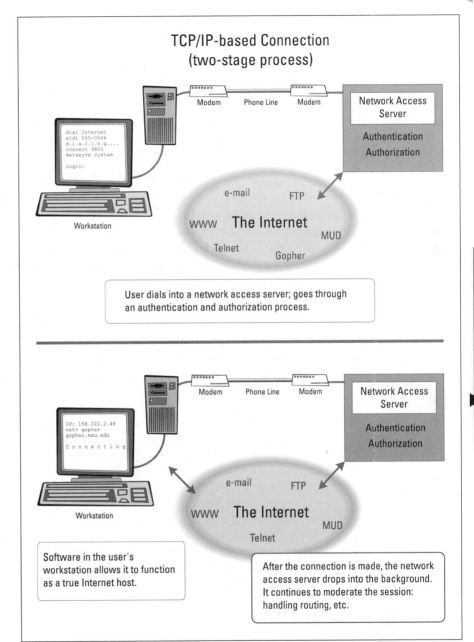

TCP/IP-based Connection (two-stage process)

Modem Phone Line Modem

Network Access Server

Authentication

Authorization

```
dial Internet
atdt 555-0546
d.i.a.l.i.n.g....
connect 9600
Netserve System

Login:
```

Workstation

e-mail FTP

www **The Internet**

MUD

Telnet

Gopher

User dials into a network access server; goes through an authentication and authorization process.

Modem Phone Line Modem

Network Access Server

Authentication

Authorization

```
IP: 158.222.2.48
net> gopher
gopher.msu.edu

C o n n e c t i n g
```

Workstation

e-mail FTP

www **The Internet**

MUD

Telnet

Software in the user's workstation allows it to function as a true Internet host.

After the connection is made, the network access server drops into the background. It continues to moderate the session: handling routing, etc.

Direct and Dialup Links

ch.
5

type that information into a configuration file. Another advantage of PPP is that it allows for better compression of the data in your session, which makes for faster throughput of your data. One final advantage of PPP is that it allows for authentication and authorization of the user as the connection is being established, rather than after the user connects to a network access box. PPP is, therefore, a more secure protocol.

▶ *Modems*

Hundreds of thousands of Internet users make their connection to the Net via a dialup modem and communications software running on their personal workstation. The purpose of a modem (*mod*ulator-*dem*odulator) is to translate the digital signals that computers use to store and transmit information into the analog signals that telephone lines (or radio data systems) use to transmit information.

Digital systems represent information in the form of discrete voltage levels (typically 0.5v is "on" and 0v is "off") that correspond to the binary (base 2) digits 1 and 0. Combined into binary numbers, these bits form the building blocks of all information stored and processed by your computer. Communications systems are designed to transmit information in the form of *analog* voltages, which vary continuously over a range of values. (If you think of a light switch, with its two states—on and off—as illustrating the concept of a digital device, then a radio volume dial, with its continuous range of settings, would be analog.) A modem, then, makes the translation so that the computers on both ends of the connection can understand each other.

A network that allows dial-in access provides one modem at its end, while a user who dials in provides the other. These modems have to be compatible to be able to communicate. When you get your account with your provider, they should tell you what modems your modem is compatible with. When you purchase your modem, look for one compatible with a wide range of modems. We'll look at other important criteria later in the chapter.

 ▶ ▶▶ N O T E

An excellent guide to modems is Sharon Crawford's *Your First Modem*, available from SYBEX.

▶ Parity

In data communications, the word *parity* refers to a simple means of checking for errors in data transmitted. Parity only provides for the detection of errors; not for their correction. (It is also possible to add mechanisms to allow for retransmission of data, but the parity mechanism itself does not specify that. Error correction is merely the combination of error detection plus retransmission when an error is detected.) Many modern communications protocols, such as PPP and SLIP, do not use parity for error checking, because the information is checked for transmission errors in other ways.

With TCP/IP-based communications software to access the Internet, you should set up your communications software to use No parity. In this kind of parity, the parity bit is used by the communications software for other purposes. (See the discussion of an 8-bit data path below.)

If you are using standard "host-dial" communications to reach the Net, you will use either No parity or Even parity.

▶ Data Bits per Character

Information sent from one computer to another is divided into pieces, known as characters (or bytes). Characters are made up of bits, and the number of bits per character depends on whether one bit per character is reserved for parity.

Most communications software used today will have one of these two settings:

- Even parity: 7 bits per character (may be listed 7-E-1).
- No (None) parity: 8 bits per character (may be listed 8-N-1).

▶ 8-Bit Data Path

If you use TCP/IP-based software, you'll need to be able to set up your software to run in what is called "8-bit" mode, or an "8-bit data path." To understand this you need to know something about how data is encoded for transmission over networks.

Most networks use ASCII (American Standard Code for Information Interchange) characters in their communications. ASCII is a means of encoding the roman alphabet, arabic numbers, and various punctuation and control information using seven data bits. Traditional ASCII defined character encodings for 7-bit values, and assumes that one bit of each character is reserved for a different purpose (such as parity). The new ASCII standard defines a way to encode the alphabet, numerals, and punctuation and control information using the eighth bit as part of the character.

Old host-dial or "dumb terminal" connections used ten bits for each character: a start bit (which signaled the beginning of the character), seven bits for the character information itself, a stop bit (which signaled the end of the character), and a parity bit (which helped in error detection).

Since modern protocols handle some of the control functions outside of the basic character set (they use a different error correction method, for example), they use the extra 8th bit to send more information, such as control or formatting characters.

To create an 8-bit data path, you need to be using no parity (because you want to free up the parity bit for use in information).

▶ Duplex

When you access a remote computer, the characters you type are displayed on your screen so that you can see what you are typing. This is called *echoing*. There are two ways to handle echoing: older terminals could display everything as soon as you typed it (Half Duplex mode), or the computer at the remote end can send each character back to your screen as soon as it is received (Full Duplex mode).

Full Duplex is used in almost every network you'll encounter. In your software you may be able to set this parameter: if so, it will usually be called something like Full-Duplex, FDX, or Remote Echo in your terminal emulator program. It will usually be set to Full Duplex as the default: you should leave it that way. If not, set it to Full Duplex and forget it.

▶ *Carriage Returns and Line Feeds*

Whenever you send a carriage return, you expect the cursor to move to the next line. The software in most networks provides a line feed (harking back to the days of printing terminals) with each carriage return sent or received. When you set up your terminal emulator program, be certain to turn auto-linefeed off, or to set the end-of-line character to just carriage return, or else all the information that prints at your screen will be double-spaced.

Usually this will be a problem only when you are using dialup, particularly into bulletin board systems. It is possible to encounter this in a LAN setup, but it is much rarer (and usually is a result of someone fiddling with the software without knowing what they are doing).

▶ *Flow Control*

Flow control is something like running a hose into a bucket. When you are filling the bucket, you want to slow down the hose early enough that the remaining water in the hose goes into the bucket rather than onto your feet. After you've emptied the bucket into your kid's pool, you turn the hose back on, and wait a few seconds for the water flow to come back up to full strength.

In a computer network, flow control tells the computer at one end to stop sending data until the computer at the other end has finished processing it.

When flow control is turned on, the workstation or modem on the receiving end can send a message to the other computer to tell it to stop sending information until the message comes to start again. These messages are called flow control signals. You can do the same thing manually with most host-dial software by pressing Control-S to stop the flow of information and Control-Q to start it again.

Two Kinds of Flow Control

In today's communications, you can get two main kinds of flow control. One kind is handled by your communications software. In this kind (sometimes called *software flow control* or *in-band flow control*), the software inserts control sequences into the data traffic itself to tell the computer at the other end to start and stop sending data. You can't get an 8-bit clear data path if you use this kind of flow control, so you can't use TCP/IP-based software with it.

The other kind of flow control is called *hardware flow control* or *out-of-band flow control*. Hardware flow control uses two of the wires in your modem cable itself to tell the modem to start or stop sending information. Since it's not in the data stream, it's called "out of band" flow control. And since it's handled by the hardware itself, it's called "hardware" flow control.

When you look for a modem to use with your TCP/IP-based software, be sure and get one that supports hardware flow control.

►► *Plugged In: Using a Direct Link*

In the past, a direct link meant a cable that ran from your dumb terminal (a terminal that couldn't do anything but be an interface to the computer) to the mainframe computer. This link didn't depend on the phone lines being up and, as long as the mainframe was up, was always connected.

Today the concept is the same: a link that plugs into the back of your computer and connects you directly to your computing resources, as shown in Figure 5.3. However, what happens on the other end of the line has changed somewhat.

FIGURE 5.3 ►

A direct link.

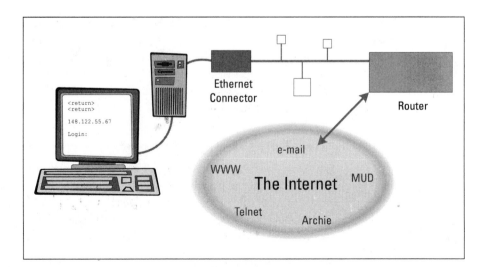

Today you are more than likely working on a personal computer or workstation that can do more all by itself on your desktop than the mainframe could twenty years ago. To link up with the network, you run special software on the workstation that handles the interface to the network. If you have a direct link, that cable plugged into the back of your workstation puts you in contact with some network instantly. You could have one of the following kinds of connections:

- Ethernet hooked into a router (the type of connection shown in Figure 5.3).

- AppleTalk hooked into a router.

- Novell, Banyan, or other LAN connection, which in turn talks to a Internet gateway.

- SLIP connection with a leased phone line that hooks you into a router connection or local network.

Direct connections tend to require moderately expensive equipment such as Ethernet installations, routers, repeaters, and so on. The phone or fiber line usually runs at higher speeds: 56,000 bits per second (also called 56K, or 56 Kilobits per second) to over a million bits per second (T1, or 1.54 million bits per second). These high-speed phone lines are very expensive, and so direct connections that use them are usually shared among several users, or they are reserved for users sending very large amounts of data (graphics, sound, and so on) over the network for long periods of time.

Direct connections are also used for file servers, Gopher servers, World Wide Web servers, FTP archives, and other services that have lots of traffic all the time.

A variation on the direct link is demand dialup (which we discussed in Chapter 4). When you are using an application on your workstation that does not require connection to the Internet, the link to the Internet is down; when you use an application that requires a link to the Internet, software in your system or your LAN server brings up the dialup link and makes a connection to a node somewhere else on the net. These links usually use a moderate-speed dialup—9600 bps to 56K—and are not usually used for systems with a great deal of traffic.

Direct and Dialup Links

ch.
5

Again, Chapter 4 discussed how to assess your needs for a connection and decide what sort of a direct connection suits you, and your organization or business, best.

▶ Troubleshooting a Direct Link

Let's start with the easy problems. Beware! Troubleshooting directly connected links can involve getting under your desk or behind a cabinet to look for wires and jacks. Wear comfortable clothes and take along an adventurous attitude. If you work your way through each of the tips here, and you still have the problem, contact your systems administrator or someone who is good at debugging these things.

 ▶ ▶ **W A R N I N G**

Checking and connecting or disconnecting network wires (and other troubleshooting techniques) have the potential to bring down your whole local network. Some network administrators prefer that no one but them or their staff touch network hardware. If you are in an environment where you have network administrators, you will most likely want to check with them before you touch any hardware.

This is by no means an exhaustive list of remedies for problems on direct links; we could write whole books just on those topics. But it should help you get started, and give you good information to give to your repair center or help service if you still can't locate the trouble.

The Connection Won't Wake Up

Particularly in corporate or group settings, you may have gotten a notice about scheduled maintenance time, changes about the network, or other happenings which may affect the network. Be sure to read and remember those notices! But assuming your system hasn't been "taken down" for scheduled maintenance, here are some possibilities:

    0. Go back to square one: Is the computer connected to the jack, plug, Ethernet box, or whatever, and are all the cables screwed or clamped securely? Is the power turned on in the computer and all your peripheral equipment?

1. **Wrong speed?** Make sure that your communications program is set for the same speed as the connection you're attached to.

2. **The network is dead.** Ask next door or in the next cubicle if they have a live network connection. If you can see your router, server or the console for your LAN, go look to see if it has any lights flashing or warning messages printed on it. If you are not the systems administrator, you may decide not to touch this equipment if it doesn't appear to be working. Once you've called for help, there's nothing much else you can do to troubleshoot this problem.

3. **Wrong settings** in your communications software. Go back to the basic instructions, and check to see that your communications software is set up correctly. Pay close attention to speed, protocols, and parity.

4. Your **network address** is wrong or has changed. Check the instructions you were given to make sure that your communications software has the correct network address for your machine. This should be in a menu called something like "Connections," "Configuration," "IP settings," or "Setup." Depending on your software, it may be in a file with the string "config" in the name. Look at that file carefully to make sure the address is correct.

W A R N I N G !

Never edit a configuration file unless you have made a copy, called a backup, first. Copy the "config" file into a file called "config.old" or "config.bak" on PC-based systems, or some helpful similar name on Macintosh or UNIX systems. This will let you restore your old configuration in case you make a mistake editing the file. If you have any doubt about undertaking this project, get someone knowledgeable to help you.

5. Someone **upstream** of you has disconnected the cable leading to you. Walk around to your co-workers and look for someone near you who has a live connection. Look for the wire that goes to your

machine. If you find a place where it has been disconnected, you can *try* reconnecting it. Warning! Most systems administrators prefer to be called if you find a loose connection.

6. Your network connection is improperly **terminated.** Some network connections, particularly AppleTalk and some Ethernet connections, go through a small box with two jack holes that look like phone jacks. These boxes connect near the wire leading to your computer. Both holes should be filled; *how* they are filled depends on your location in your network and the particular configuration of your network. The easiest to troubleshoot on your end is the Local Talk network. (Other network wiring and configurations are more difficult for end users to troubleshoot, so we do not include tips on them here.)

   - If you are the last person in line on the circuit, there will be a dummy plug, called a terminator, in one of the holes to indicate to the routing equipment that this is the end of the line. These plugs look like plastic phone jacks with little washers connected to them. If you don't have one, look to see if it's been pulled out (check on the floor around your work area). Contact your systems administrator or repair office.

   - If there is someone downstream on the network of you, you should have two wires coming out of the network connection box. One leads to your computer, and the other goes on to the next person's connection. Look for a pulled-out wire near the connection box or mixed in with the other cables. If you don't find it, contact your systems administrator or repair office.

The Connection Wakes Up but Won't Go Anywhere

Sometimes your communications software comes up and tries to make a connection, but never succeeds. Your connection is live (or awake) on your end, but there's nobody home on the other end.

You Get an Error Message That You Can't Find the Network There are several possible reasons for this:

1. The first possibility is that your **network server** is dead. Ask next door or in the next cubicle if they have a live network connection.

If you can see your server or the console for your LAN, go look to see if it has any lights turned on or warning messages printed. If you are not the systems administrator, you may decide not to touch this equipment if it doesn't look as if it is working.

2. Your network **gateway or router** has changed addresses. Check back through your e-mail and other memos to find that message you threw out from the systems administrator about DNS changes over the weekend. Check your software or network instructions to find out what the backup or default gateway address is, and reset your software to find it. (The gateway addresses are the network addresses of the routers or other computers that handle DNS, routing, and other connection mechanics. If your software isn't talking to the right box, your session won't do anything.)

3. Your **software has the wrong address** for the gateway or router. Check your setup file or configuration file for the default gateway address. (Remember to back up the configuration file before you change it!)

4. Your local connection is OK, but you are cut off from the world. Perhaps you can get to your local gateway or your local router, but there is a problem in the greater network past that point. There's nothing you can do about this, but sometimes telling your systems administrators is a blessing, because they haven't noticed yet. (Be gentle when you let them know: you may be the first person to tell them, but you could also be the hundred-and-first.)

You Can Issue Commands, and the Session Looks Like It's Working, but It Never Makes a Connection Here again there are several possibilities to consider:

1. Your software is **improperly configured.** Check to make sure that your communications software has the correct network address for your machine. This should be in a menu called something like "Connections," "IP settings," or "Setup." Depending on your software, it may be in a file with the string "config" in the name. Look at that file carefully to make sure the address is correct. Check the gateway and router default addresses, too.

2. The service you are trying to reach is **down or unreachable.** Ask a neighbor or someone else on the net if they can reach the service from their workstation. (If they can, you need to contact your support line or systems administrator for assistance.)

3. The **DNS server** or other **routing** equipment/software is down or broken. Contact your support line or systems administrator for assistance.

Garbage on the Screen

The causes and solutions here depend on what the garbage looks like.

Do You See X's, F's, Nonprinting Characters, or Graphics Characters?
You may be accessing a system that needs a different **parity** than the one you have set. This is most likely with host-dial, non-TCP/IP systems. Check the instructions for dialing in: check your modem or software settings. Most common settings are *8-N-1* (eight data bits, no parity, one stop bit) or *7-E-1* (seven data bits, even parity, one stop bit). Figure 5.4 shows an example of a connection with the wrong parity.

FIGURE 5.4 ▶

Incorrect parity on a connection.

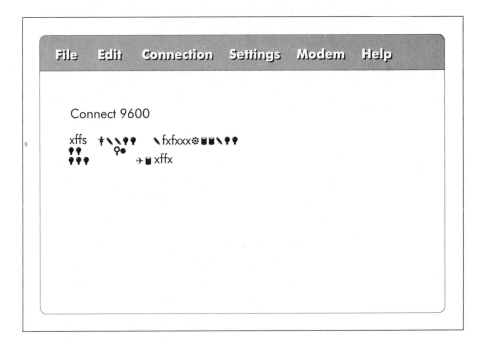

Do the Words Look Like a Foreign Language? In other words, the pattern looks like it should be words, but the characters are not in English. Check your parity and bit settings. Although most networks require you to connect the Internet using 8 data bits and no parity, some require that you use 7 data bits and even parity. Figure 5.5 shows sample data with incorrect parity and data bit settings.

FIGURE 5.5 ▶

Incorrect parity and data bit settings.

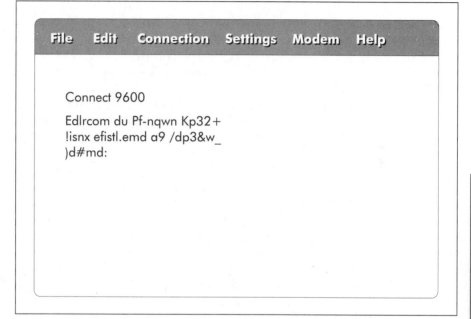

File	Edit	Connection	Settings	Modem	Help

Connect 9600

Edlrcom du Pf-nqwn Kp32+
!isnx efistl.emd a9 /dp3&w_
)d#md:

Is the Garbage Sporadic or in Rhythmic Patterns, Occurring Unexpectedly and at Random Locations on Your Screen? Although it's very unusual on a direct connection, this can happen. The most likely source is **noise** either on your physical connection wire or in the electrical system of your house or office. If you don't have a surge and noise protection power strip or control center for your computer equipment, buy one.

Figure 5.6 shows sporadic garbage in a connection.

Causes of data-corrupting noise include:

- Worn shielding on your cabling, and another cable (or heavy power line) running close to it.

- A big electric motor operating nearby (usually something like a refrigerator, a generator, or a vacuum).

FIGURE 5.6 ►

Noise in an otherwise normal connection.

File	Edit	Connection	Settings	Modem	Help

Inbox: 567

From: Harry Smith((((c(c(c
re: (c(c(c(Conference room use

Please {F{F{F{F be certain to sign up ((((
for the &&&conference room if you plan to
use it in the mornings. %R%e%c%ently we have had
pro#blemss w(i

- An incandescent or fluorescent light or a radio on the same circuit as your computer.
- Bad weather (such as high winds, rain, snow, thunderstorms, tornadoes), particularly if your network runs between buildings.

There's usually not much you can do about line noise, but here are a few suggestions:

- Buy a noise and power surge protector for your computer equipment.
- Wait until the weather clears (or move to a different climate).
- Move the electric motor, the light or radio, or the computer to a different electrical circuit.
- Check the wires and cables around your computer carefully for breaks, cracked or torn insulation, or other problems. (They may have gotten pinched, crushed, or had heavy objects set on them.)
- Ask the physical plant or help desk folks for assistance.

▶▶ *Reach Out and Touch the Net: Using a Dialup Link*

Our goal here is to help you better understand the instructions you've gotten from your dialup provider. We can't give detailed instructions on how to access every possible provider, but we *can* give you the benefit of our experience in dialing into a lot of providers to help you understand what's happening when you dial up. In this section we talk about pitfalls to avoid, tricks to get better performance, and how to troubleshoot your connection.

▶ *Choosing a Modem*

A modem is an essential link between your computer and your dialup service provider, so it's essential that you select one that meets your needs. Here are some of the most important considerations.

▶ ▶**M A S T E R   W O R D S**

One very nice feature to look for as you decide on a modem is whether it can be configured to support either host-dial or TCP/IP-based communications.

Communications Speeds

Most modern dial-in modems operate at 2400, 9600, or 14,400 bps (bits per second, sometimes incorrectly called the *baud rate*). The higher the number, the more bits it can push across your data pipe per second. In general, you want to buy the fastest modem you can afford when you buy a new modem. Technology for modems is changing so quickly that the speeds get higher and higher every year, and the older and cheaper modems (which are much less expensive) are consequently out of date almost before you get them out of the box.

The usual rule of thumb for figuring out how long it will take your file to go across a communication line is based on your communication speed. Generally, you can divide that rate by eight to find out how many characters per second are going across the line. Thus, for a

Direct and Dialup Links

▶ ▶
ch.
5

14,400 bps line, you are actually sending 1800 characters across the line every second. This is because there are roughly eight bits per character. (We'll talk later about data compression, but even with compression, this ratio holds most of the time.)

In reality, because of slow connections, line noise causing your computer to resend (retransmit) your data, and other *overhead* on the line, you'll almost never get your line to run as fast as it is rated for. But you can come close.

Modem Standards

When looking at modems, you'll find that most say they have one or more of the following attributes:

- MNP4 or MNP5
- V.42, V.fast, or V.42*bis*
- Hayes Compatible or Hayes Command Set

"V" or MNP? In general, you should look for a modem which supports error correction. Both the "V" standards and the MNP standards provide for data compression and error correction. This lets you transmit more information faster, and with fewer errors (even over a noisy line).

Although many service providers support both the MNP suite and the "V" standards, most are moving to support only the V family. MNP is a proprietary protocol promoted by the MicroCom corporation; it is becoming less popular in favor of the more widely accepted V family of standards. The V standards are those promulgated by the CCITT; they are commonly referred to by their version numbers.

One reason for the rising popularity of the V protocols is that they are more easily configured for use with TCP/IP-based software. Another is that more and more modem manufacturers are incorporating them into their modems, avoiding the use of MicroCom's proprietary software.

Hayes-Compatible The Hayes modem company created a set of commands for use in talking to the modem (the "Hayes command set") that has become accepted as a *de facto* standard. This standardization on one command set (and other commands in the same format) allows users to quickly familiarize themselves with new modems.

▶ *Starting the Link: Using the Modem*

Most modems sold now are autodialing modems—you can type commands from the keyboard to make your modem dial the telephone and establish a connection to the computer at the other end of the line. Figure 5.7 shows such a connection.

Many software packages even support dialing scripts to let you press one function key or click on one icon and make a connection to your dialup provider.

FIGURE 5.7 ▶

Making the dialup connection with a modem.

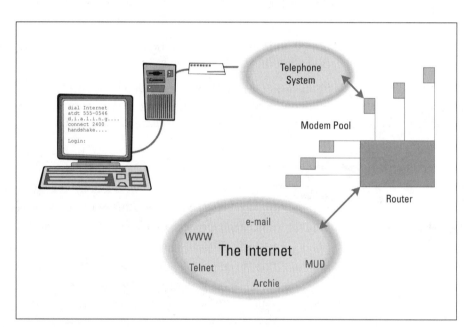

```
dial Internet
atdt 555-0546
d,i.a.l.i.n.g....
connect 2400
handshake....

Login:
```

Telephone System

Modem Pool

Router

e-mail

WWW

The Internet

Telnet   MUD

Archie

Direct and Dialup Links

▶ ▶

ch.

5

  ▶ ▶ **W A R N I N G**

Never put your password in a dialing script. That would allow anyone who sat down at your computer (or who stole it from your car, home, hotel room, or office) to access the network using your identity. Make sure you have to type your password in every time you start your script unless you are totally confident of the physical security of your computer.

The best modems indicate what is happening at every step of a dial-in session. You can track the progress of the call in any of several ways: lights that indicate the modem's status, a speaker that allows you to listen to the progress of your call, or, in graphical user interface (GUI) programs, a phone ringing or a status bar. Your modem sends signals to your software which may appear as on-screen messages or status bars.

While your modem is dialing, for instance, you may hear the dial tone and then ringing, and see something like 'Dialing...' with the periods coming one at a time as a graphic reminder of the progress.

When the modem on the other end answers, you may hear the two modems start to hiss or "sing" to one another to make the connection.

Once your modem makes the connection to another computer, you may see something like 'Connect 9600' (or whatever speed you are using).

The best source of information about your modem is the manual that came with it, and the help line or service number provided by the manufacturer. Many trouble calls can be eliminated if you just read the manual!

 ▸ ▸**M A S T E R   W O R D S**

Friends, roommates, and parents can be the death of a dialup session. If you can arrange it, don't connect your modem to a phone line someone else may try to use while you're on-line! If someone picks up another phone on the same line you're using, your session will be at best mangled (junk characters will appear on your screen) and at worst abruptly disconnected. Call Waiting is another enemy of the dial-in session. The tones used to indicate another call is coming in can completely disconnect your modem session. Either have the service removed from your phone line (or don't get it installed on your modem line), or be sure to disable it before you start a session. Instructions for disabling Call Waiting are in the front of most United States phone books or are available from your local phone provider. (In most areas, you press *70 to disable Call Waiting.)

▶ *Using a Calling Card with a Modem*

Once you figure out how to dial your modem from home, you can put it in a dialing script and more or less forget the mechanics. But you may want to use a calling card at some point to charge your call. How do you do that?

Why Use a Charge Card?

You will probably make most of your modem calls from the comfort of your own home, using your own telephone to call a local number. But you may hear of a service that is only available by a long distance telephone call, or you may live in a city that doesn't have a local dial-in system.

And there are times when you will need to make a long distance call and either not want to or not be able to charge the call to the phone number you are calling from. For instance, you've had a long commute from the office and now have to dial in to the office network to get a bit more work done. While there are other options (like paying for the call yourself), you might prefer to put the call directly on the company's calling card.

Or you might be out of town on a business trip and need to pick up the latest information for a proposal due the next morning. You could charge the call to your hotel room, but then you won't be able to control which long-distance company the hotel uses. So you will want to use your telephone charge card.

▶ ▶ **M A S T E R   W O R D S**

> **Hotel rooms are common places to make modem calls from. Some hotels and motels still have old-fashioned switchboards that do not allow you to make phone calls with your modem. Luckily, most of these hotels have installed special phone areas which have direct lines outside for you to use. If in doubt, check with the switchboard operator.**

Setting Up the Card Transaction

Charging a voice long-distance call to a card is relatively easily. You dial your long-distance company's local access number (or its 800 number,

Direct and Dialup Links

▶ ▶

ch.
5

if it doesn't have a local access number), wait for the beeps, dial the number you want to call, wait for a few more beeps, and then punch in your card number. It all goes very quickly and easily.

But you're a person. You know that you may have to wait a different amount of time this call than you did last call. Computers aren't that smart. For them, a dialing script has to be set up to work the same no matter what the phone company decides to do. A modem can't hear the beeps that would tell it to send the next string of digits. Neither is there a button we can push to tell the modem that's it time to send the next stream of digits into the telephone system. So we have to find another way to keep from entering a number before the telephone company's switch is ready to receive it. (Remember, a digit sent too early is lost, so we have to start over. And hope we get it right this time.)

So making a charge call over a modem is a process of trial and error.

Telling the Modem to Wait

Fortunately, the command set for today's modems includes the ability to tell the modem to pause. Simply adding a comma to the dial string will cause the modem to wait a bit before entering the next digit. Putting commas between the three separate number strings will allow the telephone switches sufficient time to process the preceding number before receiving the next one.

However, this solution, while simple, is not the whole story. The length of the pause will vary from one modem to the next. Some modems may pause for as long as four minutes for a comma, while others may pause for less than half a second. So you will have to look in your modem's manual to find out how long your modem pauses. (The manual may even tell you how to set the length of the pause.)

▶ ▶ **MASTER WORDS**

Again, it's important that you read the manuals. Getting familiar with your modem documentation is one of the most useful things you can do, especially if you travel a great deal.

Even with this piece of information, the quest is not yet over. There is still the question of how long the telephone system will take to respond to each number and thus be ready for your modem to send the next set. *The only way to discover this information for your telephone company is to experiment.*

To start, you might try the making the call by hand, noting how long it takes for the beeps to come back. There is no need to be extremely precise at this stage; it is better to err a little on the too-late side than on the too-soon side. Once you have an idea of how long it takes the telephone system to be ready for the next string, you can calculate the number of commas you need to add between the pieces.

MASTER WORDS

If you think you will be traveling and using your modem from many phones, be sure to buy a modem that lets you listen to the dialing process. Those little beeps, whistles, and hisses are great helpers when trying to debug a dialing script!

The Envelope, Please...

The final dial string will look something like

```
ATDT18005551234,,02025559876,,,234567890987654321
```

The first two letters, "AT", are the "attention" command, which alerts the modem to expect a command. The next two letters, "DT", tell the modem to "Dial" a "Tone" call. (If your telephone is a rotary instrument, you will probably need to change the "T" to a "P", for "Pulse-dialing.") Then comes the long-distance company's access number, a pause, the number you want to call (usually preceded by a zero to signify that it will require special processing, in this case charging to a calling card), another pause (slightly longer), and finally your calling card's authorization code. (For this example, I've chosen a random string of numbers. I hope I didn't get your number!)

▶ ▶**W A R N I N G**

> **Read the instructions that came with your calling card. Some cards require your personal access code first; some in the order that we have above. As they say in the Usenet newsgroups, YMMV (your mileage may vary). RTFM!**

Other Help

You will probably have to try several times to get the right number of commas for each pause. Once you have it right, though, you will not want to have to recreate it from scratch. Your communication software should include the capability to store numbers you dial frequently. (If it doesn't, you might consider finding a new one; there are many available, both commercially and as shareware, for every computer.) After storing a number, you will be able to make your credit-card calls quickly and easily.

Your modem may offer some other commands which would make these kinds of calls easier. For instance, it may offer a "W" command, to wait for a second dial tone. It may offer an "@" command, to wait for a period of silence (like the comma, the length of the period varies and you may be able to set it.) The "@" command may require a ring before waiting, so it might not be as useful as we could hope.

Pitfalls

If you have been working with your modem while reading this, you may have discovered that the command line given above does not work. Two eleven-digit telephone numbers, a fourteen-digit authorization code, several commas, and "ATDT," not to mention the final Return at the end of the line, total a bit more than the 40 characters most modems can accept on a command line. (Some modems may not count the "AT" and Return as part of the command line subject to the 40 character limit.) Spaces are usually ignored, but hyphens and parentheses are counted. Fortunately, a semicolon as the last command on the line (that is, the last character before the Return), tells the modem to return to command mode after dialing, so a second command line, with the rest of the command, can be entered. Thus, to use the command line given above, you would enter something like

```
ATDT18005551234,,02025559876,,;<RETURN>
ATDT23456789098765<RETURN>
```

Of course, you may need to use some of the other configuration commands for your modem, like disabling error detection or data compression, so the command line may have to be broken up into more pieces.

▶▶ *Dialup Troubleshooting*

No matter what kind of modem you have, or whether you're running TCP/IP software or traditional host-dial communications programs, these tips should help you solve most basic modem woes.

▶ *Garbage on the Screen*

As with direct connections, the causes and solutions here depend on what the garbage looks like.

Do You See X's, F's, Nonprinting Characters, or Graphics Characters?

1. You may be dialing into an **autospeed modem**. Some modems can accept calls from modems of different transmission speeds but must be told which speed to use. Synchronize your modem with the autospeed modem by:

   - setting your communications program for automatic answerback (see your software manual for instructions), or
   - pressing Enter twice a few seconds after your call is answered.

2. You may be accessing a system that needs a different **parity** than the one you have set. This is most likely with host-dial, non-TCP/IP systems. Check the instructions for dialing in: check your modem or software settings. Most common settings are *8-N-1* (eight data bits, no parity, one stop bit) or *7-E-1* (seven data bits, even parity, one stop bit).

Do the Words Look Like a Foreign Language?

See the diagnosis and solution in the direct connection troubleshooting section.

Is the Garbage Sporadic or in Rhythmic Patterns, Occurring Suddenly and at Random Locations on Your Screen?

Again, this is most likely **noise** on either your phone line or in the electrical system of your house. Data-corrupting causes of noise specific to dialup include:

- A noisy or static-filled telephone line (if it sounds static-filled when you talk on it, or people comment on it when they talk to you, the computers will be trying to make sense of the static along with your data).

- A microwave oven operating near the computer or phone jack where your modem plugs in.

- A noisy or outmoded phone switch at your telephone company.

- Bad weather (such as high winds, rain, snow, thunderstorms, tornadoes).

- Someone picking up your telephone receiver.

There's usually not much you can do about line noise, but here are a few suggestions:

- Buy a noise and power surge protector for your computer equipment, including the modem.

- Hang up and try again for a better connection.

- Wait until the weather clears (or move to a different climate).

- Remind others in your house or workplace not to use your phone while your modem connection is open.

- Turn off call-waiting, if you have it.

- Ask your telephone company to check your line (only if none of the other suggestions reduces the line noise). Remember that it may cost you money, depending on what service you are paying for.

Your Modem Dials but Doesn't Make a Connection

1. **Wrong modem speed?** Make sure that your communications program is set for the same speed as the modem you're calling into.

2. Some network providers use varying protocols on their networks. Not all are the same. You may have one (most commonly MNP) enabled when the modem on the other end is looking for another protocol. Be sure your setup is appropriate.

3. Your connection may be too **noisy.** See the section on line noise, above.

4. **Your dial script or modem initialization string is incorrect.** Your software may be waiting for a string which will never appear, or your host or network access server may be waiting for a response which your software doesn't send.

5. The problem may be with your service provider's modems. There's not much you can do about this. If you can't *ever* establish a connection, or if it's always noisy and you've tried everything else, call the help desk or consulting number for your provider.

The Modem Doesn't Dial at All

0. **Go back to square one:** Are the modem and the computer connected, and all the cables screwed or clamped securely? Is the modem connected to the wall jack? Is the power turned on in the modem?

1. Get to the **modem command level** (the place where you can type commands directly to the modem) and type the modem-ready command, **AT** (see your communications software documentation for specific instructions on how to issue modem commands). Do the characters you typed appear on your screen? Does the modem respond **'OK'** or "**0**" (zero)? If not, your workstation and modem aren't speaking to one another. Make sure that your modem is turned on and connected to your telephone line. Use the correct dialing command for your type of telephone—typically **ATDT** for a touch-tone phone, **ATDP** for a pulse-dial phone.

2. If you're working on a DOS (including Windows) computer, make sure that your modem is plugged into your computer's **serial port** and that your communications software is looking for the modem on the correct port. Do this by checking the menu for your modem or communications software settings. Most modems should be on COM1 but sometimes your computer will be configured with the modem on COM2.

3. Type your modem's dialing command all in UPPERCASE. (For example, **ATDT 555-0123** instead of **atdt 555-0123**.) Some modems require this.

4. Reset the modem to **factory defaults.** That is, reset it to the way the modem manufacturer set it up when it was sold. Sometimes there is a physical switch on external modems to do this: sometimes you have to issue a command from the keyboard. In many modems the command to type is **AT&F** or **AT&F1**. Look at the owner's manual to find out how to reset the modem, then start your communications software up and try again. (Some newer modems have factory default settings for both host-dial communications and TCP/IP-based software. Check to be certain you're set up for the right type of communications.)

5. **Swap components** with a friend. Find someone with a modem that you know works. Have her bring it over, including her power and serial cables. *One at a time,* swap the components in this order: power cable; modem; serial cable. This is a good way to see if you have a defective component.

6. Make sure that you've connected your modem to your computer using the right kind of **cable**. This is a very unlikely problem if you are working at home by yourself, but it might happen if you work in a place where lots of cables are floating around and people are regularly using various cables to connect computers and components.

7. **Call a friend** who is good at data communications and offer them dinner if they'll help troubleshoot your modem problem.

▶▶ *Working with SLIP and PPP*

Both SLIP and PPP are available from many commercial vendors and from several public-domain sources. Some common workstation packages are: from commercial sources—Chameleon, Versaterm, FTP software's various packages; from public domain archives— NCSA Telnet, and MacSamson. Check the list of public-domain archive sites in the Appendix G for a starting place to look for these software packages.

We have some troubleshooting tips for some of the packages, but you should talk to the people at your network provider about which one seems to work best for them. If you are connected via a corporate LAN or other connection in your workplace, your local network administrator or other expert will probably know what's best for you (and may already have installed everything you need in your workstation).

▶ *Before Setting Up an IP Connection*

Setting up your SLIP or PPP link can be tricky the first time or two. There are some basic pieces of information you need to get started, and it's better to gather them before you even sit down to try to start up the software. They are:

- The IP address you have been assigned.
- The default IP address (numbers, not words) of your IP gateway.
- The IP address and Domain Name (both numbers and words) of your Domain Name Server.

If you intend to use an e-mail client or read news via news reader software, you also need to know:

- The Domain Name (words, not numbers) of your e-mail server.
- The Domain Name (words, not numbers) of your Net News (NNTP) server.

Some applications also ask that you have a Net *mask,* or default broadcast address, in your configuration file. Experienced consultants suggest that the mask should be **255.255.255.0,** although users who plan to use Trumpet (a news reader) should set that mask address to **0.0.0.0.**

There are distinct differences between setting up a PPP link and setting up a SLIP link. One advantage of PPP is that you need less information to set it up: because PPP has advanced negotiation processes built into the protocol itself, it can find out what IP address you have been assigned, and what the gateway address is, without your having to preconfigure it. To configure most SLIP software, you need to build this information into the configuration script or file. (Some SLIP software has a configuration script which tries to recognize the IP address when it is written on the screen, but not all do.)

▶ ▶**M A S T E R   W O R D S**

If you are dialing in over a SLIP connection, you may or may not have an assigned IP address. Some systems assign you an IP address depending on what physical modem you connect to in the modem pool; some assign you a telephone number that corresponds to the IP address you will be given; some assign you an IP address which you configure into your software and which will be the same no matter what modem you call into. Be sure you understand how your system works before you start to place the call.

▶ *Starting Up the Dialup IP Link*

Dialing into an IP link is similar to dialing into a traditional host-dial link, except that you will see the IP protocol handshaking going on—you may well see a series of IP addresses being exchanged on your screen. (Handshaking is essentially how the network confirms the settings on your workstation and sets up everything that needs to be in place to let your workstation act as a network host. Information is exchanged and agreed upon, hence the reference to handshakes.)

It's good to take care of a few bits of business before you start to dial the phone.

- Make sure your flow control setting in your startup menu is set to **Hardware,** not software.
- Be sure you've properly entered the configuration information into your configuration file or script. Be especially certain that you

have not put your own IP address into the default gateway field, should you be required to give either one.

M A S T E R   W O R D S

When choosing a modem for the first time, or when considering upgrading your modem to one of the new faster modems, consider this: experience shows that modems running *v.fast* or *v.42bis* handle SLIP and PPP connections better than those with MNP. Whenever possible, buy the fastest modem you can afford.

▶ *Starting Up Your Direct IP Link*

In many ways a direct IP link is easier to set up than a dialup IP link because the step of correctly configuring your modem is eliminated. But you still need to have some of the same business taken care of before you start:

- Make sure your flow control setting in your startup menu is set to **Hardware,** not software.

- Be sure you've properly entered the configuration information into your configuration file or script. Be especially certain that you have not put your own IP address into the default gateway field, should you be required to give either one.

- Make sure your line speed and your software settings match.

- Be sure that the software driver for your Ethernet or AppleTalk (or whatever kind of physical wire you're tied into) is running and configured. You may well need to have had a special card installed in your workstation to handle these types of media. If you don't think this has been done, go back to square zero: call your systems administrator or local expert.

▶ *Troubleshooting a SLIP or PPP Link*

It's impossible to give a comprehensive list of troubleshooting tips here. Each network expert has her own, and some depend as much on the idiosyncrasies of a particular network or connection as any tried and true method. Some even seem to depend on what your mother may have called "holding your mouth right"—bewilderingly, some tricks may work for one person and not for another. But these will give you some hints to try in debugging your connection.

As in the modem list, this set of tips may not work for all problems, and you may need to call in a support person. But if you document what you tried and what the results were, the support person may be better able to solve the problem. For more comprehensive troubleshooting, contact your local network provider or join a newsgroup or e-mail discussion for your particular software.

 ▶ ▶**M A S T E R   W O R D S**

A fast search of available newsgroups turns up the following list where you can get help for communications software: comp.sys.amiga.datacom, comp.protocols.ppp, comp.dcom.modems, comp.emulators.announce, comp.os.ms-windows.apps.com, comp.os.ms-windows.networking.tcp-ip, **and** comp.sys.mac.comm. **You should also read** news.answers **to find the Frequently Answered Question lists for your particular software.**

My Modem Dials, but I Never Get a Connection

1. Are you using the right **parity, with hardware flow control enabled?** Rhana Jacot of CICNet says, "SLIP requires a totally transparent, 8-bit data path, and normal flow control will not work! Use RTS/CTS (Request To Send/Clear to Send) hardware flow control. If you are using a Macintosh and MacTCP, be sure your modem cable is a hardware-handshaking cable, where the limited number of serial control pins out of the Macintosh are used for handshaking, instead of detecting and controlling the flow rate of the modem."

2. Is your dialing **script** correct? Pritish Shah, a consultant for CICNet, says, "Most errors occur in the script where the script is expecting a particular string but gets some other input from the server—then it just keeps waiting and waiting. This is usually

solved by carefully matching what the server is sending and what the script is expecting (to the very last capitalization and space). To figure that out, log in via terminal software, do a manual login and then note every line sent (basically doing by hand what the script is supposed to do)." Another good way to capture this information is to send the screen to your printer, or capture the window in a file, either by a screen capture routine or by using cut and paste. If all else fails, use paper and pencil!

3. Are you **configured for SLIP?** Some new software (such as Chameleon, Versaterm, and FTP software) can run in either SLIP or PPP, and some in Host-dial mode. Double-check that you're configured for the correct protocol.

4. Do you have the right **device drivers** loaded? Most SLIP (and PPP) packages use at least one device driver, and you need to make sure that your configuration files call these drivers (and, more importantly, that they are installed on your workstation). This problem will need either a very patient phone consultant or a good friend to come and help you figure it out.

5. If you're using a DOS computer, are you using **SuperTCP** or **Chameleon** to link to an IP network, and another communications software package to link to other networks? Although they perform very well in most instances, both of these packages will take over the COM ports and not release them for use by other applications. This is a design feature of the software, and you cannot switch back and forth between other communications applications without rebooting your machine.

I Get a Connection and Everything Handshakes, but Nothing Ever Happens

1. Is *your* IP address in the **gateway address** box? Bob Williams of NetManage, the folks who make the Chameleon software, offers this tip: "If the user makes a mistake, like putting their own IP address in under default gateway, they will get very fast pings, and nothing else." If you have made this mistake, your software is trying to talk to itself instead of the network, and is getting (predictably) nowhere.

2. Do you have the correct **DNS IP address** in your configuration file? TCP-IP software talks to a server called a DNS server to get

the translation between IP addresses and domain names done. This lets you use domain names in your connection commands rather than IP addresses. If your DNS server, and your backup DNS server, are not listed correctly, your connection will spin its wheels waiting for routing assistance from the network.

3. Is your **DNS server** up? The only way to tell this is to set up an alternate DNS server in your configuration file. Be sure and back up your configuration file before making any changes. (Macintosh software users frequently have a list of alternate DNS servers in their software already; DOS and Windows users should try this solution only when extremely confident of their skills.) If you swap DNS servers, and your connection works, either you had the wrong address typed in or the original server is not responding. (If you're curious, you can *ping* the DNS server you were trying to reach once you make a solid connection, if your software supports Ping. The Chameleon Sampler, on Companion Disk 2, includes Ping. Type **ping** and you should see at least the response "<host name> is alive.") If you don't have an alternative DNS server, your only hope at this point is to call your help center.

4. Did you try to force your software to use a particular gateway? Did you write in an incorrect IP address for your workstation? PPP negotiates its IP address and the address of the gateway that it uses, so if you have preconfigured these incorrectly your session may hang.

I Get a Connection and Handshaking, but All That Ever Happens Is a Message Telling Me That Something Has "Timed Out"

1. Check your **DNS address.** It's likely that the machine you are trying to reach is listed incorrectly. If there are no typos, there's a chance that the primary machine is not up, and you'll need to try using a secondary machine.

2. Check your configuration file to see **how many times** your connection tries to get connected before giving up. If the network is really congested, you may need to increase the number of *retries*. In some applications, you may need to explicitly set a parameter to do this.

3. Check your dialing script. It may be waiting for a line it can never receive, and timing out while it waits.

I Get a Connection, but It Prints in Bursts or with a Very Slow Echo Rate

1. Make sure that you have selected the **proper modem type.** For example, selecting a Hayes modem when you actually have Telebit equipment can produce these symptoms. Another possible reason may be selecting too high a baud rate. Up to speeds of 19,200 bps, no special settings usually need to be changed. To use compression and/or modems that run above that rate, you'll need to see your documentation or call your support line.

2. Check for **line noise** (see the section on troubleshooting modems above).

3. The network itself may be very **congested**. Switch to an alternate resource (another service with the same information), or, if that is not possible, log off and try again later.

4. Is your **DNS server** up? The only way to tell this is to set up an alternate DNS server in your configuration file. See the suggestions for testing a DNS server under "Troubleshooting SLIP."

Direct and Dialup Links

▶ ▶ ▶

ch.
5

▶ ▶ ▶   CHAPTER **6**

Communication Software

►► **C**ommunication software (sometimes called "terminal emulation software") enables your computer to communicate with another computer. Communications software is commonly used in combination with a modem. The software offers you a way to give commands to the modem, to dial the other computer's modem, and then to issue commands and receive responses from the remote computer. There are many different packages available today. They fall into two categories: "terminal" (used for accessing most host/shell account systems) and "TCP/IP-based" (which let your computer become a host on the Internet). The "dumb terminal" packages, like ProComm Plus for DOS/Windows and VersaTerm for the Macintosh, use your computer as a keyboard and display attached to the remote machine. "TCP/IP-based" communication packages establish your computer as a workstation on a network.

►► *What Kind of Software Should I Buy?*

The kind of software you choose will depend upon how you want to use your computer and the services available from your service provider. Many providers expect you to have "dumb terminal" communications software and so give you a host or shell account. (CompuServe, Prodigy, and Delphi are examples of this kind of provider. Netcom and some other providers offer both host accounts and network accounts.) As "TCP/IP-based" communications software becomes more common, more network service providers will install systems that support networking. (Advanced Networking and Systems and CERFNet already offer nationwide dial-in networking. There are many others providing local or regional service.)

M A S T E R   W O R D S

The term "dumb terminal" does not impugn the CPU power or computing wizardry of your very expensive workstation. It means that the packages emulate the early network terminals, which had no smarts of their own: they were essentially a video display and a keyboard, and all the computing was handled by the computer at the remote end. If you are connecting to a host or shell account, this is all the smarts you need.

TCP/IP-based communication software uses either SLIP (Serial Line Internet Protocol) or PPP (Point-to-Point Protocol). Special-purpose software, like PC Remote, will use a proprietary protocol that only works with its own server. SLIP is older, but PPP is meeting with greater success. SLIP works only with IP, the Internet Protocol. PPP works with IP, AppleTalk, IPX (Novell's NetWare connectivity protocol) as well as others. The one you choose will depend upon which one your provider offers. If they offer both, it's a good idea to get software that supports PPP. Among other advantages, PPP's auto-configuration will probably be preferable to SLIP's hand-configuration.

There are many communication software packages available, both from commercial sources and from the public domain archives. Support is likely to be better for the commercial packages, but the public-domain software has a significant initial cost savings. You should base your choices on what you want to do, what works well with your local provider's network, and what kind of support you can get for the software. If you are good at troubleshooting, and enjoy watching e-mail or news for tidbits of information, one of the public-domain packages may suit your needs very well. If you want point-and-click with phone support and little tinkering, go for a commercial solution.

▶▶ *Looking for Features*

Different communication packages will have different features. A "terminal" communication package integrates the modem-dialing with the terminal interface. A "TCP/IP-based" communication package, however, separates the modem-dialing functions from the rest of the programs. The dialer establishes a link that the other pieces of the package can then use to request services from, and provide services to, the network.

A "terminal" package should offer at least a VT 100 emulation. It may emulate other terminals, such as the DEC VT220, as well. Since you will probably want to download files at least occasionally, it should support file transfer protocols as well. Some common ones to look for are Kermit, X-modem, Y-modem, and Z-modem.

A "TCP/IP-based" communication package should include at least a Telnet client and an FTP client. Like the "terminal" package, the Telnet client should emulate a VT 100, at least. Other terminal emulations may also be available. If the package includes an emulator of the IBM 3270 terminal, it will usually be as a separate application.

You will probably not be happy long without Gopher and WWW clients, as well. Look for a package that offers the complete suite of clients (or be sure and install the complete range if you are retrieving separate clients from the Net).

Other network clients, like Finger, Talk, and Whois, may also be provided. A complete package will also include servers for applications like Finger and FTP, and possibly others, that will let other people request information from your machine.

Some packages offer only the clients, requiring you to use another "communication" package. PC and clone client packages often use WinSock (for "Windows Sockets"), a standard networking interface for Microsoft Windows. If your TCP/IP software "supports WinSock," that means it can run any "WinSock-compatible" program you acquire.

When looking for software, whether public domain or commercial, remember to take into account the ease of installation and maintenance. If you are not a tinkerer, you should get a package that has an installation and configuration script or menu, rather than one that requires you to hand-edit a configuration file.

▶▶ *What's Available*

To get the best product for your needs, your best bet is to contact your provider and find out what their users have had good experiences with.

Ask your friends. Read the reviews in the trade journals and magazines. Some packages available are listed below.

▶ *Terminal Packages*

- VersaTerm for Macintosh
- ProComm
- winQVT

▶ *TCP/IP-based Packages*

- Internet Chameleon (NetManage Inc.)
- Internet_in_a_box (Spry, Inc.)
- SuperTCP (Frontier Technologies)
- Trumpet WinSock, trumpet suite (Trumpet)
- NetCruiser (Netcom)

▶ *TCP/IP-based Clients*

- MacPPP
- Minuet
- winQVT/Net
- NCSA Telnet (public domain)
- Fetch for Macintosh (FTP only)
- Mosaic

▶ *VersaTerm*

A full-featured terminal communication package for the Macintosh. It offers several file-transfer protocols, including Kermit, X-modem, Y-modem, Z-modem, and MacBinary. Later versions added SLIP support. It also works with the Comm Toolbox in Macintosh System 7.

Communication Software

▶ ▶

ch.

6

▶ *ProComm*

A full-featured terminal communications package for DOS/Windows. It offers several file-transfer protocols, including Kermit, X-modem, Y-modem, and Z-modem. The latest versions of VersaTerm also include SLIP as an option when connecting.

▶ *WinQVT*

A DEC VT220/102/52 terminal emulator and communications program that runs under Microsoft Windows. It offers Kermit, X-modem, Y-modem, Z-modem and CompuServe B-Plus file transfer protocols.

▶ *Internet Chameleon (NetManage Inc.)*

A suite of TCP/IP applications. Several versions are available, all of which include PPP and WinSock. The Chameleon Sampler on this book's Disk 2 includes FTP, Telnet, a Mail program, and Ping. You'll find information about ordering other versions at the back of the book. Appendix H contains detailed instructions for installing, configuring, and using the Chameleon Sampler.

▶ *Internet_in_a_box (Spry, Inc.)*

A suite of TCP/IP applications, including PPP and WinSock support. Available at computer retailers.

▶ *SuperTCP (Frontier Technologies)*

A suite of TCP/IP applications for Microsoft Windows. It includes PPP and WinSock support. Available at computer retailers.

▶ *Trumpet WinSock, Trumpet Suite (Trumpet)*

A news reader for Microsoft Windows (illustrated in Chapter 12, which discusses Usenet News). The package is available by anonymous FTP from ftp.utas.edu.au (yes, this really is in Australia), in the directory /pc/trumpet/wintrump. Trumpet's implementation of WinSock is in the directory /pc/trumpet/winsock. The most recent beta release adds PPP support; it has had SLIP for several years.

▶ *NetCruiser (Netcom)*

A SLIP-based package, available on this book's Disk 1, that includes most of the major Internet applications in the form of a Windows-based Graphical User Interface. Appendix H shows how to install and use the software, and how to register with Netcom.

▶ *MacPPP*

A PPP implementation for the Macintosh. It allows MacTCP to work over a modem. Note that MacPPP is just a dialer and PPP implementation. It requires MacTCP and other TCP/IP-based clients, which must be acquired separately. MacPPP is available by anonymous FTP from `merit.edu`, in the directory /pub/ppp/mac.

▶ *Minuet*

"Minnesota Internet Users Essential Tool" is an integrated package of TCP/IP tools, including a news reader and Telnet, electronic mail (using the POP protocol), Gopher, FTP and Finger clients, for DOS. SLIP, but not PPP, is available separately. It is available by an anonymous FTP on `boombox.micro.umn.edu`, in the directory pub/pc/minuet.

▶ *WinQVT/Net*

An Ethernet-TCP/IP version of WinQVT. It does not include its own transport, requiring a third-party packet driver or WinSock implementation.

▶ *NCSA Telnet (public domain)*

A collection of network clients, including Telnet, FTP, WHOIS and others, written at the National Center for Super-computing Applications, NCSA, University of Illinois, Champaign-Urbana. There are versions for both the Macintosh and DOS. They all require a TCP/IP connection, either over Ethernet or PPP; they do not include the communications software. Available at most large FTP archives.

Communication Software

ch.
6

▶ *Fetch for Macintosh (FTP only)*

An FTP client for the Macintosh. It requires a TCP/IP connection, such as is available with MacPPP and MacTCP. It is available by anonymous FTP from `ftp.dartmouth.edu`, in the directory /pub/mac.

▶ *Mosaic*

A World Wide Web client originally written by the National Center for Supercomputing Applications, NCSA, at the University of Illinois, Champaign-Urbana. There are versions of NCSA Mosaic for UNIX, Windows, and Macintosh. NCSA Mosaic is available by anonymous FTP from `ftp.ncsa.uiuc.edu`. Like NCSA Telnet, NCSA Mosaic requires a TCP/IP connection and does not include the communication software.

Various commercially distributed versions of Mosaic are also available; these are often enhanced versions of the original NCSA Mosaic. They also usually require separate TCP/IP and communication software.

▶ ▶ **M A S T E R   W O R D S**

Sybex's *Mosaic Access to the Internet* (Daniel A. Tauber and Brenda Kienan, 1995) provides instant access to the World Wide Web via Air Mosaic Express, a plug-and-play solution that installs itself, sets up the connection, and gets Mosaic running in seconds. No separate TCP/IP or communication software is needed.

CHAPTER 7

Observing the Rules of the Road

► ► **A**lthough a lot of people are tired of the "Information High-way" metaphor for the Internet (in part, because the Internet is so much more than just a highway system: it's the villages and libraries and newspapers and parking lots as well), we can compare traffic rules and regulations to the kinds of rules and agreements that govern the Internet.

Just as with the Interstate Highway System, there were fewer rules at the beginning, when the resource was used less; and there are more now, when all of us are competing for the same resources. While some network hackers, wizards, and cowboys lament the need for more rules, in general a little common courtesy and respect will get you most places you need to go.

► ► *Rules for Traveling the Internet*

When you drive an automobile from one town to another, you need to be aware that the rules of the road may be slightly different in each of the areas through which you travel. There may be differences in where you are allowed to park, in whether turning right after stopping at a red light is permitted, or in speed limits, for example.

When you travel the Internet, the same sorts of things can differ, depending on the network and the host systems you are using. Some hosts and services only permit a certain number of connections at one time and will refuse any more until some of the resources being used are freed. Some networks allow commercial messages; some do not allow them.

Most network providers and hosts or bulletin board services (BBS) have Terms and Conditions by which you agree to abide. Some of them are called AUPs (Appropriate Use Policies). Some are called contracts or user policies. The rules for your network are spelled out there. You may have signed such a policy as part of getting your account, or as part of your employment agreement. It is a good idea to read and be familiar with these rules.

For example, the systems administrators at Livermore Labs, a big research center, discovered that one of their employees was using Livermore file space as a place where people could exchange erotic images via the Net. This was certainly against their policies, and the employee knew it.

In general, usage policies for connected networks and services are posted on each service or host. Read the "message of the day" or "banner" messages at the entrance to each service. These messages will tell you of policy changes or locations of important information. If you don't think you're well-informed about the policies you are working under, ask your systems administrator about them.

In all cases, it is illegal (against the law) to use networks for illegal purposes. For example, child pornography and the distribution of it is illicit in the United States. Simply storing child pornography (either in text or graphic form) on your computer is not legal; if your systems administrator finds it, he or she must destroy it and contact the authorities. Or, using your computer network to arrange for the sale of drugs is not acceptable, for the same reasons.

▶▶ *Why Do I Care?*

When traveling the interstate highways in America, particularly in the high summer tourist season, you'll sometimes encounter a nasty backup that stretches for miles. As you inch your way along, you'll discover that several lanes are being condensed down, and that people are trying to merge into one lane.

Some folks merged over as soon as they saw the signs telling them to do so. Out by the warning signs, the overall speed stays up. The early mergers cheerfully wave to folks to merge in before them. And if someone lets you in, you're more inclined to let someone merge in ahead of you, as well.

As you get closer to the point where everyone *must* be funneled into one lane, the congestion and confusion get worse.

Closer in, some have waited a while, but still merge in before it becomes urgent. And some race right up to the last car-length before their lane ends, then honk wildly for others to let them in. If the driver who's currently at the head of the line is feeling generous and pleasant, a choppy merge takes place. If not, a game of chicken happens, where the guy who wanted to save a few minutes sticks his nose into the traffic, and the guy who's mad because of Guy Number 1's rudeness threatens to take his bumper off.

As a consequence, the whole line of traffic clogs up. Had everyone just merged over when the signs directing them to first appeared, it's likely that much of the traffic jam could have been avoided. And, with it, lots of steamed tempers and irritated drivers, who then go on to fight with folks at every place they stop for the rest of the day.

On the network, just as in this example, both rudeness and courtesy are contagious. Rudeness, or using outright illicit or banned behavior, can clog up the network for all of us. Just as in everyday life, there are two sorts of "rules" for the Internet: those which govern our physical access and those which govern appropriate behavior.

▶▶ *Sharing Your Toys*

Being rude about resources and physical access can lead to increased restrictions and, in some cases, to the resource being shut down. If modem access is scarce and you "lunch" a line (grab one early in the day and never break the connection, even when you're not using it), the normal pattern of use is disrupted, and even more people have problems getting a line. They complain: some of them grab lines and hold onto them, and soon the resource is tied up almost continuously. Everyone sends nastygrams to the system operators.

In some cases the systems operator can see who has been abusing the system (in highway terms, look at your license plate), and deal with that person. But in many cases, all they can do is collect statistics and figure out what to do.

Management looks at the stats to see if there really is a shortage, sees all these lines tied up all day (rather than the normal pattern of connects and disconnects), and either institutes a policy to limit continuous connect time, charges more (in order to buy more modems), or decides to limit access to folks with *legitimate* use as defined by the usage policies. Everybody loses.

Although it may be hard to believe, there really is an ocean of resources on the Internet. Most of us only "surf" or "cruise" around on the top, hardly touching the vast amount of things available. There seems to be plenty to go around, especially with the growing interest in providing services. If one service gets clogged up or overused, either they'll expand to let all the users who are trying to access it get in, or a competitor will spring up, offering a similar service. Since your biggest goal with the Internet is communication—getting or distributing information—these market forces are to your best advantage in the long run. Getting greedy isn't.

The other kinds of uses which are governed on the Internet have to do with appropriate use. They include things such as: respect of copyright, commercial use on a non-commercial system, employee privilege on business systems, and so on.

▶▶ *Copyright*

In mid-1994 Dave Barry, the humor columnist, and his publisher proposed discontinuing the distribution of his columns over the Net. Why? Because one of his publisher's employees got a copy of one of Barry's columns, passed along fourth or fifth hand in e-mail—forwarded from the Clarinet news subscription service which had been publishing them electronically. His publishers (and Barry, presumably) felt that his potential to earn money was being diluted because of promiscuous theft of his copyrighted material off the Internet. Some of us may actually have to start reading the paper again to find Barry's columns. :-)

It's hard to remember that copyright law and intellectual property law still obtain even though materials may not be represented in some physical form like paper. It's too easy to just forward the file in e-mail to your buddy, or a set of buddies, or squirrel it away in an FTP archive, or even dump it down to a newsletter or other publication.

But we must learn to respect copyrighted material in electronic format as much as we do that on paper or in broadcast media. Some day many of us may be making our livings solely from electronic publication, and the ground rules for that are being set now.

Remember that the materials obtained under license from news services, for example, may not be altered or used without permission. A shareware computer program obtained by downloading from a program archive may ask for a registration fee as part of its license agreement. You are ethically obligated to pay the fee if you use the program. If there's a copyright statement at the beginning of the document, software program, or other material, read it and respect it.

▶ *Copyleft*

You may well run into something called *copyleft* on your travels about the Internet. Copyleft is a concept which has come out of the GNU (Gnu's Not Unix) project, which is working on creating free software versions of most UNIX programs and utilities. The folks who work with the GNU project believe that the *source* code for every program ought to be available to everyone to use and modify. (This is a very simplistic description of the GNU project. For a more complete description, send e-mail to gnu@prep.ai.mit.edu.) Documentation and other works associated with the GNU project are *copylefted*, which means that the owner, while still retaining the copyright, has granted everyone the right to copy and use it, as long as acknowledgment is made, and *everyone else is free to use that material again in their own works.*

If you encounter copylefted materials and wish to use them for some purpose, be sure to read the provisions carefully to ensure that you use the materials appropriately.

 ▶ ▶ **M A S T E R   W O R D S**

Several authors have put their books up on the Internet under copylefting terms. To find them, FTP to ftp.eff.org, **log on as** anonymous, **and look in the directory. Among the writers whose work you'll find there are Bruce Sterling, Shari Steele, and William Gibson.**

▶▶ *Commercial Use*

What about commercial use of the Internet?

Commercial use is, roughly defined, traffic which supports business or trade rather than academic research or instruction. Want ads, service ads, software support, e-mail hotlines, and distribution of reports and financial data for large corporations can all be described as commercial use.

Positions on commercial use are changing as we speak. Five years ago, anything traveling the old NSFNET backbone (which was most of the traffic on the still-infant Internet) had to either be academic or in support of academic research. Some networks, primarily those funded largely with academic research funds, still have restrictions on commercial traffic. But the world is changing quickly, and you can find an alternative which will allow you to pass commercial traffic in nearly any location.

Material traversing the interconnected networks of the Commercial Internet eXchange (CIX) explicitly may contain commercial transactions. As of late 1994, commercial use of certain other networks that have significant support from the United States Federal government, particularly the NSFNET, may be restricted to only activities in support of research and education. Unfortunately, the definitions of support, commercial use, research, and education are not really clear, and the definitions that do exist are changing. In general, the best thing to do is to be aware that there are restrictions and try to abide by the Acceptable Use Policy (AUP) of each network. Consult with your systems administrator, employer, or university computing service if you are in doubt about the way you propose to use it.

▶ *For-Fee Services*

Some services use the Internet to deliver you to their front door and then begin charging for their use, others do not charge. Services that charge for their usage are well-marked. You will need to make account arrangements with these services before you can use them. There will be signs at the front door of these services to tell you how to open an account.

▶▶ *A Few Words about Netiquette*

The American Heritage Dictionary defines etiquette as "the practices and forms prescribed by social convention or by authority." It lists etiquette, propriety, decorum, and protocol as being roughly equivalent words which refer to codes governing correct behavior.

Netiquette is, if you will, the personal protocol that helps us participate in the networked society. Such protocols are not, unlike the remainder of the TCP/IP protocol suite, formally written down, but they are essential to the well-being of the society as a whole. Netiquette provides the guidelines that allow us, for example, to agree to disagree. Mostly, being a good networked citizen is being a responsible person: not wasting resources; being aware of and observing restrictions that are placed on some Internet resources; observing the posted rules; remembering that on the Net, you are in public.

Remember the angry drivers in the scenario up above? On the Interstates, usually, these drivers are content to dole out a few well-chosen words and gestures, and then the flow of traffic whisks them away.

Unfortunately, if you're going to start being rude to someone on the Internet, they can archive your words and argue with you for a long time. In Internet terms, this is called a *flame war,* and no one really benefits from it. (Some of them can be incredibly creative and take the art of subtle insult to amazing levels. Such things are better seen from the peanut gallery, though.)

One of the pluses of the growing networked community is that some of the old-timers, and some of the newcomers who had to discover all the unwritten rules themselves, have started writing down some of the rules, customs, and conventions that govern interaction on the Internet. There are even newsgroups for newcomers these days:

- news.answers (An amazing collection of Frequently Asked Questions show up here—a *must read* for everyone.)

- news.announce.newusers (This is where the Netiquette postings show up.)

- news.newusers.questions (This is where the Frequently Asked Questions lists, or FAQs, for many newsgroups are posted.)

► ►**M A S T E R   W O R D S**

**Arlene Rinaldi of Florida Atlantic University has written
an excellent piece on netiquette which reminds us that
we as users are ultimately responsible for our own
actions on the Net. We've included it as an appendix at
the end of the book. This document, or something like
it, can serve both as personal reference and as the
cornerstone of a corporate or organizational policy on
appropriate and courteous use of the Net.**

► ► *Joy in Diversity*

One of the most exciting things about the Internet is how easy it is to
communicate and really get to know folks who are not very much like
you. Glee has a regular e-mail exchange with a fellow in Europe whom
she met through her work at Netcom: he's thoroughly European and
about 5 years older than her oldest son. Through one of the mailing
lists she reads, Pat has met a woman who works as a janitor and is running for public office; this woman has six children and worked her way
off welfare. Nearly everybody hangs out on the Net.

The most exciting thing about all this communicating is that it's impossible to tell from the bits on the screen the gender, race, age, financial
status, sexual orientation, political affiliation, or class of the person
who's writing. Until they choose to reveal those details, all you know
about someone is what they are saying. And so we get a chance to
really get to know people without the barriers that our reptile-brain-
trained eyes and ears can throw up before our brains have a chance to
let the more rational side of us take over.

We can learn to like or dislike someone based on their expressed beliefs, the language they use, their sense of humor, their concern for others. We can make friends with folks in much different situations than
ourselves, and perhaps learn about the lives that other folks live away
from the Net.

There is something of the public commons soapbox about some net-work communications: if some person who is being a pest or annoy-ance—but who is *not* breaking any rules or laws—wants to keep sending out obnoxious messages, he or she can do it. Extreme views on both ends of the spectrum are very common: both extreme friendliness and civility, and extreme jerkiness and rudeness. We learn to revel in the one and ignore (sometimes aided by technological tools) the other.

▶ Honesty and Hidden Faces

There are problems with the ability to hide something of ourselves, of course. A 1994 Doonesbury cartoon series showed two of the charac-ters—good friends in the non-virtual universe—corresponding over a bulletin board *without knowing that they knew each other.* One of the characters pretended to be a gay man, and before he knew it, the two were involved in a hot romance over the Net, resulting in emotional pain for both of them. It pointed out that, because we can choose to hide those parts of ourselves we don't want to reveal, there is a poten-tial for deception.

There have been cases where pedophiles were trying to seduce school-children over the Net; where men masqueraded as women and vice versa; where thieves engaged unsuspecting victims in conversations, found out vacation plans or other information, and robbed the victim. These are the high-profile cases: they make great news stories, so we see much more of them than we do the other side. We don't hear as much about the fundraisers that happen spontaneously when the news gets out that someone has lost their home in a fire, the deep and abid-ing friendships that spring out of mutual interests on the Net, or the marriages and successful romances.

It's important to remember that the Internet is a mirror of life: there are good people and jerks; kindness and rudeness; political action and apathy; and excitement and boredom. In general, the good and positive outweigh the bad—just like in our everyday, noncomputer lives. We just don't hear about it as much.

▶▶MASTER WORDS

> **When you start reading news, or subscribe to a mailing list, you *can* post things anonymously. There is an anonymous server at** `anon.penet.fi` **(in Finland) which will strip off all machine generated identifying marks on your postings (although if you leave your real name at the bottom it doesn't do much good). For more information, send e-mail to** `help@anon.penet.fi`**.**

▶▶ *Pardon Me, You're Reading over My Shoulder*

Privacy concerns are one of the biggest controversies in the computer industry today, and now that more and more of us are living parts of our lives over the Net, privacy concerns are reaching out and touching us all:

- Do you dial into your bank to check your balance and make payments?
- Do you send confidential company reports over the network, including spreadsheets or graphics?
- Do you send e-mail to your mother, close friend, or lover?
- Do you buy products or request quotes via e-mail from on-line vendors?
- Do you read a newsgroup pertaining to your religious beliefs, sexual orientation, hobbies, or political leanings?
- Do you keep personnel records on-line in your company LAN?
- Do you participate in a MUD, MOO, or MUSE? A Chatline? A CB group? IRC?

If you can answer "yes" to even one of these questions, you need to think about how much of your privacy you want to protect from others on the Internet.

This is not meant to scare you. We all want to close the blinds from time to time, to keep other people from looking in our windows. It's easier to forget on the Net than in our living rooms that other people can see what we're doing.

Hilary Gardner (calliope@well.sf.ca.us) has published a good set of guidelines for new users of the Internet, included in Appendix B. Even some of us old-time users can benefit from thinking about these concerns.

More and more people are becoming concerned that the world is now so interlinked, with so many of our day-to-day transactions handled by computers, that no one will be able to have private interests or be able to even spend money without that expenditure being tracked. There are several key areas of privacy concerns: two of the most important are personal information and safety, and the sale of private information. We'll cover the sale of private information when we talk about setting policy in later chapters.

▶ ▶ **M A S T E R   W O R D S**

If you are interested in finding out more about computer-related privacy and civil-liberties risks, you can read the RISKS mailing list. RISKS is available on Usenet as comp.risks.

▶▶ *Who Knows What about Me?*

If you have an account on a networked machine, chances are people can find out quite a bit about you just by checking out your account remotely with a network utility called *Finger* (we talk about it in Chapter 9). Depending on what you yourself have implemented, and what your sysop has done, quite a bit can be found with just this one simple tool.

Let's take Pat as an example.

Pat's been published in several computing journals with a reference saying she works at the University of Michigan. Let's suppose that someone tries to Finger her at U-M. What do they get?

```
home>>finger pat.mcgregor@umich.edu

[umich.edu]
X.500 Finger Service

One exact match found for "pat.mcgregor":

"Patricia O Mcgregor, Information Technology Division, Faculty
and Staff"

  Also known as:
                Patricia O Mcgregor 1

                Patricia O Mcgregor

                Patricia Mcgregor

                Pat Mcgregor

  E-mail address:
                pat@lloyd.com

  Fax number:
                +1 313 747 3185

  Business phone:
                +1 313 747 0416

  Business address:
                Merit / UMnet
                2901 Hubbard - Pod G
                Ann Arbor, MI 48109-2016

  Title:
                Computer Systems Consultant II, UM-Net

  Uniqname:
                patmcg

  Description:
                Consultant for Merit Technical Support group,
                 working with MichNet and UMnet. Editor of the
```

```
MichNet News. Bradley Childbirth Educator,
amateur medievalist.
```

```
home>>
```

This entry is pretty much out of date: Pat hasn't worked for U-M since late 1993. (U-M was keeping the listing as a courtesy and as a forwarding service.) But you can see from this that anyone who wanted to find her could have found out not only her e-mail address, but her phone number and the building where she worked. They could also learn something of her personal interests.

Pat knew that this information was accessible and chose not to edit it: she decided to take the risk that someone might decide to stalk her or call her with harassing phone messages in order to make it easy for people who needed or wanted to locate her for business or personal reasons. She chose not to make her home information accessible, however, to protect the privacy of herself and her family.

 ▶ ▶ **N O T E**

> **The University of Michigan is aware that this information is available about many people connected with the University, and runs a large publicity campaign regularly to educate those associated with the school that this information is available. Because of the potential for harassment of several kinds, private information about students is not available via Finger unless the student explicitly includes it.**

We discover from this that Pat's e-mail address is pat@lloyd.com. Let's try Fingering that and see where we get.

```
home>>finger pat@lloyd.com
[lloyd.com]
Login name: pat                    In real life: Pat McGregor
Directory: /home/furry/pat
Shell:/usr/local/bin/tcsh
On since Jul  8 15:49:39 on ttyp2 from pickle.lloyd.com
No unread mail
No Plan.
```

This is a more typical UNIX-style Finger response. We can tell that Pat has a log-in ID on the machine furry and that she was, at the time the screen dump was taken, on-line. We can tell she logged into lloyd.com remotely over the Internet from a machine called pickle. Of importance for you, if you have sent her mail, is the fact that it looks like she has read everything that has been received by her mailer. You can tell that her real login ID is pat (and if you were a hacker interested in breaking into her account, this would give you a starting place to poke holes).

Not much other information is available about Pat from this Finger session. (If you're excited about the UNIX operating system, you can tell she's using a tcsh shell interface to UNIX, and what her home directory is called.) The systems administrators at lloyd.com have, for security reasons, chosen not to implement the features that would let you see what Pat has in her personal information file (called a *.Plan* file: it comes from old UNIX days when folks would store their current working information in their planning file).

Not every system administrator has disabled this feature. Many times, you'll find something like this when you Finger someone:

```
home>>finger pat@inkwell.com
[inkwell.com]
Login name: pat              In real life: Patricia McGregor
Directory: /home/users/pat  Shell: /usr/unsupported/bin/tcsh
Last login Wed May  4 18:43 on console
New mail received Fri Jul  8 15:50:08 1994;
  unread since Thu Jul  7 09:34:25 1994
Plan:


===============================================================


Pat McGregor                               Inkwell Publications

                    Speaker-to-Programmers
                    pat@inkwell.com


          1937 Pelican Drive, Mountain View, CA 94444
                    (415) 123-4567(voice)
                    (415) 777-3456 (fax)
```

```
"That's how freedom will end: not with a bang, but with a rus-
tle of file folders. If you love any of your rights, defend
all of them!"
```

`--Joe Chew, on the Net`

Again, we can learn quite a bit about how to find Pat: something she has chosen deliberately to allow. We can see her work phone, her work fax, where her office is located, and that she hasn't read her mail in the last day.

The point of this extended discussion is to remind you that *unless you take steps to prevent it,* quite a bit of information about you is casually available on the Net. If you want to find out just how much, ask your systems administrator.

 ▶ ▶**MASTER WORDS**

> **We can hear you now: "Just how do I *find* my systems administrator?" Many systems have a mailbox called "postmaster" or "admin" where a real human being reads the mail. If all else fails, send to "root."**

Some women in particular are concerned about harassing strangers finding out their work addresses, phone numbers, and so on. Hilary Gardner's advice in her column helps you make decisions about what you want to allow to be private and what to make public.

 ▶ ▶**MASTER WORDS**

> **If you are interested in finding out more about privacy and freedom on the network, send e-mail to info@eff.org. This is the general mailbox for the Electronic Freedom Foundation, an organization which has as one of its concerns the protection of personal privacy in the age of the Internet. They also have a World Wide Web page available at www.eff.org.**

▶▶ *cAsE Sensitivity and Other Operating System Differences*

Just as we discover the joy of diversity in people on the Internet, we also discover the challenges of working in a *heterogeneous networking environment.* Each computer and network in the global Internet operates in its own environment. You will see many different kinds of operating systems and commands. These days, most systems have good on-line help available; in most cases, you'll see the information on how to access it in the first screen you come to.

▶ ▶ **MASTER WORDS**

> **In many library catalog systems, the help and logoff information appears in the very first screen you access, and never again! Be sure and take note of it: copy it down if you think you'll forget.**

Case sensitivity means that it matters whether a letter is typed in upper or lowercase. Some operating systems don't care, others are particularly picky. One way to make sure that your e-mail gets through to someone on another system is to type everything in lowercase: i.e., barney@tv.org rather than Barney@TV.org. The rules that programmers must apply in accepting e-mail (if they want to be able to send and receive Internet mail) say that no matter what the internal system says, incoming mail must be accepted if it's in all lowercase.

▶ *UNIX*

In many cases, the systems and services you reach from the Internet are running the UNIX operating system. UNIX began in a time of very slow computer terminals for use by people who were impatient typists. Consequently, good command interface design consisted of maximum information conveyed in very few keystrokes. This led to the single-letter, case-sensitive command structure that makes it difficult to learn UNIX quickly. UNIX systems also are case sensitive in the Login ID or User name. The Login ID must be lowercase in most UNIX environments. File names can also be mixed upper- and lowercase letters. To retrieve a file, if you are entering the file name rather than clicking on the name in a list of files, you must enter its name exactly.

The good aspect of this is that it's easier to make your password secure in an environment where the operating system is case sensitive. A password of more than seven characters, typed with a mixture of upper and lowercase letters, is harder for someone to accidentally (or even with some deliberation) type in, even if you do use a dictionary word for your password (a big no-no, because most folks who try to crack password files do so with huge dictionaries and programs that try them all out).

The most useful help systems on UNIX systems are called *man pages,* short for manual pages. The complete documentation for many system utilities can be accessed through the man pages. To ask for help, type

`man man`

This peculiar-looking command gives you instructions on using the man facility itself.

MASTER WORDS

For help with UNIX commands, use a Web browser (see Chapter 11) to access `http://alpha.acase.nova.edu/UNIXhelp/TOP_.html`. **This Web server provides information about UNIX and how to use it.**

▶ *Other Systems*

Non-UNIX systems have their peculiar features, too. IBM MVS and VM systems, for example, cannot have file names longer than eight characters per name segment, leading to some interesting names where vowels are deleted so that the file name can convey something about the content of the file. These systems, however, treat upper and lowercase commands equally, giving the same result no matter how the command is entered.

▶▶ *Take Off and Explore*

Although using the Internet can be confusing and overwhelming when you're first getting started, if you keep the simple rules of courtesy in mind, you can feel your way along pretty easily. Just remember these few guidelines:

- Read the road signs as you come to them.

- Be polite and respectful of other's property and privacy.

- Keep a road map (a notepad) by your side to copy down the host address of fun or useful things, so you can find them again.

- Learn how to use bookmarks and hot lists in clients such as Gopher and WWW.

- Read the Help files.

- Read the Terms and Conditions.

- Remember that you probably can't break the computer—don't be afraid to explore and try something new.

## CHAPTER 8

Electronic Mail: Exchanging Messages with Other People

► ► **E**lectronic mail (abbreviated "e-mail") is the service most people use first in networking, whether they are on a local LAN or on a service connected to the global Internet. It is *the* most commonly used service on the Internet, perhaps because of how convenient it is. It's easier to send e-mail than paper mail: no stamps, no searching for an envelope—just type and send! E-mail allows us to send a message to another computer without requiring that the receiving person be "at home" (logged into the destination computer) at the time the destination system actually receives the e-mail. Thus, e-mail is more like "talking" to an answering machine or a voice mail system than it is like a telephone conversation. And it can seem like playing telephone tag, because you send a message to your friend, who reads it after you go home, and then you read the answer later before you go to bed (or even after you go back to work the next day).

Most important, as you can see in Figure 8.1, e-mail is familiar and easy because it looks like a memo, a note to a friend, or a formal report, only on screen instead of on paper.

It is called e-*mail* because it is similar to the paper mail that the postal service delivers:

- You put it into an electronic envelope and address it.
- You hand the message off to someone else (the network) to be delivered.
- You may not know when the e-mail is read.
- If you address your message incorrectly, you get it back in your mailbox.
- If the recipient leaves a forwarding address, the e-mail system will keep trying to route it to her until it runs out of forwarding locations.

FIGURE 8.1 ▶

E-mail looks much like any other note or message.

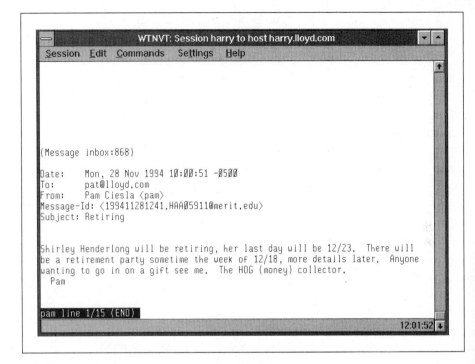

```
                    WTNVT: Session harry to host harry.lloyd.com

  Session  Edit  Commands  Settings  Help


(Message inbox:868)

Date:    Mon, 28 Nov 1994 10:00:51 -0500
To:      pat@lloyd.com
From:    Pam Ciesla <pam>
Message-Id: <199411281241.HAA059110merit.edu>
Subject: Retiring

Shirley Henderlong will be retiring, her last day will be 12/23.  There will
be a retirement party sometime the week of 12/18, more details later.  Anyone
wanting to go in on a gift see me.  The HOG (money) collector.
  Pam

pam line 1/15 (END)
                                                               12:01:52
```

- Your message will be returned if the network is unable to deliver your e-mail. (This is called *bounced* mail because it "bounces" back to you.)

There are some other similarities to the stuff the post office puts in your paper mailbox:

- Anyone who knows your address can send e-mail to you.
- Friends you haven't seen in a long time can keep in touch with you.
- You can get so much e-mail that you have trouble reading it all.
- If you subscribe to them, electronic "magazines" or mailing lists can give you a much wider point of view about the world around you.
- Commercial companies can send you advertising or "junk" mail (this is less true on academic systems, but such mail can slip through).

- If you go on vacation, your mailbox can fill up.

- Your mail can be delivered to, and read by, someone for whom it wasn't intended for.

- There's no guarantee that every piece of e-mail you get will be pleasant and friendly. (But, as of yet, there are not very many electronic bills!)

Because e-mail does travel over computers and computer networks instead of in trucks and airplanes, it's important to remember some differences between e-mail and paper mail:

- Because e-mail is so easy to handle (remember, no stamps or envelopes to hunt for), it is very easy for other people to pass around or forward on. Your e-mail may reach people you did not intend to see it.

- Because computers and computer networks have "glitches," your e-mail may end up in the hands of a computer postmaster or someone who handles bounced e-mail.

- Because e-mail is so easy to reply to, you may send off fast and snappy responses that may not say all you wanted, or you may say something you will regret later.

 ▶ ▶ **M A S T E R   W O R D S**

Remember the first rule of electronic mail: If you wouldn't want to see it posted on the lunchroom bulletin board, don't send it in an e-mail message.

▶▶ *What about Privacy?*

Although e-mail has the *potential* to be terribly public, in reality, most e-mail gets read only by the sender and the intended recipient. For example, when Pat was one of the electronic postmasters at the University of Michigan, they estimated that something like 30,000 e-mail messages were transmitted per day across campus—on a slow day. Fewer than 75 per day of those messages ended up in the postmaster's mailbox for handling. That's 0.25%—so there's very little chance your e-mail will go astray.

Even if your message bounces back to you, chances are no one but you will see it. Unless something goes terribly wrong, most bounced messages are handled by the computers involved without human intervention.

Lots of people communicate with their friends and loved ones via e-mail every day. In general, it's probably not a good idea to get graphic about your reunion with your significant other over e-mail, just in case it does bounce. But there are lots of ways to talk personally without being worried about your messages being publicly displayed.

Even if your message does get sent to a postmaster for handling, it's not likely that he or she will read it and take it home to share with friends. Most postmasters are too busy to go looking for people's private e-mail to read, and most of them have respect for your privacy. It's part of their personal ethical systems.

WARNING

Read the information you get from your e-mail service provider carefully (or ask to see the e-mail confidentiality information before you sign up). Some businesses have a policy of no private e-mail on their machines; they do not, therefore, hesitate to scan your mail. Some e-mail providers have automated programs that scan for key words (such as obscenities, root or daemon commands, hot topics such as "pornography," "cracker/hacker," and so on) in e-mail, and they will read or discard your e-mail if it contains one or more of those words. Make sure you know what you're signing up for.

▶▶ *Interconnected but Not All Alike*

There are many different electronic mail systems that use the Internet as a delivery service. Some electronic mail enters or leaves the Internet from the commercial information providers like CompuServe and MCIMail. Most e-mail enters or leaves the network from an e-mail system on a connected network node.

These e-mail systems are supported by a local computing system administration and are chosen based on criteria important to the local service area or business. Any e-mail system that allows Internet addressing can let mail traverse the Internet if the networks at either end are set up correctly and their e-mail systems can put the e-mail in Internet-compatible format.

▶▶ *How Does E-Mail Work?*

Let's review how e-mail works. As an example, we'll use the piece of e-mail between Hilary and Sue that we talked about in Chapter 1.

Hilary is in Durham, England, and he wants to get information to Sue in Seattle, Washington. Now, if these people are in the same company, using some corporate-wide e-mail system, Hilary just enters in Sue's login on the company e-mail system as her address. Hilary's address on the company system might just be `hilary`. His coworker in Seattle, Sue, would likely just be `sue`. When Hilary types or clicks the `Send` command, the corporate e-mail system delivers it to the correct mailbox without sending it outside the system. This is the easiest kind of e-mail addressing.

 ▶ ▶ **MASTER WORDS**

Not all e-mail user IDs or addresses are first names or initials. On some systems it will be your account number, your employee number, or some other randomly assigned user ID. Smaller systems tend to use names or initials; larger ones have to find a way to provide each user with a unique identifier.

In fact, people on CompuServe, GEnie, NETCOM, America Online, and many other large providers can use this simple form of addressing, because even though they do not all work together, or live in the same town or country, their mailboxes are all handled by one single e-mail system.

MASTER WORDS

Hilary and Sue's messages might well have to go over the Internet in order to reach each other, since they are so far apart. If they were in the same building, their messages might not leave the building's computer system to be delivered. But because they are part of the same corporate e-mail system, Sue and Hilary usually don't have to know anything but each other's login name to exchange mail. The corporate e-mail system handles the routing and more complicated addressing, if any.

However, it is likely that Sue and Hilary are *not* on the same e-mail system. They need to know more in order to get e-mail to one another. They have to add something onto the login name to indicate what machine the e-mail is to go to. This address extension, found following the @ (at) sign in an Internet e-mail address, is called the *fully qualified* address—this means that it has all the parts it needs in order to be delivered from anywhere on the network.

MASTER WORDS

If you send messages to people, but they can't *reply* to those messages, your e-mail system might not be putting your fully qualified address on the FROM line: It might say `joe` instead of `joe@aol.com`. Ask your correspondents to dump your message, including the headers and all the incomprehensible bits, into a new message back to you, with your full address in the TO line. When it comes back, you can see what is going out to your friends.

Let's go back to Hilary and Sue. Hilary's full address might be: hilary@durham.ac.uk. Sue's full address is: sue@seattle.org. (These are fictitious addresses used for example only. The ac.uk is a British addressing convention that means "Academic, United Kingdom." It corresponds to the .edu and .us extensions in the United States.)

Once a message has an address on it, the interconnected Internet systems take over. The e-mail handling system on the sender's computer packages the message and prepares it for "shipping." The message is broken up into small pieces and put into envelopes called "packets." The packets are all addressed to the final destination. No matter what path or paths the packets with the bits of Hilary's message in it take, they are all reassembled in the correct order by the e-mail machine at Sue's end. Figure 8.2 illustrates the process.

FIGURE 8.2 ▶

An e-mail message, broken into packets, takes many routes to destination.

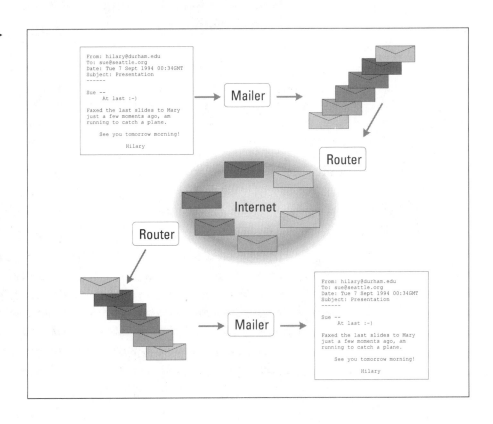

▶ *Understanding the Mail*

Let's look at an e-mail message and dissect the bits. This is e-mail from Jeff Marraccini, who helped us on the book.

```
(Message inbox:398)
Date:  Sun, 14 Aug 1994 22:58:35 -0400 (EDT)
To:    pat@lloyd.com (Pat McGregor)
From:  Jeff Marraccini <jeff@Vela.ACS.Oakland.Edu>
Subject: Re: IRC!

Return-Path: Vela.ACS.Oakland.Edu!jeff
Return-Path: <jeff@Vela.ACS.Oakland.Edu>
In-Reply-To: <mOqZgtJ-0005awC@lloyd.com> from "Pat McGregor" at
Aug 14, 94 07:50:29 am
Organization: Oakland University, Rochester, MI U.S.A.
X-Mailer: ELM [version 2.4 PL21]
Mime-Version: 1.0
Content-Type: text/plain; charset=US-ASCII
Content-Transfer-Encoding: 7bit
Content-Length: 588


--------------------------------------------------------

Pat McGregor (pat@lloyd.com) writes:
>I haven't had a chance to get it out of the FTP archive but
>I'll do that today and let you know.

I may be hard to reach starting on Tuesday and ending on next
Sunday, as I'm going on a small vacation before the crunch
hits. If you need to reach me, I'll hopefully be able to check
e-mail every other day, or leave a message on my cellular
phone.

Thanks,

Jeff
--
Jeff Marraccini          jeff@vela.acs.oakland.edu <- Work
Senior Computing Resource Admin  jeff@nucleus.mi.org<-Home
Oakland University               +1 810 370-4542
Rochester, MI 48309 "The Computer is your Friend." --Paranoia
```

Electronic Mail

▶ ▶

ch.

8

Addressing

The first section is just like a memo or paper mail letter: it tells us who the message is from, who it goes to, what it's about, and when it was sent.

```
Date:  Sun, 14 Aug 1994 22:58:35 -0400 (EDT)
To:    pat@lloyd.com (Pat McGregor)
From:  Jeff Marraccini <jeff@Vela.ACS.Oakland.Edu>
Subject: Re: IRC!
```

Jeff's mailer is more user-friendly than some; it inserts real names with the e-mail addresses. This isn't so necessary with the kind of addresses that Jeff and Pat have: you at least can tell something of their names from the user name.

▶▶ **MASTER WORDS**

User names (the part before the @ sign) can be pretty obscure. For example, take `MS04147@med.ge.com`—we can't tell who this is from without a translation. Or the standard CompuServe address:

`7041.89321@compuserve.com`.

Both GE and CompuServe (and many others systems) use account numbers or employee numbers or some other gibberish string as user names. For this reason, you'll want to use your mailer's "alias" or "address book" functions to help you remember how to reach your friends. We'll talk about that soon.

You may also see these cryptic items in the address block of a message: CC and BCC. CC means "carbon copy," and it's pretty much the same as in a paper letter or memo. You are including the person listed in that line as a courtesy or for their information. Be careful about CC-ing the world on an e-mail message. Some people regard this as rude or excessive. Worse, they may not want to see all the responses that are generated by a mass mailing (or, if they are on CompuServe, they will be charged for this mail which they did not solicit and may not want).

BCC means "blind carbon copy." It's like making an extra photocopy of a memo or letter and dropping it in someone's in-box without letting the official recipients know you did it. Some people always BCC themselves in order to have a copy of everything they send out. BCC recipients usually get a notice that this is a blind carbon. Most mailers strip out the BCC line even for the recipients, so they can't tell who else may have gotten a blind carbon. The official recipients, of course, don't know that anyone else has gotten a copy.

Think carefully before BCC-ing someone on a message. It's possible to encourage gossip or to spread information indiscriminately with BCC, and hurt someone else. Additionally, if you spread information that is incorrect, and don't send the BCC recipient any follow-up messages correcting the information, you could be responsible for whatever bad results follow.

We can tell from the Subject line that this is a reply or a forwarded message: many mailers add "Re:" to indicate that this message *refers* to another.

Deciphering Headers

The next part of the message is where e-mail is different from paper mail. With e-mail, you can tell exactly how the message got to you from your correspondent. With paper mail, you only know that the carrier delivered it. You don't know what happened in the middle (and usually, with paper mail, you don't much care).

With e-mail, you know a lot. For example, you can see, perhaps, that an intermediate mailer held onto your message for several days before passing it along, which might explain why a message was delayed. You can see who handles the mail exchanges for your correspondent (which is sometimes more esoterically interesting than useful).

You can read even more in bounced messages, which we'll look at next.

```
Return-Path: Vela.ACS.Oakland.Edu!jeff
Return-Path: <jeff@Vela.ACS.Oakland.Edu>
In-Reply-To: <mOqZgtJ-0005awC@lloyd.com> from "Pat McGregor" at
Aug 14, 94 07:50:29 am
Organization: Oakland University, Rochester, MI U.S.A.
X-Mailer: ELM [version 2.4 PL21]
Mime-Version: 1.0
Content-Type: text/plain; charset=US-ASCII
Content-Transfer-Encoding: 7bit
Content-Length: 588
```

These lines, called "*headers,*" tell us, in order:

- How to get reply mail or bounced messages back to Jeff (the "Return-path"):

  `Return-Path: Vela.ACS.Oakland.Edu!jeff`

- The machine name or number of the message that Jeff replied to:

  `In-Reply-To: <mOqZgtJ-0005awC@lloyd.com> from`
  `"Pat McGregor" at Aug 14, 94 07:50:29 am`

  and what time Pat sent the message.

- What organization or company Jeff works for and where it's located:

  `Organization: Oakland University, Rochester, MI U.S.A.`

- What kind of mailing software he's using:

  `X-Mailer: ELM [version 2.4 PL21]`

- What version of MIME his mailer is using (an emerging mail standard, MIME lets some of us include audio and other interesting material in e-mail):

  `Mime-Version: 1.0`

- And, in context of the MIME version, what kind of encoding the message is in (in this case it's plain text):

  `Content-Type: text/plain; charset=US-ASCII`
  `Content-Transfer-Encoding: 7bit`

- Finally, how many characters are in the message:

  `Content-Length: 588`

▶▶ **M A S T E R   W O R D S**

> Along with FTP and other Internet tools, MIME and e-mail played a role in the creation of this book. MIME-capable mailer software made it possible for Pat and the SYBEX editors to send chapters back and forth in the form of Microsoft Word files (attached to e-mail messages) containing text formatting, editing marks, and footnoted comments and questions—information that can't be included in a simple ASCII file.

Scoping the Body

Next comes the body of the message. First, a line of hyphens (–) to tell the computer that all the headers are done. Then, Jeff's message.

```
---------------------------------------------------------
Pat McGregor (pat@lloyd.com) writes:
>I haven't had a chance to get it out of the FTP archive but
>I'll do that today and let you know.

I may be hard to reach starting on Tuesday and ending on next
Sunday, as I'm going on a small vacation before the crunch
hits. If you need to reach me, I'll hopefully be able to check
e-mail every other day, or leave a message on my cellular
phone.

Thanks,

Jeff
```

MASTER WORDS

Two important rules for composing text in your messages: (1) Keep your line length down below 75 characters. Some mailers truncate longer lines. (2) DON'T SHOUT AT YOUR FRIENDS IN E-MAIL! (That is, don't use ALL CAPS.)

Here we see one of the ways that people in the Internet keep track of what they are talking about.

In this message, Jeff repeats part of Pat's message so that she can re-member the *context* of these messages. The greater-than signs (>) show the text that came from Pat's message. This method of including con-text can be accomplished on almost any mailing system. The documen-tation (or a consultant or systems administrator) can help you figure out the automated way to do it. If all else fails, you can do it by hand using your editor.

▶ ▶ **M A S T E R   W O R D S**

Too much quoted material can drive your recipient nuts. Try not to quote an entire message in your message and just say, "Thanks!" or "I agree." at the end.

Signing Off

Many systems let you append a signature block to your message automatically. Jeff's looks like this:

```
--
Jeff Marraccini          jeff@vela.acs.oakland.edu <- Work
Senior Computing Resource Admin  jeff@nucleus.mi.org<- Home
Oakland University               +1 810 370-4542
Rochester, MI 48309 "The Computer is your Friend." -- Paranoia
```

This is an ideal Internet signature block: four lines or less, with Jeff's real name and his e-mail address(es), how to reach him should e-mail fail, and a saying that expresses something of his personal philosophy. This block of text, also called a *sig*, can be used in both e-mail and net news.

We use signature blocks because of the hazards of computerized e-mail. Even though your mailer may start off with your correct address in the headers, that address may get corrupted or changed as it passes through several other mail machines on the way to the final destination. As a precaution, always include your real name and e-mail address at the bottom of your mail. This way, your correspondents know the right way to reach you.

Signatures are as individual as the people who send the messages. Some include "ASCII Art," pictures of airplanes or the state the person is from or some other symbolic representation of the person. Some include a funny saying or meaningful quote. It's best not to let your sig get out of hand: 4–6 lines is probably enough.

Electronic Mail

ch.
8

M A S T E R   W O R D S

"So, how do I get a signature block included in my message?" As the surlier tech-support people like to snarl behind our backs, RTFM (read the ... manual). The exact technique for creating a signature block depends on the mailer software you're using, and there are far too many such programs in common use for a single book to cover each one. If you can't find the information you need, either on-line or in paper form, you can at least demonstrate that you've attempted to do so.

▶ Bounce-O-Grams

Sometimes a message bounces (or is returned) right back to you. Sad, but true. Most commonly the cause is either a wrong user name or a wrong host name. Most mail bounces come from typos and misspellings.

Unknown User

Let's look at a bounce message where we typed the wrong user name.

```
Date:  Mon, 15 Aug 94 07:55 PDT
To:    pat
From:  <MAILER-DAEMON@lloyd.com>
Subject: mail failed, returning to sender

Return-Path: MAILER-DAEMON
Return-Path: <MAILER-DAEMON>
Reference: <m0qa3Ri-0005awC@lloyd.com>


--------------------------------------------------------------
--
¦------------------- Failed addresses follow: --------------¦
pam@cluebus.com .. transport smtp: 550 <pam@cluebus.com>...
User
 unknown
¦------------------- Message text follows: -----------------¦
Received: by lloyd.com (Smail3.1.28.1 #3)
id m0qa3Ri-0005awC; Mon, 15 Aug 94 07:55 PDT
```

```
Message-Id: <mOqa3Ri-OOO5awC@lloyd.com>
Sender: pat (Pat McGregor)
From: "Pat McGregor" <pat@lloyd.com>
To: pam@cluebus.com
Subject: Test message
Date: Mon, 15 Aug 1994 07:55:30 -0700
Sender: pat

This is a test.
```

The first part of this message looks a lot like the good message from Jeff earlier. That's because this is a well-designed message from a computer personality: the mailer daemon (pronounced "DEE-mon").

▶ ▶**M A S T E R   W O R D S**

The term "daemon" is an example of programmer humor. Daemons are the servants in the afterlife. For a programmer, the worst punishment imaginable would be to handle repetitive support tasks day after day after day. So they write little helper programs to do these horrible things for them. Daemons return bounced mail, make sure that programs that are supposed to run at certain times "wake up" and run, and so on.

Mailer daemons are getting more sophisticated these days. Many tell you what the problem is, as this one does:

```
-------------------------------------------------------------
|------------------- Failed addresses follow: ----------------
|
pam@cluebus.com ...transport smtp: 550 <pam@cluebus.com>...
User   unknown
|------------------- Message text follows: --------------------
|
```

This error message tells you several things. First, there is the address we typed in: pam@cluebus.com. There is no pam user ID on the cluebus machine. This is probably where the error is: we either mistyped the name or didn't use the correct user ID.

Second, we know how the message got sent to the destination machine. Our machine used a network protocol called SMTP, or Simple Mail Transfer Protocol. The SMTP server on our machine talked to the SMTP server on cluebus to ask if there was a user named pam. And cluebus replied:

```
550 <pam@cluebus.com>... User unknown
```

Whenever you see a line in a bounced message that starts with 550, you know it's an error message, telling you what went wrong with the delivery.

So, our mailer returned the message to us. You'll notice that this message is from the daemon on our own system. That's because it queried cluebus before it sent the message over. When it heard back from cluebus that the user name pam was wrong, it didn't even send the message out, just returned it to our mailbox.

This mailer did something user-friendly—it gave us our whole message back. That doesn't always happen: sometimes the postmaster who programmed the mailer daemon didn't think the message, no matter what it was, should be retransmitted (in case there was a bigger problem and a second or third postmaster would have to see the message). This is to protect your privacy.

MASTER WORDS

With e-mail, if you can't afford to lose the message—if you need to know what you sent, or you are paranoid about losing it if it bounces or your system goes down, write the message in a file first. Save the file carefully, either with your word processor or in a plain text file on your computer system. Then load the message into your mailer and send it. You still have a copy in case of calamity. In the last section of this chapter you'll see how to use your word processor to create and save e-mail messages.

Electronic Mail

ch.
8

Unknown Host

The second most common problem is sending a message to a host that doesn't exist. Unfortunately, most mailer daemons can't tell what you mean when you type something incorrectly, so they just return the message:

```
Date:  Mon, 15 Aug 1994 11:00:40 -0400
To:    <bruce@wayne.com>
From:  MAILER-DAEMON@uunet.uu.net (Mail Delivery Subsystem)
Subject: Returned mail: Host unknown (Name server: gothom.gov:
host not found ***)

Return-Path: uunet.uu.net!MAILER-DAEMON
Return-Path: <MAILER-DAEMON@uunet.uu.net>


-----------------------------------------------------------------
The original message was received at Mon, 15 Aug 1994 11:00:38
-0400 from boss.wayne.com [225.225.225.0]

   ----- The following addresses had delivery problems -----
<gordon@gothom.gov> (unrecoverable error)

   ----- Transcript of session follows -----
501 <gordon@gothom.gov>... 550 Host unknown (Name server:
gothom.gov: host not found)

   ----- Original message follows -----
Return-Path: <bruce@wayne.com>
Received: from wayne.com by relay2.UU.NET with SMTP
id QQxdbo05621; Mon, 15 Aug 1994 11:00:38 -0400
Received: by wayne.com (Smail3.1.28.1 #3)
id mOqa3Wf-0005awC; Mon, 15 Aug 94 08:00 PDT
Message-Id: <mOqa3Wf-0005awC@wayne.com>
Sender: bruce@wayne.com (Bruce Wayne)
From: "Bruce Wayne" <bruce@wayne.com>
To: gordon@gothom.gov, kent@dailyplanet.com
Subject: Test message
Date: Mon, 15 Aug 1994 08:00:36 -0700
Sender: bruce@wayne.com

Hi, Commissioner
```

```
Here's another test.

  bruce
```

In this rejection, the mailer daemon couldn't find the host `gothom.gov`, so it passed it along to a system whose DNS server knows more addresses: `uunet.uu.net`. The `uunet` machine had never heard of "gothom," either, so it returned the message directly to the sender, with this error message:

```
----- The following addresses had delivery problems -----
<gordon@gothom.gov> (unrecoverable error)
```

```
----- Transcript of session follows -----
501 <gordon@gothom.gov>... 550 Host unknown (Name server:
gothom.gov: host not found)
```

The "unrecoverable error" simply means that the mailer couldn't pass the message along to a machine that could fix the problem or further deliver the message, and so it bounced.

However, we also know that the message probably *did* get through to `kent@dailyplanet.com`, since that address was not listed in the list of problematic hosts.

Now, since the mailer daemon doesn't know what Bruce was trying to do, it can't tell him that he sent to "*gothom*" instead of "*gotham*." Bruce will have to puzzle that out for himself. Sometimes these typing errors are the easiest ones to miss.

"It's Not My Fault!"

The third most common cause of a bounce is a problem at the other end. For example, some systems have limits on the amount of disk space a user can have. If your friend has not cleaned out his mailbox recently, and has exceeded his allotment of space, your message to him may bounce.

Or, the system may be down. Most systems administrators make arrangements with another host to "spool" or hold their mail for three to seven days in case the first machine goes down. After that, the mail is returned.

MASTER WORDS

Some systems have very eccentric hours. One United States governmental machine is turned off every evening at 7 P.M. and is not turned back on until 6 the next morning, and it's shut down over weekends. Mailing list administrators with many subscribers on that machine have learned not to send messages that will arrive during this machine's down time, so that they will not be flooded with bounced messages. If you repeatedly send messages to a friend on Friday and they bounce, but messages sent on Mondays go through, suspect a weekend shutdown.

Another common problem at the other end is a DNS (Domain Name System addressing) problem. Perhaps the destination machine has changed its IP address and the DNS servers haven't been updated. Perhaps the destination machine is OK but the DNS server for it is down. There isn't much you can do about these except try again.

▶ *Fixing the Problem*

As you're probably guessing, there isn't much you can do about bounced mail, although the more you learn about why it happens, and how to read bounced mail messages, the better you get at correcting what you can correct.

Here are some hints to help you with e-mail.

- Before you send the message off, look carefully at the TO line or the CC line. Make sure you've spelled things right.

- Use the address book or aliases feature for your mailer. This way you don't have to remember those long complicated e-mail addresses every time—you can just type joe or sally.

- Don't be discouraged. Try again. Sometimes bounces come from temporary outages or glitches. (That's why it's good to save your message if it's critical.)

- Send a copy to yourself of any important messages.

▶ *Mail Software*

There are half a hundred different kinds of e-mail software available these days. They are generally of two kinds: e-mail services that are available on a host you access either by Telnet or a direct link; and e-mail software that runs on your personal workstation.

There are blends of these two kinds of services: some people use e-mail software that lets them store and handle their e-mail in their workstations (or their laptops), but they need to connect to a host where their e-mail is delivered. The host waits for them to call for it to be downloaded to their personal computer.

We're going to talk about just two kinds of e-mail software: *Pine*, which is a user-friendly mail interface found on lots of BBSes and hosts, and *mh*, a UNIX mailer used all around the world. There are many other kinds of interfaces and software. But these two illustrate the two main differences in mail handling.

The mh program lets you intersperse your mail handling in with other commands in your session. That is, you can be compiling a program and check to see what new mail has come in, without leaving the interface where you are running your program. (*mh* now also comes in a window-oriented version, but its most common incarnation works from the command line).

With pine, you explicitly run the Pine interface and deal with your mail. If you have multiple windows, you can leave a Pine window running, but otherwise you go into Pine, handle your mail, and go back out to your other tasks.

▶ ▶MASTER WORDS

Mail software is included in NetCruiser, on this book's Companion Disk 1, and the Chameleon Sampler, on Companion Disk 2.

Electronic Mail

▶ ▶

ch.

8

Basic E-Mail Functions

There are only a few basic functions in e-mail, and almost all mailers handle them. They are:

- Read
- Compose (new messages)
- Reply (to messages you've received)
- Forward (messages you've received)
- Refile (save the message away)
- Delete

Other handy functions allow you to work more efficiently:

- Include (other files in your work)
- Address book or aliases (remember human names for common addresses)
- Sort your mail by any given category: sender, date, subject, and so on.

We'll talk about the most basic of these commands with our two chosen mailers.

UNIX Mail and mh

Using mh, you have three basic operations: receiving mail, composing mail, and disposing of mail.

Receiving Mail Using Inc and Show You receive mail by typing **inc**, which incorporates your mail into your in-box folder, as shown in Figure 8.3.

As you can see, mail is listed with the sender's name and either the subject or the first line of the message. You can then type the **show** command, which puts the message up on your screen, as illustrated in Figure 8.4.

If you have set things up to do this (RTFM!) you can have your mail go through a "*pager*"—a UNIX utility that gives you the text one screenful at a time. This makes your mail more convenient to read.

FIGURE 8.3 ▶

Incorporating new e-mail into the in box.

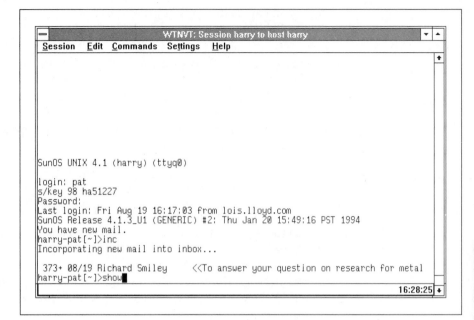

```
┌─ WTNVT: Session harry to host harry ──────────────────── ▼ ▲
│ Session   Edit  Commands  Settings   Help
│                                                              ↑
│
│
│
│
│
│
│ SunOS UNIX 4.1 (harry) (ttyq0)
│
│ login: pat
│ s/key 98 ha51227
│ Password:
│ Last login: Fri Aug 19 16:17:03 from lois.lloyd.com
│ SunOS Release 4.1.3_U1 (GENERIC) #2: Thu Jan 20 15:49:16 PST 1994
│ You have new mail.
│ harry-pat[~]>inc
│ Incorporating new mail into inbox...
│
│  373+ 08/19 Richard Smiley    <<To answer your question on research for metal
│ harry-pat[~]>show█
│                                                    16:28:25 ↓
```

FIGURE 8.4 ▶

Showing the mail message.

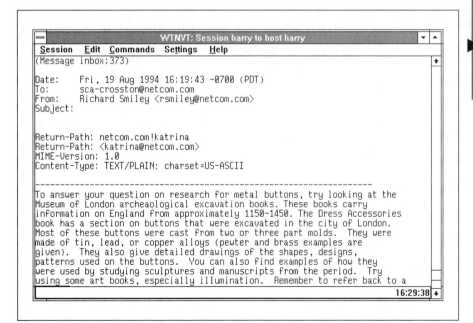

```
┌─ WTNVT: Session harry to host harry ──────────────────── ▼ ▲
│ Session   Edit  Commands  Settings   Help
│ (Message inbox:373)                                          ↑
│
│ Date:     Fri, 19 Aug 1994 16:19:43 -0700 (PDT)
│ To:       sca-crosston@netcom.com
│ From:     Richard Smiley <rsmiley@netcom.com>
│ Subject:
│
│
│ Return-Path: netcom.com!katrina
│ Return-Path: <katrina@netcom.com>
│ MIME-Version: 1.0
│ Content-Type: TEXT/PLAIN; charset=US-ASCII
│
│ ----------------------------------------------------------------
│ To answer your question on research for metal buttons, try looking at the
│ Museum of London archeaological excavation books. These books carry
│ information on England from approximately 1150-1450. The Dress Accessories
│ book has a section on buttons that were excavated in the city of London.
│ Most of these buttons were cast from two or three part molds.  They were
│ made of tin, lead, or copper alloys (pewter and brass examples are
│ given).  They also give detailed drawings of the shapes, designs,
│ patterns used on the buttons.  You can also find examples of how they
│ were used by studying sculptures and manuscripts from the period.  Try
│ using some art books, especially illumination.  Remember to refer back to a
│                                                    16:29:38 ↓
```

Now you can either reply to the message, refile it into another folder, forward it to someone else, or delete it.

Composing Mail Using Comp or Repl   Composing and replying to mail in mh are very similar processes. They both require that you know how to use at least one of the editors on a UNIX machine. They both use a template that lets you fill in the blanks with the name of the person you are sending to, and other information. And they leave you a blank space to type your message in.

To compose a new message, type **comp**. As shown in Figure 8.5, *mh* will put up a blank template on your screen for you to type into.

Many people use mh's capabilities to fill in some of the blanks for them automatically, particularly in a reply. You can also add a signature block, or have the text of the message you are replying to show up indented or prefaced with greater-than signs (>) so that the text you write will be distinct from the message you are replying to. To find out how to do this, either ask your systems administrator or copy a cool template from a friend.

FIGURE 8.5 ▶

Composing a message in mh.

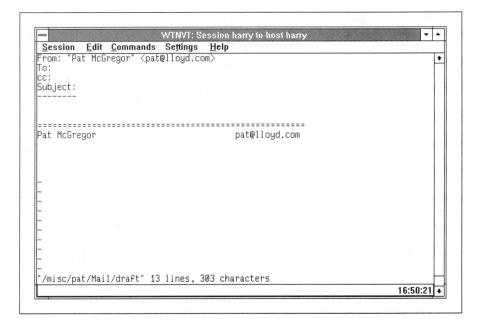

MASTER WORDS

Using any kind of mail on a UNIX system requires that you know how to use some sort of system editor. As part of getting up to speed on any new system, find out where you can get a personal tutorial on the editor, or take an introductory or other class on using the editor. You'll be glad you did.

When you type **repl** to reply to a message, the system automatically fills in the name of the person who sent you the message. You can teach the mailer to fill in other things—for example, to recopy the subject into the subject line, or to include the date and time the other message came in.

To send the message, you end your edit session and type **send**.

MASTER WORDS

***mh*, like most other mail handlers, gives you the option to view and then edit your message. Use it! Taking one last glance over the message before you send it gives you the chance to catch typos and funny phrases, or even to change your mind about the message.**

Disposing of Messages: Refile, Or Delete? Just as with paper mail, the big dilemma with e-mail is what to do with it once you've gotten it. Do you print it? Throw it away? File it electronically?

Saving it on paper means you probably can't forward it or do anything else electronically unless you also save it electronically. Deleting it means you'll no doubt urgently need to have it again next week. Refiling it will fill up your available disk space in no time flat.

There is no reasonable answer, of course.

mh offers you the facility to refile your messages: to move them from the in box into a file folder. This lets you access them through the mailer again; to harass someone who hasn't answered you yet, or reply to something later if you have a better answer or more information, or forward something juicy to a pal. Figure 8.6 illustrates a filing session in mh.

Of course, if you do decide to delete the message, you can't type **delete** (this is UNIX, remember?). Type **rmm** to remove the message.

Aliases Mh uses a text file to store aliases in. When you type a familiar name into the blank template, mh goes and looks up the name in the file and substitutes the e-mail address. You can make simple mailing lists (more than one recipient) in your alias file. You can also use an alias file to store a nickname that you will remember instead of a formal user name.

An *mh* alias file looks like this:

```
lisa:   lprg1@uniface.com
joe:    8023.45689@compuserve.com
sales:  marie,tom@denver,mark,sarah,admin
tj:     tom
mom:    macoleman@aol.com
malcolm:  rsmiley@netcom.com
glee:   glee@netcom.com
```

FIGURE 8.6

Squirreling a message away for later use via refile.

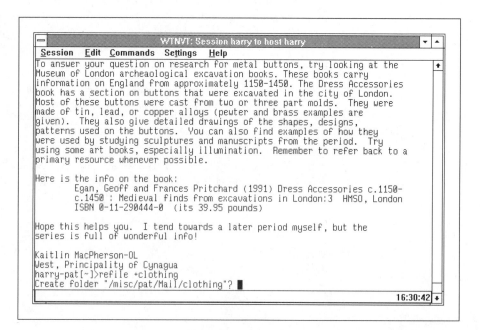

▶

RECOVERING DELETED MAIL

So you deleted a message you desperately wish you hadn't? If you are on a UNIX system, move to the directory /Mail (careful: that capital letter is important) and then to /inbox. The command should look something like:

```
cd ~/Mail/inbox
```

Then list your files. Look for the ones with commas (,) in front. These are your deleted messages. Rename them and put them back in your mailbox with the command:

```
mv ,n n
```

where *n* is the number of the message you trashed.

Using Pine to Handle Your Mail

Pine is a very nice mailer. It's easy to learn, it has familiar controls (menus, graphic presentations), and it simplifies many of the tasks of handling e-mail. It runs on many UNIX machines, as well as many BBSes and other hosts. Pine has a graphic user interface, which lets you see your menus and all your choices of options at once.

Pine lets you use all the same mail functions as mh, but you don't have to remember what the commands are, as Pine is menu-driven. Figure 8.7 illustrates the Pine main screen.

Receiving Your Mail with Pine When you call Pine (by typing **pine** at the command prompt in your main session), your mail is automatically incorporated into your in-box, as illustrated in Figure 8.8. Then, you can call up a menu of available mail to choose which ones you want to read. When you highlight and choose a message, it appears in a new window.

Composing Mail to Send New Messages or to Reply Once you've selected either compose or reply options, Pine, like mh, gives you a template to fill in.

FIGURE 8.7

The Pine main screen.

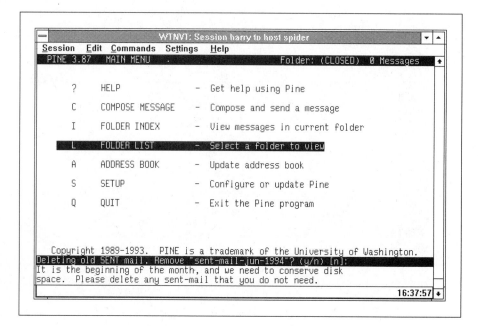

FIGURE 8.8

The Pine in-box.

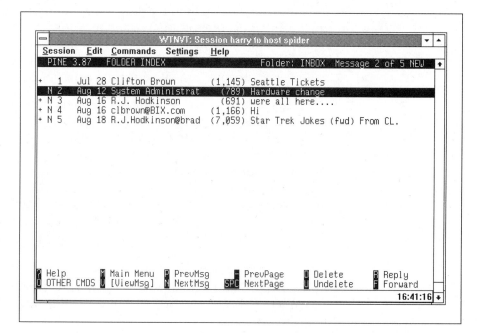

Unlike mh, however, Pine lets you go to a menu driven "address book" (Figure 8.9) to choose from folks you have saved addresses for. You can, of course, type in a new name and address if you wish.

Once you have chosen a recipient, or typed in a new address, composing the rest of your message in Pine is much like any other editing task, as you can see in Figure 8.10.

To send the message, you choose the Send option and away it goes!

You can then delete or refile messages using menu choices.

FIGURE 8.9 ▶

The Pine address book.

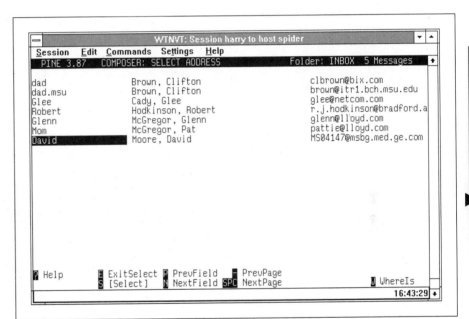

▶ Addressing E-Mail Messages

The exact format for addressing e-mail depends on the network or mail service your correspondent is using. The information that follows came from *The Inter-Network Mail Guide* modified and ©1993 by Scott Yanoff (yanoff@csd4.csd.uwm.edu), original copyright ©1992 by John J. Chew. It represents the aggregate knowledge of the readers of the newsgroup comp.mail.misc and many contributors elsewhere.

FIGURE 8.10 ▶

Composing a message in Pine.

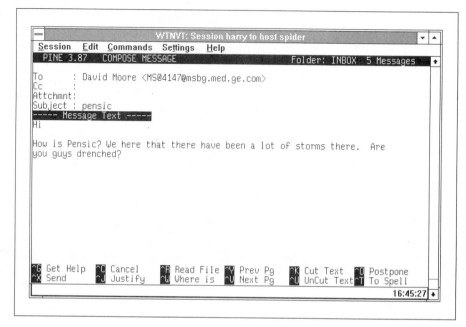

To Another Internet User

If the person to whom you wish to send e-mail is known as p.leia at base.endor.org, you put the address p.leia@base.endor.org in the To: line of your electronic mail message.

To an America On-Line User

If the person to whom you wish to send e-mail is known as H Solo, you put the address hsolo@aol.com in the To: line of your electronic mail message. Be sure to use all lowercase letters and remove all spaces from the name. AOL may shorten messages to 32,000 characters (8000 characters for PCs). AOL changes all nonalphabetic and numeric characters to spaces except for the newline character. AOL users are limited to 75 pieces of Internet mail in their mailbox at one time. In an emergency, you can request assistance by sending electronic mail to postmaster@aol.com.

To an At&T Mail User

If the person to whom you wish to send e-mail is known as `solo`, you put the address `solo@attmail.com` in the To: line of your electronic mail message.

To a Bitnet User

If the person to whom you wish to send e-mail is known as `chewie@site`, you put the address `chewie@site.bitnet` in the To: line of your electronic mail message.

To an MCI Mail User

If the person to whom you wish to send e-mail is known as `Han Solo` (123-4567), you can send to `1234567@mcimail.com` or `HSolo@mci-mail.com` (if HSolo is unique) or `Han_Solo@mcimail.com` (if Han Solo is unique), or to `Han_Solo/1234567@mcimail.com` (if Han Solo is NOT unique). Be sure to use the underscore (shifted hyphen) character between the first and last names.

To a CompuServe Mail User

If the person to whom you wish to send e-mail has the CompuServe account number 71234,567, enter the address as `71234.567@compu-serve.com` in the To: field. You can enter *compuserve* as any combination of upper- and lowercase letters.

To a GEnie User

If the person to whom you wish to send e-mail is known as `solo`, enter the address as `solo@genie.geis.com` in the To: field. To reach the GEnie postmaster in an emergency, send to `postmaster@genie.geis.com`.

To a Prodigy User

If the person to whom you wish to send e-mail is known as `1234AB5`, enter the address as `1234AB5@prodigy.com` in the To: line. In an emergency, you can reach the Prodigy system postmaster by sending e-mail to `postmaster@prodigy.com`.

Electronic Mail

ch. **8**

To a Sprint-Mail User

If the person to whom you wish to send e-mail is known as Han Solo at Millennium, enter the address as `/G=Han/S=Solo/O=millennium/ADMD=TELE-MAIL/C=US/@Sprint.COM` in the To: field. You can obtain help by telephoning +1 800 827 4685.

► For Information on Sending Mail to Other Networks

If the network you need to reach isn't listed here, try looking it up in the complete *Inter-Network Mail Guide* on-line. The guide is available via anonymous FTP to `csd4.csd.uwm.edu` in the pub directory. The file is named internetwork-mail-guide.

►► Using Your Word Processor for E-Mail

There are two main reasons why you may want to use your word processor to write the messages you send via e-mail. The first is familiarity. If you are like most people, one of the first applications you installed on your machine was a word processor. You have probably become very familiar with its strengths and weaknesses. The second reason is that it's cheaper to write your messages off-line. Most dial-in services charge for *all* of the time you spend connected. Drafting and revising messages can consume a lot of time, so you will probably prefer to spend that time while *not* connected. Moreover, your mailer's built-in word processing options are likely to be fairly limited; without those shortcut keystrokes, your message may take even longer to write.

► Avoiding Common Problems

There are a few features of your word processor that you should avoid using in text destined for e-mail, because they probably won't be translated successfully. You have probably discovered many ways to enhance text with your word processor. You might underline important ideas or italicize titles. Perhaps you even use boldface occasionally. Unfortunately, you can't know what kind of machine your correspondent will be using to read your e-mail missive, so most of these features will not be available in your e-mail. Your correspondent may not have the correct software to display the beautiful effects you have included. Some of the effects may even backfire. For instance, "smart" quotation marks get mistranslated and show up as capital letters, R, S, and U, when the file is saved as plain text.

Another feature that often causes trouble is the Tab key. While tabs are very useful for aligning text, the tab character is sometimes interpreted as an instruction to ring the terminal's bell. If you have ever received a message that made your machine beep madly, tab characters were probably the cause.

Fortunately, there are alternatives to using these features. You can use spaces to align your tables. Leading and trailing underscore characters ("_") will indicate _underlined_ words. You might use asterisks to mark *boldface* or *italicized* phrases.

Also, you may want to set the left and right margins to allow no more than 70 characters on a line, including spaces. This way, you can be sure your message will appear on your correspondent's screen with the same line breaks as on your screen.

▶ Saving the Text

Once you've written your message, the next step is to save it in a format that can be sent as e-mail, to avoid mistranslation problems. Your word processor's proprietary format includes information about the typeface, the size of the letters, and so forth. None of this information will be needed for your e-mail, and your mailer program will probably not be able to understand your word processor's codes. So you will have to save your text without them.

Your word processor should offer a "Save As" or "Save File As Type" option for specifying different file formats. Once you've located this option and its list of available formats, select "text with line breaks." Many word processors treat a paragraph as simply one long line of characters. Since most modern computers can display only 80 characters on a line (and some older ones can display even fewer), these long "lines" may be truncated (cut off at the 81st character) or "wrapped" at odd places. Your correspondents will find these lines hard to read.

By choosing "text with line breaks", you are telling your word processor to treat each line displayed on your screen as a separate paragraph. If your document is displayed nicely on your screen, it should be displayed in much the same way on your correspondent's screen.

▶ Transferring the Text

The next step is to get your missive into an e-mail message. What you do at this point depends on your type of Internet connection and the software environment you're working in.

Macintosh and Windows users connected directly to the Internet (probably on a LAN) can use the clipboard to copy the word processor text and paste it into a message in the mailer program, or use whatever technique the mailer program provides for attaching a file. (These techniques vary from program to program; see your documentation.) DOS users with a dedicated link can also use the mailer's "attachment" commands. Once you've done that, your message is ready to send.

With a dialup connection to a service provider, however, you need to transfer the file from your machine to the service provider's host computer.

If you have downloaded files via your service provider, you will only need to reverse that process to upload your files. If you are not familiar with downloading files, you will first have to find out which file transfer systems are available from your service. Some common options are Kermit, X-modem, Y-modem, and Z-modem. If you are using PPP or SLIP, and so have a TCP/IP connection, you will use FTP, the Internet's File Transfer Protocol, to move your files between machines. Let's take the easy one first; we'll start with FTP.

FTP

One of the pieces of your PPP (or SLIP) package should have been an FTP client. Although FTP clients have many names, a common one is "FTP" or some variant. For instance, the MS-DOS Telnet package available from the National Center for Supercomputing Applications (NCSA) at the University of Illinois—Urbana/Champaign calls its FTP client "ftpbin." Novell has named the FTP client included with their

LAN WorkPlace for DOS package "Rapid Filer." The Macintosh FTP client from Dartmouth College is called "Fetch." Both Fetch and Rapid Filer automate many of the processes of transferring a file by FTP, so we will use NCSA's FTPBIN to describe FTP, which doesn't offer automation.

After your PPP (or SLIP) connection is established, change directories ("cd") to the one containing the NCSA software. Then, enter the command

`ftp host.domain`

replacing `host.domain` with the name of the machine you log on to. FTP will start up; when the connection is established, you will see a Name: prompt. Enter your user name on that machine. You will then be prompted for your password. After your password is accepted, you should be in your usual file space on that machine. Enter the FTP command type `ascii` to set the type of file transfer to plain text. The remote machine will report that the file type has been set to either "ASCII" or "text", depending upon how the system administrator has set it up. Enter the command

`put filename1 filename2`

replacing *filename1* with the name of the file you saved in your word processor (using the full pathname, for example, C:\DOCS\MES-SAGE.TXT) and *filename2* with the name you want it to have on the remote machine. When the file transfer is completed, type **bye** or **quit** to close the connection. Your file has now been copied to the machine you use for e-mail. You can now log on to the remote machine in the usual way (with Telnet, for instance) and use the file in an e-mail message.

Kermit, X, Y, and Z-Modem

Kermit, X-modem, Y-modem and Z-modem are all similar to each other. First you establish a connection to your e-mail service. Next you start the file transfer program on the remote machine (that is, your e-mail service's machine), specifying the kind of transfer (text, or ASCII, rather than binary) and the name of the file to receive. Then you start the file transfer program on your local machine, specifying the kind of transfer (text again), and finally you specify which file you want to transfer. When the transfer is completed, you can shut down

Electronic Mail

ch.
8

the file transfer programs; your file has now been copied to the machine you use for e-mail. Let's look at VersaTerm, a communications program for the Macintosh, and Kermit for a specific example.

After dialing in to your service with VersaTerm and logging on in your usual fashion, enter the command to start Kermit, probably something like

```
Kermit
```

to begin the file transfer process. Next, enter set file type *text*. The remote machine should respond Text filetype set. Now that the type of file to be transferred has been specified, enter the command *receive filename2*, replacing *filename2* with the name you want the file to have on the remote machine. The remote machine is now ready to accept your file.

Go into VersaTerm's File menu and make sure that the option Text Kermit is available. If it isn't (and some of the other choices are Mac XModem, Text XModem, Binary XModem and MacBinary XModem), select whatever is showing and then, from the resulting dialog box, choose Text Kermit and click OK.

Now go back into the File menu and select Send File. VersaTerm's next dialog box will let you browse the disk to find the file you want to transfer. After selecting the file, and clicking the Add button to put it in the Send Files window, click the Send button to begin the transfer. When the transfer is complete, all of the dialog boxes close, and you will again be at your service's prompt. You can now enter quit to close the Kermit program. Your file has been copied to the remote host.

▶▶ *Interesting E-Mail Addresses*

Now that you know a little bit about e-mail, here are some fun places to send mail.

E-Mail to the White House

For those of you who would like to communicate with the current United States executive officer, the Clinton administration has encouraged you to e-mail the president or the vice president with your thoughts on the issues that affect us all. Do not expect to get anything but a form reply yet, but you can address your comments to

`president@whitehouse.gov`

or

`vice.president@whitehouse.gov`

You can receive a summary of White House press releases. To find out more, send e-mail to `publications@whitehouse.gov` with the body of the message containing `send info`.

Almanac E-Mail Information Service

The United States Department of Agriculture operates an e-mail information service called Almanac. To find out more about it, send e-mail to `almanac@esusda.gov` with the message `send guide`. The message `send catalog` will ask the server to send you a catalog of available information. The USDA also operates a Gopher server at `esusda.gov`. Figure 8.11 shows typical information available from the Almanac service.

FIGURE 8.11 ▶

Almanac service information from the USDA.

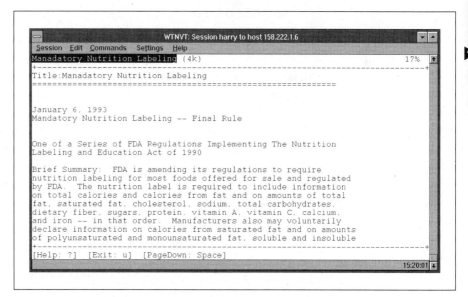

Books for Young People

Scholastic Press, a publisher of books for young people, maintains a mailing list for reviews of new and interesting books. (E-mail mailing lists are discussed later in this chapter.) It is called the `BookBrag` mailing list. The address for the mailing list server is `bookbrag-request@scholastic.com`. Send an e-mail message to this address with the body of the message as follows:

`subscribe bookbrag` *yourfirstname yourlastname*

Talking Back to National Public Radio

If you have wanted to talk back to NPR, here are a few addresses of specific programs:

Talk of the Nation	`totn@npr.org`
All Things Considered	`atc@npr.org`
Science Friday (Ira Glass)	`scifri@aol.com`
Fresh Air	`freshair@hslc.org`
Weekend All Things Considered	`weekend@npr.org`
Weekend Edition/Sunday	`wesun@clark.net`

Shakespeare Online

Michael Conner recently announced, to the newsgroup `rec.arts.books`, the formation of a Shakespeare reading group. The group reads one play per month. The first half of the month is spent in reading the play individually; the second half of the month the play is discussed by e-mail. Volunteers take turns leading the discussion. Feel free to join, volunteer as a leader or just lurk and learn. Everyone is welcome. e-mail `YORTMTC@henson.cc.wwu.edu` if you are interested.

Using Address Directories in Gopher

Many Gopher menus includes selections that point to various types of electronic address directories. Choose WorldWide Directory Services. Look at the choices, read the descriptions and the help information provided to see if one might fit your needs. Choose among the entries for the directory most likely to fit your needs.

Searching for Usenet Addresses

If you think your correspondent has ever posted to Usenet News, you might be able to find their address if you know a little about their name and address. Send e-mail to `mail-server@rtfm.mit.edu` with the message

`send ` *`usenet-address/name`*

where *name* is one or more words separated by spaces. For example, if you were interested in finding out whether award-winning Star Trek writer Peter David has ever posted to a Usenet news group, you would send this message:

`send pdavid@/peter david`

You would discover that David has, indeed, posted many times to news groups. This server works better when you give it more material with which to work, so you should list all the words you think might appear in the address. Neither the order of the words nor their case is important to the server. You can send multiple requests in one e-mail message. Each request should appear on a separate line. The server may return more than one match, but it will never return more than 40 matches.

For more information, send a message containing

`send usenet-addresses/help`

Electronic Mail

▶ ▶

ch.
8

▶ ## LURKING

Lurking describes the activity of reading mailing list posts and newsgroup articles without participating in the group. In spite of the name, lurking is a recommended activity, at least for the first few weeks that you read in a particular area. Taking the time to see the kind of discussion that occurs in a particular networked community will give you an idea of the type of posting to which the community likes to respond. For more on appropriate posting, see the discussion of netiquette in Chapter 7. For more on newsgroups, see Chapter 12.

▶ The IBM Mail Exchange Directory

Advantis and the IBM Information Network provide e-mail access to the IBM Mail Exchange directory server. The IBM Mail Exchange allows its subscribers to exchange mail with a wide range of office systems. The directory contains address book details of those subscribers to the service who have granted public access to that information. It contains entries for users (typically commercial users) in more than 60 countries.

You can search on any of the following items:

- Name (last name, first name or initial)
- User ID (IEA)
- Organization name
- Telephone number
- Country

You specify one or more keywords and parameters in the body of an e-mail message to

whois@ibmmail.com

The server answers several basic styles of query:

WHOIS Sm*

will retrieve results for names beginning with the characters Sm.

WHOIS !*userid*

will retrieve results for the user ID *userid*. Note that user ID searches need to begin with the ! character.

WHOIS Smith
Phone 813*

will retrieve results with the name Smith and a telephone number beginning with 813. The wildcard character (*) can be used at the beginning or the end of a telephone number, but not in both places.

WHOIS Smith
ORGANIZATION ABC

will retrieve results with the name Smith from the ABC organization.

```
WHOIS Smith
COUNTRY US
```

will retrieve results with the name Smith and the country code US. Send HELP in the body of your message for more instructions.

►► *Mail Reflectors, Mailing Lists, and List Servers*

Mailing lists are a specialized type of e-mail, a hybrid of e-mail (which is individual) and net news (which is seen by many). Lists are delivered specifically via e-mail to the individual mailboxes of the individuals who subscribe to the list. You can choose to participate in many mailing list communities on the Internet. When you find a list you like, you "join" it by sending mail to the list administrator. A mail reflector is the name of the mailbox to which you send e-mail when you want to send it to all of the people who read the list. The reflector receives the e-mail and "reflects" it to the members of the mailing list. Maintaining mailing lists is one of the many tasks of a systems administrator. When the list administrator is aided by a computer program that helps with list management, that program is called a *list server*. LISTSERV is a representative example.

► *About LISTSERV*

LISTSERV is the name of a specific program developed by Eric Thomas. Like other list servers, it allows a user to send electronic mail to addresses like these:

```
listserv@kentvm.kent.edu
listserv@cunyvm.cuny.edu
listserv@is.internic.net
```

Sometimes the lists are *moderated*. This means that the messages sent by the subscribers to the rest of the list are read by a person before they are forwarded on to the remainder of the list. The moderator may choose not to send a message on to the list. Large lists are frequently moderated so that mailing errors do not get sent on to all the people reading the list, or so that messages that are "off the topic" of the list are not sent to the list.

▶ *Using a "–request" Petition*

Another style of list subscription is the "–request" petition. This is an address constructed from the name of the mailing list, the –request modifier and the `@fully.qualified.domain` Internet address. This message may be read by a person or by a program; the address does not tell you which. Your e-mail message would be something like

```
To: starwars-request@academy.endor.org
```

in the address portion of your message. In the body of the message you put

```
subscribe starwars yourfirstname yourlastname
```

This would subscribe you to the mailing list.

Do not assume that because a mailing list is served from a particular host computer, the list will always remain there (or that the organization that owns the computer necessarily supports or agrees with the discussion on the mailing list). Sometimes people start lists from a particular computer and the goals of the list do not match the goals of the host organization. In that case the list will move or change its nature. Sometimes list traffic becomes too heavy for the original list server to adequately handle, so the list is either moved or the traffic becomes restricted in some way.

▶ *How to "Talk" to List Servers*

If the address for subscribing to a mailing list begins with the words LISTSERV, LISTPROC or MAJORDOMO, you should assume that you are communicating with a program that manages the list, not a person. This means you should not include extraneous information, like punctuation or signature files. These can confuse the programs. These programs usually ignore anything you put in the subject line of your e-mail message.

Always be careful to send your electronic mail requests to the list server, not to the list itself; that is, to `listserv@nodename`, *not* `list@nodename`.

When you *unsubscribe* from the list, you must unsubscribe from the same e-mail address that you subscribed from. If you are no longer able to do that, you will need help from the list owner. You can find out

COMMON LISTSERV COMMANDS

```
SUB(scribe) <listname> <yourfirstname> <yourlastname>
UNSUB(scribe) <listname>
Signoff <listname>
set nomail <listname>
```

When this command is accepted, the listserver will not send you mail. To receive mail again, send the `set mail <listname>` command.

```
set conceal <listname>
```

Similar to an unlisted telephone number, this command hides your name on the subscription list. Sending the command `set no conceal` will reset the default.

Sending the command `Info Refcard` will cause the ListServ program to send you a list of commands.

about the owners of the list by sending the command `review <list-name>` to the LISTSERV program.

▶ *How to Search for Mailing Lists*

There is a searchable list of BITNET mailing lists maintained at Nova University. Use the Web to go to `http://alpha.acast.nova.edu/cgi-bin/lists`. This link opens a search. Enter your search word into the dialog box and press Enter. This search returns literal matches. For example, entering the word **bird** will return citations for the mailing lists about bird-watching (BirdChat, and so on), and mailing lists that feature discussion of cars (T-Birds and Firebirds), and a mailing list that deals with the Blackbird fighter plane.

How to Get the BITNET "List of Mailing Lists"

The BITNET network maintains a list of all the BITNET mailing lists that are known to its network nodes. You can request that the BITNIC (BITNET Network Information Center) computer send you that list.

To do so, send e-mail to `listserv@bitnic.educom.edu` with the message:

`get bitnet userhelp` *to receive a longer explanation of BITNET*

`help` *to receive a short list of commands*

`info refcard` *to receive a command reference card*

`info ?` *to receive a list of ListServ information guides*

`list global` *to receive the complete list of BITNET mailing lists*

▶ Publicly Accessible Mailing Lists

The FAQ "Publicly Accessible Mailing Lists" is posted in multiple parts to the newsgroup `news.announce.newusers`. This FAQ has a list of all the Internet mailing lists (it is a companion list to the BITNET list of lists, above.) See Chapter 12 on reading network news if you need help reading these news groups. There is also a World Wide Web page that reflects these lists. You can use the Web to jump there by entering `http://www.ii.uib.no/cgi-bin/paml` in the center dialog box from the display of any Web page. For more information about using the Web, see Chapter 11.

▶ New Patent Titles Mailing List

Greg Aharonian offers a free service to anyone who can receive e-mail from the Internet. The service is a weekly mailing of all patents issued by the Patent Office during the last week (or more specifically, all of the patents listed in the most recent issue of the USPTO Patent Gazette).

Please include some information on what you do and how you might use this patent information. Send your requests to: `patents-request@world.std.com`.

Here's a sample list of patents as distributed to the mailing list:

5177805	Optical sensors utilizing multiple reflection
5177804	Waveguide-type optical switch
5177802	Fingerprint input apparatus
5177801	Cross-fader for editing audio signals

| 5177799 | Speech encoder |
| 5177798 | Sound reproducer for high definition television |

▶ *Other Special Interest Mailing Lists*

You can subscribe to these lists using the "-request" technique described above.

For people who enjoy leisure reading: `SFLOVERS@uga.edu` and `DOROTHYL@kentvm.kent.edu` are discussions of science fiction and mystery fiction respectively.

For people who enjoy discussing computer gaming:

`GAMES-L@brownvm.brown.edu`

For people who enjoy discussing the game of golf:

`GOLF-L@ubvm.buffalo.edu`

For people who enjoy discussing the game of chess:

`CHESS-L@GREARN.bitnet`

For people who are interested in genealogy:

`ROOTS-L@ndsuvm1.nodak.edu`

► ► ► CHAPTER **9**

FTP and Telnet

► ► **F**TP and Telnet are two of the most common tools you'll use on the network. FTP (File Transfer Protocol) lets you move files around: either files that are specifically intended for you, or files that are placed for general consumption. Telnet connects you to other computers. Implementations of both tools can be found in NetCruiser, on Companion Disk 1, and the Chameleon Sampler, on Companion Disk 2.

► ► *About FTP: the File Transfer Program*

FTP is the abbreviation used for the *file transfer protocol* and the file transfer programs that use the protocol. File transfer simply means sending a file (not a message) from one computer to another. Examples of files include spreadsheets, sounds, compiled programs, or document files from a word-processing program. If you want to send a file from your computer to another computer, you use the FTP program to *upload* or *put* the file. More frequently people use FTP to *download* or *get* something, for example, to retrieve public domain computer programs.

There are two modes, basically, for using FTP. In one mode, you sign on with your own account or ID and transfer files. In the other, you sign on as a guest or as an anonymous user and transfer files. With this anonymous FTP, your privileges on the host system will be severely limited for security reasons. That's because hosts that provide anonymous FTP do so specifically to make certain files available to anyone who wants them. To use it, you select the login ID anonymous and use your e-mail address as a password. The use of your e-mail address helps the

FTP provider track who is interested in which materials, and it provides a trace in case of a security problem.

You can find a FAQ on Anonymous FTP via anonymous FTP itself at `rtfm.mit.edu`, and it is regularly posted to `news.newusers.questions` and several `*.answers` newsgroups. (See Chapter 13 for more information about FAQs.) The specific way to get this FAQ is:

```
ftp rtfm.mit.edu
hash
cd pub/usenet-by-group
cd news.announce.newusers
get Anonymous_FTP:_Frequently_Asked_Questions_(FAQ)_List
quit
```

(If you are FTPing this to a DOS machine, the file name will be truncated to something like "Anonymou".)

Anonymous FTP is a convenient tool for making information and other files available to the public. More than 1000 sites currently use it to provide resources; you can find a listing of selected sites in Appendix G.

▶ *File Modes, or What's a Binary File?*

Many files stored for FTP are in ASCII, or plain text format. But some are programs, visual images, or sounds. It's important that you know what kind of file you are getting, because you have to tell the FTP client what *mode* to transfer the file in.

There are two modes for transferring files in FTP. ASCII mode is used for plain text, BinHex (Macintosh transfer format), uuencoded (UNIX transfer encoding), and PostScript files. Binary mode (also, confusingly, called I mode on some servers) is for everything else. Here's a list of the common types of files and the modes in which you should retrieve them. As you'll see, most files you are likely to encounter should be transferred in binary mode.

- **.Z** files are UNIX files that are compressed and require you to execute the UNIX uncompress utility before you can use them. Retrieve these files in binary mode.

- **.gz** files are UNIX files that are compressed by the UNIX GNU gzip utility program and will need to be processed before you can use them. Retrieve these files in binary mode.

FTP and Telnet

▶ ▶

ch.
9

- **.tar** files are UNIX files that are in the UNIX tape archive format and need to be processed with the UNIX tar utility before you can use them. They should be retrieved in binary mode.

- **.tar.Z** files are compressed UNIX tar files that require application of the uncompress utility followed by the tar utility. Retrieve these files in binary mode.

- **.hqx** files are compressed Macintosh files. These files should be retrieved in binary mode and then processed by a Macintosh decompression program.

- **.sit** files are Macintosh files processed by the Stuffit program. Retrieve them in binary mode.

- **.zip** files are DOS files compressed by a zip utility. These files need to be decompressed (unzipped) before you can use them. Retrieve these files in binary mode.

- **.com** files are executable files for DOS computers. They should be retrieved in binary mode.

- **.exe** files are executable files for DOS or VAX/VMS computers. They should be retrieved in binary mode.

- **.ps** files are PostScript files that must be viewed with a PostScript viewer or printed on a PostScript printer. These files should be retrieved in text/ASCII mode.

- **.c** files are C programming language source code. These files should be retrieved in text/ASCII mode.

- **.h** files are C programming language header files. These files should be retrieved in text/ASCII mode.

- **.gif** files are files in Graphics Interchange Format. These files should be retrieved in binary mode.

- **.mpeg** files are video files. They need to be played with a video player. These files should be retrieved in binary mode.

- **.jpg** files are graphics files in a compressed format. These files should be retrieved in binary mode.

- **.txt** files or files with no special suffix are plain text files that can be displayed or printed without requiring processing by any utility. These files should be retrieved in text/ASCII mode.

▶ *How to Use FTP*

Except for the act of signing on, regular FTP and anonymous FTP are almost identical in the way you use them. With regular FTP, you sign on to the host site with your account or user name and password. With anonymous FTP, you type the word **anonymous** as your user name and your e-mail address for the password.

There are two basic kinds of FTP clients these days: line mode and GUI (Graphic User Interface) clients. In line mode you type the commands at a system or FTP prompt. With a GUI client you can use the mouse or arrow keys to manipulate the transaction.

▶ *Line-Mode FTP*

The most common way to use FTP is with a command or line mode FTP client. These clients do not have pull-down menus, or point-and-click buttons. You call them from the regular system prompt on your host account.

To access an FTP site, you type:

```
ftp hostname.domain
```

Many FTP sites have the prefix *ftp.* in front of their regular host name, so that you can access the FTP server directly. For example, to access Merit, Inc.'s anonymous FTP server and get the NSFNET statistics stored there, you would type:

```
ftp nic.merit.edu
```

Once you are connected, you will see a screenful of introductory information, as in Figure 9.1, and then be asked for your user name and password. Type (your responses are in **bold** type):

```
Login: anonymous
password guest
```

Most FTP clients will give you a list of available commands if you type **help** or **?** at the FTP> prompt.

FTP and Telnet

▶ ▶

ch.
9

FIGURE 9.1 ►

*Starting an anony-
mous FTP session to
venera.isi.edu.*

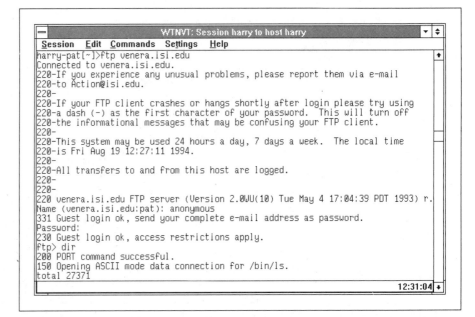

```
WTNVT: Session harry to host harry
Session  Edit  Commands  Settings  Help
harry-pat[~]>ftp venera.isi.edu
Connected to venera.isi.edu.
220-If you experience any unusual problems, please report them via e-mail
220-to Action@isi.edu.
220-
220-If your FTP client crashes or hangs shortly after login please try using
220-a dash (-) as the first character of your password.  This will turn off
220-the informational messages that may be confusing your FTP client.
220-
220-This system may be used 24 hours a day, 7 days a week.  The local time
220-is Fri Aug 19 12:27:11 1994.
220-
220-All transfers to and from this host are logged.
220-
220-
220 venera.isi.edu FTP server (Version 2.0WU(10) Tue May 4 17:04:39 PDT 1993) r.
Name (venera.isi.edu:pat): anonymous
331 Guest login ok, send your complete e-mail address as password.
Password:
230 Guest login ok, access restrictions apply.
ftp> dir
200 PORT command successful.
150 Opening ASCII mode data connection for /bin/ls.
total 27371
                                                                  12:31:04
```

► ►**M A S T E R   W O R D S**

**The FTP programs have a utility built in that will let
you track the progress of your file transfer in line
mode. It's called** *hash,* **because it prints out # signs
(***hash marks***) to show you how much of your file has
transferred. It's a good idea to enter the hash
command as the first thing you do when you start a
line-mode FTP session. Simply type** *hash* **at the FTP>
prompt. Some systems will respond with the number
of transferred bites each hash mark represents; some
simply return you to the FTP> prompt.**

Finding Things

Once you have connected to a host via anonymous FTP, you can usually get a listing of the materials available by typing the UNIX directory command:

dir

Figure 9.2 shows such a listing.

This will give you an idea of what's available on the system. If you see a file called "index" or "Read.Me" (or some variant), it is usually a general information document.

FIGURE 9.2

A typical directory listing.

```
─                        WTNVT: Session harry to host harry              ▼ ▲
 Session   Edit   Commands   Settings   Help
230 Guest login ok, access restrictions apply.
ftp> dir
200 PORT command successful.
150 Opening ASCII mode data connection for /bin/ls.
total 27371
drwxrwxr-x  2 root     0            512 Nov 19  1993 Intermail
drwxrwxr-x  2 1130     106          512 Nov 19  1993 Valid-Code
drwxrwxr-x  2 1130     106         2048 Nov 19  1993 Valid-Tests
-rwxrwxrwx  1 root     1          33420 Jul 29 17:28 amy.log
-rwxrwxrwx  1 root     1       26763264 Jul 29 17:25 amy.tar
drwxrwxr-x  2 1204     135          512 Aug  2 15:14 arts
drwxrwxr-x  2 1215     104          512 Nov 19  1993 atomic
drwxrwxr-x  2 1047     10          1024 Jul 18 17:18 atomic-doc
dr-xr-sr-x  2 root     0            512 Aug 15 11:37 bin
-rw-rw-r--  2 root     0         173156 Jan 18  1992 boot-csc2
-rw-r--r--  1 1129     10         30570 Jan 23  1991 bos9.sav
drwxr-xr-x  2 root     10           512 Nov 19  1993 bromine
drwxrwxr-x  2 1204     135          512 Nov 19  1993 bytecounters
drwxr-xr-x  5 2007     10           512 Nov 19  1993 choy
drwxrwxr-x  6 1215     134          512 Apr 14 10:42 confctrl
-rw-r--r--  1 root     10         46537 Jul  2  1990 cps.msgs
dr-xr-xr-x  2 root     0            512 Nov 19  1993 dev
drwxr-xr-x  2 root     10           512 Nov 19  1993 dist
d--x--x--x  2 root     0            512 Nov 19  1993 etc
                                                       12:31:35 ▲
```

What a UNIX File/Directory Listing Tells You

Here is a sample directory listing from a file archive hosted on a remote computer using the UNIX operating system. Many of the archive sites are hosted on UNIX machines, so this may help you understand what the directory listing says:

```
drwxr-xr-x   2  glee      512      Jan  8 22:92      foom
-r--r-xr--   1  brian   165418     May  3 92         game.zip
```

Left to right: the first series of letters describes (cryptically) the file type and permissions set for the directory or file. If the first character is a **d**, it is a directory. A file will have a - (hyphen) in this position.

The next characters describe the security permissions. They are in three groups of three characters. The **r** indicates permission to read. The **w** indicates permission to write. The **x** indicates permission to execute from. The first group of three characters describes the permissions set by the owner. The second group of three characters describes the permission set for a group of login IDs in which the login ID is a part. The third group of three characters describes the permission set for the world, that is, everyone who has access to this host computer.

For example, take our sample directory:

```
drwx-r-x--x   2  glee      512     Jan  8 22:92     foom
-r--r-xr--    1  brian   165418    May  3 92      game.zip
```

The first entry, foom, is a directory (that's what the d means). It can be written (that is, changed) by the owner, who can read every file in the directory and can also execute (run) programs stored in it. So the second, third, and fourth letters are rwx. Next we have r-x. This means that the owner's group can read files and execute the programs, but not write or change anything. Finally, we have --x. This means that the rest of the users on the system can execute any programs stored in the directory, but can't read the files or change anything. In fact, general users can't even get a directory listing of what's stored in this directory: they have to know a program is there to use it. (This isn't as strange as it sounds: UNIX lets you link files together and so users might think they were executing a file stored elsewhere when it really lives in this directory.)

The second entry, game.zip, has more limited permission. It is a file, not a directory (there is a hyphen in the first position). The owner can read it, but not change or execute it. The group can read and execute it. The rest of the world can read it but not change or execute it.

For anonymous FTP to work, the **r** must be present in the eighth character position. That is, the world must have permission to read the file. If you are the file owner, or your login ID is part of the defined group with the file owner login ID, you may transfer the file if the **r** is present in the second or fifth character.

To be able to write a file to a directory, there must be a **w** in the appropriate character position.

The name of the file owner is the next piece of information. If the file owner is named something like root or wheel, you are looking at the description of a file or directory managed by the system administrator for that system. Such files typically include those placed for anonymous FTP, the password files for the system, and your network directory entry. (Even though you control everything within your home directory, the directory itself is managed by the system administrator.) The size of the file in bytes is listed. The date that the file was last stored appears next. If the file was modified in this calendar year, the time that the file was stored may be listed. Otherwise, the year that the file was modified is displayed.

Finally, the name of the file finishes up the description line.

Most FTP archive owners want you to be happy using their resource, and so they use the conventions listed earlier in naming their files. However, a few rogues do exist, and so it's important to check the INDEX or README files when you access a new archive.

MASTER WORDS

The file doc/pcnet/compression **at** ftp.cso.uiuc.edu, **available via anonymous FTP, contains a comprehensive table listing the available file compression software and naming conventions. It is updated when new tools become available.**

To turn ASCII mode on in a FTP session, type **ascii**. To turn BINARY on, type **bin.** Most FTP sessions start up by default in ASCII mode.

Moving Around with FTP

After you see the top-level directory of materials available (and you read the index or the README), you may need to move into a lower-level directory to retrieve your file. The command to change directories is:

cd *directory-name*

To find out where you are, you can always use the UNIX "print working directory" command. Type **pwd** to find out what directory you are in.

FTP and Telnet

ch.
9

Getting Files to You

Most commonly, you will be bringing files down to your local work-station or the host on which you have an account. You will use the get or mget commands.

get To bring a single file down to your local host or workstation, type the command:

```
get filename
```

This will initiate the file transfer from the server to your local system. Don't forget to include the extension (if any) after the filename.

▶▶ **M A S T E R   W O R D S**

> **If you want to look at a short file, such as a README or an index file, you can use UNIX syntax and your pager to look at it right from your FTP session. Type** get **filename ¦more to "pipe" (that's the UNIX name for the vertical rule [¦]) the file into the UNIX page reader,** *more.*

If you want to change the name of the file on your local system, you can do that right in the same transfer process. Type:

```
get remotename localname
```

For example, if you are retrieving the Anonymous FTP FAQ and put-ting it on your DOS system, you will want to rename it to fit within the DOS naming convention. You might type (all on one line):

```
get Anonymous_FTP_Frequently_Asked_Questions_(FAQ)_List
anoftp.faq
```

The principal of renaming holds for all the single get and put com-mands, but not for multiple files at a time.

mget Sometimes you want to get a whole bunch of files. For example, if you are transferring JPEG images, they frequently are broken up into linked but separate files, because of their size. Or you may want to get several PostScript files at once.

mget is a program that will do Multiple GETs for you. You use it almost like you use get, except that mget takes advantage of the UNIX (and DOS) *pattern matching* facility. You can use the asterisk (*) in place of the variable parts of the filename.

For example, if you want a bunch of JPEG files about tigers, you might want to look for all the files that match the pattern tigr*.jpeg. The asterisk will usually stand in for a number or a series of letters.

Once you have examined the directory and decided which files you want, type:

mget *filepattern*

WARNING

> It is extremely important to know whether you want to use ASCII or binary mode when you are transferring files with mget, or you will waste time and bandwidth and end up with files filled with gibberish. *Always* transfer all the files that need the same mode in the same mget operation; if you need both ASCII and binary transfers, you'll need to run mget twice. Some FTP clients are smart enough these days to read the extension and guess the file type, but not all are. Be sure and set the mode before you begin the mget.

Figure 9.3 shows an mget session, requesting files with the pattern *audio*.* and using hash to measure the transfer's progress.

Moving Files from You to Somewhere Else

Sometimes you will want to place a copy of a file on another host, either to share it with someone or to put it into a public archive. Then you use the put or mput commands.

FIGURE 9.3 ▶

The mget command in operation.

```
─                    WINVT: Session harry to host harry           ▼ ▲
Session  Edit  Commands  Settings  Help                              ▲
ftp> hash
Hash mark printing on (8192 bytes/hash mark).
ftp> mget *audio*.*
mget ietf-audiocast-article.ps? y
200 PORT command successful.
150 Opening ASCII mode data connection for ietf-audiocast-article.ps (177682 by.
#########################
226 Transfer complete.
local: ietf-audiocast-article.ps remote: ietf-audiocast-article.ps
184247 bytes received in 57 seconds (3.2 Kbytes/s)
mget ietf-audiocast.txt? y
200 PORT command successful.
150 Opening ASCII mode data connection for ietf-audiocast.txt (21761 bytes).
###
226 Transfer complete.
local: ietf-audiocast.txt remote: ietf-audiocast.txt
22123 bytes received in 19 seconds (1.2 Kbytes/s)
ftp>
ftp>
ftp>
ftp>
ftp>
ftp>
ftp> █
                                                         12:41:25 ▼
```

> ◎ ▶ ▶ **W A R N I N G**
>
> **You will not be able to copy a file into a directory or onto a host if you do not have *write permission* for that host or directory. Some FTP sites do not allow any anonymous FTP users to write (copy) files into their archives. You will need to have a real user ID to *put* files on such hosts.**

put The put command works just like get, only in reverse. Check what your file mode should be (ASCII or binary), set the appropriate type, and then send it away. For example,

```
hash
set binary
put irc.zip
```

The little hash marks will march across the screen, and your file will slip away across the Internet to its new home.

Remember, however: unlike the DOS command MOVE or the UNIX mv, put and mput do not *move* the file from one place to another: they merely *copy* it.

mput Just as mget retrieves multiple files with one command, mput sends multiple files. Again, you check what your file mode should be (ASCII or binary), set the appropriate type, and then send them away. Figure 9.4 illustrates a typical mput session.

FIGURE 9.4 ▶

Using mput from a VT100 terminal session.

```
FTP session 1 connected to ftp harry.lloyd.com.
220 harry FTP server (Version wu-2.4(6) Fri Aug 5 15:22:21 PDT 1994) ready.
Enter user name: pat
331 s/key 98 ha51227
Password:
230-Welcome to the Lloyd Internetworking FTP server.
230-Local time is Thu Aug 18 08:18:41 1994.
230-There are 1 out of a possible 8 users signed on.
230-
230 User pat logged in.
ftp> syst
215 UNIX Type: L8
ftp> hash
ftp> bin
ftp> mput *.doc
200 Type set to I.
200 PORT command successful.
150 Opening BINARY mode data connection for 16450c02.doc.
##########################################################
226 Transfer complete.
STOR 16450c02.doc: 56600 bytes in 43 sec (1287/sec)
200 PORT command successful.
150 Opening BINARY mode data connection for email.doc.
######
▓▓▓▓ 1: ftp harry.lloyd.com.              Unack: 1024  F6:nxt F8:cmd
```

▶ *Using GUI FTP Clients*

Many of the most modern TCP/IP-based Internet clients that you run from your desktop have GUI interfaces. That is, they will run in either the standard Macintosh or Windows-like formats. These clients are extremely easy to use, because they have menus that help you remember how to do things.

Signing On

Most of these clients have a menu of hosts you have used regularly, or they let you type the name of the FTP service you wish to use into a response box. You can also type in your user name and password at the

FTP and Telnet

▶ ▶

ch.
9

same time. The client generally handles passing along these bits of information for you.

One such client program is FTP Software's WFTP. Figure 9.5 shows the start of a WFTP session.

FIGURE 9.5

Starting an FTP session with a Windows client.

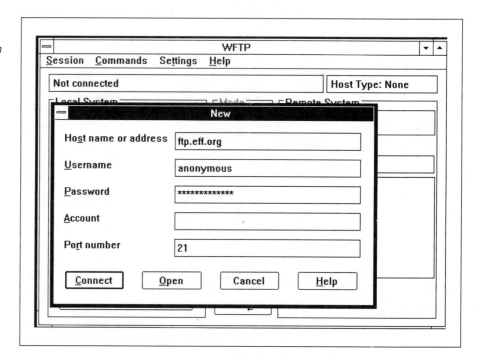

Getting Files

When you sign on, you will see a list of files available. Some clients show you both the available files on your local workstation or host as well as those on the remote host; some show you only the remote host unless you explicitly ask for a local listing. (By checking your local file system, you can make sure you aren't going to overwrite a local file with a file of the same name that you're bringing over by FTP.)

MASTER WORDS

Remember that DOS systems truncate file names to eight characters. If you're bringing over several files with the first eight characters the same (such as MASTERING_FTP, MASTERING_TELNET, and MASTERING_GOPHER), you'll need to rename each file on the local system as soon as you bring it down, or you'll end up with one file called MASTERIN, and it will contain only the last file you transferred.

In general, you select the file mode in which you want to transfer the files, highlight the names of the file or files you want to transfer, and then click on the direction you want to send the files (in this case, to you). Figure 9.6 shows a typical WFTP transfer session. In this illustration, because we have highlighted files on the remote host, the "Copy" box arrows are pointing at the local host. If we had highlighted files on the local host directory, the arrows would be pointing at the remote host.

FIGURE 9.6

Transferring files using FTP Software's Windows client.

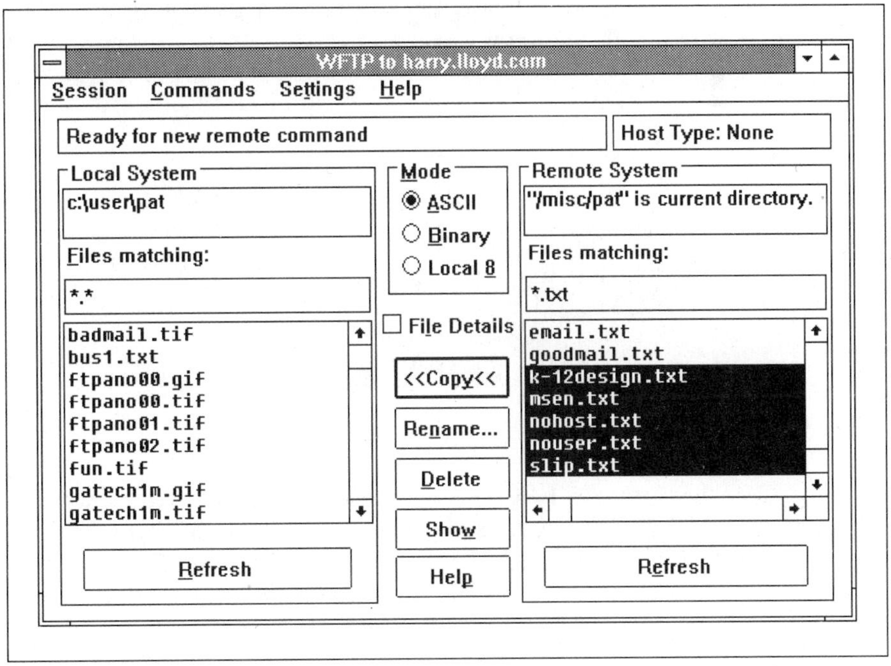

Placing Files

Putting a file on a remote host is very simple with these GUI clients: you click on the arrows for the direction in which you want to copy the files (from you to the remote host) or on a button labeled something like Put.

Remember, you must have write permission on the remote host to place files there. If you have signed on with a regular user name and password, you generally have write permission. If you're using anonymous FTP, you may need to write into a special directory (such as *pub* or *incoming*), if you have write permission at all.

Again, you can transfer either a single file or multiple files with most clients. But remember that the file *modes* must be identical for all types if you are transferring several files.

▶ NCFTP

NCFTP is a new program for anonymous FTP that doesn't even require you to be able to spell *anonymous*. It also automatically enters the e-mail address (derived from the user ID and host name) as the password. It's intended to be an easy and efficient "front end" to the traditional FTP programs.

Figure 9.7 shows a typical NCFTP session. You simply type

ncftp *hostname*

and the program makes the connection and logs you in anonymously.

Check with your systems administrator to see if NCFTP has been installed on your host or site.

▶ Interesting FTP Sites

Some places to go with FTP include:

- **Extensive archives of computer source code:** for Windows at ftp.cica.indiana.edu (Indiana University); for Macintosh computers at the SUMEX-AIM system in the Stanford University in California domain (sumex-aim.stanford.edu); for DOS and

FIGURE 9.7

An NCFTP session to
oak.oakland.edu.

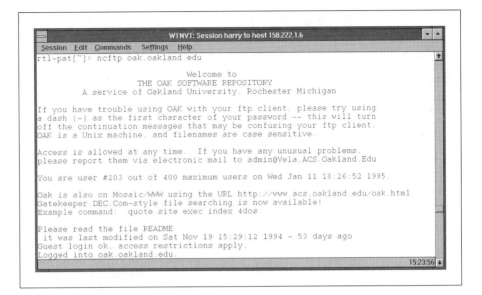

Amiga machines (among others) at `wuarchive.wustl.edu` (Washington University in St. Louis, Missouri) or `oak.oakland.edu` (Oakland University in Rochester, Michigan).

- **Information Source Lists:** The Internet and Computer-Mediated Communication (AKA The December list), compiled by John December (`decemj@rpi.edu`) at host `ftp.rpi.edu` (Rennselaer Polytechnic Institute, Troy, New York); also available via the Web at Uniform Resource Locator *(URL)* :

`http://www.rpi.edu/Internet/Guides/decemj/text.html`

(For more information on URLs and the World Wide Web, see Chapter 11.) This file lists pointers to information describing the Internet, computer networks, and issues related to computer-mediated communication (CMC). Special Internet Connections (AKA the Yanoff list) is another list that contains many resources of potential interest. Scott Yanoff compiles and updates it and the list is posted frequently across the Net. It can be reached via anonymous FTP from the host `csd4.csd.uwm.edu` (University of Wisconsin, Madison, Wisconsin) or via the World Wide Web. One place you can find it is at the Stanford Linear Accelerator Center:

`http://slacvx.slac.stanford.edu:80/misc/internet-`
`services.html`

FTP and Telnet

ch.
9

- **Connected countries:** If you'd like to know what countries are connected to the global Internet and how, you can get a file of information collected by Larry Landweber. It's in the directory connectivity-table on the host `ftp.cs.wisc.edu` (University of Wisconsin). The same information is also available via the InterNIC Information Services InfoSource Gopher server. Gopher to `is.internic.net` or use the Web by opening a URL to `gopher.is.internic.net`. Choose Internet Information for Everybody, then choose Internet Statistics, Size and Connectivity.

- **State Government:** For information from the Legislature of the State of California, FTP to `leginfo.public.ca.gov` or Gopher the University of California at Santa Cruz's InfoSlug system (`scilibx.ucsu.edu`). From their main menu, choose "The Community" then "Guide to government" then "US, State and Local." This menu will present a number of choices for government information. (Many states now have public archives available. Call your state librarian or a local state-supported university or college computing center to see if your state has such a service.)

- There is an archive of USENET newsgroups at `rtfm.mit.edu`. You can use the directory feature in FTP to find out more about what is there.

- Author Bernard Aboba has edited an **online magazine** for users of the Internet. You can find it at

  `ftp://ftp.netcom.com/pub/mailcom/internaut/`

  The first issue has the filename internt1.zip.

► More FTP Archive Locations

In Appendix G you will find a long list of FTP archives around the world, with a brief description of what they contain. You will also find information on how to get a copy of a regular posting called "the Monster List," which contains over one thousand FTP sites.

►► Telnet

People who are in one location frequently want to use a computer in another location. Perhaps they are on a business trip and want to read their e-mail. Perhaps they want to access data on the computer in another branch or in the main office. Perhaps they want to look at a library catalog to see if a certain book has been published. Perhaps they want to use one of the services of the Information Providers such as Dialog or Mead Data Central. Telnet is the Internet tool that lets you travel from your own workstation out into cyberspace.

You can also use Telnet to get to services, such as Gophers, line-mode Web servers, libraries, and WAIS servers, even if you do not have clients for those servers on your own host system. (See Chapters 10 and 11 for information about Gopher, the Web, and WAIS.)

▶ *Using Telnet*

Telnet is one of the simplest tools on the Internet. To open a session with a remote host from a system prompt, type:

`telnet hostname`

You should see the welcome or login banner for the host.

If you are already in a Telnet session, you may see a prompt for the Telnet program itself: `telnet>`. If you are at such a prompt, type:

`open hostname`

and, again, you should see the login prompt. Figure 9.8 shows the beginning of a Telnet session.

If you are using a GUI Telnet client, you may be able save short names for commonly used hosts or services, as in Figure 9.9.

Telnet sessions may be established directly by typing the command explicitly, or through an intermediary such as Gopher or WWW. There are directories that you will find on the Internet that list remote services. (For example, if you Telnet to `hermes.merit.edu`, you will find a number of remote services listed.) These directories will list the appropriate command to use, including the appropriate domain and/or Internet address. If a remote service is a publicly accessible one, you may not need a user account on the remote system.

FIGURE 9.8

*Beginning a simple
Telnet session to the
NameFLOW directory
service.*

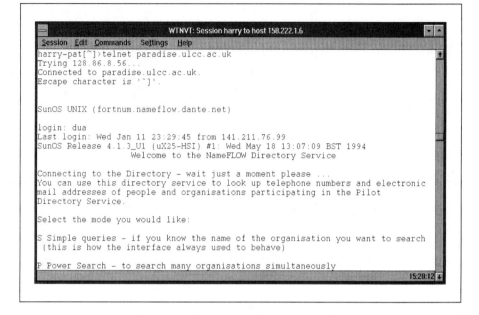

FIGURE 9.9 ▶

*Opening a connection
with a GUI Telnet
client.*

▶ *tn3270*

Some remote systems (some library public catalog systems, in particular) require you to use a different Telnet program to connect properly. This program, called tn3270, causes your computer to appear to be ("emulate") an IBM 3270 computer terminal (instead of using the more common VT100 emulation). If you need to connect to one of these systems, and if your host or service does not offer tn3270, you need to Telnet to a public site that offers a tn3270 program.

Two clues will tell you that you might need to use tn3270. The first is a message that says

```
Connection closed by foreign host.
```

consistently. This message indicates there is trouble between your two systems. Naturally, there are many reasons you might receive this message including that the remote host is not currently available. However, if you suspect that the host is an IBM system, think about trying tn3270.

The second clue is a ...connected ... message returned from the remote host, containing the letters VM or MVS in the welcome message. This indicates that you are connected to a IBM system. If the interaction between your computer and the remote host doesn't go well, you probably need to use tn3270.

MASTER WORDS

Many hosts will ask you what kind of terminal emulation you are using when you first make a connection. Usually these hosts tell you what kind of emulator they think you are using and ask you to confirm (or enter a different emulation). It is particularly important to respond correctly to these prompts, because otherwise your screen will not look correct, and your keyboard commands will probably not behave in an expected way. If you don't know how to respond, type a question mark (?) and see the online help.

Once you are connected to this type of system, you will be presented with menus and forms that expect you to "fill in the blanks." When you have completed your form, send it to the remote host by pressing Enter. tn3270 maps your keyboard to the keyboard of the 3270 terminal. Many systems that use these terminals use the Program Function (PF) keys and the Clear key to communicate special commands to the program. It is particularly important to tell the tn3270 program that you have a VT100 terminal when you start the program. Then, once you are connected, you will need to figure out how the keys on the 3270 keyboard are represented. Usually Tab will move you through the input areas. Try the arrow keys. If they don't work, you can use Tab. Usually the tn3270 Enter is the Enter key on your keyboard and also the one on your numeric keypad.

For the function keys, try the F1, F2, … keys across the top of your keyboard. If they work, the screen display will change or you will get a message like "PF4 undefined." If they don't work, try Escape+1 for PF1, and so on.

To clear the screen, try Ctrl-Home, Ctrl-l, or Ctrl-z.

Any Port in a Storm

A *port* is rather like a transmission channel on a radio. It is the place at which the application on the remote or host computer "listens" for connection requests to a particular application. Gopher usually uses port 70. Telnet usually uses port 23. FTP usually uses two ports, one of which is port 21. Services can use other port numbers to direct connections to specific applications. If you are given a specific port number, place the number after the host name in a command-line interface, or in the "port" box in a GUI or dialog box interface.

 ▶ ▶**M A S T E R   W O R D S**

> **Curious about geographic location as well as location in cyberspace? Can't remember your mother's zip code? Need to find out the longitude and latitude of your office building? Telnet to** `martini.eecs.umich.edu` 3000, **where you will be connected to the machine called** `martini` **in the Electrical Engineering Computer Science domain at the University of Michigan, using port 3000. This is the Geographic Name Server. Once connected, you can enter a place name or a zip code. In return, you will receive a short display of information available about that place. No special login sequence is needed. There is online help.**

► *HYTELNET*

An important tool for working with Telnet is HYTELNET. Peter Scott of the University of Saskatchewan has designed and implemented this program, which presents menus of library catalogs and other resources that allow public access through Telnet. The particular advantage of HYTELNET for the user is that the specific information about a library or service is remembered by the program, and you need not keep track of it. If HYTELNET is not already on your system, you can try it out by connecting via Telnet to `herald.usask.ca`. Use the login ID `hytelnet`. Mr. Scott makes the program available for others to run on their own host systems and also maintains a mailing list of people who are interested in updates to the system.

► *Interesting Telnet Sites*

These sites offer products, services and/or discussions. When you Telnet to these sites, use the login name specified for the service. Be prepared to register your name, address, and perhaps e-mail address on entry to these services.

- Argonne National Laboratory in Illinois offers an educational service called Newton. To reach it, Telnet to `newton.dip.anl.gov`.

- There is a backgammon server at `fraggel65.mdstd.chalmers.se` on port 4321.

- You can play bridge by Telnetting to `irc.nsysu.edu.tw`. Log in as `okbridge`. This is an IRC (Internet Relay Chat, discussed in Chapter 14) system in Taiwan that has been adapted for playing bridge. Enter **/help for instructions.**

- MichNet and its members maintain several interesting Gophers as well as other interesting services. Telnet to `hermes.merit.edu`, and then, at the "Which Host?" prompt, type HELP. Some of the most interesting services include UM-Weather, which has forecasts and current information as well as educational programs and curriculum ideas for teachers; the MSU Gopher, which has a library of voice recordings; the libraries of many of Michigan's colleges and universities; and many others.

FTP and Telnet

ch. **9**

- Telnet to `books.com` to find a bulletin board system (BBS) that is a bookstore.

- Telnet to `career.com` to find a bulletin board system with a career service.

- Telnet to `classroom-earth.ciesin.org` port 2010 to find the Global Change Education bulletin board.

- Pilots! Telnet to `duats.fsd.gte.com` to get a complete weather briefing; with your pilot's certificate number, you can even file your flight plan.

► ► **CHAPTER** **10**

Resource Discovery — Finding Things on the Internet

►► ***T**he* Internet basic tools, FTP, e-mail, and Telnet, discussed in previous chapters, give you the necessary information to transfer files to your machine, to send and receive e-mail, and to log in to a remote computer on which you have an account. These are wonderful things to know, but if you want to find the address of a specific person to whom you want to send e-mail, what do you do? How do you know where a file you want to transfer might be found? How can you find some specific services or Internet presence in which you are interested? This chapter attempts to address these questions.

 ► ►**MASTER WORDS**

> **When you navigate the Internet, be sure and keep a notepad by your computer. This way you can note down the address or URL of interesting items; there's nothing worse than finding a gold mine and not being able to get back there again! Some Internet tool client programs, particularly for the navigation programs like Web browsers and Gopher (both discussed in Chapter 11), provide a bookmark facility to store markers. These facilities let you leave a signpost for a page or Gopher menu where you think you'd like to come back again. When you use a bookmark, your computer makes the notes for you.**

►► *Finding People*

It remains true that the very best method to discover the e-mail address of a particular person is to ask him or her. This method guarantees that you have found the preferred e-mail address for your proposed correspondent (some people have several e-mail addresses, and they use these addresses for different things).

It also confirms that your correspondent will sometimes participate in an e-mail correspondence. Some people have e-mail addresses and don't use them. One sure sign of this is the response "Hmm, I don't really have that at my fingertips. I'll let my secretary get back to you with that information." (Glee actually heard a United States Representative say that to a roomful of constituents who had just listened to him speak on the virtues of "The Information Superhighway.") This example does illustrate the second-best method, though, which is to ask someone *else* who would know the address you need.

Occasionally, however, it is difficult or inconvenient to ask for an e-mail address. You may want to correspond with an expert in a field about which you need information. Or you may want to send e-mail to an address representing a functional position, rather than a specific person. In the first case, you'll want to choose methods of determining the exact e-mail address for a person. In the second case, you'll be looking more for a specific Internet domain to which to send your message.

Let's take a really easy case. Suppose you want to send a message to the President of the United States giving your opinion about, say, a proposed executive position on taxation. This example is one of the "ask someone" variety. It's included in practically every book about the Internet and every basic e-mail training class; and virtually everyone who has used the Internet in the United States knows it. Address your e-mail to:

```
president@whitehouse.gov
```

But suppose for a moment that we are stuck at home without immediate access to our friends and colleagues who already know this information, so we will use a few Internet tools to identify the appropriate address.

▶ *Finger*

Finger is an Internet standard tool that lets you "reach out and touch" a computer on the Internet with your "finger" to find out information about "accounts" that are registered on that host. Each Finger client (as you would expect) uses similar syntax to say "touch the account named *user* at the host computer *hostname*." For UNIX systems, the command looks like

`finger user@hostname`

Some hosts will return a list of all the accounts on the system if you send the command

`finger @hostname`

Note that in this case, you left the user ID part of the command blank.

If you try the command

`finger clinton@whitehouse.gov`

you will see one of the first problems with this particular facility. Not all sites support the command. Some sites choose not to support it for security reasons, not wanting everyone who can connect to the Internet and issue the command to be able to access a particular user or a user list at the site. Others make the same decision for considerations of privacy rather than security. So, in late 1994, you receive the message shown in Figure 10.1, to the effect that Finger is not supported for arbitrary addresses within the `whitehouse.gov` domain.

FIGURE 10.1 ▶

Results from Fingering the White House.

The message continues with the information that electronic mail may be sent to the addresses

president@whitehouse.gov

and

vice-president@whitehouse.gov

The command did tell us that we have the correct domain identifier, though. With that information we can use the Whois service to obtain more information about this domain.

On some systems, Finger will return more information than a simple association of user ID and "full name." Finger will display some information about the system which is associated with the domain in question and some information about the user. On UNIX systems in particular, Finger can be configured by the host administrator to display the user ID, the full name of the user, the last time the user was logged in to the system, whether mail is waiting, and the arrival time of the last received message. Figure 10.2 shows a Finger response with all of this information.

Some systems will respond to a blank user ID. Finger will then answer with a display of all the active users on that host system. Sometimes

FIGURE 10.2 ▶

A typical Finger response.

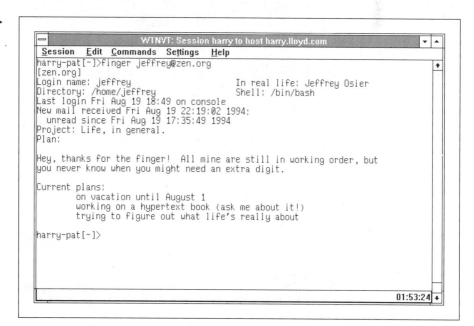

that response contain many users, and therefore, will be quite long. When you try this you may want to send (or "pipe" on a UNIX system) the results of your Finger command through a paging command like more or you may want to send the results to a file. To "pipe" your answer through the more command, enter

```
finger @hostname ¦ more
```

To send the results to a file, enter

```
finger @hostname > filename
```

Figure 10.3 shows the result of a Finger command on a large system. You can see that more users are signed on than we can see in a whole screenful.

From this discussion, you will no doubt have noticed that you need to have the name of the appropriate Internet host in order to use the Finger command to find a user on another system. On most systems if you just enter the command finger *userid*, you will only be looking on the system to which you are connected. Naturally, the information you can retrieve is no less valuable for being local. It's about other users of your

FIGURE 10.3 ▶

Using Finger to see who is signed onto a large system.

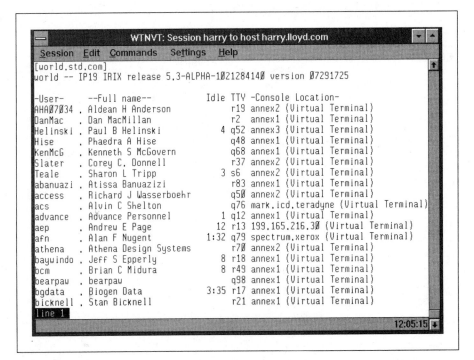

host system. Are they connected now (so you can perhaps try the Talk command, described in Chapter 14)? Have they read all their mail?

But let's say you want to find our friend, Sue Joiner, and someone told you only that she is working now for the Merit Network. Finger won't yet be the appropriate tool to use. You need more information than you have now. You need to find out what host name would be appropriate to use. The Whois database is a good place to look for that information.

▶ *Whois—Searching for Registered Domains*

The Whois service is a client/server program where the client queries the distributed Internet database of domains. If you are logged on to a machine that supports Whois queries, you may get a response simply by entering

```
whois domain-identifier
```

at a command prompt. On some host systems, for example, if you enter

```
whois whitehouse
```

or

```
whois merit
```

the client program will check the nearest copy of the database (that is, nearest in network geography, not in physical geography) and return what information it can. If the server is not the "official" domain database, which is kept by the InterNIC, the information will be accompanied by a disclaimer stating that you might want to check the information with the official listing before you consider it valid. Normally, the only reasons to check the official data would be to determine if a domain had been assigned but not yet completely distributed throughout the domain name system, or to confirm an IP address if you were going to do something that required an absolute IP address. If you were planning to register a domain name, you would want to make sure it had not already been used. With the acceptance of the domain name system and more and more implementations of it among TCP/IP software vendors, there are fewer and fewer reasons to need to know the IP address of a particular site.

At this writing, the *whitehouse* search returns the display shown in Figure 10.4. It shows that *whitehouse.gov* is the relevant domain and that

FIGURE 10.4 ▶

Results of the command "whois whitehouse."

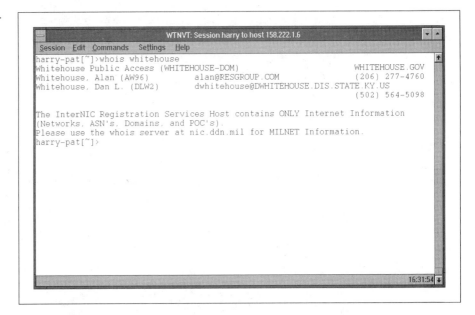

the IP address is 198.137.240.100. If you continue searching by entering *whitehouse.dom* as the argument to your Whois search, you'll find that there is a domain called EOP.DOM. (We assume that EOP stands for Executive Office of the President.) Anyway, should you be interested, you can find out who the administrative and technical coordinators are for the Executive Office's IP network this way. The same is true of the merit.edu domain.

MASTER WORDS

The Whois database also contains information about a number of registered individuals. Unfortunately, the Whois database contains only the people who have voluntarily registered themselves. If you don't find an entry here for a particular person, all you know is that the person is not registered with the InterNIC. You'll need to look elsewhere for information that is missing. Most Internet users are not individually registered.

If you do not have direct access to the Whois database (by entering the command Whois at a command prompt or by using a whois function on your local system), you can use one of the public Whois servers by using Telnet to login to the remote server. The authoritative server is located at `rs.internic.net`. If you connect to this host via Telnet, you will receive instructions that will tell you how to search the Whois database.

If you prefer not to use Telnet, you can use one of the Internet navigator programs (described in the next chapter) like Gopher or your favorite World Wide Web browser to connect to the InterNIC site. Gopher to `rs.internic.net`. Or, in the Web, enter the URL `http://rs.internic.net`.

To find the appropriate domain for Sue Joiner takes a bit more work. A search for the word "joiner" returns some results, but none of them are Sue. She's not registered in the Whois registration database. So you need to search for "merit." If you enter a search for that word, as in Figure 10.5, you'll see a number of entries, some of which are names of people, some of which are names of domains. Since you are pretty sure that Sue is still in Michigan, you look among the entries for Merit Network and find the primary domain record for Merit. Now you can go

FIGURE 10.5 ▶

Results of "whois merit" command.

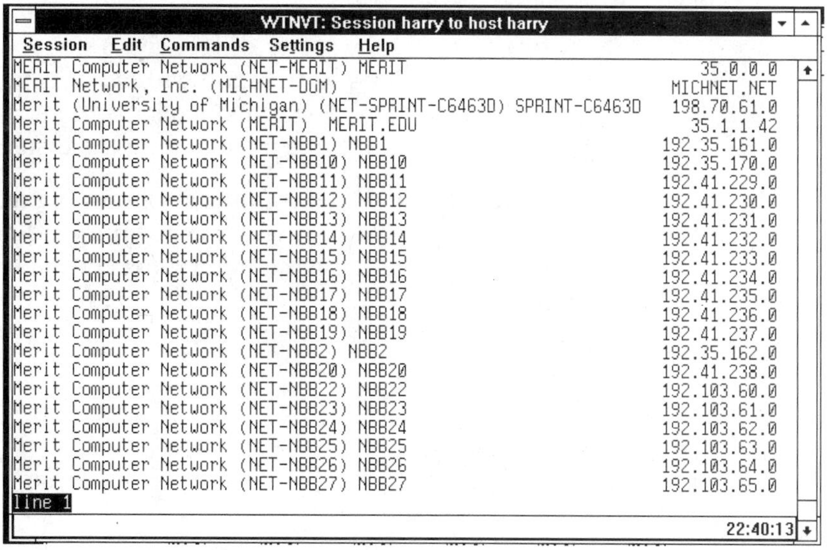

```
 ═                       WTNVT: Session harry to host harry            ▼  ▲
 Session   Edit   Commands   Settings   Help
 MERIT Computer Network (NET-MERIT) MERIT                          35.0.0.0    ↑
 MERIT Network, Inc. (MICHNET-DOM)                                 MICHNET.NET
 Merit (University of Michigan) (NET-SPRINT-C6463D) SPRINT-C6463D  198.70.61.0
 Merit Computer Network (MERIT)   MERIT.EDU                        35.1.1.42
 Merit Computer Network (NET-NBB1) NBB1                            192.35.161.0
 Merit Computer Network (NET-NBB10) NBB10                          192.35.170.0
 Merit Computer Network (NET-NBB11) NBB11                          192.41.229.0
 Merit Computer Network (NET-NBB12) NBB12                          192.41.230.0
 Merit Computer Network (NET-NBB13) NBB13                          192.41.231.0
 Merit Computer Network (NET-NBB14) NBB14                          192.41.232.0
 Merit Computer Network (NET-NBB15) NBB15                          192.41.233.0
 Merit Computer Network (NET-NBB16) NBB16                          192.41.234.0
 Merit Computer Network (NET-NBB17) NBB17                          192.41.235.0
 Merit Computer Network (NET-NBB18) NBB18                          192.41.236.0
 Merit Computer Network (NET-NBB19) NBB19                          192.41.237.0
 Merit Computer Network (NET-NBB2) NBB2                            192.35.162.0
 Merit Computer Network (NET-NBB20) NBB20                          192.41.238.0
 Merit Computer Network (NET-NBB22) NBB22                          192.103.60.0
 Merit Computer Network (NET-NBB23) NBB23                          192.103.61.0
 Merit Computer Network (NET-NBB24) NBB24                          192.103.62.0
 Merit Computer Network (NET-NBB25) NBB25                          192.103.63.0
 Merit Computer Network (NET-NBB26) NBB26                          192.103.64.0
 Merit Computer Network (NET-NBB27) NBB27                          192.103.65.0
 line 1
                                                                  22:40:13  ↓
```

on and use Netfind to find out if there is information about Sue in that domain.

▶ Netfind

Netfind is another tool for finding individuals on the Net. The original Netfind server is located at `bruno.cs.colorado.edu`. To find if this program is available on your host, enter the command `netfind` at the command prompt. If you receive an error message, like

```
Command invalid
```

or something similar, you know that you'll need to look elsewhere for this service.

To use Netfind to find an e-mail address for a person, you will need two pieces of information about them—one distinguishing part of their name and one part of a domain in which you might expect to find them. Mike Schwartz of the University of Colorado began the development of Netfind with the idea that with these two pieces of information, it should be possible to determine possible (and then best-possible) e-mail addresses for people.

Let's continue with our example of Sue Joiner at Merit. On a system that is running Netfind, enter

```
netfind joiner merit
```

As Figure 10.6 shows, you will receive a message that tells you that too many possible hosts were found with *merit* as part of their domain name. The possible hosts will be displayed and you will be asked to pick not more than three from among the displayed names.

Let's pick the host *merit.edu*. As shown in Figure 10.7, we enter the number of that host listing at the prompt, and Netfind will continue processing. Using Finger among other tools, Netfind displays the information for Sue Joiner. By looking at the fully qualified domain name for the machine that Sue used to connect to merit.edu, Netfind recommends the e-mail address

```
smj@pony.merit.edu.
```

FIGURE 10.6 ▶

Results of the command "netfind joiner merit."

```
┌──────────────────────────────────────────────────────────────────────────┐
│           WTNVT: Session bruno to host bruno.cs.colorado.edu      [▼][▲]   │
│  Session  Edit  Commands   Settings   Help                                 │
│ Enter person and keys (blank to exit) --> joiner merit                  [↑]│
│ Please select at most 3 of the following domains to search:                │
│       0. k12.edu (merit network, inc, ann arbor, michigan)                 │
│       1. merit-tech.com (merit technology, inc, plano, texas)              │
│       2. merit.com (merit medical systems, inc, salt lake city, utah)      │
│       3. merit.edu (merit computer network, inc, ann arbor, michigan)      │
│       4. merit.net (merit computer network, inc, ann arbor, michigan)      │
│       5. meritsoftware.com (merit software, dallas, texas)                 │
│       6. mich.net (merit computer network, inc, ann arbor, michigan)       │
│       7. michnet.net (merit computer network, inc, ann arbor, michigan)    │
│       8. mspb.gov (us merit systems protection board, washington, d.c.)    │
│       9. archive.merit.edu (merit computer network, inc, ann arbor, michigan)│
│      10. archive.merit.net (merit computer network, inc, ann arbor, michigan)│
│      11. baker.mich.net (merit computer network, inc, ann arbor, michigan) │
│      12. bc-epa.mich.net (merit computer network, inc, ann arbor, michigan)│
│      13. bhsj.merit.edu (merit computer network, inc, ann arbor, michigan) │
│      14. ciesin.mich.net (merit computer network, inc, ann arbor, michigan)│
│      15. dialip.mich.net (merit computer network, inc, ann arbor, michigan)│
│      16. dsf4.merit.edu (merit computer network, inc, ann arbor, michigan) │
│      17. econ.merit.edu (economics department, merit computer network, inc, )│
│      18. el01.merit.edu (merit computer network, inc, ann arbor, michigan) │
│      19. elf.mich.net (merit computer network, inc, ann arbor, michigan)   │
│      20. emu-yp.mich.net (merit computer network, inc, ann arbor, michigan)│
│      21. erim.mich.net (merit computer network, inc, ann arbor, michigan)  │
│                                                          16:37:45 [↓]       │
└──────────────────────────────────────────────────────────────────────────┘
```

FIGURE 10.7 ▶

Netfind yields Sue Joiner's whereabouts!

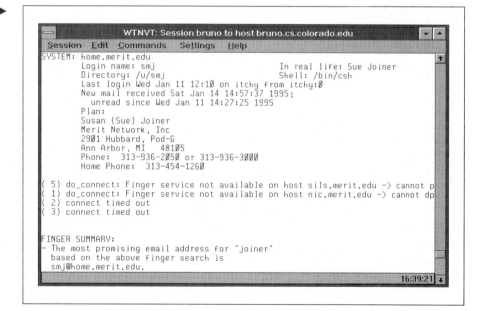

```
┌──────────────────────────────────────────────────────────────────────────┐
│           WTNVT: Session bruno to host bruno.cs.colorado.edu      [▼][▲]   │
│  Session  Edit  Commands   Settings   Help                                 │
│ SYSTEM: home.merit.edu                                                  [↑]│
│        Login name: smj                      In real life: Sue Joiner       │
│        Directory: /u/smj                    Shell: /bin/csh                 │
│        Last login Wed Jan 11 12:10 on itchy from itchy:0                    │
│        New mail received Sat Jan 14 14:57:37 1995;                          │
│          unread since Wed Jan 11 14:27:25 1995                              │
│        Plan:                                                                │
│        Susan (Sue) Joiner                                                   │
│        Merit Network, Inc                                                   │
│        2901 Hubbard, Pod-G                                                  │
│        Ann Arbor, MI   48105                                               │
│        Phone:  313-936-2050 or 313-936-3000                                 │
│        Home Phone:  313-454-1260                                            │
│                                                                            │
│ ( 5) do_connect: Finger service not available on host sils.merit.edu -> cannot p│
│ ( 1) do_connect: Finger service not available on host nic.merit.edu -> cannot dp│
│ ( 2) connect timed out                                                     │
│ ( 3) connect timed out                                                     │
│                                                                            │
│ FINGER SUMMARY:                                                            │
│ - The most promising email address for "joiner"                           │
│   based on the above finger search is                                     │
│   smj@home.merit.edu.                                                      │
│                                                          16:39:21 [↓]       │
└──────────────────────────────────────────────────────────────────────────┘
```

▶ TELNETTING TO NETFIND

If the host to which you are connected does not run Netfind, you can Telnet to one of the publicly accessible Netfind servers. The original server is at the University of Colorado. Telnet to bruno.cs.colorado.edu, as we've done here:

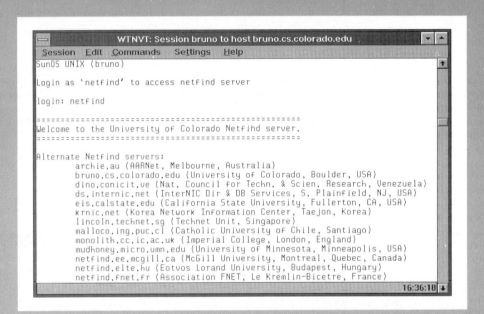

```
WTNVT: Session bruno to host bruno.cs.colorado.edu
Session  Edit  Commands  Settings  Help
SunOS UNIX (bruno)

Login as 'netfind' to access netfind server

login: netfind

========================================================
Welcome to the University of Colorado Netfind server.
========================================================

Alternate Netfind servers:
        archie.au (AARNet, Melbourne, Australia)
        bruno.cs.colorado.edu (University of Colorado, Boulder, USA)
        dino.conicit.ve (Nat. Council for Techn. & Scien. Research, Venezuela)
        ds.internic.net (InterNIC Dir & DB Services, S. Plainfield, NJ, USA)
        eis.calstate.edu (California State University, Fullerton, CA, USA)
        krnic.net (Korea Network Information Center, Taejon, Korea)
        lincoln.technet.sg (Technet Unit, Singapore)
        malloco.ing.puc.cl (Catholic University of Chile, Santiago)
        monolith.cc.ic.ac.uk (Imperial College, London, England)
        mudhoney.micro.umn.edu (University of Minnesota, Minneapolis, USA)
        netfind.ee.mcgill.ca (McGill University, Montreal, Quebec, Canada)
        netfind.elte.hu (Eotvos Lorand University, Budapest, Hungary)
        netfind.fnet.fr (Association FNET, Le Kremlin-Bicetre, France)
                                                              16:36:18
```

Login as netfind. The server limits Netfind connections, so your connection may be refused (although the one shown here was successful). However, the server lists all other Netfind servers that can be used. Select one that is reasonable for you. Remember that sometimes servers that are geographically nearby may not be good choices. Consider how much activity there is likely to be in your time zone. It might be less load on the Internet as a whole to connect to a machine that is 9 or 10 hours away, because that computer is not as busy serving its local users. (If your geography is a little rusty, you can use Gopher to find the 'Local time' displays from around the world.)

> **N O T E**
>
> **Netfind will not find everybody who can receive e-mail via the Internet. For example, there is no way to inquire about the e-mail addresses of people who are connected to the Internet through an e-mail gateway. If your correspondent uses GEnie, for example, there is no way for Netfind to discover and recommend an address for that person. If your correspondent is in a location where the X.500 directory standard has been implemented, you can use the Gopher to X.500 address gateway or you can use the Paradise system directory.**

▶ *Paradise*

Paradise is a directory user agent (dua) for an X.500 server that is located in the United Kingdom. A *user agent* is another name for a client program—just differing terminology for the same concept. In this case, the client program is an agent that consults the directory on behalf of the user (you). X.500 is an international standard for geographically hierarchical directories. The concept behind X.500 is the same as your telephone directory: you need to know the geographical location of the person you are trying to reach. Without that information, you don't know in what part of the directory to look. This is the same as needing to know the city in which your friend resides before you can consult the telephone directory for her telephone number.

X.500 is used much more in Europe than in the United States at this time. To use it, Telnet to `paradise.ulcc.ac.uk` and enter **dua** at the login prompt. You'll see the display shown in Figure 10.8.

The Paradise directory service helps you to find out information about people and the organizations they work for. The introductory material displayed when you connect reminds you that once you have provided information about a person's NAME and where they are based, the directory service will search various local and remote databases to try and find information about people with a name matching the one you have given.

FIGURE 10.8 ▶

The main Paradise instruction screen.

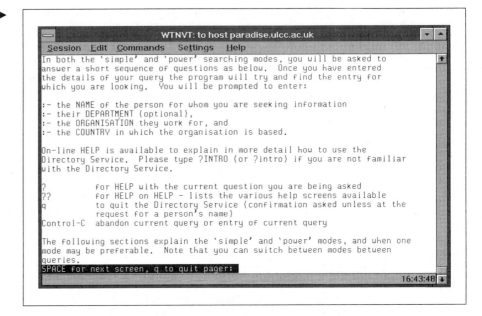

Like all services of this kind, the directory service can, of course, only find entries for people who work for organizations that are participating in this pilot service. Paradise is a good place to look for e-mail addresses for people who work for organizations concerned with international standards because the directory itself is an early implementation of the X.500 distributed directory standard.

▶ CSO Phone Books

This brief list wouldn't be complete without mentioning the CSO phone books that are kept at some university Internet sites. CSO is another client (paired with the *ph* server) program named for its original developer, the Computing Services Organization of the University of Illinois. These are searchable databases that allow you to search by name, user ID, or department. The searchable fields vary with each implementation of the database. For universities, the academic department can be a search term. This field is not usually relevant if the organization is not an academic institution and other fields may be used instead. A CSO phone book is frequently the faculty-staff directory for an institution. You can find the list of current servers relatively easily by Gophering to Notre Dame University in Indiana and choosing menu items that lead you to the World Wide "telephone" book list, as in Figure 10.9.

The methods we've just described depend upon your knowing the site through which your correspondent is connected to the Internet. This is the same problem as trying to use the directory services provided by the telephone companies in the United States. If you know approximately where the person you want to reach lives, your chances of being able to discover their number are pretty good, unless they choose to be unlisted. Pretty much the same is true of directory services available on the Internet. While the Internet itself allows you to break the barriers of time zones and geographical location, the directories haven't caught up quite yet.

FIGURE 10.9 ▶

*A Gopher search of all
the connected phone
books.*

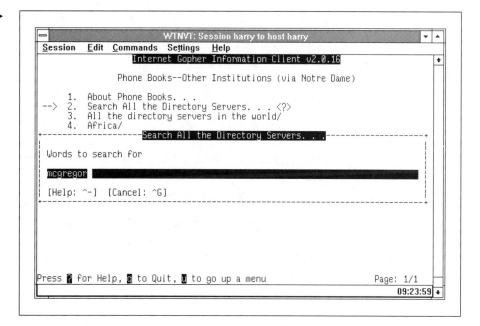

▶▶ *Finding Stuff: Files, Menus, Pictures, and Libraries*

Finding "stuff" that interests you on the Internet can be even more challenging than finding people. There are many tools, and selecting the appropriate tool may be as difficult as deciding upon the search criteria. Sometimes we think the directories for resources are even more primitive than the directories for people. In general, discovering and defining appropriate attributes to describe people and their addresses is a simpler task than defining a paradigm to describe all of human knowledge.

A number of information and library scientists have worked on describing the collections of knowledge on the Internet similarly to library collections. Library collections, however, have the advantage of being descriptions (usually) of material that is not quite as ephemeral as the collections on the Internet. We've had to change the examples used in this book several times, for example, because sites that nicely illustrated some point reorganized their collections, changed their focus, or even ceased to exist. Library collections don't usually change quite that drastically in so short a time.

There is work being done under the auspices of the Internet Engineering Task Force and similar bodies to consider the volatility of the information on the Internet and to build directories of material that include "self-identifying" and classifying attributes. At this writing, the expansion on the ideas from the Universal Resource Locators (URLs) and similar tagging mechanisms (generally called Uniform Resource Identifiers (URIs)) haven't been completed. Discussion includes concepts like Uniform Resource Names or Naming that would serve as an identifier like the International Standard Book or Serial Numbers for books and periodicals. As the ideas become more refined and as more ideas for directories are proposed, built, tested, and refined, the process of resources discovery will become more like driving the highway and less like trying to find a new sea route to India—"Beyond this point be dragons."

The Center for Networked Information Discovery and Retrieval (or CNIDR) is among the groups available to help discover and distribute appropriate tools. You can find more information about their activities via the Web at `http://kudzu.cnidr.org`.

In the meantime, here are a few tools that will help with specific tasks. Two of the most important tools for finding information on the Net, Gopher and the World Wide Web, are covered in Chapter 11.

▶ Finding Files—Archie

Archie is a program written to help you find files and the hosts upon which they are stored. The idea originated with Peter Deutsch and Alan Emtage, then of McGill University and now with Bunyip. The name Archie refers to both the client program running on many host computers and to the several Archie servers located in geographically

▶ IF ARCHIE IS NOT ON YOUR HOST

If your host does not have an Archie client, you can use it via several other methods: its World Wide Web or e-mail interfaces, for example.

To use the e-mail interface, send e-mail to any Archie server (like archie.internic.net) with the body of your message containing Archie commands. To obtain a complete list of Archie servers, send e-mail to archie.internic.net with the body of the message containing the command servers. The command help, sent to an Archie server as an e-mail message, will cause the server to send a return message, listing the commands that the Archie server supports.

You also can use Telnet to access a public Archie server. Some Archie public sites are archie.internic.net, archie.unl.edu, archie.uqam.ca, archie.ac.il, and archie.nz. Once you are connected to an Archie server, enter help to have the program display a list of the commands it will process. Be warned, however, that these sites are heavily used and consistently overloaded. To exit the help system within Archie, enter a period (.) and then press the Enter key.

separate places around the world. When you use Archie, you are using a client program to access one of the server programs. The server programs contain a directory (database) of the names of files available in directories accessible via anonymous FTP. This directory is periodically updated. To use it, you think of a word that might be used to describe what you need to find. For example, if you're looking for the program pkunzip.exe for your Windows system, you would search for the program name *pkunzip.exe*. If you are using an Archie client on a UNIX system, you would enter

```
archie pkunzip.exe
```

Figure 10.10 shows the beginning of the resulting display.

A search like this may return too many locations to process, so you might want to limit the number of sites returned by entering

```
archie -m10 pkunzip.exe
```

This will return the names of up to ten sites that have directories containing the program pkunzkip. You can then use anonymous FTP to

FIGURE 10.10 ►

Results from the command "archie pkunzip.exe."

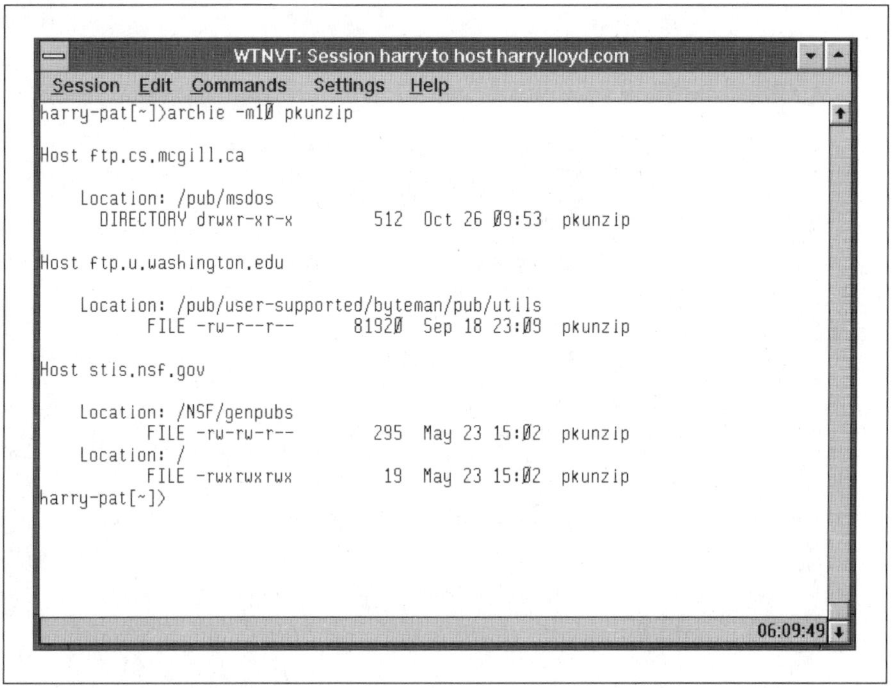

```
WTNVT: Session harry to host harry.lloyd.com
Session  Edit  Commands  Settings  Help
harry-pat[~])archie -m10 pkunzip

Host ftp.cs.mcgill.ca

        Location: /pub/msdos
          DIRECTORY druxr-xr-x          512  Oct 26 09:53  pkunzip

Host ftp.u.washington.edu

        Location: /pub/user-supported/byteman/pub/utils
              FILE -rw-r--r--         81920  Sep 18 23:09  pkunzip

Host stis.nsf.gov

        Location: /NSF/genpubs
              FILE -rw-rw-r--           295  May 23 15:02  pkunzip
        Location: /
              FILE -ruxruxrux            19  May 23 15:02  pkunzip
harry-pat[~]>

                                                            06:09:49
```

connect to those sites and see if they have what you want. You can, of course, use the information returned from your Archie search to decide which among the possible copies might be the one in which you are most interested. In UNIX systems, which constitute most of the program archives that are being searched in the Archie database, the date that the file was last modified and the number of bytes used in storing the file are displayed as part of the file information. In general, you will want to obtain the latest copy of a file. You can use the date to decide which program among the multiple ones found might be the latest copy. If there is more than one copy with the same date, or if they take the same number of bytes of storage, they are probably the same file stored in multiple places. If there are multiple files with the same date, but with differing sizes, you probably should choose the larger of the files available.

▶ *WAIS*

WAIS (pronounced "ways") is the Wide Area Information Server—a client/server application for performing full-text searches on databases containing indexed documents. Its concepts were formulated by Brewster Kahle, then of Thinking Machines Corporation, as an application for parallel-processing computers.

As with other Internet tools, the term WAIS has several overlapping meanings. It's used to describe databases of documents that have been processed for searching by the WAIS search engine, the structure of the distributed servers that form part of the WAIS technology demonstration, and the searching process itself. The directory of WAIS servers, the registry of public WAIS databases, lists 526 databases at this writing. Of course, there are other WAIS databases that are "hidden" behind gopher servers all around the Internet, because WAIS tools are a reasonable method of providing searching and indexing tools in many environments. In addition to its usefulness as a tool for finding information, WAIS is also important because it was the first demonstration of the Z39.50 information retrieval protocol in use outside the library automation community. (Z39.50 is the transport medium for data from databases of differing structures, so that a user can request data from a remote database and display it in the format he/she finds familiar. Potentially, this is a big step toward erasing the invisible boundaries between different database formats. Full implementation of Z39.50 in the library community will make it possible for the different catalog systems to exchange information.)

To be made into a WAIS-searchable database, documents are indexed—processed by WAIS programs. Each word is counted, its location to other words encoded, and the information is stored with the document itself in a database. This database is then announced to the WAIS server community and becomes part of the servers accessible using the WAIS searching mechanism throughout the Internet.

A special strength of a WAIS database is that full text documents retrieved by searching a WAIS database can be rated for their "relevance" to your search query. Weighting is determined by the number of times the search argument appears in the document as well as the particular placement of the word or words in the document. If more than one document meets your search criteria, WAIS presents the result set in the order it believes is most relevant.

Many Gopher servers provide WAIS-based searches of their menu items or document collections to enable you to much more quickly find a menu item of interest.

The WAIS directory of servers, the list of available databases, can be found at `quake.think.com`. With your WAIS client (or by using Telnet to connect to the public WAIS client at `quake.think.com`), you select a server from this list in which to search. Judicious selection of servers is important. You won't want to send a search for something in a speech by President Clinton against a database containing weather data. You can run searches against multiple databases, however. You might well want to check both the database with President Clinton's speeches and the database of agricultural market news if the topic in which you are interested is a speech of President Clinton's about agriculture and the economy.

Using WAIS

To try out WAIS, use Telnet to connect to

`quake.think.com`

When you receive the "login:" prompt, enter

`wais`

and then press the Enter key. You will be asked to supply your login name and host. Just as with anonymous FTP connections, you don't have to enter your name, but it is considered good netiquette.

Because the number of possible databases to search is large, the administrators at quake.think.com have pointed the user community to the "directory of servers" database (dofs). You can enter a search and this database will be searched to present you with a reasonable choice among the possible databases. Let's enter

```
federal text
```

as our search. The search results will be presented as a table. The WAIS "number" of the database will be presented in the upper-left corner of your display. You'll also see the "score," which describes the measured relevance of this document to your search term with 1000 being the highest score, the database from which the result came (not too useful, of course, if you are searching only one database, but very useful if you are running your search against multiple databases), the title of the document found, and the number of lines in the document.

In our example, the search on "federal text", the highest score is achieved by the database USHOUSE Bill Text. This database, maintained by the United States House of Representatives, contains the complete text of all the bills introduced into the United States Legislature. If you retrieve the document you'll see a description of this database, its hours of availability, the search operations supported by the server, and so on.

WAIS software itself, the servers and the clients, is available from WAIS, Inc. A public-domain version, called FreeWAIS, is supported and dispensed by the Center for Networked Information Directory and Retrieval (CNIDR).

▶▶ *Lost at Sea? There's Help on the Way*

Although the most common metaphor for the Internet is the "Info-Bahn" or "Information Superhighway," looking for resources can make you feel more like a Renaissance seaman instead of the confident highway driver you probably are. The sea of resources is vast and ever changing; the landmarks are sometimes distant, and sometimes seemingly not related to the landscape about you. You need to learn to navigate from point to point and to be willing to explore no matter where you come ashore. Sometimes it feels like the Internet is full of sharks, as well!

In the next chapter we'll explore two of the most important tools for finding information on the Internet, Gopher and the World Wide Web. As you'll see, these services make navigating cyberspace much easier (and fun, too).

## CHAPTER 11

Cruising the Net with Gopher and the World Wide Web

►► **T**he tools we have talked about so far have a significant limitation: in order to use them you must already have an address for a host computer or the name of the file or person you're interested in. This next chapter is about serendipity and starting points: Gopher and the World Wide Web. These two tools have done the most to excite the interest of ordinary, nontechnical people in the possibilities of the Internet. Both Gopher and the World Wide Web offer views of cyberspace that don't require you to have an exact address, to know exactly what you are looking for, or to type a command with exactly the right characters in order to find something. You start from some point (and it doesn't really matter too much which point), and you can wander around in cyberspace just by taking "jumps" or links to connections that interest you from the display at which you are looking.

NetCruiser, on this book's Companion Disk 1, gives you access to both Gopher and the Web.

Internet users have coined the term *gopherspace* to describe the whole set of computers with Gopher servers and the information they contain. Once you've connected to any Gopher site, the information at all of the sites is available to you, through a hierarchical system of menus. These menus are lists of pointers or links. If you choose to exercise a link, you are "transported" to the next menu until you are viewing a document or downloading a graphical image file, for example. The links may point you to other files on the Gopher server you're connected to, or to files stored on computers halfway around the world. The strength of gopherspace is that you, as a gopherspace-traveler, do not need to know where any of the files are stored.

The Web is similar to gopherspace in that you don't need to know the address of the page that you wish to reach as long as you can find a page to which it is linked. When you are viewing a Web page, you see visually distinct "links" to other Web pages. The links may be underlined, for example, or displayed in a second color. The main difference between a Web page and a Gopher menu is that on a Web page the designer is free to give more information about the linked item.

Of course, if you do have an exact citation, Web browsers and Gopher clients allow you to enter these addresses directly. And most Web browsers and Gopher clients have a bookmark facility. A bookmark is a link, stored with your client, that "remembers" the address of the page or menu where you placed it. Ever after, when you call up the bookmark, the stored link takes you directly to the specific place that you wanted to remember. For example, if you place a bookmark in the Global Schoolhouse Gopher server (`gopher.cnidr.org`), every time you select that bookmark your client will open the Global Schoolhouse page. This feature allows you to keep special Internet sites that are particularly useful to you at your fingertips.

►► *Gopher*

Gopher is one of the most exciting developments in Internet tools to come along. Gopher allows novice users to find many of the cool things we Internet fanatics rave about, without having to be a technical expert to do it. More than that, a Gopher server is easy to build and maintain, and many people and organizations are finding it easier to become Internet information providers.

Gopher is an Internet navigation tool that allows you to find and retrieve information using a hierarchy of menus and files. Your Gopher client connects to a Gopher server (like the Michigan State University Gopher illustrated in Figure 11.1) and, using the menu structure, displays another menu, a document or file, an index, or a connection to another remote application using Telnet. The Gopher protocol allows all the Gopher clients on the Internet to talk with all the other "registered" Gopher servers on the Internet. Each time you select another menu, Gopher connects to the linked server, retrieves the next menu level or the file wanted, and returns control to your local client. Gopher both uses Internet resources efficiently and allows you to find and use information dispersed throughout the world.

Gopherspace is the universe of Gopher servers connected to the Internet. Each server has a location (Internet address and port number)

FIGURE 11.1 ▶

The main Gopher menu at Michigan State University (gopher.msu.edu).

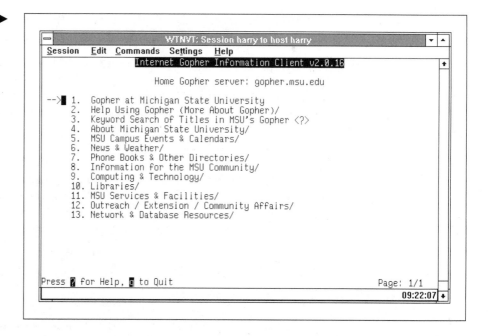

of its own and links to other Gopher servers. (A port number is just the equivalent of a telephone at which the Gopher server will listen for connection requests.) Most Gopher servers are registered with the Mother Gopher at the University of Minnesota. Its menu contains the option All The Gopher Servers In The World, which you can select to see a list of all the registered Gopher servers. With Gopher you can connect to each and every one of them, regardless of their physical location in the world. A Gopher server must be "up" to listen for your connection, however. Sometimes computers break down or Net connections are lost, and sometimes people just turn off their computers. When this happens, of course, you can't connect to the Gopher.

In general, gopherspace is organized geographically. For example, if you want to see information from South America, from a Gopher menu with links to other servers, choose

```
Other gophers
South America
```

Gopher will display a menu that gives you access to South American Gopher servers.

Gopher clients have been written for most of the computing platforms that support the TCP/IP protocol suite. Some of these clients really take advantage of the available user interface. For example, TurboGopher offers the familiar Macintosh point-and-click interface, with buttons and menus. Others run on host computers and operate using the VT100 terminal emulation interface. Note that some Gopher objects (the type of files that Gopher can access) cannot be displayed on all clients. If you are attached as a VT100 terminal to a host computer, you will not be able to see the pictures or hear the audio that can be stored on a server and transmitted by choosing a particular Gopher menu item. But VT100 Gopher clients do serve to connect the user to information located all over the Internet, and they have the advantage that the network connections of many host systems are much better than those of most home systems. This means that you will be able to move large amounts of information to your site more quickly if you are using a Gopher client on a larger host system.

Many Gopher clients will also let you send material back to yourself or to anyone you choose by e-mail or file transfer, right from the Gopher session.

▶ *A Brief History of Gopher*

Gopher was developed at the University of Minnesota to provide a better interface to distribute campus information for local users. As with many good ideas, the charm and simplicity of Gopher appealed to many people. Gopher servers and Gopher clients soon began to pop up all over the Internet. To find more information about Gopher development and to obtain program source code for Gopher servers and clients, you can look in the computer called boombox.micro.umn.edu. This computer supports both FTP and Gopher access. You can Gopher there directly by entering boombox.micro.umn.edu with an "open a connection" command that you can find in most Gopher clients; or, from any Gopher, you can choose

```
Other gophers
North America
USA
Minnesota
University of Minnesota
```

Gopher and the
World Wide Web

ch.
11

This path, while not direct, demonstrates one of the nicest things about Gopher—the ability to pilot around through many locations and still end up with something useful. Not all people find (or want to find) information in the same manner.

▶ *Finding Gopher Clients*

If you have a host-dial account on a BBS or other service, chances are you already have access to a VT100-style Gopher client. Type **gopher** at the main system prompt to call up your local Gopher client.

However, if you are working with TCP/IP-based software on your personal workstation, you will want to install a Gopher client on your workstation. As the originator of Gopher, the University of Minnesota maintains an excellent anonymous FTP site (listed above) with the clients they support, as well as newly submitted clients from contributors in the worldwide Gopher community.

In Appendix G you will also find a list of FTP archives across the world, many of which have Gopher clients available.

Most popular Gopher clients are capable of dealing with flat ASCII files, folders, and index searches under Gopher. Many clients are also capable of handling the common still-image format GIF (popularized by CompuServe). The NeXT and Sun workstations can play sound (.SND) files, which means they can play audio files delivered over the network.

Most of the clients come bundled with several files in an archive format appropriate to the computer and operating system you will be using them on. Most also have DOC or READ ME files that assist in using the clients.

Gopher Clients for DOS Systems

Ugopher This DOS Gopher client was developed at the University of Texas. It presents a very simple full-screen interface, needs little memory, and can launch user-specified file browsers and GIF (still-image) viewers. You should retrieve Ugopher as well as a shareware file browser (LIST) and a shareware GIF viewer (VPIC). Ugopher will function without these tools but will use a limited browser and will be unable to view GIFs.

PC Gopher II   This is the standard PC client from the University of Minnesota. Unlike Ugopher, PC Gopher II presents a colorful, pseudo-Windows environment, complete with multiple windows and scroll bars. (However, it is a TurboVision application that runs under MS-DOS; it is not a Windows program.) It also supports bookmarks. PC Gopher II takes up a fair amount of memory and there have been reports of users running out of memory with it.

▶ *Windows Gopher Clients*

There are two clients available for IBM PC under Windows. Goph-Book and HGopher both need Windows 3.1 and WINSOCK.DLL. These two clients have been tested using Windows 3.1, WIN-SOCK.DLL, and PCTCP software 2.2.

GophBook   This client is available via FTP from Minnesota at `boom-box.micro.umn.edu` in /pub/gopher/Windows/gophbook. Items in this gopher client are displayed as pages in a book. GophBook can display images when used in conjunction with a Windows viewer. You can also play sound, and save and edit bookmarks.

HGopher   This client is available via FTP from `lister.cc.ic.ac.uk` in pub/wingopher. It uses a familiar Windows interface. In addition to the common features found in GophBook, HGopher can support user-specified "viewers" for displaying almost any type of document. The `lister.cc.ic.ac.uk` FTP site also includes several Windows viewers in the pub/wingopher/viewers directory.

Apple Macintosh Gopher Clients

Our favorite client for the Macintosh is Turbogopher, from the University of Minnesota. It is faster than earlier Macintosh clients, uses icons to distinguish document types, and opens multiple windows on screen as necessary. Turbogopher is capable of launching GIF viewers installed on your Mac.

Generic UNIX Gopher Clients

Curses   This client, from the University of Minnesota, provides a simple full-screen interface (but can also support display of GIF files).

Xgopher The other UNIX client is Xgopher, by Allan Tuchman of the University of Illinois. This client supports the X Windows user interface. The client is available on `ftp.x.org`.

Using a Web Browser as a Gopher Client

You can, of course, use your Web browser as a gopher client: open the URL `gopher://`*gopher name*, and the Web browser will connect you to the appropriate Gopher server.

▶ How to Use Gopher

To use Gopher from a UNIX host system Gopher client, type:

```
gopher
```

This command will connect you to the local or default Gopher server for your host. On the Netcom host systems, for example, this command is the same as entering

```
gopher gopher.netcom.com
```

The Netcom Gopher server will then display the top-level menu, as shown in Figure 11.2.

As an example, we will find and retrieve the local access numbers for Netcom's network. From the displayed menu, we see that the second menu entry is

```
Information about NETCOM
```

This looks like a reasonable place to find information about the access numbers, so we select the item (using the arrow keys) and press Enter. This connects the Gopher client to the Gopher server and requests a connection to the link specified by this menu entry.

When this connection is made, you'll see the menu shown in Figure 11.3.

From here, you can move your cursor to the Netcom Local Access Numbers entry and press the Enter key. Again, this connects the Gopher client to the Gopher server and requests a connection to the link specified. The server will then pass the specified file of access numbers to your client, which will display them on your screen (Figure 11.4).

FIGURE 11.2 ▶

*The Netcom Gopher's
top-level menu.*

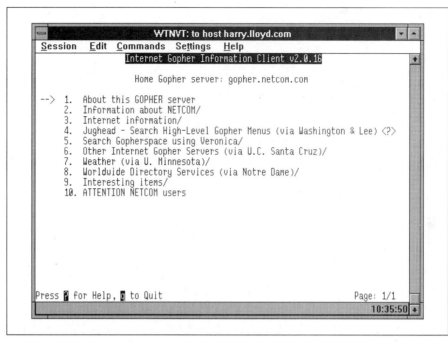

FIGURE 11.3 ▶

*The Information about
Netcom menu.*

FIGURE 11.4 ▶

The Netcom access numbers located by our Gopher search.

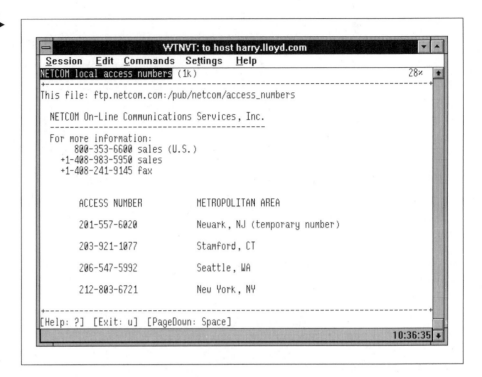

```
┌─────────────────────────────────────────────────────────────────────┐
│ ─        WTNVT: to host harry.lloyd.com                        ▼ ▲ │
│ Session   Edit  Commands  Settings   Help                          │
│ NETCOM local access numbers (1k)                             28%  ▲ │
│ +--------------------------------------------------------------+    │
│ This file: ftp.netcom.com:/pub/netcom/access_numbers               │
│                                                                    │
│   NETCOM On-Line Communications Services, Inc.                     │
│   -------------------------------------------                      │
│                                                                    │
│   For more information:                                            │
│       800-353-6600 sales (U.S.)                                    │
│     +1-408-983-5950 sales                                          │
│     +1-408-241-9145 fax                                            │
│                                                                    │
│        ACCESS NUMBER            METROPOLITAN AREA                  │
│                                                                    │
│        201-557-6020             Newark, NJ (temporary number)     │
│                                                                    │
│        203-921-1077             Stamford, CT                       │
│                                                                    │
│        206-547-5992             Seattle, WA                        │
│                                                                    │
│        212-803-6721             New York, NY                       │
│                                                                    │
│ +--------------------------------------------------------------+    │
│ [Help: ?]  [Exit: u]  [PageDown: Space]                            │
│                                                      10:36:35  ▼  │
└─────────────────────────────────────────────────────────────────────┘
```

▶ Things You Can Expect to Do

Gopher clients offer some other features besides connecting you to documents and other files. The most important of these is saving the item you've retrieved. Some clients move the desired files to a host system and you will need to download them to your local machine. Others save directly to the local machine. Some send them to you via your e-mail account. Again, you will need to consult the help files in your Gopher client software to see how it can best serve you.

Sometimes your don't really want the file itself, you just want to be able to get to this "gopherhole" again directly. Consider the electronic books stored in various servers on the Internet. Or the size of the CIA World Factbook, a reference work with information gathered about countries all over the world (see Chapter 23). You don't really need a personal copy of the material—you just need to get to it again promptly when you want. This is perhaps the most wonderful feature of gopherspace—the fact that multiple copies of the same work don't need to be made and yet many, many people can read the material. It is a magnificent saving in time, disk space, and resources.

To keep your own personal reference pointer to the Factbook, investigate the ability of your client to store "bookmarks." These are files that contain pointers that link information to a specific item in a specific Gopher server menu. Unfortunately, bookmarks work at the item level; there is not yet a way to go to exactly the line you were reading when you stopped reading.

In large documents, like the country entries in the CIA World Factbook, it is nice to be able to go quickly to a specific known point. Or to find whether a specific point is present in the file. To serve this function, many Gopher clients have a search capability. You select the Search option, enter the word or words you are looking for, and the Gopher client moves your cursor to the point in the document where that word appears.

For navigation within a menu and a server, Gopher uses the command Back or Up. The spatial metaphor refers to what you've done before arriving at your current point. If you choose this command, you will be returned to the last menu you viewed before this one. You can continue to choose Back until you reach the menu at which you entered gopherspace for this session. Sometimes this "gopherhole" is called "home." To go back to the previous spot, most Gopher clients use the left-arrow key.

▶ *What Kinds of Information Will I Find in Gopherspace?*

Information in gopherspace can be any of the following:

- another menu (sometimes represented by a folder icon).
- a document, a graphic file, or a text file (sometimes represented by a document icon).
- a search entry (sometimes represented by a magnifying glass icon).
- a pointer to a text-based remote login (Telnet).
- a pointer to a software gateway to another service (Usenet or FTP).

▶ *Veronica and Jughead*

Veronica (Very Easy Rodent-Oriented Net-wide Index to Computer Archives) and Jughead are the Archie services of gopherspace. They construct menus for you, based on "keywords" you enter. To try either of these tools, bring up the main Veronica Gopher, at `gopher.scs.unr.edu`. From the main menu, select either Veronica or Jughead. As in Figure 11.5, you'll be asked to enter the word or words you would like to find—the *search argument*. Veronica searches the menu titles of the Gopher servers that are known in gopherspace and constructs a personal menu showing the titles available for you to access. Figure 11.6 shows the "personal Gopher" displayed for the word *business*.

Jughead does much the same thing, but it looks only at the higher level Gopher menu titles rather than all the available menus on all levels. Jughead searches are occasionally restricted to searching the menus

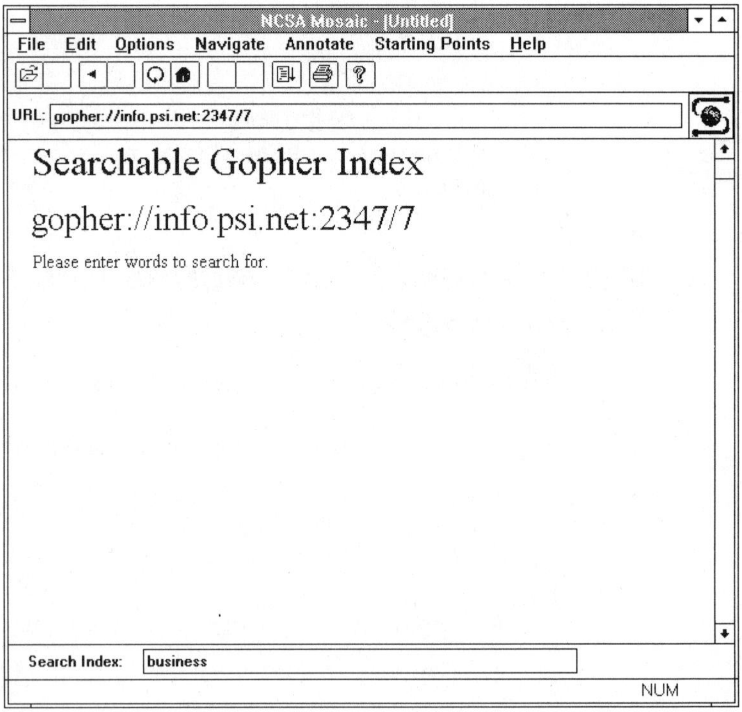

FIGURE 11.5 ▶

Starting a Veronica search through the World Wide Web.

FIGURE 11.6 ▶

Results of a Veronica search on the word "business."

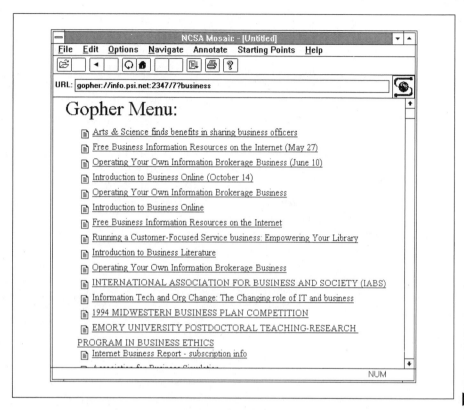

that appear in a particular Gopher. This service is offered by the particular Gopher server and must have been set up by the Gopher administrator or designer at the site. Once you have received the search results from your Veronica or Jughead search, you interact with the Jughead- or Veronica-built menu just the way you would with any other Gopher.

 ▶ ▶ **M A S T E R   W O R D S**

> **Sometimes Jughead searches are called "Search Gopherspace by Top-Level Menus" rather than Jughead.**

As an example of such a menu, from the Netcom Gopher, choose the Jughead search menu item. When you receive the prompt asking for your search term, enter the word **telecommunications**. At this writing, using the UNIX client on the Netcom host systems, this search returned a menu with 11 screens of entries with the word "telecommunications" in their menu title. (Figure 11.7 shows the first of these screens.) From this menu, you can move your cursor to an item in which you might be interested and press Enter. The Gopher client will then connect to the Gopher server and, using the link provided by the menu, retrieve the item you have chosen. If the item is a document, you can use e-mail to send it to an e-mail address or you can download it. You work with a menu built by Jughead the same way you would with any other Gopher menu.

FIGURE 11.7 ►

Results of a Jughead search on the word "telecommunications."

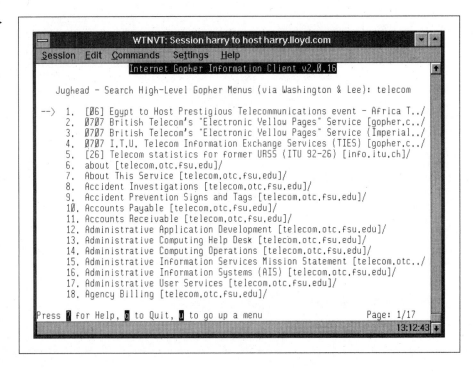

Many Gophers display pages that are not self-identifying. That is, you cannot tell by looking at the page where the information came from. Usually, that is not important. But if you see an announcement of a lecture you would like to attend, for example, it would be nice to know in which town, state and country the lecture is being given. Most clients have a way to display the fully qualified name and address of the server from which information is being shown. Using the help screen (press "?" in most clients), you can discover how your client displays this information. In some clients it's called "technical info about this item or directory." In most line-mode clients, press ^ to show the fully qualified name. This name might help you locate the site from which the information is being displayed.

► *Taking Advantage of Geography*

With its easy-to-use navigation tools and hierarchical structure, Gopher lends itself to browsing. This is particularly true if there's a geographical focus to your interest. If you want information about South America, for example, you might just wander through the

```
All the gophers in the World
South America
```

hierarchy. By selecting links that look promising, and using the Up and Back options, you can move around the globe, looking for information in a quick, but relatively unstructured way. Sometimes, browsing in this manner will help you find information about a topic that you wouldn't have thought about, or whose specific category name you didn't know. Not to mention, of course, that it's fun!

▶▶ *The World Wide Web*

The World Wide Web (also called WWW, or W3, or simply the Web) is another Internet navigation tool that helps you to find and retrieve information, using links to other WWW pages. Web links are stored within the page itself and when you wish to "jump" to the page that is linked, you select the "hotspot" or "anchor." This technique is sometimes called *hypermedia* or *hypertext*. If you've used a Windows-based help system in which you click on an underlined phrase to jump to that topic, you're already familiar with hypermedia. Figure 11.8 shows the "home page" (starting point) for the Web presented by CERN, the organization that created this tool.

The Web is a "sister" service to Gopher. The basic difference between the two tools is that a Gopher link can only be represented by a relatively short title on a menu and a Web link doesn't have this restriction. Sometimes it is very difficult to organize your information into a series of menus. Sometimes your information is best represented by lists within paragraphs of description, or by an image, or by a list of items

FIGURE 11.8 ▶

The CERN Web "home page."

that have associated paragraphs of description. And sometimes, it's nice to just click on a map of the world to select the information servers located in Italy.

WWW, because of its ability to incorporate FTP, Gopher, and other tools, is fast becoming the most widely used Internet navigation tool. Add to this a snazzy graphic interface and point-and-click capability, and we see the beginnings of a truly democratic Internet interface.

WWW clients on the Internet can display pages from any of the nearly 5000 Web servers. Each time you choose a link, WWW connects to the appropriate server, retrieves the next page wanted, and returns control to the local client. Once the document has been retrieved, the link is broken. This means that the server does not have to keep the link open while you read the document. WWW is thus an efficient method of finding and using information widely dispersed throughout the world. Figure 11.9 shows the beginning of the geographically organized list of Web servers.

FIGURE 11.9 ▶

A listing of known Web pages in the world.

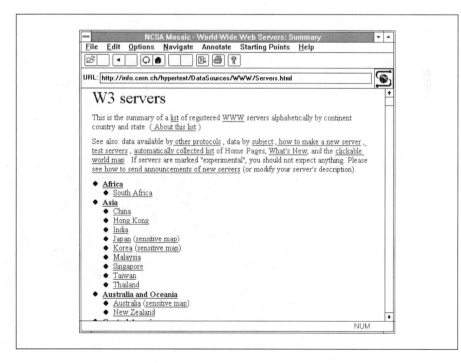

Web pages are truly multimedia: they may contain text, graphic images, moving pictures, sound files, and other types of electronic information. Figures 11.10 through 11.13 show the variety of graphic images available on the Web.

Not all Web clients can handle all the various media available. Even if your client can process the information, your particular configuration may not be able to display it. For example, Figure 11.14 is a display of the White House home page, only shown through the line-mode browser Lynx rather than the graphic display tool Mosaic. You can see text only, rather than the pictures (although you can download the pictures and display them if you have a local GIF viewer).

Fortunately, the designers of the clients know about this limitation and make allowances for differing configurations. If a page contains something that the client cannot process, it will not attempt to display it. Some well-known Web clients include Cornell Law's Cello, University of Kansas' Lynx (a very nice text-based client, illustrated in Figure 11.15), NetScape Communications Corporation's NetScape, and the National

FIGURE 11.10 ►

A map from the National Estuary program.

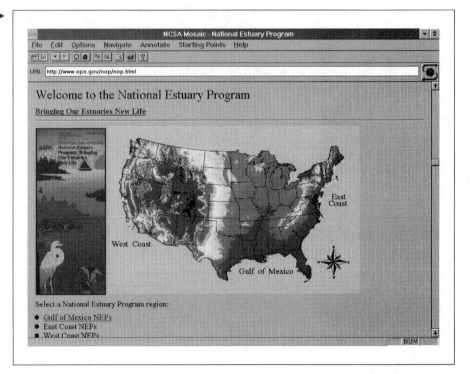

FIGURE 11.11

The Future Fantasy Bookstore in Palo Alto, California.

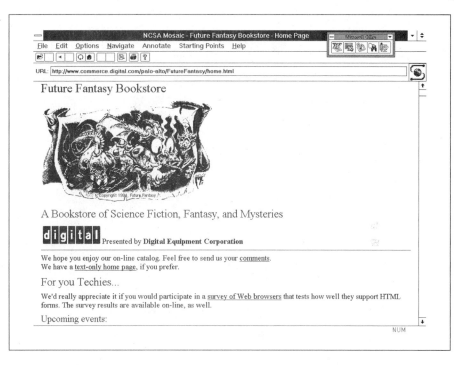

FIGURE 11.12

Virtually Reality, the 3-D rendered Cyberspace Comic ("Orca Winfrey"). Artwork by Eric Scroger.

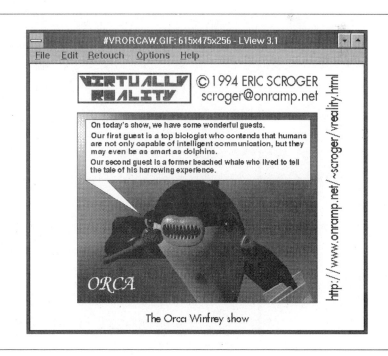

FIGURE 11.13 ▶

*An Interactive Citizens'
Handbook: the White
House.*

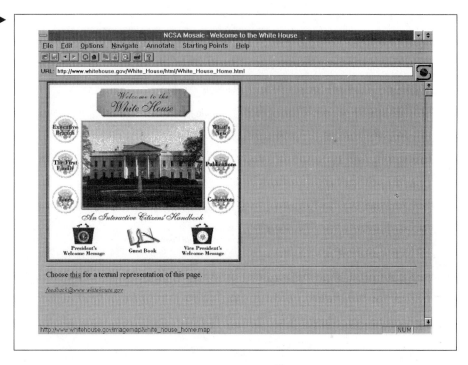

FIGURE 11.14 ▶

*White House Web
page through a Lynx
Web browser.*

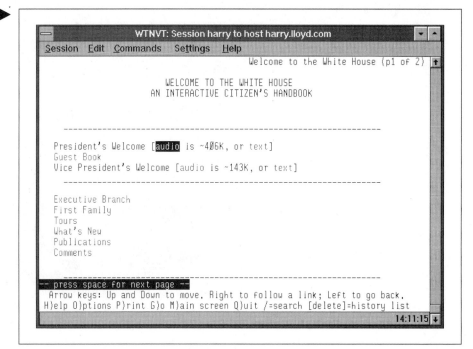

FIGURE 11.15

Reading a home page with Lynx.

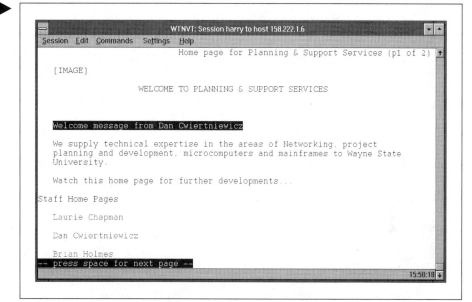

```
┌──────────────────────────────────────────────────────────────┐
│ ▭              WTNVT: Session harry to host 158.222.1.6    ▼ ▲ │
│ Session  Edit  Commands  Settings  Help                       │
│                     Home page for Planning & Support Services (p1 of 2) ▲│
│      [IMAGE]                                                    │
│                  WELCOME TO PLANNING & SUPPORT SERVICES        │
│                                                                │
│      Welcome message from Dan Cwiertniewicz                    │
│      We supply technical expertise in the areas of Networking, project │
│      planning and development, microcomputers and mainframes to Wayne State │
│      University.                                               │
│                                                                │
│      Watch this home page for further developments...          │
│ Staff Home Pages                                               │
│      Laurie Chapman                                            │
│      Dan Cwiertniewicz                                         │
│      Brian Holmes                                              │
│ -- press space for next page --                                │
│                                                      15:58:18 ↓ │
└──────────────────────────────────────────────────────────────┘
```

Center for Supercomputer Application's (NCSA) Mosaic. You'll see how to find these programs shortly. Netcom's NetCruiser package also includes a Web browser.

Some newer Web pages include forms you can fill out or database front ends to let you search for specific patterns or words. Some even let you send e-mail or comments on the Web page itself. Not all browsers can handle the forms in these pages: most of the graphical front ends are "forms-capable," but many of the simple line-mode interfaces (like the "www" tool) are not.

World Wide Web was originally developed at CERN, the high-energy physics research center in Switzerland. The Web interface is designed so that you can choose to follow a Web "filament" around the Web as far as you like by selecting a spot on the "page" displayed on your screen. The locus of the WWW system is the "home page." This is the place from which the server to which you are connected starts. The ultimate home page for WWW is the home page at CERN (http://info.cern.ch). Giving Web page citations, called URLs (Universal Resource Locators), lets you indicate the filament of the Web you wish to follow or you may jump directly to particular points on the Web.

► **UNIVERSAL RESOURCE LOCATORS**

URLs are the resource locators used by the World Wide Web as explicit addresses for information. Each one contains an access method/resource type (file, or Gopher, or http, for example); a host name; perhaps a TCP/IP port number; and perhaps a directory/file path. These explicit strings are used by the Web-traversing programs to connect the user directly to a particular document or page. Some examples of URLs follow. Use this form to describe a specific file of text:

```
file://FTP.yoda.edu/pub/doc/file.txt
```

or

```
FTP://FTP.yoda.edu/pub/doc/file.txt
```

Use this form to describe a specific directory:

```
file://FTP.empire.mil/pub
```

Use this form to describe how to get to a Gopher using a specific port number:

```
gopher://swamp.dagoba.edu:1234
```

And use this form to connect to a specific document (the complete directory path is specified) using the specific port

```
http://www.ice.hoth.org:1234/pub/doc/force.html
```

If you have never used the Web, the easiest way to find out more about it is to take a tour. You could try the Guided Tours page that Glee put together for Netcom's NetCruiser. Start whatever client you have available by opening the NetCruiser Homeport page (`http://www.net-com.com/netcom/cruiser.html`). From this page, you can jump to a Web overview, view and jump to a list of home pages, and learn more about services available via the Web. You will also find demonstrations of the interconnections among Gopher, FTP sites, and the Web. You can go to and use Gopher and FTP servers with your Web client by simply indicating the type of server in the URL. To go to a Gopher, for example, enter gopher://gopher.netcom.com/ or gopher://gopher.isoc.org/ wherever your client allows you to specify a particular URL. To go to an FTP server, for example, enter ftp://ftp.netcom.com/ in the dialog box.

More introductory information about the Web can be found at the CERN laboratory in Switzerland. You might want to see how many ways there are to reach that page by using the information you have so far to navigate.

▶ Finding Web Clients

As with Gopher, you may already have access to a WWW browser client. If you have a host account on someone else's system, try typing **lynx** or **www** at the main system prompt.

Below is a list of WWW client software available for most common systems. You will need to bring them to your computer via anonymous FTP, and install them (following the instructions in the README and doc files). Unless otherwise listed, the following browser clients are available via anonymous FTP from the archive at info.cern.ch.

Terminal-Based Browsers

You will probably already find these installed on your host-based account; if not, consult your local systems administrator to get them installed.

WWW Line Mode Browser The CERN Line Mode Browser is a character-based World Wide Web Browser. It is developed for use on hosts that support VT100 terminal emulation. Binaries are available for most UNIX varieties and many other platforms as www*.tar.Z.

"Lynx" Full Screen Browser This is a hypertext browser for VT100s using full screen, arrow keys, highlighting, and so on. It is much preferred over the www line mode browser. Sources and precompiled binaries are available for rs6000, sun3, sun4, NeXT, VMS(multinet). Code is available by anonymous FTP from ftp2.cc.ukans.edu.

Windows Web Browsers

Cello This program allows you full access to the information resources of the Internet. It can run World Wide Web, Gopher, FTP, CSO/ph/qi, and Usenet News retrievals, and it runs other protocols (WAIS, Hytelnet, Telnet, and TN3270) through external clients and public gateways. It can be used to view hypermedia documents, including inline images, text, and digital sounds and movies. Cello runs under Microsoft Windows on any IBM PC with a 386SX chip or better. You will get better performance with at least 4 Megabytes of RAM and a 16 MHz or faster chip. You'll also need Winsock software from another source, either software supplied by your network vendor or a publicly available package such as Peter Tattam's Trumpet Winsock. Cello has been used successfully with Winsocks from all leading software vendors. Winsock and Cello are available via anonymous FTP from `ftp.cica.indiana.edu.`

Mosaic for Windows NCSA Mosaic is a full-featured, forms-capable WWW browser. It supports World Wide Web, Gopher, FTP natively, and other protocols either by emulation or through public gateways. Mosaic for Windows runs under Microsoft Windows on any IBM PC with a 386SX chip or better. You will have better performance with at least 4 Megabytes of RAM. You'll also need Winsock software from another source, either software supplied by your network vendor or a publicly available package such as Peter Tattam's Trumpet Winsock. Mosaic for Windows is available via anonymous FTP from ftp.ncsa.uiuc.edu in PC/Mosaic. Other forms of Mosaic are available commercially; see Chapter 6.

WinWeb A full-featured, graphic WWW browser employing standard Windows interface. To install it you will need Windows 3.1, and 4 Megabytes of RAM. You should also have 5 Megabytes of space free on your hard drive to install the software. EINet WinWeb is available by anonmyous FTP from `ftp.einet.net.`

Netscape The newest addition to the Windows-based WWW browsers. It is a full-featured, forms-capable browser, and in addition many users like the way it handles inline graphics and other media better than the other three browsers. To install it you will need Windows 3.1 and 4 Megabytes of RAM. You should also have 5 Megabytes of space free on your hard drive to install the software. You'll also need Winsock software from another source, either software supplied by your network vendor or a publicly available package such as Peter Tattam's Trumpet

Winsock. Netscape has been used successfully with Winsocks from all leading software vendors. Winsock and Netscape are available via anonymous ftp from `ftp.cica.indiana.edu`.

Sybex's *Surfing the Internet with Netscape* (Daniel A. Tauber and Brenda Kienan, 1995) provides complete information for getting and using the Netscape Web browser and includes TCP/IP software on disk in the form of Chameleon Sampler.

Macintosh Web Browsers

Mosaic for Macintosh Like its cousins, NCSA Mosaic for Macintosh is a full-featured, forms-capable browser. It is available via anonymous FTP from `ftp.ncsa.uiuc.edu`.

Samba A basic browser, available from CERN. It does not support many of the advanced WWW features. To install Samba on your system, you must install Mac-TCP (at least version 1.1.1, to avoid a bug in earlier versions). The binary can be picked up from `info.cern.ch` on /ftp/pub/www/bin/mac by anonymous FTP.

MacWeb This is EINet's full-feature World Wide Web client. EINet MacWeb is available by anonymous FTP from the host named `ftp.einet.net`, in the file named /einet/mac/macweb/macweb.lat-est.sea.hqx. In order to run MacWeb, your Macintosh must be configured with System 7 and MacTCP 2.0.2 (MacTCP 2.0.4 is recommended). Use StuffIt Expander (or an equivalent program) to de-binhex and expand the archive.

▶ How to Navigate within the Web

When you start most Web clients, you begin with the display of a home page. This page could be one that points to descriptions of the organization that sponsored the development of the client. Or it could be one you constructed from links that are meaningful and useful to you. If your organization has a home page, displaying it when each client is called up onto the display screen is a good way to remind people where they "are" in the Web. (If your organization doesn't have a home page, you might want to recommend constructing one. Every organization on the Internet should have a home page. Presenting a home page allows you to tell other Internet users who you are and where you are and what your organization does. You can list the products or services that you provide and present links to information about your organization. Chapter 4's discussion of options for connecting to the Internet includes a list of "information publishers"—companies that will construct and maintain a Web page for your organization. The fees they charge vary widely. Chapter 19, "Building the Resource," shows how to construct your own Web page and offers examples of well-designed Web pages.)

From the home page you can select to move to any link by moving your cursor to the hotspot or anchor. To take the jump, click your mouse or Press Enter.

Most Web clients also provide a method of moving directly to a specific page. This is called "Opening a URL" (pronounced *Yew-R-El*). To do this, you use the command or action required by the client to open, and then enter the URL in the space provided. If you are using Net-Cruiser, enter the URL in the center dialog box at the top of the screen page. If you are using Lynx, type **g** for "go," followed by the URL.

MASTER WORDS

URLs are frequently case-sensitive. Remember that the part after the host name is the complete file name for the file you want to retrieve. If you fail to connect to a specific Web page on a direct jump, chances are you've mistyped the URL.

▶ Things You Can Expect to Do

Web clients offer some other features besides connecting you to documents and other files. At its simplest, each variety of Web server will let you print a file. You can choose to print it to a printer, to a file, or you can send it to yourself by e-mail. All of these are in the Print menu on most clients. You can also choose to save these items as PostScript files, HTML (Web source format), or just plain typescript. Some clients move the desired files to a host system, and you will need to download them to your local machine. Others save directly to the local machine. Again, you will need to consult the help files in your client software to see how it can best serve you.

MASTER WORDS

Some clients save the pages in HTML format—that is, containing the HyperText Markup Language codes—so that you can use the page locally as a jump point, either as you saved it or as you modified it.

Sometimes your don't really want to store the page itself, you just want to be able to get to it again directly. In large documents, it is nice to be able to go quickly to a specific known point, or to see whether a specific word or string is present in the file. To serve this function, many Web clients have a search capability. You select the Search option and enter the word or words you want to find, and the Web client moves your cursor to the point in the document where that word appears.

You can also add to your bookmark list. In many Web browsers this called the "hot list." Under the Navigation menu in most browsers, look for an item that lets you add the current displayed page to the hot list.

For navigation within a page and within a server, Web clients use commands like Forward or Down as well as Back or Up. This means you can move around in the "history" of your recent Web travels. Back returns you to the page from whence you just came. Forward will take you to the next page in your history of Web travels, if you have returned back along the path; it's meaningless unless you have a history path to travel. You can continue to choose Back until you reach the point at which you entered the Web for the current session. This page is called "home" for the session.

The final important thing to learn how to do with your Web client is to stop the display of a very long page. Sometimes you will start the display of a page that contains so much information that you decide you don't want to wait for it to be delivered to your client. You should be able to choose some sort of Halt, Stop, or Abort command that will stop the current activity and redisplay the currently loaded page. Look for a "stop sign" or something like that at the top of the page.

▶ *Global Links*

Here are some fun links and interesting entries from around the Globe.

Clickable Map of the World:

`http://wings.buffalo.edu/world`

An Entry Point for Asia:

`http://coombs.anu.edu.au/WWWVl-AsianStudies.html`

Australia's Matilda in Cyberspace:

`http://info.anu.edu.au:1066/pubs/Matilda/index.html`

Pictures from Brazil:

`http://guarani.cos.ufrj.br:8090/Rio/Todas.html`

Information about Italy:

`http://www.mi.cnr.it/NIR-IT/NIR-map.html`

Information about Japan:

`http://fuji.stanford.edu/japan_information/japan_informa-tion_guide.html`

Information about the Netherlands:

`http://www.tno.nl/NL-www/nl-info.html`

Information about Norway:

`http://www.service.uit.no/homepage-no`

Information about Peru:

`http://www.rcp.net.pe/rcp.html`

Information about Portugal:

`http://s700.uminho.pt/Portugal/general_info.html`

Russian and Eastern European Studies:

`http://www.pitt.edu/~cjp/rees.html`

United Nations UNICEF:

```
gopher://hqfans.unicef.org/
```

Le WebLouvre:

```
http://mistral.enst.fr/~pioch/louvre
```

▶▶ *Special Indexes*

A number of specially constructed indexes that are available through-out the Internet are particularly helpful in finding things via Gopher and the Web. Many of these indexes are used as references throughout this book. The people who have constructed them have provided a service that is almost without parallel. It is efforts like these that show how effective a collaborative environment the Internet can be. Someone needed to provide a list that either demonstrated many of the features of the Internet, or a list that gathered information about one specific topic, or that attempted to make a general survey of one corner of cy-berspace. So here are a few of the famous efforts along with references to where to find them and a word of thanks to the people behind the index.

▶ *The University of Geneva's W3 Catalog*

The University of Geneva has developed a particularly useful catalog that collates information from around the World Wide Web and allows searching for words that may be associated with specific pages and ser-vices. We've enclosed here a description from the information about the catalog that lists the sources used to build the catalog. The sources in-clude many of the descriptive services available through the Web; you may want to explore each of them when you are browsing. Each service brings another view of the Web. We find each perspective to have value. You'll need to explore to see which of them best fits your needs and interests.

To use the catalog, use your Web browser to connect to

`http://cuiwww.unige.ch/w3catalog`

You'll see the screen shown in Figure 11.16. If you have a forms-capable browser, you can enter your search term into the appropriate place on the form.

If your browser doesn't have this feature, you should choose the alternative entry paths and follow the instructions. When you send your search term to the database, a program compares your term to all the entries in the database. The program builds a Web page, with appropriate links, which is displayed as a result of your search. You can then use this Web page to move to any (or all) of the pages whose references met your search criteria. If you would like to save the results of your search, you can do so using your Web browser's bookmark or hot list facility, or download or save the page to your computer.

FIGURE 11.16 ▶

Starting a search on the catalog.

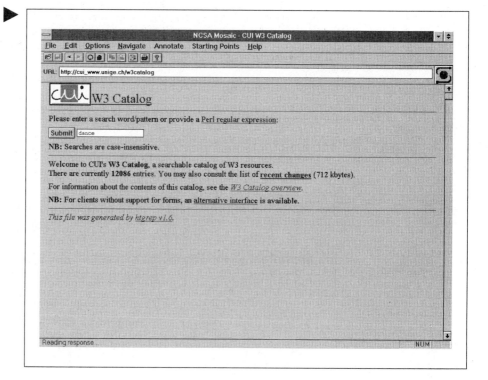

FROM THE "ABOUT CUI W3 CATALOG" PAGE

W3 Catalog is a searchable catalog of W3 resources built up from a number of manually maintained lists available on the WWW. There is some redundancy amongst the various sources, but a bit of noise seems acceptable to increase your chances of finding what you're looking for.

The following sources are copied and local mirrors of these pages are consulted daily and used to update the catalog:

NCSA What's new:

(http://www.ncsa.uiuc.edu/SDG/Software/Mosaic/Docs/whats-new.html)

NCSA's NCSA Starting Points:

(http://www.ncsa.uiuc.edu/SDG/Software/Mosaic/Starting-Points/NetworkStartingPoints.html)

CERN's W3 Virtual Library Subject Catalog:

(http://info.cern.ch/hypertext/DataSources/bySubject/Over-view.html)

Martijn Koster's Aliweb—Archie-like Indexing for the Web:

(http://web.nexor.co.uk/aliweb/doc/aliweb.html)

Scott Yanoff's Internet Services List:

(http://slacvx.slac.stanford.edu:80/misc/internet-serv-ices.html)

Simon Gibbs' list of Multimedia Information Sources:

(http://cuiwww.unige.ch/OSG/MultimediaInfo/index.html)

John December's list of Computer-Mediated Communication Information Sources and his Internet Tools Summary:

(http://www.rpi.edu/Internet/Guides/decemj/internet-cmc.html)

and

(http://www.rpi.edu/Internet/Guides/decemj/internet-tools.html)

Marcus Speh's User Documents for DESY and HEP:
(`http://info.desy.de/general/users.html`)

Other searchable catalogs can be found on the University of Geneva's list of W3 Search Engines (`http://cui_www.unige.ch/OSG/MultimediaInfo/meta-index.html`) **and CERN's list of Virtual Libraries** (`http://info.cern.ch/hypertext/DataSources/bySubject/Virtual_libraries/Overview.html`). **You might also want to consult the University of Geneva's list of W3 FAQs and Guides** (`http://cuiwww.unige.ch/OSG/FAQ/www.html`).

▶ Special Internet Connections

Special Internet Connections (AKA the Yanoff List) is one of the lists used to construct the W3 Catalog. It contains many resources of potential interest. Scott Yanoff compiles and updates it, and the list is posted frequently across the Net. It can be reached via anonymous FTP from the host `csd4.csd.uwm.edu` (University of Wisconsin, Madison, Wisconsin) as well as via the Web at `http://cui_www.unige.ch`.

▶ Oliver McBryan's World Wide Web Worm

This award winning Navigational Aid (Winner, Best of Web '94) is among the experimental search tools being built for the World Wide Web. The "Worm," located at

`http://www.cs.colorado.edu/home/mcbryan/WWWW.html`

and its companion, Oliver McBryan's "Mother of All Bulletin Boards," located at

`http://www.cs.colorado.edu/homes/mcbryan/public_html/bb/summary.html`

represent two possible approaches to finding things in the Web's truly distributed information base. The Worm searches for you by following links and looking for the search pattern you give it. Figure 11.17 shows

FIGURE 11.17

McBryan's Worm.

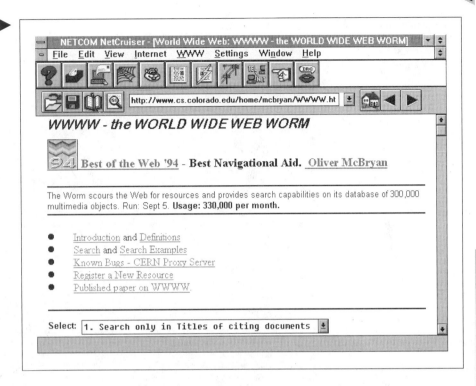

the home page for the Worm. The Bulletin Board presents an organization of the Web itself. Figure 11.18 shows the home page for the mother of all bulletin boards.

Neither approach is ideal, because there is not yet a reasonable way to capture all the pages that might possibly be of interest to you. Great ideas, both of them. Explore and use them to your advantage.

M A S T E R   W O R D S

You can find all the winners in the Best of the Web '94 at `http://wings.buffalo.edu/contest.`

▶ *The Virtual Reference Desk*

As part of the University of California at Irvine's Campus Wide Information Service (CWIS), Cal Boyer of UCI's Office of Academic Computing has built an excellent Gopher that includes what he terms the

FIGURE 11.18 ▶

The mother of all bulletin boards.

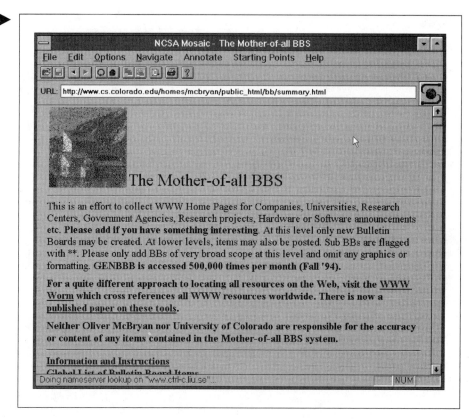

Virtual Reference Desk. These references are a collection of valuable Gopher links you can use to access information about the Internet and how to use it from the Internet itself. Connect to

```
gopher peg.cwis.uci.edu 7000
```

then choose Virtual Reference Desk. Figure 11.19 shows what you'll see there.

If you want to navigate here via the Web, the reference is

```
gopher://peg.cwis.uic.edu:7000/11/gopher.welcome/peg/VIRTUAL%20
REFERENCE%20DESK
```

(The "%20" characters are the ASCII code for the space character. They are recorded this way because URLs can't contain internal spaces.)

FIGURE 11.19 ▶

The Irvine Campus Wide Information Service Gopher, with the Reference Desk highlighted.

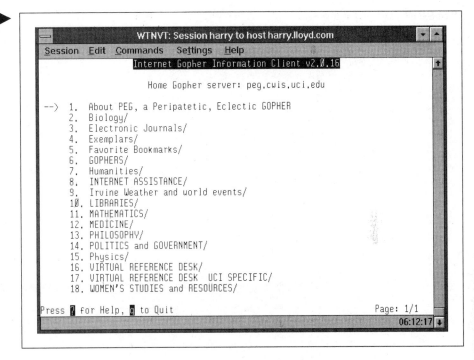

```
┌─────────────────────────────────────────────────────────────────┐
│              WTNVT: Session harry to host harry.lloyd.com      ▼ ▲│
├─────────────────────────────────────────────────────────────────┤
│  Session  Edit  Commands  Settings  Help                         │
│ ┌─────────────────────────────────────────────────────────────┐ ↑│
│ │          Internet Gopher Information Client v2.0.16          │ │
│ │                                                             │ │
│ │             Home Gopher server: peg.cwis.uci.edu            │ │
│ │                                                             │ │
│ │  -->  1.  About PEG, a Peripatetic, Eclectic GOPHER         │ │
│ │       2.  Biology/                                          │ │
│ │       3.  Electronic Journals/                              │ │
│ │       4.  Exemplars/                                        │ │
│ │       5.  Favorite Bookmarks/                               │ │
│ │       6.  GOPHERS/                                          │ │
│ │       7.  Humanities/                                       │ │
│ │       8.  INTERNET ASSISTANCE/                              │ │
│ │       9.  Irvine Weather and world events/                 │ │
│ │      10.  LIBRARIES/                                        │ │
│ │      11.  MATHEMATICS/                                      │ │
│ │      12.  MEDICINE/                                         │ │
│ │      13.  PHILOSOPHY/                                       │ │
│ │      14.  POLITICS and GOVERNMENT/                         │ │
│ │      15.  Physics/                                          │ │
│ │      16.  VIRTUAL REFERENCE DESK/                          │ │
│ │      17.  VIRTUAL REFERENCE DESK  UCI SPECIFIC/            │ │
│ │      18.  WOMEN'S STUDIES and RESOURCES/                   │ │
│ │                                                             │ │
│ │ Press ? for Help, q to Quit                    Page: 1/1    │ │
│ └─────────────────────────────────────────────────────────────┘ │
│                                                       06:12:17 ↓ │
└─────────────────────────────────────────────────────────────────┘
```

▶ *Distributively Administered Categorical List of Documents*

This index, started by Sam Sengupta at Washington University in St. Louis, is a truly distributed list. Project DA-CLOD wants each of us to contribute to this list of topics within Web pages. To use this "index," navigate via the Web to

`http://schiller.wustl.edu/DACLOD/daclod`

Figure 11.20 shows the DA-CLOD index reached via the Web.

▶ *Galaxy*

Another distributed index organized by topic is the one at Galaxy, started at EINet within their Manufacturing Automation and Design Engineering project. This index uses volunteer "editors" with particular

FIGURE 11.20 ▶

The DA-CLOD index.

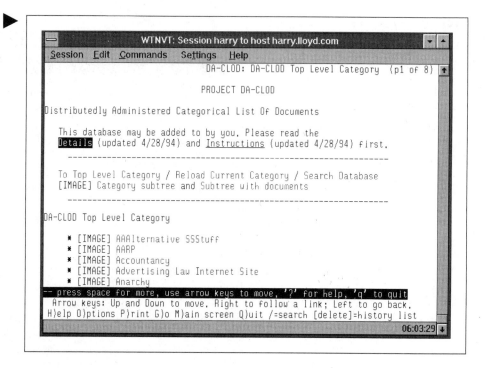

expertise to construct pages that provide links to other pages. To try this one, navigate to

`http://galaxy.einet.net/galaxy.html`

▶ The Virtual Tourist

We can't leave navigational aids for the Web without a pointer to a very special tool: Brandon Plewe's "Virtual Tourist" page. This "index" is graphical and geographical. Go there to use your graphical Web browser to point and click your way around the world, starting from a world map. Figure 11.21 shows the world map for the Virtual Tourist. You can reach it at:

`http://wings.buffalo.edu/world`

FIGURE 11.21 ▶

The Virtual Tourist World Map.

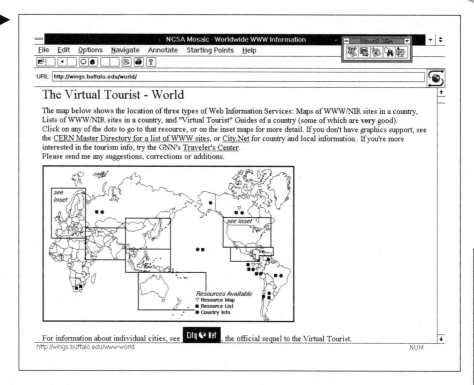

▶ *Collaborative Efforts at University of Michigan*

This list of indexes should not be closed without reference to the fine work done in indexes being built and maintained by classes in the School of Information and Library Science at the University of Michigan. These topical and subject indexes cover the humanities and the sciences in specific subject areas and are made available through Gopher. There is a Web page as an entrance into the collection. Figure 11.22 shows the list of indexes available at the SILS database. To reach it, open the URL:

```
http://http2.sils.umich.edu/~lou/chhome.html
```

FIGURE 11.22 ▶

The SILS indexes, avail-able through the Web.

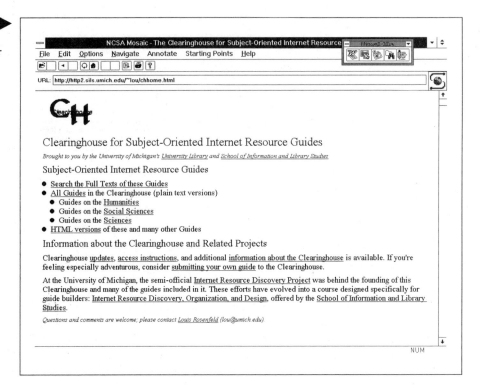

▶▶ *Now It's Time to Explore...*

As we said at the beginning of this chapter, Gopher and Web are bring-ing the resources of the Internet to computer users at all levels of tech-nical sophistication. Gopherspace, although not growing as quickly as the Web, is a mature, well-developed facility which allows a wide range of materials to be accessed easily.

The Web is the fastest growing area on the Internet. More and more organizations are announcing more and more servers and pages each week. The NCSA What's New Page (you can get there from the Net-Cruiser Home Port page) gets bigger and bigger each week. The num-ber of new Web servers each month is bigger than the number of new Gopher servers and new services that you can reach via Telnet and FTP, although those are all growing, too. The Web allows you to illus-trate and describe, to teach and let interested people interact with the information an organization can provide. (In Chapter 19 you'll learn how to create a Web page for your organization.) The Web and the possibilities it presents have truly captured the imagination of many potential information providers.

With so many good client programs readily available and the servers relatively easy to install on many differing platforms, Gopher and the World Wide Web are truly linking threads of information around the globe. Now it's time to start exploring them on your own.

Gopher and the
World Wide Web

ch.
11

## CHAPTER 12

Usenet
Newsgroups

► ► **A***fter* e-mail, Net News is the single largest information-sharing mechanism on the Internet. Net News is asynchronous, one-to-many communication—in other words, someone makes an article or message available, and anyone who is interested can read it whenever they like. The information can be authoritative or untrustworthy, detailed and official or chatty (or catty!). News covers every conceivable category; if you don't find what you like, you can start a new group to talk about it.

Net News or *Usenet News* or *News* are all names for the same concept: the broadcast of "posted" messages to a newsgroup. The original News software was developed for UNIX systems in 1979 by two graduate students at Duke University, as an early information-sharing and conferencing method. As good ideas on the Net tend to do, it spread like wildfire. Within a year, fifty UNIX sites, including Bell Labs, were participating.

Some newsgroups get hundreds of messages per day; some, only a few. Figure 12.1 shows what was available on a given day in the `misc.kids` newsgroup.

A News item looks much like an e-mail message; it has headers and a body of text. But News items are stored and handled by a different set of programs, and there are specialized *newsreaders*—programs to let you more easily handle the volume of news available. Newsreaders let you select what you want to read, discard what you don't want (or filter it out altogether before you even see it), and keep items in a single discussion or *thread* together.

FIGURE 12.1 ▶

*A typical News menu
(from misc.kids).*

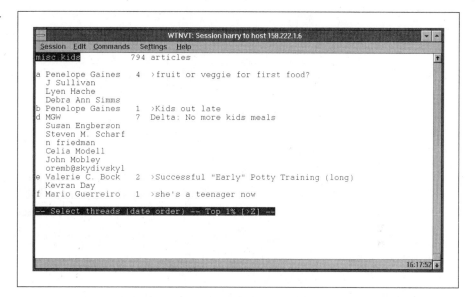

MASTER WORDS

Networks and host systems agree to accept News in certain groups and to feed postings to certain groups. They need not accept all possible newsgroups. This is particularly important for communities that include people such as young students or college students for whom some of the material in newsgroups is not appropriate. We have included an article on issues of censorship and college students as Appendix F.

There are over 9000 newsgroups worldwide as of late 1994. New ones are added each day. The groups are arranged in hierarchies and sub-hierarchies roughly according to subject. The groups reflect the diversity of the Internet community. For example, fans of Robert Jordan, a writer of speculative fiction or sci-fi, can discuss his work in the newsgroup alt.fan.robert.jordan; soccer fans have rec.sport.soccer, and programmers can discuss particular technical points in compilers or networking protocols in groups with names like comp.infosystems.*. New Net users should look at the groups news.newusers or news.newusers.announce.

Not all newsgroups are available in all countries. In the United States, for example, over one thousand foreign groups cannot be accessed.

A specialized kind of Net News is the commercial subscription service ClariNet, which broadcasts news from United Press International (UPI) to its subscribers. You can read ClariNet if your News provider has paid to deliver it to you.

▶ ▶ **W A R N I N G**

ClariNet is a subscription service, and if you receive it, your provider has signed an agreement that they will not redistribute it. DO NOT pass along items from ClariNet in e-mail to your buddies.

▶▶ *Newsgroup Hierarchies*

With thousands of newsgroups available, how do you find the ones you're interested in? Usenet newsgroups are organized into hierarchies, either by subject matter or geographically; and newsgroup names reflect this hierarchy. The first part of the name is the top-level hierarchy, the broadest category; and the following parts refer to more specific topics. For example, in the name `rec.sports.soccer`, it's not hard to see that the specific topic of soccer is part of the broader category of sports, which is in turn part of the `rec` (recreational activities) hierarchy. The top-level subject hierarchies are as follows:

`comp`	Computer-related topics
`news`	News about the Usenet network itself and the News system
`rec`	Recreational subjects such as music, art, hobbies, etc.
`sci`	Science and engineering discussions
`soc`	Social groups and societal issues
`talk`	Random discussions

misc　　　Miscellaneous topics

alt　　　New groups that have not yet passed the
newsgroup addition process or topics that do not
fit into other categories

Almost all sites that take News carry the top-level hierarchies. When someone wants to begin a new newsgroup within one of these hierarchies, they submit a proposal to the Usenet community (in the group news.announce.newgroups), and a discussion period begins, followed by a formal vote. This process is designed to ensure that the new group will have enough users to remain active and will not waste network resources. The alternative (alt.) newsgroups are not governed by the formal evaluation process.

The names of the organizational and geographical hierarchies reflect the diversity of the organizations and geographical areas that are organized into the Usenet. Some of the hierarchies include:

de　　　for a group of systems in Germany

fj　　　for a group of systems in Japan

ba　　　for a group of systems in California's Bay Area

atl　　　for a group of systems in Atlanta, Georgia

umn　　　for a group of systems at the University of
Minnesota

In addition, local organizations frequently have a local News hierarchy that runs only on their machines, and it is used to keep members of the organization in touch. Some large companies and universities have extensive internal hierarchies, including some that mirror topics on the larger News hierarchies, for internal discussion only. Figure 12.2 illustrates a posting on one such newsgroup.

▶▶ *How Does It Work?*

News is propagated, or distributed, cooperatively. Starting with a site with a full *feed* (all the possible newsgroups), other sites get this feed shipped over the Net to them daily. A full feed of the approximately 10,000 newsgroups that are distributed in the United States will take

FIGURE 12.2 ▶

A local newsgroup for staff information sharing.

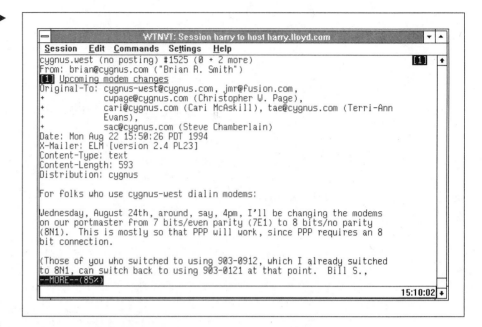

```
┌─────────────────────────────────────────────────────────────────┐
│ ▬        WTNVT: Session harry to host harry.lloyd.com      ▼ ▲   │
├─────────────────────────────────────────────────────────────────┤
│ Session   Edit  Commands  Settings   Help                        │
│ cygnus.west (no posting) #1525 (0 + 2 more)            [1]   ↑   │
│ From: brian@cygnus.com ("Brian R. Smith")                        │
│ [1] Upcoming modem changes                                       │
│ Original-To: cygnus-west@cygnus.com, jmr@fusion.com,             │
│ +            cwpage@cygnus.com (Christopher W. Page),            │
│ +            cari@cygnus.com (Cari McAskill), tae@cygnus.com (Terri-Ann│
│ +            Evans),                                             │
│ +            sac@cygnus.com (Steve Chamberlain)                 │
│ Date: Mon Aug 22 15:50:26 PDT 1994                              │
│ X-Mailer: ELM [version 2.4 PL23]                                │
│ Content-Type: text                                              │
│ Content-Length: 593                                             │
│ Distribution: cygnus                                            │
│                                                                  │
│ For folks who use cygnus-west dialin modems:                    │
│                                                                  │
│ Wednesday, August 24th, around, say, 4pm, I'll be changing the modems│
│ on our portmaster from 7 bits/even parity (7E1) to 8 bits/no parity│
│ (8N1).  This is mostly so that PPP will work, since PPP requires an 8│
│ bit connection.                                                 │
│                                                                  │
│ (Those of you who switched to using 903-0912, which I already switched│
│ to 8N1, can switch back to using 903-0121 at that point.  Bill S.,│
│ --MORE--(85%)                                                   │
│                                                 15:10:02  ↓     │
└─────────────────────────────────────────────────────────────────┘
```

about 200 megabytes of file storage per day. In turn, these secondary sites may feed other sites downstream from them.

Many sites get their News feed from a central News hub, which makes for efficient distribution.

Each site administrator can make the decision about what groups to receive. Many sites receive only the main groups (that is, everything but the `alt.` hierarchy). Others, because of site storage limitations or policies about personal use of computing resources (see Chapter 18), may only get certain specific groups.

News items are *expired* in order to keep the amount of file space consumed by this monster at a minimum. Most sites expire News items in 5–7 days. Some keep things around a little longer; some for only 48–72 hours.

A News message is called, in newsgroup jargon, a *posting*. A posting and all its responses are called a *thread*. If you read a posting and want to post a reply, you will compose it in much the same way as writing an e-mail message. Once you send or post the message, it will appear instantly in the menu for that newsgroup hierarchy on your machine. Then it will go out to the Net to be gathered into the feed for your site, and will propagate across the rest of the sites receiving that group. It can take about a week for postings to show up at all the sites that get your group. This delay can make it difficult to keep track of which thread a given message was intended for. In response, News enthusiasts have developed both the social practice of "context quoting," as in e-mail, and newsreader software designed to sort and distribute mail.

Each News posting or article has "tags" that help the News software sort and distribute it. They are:

`Subject:`	The subject or title of the article.
`From:`	The author's name and electronic address.
`Date:`	The date posted.
`Organization:`	The organization from which the article was posted.
`Keywords:`	Important words chosen by the author, which allow some newsreaders to do keyword searching.
`Summary:`	A summary of the article, written by the author.
`Newsgroups:`	The newsgroups to which the article was posted.
`Distribution:`	An indication of how widely the article is distributed.

Your particular News software may not show or use all of these tags, but most newsreaders and posting software will let you edit them into your posting before you send it off. Tags have the format <tag>: <space> <word or words>. For example, an Organization tag might say:

`Organization: Acme Properties, Inc. Coyote, Wyoming.`

Or, the newsgroup tag might look like this:

`newsgroups: rec.org.sca, rec.food.historic`

Usenet Newsgroups

ch.
12

▶▶ *Caveat Emptor*

If you have seen a screaming headline like "*Local high-school student finds pornography on school computer,*" chances are the student (or his parents) was reading it on Net News. Among the posted items, it is possible to find material, including erotica, that may offend some people. All people who read News should be aware that such material exists and that *they can choose* whether to look at it.

On the Internet, there are all sorts of people posting all sorts of information and opinions. Some newsgroups contain material that is sexually explicit and potentially offensive to some adults and perhaps dangerous for children to see. This may not simply be what is called "soft pornography." You will find newsgroups and articles that explore (and illustrate, because systems on the Internet are not restricted to text) issues of bondage, sadomasochism, bestiality and many other sexually explicit topics.

There are also materials that offend people in other ways. There are discussion groups for every political point of view, for every possible lifestyle and belief system, and for many other topics to which some people (particularly parents of young children) wish to control access.

In general, sexually explicit discussion groups can be found in the `alt.sex` newsgroup hierarchy. You can also find a lot of new and interesting ideas being discussed in the `alt.` hierarchies, so you should not assume that all `alt` newsgroups are sexually oriented. Nor should you assume that all other groups are clear of any potentially offensive material. (For example, the group `rec.arts.erotica` is a moderated group for erotic fiction and poetry.) Appropriate caution should be taken.

You will also find discussions from people who are very angry at or pleased with other persons, groups or the world in general. Do not be surprised if you find comments that are sexist, racist, or otherwise offensive. The Internet, particularly in the Usenet newsgroups, is a free-form exchange and there is little or no censorship other than the kind imposed by peer pressure. There have been instances where illegal files, such as child pornography, were posted to News. In cases like this, as many systems operators as possible are notified through the Net, and those files are removed. Attempts are usually made to prosecute the persons who post illegal materials.

In news.announce.newusers, you will find the periodic posting *A Guide to Social Newsgroups and Mailing Lists*, by Dave Taylor. This important and useful document describes the socially oriented newsgroups and some of the netiquette you will find useful for reading and posting to them.

We discuss policies for helping children who work on the Net in Chapter 17, on the K-12 presence on the Net.

▶ ▶ *Moderated or Unmoderated?*

Although for the most part Usenet is a free-for-all, governed only by peer pressure and consensus, some newsgroups have decided to filter the content and tone of the group by the use of a mechanism called moderation.

Moderated newsgroups (and mailing lists, for that matter) have strict guidelines for content, following the topic, and tone (emotionality and flames are not tolerated). A single individual (in lower-traffic groups) or a group of people handle the moderation tasks. They are called, not surprisingly, the moderators.

Here's how moderated groups work: when you post an article to a moderated newsgroup, the message is intercepted by the News distribution software and sent to the moderator(s). The moderator will decide whether to allow the posting to be distributed further. Sometimes the moderator will add comments or further headers to show that the posting has been passed.

Moderators usually "rule" with an even hand. They will tolerate a little bit of horseplay, but topics seldom stray for more than a few postings (or a couple of days).

You can tell if a group you are reading is moderated by reading the headers carefully, looking for postings from the moderator. You should also read the FAQ for any newsgroup you are interested in participating in before leaping into the fray.

▶▶ *Reading News*

Newsreader software exists for most computing environments. The Net-Cruiser package on Companion Disk 1 includes a newsreader; and Table 12.1 lists the most common public domain programs and the FTP sites where you can get them. This list is stored in the Gopher server at `cwis.usc.edu`; check there for the most current version.

▶ **TABLE 12.1:** *Guide to Usenet Newsreader Software*

ENVIRONMENT	FTP SITE	READER	COMMENTS
UNIX	lib.tmc.edu	rn	Also available via e-mail to `archive-server@bcn.tmc.edu`.
	ftp.coe.montana.edu	trn	
	dkuug.dk	nn	
	ftp.germany.eu.net	tin	
VMS	kuhub.cc.ukans.edu	ANU-NEWS	
	arizona.edu	VMS/VNEWS	
VM/CMS	psuvm.psu.edu	NetNews	Also available from `LISTSERV@PSUVM`.
	ftp.uni-stuttgart.de	NNR	
	cc1.kuleuven.ac.be	VMNNTP	
MVS	ftp.uni-stuttgart.de	NNMVS	
Mac	ftp.apple.com	News	
MS-DOS	ftp.utas.edu.au	Trumpet	
MS-Windows	ftp.utas.edu.au	WTrumpet	
X-Windows	ftp.x.org	xrn	
	export.lcs.mit.edu	xvnews	
EMACS	Most GNU sites.	GNUS	For use with GNU EMACS editor.
	Most GNU sites.	GNEWS	For use with GNU EMACS editor.

▶ *rn and nn*

With the simple UNIX newsreaders—rn (read news), nn (no news), and trn (threaded read news), you can read News happily without anything more than a spacebar. But if you do that, you'll read every item in every group, and it can become pretty overwhelming pretty quickly.

▶ ▶ **M A S T E R   W O R D S**

> nn, tin, **and** trn **all let you use the "+" symbol to display a listing of the available News articles. Display the list, select (by letter or number) the articles you want to read, and then, if you are pretty sure you won't want to come back and read something else, use the "c" command to mark everything else as read. This keeps the newsgroup manageable.**

With these three, you type the name of the reader at the UNIX system prompt, and follow the prompts. nn, tin, and trn have nice menu-based and configurable interfaces, which let you read the groups you want and the specific items you want without having to read everything. For example, Figure 12.3 shows how trn lets you select a newsgroup in which to explore. In Figure 12.4, an item from the rec.org.sca group has been selected.

Enter **h** at almost any prompt to get a help menu. Typing **q**, or Shift-**q**, or Ctrl-**q**, will almost always get you back out to either the main News prompt or the system prompt.

▶ ▶ **M A S T E R   W O R D S**

> nn **is a nice interface to use for several reasons, not least of all because if there are no new items, it tells you "No news is good news!" and automatically exits.**

There are other UNIX newsreaders: GNUS and GNEWS within EMACS. Both require knowledge of the complexities of the EMACS editor, and are not for the faint of heart or the beginning UNIX user.

Usenet Newsgroups

ch. **12**

FIGURE 12.3 ►

*Entering trn from a
system prompt.*

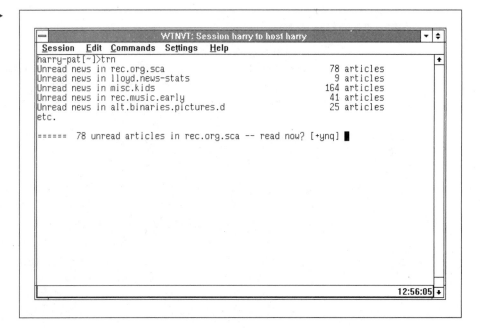

```
harry-pat[~]>trn
Unread news in rec.org.sca                           78 articles
Unread news in lloyd.news-stats                       9 articles
Unread news in misc.kids                            164 articles
Unread news in rec.music.early                       41 articles
Unread news in alt.binaries.pictures.d               25 articles
etc.

======   78 unread articles in rec.org.sca -- read now? [+ynq]
```

FIGURE 12.4 ►

*Reading a News item
(notice the quote from
a previous message).*

```
rec.org.sca #3 (4 + 72 more)                    -( )+-( )--( )+-(1)
From: gray@ibis.cs.umass.edu (Lyle Gray)         |       |-(1)--[1]
[1] Re: Things we tolerate                        |        \-[1]
Date: Wed Aug 17 12:41:48 PDT 1994                \-( )--( )--( )--( )--[1]
Organization: Dept. of Computer Science, Univ.  -( )--( )--[1]
+            of Mass., Amherst, MA
Lines: 33
Distribution: world
X-Newsreader: TIN [version 1.2 PL0]


Robert G. Gleason (gleason@scf16.scf.loral.com) wrote:
: In article <32t6p9$moo@opine.cs.umass.edu>
: gray@ibis.cs.umass.edu (Lyle Gray) writes:

: > Sorry, [bar grills] are period, depending on the helm style.
: >

: I knew someone was going to say this.

And I had a strong feeling that someone would comment. ;-)

: This is true to a point but we take the use of bar grills
--MORE--(48%)
```

► *Workstation-Based News Readers*

Many modern newsreaders use GUI clients, just like the Telnet and FTP clients we discussed in earlier chapters. These newsreaders make accessing and reading Net News even simpler.

When you install your client software, you will need to know a news server host to "point" your newsreader at. You'll be asked to supply the host name (and sometimes the IP address) of the news server. Ask your service provider for this information; there are very few public News servers available to nonsubscribers.

Subscribing to Groups

After you've installed your client, you'll still need to subscribe to the newsgroups you are interested in. Usually you will double-click on the name of a group or drag it from the Unsubscribed list to the Subscribed list. Figure 12.5 shows this step using Trumpet, a popular newsreader.

Unsubscribing from groups is just as easy.

FIGURE 12.5 ►

Subscribing to newsgroups using Trumpet.

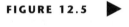

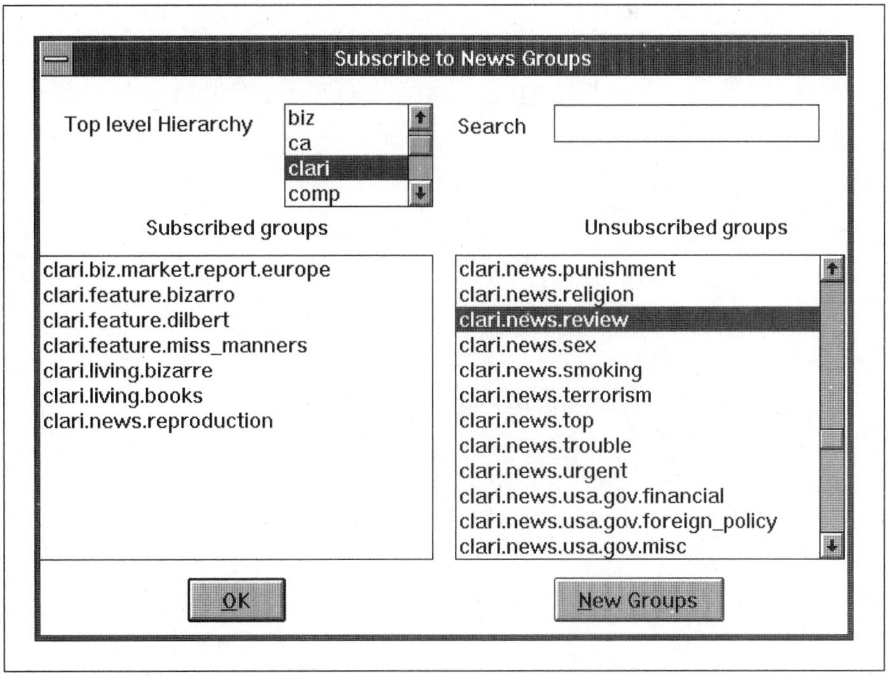

Subscribe to News Groups

Top level Hierarchy

biz
ca
clari
comp

Search _____

Subscribed groups	Unsubscribed groups
clari.biz.market.report.europe	clari.news.punishment
clari.feature.bizarro	clari.news.religion
clari.feature.dilbert	**clari.news.review**
clari.feature.miss_manners	clari.news.sex
clari.living.bizarre	clari.news.smoking
clari.living.books	clari.news.terrorism
clari.news.reproduction	clari.news.top
	clari.news.trouble
	clari.news.urgent
	clari.news.usa.gov.financial
	clari.news.usa.gov.foreign_policy
	clari.news.usa.gov.misc

[OK]   [New Groups]

Usenet Newsgroups

►►

ch.
12

Choosing Which Articles to Read

Once you pick a newsgroup to read, the names of the articles will appear in your window, as shown in Figure 12.6.

FIGURE 12.6 ▶

Choosing articles to read.

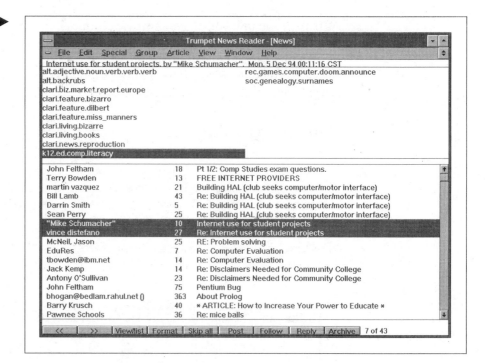

Reading Articles

After you click on the article you want, the text will appear in a new window, as shown in Figure 12.7. You can scroll back and forth through this text at your leisure.

Replying to a Posting

Replying (posting a follow-up) to a posting is easy with GUI newsreaders. You can click on a Reply button and a News template will appear. This process is shown in Figure 12.8.

FIGURE 12.7 ▶

Reading an article in Trumpet.

FIGURE 12.8 ▶

Posting a follow-up to an article.

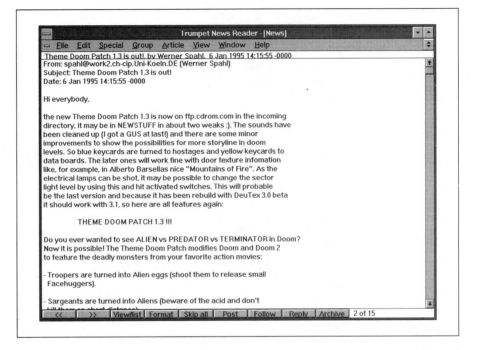

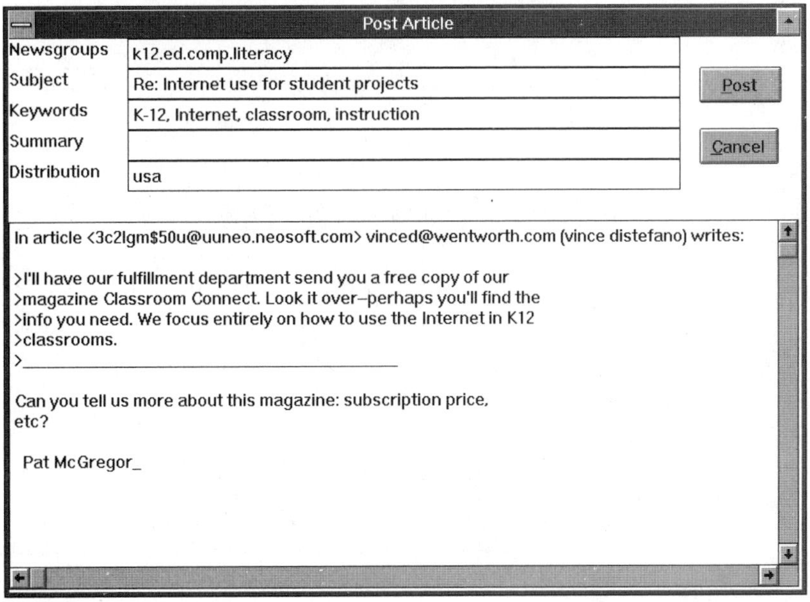

Saving to a File

Click on the Save or Archive button or menu item to save an article to a file on your workstation. You will be prompted for the directory and file name. Saving is shown in Figure 12.9.

FIGURE 12.9 ►

Saving an article to a file in Trumpet.

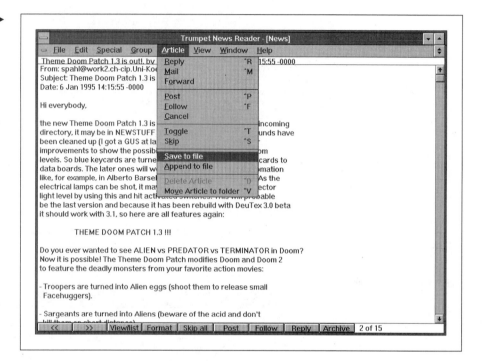

►► Non-Text Files on News

The News mechanism is used to transfer all kinds of information. Not all of it is simple text. Other things you can get (or post) on News include:

- public domain programs in binary format.
- pictures and images of all sorts (including maps, satellite images, and clip art).
- PostScript files of documents and other materials.

Images and other binary files require special processing to get them out of News and into your computer.

▶ ►WARNING

> ***Practice Safer Computing!* Just as with any file you download, or any diskette you accept from anyone else, you must be cautious about loading any file into your workstation and running it without checking for viruses and other hostile agents. Always run your protection software; always check any file before you install and run it!**

▶ *Getting Images off the Net*

The most comprehensive information available about getting pictures and other compiled binary information out of newsgroups is in the `alt.binaries.pictures.d` newsgroup. The FAQ for this group comes in three parts. The second and third parts are named `pictures-faq/part2` and `pictures-faq/part3`.

This FAQ is posted every other Monday to the `alt.binaries.pictures` newsgroups and to `news.answers`. It is also available by anonymous FTP or through e-mail by using the services available from at least two mail servers. For anonymous FTP access, you can look on either `rtfm.mit.edu` in /pub/usenet/news.answers/pictures-faq in files "part1.Z," "part2.Z," or "part3.Z," on `ftp.cs.ruu.nl` in /pub/NEWS.ANSWERS/ pictures-faq for "part1," "part2," or "part3," or on `ftp.uu.net` in /usenet/news.answers/pictures-faq as the files "part1.Z," "part2.Z," or "part3.Z."

For e-mail access, send a message to `mail-server@rtfm.mit.edu`, with the single-sentence body

```
send usenet/news.answers/pictures-faq/part1
```

to get the first part,

```
send usenet/news.answers/pictures-faq/part2
```

for the second, and

```
send usenet/news.answers/pictures-faq/part3
```

for the third. You can also send e-mail to `mail-server@cs.ruu.nl` with

`send NEWS.ANSWERS/pictures-faq/part1`, `send NEWS.ANSWERS/pictures-faq/part2`,

and/or send `NEWS.ANSWERS/pictures-faq/part3` in the body of the message.

Most people post to the `pictures` newsgroups in the UUENCODE encoding standard. This program, included with most implementations of UNIX, converts binary files into plain-text ASCII files, which can be handled by the mail system. In the past, you had to use the UUENCODE program yourself to convert the encoded files out of ASCII back into binary.

In addition, the pictures are generally split into two or more articles in the newsgroup to keep the size of the posting small. Somehow, you have to recombine the parts of the pictures and also decode them.

Luckily, some newsreaders have an "extract" capability that automatically decodes articles—this means you don't have to save the postings to a file and then decoding them. `rn`, `nn`, and `trn` can handle this.

Using Your News Reader to Decode the Pictures

Select the articles you want to decode. You need to make sure you get the entire sequence of articles. Most people post picture sequences with subject lines that let you know which one in the sequence it is and how many you can expect, for example,

```
Mel Gibson as Hamlet JPEG part 1 of 24
Mel Gibson as Hamlet JPEG part 2 of 24
Mel Gibson as Hamlet JPEG part 3 of 24
Mel Gibson as Hamlet JPEG part 4 of 24
Mel Gibson as Hamlet JPEG part 5 of 24
Mel Gibson as Hamlet JPEG part 6 of 24
Mel Gibson as Hamlet JPEG part 7 of 24
Mel Gibson as Hamlet JPEG part 8 of 24
Mel Gibson as Hamlet JPEG part 9 of 24
```

and so on. Figure 12.10 shows a group of articles that make up a single picture selected.

After you've chosen all the pictures you want to decode and display (or download), type this sequence:

`:e`

FIGURE 12.10 ▶

Selecting a group of files that make up a single picture.

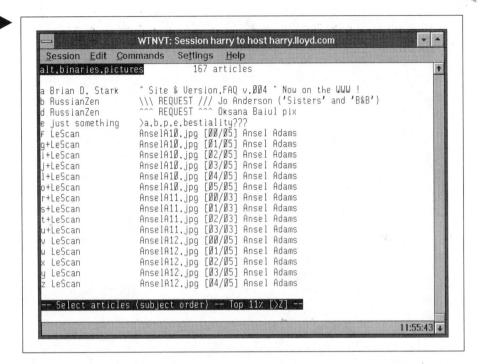

PICTURES ON EXHIBITION

The most common type of picture is the GIF format (which usually has a .GIF or .gif file suffix). GIF stands for Graphic Interchange Format. GIF is a standard format for images. It was developed by CompuServe to store pictures independent of the type of computer on which they originated. The GIF format includes Lempel-Ziv-Welch (LZW) compression, which makes the files fairly small. In early 1995, CompuServe annouced that it will require a licensing fee from companies using the GIF format. GIFs are expected to become less available on the Net, in favor of the free JPEG format.

JPEG is another standardized image compression mechanism. JPEG stands for Joint Photographic Experts Group (the original name of the committee that wrote the standard). More and more JPEG-type pictures (.JPG or .jpg file suffix, usually) are getting posted to the Net. Some Net watchers claim that JPEG is destined to overtake GIF format in popularity, because it uses much less space to store the same picture. JPEG may well take over from GIF, but that will probably take a while to happen, as more people have GIF software and viewers, but lack the JPEG equivalents. Undoubtedly, and probably faster than we expect, JPEG utilities will spread to more home computers, but at this point, JPEG is still in its infancy.

The latest and greatest info about JPEG is included in the Tom Lane's "JPEG image compression: Frequently Asked Questions" (archive name is `jpeg-faq`), posted on a regular basis to the `alt.binaries.pictures.d`, `alt.graphics.pixutils`, `alt.binaries.pictures.erotica.d`, `alt.sex.pictures.d`, and `news.answers` newsgroups.

The newest and most fun picture format on the net is MPEG, a format named for the Moving Pictures Experts Group. As the name implies, MPEG is movies on the Net. Some are extremely sophisticated; most are somewhat jerky, and the picture quality is somewhat poorer than with GIF or JPEG. However, it's a start. Most MPEG postings come in the form of movie loops. You'll need to have a MPEG viewer to see these movies.

Most PC and Macintosh FTP archives (see Appendix G for a list of anonymous FTP sites) have several shareware viewers for GIF, JPEG, and MPEG. Try them out and see which one works the best for you.

This command means "extract the selected items." Your newsreader will extract the articles, reconnect them into one file, and let you know what file they are stored in. Figure 12.11 shows the result of extracting the pictures we selected in Figure 12.10.

FIGURE 12.11

Recombining and extracting the image.

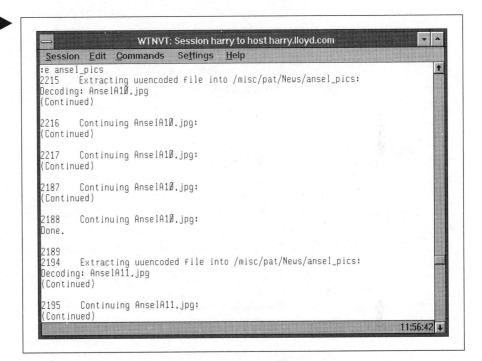

```
         WTNVT: Session harry to host harry.lloyd.com

Session   Edit   Commands   Settings   Help
:e ansel_pics
2215    Extracting uuencoded file into /misc/pat/News/ansel_pics:
Decoding: AnselA1Ø.jpg
(Continued)

2216    Continuing AnselA1Ø.jpg:
(Continued)

2217    Continuing AnselA1Ø.jpg:
(Continued)

2187    Continuing AnselA1Ø.jpg:
(Continued)

2188    Continuing AnselA1Ø.jpg:
Done.

2189
2194    Extracting uuencoded file into /misc/pat/News/ansel_pics:
Decoding: AnselA11.jpg
(Continued)

2195    Continuing AnselA11.jpg:
(Continued)
                                                      11:56:42
```

Viewing the Picture

You can view the picture on the most convenient machine for you. Sometimes this will be a remote host machine; sometime it will be your home or office computer.

If you're going to download the decoded picture file to a home machine, or move it around a network, remember that most decoded file outputs are stored in binary files. Be sure to set your transfer protocol accordingly. If you are moving around the uuencoded data, an ASCII transfer will work just fine, however. (You'll have to decode it eventually, of course.) For most of us it's more convenient to decode the images with a newsreader and then transfer it to the home machine.

Usenet Newsgroups

ch.
12

▶ ▶**M A S T E R   W O R D S**

If you *don't* transfer the decoded file in binary mode, your transfer will appear to work just fine— *until* you attempt to view the picture. You'll get error messages and peculiar looking images, but not the pictures you want to see. Some FTP clients will warn you if the file appears to be binary and you're transferring in ASCII (or vice versa), but not all will. You'll need to remember.

▶▶ *Posting to News*

There are two ways to post to News. One is to post a reply or response (or even a new item) while you are reading items. The exact command to do this varies: with line-mode readers usually it is **F** to follow-up (and include the quoted material) and **f** to follow-up without any preceding material (or to start a new thread). Graphic interface newsreaders may have a button or pull-down menu to start this process.

The other way to post News is from the system prompt. In UNIX systems the tool you will use is likely to be the Pnews program. Other operating systems have other programs; you'll need to ask your local News junkies. Figure 12.12 shows the first steps in preparing to post a item from the Pnews program, Figure 12.13 shows a typical editing session for a News item, and Figure 12.14 shows the stage of actually posting the article.

The easiest way to prepare a News posting is to edit it in a file, separate from the News process itself. This lets you think carefully about what you are writing. You can save the posting which prompted your response to a file, edit in your response, and then post it.

To save a posting from a line-mode newsreader like tn**,** follow these steps:

1. Select and read the article you want.

2. At the command prompt at the bottom of the item, type the command

   :s *filename*

FIGURE 12.12 ▶

Starting a News posting in Pnews.

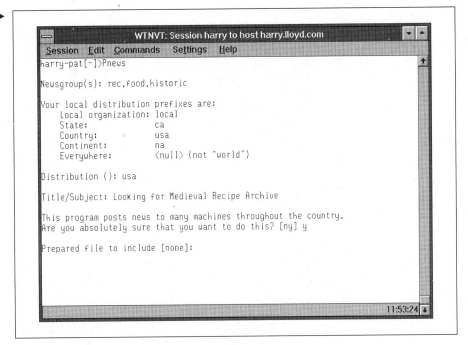

FIGURE 12.13 ▶

Editing a posting.

FIGURE 12.14 ▸

Posting the article.

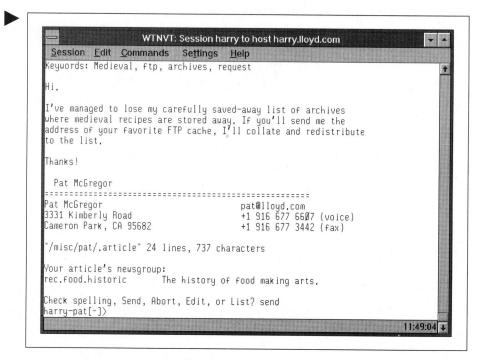

```
┌─────────────────────────────────────────────────────────────────┐
│ ⊟            WTNVT: Session harry to host harry.lloyd.com    ▼ ▲ │
├─────────────────────────────────────────────────────────────────┤
│ Session  Edit  Commands  Settings  Help                         │
│ Keywords: Medieval, ftp, archives, request                    ↑ │
│                                                                 │
│ Hi,                                                             │
│                                                                 │
│ I've managed to lose my carefully saved-away list of archives  │
│ where medieval recipes are stored away. If you'll send me the  │
│ address of your favorite FTP cache, I'll collate and redistribute│
│ to the list.                                                    │
│                                                                 │
│ Thanks!                                                         │
│                                                                 │
│   Pat McGregor                                                 │
│ =================================================               │
│ Pat McGregor                      pat@lloyd.com                 │
│ 3331 Kimberly Road                +1 916 677 6607 (voice)       │
│ Cameron Park, CA 95682            +1 916 677 3442 (fax)         │
│                                                                 │
│ "/misc/pat/.article" 24 lines, 737 characters                  │
│                                                                 │
│ Your article's newsgroup:                                      │
│ rec.food.historic       The history of food making arts.       │
│                                                                 │
│ Check spelling, Send, Abort, Edit, or List? send               │
│ harry-pat[~]>                                                  │
│                                                      11:49:04 ↓ │
└─────────────────────────────────────────────────────────────────┘
```

3. You will be prompted about whether you want to save this in mailbox format: enter **no**.

4. The file will be save in the News directory, with the filename you have entered.

Figure 12.15 shows the step of saving a posting to a file using tn.

With a GUI newsreader, saving a file is easier. You press the "Save File" button (or pull down a menu and click on the item) and you'll be presented with a dialog box asking you what file you want to save it in. Type in the name, and the article will be saved in that file.

The third way to save a posting is to select it (if your terminal emulator supports copy and paste for text on the screen) and copy the selection to a file.

Once you've edited your file to include the old posting, and the new information you want to add, you can post it to the newsgroup. You should remember to make sure that you've added more new material than you quote: most newsreader and posting software will keep you

FIGURE 12.15 ▶

Saving an article to a file.

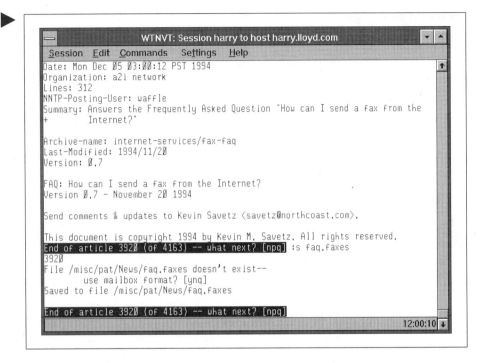

```
┌─────────────────────────────────────────────────────────────────┐
│ ─        WTNVT: Session harry to host harry.lloyd.com      ▼ ▲  │
├─────────────────────────────────────────────────────────────────┤
│ Session  Edit  Commands  Settings  Help                         │
│ Date: Mon Dec 05 03:00:12 PST 1994                          ↑   │
│ Organization: a2i network                                       │
│ Lines: 312                                                      │
│ NNTP-Posting-User: waffle                                       │
│ Summary: Answers the Frequently Asked Question "How can I send a fax from the│
│ +        Internet?"                                             │
│                                                                 │
│ Archive-name: internet-services/fax-faq                         │
│ Last-Modified: 1994/11/20                                       │
│ Version: 0.7                                                    │
│                                                                 │
│ FAQ: How can I send a fax from the Internet?                    │
│ Version 0.7 - November 20 1994                                  │
│                                                                 │
│ Send comments & updates to Kevin Savetz <savetz@northcoast.com>.│
│                                                                 │
│ This document is copyright 1994 by Kevin M. Savetz. All rights reserved.│
│ End of article 3920 (of 4163) -- what next? [npq] :s faq.faxes  │
│ 3920                                                            │
│ File /misc/pat/News/faq.faxes doesn't exist--                   │
│         use mailbox format? [ynq]                               │
│ Saved to file /misc/pat/News/faq.faxes                          │
│                                                                 │
│ End of article 3920 (of 4163) -- what next? [npq]               │
│                                                        12:00:10 ↓│
└─────────────────────────────────────────────────────────────────┘
```

from posting anything which does not make significant additions to the information on the Net.

As part of posting to News, you'll likely be asked questions to help the posting software distribute your News properly, and to put the proper tags and headers on your posting.

When you post from a GUI newsreader, you select the "post" button or select posting from a pull-down menu. You'll be prompted for the filename you want to include in your posting. Figure 12.16 shows posting from the Trumpet newsreader software.

▶▶ **MASTER WORDS**

At the end of the editing process, you will be offered a chance to list or reread your article. *Do it!* Make sure you've said what you intended, and that you really want to say it publicly.

Usenet Newsgroups

▶▶
ch.
12

FIGURE 12.16 ▶

Posting from Trumpet.

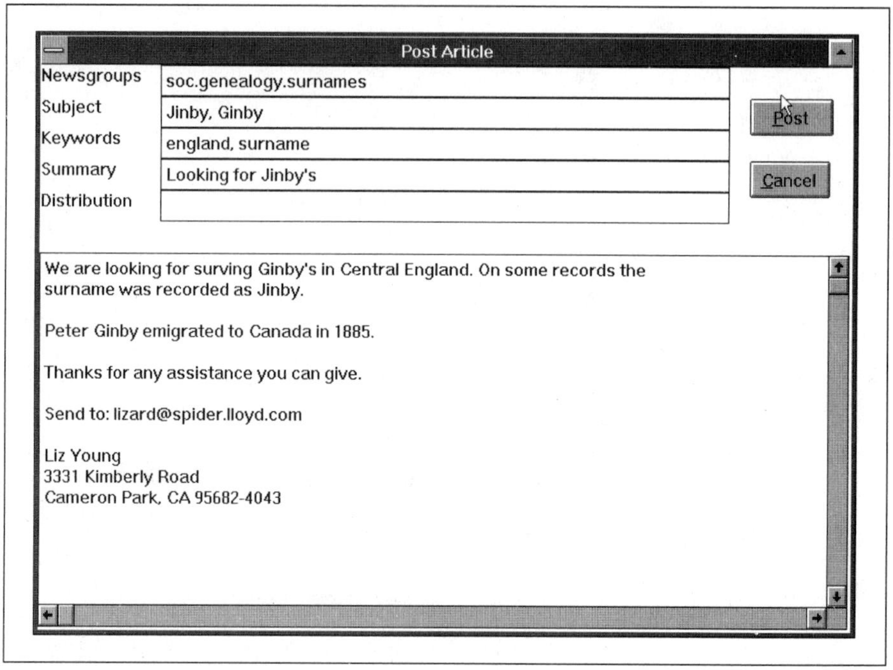

Posting from Trumpet.

▶ *Appropriate Distribution, or "Who Cares?"*

As unlimited as the Internet may seem, its resources are limited. With the vast amount of Usenet traffic that traverses the Net each day, it is expensive to post items of local interest to the whole world. Some articles (such as an announcement of a car for sale) are obviously not of interest to users at distant sites. In fact, you may get unpleasant responses from readers in far-away places if you post items meaningful only in your backyard. To help manage this, you can use the `Distribution:` line to limit where an article is sent. To attempt to limit distribution, add this line to the article header:

`Distribution: area`

You will be prompted (with an intimidating message about wasting Net resources) about distribution when you start a new posting. Take it seriously: think carefully about whether what you are posting adds anything to the conversation. If all works well, the distribution mechanism will keep your posting limited to the folks who are most likely to be interested in it.

MASTER WORDS

> The News distribution hierarchy is supposed to ensure that geographic distributions—ba **for the Bay Area,** atl **for Atlanta, or** oh **for Ohio, for example—stay in their geographic region. When you post a response or new item, you will be asked if you want to limit distribution. Unfortunately, because newsfeed software is not very efficient at screening out distribution codes (and because some systems administrators do not activate distribution filtering), it usually does not work. Be careful about posting items of local interest only to world-wide newsgroups.**

▶ Steering Responses to the Right Place

Sometimes you post to several groups but intend that follow-up discussion take place only in one group (it's easier to follow that way). Along with mentioning this in your article, you can get the News software to help you. Specify that follow-ups to your article are to go to a specific newsgroup by adding this line to the article header:

```
Followup-To: groupname
```

Replace *groupname* with the name of the group to which responses will be directed. If you want responses to come to you by e-mail, you can add the line

```
Followup-To: poster
```

Enter this line exactly as shown, including the word poster. All responses to your posting will be sent to you via e-mail, and will not be posted to News.

▶ Organization Name

This tag shows what organization the machine you are posting from is affiliated with. Usually this is automatically filled in from a standard template placed on the system by the system's administrator.

Usenet
Newsgroups

ch.
12

However, you may sometimes want to change this. For example, if you are posting from your work machine to a newsgroup discussing, say, gay rights, you may not want your company or organization name on the posting.

Edit the "Organization:" line to say which organization you want, or delete the line entirely.

► Where's the Beef?—Making Your Content Count

You have an objective in posting to News: you want to distribute information. Other people have their own objectives: they want to waste as little time as possible reading News in order to glean the most possible information. The quality of your message and its content are important. Following are some guidelines that will help you get your message to its widest appropriate audience.

Flames

Practically everyone has heard of flames—wildly inappropriate, highly personal, overreactions to something that someone else has said on the Internet. Some flames will be very vituperative and scurrilous.

But not all angry responses are flames. Consider the following (remember, '>' shows a previous message for context):

```
On Tuesday, Dennis wrote:
> Barbara Bush should have stayed at home and minded the
>puppies instead of pretending to know anything about
>literacy campaigning. We made no progress whatsoever during
>the Reagan-Bush years in stamping out illiteracy.

Dennis, that kind of statement makes me really mad.
Barbara Bush brought a visibility to the literacy problem
that we hadn't achieved in thirty years with conventional
attacks. What kind of evidence do you have??
Janet
```

Nothing inappropriate or offensive here. But if Janet had said:

```
Dennis, you are a sexist jerk. Any one who would
slam Mrs. Bush has got to be one of those stupid
```

```
Democrats. You probably learned to read from a cereal
box.
Janet
```

we could label Janet's response as a flame on Dennis. When Janet took the argument to the personal—when she said something unpleasant about Dennis, rather than disputing his ideas—then this became the match for a flame war.

This kind of behavior is discouraged. Some people will enter something like `<flame on>` to indicate that they are responding emotionally to a particular topic. Emotional responses are not discouraged, but attacks on people rather than ideas will in turn incur flames from others. These *flame wars* can be unpleasant—but they sometimes can turn a misunderstanding into a new understanding shared by the group. Flames can therefore be an interesting group process.

Some people enjoy causing flame wars. They respond with emotional or harassing statements in order to stir things up. One particularly obnoxious poster said to Pat, "I like a good flame war. The Internet is for those who are tough. If you can't take it, don't read News." Luckily, this sort of participant is rare, and becoming rarer as more people use newsgroups as widespread discussion groups and support groups.

One way to avoid a flame war is to ostracize the folks who are trying to stir one up. If, after several requests to stop the flaming a poster keeps it up, you can just ignore that person's postings.

Flames and FAQs A good way to avoid being flamed if you're looking for specific information about something is to first see whether the answer to your question isn't already written down somewhere, perhaps in a FAQ (Frequently Asked Questions) document. Frequently asked questions are just that—questions that every newcomer to a subject (whether it's azaleas or C programming) asks. Old-timers get tired of answering the same questions over and over again, so they write down the answers and post them where any interested person can find them. FAQs are the subject of Chapter 13, but the important point here is that if there's a FAQ on your topic and you've ignored it, someone may tell you—perhaps unpleasantly—that you've wasted the entire group's time.

▶

KILL FILES

Most newsreader software has something called a "kill file" function. This lets you sort your incoming News items—to autoselect things you want to read, and reject things you don't. Kill files are great for ignoring people whose postings are obnoxious. Once you put them in your kill file, it is as if they disappeared off the Net. Check the man pages for your newsreader to find out how to create a kill file entry. Most newsreaders either respond to a Shift-K or have a pull-down menu item to let you select or deselect certain strings (letter patterns) in News headings. Here's a list of items marked for deletion in trn.

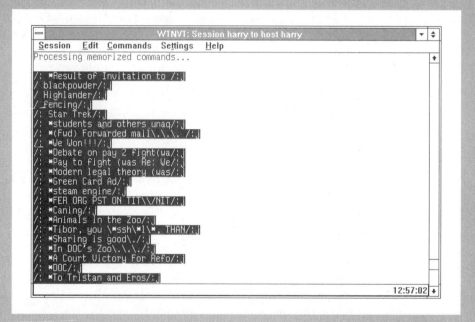

Chapter 7, which discusses "netiquette," includes a basic guide to appropriate behavior on newsgroups as well as mailing lists and other general Net citizenship. We suggest you read it, and any other related material you come across, if you are new to newsgroups.

Brevity Is the Soul of Wit

Chuq von Rospach, a respected Net veteran, says, "Never say in ten words what you can say in fewer. Say it succinctly and it will have a greater impact. Remember that the longer you make your article, the fewer people will bother to read it."

Make Sorting Easier: The Subject Should Be Descriptive

Remember that time on the Internet costs something: either your money paid to your provider, money spent by your company; or the reader's time. Most people make decisions on what to read based on the subject line.

That line lets people with limited time quickly decide whether to read your article. Tell people exactly what you are talking about. A title like "Safe Kids" doesn't help as much as "Tips for Fire-Safe Children." Most people won't bother to read your item to find out what it's about: they expect the subject to tell them.

MASTER WORDS

Chuq says, "Some computers truncate the length of the subject line to 40 characters, so keep your subjects short and to the point."

To Know You Is to Love You

There are over a million computers on the Net, and many of those have more than one person using them. It's unlikely that most of the people who read your postings know you personally. Most will come to know you only by your words—what you say and how well you say it. Your writing, your posting, and the quality of what you have to say represent you. Make sure your postings will not embarrass you. Before you send the posting out, check for:

- spelling errors
- clarity
- civility (see *Flames* above)

- context (and that you aren't quoting too much)
- signature

This isn't to say you have to be an award-winning author to write on the Net. Most of us aren't. But you should make sure that your writing is clear, concise, and as mechanically correct as you can make it.

▶ ▶**MASTER WORDS**

Not certain if your software is working? Want to see if the text or image file you just converted really goes over the Net? If you want to test something, *don't* use a Net-wide newsgroup! Messages with subjects that say "This is a test" are likely to provoke many irritated messages. Post those messages to misc.test**. You'll also get a surprise back: many hosts that receive** misc.test **send back an automated response. You'll get messages from all over the globe.**

Context, or What Are You Talking About?

Because it can take a week for a posting to get to all the machines on the Net, helping your readers keep track of context is particularly important. Some of them may get your response before they get the original posting! When you follow up someone's article, it helps to summarize the parts of the article to which you're responding. This lets others spend time thinking about what you said rather than trying to remember what the original article said.

The easiest way to summarize what's gone before is to include appropriate quotes from the original article. Don't include the entire article, since it will irritate the people who have already seen it. Even if you're responding to the entire article, summarize only the major points you are discussing.

If you want to include points from more than one person, you should label their individual comments in some way. There are a couple of conventions for labeling. One is to put the all comments from the same person together:

```
Jennifer (wander@taliesen.com) said on Tuesday:
> We have six databases to consolidate. I think the best
> thing is to pick the one which is set up most efficiently,
> and then just trash the others.
<design criteria snipped>
> This will keep us from having to re-enter the data. I'm
> not interested in spending several weeks typing 30,000
> entries in again.
>

Christian (jfh@carlyle.edu) replied:
> None of them is particularly well-designed. It would be
> better to redesign from the ground up and then transfer
> all the information into the new database. We have money
> in the budget to pay for data entry personnel.
```

The other convention is to use the person's initials at the front of their comments to distinguish who is saying what:

```
Jennifer (wander@taliesen.com) and Christian
(jfh@carlyle.edu) are discussing what to do about the
databases:

>J: We have six databases to consolidate. I think the best
>J: thing is to pick the one which is set up most
>J: efficiently, and then just trash the others.

>C: None of them is particularly well-designed. It would be
>C: better to redesign from the ground up and then transfer
>C: all the information into the new database.

>J: This will keep us from having to re-enter the data. I'm
>J: not interested in spending several weeks typing 30,000
>J: entries in again.

>C: We have money in the budget to pay for data entry
>C: personnel.
```

Summarizing the discussion that came before does take thought and editing. It's worth it, however, to make sure that your information gets respect from those you are writing to.

Mail or News: How Best to Respond to a Posting?

Since so many of us read and respond on the Net, chances are we all know the right answer to any given question. Often, someone will ask a question over Net News, and for a couple of weeks identical answers will clutter up the newsgroup. This is very irritating to everyone and can set off further clutter as irritated people send off snappish follow-ups telling people not to answer such questions on the Net. (You're right. It's not logical.)

You can help prevent such silliness. Before answering such a question, mark it to show up again in your newsgroup (in most readers the command will be **m** or a menu choice). Scan the rest of the day's items and see if someone else has answered it correctly. If so, don't duplicate the information. If you do want to respond, e-mail your answer to the person instead of posting a follow-up, and suggest that they summarize the answer or answers in a single posting (see next section). This way, only a single copy of the answers goes out, no matter how many folk answered the question.

If you post a question, please remind people to send you the answers by e-mail and offer to summarize them to the network.

Gathering In the Harvest

If you request information from the network, it's common courtesy to report your findings so that others can benefit as well. The best way of doing this is to take all the responses you receive and edit them into a single article that's posted to the places where you originally posted your question.

Take the time to strip headers, combine duplicate information, and write a short summary. Credit the information to the people that sent it to you (if you keep track of the original mail carefully, it is easy to do this).

Keep It Clean and Legal

The laws of the country in which you live (and possibly of every country where your article is received!) apply to your postings. Once something is posted onto the network, it effectively goes into the public domain. No matter how carefully you copyright your work, others may well copy it or post it elsewhere.

Additionally, remember that copying or retyping movie reviews, song lyrics, or anything else published under a copyright and putting them in a posting could cause you, your company, or the Net itself to be held liable for damages, so consider carefully whether you want to use this material.

It's legal to reproduce short extracts of a copyrighted work for critical or review purposes, but reproduction in whole is strictly and explicitly forbidden by US and international copyright law. Remember that people make their living by these words; if you steal them and give them away, the writer's ability to make a living may well be damaged.

MASTER WORDS

> **There are a great many people in the world who believe that copyright laws are, in themselves, an abridgment of their rights. Some of these people hold that breaking laws which they feel are unjust is the appropriate way to combat them. If you choose to post to the Net something you later hope to publish, think carefully about whether you are limiting your options by this publication.**

Many people read News from company or organization machines. Most companies and organizations do not have official opinions on most of the topics represented in newsgroups. You should consider all opinions or statements made in News articles as the opinions of the person who wrote the article. They don't necessarily represent the opinions of that person's employer, of whoever owns the computer from which the message was posted, or of anyone involved with News or the underlying networks which comprise News.

At the same time, some people do respond to News as official representatives of their companies. You can take what they say as authoritative.

Legal precedents view posting on News as being similar to publishing your own books or magazines. You are legally responsible for the content of your postings. Don't post instructions for how to do some illegal act (such as jamming radar or obtaining cable TV service illegally); also don't ask how to do illegal acts by posting to the Net. Authorities are particularly sensitive to pornographic material on the Net.

Usenet Newsgroups

ch.
12

Don't Ruin the Ending!

Many newsgroups discuss movies, books, and other material. Some people like to talk about these items in detail, including plot information and (sigh) the endings. Lots of people don't want to know the endings or other surprise information: it really upsets them and may cause them not to see the film or read the book. Such information, in News jargon, is called a "*spoiler.*"

If you choose to post something that might spoil the surprise for other people, please mark your message with a warning so that they can skip the article. When you post a message with a spoiler in it, make sure the word "spoiler" is part of the Subject line. You can also insert a Ctrl-L (or several of them) in your text just above where you start to talk about the surprise material. This pauses the newsreader and lets folks stop reading the article at that point.

▶▶ *Women on the Internet*

There has been a great deal of publicity in the past few years about women feeling threatened on the Net. Anecdotes tell of women who started responding to a newsgroup, or participating in other kinds of exchanges (IRC, or MUDs), and who received unwanted sexual offers.

It's hard to say how threatening the Internet is. For many years, the Internet was almost exclusively a male domain, because so many men were in the professions that used or were exposed to the Net. But increasingly, women as well as men are coming to the Net to find or provide information, exchange e-mail, and so on.

It's also true that there are a lot of immature males on the Net. Most users of social interaction groups (other than those limited to women only) on community bulletin boards and on college campuses tend to be young males, some of whom are not very socially adept. Why aren't there more women in these groups? Some theories point to social conditioning of women as a barrier to computing fluency.

When you add to this the feeling of safety that the Net's anonymity provides, it's easy to see why some men feel they can say *anything* to a woman, even a stranger, over this communication medium.

It's also true that some newsgroups have a more argumentative style than others, and that many women do not feel comfortable in the sort of rough-and-tumble give-and-take that occurs in these groups.

Obviously, both authors of this book work on the Net, and a great many other women do. Some women feel that only female-restricted conversation will help women new to networking gain the confidence they need: so private mailing lists and other resources have been set up.

Other women feel that a slightly thicker skin and a willingness to speak up if you think a behavior is inappropriate is the best armor.

What we can say to you is this: The Internet is full of a great many people, most of whom have something valuable to offer. Not everyone knows how to offer that information in an appropriate way. Some learn; some don't. You have the choice, and the technology, and the policy backups, to keep these people from bothering you.

▶ Protect Yourself

If you get e-mail or contacts in other ways from people you don't want to hear from, take these steps to protect yourself:

- Tell the person you do not want any further contact of this nature. Be firm. (For example, you might say, "I do not wish to get any more mail with sexually explicit content in it from you.") Keep a copy of the correspondence, and a copy of your request, for evidence if it continues.

- If the inappropriate contact does not stop, contact your systems administrator or postmaster, and the postmaster at the sender's host. To reach the postmaster, send to postmaster@*host*. All Internet sites are required to have a live human being reading and responding to mail addressed to "postmaster."

- Compute smart. Find out how to use kill files. Read headers, or use other ways (such as asking your local systems administrator or postmaster) to find out who is sending you the material.

- Check to see if your personal information (available via finger and other sources) has information you do not want the world to see; fix any problems.

- Use peer pressure. If a responder on a newsgroup is behaving inappropriately, ask your fellow Net citizens to either ignore the responder or let the responder know why they are unhappy.

The Internet is *your* resource, too. Don't let anyone drive you away from it.

▶▶ *Adding Emotional Bandwidth*

When we speak, our tone of voice and facial expression may convey as much of our meaning as the words we use. In a brief written message, these connotations may be lost or blurred—Was that a joke? Is he really angry? Is she sad?

Because of this lack of *emotional bandwidth* (we just don't have full video and audio capability over the Net yet), people have invented ways to let the reader know how they are feeling.

▶ *Word Shorthand*

We mentioned `<flame on>` as a signal that the poster was getting hot under the collar (and knew it). Other signals include:

`<hug>`	Sends a hug to the reader/readers
`<smile>`	The poster is smiling
`<wink>`	The poster is winking
`<sigh>`	Sadness, exasperation, resignation (must be read from context)

These are word signals. Other shorthand includes:

RTFM	Read the (fine) manual
IMHO	In my humble opinion
YMMV	Your Mileage May Vary (in other words, people's experiences differ)
ROTFL	Rolling on the floor laughing

| TANSTAAFL | There ain't no such thing as a free lunch |
| `<std.dis>` | Insert standard disclaimer (that is, these are my opinions, not my employer's). |

▶ *Smileys*

Probably the best-known form of shorthand signal is the set of symbols called "emoticons" or "smileys." This is a simple smiley:

:-)

If you haven't ever seen one, turn the page sideways. The characters **:-)** should look like a simple "happy face" sort of figure. Here are some more:

:-(	Frown
:-o	Surprise (or shout)
:-|	Grim expression (or null face)
;-)	Wink
:-J	Wry smile (or licking lips, in some vernaculars)
<:-)	Spock-like raised eyebrows
:-P	Tongue in cheek

You may see people who have distinctive "smileys" in their postings, as well.

▶▶ *Signatures*

As in e-mail, your *signature* is a standard text block that you append to any posting you send out. These are important, because some News software mangles your address so that people can't tell who you are or how to send a message to you in response to your posting (or e-mail). Most e-mail and News software has some way to set up an automatic process to append your signature. You can also read it in from a file (retyping it every time gets very wearisome).

Signature blocks are a source of both amusement and frustration for Net News readers. Some folks, particularly newbies, discover signature blocks and just go wild, including ASCII art (pictures made of standard characters), quotes, and the like, so that their signature blocks sometimes are longer than their postings!

The standard netiquette asks that you keep your signature block to four lines or less. A basic signature block includes:

- Your name
- Your e-mail address

Some people also include:

- A Phone number where strangers can call
- A paper mail address
- A fax phone number
- Company or affiliation

And, of course, there are signature quotes.

▶ ▶**M A S T E R   W O R D S**

Interested in seeing a wild collection of signature quotes? Try `finger ambar@cygnus.com.` **Ambar (Jean-Marie Diaz) has collected a hilarious collection of quotables.**

So, let's make up a good sample signature (called a *sig* in Internet lingo):

```
-----------------------------------------------------------------
Hilary St. Montain (hilary@everest.org) +1 901 555 1234 (v)
Explorer's Hut, Mt. Washington, NH 00000 +1 901 555 1222(f)

"On the mountain, there is only the rock, the summit, the
rope, and you."
```

(Some folks would quibble that the dashed line is part of the sig, and that it is therefore five lines long. YMMV.)

Trusted signatures and signatures that include an public encryption key are likely to be the next improvement in signatures. These will let you verify that the person whose signature is on the bottom of any message is really the person who they claim to be.

▶▶ *Do I Trust It?*

Hundreds of thousands of words go out over News every day. Most of those words are the opinions of the people writing them. Some of those people are experts in their field; some are just folks who read newspapers and other newsgroups. Some postings contain verifiable facts, some contain rumors. How do you tell whether the information is authoritative?

Well, how do you tell at a cocktail party, a staff luncheon or meeting, or any other way that you get information? You depend on several things:

- The speaker's sources
- The speaker's credentials
- The speaker's presentation
- Your past history with the speaker's information

The same criteria can hold true in evaluating News postings. For example, if you see a posting that says:

```
John asked about how to get chickens to lay more eggs in the
winter. Increasing the hours the lights are on in the hen
house, keeping the temperature up (and reducing drafts), and
adding extra green bits to the food mixture are all ways to
stabilize egg production seasonally.
You can get more detailed information on this from your local
county extension agent. Look for them in the phone book under
your county government listings. There are several publica-
tions out which have detailed instructions on how to stabilize
your egg production.
If you don't get good answers, please send me e-mail and I'll
try and help.

Martha Hart, Extension Poultry Specialist, Bucks County
(hart@ces.bucks.gov)
```

you can probably be sure that Martha knows her stuff. You judge her information to be trustworthy because:

- Her language is professional and factual.
- Her credentials are in the right field.
- Her e-mail address looks legitimate (and it comes from a .gov domain, which means she is at least affiliated with the government).
- She offers more information and further contacts.

By contrast, you might be suspicious of the quality of information in a posting like this:

```
Hey, John!
Somebody was talking the other day at a party about this, and
I think they said that you had to change the lights and make
sure the chickens are warm. You have to do something with the
food, too.
Maybe you need to buy a new rooster!

Pam
```

"Somebody said," "I was reading in the paper," "A book I once read," and other nebulous sources are what Internet cynics call "Standard Internet Sources." Some folks even quote these sources if they know their information is hearsay. Treat such information just as you would the same information in a conversation or paper letter.

 ► ►**W A R N I N G**

We made this example up from remembered fragments of a talk on poultry farming. It may have no bearing on the realities of chicken farming. Standard Internet Sources apply! ;-)

► ► **CHAPTER 13**

Just the FAQs, Ma'am—
Nothing but the FAQs

One of the hardest things about gathering information from public Internet sources is determining how authoritative the information is. Since anyone can post to newsgroups or put up an information server, how do you know what information to trust?

About the most public and most authoritative Usenet postings that can be found are the FAQs—lists of Frequently Asked Questions (and their answers).

In Chapter 2 we introduced a way of classifying types of communication on the Internet. According to that classification, FAQs are Type III communications—they are public, they come from many contributors and go to many recipients, and they are authoritative. They are published in the Internet manner: they are posted periodically (usually once a month) to the newsgroups that discuss their specific topics. FAQs also are found in the *.answers newsgroups. As the list at the end of this chapter shows, there are more than 500 FAQs available, and the list grows daily. Note the varied topics—everything from FAQs about specific computers and programs that run on them, to the description of the Society for Creative Anachronism (S.C.A.) illustrated in Figure 13.1, to a FAQ about Social Security Numbers. But what makes the information in a FAQ authoritative? As you'll see shortly, that comes from the collaborative process of producing the document.

The idea of collecting common information and distributing it is not new: any organization or group of people with common interests can do this by preparing a flyer or leaflet or even a book about their topic. But the difference between those items and FAQs on the Internet is accessibility, timeliness, and availability. For little or no charge in most instances, you can access the archives for a newsgroup or send e-mail to get a FAQ whenever you want, from anywhere in the world. The FAQ can be updated and new information distributed in less than a day. Fresh copies are always available: FAQs usually don't go out of print.

FIGURE 13.1

The SCA FAQ as it appears in Usenet news.

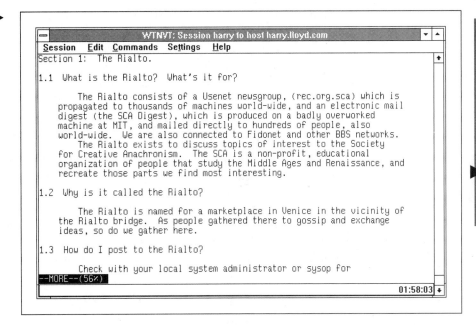

```
WTNVT: Session harry to host harry.lloyd.com

 Session  Edit  Commands  Settings  Help
Section 1:  The Rialto.

1.1  What is the Rialto?  What's it for?

      The Rialto consists of a Usenet newsgroup, (rec.org.sca) which is
  propagated to thousands of machines world-wide, and an electronic mail
  digest (the SCA Digest), which is produced on a badly overworked
  machine at MIT, and mailed directly to hundreds of people, also
  world-wide.  We are also connected to Fidonet and other BBS networks.
      The Rialto exists to discuss topics of interest to the Society
  for Creative Anachronism.  The SCA is a non-profit, educational
  organization of people that study the Middle Ages and Renaissance, and
  recreate those parts we find most interesting.

1.2  Why is it called the Rialto?

      The Rialto is named for a marketplace in Venice in the vicinity of
  the Rialto bridge.  As people gathered there to gossip and exchange
  ideas, so do we gather here.

1.3  How do I post to the Rialto?

      Check with your local system administrator or sysop for
--MORE--(56%)
                                                         01:58:03
```

And the group putting out the FAQ doesn't need to spend money finding out what newspaper you read, or printing the FAQ, or mailing it to you. (As discussed in earlier chapters, there are costs associated with the Internet; nothing is free. But these costs generally are less to all concerned than the costs associated with print publication.)

▶▶ *Newsgroup-Related FAQs*

FAQs frequently describe the charter (discussion rules) of a particular newsgroup. Other kinds of information you'll find include:

- Rules about commercial postings (most commonly, the rule is that they are not allowed).

- Suggestions for appropriate topics for discussion in the group.

- Information about format of postings.

- Newcomer questions, such as "How do I find *X*?" (*X* being some item related to the topic, such as a shareware program if it's a computer news group).

A moderated group will include information about how to post to the newsgroup: where the article should be sent and what criteria the moderator will use to judge how appropriate the posting is for the group. Usually there is only one FAQ per newsgroup, but some newsgroups have gathered extensive archives and make pointers to the archives available through the FAQ and periodic posting mechanism.

A good example of a thorough FAQ that pertains to a specific newsgroup is the one written by Diane Lin for the `misc.kids` newsgroup. Ms. Lin first describes the discussion topics accepted in this active group. She points people to discussions of newsgroup posting netiquette which can be read elsewhere, and she expands from the general netiquette rules to the specific ones used for `misc.kids`. Then she writes about "de-lurking"—introducing yourself to the group as a whole after you've read the group for a while. `Misc.kids` has a special "de-lurking" time where introductions of new readers are especially welcome.

The `misc.kids` FAQ contains further pointers for more information: to World Wide Web pages maintained by readers of `misc.kids`; to the e-mail addresses of specific people who have volunteered their expertise on particular topics like adoptive children, or car seats, or nannies; and to mailing lists that discuss special points.

Not all newsgroups have FAQs. In late 1994, there are 500 or so FAQs. There are 8000 or so newsgroups available in the United States, and approximately 9000 world-wide. Thus, more than 90% of the newsgroups don't have a compiled FAQ. You may find that a group in which you are particularly interested lacks a FAQ. After you have participated in the newsgroup for a while, consider offering to compile a FAQ for the group yourself. You can learn a lot about the topic that way, and more about using the Internet effectively.

▶▶ *Who Knows All the FAQs?*

FAQs are written by people like you—volunteers, from the community that reads a newsgroup, who want to offer their help to other members of their community. Frequently the FAQ development process goes like this:

1. Someone begins writing down information about a specific topic for personal use.

2. The writer posts it to the newsgroup and offers to accept comments on the work.

3. Readers from the newsgroup will offer suggestions for improvement of the work.

4. The author may accept and add to the work. Individual contributions are often specifically noted.

5. The community agrees that the work is complete and accurate within the scope defined by the community itself; the work is accepted as authoritative.

6. The writer/maintainer then keeps the authoritative copy and posts it to the group about once a month.

Legally, a FAQ about a newsgroup is generally the intellectual property of its writer/maintainer. (When you read FAQs, note their copyright notices. They range from extremely liberal to very restrictive.)

▶ ▶ **M A S T E R   W O R D S**

Legally, publication on the Internet is a very slippery topic. If you have signed a contract with your employer concerning the rights to anything you produce on the job, you may need to discuss works published on the Internet with them.

▶▶ *Topical FAQs*

Another type of FAQ is one that discusses a topic, not how to participate in a particular newsgroup. The meditation FAQ is an example of this type. This FAQ discusses meditation itself and presents answers to questions like: "What is meditation?"; "Should I meditate with my eyes open or closed?"; or "What is the best time of day to meditate?" Figure 13.2 shows the opening screen of the meditation FAQ.

FIGURE 13.2 ►

The meditation FAQ.

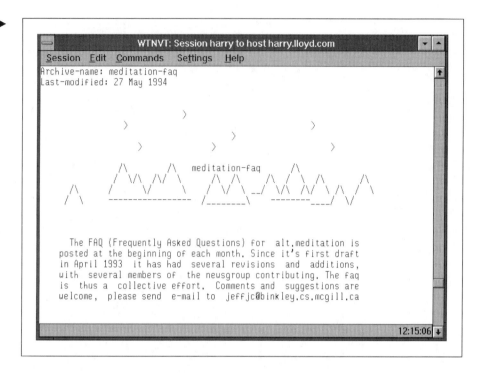

More and more topical FAQs are becoming available on the net, as shared expertise and information is being collected. Topical FAQs are generally validated in much the same way as newsgroup FAQs: that is, they are posted, the authors accept comments and make revisions, and then they are acceped. If the author is a recognized authority in the topic, the process may be shortened somewhat.

►► *Business and Commercial FAQs*

The FAQ format has become so useful and so widespread among Internet users that many other organizations besides newsgroups have started using them. Many software manufacturers prepare FAQs that you can get by sending to special e-mail addresses, or that are posted (if permissible) to newsgroups devoted to their product; computing consultants prepare them to give to users who ask about a common problem; a midwifery organization on the Net has a FAQ about becoming a midwife.

▶▶ *Keeping Up the Information*

Maintaining a FAQ is relatively easy. As new information becomes available, the writer/maintainer simply adds it to the FAQ, amends the "date-last-changed" statement that every good FAQ should have, and posts the FAQ.

New information can come from nearly anywhere: printed material from a manufacturer or software house, the government, volunteer researchers, anecdotal histories, or testing results. Many FAQ maintainers attempt to confirm new information before adding it into the list. (As you might expect, some FAQs are likely to be more rigorously fact-checked than others. Consider the source—is the FAQ maintained by an advocacy group presenting its view of a controversial issue, for example, or by academic researchers summarizing current work in their discipline?)

Many FAQs have a summary section at the top where changes since the last posting are listed. Sometimes changes are listed with plus signs (for new information) and minuses (to show where information has been deleted. In some instances, these + and – symbols can be run through a text processor to update the old files automatically. In most instances, however, it's easier to discard the old one and keep the new one.

▶▶ *How Is a FAQ Different from a Book?*

The publication process for a FAQ is quite different from that of the printed work—but it's a very common method of publication on the Net. The development process for a printed work (like this book, for example) goes something like this:

1. The author submits a proposal.
2. The author's proposal is accepted by the publisher, whose marketing staff has determined that there is sufficient interest in the subject matter for a book of the proposed scope to be published profitably.

3. A general outline and schedule are agreed upon.

4. The work is written and submitted to an editor. In the course of writing, the author may have circulated some or all parts of the work to colleagues for comment, but those people are not held responsible for the accuracy of its content.

5. Editors and technical editors amend or suggest amendments to the work. Technical editors attempt to verify the accuracy of all the information in the work, with varying degrees of thoroughness.

6. The manuscript is prepared for printing.

7. It is printed and sent through distribution channels.

Early in the distribution stage, the work is sent to various publications in the field for review. Editors of these publications then send the work to reviewers whom they consider authoritative in the subject area. The reviewers then read and construct their comments for publication or broadcast. The authors and publishers of the work hope the reviewer's comments will be positive and in turn will encourage potential readers/consumers to purchase the work. The comments of the reviewers do not affect the content of the work itself—it's already written—but they can certainly affect its acceptance by the intended audience. Ultimately, no matter how much or how little the author and publisher may have done to verify the information, authoritativeness is bestowed (or not) after the actual publication—if the consensus of the reviewers is positive, then the work is considered authoritative. The ownership of the intellectual property of the work is dictated by the contract between the author and the publisher.

With a FAQ, authoritativeness arises from the collaborative nature of the FAQ development process itself—the community has agreed that the work is good and true. If the community does not agree, the FAQ is rejected. If someone thinks the information wasn't helpful, or was wrong, you are likely to not only receive e-mail telling you your work was wrong, but your more opinionated fellow Net News readers will no doubt post an incisively worded critique of your work to related newsgroups.

An important difference between the two types of publication, of course, is the signficant financial investment behind the print publication of any work. Publishers employ people and use equipment to prepare a work for publication, to print it, to distribute it, to market it, and so on. If they are to recover these costs (and make a profit), a sufficient number of people need to buy the work. Many, if not most, books fail to earn a profit; a few "blockbusters" may account for most of the publisher's sales. In the case of the FAQ, there are no editing costs (because the editors work for free), the printing costs (if any) are borne by the reader, the distribution channel already exists as part of another service, and the marketing costs are nil, because the marketing is limited to a simple announcement.

All of this is intended only to show that the publication of a FAQ is a lot less complex than that of print publication, with significant benefits. Because the costs are so much less, the information can be updated much more frequently. Moreover, information that's of interest to an unprofitably small audience can be published in this way. On the other hand, the only recompense is the (usually unstated) appreciation of the information seeker who needed to know what is in the FAQ. Sometimes the information seekers will send you a brief e-mail of thanks if your information was helpful.

▶▶ *I'm Ready, Show Me the FAQs*

You can find the FAQs in several places on the Internet. FAQs are available most easily to everyone with access to the full set of Internet tools, because you can use FTP, Gopher, and the Web to locate them. People who are restricted to e-mail access can get them, too. Here's a quick guide to locating them.

▶ *Using News Itself*

Read the groups news.announce.newusers and news.answers (and any *.answers group). Watch the postings in any newsgroup you might read for an article labeled FAQ or Periodic Posting.

(We can't emphasize this one enough: news.answers is probably the single most interesting and useful newsgroup you'll ever read.)

▶ Using the News Archive at MIT

Use FTP to connect to the server `rtfm.mit.edu`. You'll find the FAQs in the pub/usenet directory. Use the Get command in FTP to bring the FAQ to you.

▶ Using the World Wide Web

Using your favorite Web browser, connect to

```
http://www.cis.ohio-state.edu/hypertext/faq/usenet/faq-
list.html
```

You'll see the list shown in Figure 13.3.

FIGURE 13.3 ▶

The FAQ list as seen through a Web browser.

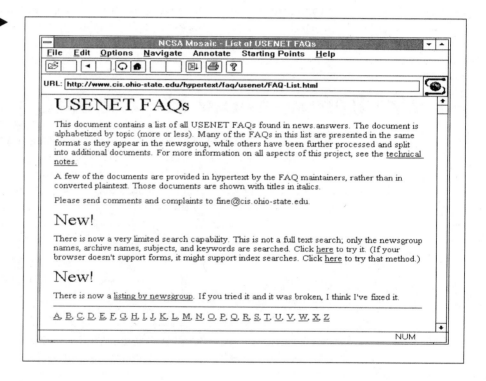

▶ *Using E-Mail*

Send e-mail to `mail-server@rtfm.mit.edu`. The body of the message should look like this:

```
help
index
```

Do not add signature lines. The mail server will send further instructions in response to the command word *help* and a list of available files in response to the command word *index*.

▶ *Using Gopher*

The FAQs are available at `jupiter.sun.csa.unb.ca` or at `gopher.germany.eu.net`. Once you get there, select this series of menu items: Direct archive access ➤ News archive ➤ news.answers. Once in the `news.answers` Gopher menu, select the FAQ you are interested in reading.

 ▶ ▶ **W A R N I N G**

> If the FAQ you want has a file name ending with the characters ".Z", it means that the file has been compressed with the UNIX compression utility. To read the contents of the file, you will need to move the file to a UNIX machine where you can run an uncompression utility before you can read it.

▶▶ *List of Usenet FAQs*

The remainder of this chapter is a list of the Usenet FAQs found in the newsgroup `news.answers`. It is derived from a similar list prepared by `fine@cis.ohio-state.edu` for the hypertext list of FAQs maintained at

```
http://www.cis.ohio-state.edu/hypertext/FAQ/usenet/faq-
list.html
```

You can use your favorite World Wide Web browser to find this hypertext list.

▶ ▶**N O T E**

> **This list changes quickly: it is up-to-date as of late 1994, but it may have additions or deletions by the time you read this. We include it to show the range of FAQs possible, and to get you started looking for good factual information on the Net. Use one of the methods outlined above to get the most up-to-date list.**

386bsd FAQ

3b1 FAQ

3b2 FAQ

3-D Information for the Programmer

68hc11 microcontroller FAQ

A

Abdominal Training FAQ

ACEDB Genome Database Software FAQ

Acorn

Active Newsgroups

Address Book

AFS distributed filesystem FAQ

Ai FAQ

AIDS FAQ part1of4: Frequently Asked Questions with Answers

AIDS FAQ part2of4: Frequently Asked Questions with Answers

AIDS FAQ part3of4: Frequently Asked Questions with Answers

AIDS FAQ part4of4: Frequently Asked Questions with Answers

Aix FAQ

alt.2600 (Newsgroup for the Hacker Quarterly) FAQL

Alt.beer FAQ 940117 revision

Alt Buddha Short Fat Guy

So You Want to Create an Alt Newsgroup

Alt Games Gb FAQ

Alt Hierarchies

Alt Sex

Welcome to alt.sources! (biweekly posting)

Alt Support Depression

ADMIN: Amethyst Coffeehouse Frequently Asked Questions

Amiga

Amiga Related Books FAQ

The alt.angst FAQ—Monthly Posting

[rec.arts.animation] Frequently Asked Questions v. 1.26

Anime

FAQ: news.software.anu-news

Apollo FAQ

Apple2

FAQ—ASCII Art Questions & Answers (3.1 - 53 K)

Astrology FAQ

Astronomy

Atari 8 Bit

Atheism

Audio Fmts

AudioFAQ

Australia

Australian FAQ

Autos

Aux FAQ

Aviation

B

Backcountry FAQ

Backrubs

[alt.backrubs] FTP archive site

Bahai Faith

rec.food.drink.beer FAQ

Benchmark FAQ

FAQ: BETA Programming Language

Bicycles FAQ

Bigfoot

Pool & Billiards Frequently Asked Questions

Biology

Birds FAQ

Bisexual

Bit (BitNET LISTSERV newsgroups)

[bit.listserv.muslims] Frequently Asked Questions

[bit.listserv.pakistan] Frequently Asked Questions

[bit.listserv.pns-l] Frequently Asked Questions

Biz.* Frequently Asked Questions (FAQ)

FAQ: biz.sco.* newsgroups/mlists (periodic posting)

Boats FAQ

Bodyart

FAQ: alt.netgames.bolo

Bonsai FAQ

Books

Soc.Culture.Brazil Frequently Answered Questions [FAQ]

rec.crafts.brewing Frequently Asked Questions (FAQ)

Bulgaria FAQ

C

C++ FAQ

C FAQ

California Driving FAQ

Caffeine's Frequently Asked Questions

Callahans

Canada FAQ

Canadian Football (CFL/CIAU) Frequently Asked Questions

Car Audio

Cats FAQ

COMP.SYS.CBM: General FAQ, v2.0 Part 1/2

COMP.SYS.CBM: General FAQ, v2.0 Part 2/2

COMP.SYS.CBM: General FAQ, v2.1 Part 1/4

COMP.SYS.CBM: General FAQ, v2.1 Part 2/4

COMP.SYS.CBM: General FAQ, v2.1 Part 3/4

COMP.SYS.CBM: General FAQ, v2.1 Part 4/4

CDrom FAQ

comp.dcom.cell-relay FAQ: ATM, SMDS, and related technologies

Chinese Text

How to Read Chinese Text on Usenet: FAQ for alt.chinese.text

Church of All Worlds FAQ

Church_all_worlds

ADMIN: Rec.Arts.Cinema FAQ Answers

Civil War Usa

Clarinet

sci.classics FAQ

Co-operatives—Frequently Asked Questions

COBOL FAQ

Coffee Resources Guide

Coherent Files

Comics

Communication Net Resources

comp.constraints FAQ Frequently Asked Questions [Monthly posting]

Comp Groupware FAQ

Comp Home Misc

comp.home.misc Welcome and FAQ

Comp Lang Ada

Icon Programming Language FAQ

Comp Speech FAQ

FAQ: Sun Computer Administration Frequently Asked Questions

comp.compilers monthly message and Frequently Asked Questions

Compression FAQ

Computer Security

VIRUS-L/comp.virus Frequently Asked Questions (FAQ)

alt.fan.conan-obrien FAQ (6/22/94)

Consumer Credit FAQ

Contract Jobs

rec.food.cooking FAQ and conversion file

Copyright FAQ

Crafts

Historical Costuming FAQ

Textiles FAQ

Crafts Textiles Books

Creating Newsgroups

Crossword FAQ

Cryonics FAQ

Cryptography FAQ

Atari ST FAQ

FAQ: CSH Coke Machine Information

Culture French FAQ

Soc.culture.japan references [Monthly Posting]

alt.cyberpunk Frequently Asked Questions list

D

Databases

alt.fan.dave_barry Frequently Asked Questions

De Amiga FAQ

De Answers

GATEWAY FAQ: Fragen & Antworten zur Mail-Adressierung

TCP/IP over ISDN. Frequently Asked Questions in German

De Newsgroups

De Rec Fahrrad FAQ

De Studium

Netzwerk-Infos fuer Studierendenvertretungen [FAQ]

de.talk.chat FAQ (Haeufig gestellte Fragen, mit Antworten)

de.comm.misc FAQ Fragen und Antworten rund ums Telefonieren

Dec FAQ

DESQview/QEMM Frequently Asked Questions: READ BEFORE POSTING

Devilbunnies FAQ

Diabetes

Dieting

Dieting FAQ

Disc FAQ

Disney FAQ

Distributions

Dogs FAQ

alt.fan.douglas-adams FAQ

Dreams FAQ

GROUPS: Anti War-on-Drugs Activists' List

Drugs

Drumcorps FAQ

Dsp FAQ

alt.fan.dune Introduction and FAQ

E

Welcome to alt.religion.eckankar

Economists' Resources on the Internet

Editor FAQ

comp.lang.eiffel Frequently Asked Questions (FAQ)

Electrical Wiring

Elm

Emacs implementations, list of, regular post [long, FAQ]

Emily Postnews

Apple2 Emulation Frequently Asked Questions (FAQ)

Epoch FAQ

ADMIN: rec.arts.erotica introduction

soc.culture.esperanto Frequently Asked Questions (Oftaj Demandoj)

F

FAQ Format

Fax FAQ

Feminism

Fencing FAQ

Ferret FAQ

Filipino FAQ

FAQ: How to find people's E-mail addresses

How to find the right place to post (FAQ)

How to find sources (READ THIS BEFORE POSTING)

Firesign Theatre

Firewalls FAQ (Rev 3, updated Mon Jun 6 10:17:59 1994)

Fleas, Ticks, and Your Pet: FAQ

Folklore FAQ

Fonts FAQ

ForthFAQ

Fortran FAQ

Fractal Questions and Answers

FrameMaker

Free Compilers

Catalog of free database systems

FSP Frequently Asked Questions (Read This Before Posting!)

Ftp List

comp.lang.functional Frequently Asked Questions
(monthly posting)

Fuzzy Logic

G

G++ FAQ

Gambling FAQ

Games

Garnet Toolkit Frequently Asked Questions

Geology FAQ

FAQ: soc.culture.german Frequently Asked Questions (posted
monthly)

Globewide Network Academy FAQ, plain text version [Last Revised 1994/05/01]

Gnosis

GNU Emacs FAQ

rec.sport.golf Golf FAQ

Gopher (comp.infosystems.gopher) Frequently Asked Questions (FAQ)

FAQ alt.gothic Frequently Asked Questions

Graphics

alt.fan.greaseman FAQ

Greek FAQ

Introduction to comp.groupware (Periodic informational Posting)

H

History

Hockey FAQ

Holocaust

Hongkong FAQ

misc.consumers.house FAQ (frequently asked questions)

alt.housing.nontrad Frequently Asked Questions (FAQ)

Howard Stern

comp.sys.hp.hpux FAQ

Hp48 FAQ

Hungarian electronic resources FAQ

I

bit.international.software FAQ

Ibm Rt FAQ

comp.protocols.tcp-ip.ibmpc Frequently Asked Questions (FAQ)

Ibmpc Tcp Ip FAQ

IDL (Interactive Data Language) FAQ

Image Processing

[soc.culture.indian] FREQUENTLY ASKED QUESTIONS

Info Vax

INN FAQ

X on Intel-based Unix Frequently Asked Questions [FAQ]

soc.couples.intercultural FAQ: Frequently Asked Questions

Interleaf FAQ—Frequently Asked Questions for comp.text.interleaf

Internet Access

Internet Services

Internet Talk Radio

Investment FAQ

soc.culture.iranian: Frequently Asked Questions [monthly posting]

Irc

IRC Frequently Asked Questions (FAQ)

comp.dcom.isdn Frequently Asked Questions

[alt.religion.islam] Frequently Asked Questions

[soc.religion.islam] Frequently Asked Questions

J

Japan

Journalism Resources on the Internet

JPEG image compression: Frequently Asked Questions

Judaism

Junk Mail FAQ

K

Kerberos FAQ

rn KILL file FAQ

Klingon Language FAQ

L

LANs

Law

Law Net Resources

Lebanon FAQ

LEGO frequently asked questions (FAQ)

Lemur FAQ

Letterman

FAQ: alt.fan.letterman Frequently Asked Questions (read before posting)

Libertarian

Linear Programming FAQ

Linux

Linux FAQ

Lisp FAQ

comp.programming.literate FAQ

alt.locksmithing answers to Frequently Asked Questions (FAQ)

Lsi Cad FAQ

M

comp.os.mach Frequently Asked Questions

Macintosh

Magic FAQ

Mail

Mailpaths

Manga

Martial Arts

comp.soft-sys.matlab FAQ (Frequently Asked Questions)

Medical Image FAQ

Medicine

Meditation FAQ

Mensa

Comp.Lang.ML FAQ [Monthly Posting]

[comp.text.tex] Metafont: All fonts available in .mf format

soc.culture.mexican FAQ Periodic Posting

MH Frequently Asked Questions (FAQ) with Answers

Mil Aviation FAQ

MINIX Frequently Asked Questions (Last Changed: 30 April 1994)

Minix Information Sheet (Last Changed: 30 April 1994)

misc.forsale.computers FREQUENTLY ASKED QUESTIONS (Periodic post)

HOW TO POST/BUY/SELL on MISC.FORSALE.* (FAQ)

Welcome to Misc.kids/FAQ File Index (Updated 7/15/94)

alt.business.multi-level FAQ (Frequently Asked Questions)

Model Railroad FAQ

Modems

Moderator List

comp.lang.modula2: Answers to Common Questions - v1.5 93.06.02

comp.lang.modula2: Answers to Common Questions - v1.8 94.04.11

Modula-3 Frequently Asked Questions (FAQ)

Motif FAQ

Motss

Movies

Mpeg FAQ

Message Passing Interface (MPI) FAQ

Msdos Archives

Msdos Mail News

Msdos Programmer FAQ

Music

N

Net Anonymity

Net Community

Net Privacy

Network Info

FAQ in comp.ai.neural-nets—monthly posting

FAQ: Top-level international planet domain names

Welcome to comp.newprod [periodic posting]

News

News Announce Intro

News Answers

Welcome to news.newusers.questions! (weekly posting)

news.groups.reviews guidelines

Net-Letter Guide 7/10

NN Frequently Asked Questions (FAQ) with Answers

Nonlinear Programming FAQ

alt.tv.northern-exp Frequently Asked Questions

Nude FAQ

sci.med.nursing FAQ

O

Oberon FAQ

Comp.lang.oberon FAQ (monthly) 2/3

Comp.lang.oberon FAQ (monthly) 3/3

Object FAQ

Objective C

Objectivism

Open Look

Os Research

Os2 FAQ

comp.protocols.iso FAQ

Ozone Depletion

P

rec.boats.paddle frequently asked questions and answers

ALT.PAGAN Frequently Asked Questions (FAQ)

Pagemaker FAQ

[soc.culture.pakistan] FREQUENTLY ASKED QUESTIONS

comp.databases.paradox Frequently Asked Questions

ADMIN: comp.sys.ibm.pc.games - Frequently Asked Questions - Read before posting

PC Games FAQ

Pc Hardware FAQ

Pc Unix

Pcgeos FAQ

Pcnfs FAQ

PCsoundcards

PDIAL #015: Public Dialup Internet Access List

Periodic Postings

Perl FAQ

Pern Intro

Pet Ferret FAQ

Pets Birds FAQ

(28mar94) Welcome to comp.windows.x.pex! (FAQ)

Pgp FAQ

ph (cso nameserver) Frequently Asked Questions (FAQ)

Physics FAQ

Pictures FAQ

Playboy Enterprises, Inc. FAQ

sci.polymers FAQ 7-8-94

Portable GUI Software

Portable GUI Software Diffs

Posting Rules

Postscript

Powerlines Cancer FAQ

PowerPC Frequently Asked Questions (FAQ)

PPP FAQ

Pratchett

Pro Wrestling

Project Management Programs - Frequently asked Questions (FAQ)

Prolog

ADMIN: Amethyst Coffeehouse Frequently Asked Questions

Puzzles

rec.pyrotechnics FAQ

Python FAQ

Q

soc.religion.quaker Answers to Frequently Asked Questions

Quotations monthly FAQ v1.01 08-02-93

Quotations monthly FAQ v1.00 04-13-93

R

Radio

RC Flying FAQ

Realtime Computing

Rec Autos

rec.guns FAQ Pointer

Rec Photo

rec.photo FAQ and answers

Rec Skate FAQ

Rec Video

Red Dwarf Frequently Asked Questions List (FAQ)

Ren N Stimpy

news.groups.reviews guidelines

Introduction to REC.HUMOR.FUNNY—Monthly Posting

Ripem

Robotics FAQ

Roller Coaster FAQ

Romance FAQ

Soc.roots Frequently Asked Questions (FAQ)

Running FAQ

S

Satellite TV

S.C.A. FAQ

Scf FAQ

Scheme FAQ

Scientific Data Format Information FAQ

sci.lang FAQ (Frequently Asked Questions)

Sci Math FAQ

Scientology

alt.religion.scientology Frequently Asked Questions (FAQ)

SCItalian FAQ

Welcome to comp.unix.xenix.sco [monthly FAQ posting]

Scouting

Scsi FAQ

comp.periphs.scsi FAQ (TOC & Volume I)

comp.periphs.scsi FAQ (Volume II)

[rec.scuba] FAQ: Frequently Asked Questions about Scuba, Monthly Posting

Sea Level, Ice, and Greenhouses—FAQ

FAQ: Computer Security Frequently Asked Questions

Sci.Engr.Semiconductors FAQ

Science Fiction

Sgi

Shamanism

Shamanism-General Overview-Frequently Asked Questions (FAQ)

alt.shenanigans - FAQ and guidelines for posting

Ship Models FAQ

Signature and Finger FAQ

Simpsons

soc.singles Frequently Asked Questions (FAQ); monthly posting

How to become a USENET site

sci.skeptic FAQ: The Frequently Questioned Answers

rec.skydiving FAQ (Frequently Asked Questions)

Smalltalk Frequently-Asked Questions (FAQ)

comp.protocols.snmp [SNMP] Frequently Asked Questions (FAQ)

Social Newsgroups

Software Eng

Solaris2

Solaris 2.1 Frequently Answered Questions (FAQ)

comp.sources.testers - Frequently Asked Questions (FAQ)

Southern US Skiing FAQ

Space

Sports

Sri Lanka FAQ - Monthly posting to soc.culture.sri-lanka

Social Security Number FAQ

Standards FAQ

Star Trek

More Star Trek

Stretching

Suicide - Frequently Asked Questions (monthly posting)

alt.suicide.holiday periodic Methods File posting (FAQ, sort of)

alt.supermodels FAQ

Sw Config Mgmt

comp.databases.sybase Frequently Asked Questions (FAQ)

T

Table Soccer

Table Tennis

Welcome to talk.bizarre! (Monthly Posting)

Talk Origins

Welcome to alt.tasteless! (Monthly Posting)

Tattoo FAQ

Tcl FAQ

Team OS/2 Frequently Asked Questions

Techreport Sites

Tennis FAQ

TeX, LaTeX, etc.: Frequently Asked Questions with Answers [Monthly]

Tex FAQ Supplement

comp.text Frequently Asked Questions

Thai

Theatre

alt.tv.tiny-toon Frequently Asked Questions (read before posting)

FAQ: alt.music.tmbg

Toastmasters FAQ

Tolkien

FAQ: Top-level international country domain names

Configuring the Telebit Trailblazer for Use with UNIX

bit.listserv.transplant FAQ, Organ transplantation newsgroup

Travel

Turbo Grafx

[FAQ] Soc.Culture.Turkish Frequently Answered Questions

alt.culture.tuva FAQ Version 1.07 [1 of 1]

Television

Typing Injury FAQ

U

Uk Telecom

Unix FAQ

Uninterruptible Power Source FAQ

Us Govt Net Pointers

Us Visa FAQ

Usenet FAQ

[rec.humor.oracle] Intro to the Usenet Oracle (Monthly Posting)

Usenet Primer

Usenet Software

ADMIN,DOC: Usenet University FAQ

Usenet Writing Style

Known Bugs in the USL UNIX distribution

UUCP Internals Frequently Asked Questions

V

Vegetarian

Virtual Worlds

Visual Basic FAQ

comp.lang.basic.visual VB/DOS Frequently Asked Questions

comp.lang.basic.visual General Frequently Asked Questions

comp.lang.basic.visual VB/Win Shareware VBX List

comp.lang.basic.visual VB/Win Frequently Asked Questions

rec.sport.volleyball Frequently Asked Questions (FAQ)

comp.os.vxworks Frequently Asked Questions (FAQ) [LONG]

W

Waffle Frequently Asked Questions (FAQ)

WAIS FAQ

Weather

What Is Usenet

alt.whistleblowing FAQ v1.1 (Jan 94)

Whitewater outfitter/dealer address list

MS-Windows COM and Ns16550A UART FAQ

Windows Emulation

Comp.windows.misc Frequently Asked Questions (FAQ)

Wireless Cable Television FAQ

Wireless Cable Television FAQ

Woodworking

[soc.history.war.world-war-ii] Frequently Asked Questions

Writing

World Wide Web FAQ

X

X11 FAQ

Xanadu

Xanadu World Publishing Repository Frequently Asked Questions

comp.windows.x.intrinsics Frequently Asked Questions (FAQ)

Z

comp.specification.z Frequently Asked Questions (Monthly)

ZyXEL Modems

ZyXEL U1496 series modems resellers FAQ (bi-monthly)

► ► CHAPTER **14**

Instantaneous Personal Communication: IRC and Talk

▶▶ **O**ne of the most exciting things about the Internet is how fast you can communicate with folks: sometimes we've exchanged over 20 messages with people in England in the course of an hour! The communication is fast and fun.

The most personal and instantaneous methods of communication are Internet Relay Chat (IRC) and Talk. Both let you communicate with others right from the keyboard. IRC lets you talk to multiple people at once, almost like a CB radio or cocktail party. Talk is more personal; it's just two people chatting together on screen. Even the keystroke corrections show up.

▶▶ *Internet Relay Chat: Keeping a Finger on the Pulse of the Internet*

Popularly known throughout the Internet as IRC, Internet Relay Chat offers the ability to communicate interactively with many thousands of people around the world about nearly any subject imaginable. Unlike any other Internet service, IRC enables you to hold a spontaneous conversation, in real time, with a group of individuals who may never physically meet. Moreover, your conversation is transmitted using more than 125 interconnected servers, which means that you can talk with a wide variety of people from every interconnected country in the world at the same time.

But if you think Usenet newsgroups are anarchic, wait until you try IRC. When groups of individuals from widely disparate backgrounds come together in a physical meeting, the topics discussed are usually constrained by each participant's perception of what would be allowed

IRC AND TALK BRING THE WORLD HOME

IRC and Talk are two of the Internet applications that show most clearly the great potential for the Internet to bring communication and fellowship to the lives of some disabled or, the house-bound, senior citizens, and others who for whatever reason cannot engage in face-to-face personal communications.

For example, a deaf teen in California got an Internet account and began to use IRC to chat with teens in Australia. Her father reports that before the Internet came into her life, she had been withdrawn and sullen, often missing school for mysterious ailments. In the four months since she began using IRC, the teen has improved her outlook on life, had regular attendance at school, and improved her writing skills. She has written several papers on life in Australia based on her discussions with her overseas friends. The teen spends close to four hours a day on the Net.

Senior citizens in Atlanta who are house-bound use Talk to check in with their adult children in other parts of the country during the day. Several of them have organized regular check-in times for those who are ill or on sensitive medications. A public health nurse uses Talk to "call up" each senior in turn and assess his or her condition.

One young woman who has cystic fibrosis cites another benefit of IRC and Talk for disabled people—no one you meet online can be distracted by your physical appearance. She has had problems in the past getting new acquaintances to look past her facial tics and uncontrolled body movements and see the personality inside. Using her special computer keyboard, this bright, clever woman is making new friends around the world to whom her online persona is the more important aspect of her being, not her looks or physical condition.

or generally accepted by the other participants. In Internet Relay Chat, anarchy reigns.

There are no constraints on the topics that may be discussed. Topics range from the serious (an oft-mentioned example is the successful use of IRC to relay information into and out of Russia during the 1993 Boris Yeltsin coup), to the inevitable computer-speak, to the recreational topics of international society, such as sports, movies, books, gossip about the rich and famous, and political debate. Topics may be controversial or mainstream at the whim of the participants, and anyone can create a topic (known as a *channel* within IRC).

Those of us old enough to remember the 1970s may be reminded of the Citizen's Band (CB) radio phenomenon. But comparing Internet Relay Chat with CB radio reveals more differences than similarities. Like CB, Internet Relay Chat is spontaneous—you can enter IRC, choose an existing channel or create a new one, and begin talking. Yet IRC does not have the limitations of CB: whereas CB users must be geographically close because the medium is radio waves, IRC works over the Internet, a world-wide collection of thousands of interconnected computer networks. Participants in an IRC channel may be from Michigan, California, London, Moscow, Taipei, or virtually any location where Internet service is available. IRC topics and language are also not constrained by FCC regulation.

A striking similarity with CB is the fact that IRC has developed its own culture and etiquette. (Members of the CB subculture pretended to be truck drivers and often spoke in fake-Southern accents. Everyone had a "handle"; Betty Ford's was "First Mama." If you disagreed with what someone said, you told them to "Lay down 'cuz yer tired." More seriously, an informal protocol arose so that people did not interrupt each other, recreational conversations did not interfere with actual truckers' business, and so on. As in other subcultures, this protocol was enforced by peer pressure.) Similar cultural evolution has happened with IRC. Obnoxious characters are ignored or cut out of the conversation. Those who are dealing with serious topics (depression, abuse, and so on) receive support but not the sometimes raucous banter encountered in the less serious channels. Each person on an IRC channel has a "nickname," just like handles on CB, which lets them develop an online persona.

Learning (and if desired, becoming a part of) the IRC's culture is one of the more challenging and entertaining aspects of using this Internet service. Fortunately, documents are available from Internet Relay Chat experts that explain the workings of the IRC programs and provide a glimpse into its culture. (See "IRC Resources" later in this chapter to locate the IRC Frequently Asked Questions.)

Internet Relay Chat has proven to be an effective tool during emergencies, natural disasters, and political upheavals. In addition to the Boris Yeltsin incident, IRC was used to convey current information during the 1991 Persian Gulf war, in several earthquakes, and during Hurricane Andrew. Because the IRC (and the underlying Internet) are carried over such widely distributed computers, information can arrive from areas where conventional communications may have failed. Also, since these current topics can be discussed in real time, with information coming in from different sources simultaneously, an IRC user can learn a great deal about a situation very rapidly.

Unfortunately, the *scroll rate* (the speed that incoming text from IRC flows off the screen) can be incredible when many IRC users are "talking" (typing text into) an IRC channel. To solve this problem, IRC client programs usually have the capability to log all text from one or more channels into a file for later reading. We'll talk about using this client software next.

▶ *Accessing Internet Relay Chat*

Internet Relay Chat works as a client/server application, and the IRC servers are interconnected to form, from the user's perspective, one large service. Each IRC user must use a client program on their Internet host. You instruct the client to connect to at least one IRC server, preferably a server nearby to minimize network delays and inefficiencies. Internet Relay Chat clients are available for IBM mainframes running VM, most UNIX systems, VMS with a TCP/IP package, Microsoft Windows-equipped PCs with Winsock support, and the Macintosh. IRC clients must run on a computer attached directly to the Internet.

Some of you will find that IRC is already installed and popular on the computer where you have a host account. Others may need to install an IRC client on your home computer, to run over your dialup IP link.

IRC and Talk

▶ ▶

ch.
14

▶ ▶ **M A S T E R   W O R D S**

You'll find an IRC client in the NetCruiser package on this book's Companion Disk 1. NetCruiser is intended for users at the service provider Netcom (with the disk you get a 30-day trial subscription); the following instructions are for readers connected to the Internet in some other way.

These steps will get you started, letting you collect the necessary software and documentation:

1. Obtain the latest Frequently Asked Questions (FAQ) files regarding IRC. These files are indispensable, as they contain updated information on how to configure the software and include the latest list of publicly-available IRC servers that are available for clients to connect to. FAQ files for IRC are available via anonymous FTP from `rtfm.mit.edu` (`18.181.0.24`). They are also frequently posted to the Usenet news groups `news.answers` and `alt.irc`. A collection of IRC clients and servers for many different machine types is available via anonymous FTP from `ftp.undernet.org` (`140.104.4.169`).

2. *Read* the Frequently Asked Questions in their entirety. This saves considerable time and trouble later; you'll be sure you don't have an obsolete client, and you'll understanding the developed culture and etiquette of Internet Relay Chat.

3. On a UNIX or VMS host, try the `irc` command. If that command is not available, you'll need to obtain and build the IRC client. Personal computer users will also need to obtain the client. If the command does work, and a screen similar to Figure 14.1 appears, proceed to "Using Internet Relay Chat" below.

4. Use the list of IRC client sources in the Frequently Asked Questions file to obtain the appropriate client. UNIX system users will find that the ircII (irc2) client is most commonly used.

5. Select an initial server to connect to. The Frequently Asked Questions files list a number of public servers that are useful to use. Later, by asking IRC server operators for leads on nearby servers, you may be able to find a server that is faster and less heavily used

than the well-known public servers listed in the Frequently Asked Questions files. Most clients require the host name or IP address and the port number (usually 6667) of the IRC server prior to compiling the software.

6. Install the client software following the instructions in the README file. When the client is started, a screen similar to Figure 14.1 should appear. If the connection to the server fails, try another from the public server list.

FIGURE 14.1 ▶

Initial connection to IRC server irc.uiuc.edu using ircII client.

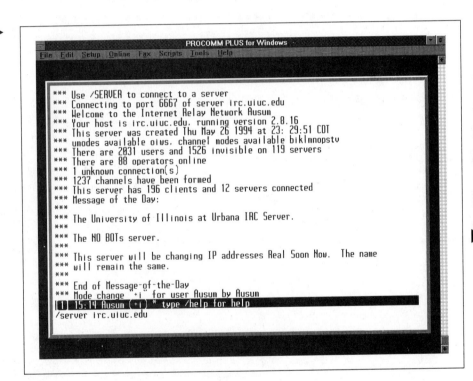

▶ *Using Internet Relay Chat*

Each IRC user has a nickname, a unique word chosen by the user. Other IRC users may send private messages to the nickname, and users within channels refer to participants generally by their nickname. Nicknames must be unique and are not owned or permanently recorded in IRC. The nickname should be nine characters or less. IRC users often use a whimsical name, their first name, or some other unique word that has special meaning.

▶ ▶**M A S T E R   W O R D S**

When you want to join an IRC channel, you cannot take the same nickname as someone already in the channel. You may need to change your nickname to something else. When you start a channel and are the first one there, of course, other people will have to choose their nicknames so as not to conflict with yours.

▶

IRC COMMANDS

Commands listed are for the ircII client.

Command	Description
/help	Lists ircII commands.
/help *command*	Displays an explanation of *command*.
/nick *nickname*	Changes the IRC nickname.
/list	Lists all IRC channels.
/join *channel*	Joins an existing channel or creates a new one.
/part *channel*	Disconnects from a channel.
/who *channel*	Lists users on a channel, use ⋆ for current channel.
/whois *nickname*	Shows e-mail address and current server of an IRC user.
/msg *nickname message*	Sends a message to the IRC user *nickname*.
/quit	Disconnects from IRC and exits the client program.

Most IRC clients will prompt for a nickname, or the nickname may be specified on the command line or environment variable. For example, the ircII client accepts the command:

```
irc Annette irc.uiuc.edu
```

This command sets the nickname to "Annette" and connects to the IRC server `irc.uiuc.edu`. There may be other, more convenient methods of setting the nickname described in the client documentation. Figure 14.1, in the previous section, shows a connection to an IRC server with a selected nickname.

Selecting and Creating Channels

Once you've connected to an Internet Relay Chat server and chosen a nickname, finding or creating a channel of interest is the next step. There are often over 1000 channels active on IRC, but most users find a few that are of interest and regularly use them. Listing channels the first time may be a mind-numbing experience, and it helps to have a small notepad handy to write down the names of channels that sound interesting for future use. The `/list` command will list all channels currently active within IRC.

Again, recall that IRC is anarchic and freewheeling, so do not be surprised if some of the channels sound unsavory or are unconventional. Channel names that begin with a # are IRC-wide channels available to any IRC user. Channels beginning with & are available only from the current IRC server. You will almost always find at least one interesting IRC-wide channel (and often many more).

To access a channel, type `/join name`, where *name* is the channel's name. The command `/join #sports` would join the sports channel within IRC. If there is no channel of immediate interest, you can easily create a new channel. Type `/join #name`, where *name* is a word describing the channel's topic. For example, the command `/join #karate` would join the #karate channel if one existed in IRC; but if there was no such channel, one would be created. You can use the `/topic` command to add a short phrase describing your new channel:

```
/topic Interested in Karate?
```

When IRC users use the `/list` command to list channels, the topic helps identify the channel as new, and provides an insight into what you propose to discuss in the channel.

After you select or create a channel, any text you type will be sent to participants of the channel. (If you are the first one there, no one will answer you, of course.) IRC shows the user that typed each line of text in the channel. A typical dialog might look like Figure 14.2.

The IRC nickname is shown in angle brackets (<>) when the typed message is directed to every participant in the channel. When the name is shown in asterisks (*), the message is private and is only seen by the recipient (in Figure 14.2, Wynter sent a message to Ausum). Thus, both public (to all channel viewers) and private messages may be sent and read simultaneously while using IRC.

See "IRC Commands" for a summary of the commonly used commands within IRC, including those for sending private messages to other IRC users.

FIGURE 14.2 ▶

An IRC conversation in a newly created channel.

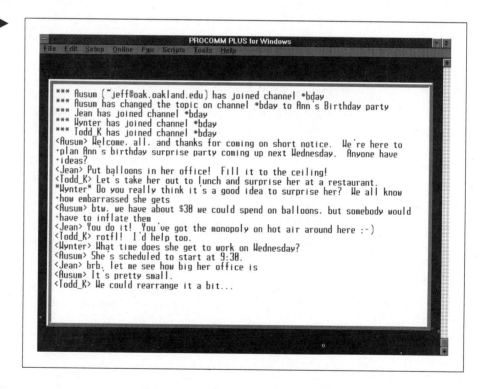

```
                         PROCOMM PLUS for Windows
  File  Edit  Setup  Online  Fax  Scripts  Tools  Help

  *** Ausum (~jeff@oak.oakland.edu) has joined channel *bday
  *** Ausum has changed the topic on channel *bday to Ann's Birthday party
  *** Jean has joined channel *bday
  *** Wynter has joined channel *bday
  *** Todd_K has joined channel *bday
  <Ausum> Welcome, all, and thanks for coming on short notice.  We're here to
  *plan Ann's birthday surprise party coming up next Wednesday.  Anyone have
  *ideas?
  <Jean> Put balloons in her office!  Fill it to the ceiling!
  <Todd_K> Let's take her out to lunch and surprise her at a restaurant.
  *Wynter* Do you really think it's a good idea to surprise her?  We all know
  *how embarrassed she gets
  <Ausum> btw, we have about $30 we could spend on balloons, but somebody would
  *have to inflate them
  <Jean> You do it!  You've got the monopoly on hot air around here :-)
  <Todd_K> rotfl!  I'd help too.
  <Wynter> What time does she get to work on Wednesday?
  <Ausum> She's scheduled to start at 9:30.
  <Jean> brb, let me see how big her office is
  <Ausum> It's pretty small.
  <Todd_K> We could rearrange it a bit...
```

▶ *The Undernet*

Recognizing that the current Internet Relay Chat network (known as EFnet by IRC users) is overcrowded, a group of IRC server administrators came together within the past two years to create a new IRC network known as the Undernet. Using the same software and servers, accessing the Undernet just requires connecting to a different server, usually known as *country*.undernet.org, where *country* is the two-letter country code for the nearest country with an Undernet server.

In late 1994, the us.undernet.org server was very quiet compared to the EFnet, but the Undernet promises to be a well-organized Internet Relay Chat network as it matures. Most IRC client programs allow a connection to two servers, so it's possible to participate in the bustle of the EFnet while simultaneously enjoying a clutter-free, fast connection to world-wide users on the Undernet.

Using the ircII client software, to open a new window to the Undernet you would type:

```
/window new server country.undernet.org
```

Thus, the ircII command to open a new window to the United States Undernet server would be:

```
/window new server us.undernet.org
```

To switch between the two windows (EFnet and Undernet) press **Ctrl-x, p.** The window currently active will have a row of carets, or ^ symbols, in its status line. Any text that is typed will be sent to the server in the currently active window only, so if you want to follow and contribute to the conversations in both windows, you'll need to become proficient with this window-switching keystroke combination. Figure 14.3 illustrates the ircII client in two-window mode, with connections to an EFnet server and an Undernet server simultaneously.

Because the Undernet uses the same client and server software as the rest of Internet Relay Chat, you'll use the same techniques described in "Using Internet Relay Chat" above to join channels, create new channels, and communicate over Undernet IRC.

IRC and Talk

ch.
14

FIGURE 14.3 ►

IRC connection to both Undernet (us) and EFnet (irc) servers.

►► *Talk: Person to Person*

Like IRC, Talk happens on screen and instantaneously. The talk command is supported on most UNIX hosts, and a great many LANs have an analogous command, sometimes called CHAT or WRITE. There is even a Macintosh TCP/IP client called "talk," which simply lets you talk to folks over the Net.

Talk is much less formal than IRC, if you can believe it, because it is simpler. Talk is just two people instead of an endless number. Talk can happen between two folks on the same host or between people on differing hosts. Pat, logged on at home, can talk to Glee, logged into a Netcom machine. If you know the person's address, you can attempt to talk to them.

You need two things to have a successful talk session: a terminal emulator running a VT100 (visual) terminal emulation (or a more advanced visual terminal), and the person's e-mail address.

Starting a Talk Session

To start a Talk session, generally you type the `talk` command and the person's address, like:

`talk sue`

or, if sue is on a different host than you are,

`talk sue@seattle.org`

Sue will hear a bell and see your Talk request on her screen, as in Figure 14.4.

►M A S T E R   W O R D S

Sometimes the e-mail address you have for someone is an alias. You will need to find out what their real login is and what machine they are working on. The easiest way to find this information is to have them start a Talk session with you. Then you will see on your screen exact instructions on how to respond.

IRC and Talk

ch.
14

FIGURE 14.4 ►

A Talk request appearing on your screen.

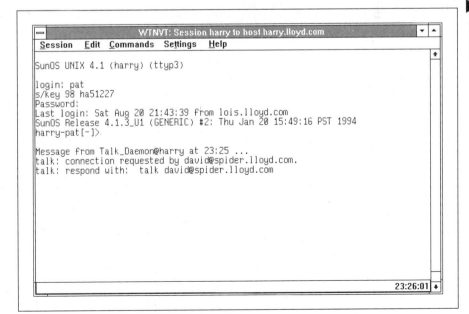

```
                    WTNVT: Session harry to host harry.lloyd.com
 Session   Edit   Commands   Settings   Help

SunOS UNIX 4.1 (harry) (ttyp3)

login: pat
s/key 98 ha51227
Password:
Last login: Sat Aug 20 21:43:39 from lois.lloyd.com
SunOS Release 4.1.3_U1 (GENERIC) #2: Thu Jan 20 15:49:16 PST 1994
harry-pat[~]>

Message from Talk_Daemon@harry at 23:25 ...
talk: connection requested by david@spider.lloyd.com.
talk: respond with:  talk david@spider.lloyd.com




                                                            23:26:01
```

If you try to initiate a Talk session with someone, your screen will divide in half and the Talk daemon will tell you that it's trying to reach your friend. If the person is on a different host, you will see a note that the daemon is trying to talk to a remote daemon, as in Figure 14.5.

While on your end you see a series of notes that your daemon is "Ringing your party again," your friend will get a series of requests, like the one shown earlier in Figure 14.4, accompanied by a bell sound. (If your friend should have her session set to reject Talk requests, or if she is not logged in, you'll get a message to that effect, and you'll go back to the regular system prompt.)

Once your friend has responded, and the connection is established, you can start typing, and your friend will see every keystroke—including the typos and the backspaces!

Don't Everyone Talk at Once!

One convention is that only one person writes at a time. In practice, you will frequently be writing at the same time. When that happens, you just pause and wait for the other person to continue.

FIGURE 14.5 ►

What the person initiating the Talk session sees.

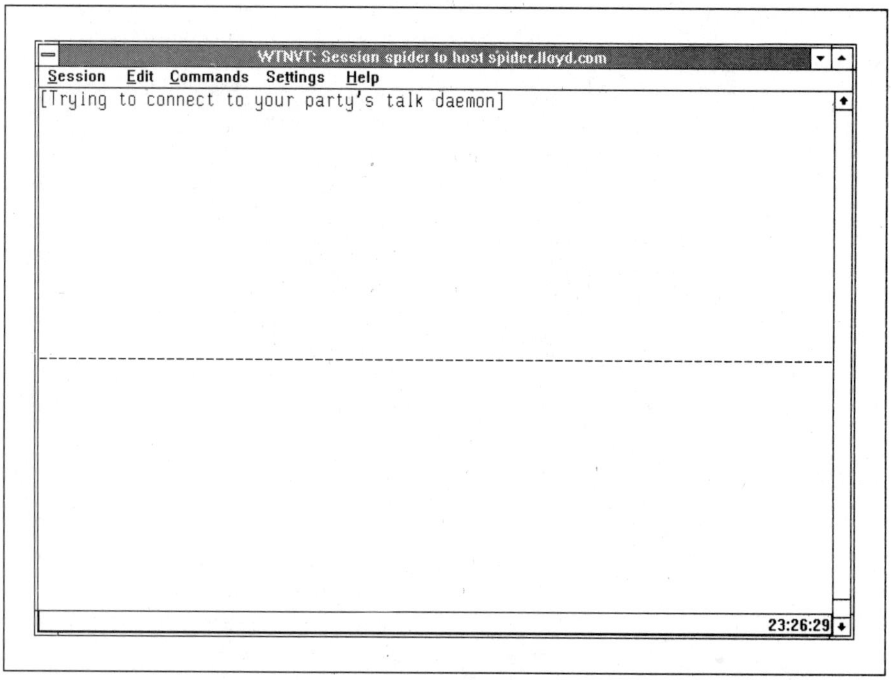

```
┌─────────────────────────────────────────────────────────┐
│ ─    WTNVT: Session spider to host spider.lloyd.com  ▼ ▲ │
│ Session  Edit  Commands  Settings  Help                  │
│ [Trying to connect to your party's talk daemon]        ▲ │
│                                                          │
│                                                          │
│                                                          │
│                                                          │
│                                                          │
│ - - - - - - - - - - - - - - - - - - - - - - - - - - - -  │
│                                                          │
│                                                          │
│                                                          │
│                                             23:26:29   ▼ │
└─────────────────────────────────────────────────────────┘
```

Some folks end each "transmission" from their side with two carriage returns, to show that they have stopped "speaking" and the other person can go ahead.

People use Talk for everything from personal (and sometimes intimate) chat to quick business conversations. Since Talk is unmonitored and not recorded, it has the greatest potential for truly private conversation over the Net.

It might seem that using Talk demands someone's attention immediately, in a way that e-mail does not. It's true that a Talk request repeats endlessly (and somewhat obnoxiously) until the sender terminates it. But if you do not want to be bothered with Talk requests, you can set up your terminal session to refuse Talk connections (ask your systems administrator or other guru how to do this for your particular system). Courtesy says that if you initiate a Talk session with someone, and they tell you that it's not convenient right now (or that they do not want to talk to you at all), you terminate the connection and send your urgent communications (if any) via e-mail.

Figure 14.6 shows the beginning screen for a Talk session.

FIGURE 14.6 ▶

Starting a Talk session.

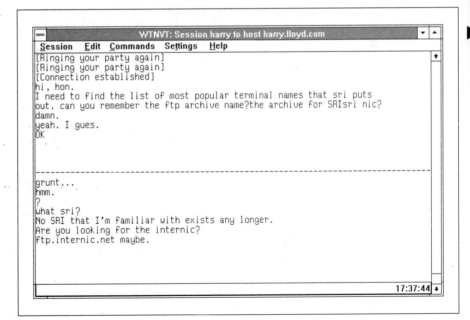

▶ ▶**M A S T E R   W O R D S**

"Unmonitored" is a relative term. No one is recording the talk sessions on either host, in general. However, if someone happens to be monitoring the physical connection (for example, if they are attempting to troubleshoot a network problem, or if they are crackers attempting to catch passwords transmitted without encryption over the network) and catches your Talk session, it can be recorded—along with the hundreds of other trans-missions going over that connection at the same time.

Your words will appear at the top of the screen, and your friend's at the bottom. At her end, things are reversed: her words are on top and yours on the bottom.

As the conversation goes on, you may type more than the ten lines or so allotted to each party. If that happens, the Talk daemon will just scroll your lines back to the top of the screen, and you will overwrite your old conversation. This may take a little getting used to. Figure 14.7 shows the overlapping nature of a long-running Talk session.

Hanging Up

To end your Talk session, let your partner know you need to go, and then type **Ctrl-C.** This will close the session down. Your words go off the screen and are gone, just like when you hang up from a telephone call.

FIGURE 14.7

A long-running Talk session.

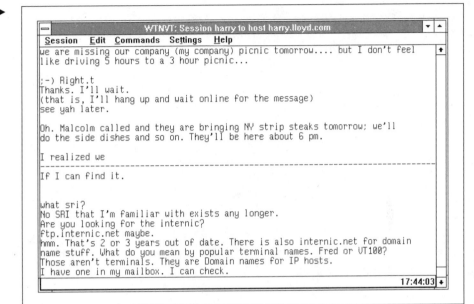

```
─ | WTNVT: Session harry to host harry.lloyd.com | ▼ ▲
  Session  Edit  Commands  Settings  Help
 we are missing our company (my company) picnic tomorrow.... but I don't feel   ▲
 like driving 5 hours to a 3 hour picnic...

 ;-) Right.t
 Thanks. I'll wait.
 (that is, I'll hang up and wait online for the message)
 see yah later.

 Oh. Malcolm called and they are bringing NY strip steaks tomorrow; we'll
 do the side dishes and so on. They'll be here about 6 pm.

 I realized we
 ──────────────────────────────────────────────────────────
 If I can find it.


 what sri?
 No SRI that I'm familiar with exists any longer.
 Are you looking for the internic?
 ftp.internic.net maybe.
 hmm. That's 2 or 3 years out of date. There is also internic.net for domain
 name stuff. What do you mean by popular terminal names. Fred or VT100?
 Those aren't terminals. They are Domain names for IP hosts.
 I have one in my mailbox. I can check.
                                                           17:44:03  ▼
```

IRC and Talk

▶ ▶

ch.
14

▶ ▶ ▶ CHAPTER 15

Living Out
Your Fantasies:
MUDs

▶▶ **A** **MUD** (Multiple User Dimension, Multiple User Dungeon, or Multiple User Dialogue; also known as a MUSE, or Multiple User Simulated Environment) is a computer program in which many users interact. As the various interpretations of the acronym suggest, MUDs can take many forms, but most are fantasy games. Most are available via Telnet, but many are becoming available with WWW.

 ▶ ▶**M A S T E R   W O R D S**

MUD is the generic term for a whole range of interactive environments. Other names are MOOs, MUSHes, MUCKs, TinyMUDs, AberMUDs, and so on. The name varies depending on the software underlying the shared environment. In this chapter we use the term MUD unless a specific software is intended.

▶▶ *What's Special about a MUD?*

Many computer users enjoyed playing a game called Adventure in the late 70s and early 80s, where they rambled through a cave, solving problems and interacting with various creatures in the cave. Many newer computer users have played Dungeons and Dragons or other fantasy role-playing games. MUDs combine several elements of each of these experiences.

In a MUD, you type commands to manipulate objects, make a general announcement, or whisper in a friend's ear. You read descriptions of your locale, and can wander at will, exploring your environs. There are rooms, or caves, or conference rooms. You can read papers. You can change your clothes, perform actions on other object (jump on a table, break an egg, eat breakfast). All these actions and experiences are familiar to folks who've played games like Adventure or Zork on a computer.

However, when you played Adventure your friends were clustered around you in chairs, watching the screen and shouting suggestions about what to do next. No one was in the game with you. Every time you went through a certain part of the cave, everything behaved predictably.

Role-playing games, on the other hand, are ensemble expeditions. Random chance (the toss of a die or the whim of the game's master) changes the behavior of both villains and friends. You can experience the action together, from each of your individual viewpoints. It's a group experience, and has more similarity to the unpredictability of real life than a game of Adventure.

In a MUD, you have the on-screen descriptions, the typing of commands, and the manipulation of objects. You also have dozens of other autonomous beings in the environment with you, real humans taking a role in your experience and interacting with you according to their personalities, abilities, and whim. You can flirt, dance, design a marketing program, hold a meeting, explore an adventure game, or just chat.

Across the world, hundreds of thousands of MUDders are doing just that. Figure 15.1 shows an internationally popular MUD, called the Imperial DikuMUD or simply the Imperial. You can Telnet to the MUD at `supergirl.cs.hut.fi` (130.233.40.52), port 6969, or reach it (as we did) via the Web. Connect to the CERN home page, look for Information by Subject, and then choose Games. The Imperial appears among the huge list of available MUDs.

▶▶ *A Short History of MUDs*

Historically, MUDs derive from an artificial intelligence (AI) experiment by Richard Bartle and Roy Trubshaw at the University of Essex (England) in the early 1980s. MUD1, written in 1979–80, is generally accepted as the first MUD. One of the goals of the experiment was to see if a program could be developed that would respond to the actions of multiple users with appropriate environmental responses. For example, if you dropped a vase, could the program decide if it would break

Living Out Your Fantasies: MUDs

ch.
15

FIGURE 15.1

The main room of the Imperial DikuMUD.

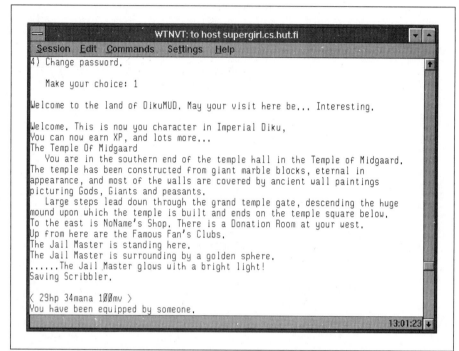

depending on what you were standing on, or random chance? The name MUD was trademarked to the commercial MUD run by Bartle on British Telecom (the motto was: "You haven't *lived* 'til you've *died* on MUD!"). Like most other fascinating concepts, this one became popular with students, and many new and improved MUD-like programs sprang up on the European academic networks. Most of these had associated bulletin-board systems for social interaction. Because Usenet feeds were spotty and difficult to get in the UK, and the British JANET network (a cousin of the US BITNET) didn't support FTP or remote login via Telnet, the MUDs became major focal points for social interaction among hackers there before Internet connections became plentiful.

MUD variants crossed the Atlantic around 1988 and quickly gained popularity in the US; they became nuclei for large network communities with only loose ties to traditional hackerdom. A second wave of MUDs (TinyMUD and variants) arose; these games tended to emphasize social interaction, puzzles, and cooperative world-building as opposed to combat and competition.

▶▶ *Enter a New Reality*

In a typical MUD, each user takes control of a computerized being (also sometimes called persona, incarnation, avatar, or character). You type commands and the affected users or objects respond. Your persona can walk around, chat with other characters, explore dangerous territory, solve riddles and puzzles, and even create your very own space. Many MUDs are live, role-playing games in which you assume a new identity and enter an alternate reality through your keyboard.

Each MUD has its own personality, which largely comes from the creator who developed its rules, laws of nature, and information databases. Some MUDs stress the social aspects of on-line communications—users frequently gather on-line to chat and join together to build new structures or even entire realms. Others are closer to "Dungeons and Dragons" and are filled with sorcerers, dragons and evil people out to keep you from completing your quest—through murder if necessary. Several have themes—such as a world based on the fantasy *Pern* series, or on the *Worlds of Amber* series.

In the Imperial, you are entering a typical role-playing environment. You equip yourself with items to prepare you to start an adventure, you gather companions, you learn magic spells and increase your skills and potentials. This is a magic-users world. By contrast, the SchMOOze, a MOO (MUD, Object Oriented) sponsored by Canadian schools, recreates a school campus. Newcomers take beginning classes, go to seminars, explore the campus. Later in this chapter, you'll see how these very different MUDs handle similar operations.

The advantages of MUDs for conversation and communication have not been lost on the business and research worlds. Several firms have "virtual conference rooms"—really MUDs—where participants scattered across the globe can meet to talk, in the same way they would talk if they were all in the same room. The meeting planner can even develop agendas, AV displays (participants download GIFs and MPEGs to display on their own workstations), and so on, which the participants can manipulate and display for themselves.

Living Out Your Fantasies: MUDs

▶▶
ch.
15

▶ ▶ M A S T E R   W O R D S

Geologists unite! There is a Geology MUD at Miami University in Ohio. Telnet to: 134.53.3.230 3000 (**3000** is the port number). You will be prompted for a name and password (which you can make up, so that you can get back in again). Try out the Geology Lab in the south, which has rock hammers, streak plates, and so on, and a lab assistant to hand you specimens of the minerals to test. There is also a card file that lets you look up a page on each mineral, with formulae, lattice constants, cleavage, color, and optics. Graduate student Erich Boring is the creator of this MUD, which is part of his Master's research.

Other creative firms use MUDs and other shared environment software similar to MUDs for brainstorming, creative development work, and so on. Oklahoma State University uses a MUD for conversations among its varied systems administrators.

▶ ▶ W A R N I N G

MUD playing and other game playing is not acceptable behavior at many companies and institutions, particularly when players are connecting from shared labs or other public work space. One problem (besides the obvious waste of employee time) is that MUDders use up resources intended for study or business use. If in doubt, contact your systems administrator to see what the appropriate use rules are for your site.

▶▶ *Different Types of MUDs*

Along with the original MUDs, there are a number of variants. Each has its own flavor, and the underlying basic game and databases of objects and commands are focused on or modified to reflect the flavor of the game. The four major variants are described below.

▶ LPMUDs

LPMUDs are free-form MUDs. In these environments each room is an independent universe and may be created by different individuals. Each has its own rules and realities. Anything can happen. Most LP-MUDs are puzzle-oriented or social rather than combat games. LPMUDs are the most sophisticated MUDs. LPMUDs have similar programming bases, but each room is limited only by its creator's imagination.

▶ TinyMUDs

TinyMUDs are an offshoot of LPMUDs, which use less disk space and frequently have a smaller number of rooms (although they are still quite extensive).

▶ DikuMUDs

DikuMUDs are role-playing adventure games, based on the "kill, kill, kill" principle. Characters kill monsters and evil characters created by the gods, wizards, and other players. Killing off monsters lets characters gain status, experience, equipment, and (fake) money. DikuMUDs have many social-interaction commands, as well, and some have evolved into places where participants can go to chat and socialize with each other. DikuMUDs are based on one stock game and database setup, with rooms radiating from a central hall, which is usually called Midgaard.

▶ AberMUDs

AberMUDs are much like DikuMUDs except that they are based on players killing each other rather than monsters or other artificial denizens of the game. In essence, the players hunt one another.

▶ MUSHes

All MUSHes are theme-based: for example, many are based on science fiction or fantasy books such as Frank Herbert's *Dune* or Anne McAffrey's *Pern* series. The creators of these games start off with a standard game program and database, and customize it to reflect the environment, customs, and characters from the books. In the *Dune* MUSHes, for example, they have imported the Houses Royal, Houses Major, and the Spacer's Guild, as well as the physics and the magic systems from Herbert's novels. Similarly, in one of the *Pern* MUDs, characters take on personas based on characters in that series: they become weyrwomen, dragon riders, holders, guild members. They interact in games designed around the geography and customs of the books. If you wish to be a dedicated player in one of these games, you will be assigned a character and role by the wizards or gods. Reading all the books about your theme-world is critical to your success there. Guests take minor roles and wander in and out of the action. Frequently the MUSH's creators will create a crisis, which the participants must resolve—in character.

▶▶ *How Do I Connect to a MUD?*

There are several ways to hook yourself up to a MUD. We'll start with Telnet.

▶ Telnet

You can use Telnet once you know the MUD's network address and port number. If, for instance, we knew that PernMUSH was at the network address `cesium.clock.org` at port 4201, we could type:

`telnet cesium.clock.org 4201`

On some VMS systems you will need to type:

`telnet cesium.clock.org/port=4201`

And you arrive in a new reality!

MASTER WORDS

If you get back an error message like "host unknown," you'll need to use the IP address rather than the domain address. Most MUD directories, including the list we present in Appendix D, have both the domain name and IP address listed.

If you're using Telnet on a VMS system, you may need to make sure that your terminal has "newlines" turned on. If it doesn't, the MUD's output will scroll across the screen without any carriage returns, making it very difficult to decipher and interact with.

▶ *MUD Clients*

Telnet is a low-tech and unpleasant way to connect to most MUDs, since it doesn't handle text wrapping. Even worse, if someone speaks to you and you are typing at the same time, your lines will become horribly intermingled, making it hard to see what you're typing and hard to keep track of what's going around you in the MUD. A better way to connect is via client software. MUD client programs provide:

- Access or transport to the MUD

- Pre-formatted macros that let you change MUDs conveniently

- Macros to either "gag" (suppress) or highlight certain MUD output.

Most clients use BSD UNIX, although many also run under System V (SysV) UNIX. Other operating systems for which there are MUD clients include VMS with either MultiNet or Wollongong networking, Macintosh, and IBM's VM. Only a few are available for DOS.

Where Do I Find Clients?

The following list of clients came from the MUD FAQ, and the commentary is taken from the contributors to that list. (Because this commentary was originally written for experienced MUDders, it's pretty terse. The accompanying glossary will help to clarify the more cryptic terminology.) You should use Archie or Veronica to look for the latest versions of these clients.

Living Out Your Fantasies: MUDs

ch.
15

According to experienced players, TinyTalk and TinyFugue are among the easiest to learn; Tcltt and VT are more professional. Some of these clients have more features than others, and some require a fair degree of computer and programming experience to use. Since many MUDders write their own clients, this list can never be complete. Your best bet is to try out a couple, and ask more experienced folk for their recommendations.

In this list, UNIX clients appear first, VMS clients next, miscellaneous clients last. EMACS (LISP) clients for UNIX appear after those written in C.

You'll notice that for many of the MUD clients listed here, the location on the Net includes an IP address (such as 13.1.64.94) as well as the equivalent domain name (for this address, parcftp.xerox.com). This practice is widespread in the MUD community; you'll also see it in Appendix D. In the early days of MUDs in the US, most MUDding was restricted because of bandwidth problems, and so MUDders used hidden or frankly illegal resources to run their games. Even though many MUDs are now acceptable to the owners of the resources, the tradition of using IP addresses continues.

▶

GLOSSARY OF CLIENT TERMS

Here's what those cryptic notes on the MUD list mean:

Auto-login: The client automatically logs into the game for you.

Hiliting: The client allows boldface or other emphasis to be applied to some text. It's often allowed on particular types of output (for example, whispers), or particular players.

Regexp: The client lets you use UNIX-style regular expressions to select text to highlight.

Gag: The client allows some text to be suppressed. The choice of what to suppress is often similar to hiliting (players or regular expressions).

Macros: The client allows new commands to be defined. How complex a macro can be varies greatly between clients; check the documentation for details.

Logging: The client allows output from the MUD to be recorded in a file.

Cyberportals: The client supports special MUD features that can automatically reconnect you to another MUD server.

Screen mode: The client supports some sort of screen mode (beyond just scrolling your output off the top of the screen) on some terminals. The exact support varies.

Triggers: These are events that happen when certain actions on the MUD occur (for example, waving when a player enters the room). The notation means that the client supports them automatically. However, if the client is programmable (see the next item), you can nearly always add this capability, even if it isn't built in.

Programmable: The client allows you to customize it to some extent. Read the client's documentation for programming details.

File and command uploading: The client supports using FTP or similar Internet tools from within the MUD. This feature allows you to download files (including graphics images) from other players. This will also allow you to read mail and do other activities from within the game.

Multiple connects: Lets you connect to the same game more than one time. For example, you could run more than one character or persona at a time using multiple connections. Or, you and a friend could play in the same game from the same terminal.

History buffer: Keeps a listing of the commands you have issued so that you can keep track of what you have done, or go back and easily repeat sequences.

TinyTalk Runs on BSD or SysV. Designed primarily for TinyMUD-style MUDs. Features include line editing, command history, hiliting (whispers, pages, and users), gag, auto-login, simple macros, logging, and cyberportals. Sources: at `ftp.math.okstate.edu`, go to /pub/muds/clients/UnixClients; at `parcftp.xerox.com` (`13.1.64.94`), go to /pub/MOO/clients; at `ftp.tcp.com` (`128.95.10.106`), go to /pub/mud/Clients.

TinyFugue Runs on BSD or SysV. Commonly known as 'tf'. Designed primarily for TinyMUD-style MUDs, although will run on LPMUDs and DikuMUDs. Features include regexp hilites and gags, auto-login, macros, line editing, screen mode, triggers, cyberportals, logging, file and command uploading, shells, and multiple connects. Sources: at `ftp.math.okstate.edu`, go to /pub/muds/clients/UnixClients/tf. At `ftp.tcp.com` (`128.95.10.106`), go to /pub/mud/Clients.

TclTT Runs on BSD. Designed primarily for TinyMUD-style MUDs. Features include regexp hilites, regexp gags, logging, auto-login, partial file uploading, triggers, and programmability. Sources: at `ftp.white.toronto.edu` (`128.100.2.220`), go to /pub/muds/tcltt. At `ftp.math.okstate.edu`, go to /pub/muds/clients/UnixClients.

VT Runs on BSD or SysV. Must have VT102 capabilities. Usable for all types of MUDs. Features include a C-like extension language (VTC) and a simple windowing system. Sources: at `ftp.math.okstate.edu`, go to /pub/muds/clients/vt. At `ftp.tcp.com` (`128.95.10.106`), go to /pub/mud/Clients.

LPTalk Runs on BSD or SysV. Designed primarily for LPMUDs. Features include hiliting, gags, auto-login, macros, logging. Source: at `ftp.math.okstate.edu`, go to /pub/muds/clients/UnixClients.

SayWat Runs on BSD. Designed primarily for TinyMUD-style MUDs. Features include regexp hilites, regexp gags, macros, triggers, logging, cyberportals, rudimentary xterm support, command line history, multiple connects, and file uploading. Sources: at `ftp.math.okstate.edu`, go to /pub/muds/clients/UnixClients.

PMF Runs on BSD. Usable for both LPMUDs and TinyMUD-style MUDs. Features include line editing, auto-login, macros, triggers, gags, logging, file uploads, an X-window interface, and ability to do

Sparc sounds. Sources: at `ftp.lysator.liu.se` (130.236.254.153),
go to /pub/lpmud/clients. At `ftp.math.okstate.edu`, go to /pub/muds/
clients/UnixClients.

TinTin Runs on BSD. Designed primarily for DikuMUDs. Features include macros, triggers, tick-counter features, and multiple connects.
Source: at `ftp.math.okstate.edu`, go to /pub/muds/clients/UnixClients.

TinTinTwo Runs on BSD. Derived from and improved from TinTin.
Additional features include variables and faster triggers. Source: at
`ftp.math.okstate.edu`, go to /pub/muds/clients/UnixClients.

TUsh Runs on BSD or SysV. Features include hiliting, triggers, aliasing, history buffer, and screen mode. Sources: at `ftp.warwick.ac.uk`
(137.205.192.14), go to /tmp. At `ftp.math.okstate.edu`, go to
/pub/muds/clients/UnixClients.

LPmudr Runs on BSD or SysV. Designed primarily for LPMUDs. Features include line editing, command history, auto-login and logging.
Source: at `ftp.math.okstate.edu`, go to /pub/muds/clients/UnixClients.

MUD.el Runs on GNU EMACS. Usable for TinyMUD-style MUDs,
LPMUDs, and MOOs. Features include auto-login, macros, logging,
cyberportals, screen mode, and programmability. Sources: at
`parcftp.xerox.com` (13.1.64.94), go to /pub/MOO/clients. At
`ftp.math.okstate.edu`, go to /pub/muds/clients/UnixClients.

TinyTalk.el Runs on GNU EMACS. Designed primarily for Tiny-
MUD-style MUDs. Features include auto-login, macros, logging,
screen mode, and programmability. Sources: at `ftp.tcp.com`
(128.95.10.106), go to /pub/mud/Clients. At `ftp.math.okstate.edu`,
go to /pub/muds/clients/UnixClients.

LPmud.el Runs on GNU EMACS. Designed primarily for LPMUDs.
Features include macros, triggers, file uploading, logging, screen
mode, and programmability. Sources: at `ftp.lysator.liu.se`
(130.236.254.153), go to /pub/lpmud/clients. At `ftp.math.ok-`
`state.edu`, go to /pub/muds/clients/UnixClients.

CLPmud Runs on GNU EMACS. Designed primarily for LPMUDs.
Similar to LPmud.el, but with the added capability for remote file

Living Out Your
Fantasies: MUDs

ch.
15

retrieval, editing in EMACS, and saving, for LPMud wizards. Source: at `mizar.docs.uu.se` (130.238.8.6), go to /pub/lpmud.

MyMud.el Runs on GNU EMACS. Designed primarily for LPMUDs and DikuMUDs. Features include screen mode, auto-login, macros, triggers, autonavigator, and programmability. Sources: at `ftp.math.ok-state.edu`, go to /pub/muds/clients/UnixClients. At `ftp.tcp.com` (128.95.10.106), go to /pub/mud/Clients.

TINT Runs on VMS with MultiNet networking. Designed primarily for TinyMUD-style MUDs. Features include hiliting (whispers, pages, users), gags, file uploading, simple macros, screen mode. See also TINTw. Source: at `ftp.math.okstate.edu`, go to /pub/muds/clients/VMSClients.

TINTw Runs on VMS with Wollongong networking. Same features as TINT. Sources: at `ftp.math.okstate.edu`, go to /pub/muds/clients/VMSClients. At `ftp.tcp.com` (128.95.10.106), go to /pub/mud/Clients.

FooTalk Runs on VMS with MultiNet networking and BSD UNIX. Primarily designed for TinyMUD-style MUDs. Features include screen mode, and programmability. Source: at `ftp.math.okstate.edu`, go to /pub/muds/clients/VMSClients or /pub/muds/clients/UnixClients.

REXXTALK Runs on IBM VM. Latest version is 2.1. Designed primarily for TinyMUD-style MUDs. Features include screen mode, logging, macros, triggers, hilites, gags, and auto-login. Allows some IBM VM programs to be run while connected to a foreign host, such as TELL and MAIL. Source: at `ftp.math.okstate.edu`, go to /pub/muds/clients/misc.

MUDDweller Runs on any Macintosh. Latest version is 1.2. Connects to a MUD through either the communications toolbox or by MacTCP. Usable for both LPMUDs and TinyMUD-style MUDs. Current features include multiple connections, a command history and a built-in MTP client for LPMUDs. Sources: at `rudolf.ethz.ch` (129.132.57.10), go to /pub/mud. At `mac.archive.umich.edu` (141.211.32.2), go to /mac/util/comm. At `ftp.tcp.com` (128.95.10.106), go to /pub/mud/Clients.

Mudling Runs on any Macintosh. Latest version is 0.9b26. Features include multiple connections, triggers, macros, command line history, separate input and output windows, and a rudimentary mapping system. Sources: at `imv.aau.dk` (129.142.28.1), go to /pub/Mudling. At `ftp.math.okstate.edu`, go to /pub/muds/clients/misc.

MUDCaller Runs under MS-DOS. Latest version is 2.50. Requires an Ethernet card, and uses the Crynwr Packet drivers. Does NOT work with a modem. You need to be able to Telnet from your desktop directly into the network to use this. Features include multiple connections, triggers, command-line history, scroll-back, logging, macros, and separate input and output windows. Sources: at `ftp.tcp.com` (128.95.10.106), go to /pub/mud/Clients. At `ftp.math.okstate.edu` (138.78.10.6), go to /pub/muds/clients/misc. At `oak.oakland.edu` (141.210.10.117), go to /pub/msdos/pktdrvr.

BSXMUD Clients These clients run on various platforms, and allow the user to be able to see the graphics produced by BSXMUDs. BSXMUDs are generally LPMUDs (but not necessarily) that have been modified so that polygon graphics coordinates can be sent to BSX clients, thus letting you play a graphic MUD instead of just a text-based one. For more information, contact `vexar@watserv.ucr.edu`. Sources: at `ftp.lysator.liu.se` (130.236.254.153), go to pub/lpmud/bsx. At `ftp.math.okstate.edu`, go to /pub/muds/BSXstuff. The filenames you need to search for are:

- For Amiga: AmigaBSXClient2_2.lha.
- For DOS: msclient.lzh and x00v124.zip
- For X11: sources, version 3.2—bsxclient3_8c.tar.Z
- For Sun4: binary—client.sparc.tar.Z

Also available are programs to custom-draw your own graphics for a BSXMUD, muddraw.tar.gz and bsxdraw.zoo.

▶ Connecting to MUDs via the Web

Many MUDs are now available from WWW clients, many of which use a Telnet intermediary to get you to the MUD. To find the MUDs via

Living Out Your Fantasies: MUDs

ch.
15

the Web, go to the Mother of All Webs at CERN (almost all Web clients have this listed in their STARTING POINTS directory). Select Information by Subject ➤ Games ➤ MUDs.

▶▶ *Once You're In, What Do You Do?*

Watch and learn is the first rule for MUDding, unless you have an experienced player sitting at your shoulder telling you what to do. Carefully read the login screens and instructions for new users, and find out how to get help.

In a role-playing MUD, and for many people in social MUDs, the character is the thing. You'll want to create a character you enjoy playing, and in which you can comfortably interact with the people around you. Some MUDs allow you to create your own character, and others require you to send off for an assigned role via e-mail. If you have to send off for one, send one e-mail request and then wait for the Powers That Be to reply.

The first steps, then, are these:

- Connect to the MUD and register. You can usually register as a guest to try things out; many MUDs let you give yourself a persona name to help you feel comfortable. Figure 15.2 shows the registration procedure for the Imperial, which is pretty standard.

- Read the opening screens carefully. They will give you something of the flavor of the game, and where important information can be found. Figure 15.3 shows the opening screen in the Imperial.

- Type **help**, read the instructions and directions, and make sure you understand them. Keep asking questions until it's clear how each instruction or command works. Figure 15.4 shows the help screen in the Imperial.

- Read the current news (type **news**), because it will tell you about policies, changes, and the like. It's also a lot of fun! Figure 15.5 shows the news on the Imperial.

FIGURE 15.2 ▶

Registering in the Imperial DikuMUD.

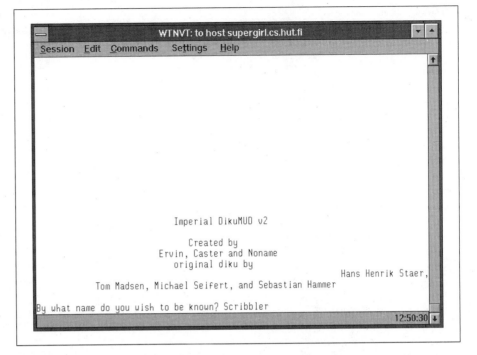

FIGURE 15.3 ▶

The Imperial opening screen.

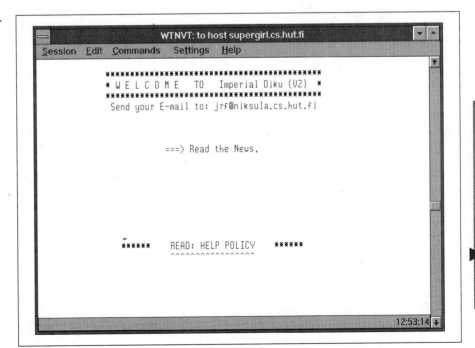

Living Out Your Fantasies: MUDs

ch.
15

FIGURE 15.4 ▶

Getting help in the Imperial.

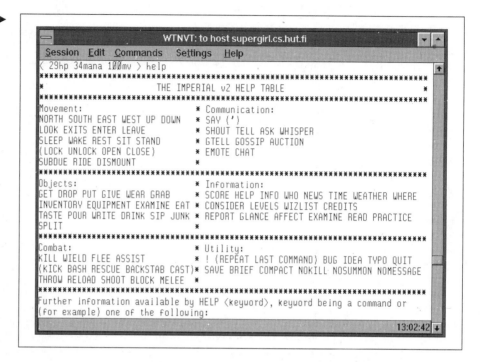

FIGURE 15.5 ▶

Reading the news.

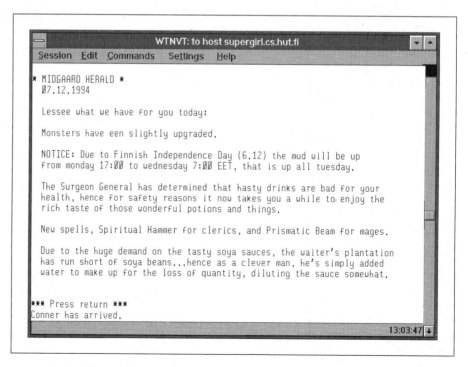

- Read the policy statement (type **policy**). This will tell you the restrictions and agreements the game operates under. It's important to know and agree to these policies. Figure 15.6 shows the policy statement for the Imperial.

- Some MUDs have a newcomer's guide, to help you get started. Reading it will prevent stumbling around and feeling frustrated while you're getting started. Instructions for finding it will usually be somewhere in one of the documents you've already read. Figure 15.7 shows the newbie guide for the Imperial.

- Practice using the commands you've learned to get comfortable with the movement in the game. Figure 15.8 shows a series of movements in the Imperial.

FIGURE 15.6 ▶

The Imperial policy statement.

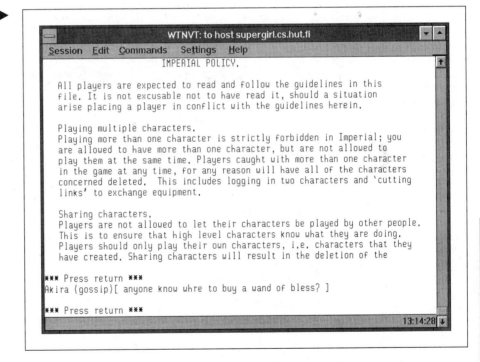

```
                    WTNVT: to host supergirl.cs.hut.fi
  Session   Edit   Commands   Settings   Help
                        IMPERIAL POLICY.

  All players are expected to read and follow the guidelines in this
  file. It is not excusable not to have read it, should a situation
  arise placing a player in conflict with the guidelines herein.

  Playing multiple characters.
  Playing more than one character is strictly forbidden in Imperial; you
  are allowed to have more than one character, but are not allowed to
  play them at the same time. Players caught with more than one character
  in the game at any time, for any reason will have all of the characters
  concerned deleted.  This includes logging in two characters and 'cutting
  links' to exchange equipment.

  Sharing characters.
  Players are not allowed to let their characters be played by other people.
  This is to ensure that high level characters know what they are doing.
  Players should only play their own characters, i.e. characters that they
  have created. Sharing characters will result in the deletion of the

  *** Press return ***
  Akira (gossip)[ anyone know whre to buy a wand of bless? ]

  *** Press return ***
                                                          13:14:28
```

FIGURE 15.7 ▶

*The newcomer's guide
at the Imperial.*

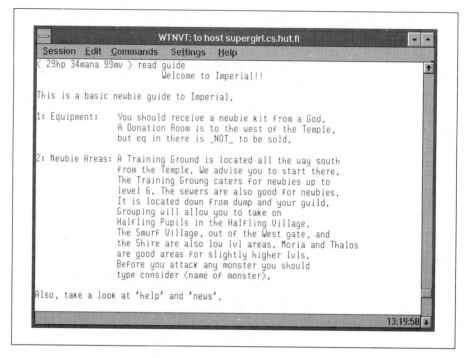

FIGURE 15.8 ▶

*A series of movements
in the Imperial.*

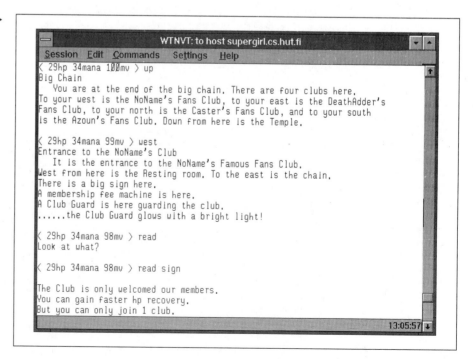

▶ *Why Not Jump Right In?*

Jennifer "Moira" Smith (jds@math.okstate.edu), editor of the MUD FAQ, says, "Some people are easily annoyed when other people clearly have no idea what they are doing, even if they were recently in that position themselves. It'll be much easier for you to cope without some fella saying things you don't understand to you and possibly killing you. However, many MUD players are helpful, and asking them, 'excuse me, are you busy? I'm a brand new player, and I have a question,' will often work just fine."

▶ *Feeling Secure*

Unless you are perpetually a guest, you will want to create a password for your character on every MUD you play on. Choose that password as carefully as you would one for your host system: there are MUD crackers who enjoy trying to break into other people's MUD accounts. **Never** use the same password as the one you use on your host system! Changing it regularly might be a good idea, as well.

Why would anyone want to break into your account? Posing as you, they could send messages from your account which would be traced to you, or simply get all your characters into weird and unpleasant situations. Obviously, the consequences would be less serious than if they broke into your company databases, but if they crack your MUD password, hackers could then try that same password on your company computers.

▶ *Common Commands Used on MUDs*

Most MUDs have a core set of commands that players use to move around and interact with each other. Here are a few to help you get started:

say *X*	Sometimes "X". Your character speaks the word *X*.
look	Your character looks around.
go *X*	Your character goes to point X
home	Takes your character home (in TinyMUDs)

help	Displays a help document
news	Displays important things the creator wants you to know.
who	Lists all the other characters in the MUD at that time.

Some MUDs allow you to alter certain things in the database, by using commands prefixed with "@": @describe, @create, @name, @dig, and @link allow you to expand the universe, change it, or even, perhaps, @destroy it.

Most MUDs have documentation on-line, although better documentation can be gotten via FTP from other sites. Standard sites to check are ftp.tcp.com (128.111.72.60) and ftp.math.okstate.edu, in /pub/muds/misc.

▶ Asking for Help

According to real MUD veterans, the most dangerous time for a budding MUDder is when you think you know what's going on. That's when you are most annoying (and, in adventure MUDs, possibly most likely to be killed by players you've annoyed). You can, however, ask for help nicely. Wizards are usually helpful; if you know that someone is a wizard, you can usually ask them a question, as long as you make sure they're not busy first. Also, players who have been logged on for a long time (which you can check using the who command) are often helpful. In combat MUDs, ask relatively high-level characters.

▶▶ *SchMOOze University: A Different Kind of MUD*

Schools in Canada have taken the MUD concept and created an interactive campus. SchMOOze University is an experiment in bringing the K–12 environment to the MUD world.

MASTER WORDS

SchMOOze is a MOO—MUD, Object-Oriented. This means that the underlying programs are object-oriented (like C++), rather than using older programming styles (like Fortran). This lets the programmer build modules or sections of the code and interconnect them more flexibly. In practice the players should see few differences deriving from this programming style. SchMOOze U differs from combat-style MUDs in its content and purpose rather than its programming techniques.

Schmooze U has a different flavor than the combat-oriented Imperial MUD; Figure 15.9 shows the opening screen. It also has a map of the campus to help you get oriented; Figure 15.10 shows this map. Even the news has a different flavor at SchMOOze U, as you can see in Figure 15.11. And instead of reading a newcomer's guide, participants go

FIGURE 15.9 ▶

The SchMOOze University opening screen.

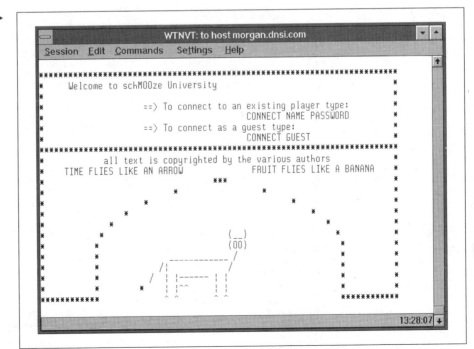

FIGURE 15.10 ▶

*The SchMOOze
U map.*

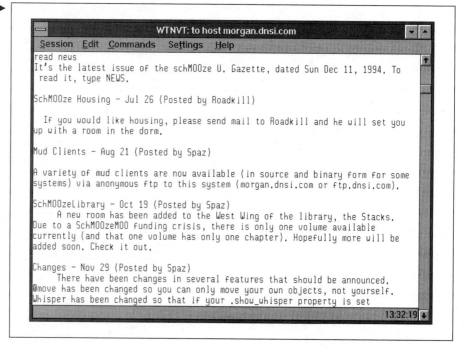

```
                    WTNVT: to host morgan.dnsi.com
   Session   Edit   Commands   Settings   Help
map
Pat [Guest] looks at a map

  .-------------------.  .----.  .------------------------.
  |                   |  | Library |  |                        |
  |      yard         |  | .-------. |  |    yard        yard   |
  |   .--------.      |  |         |  |  .==========.           |
  |  / Student \      |  |         |  |  | Class-   |   yard    |
  |  |  Union  |      |  | North Mall |  | rooms    |           |
  |  .--------.       |  |         |  |  .==========.  /------\ |
  |     *             |  |         |  |     *         | D      |
  |   *   *           |  | Central Mall |  |  *   *    | O   P |
  |   | |             |  |         |  |  | |          | R   A |
  |  West Mall        |  |         |  | East Mall     |_M_  S |
  |  .--------------. |  |         |  | .==========.  |    T  |
  |  | Administration||  | South Mall |  | Conference | |  U  |
  |  .--------------. |  |    --      |  | Center     | |  R  |
  .-------------------.  |   / Arch \ |  .==========.   |  E  |
                         .--|       |--.                .------.
                            | Entrance Gate |
                            .----    ----.

                                                        13:30:42
```

FIGURE 15.11 ▶

*The news at
SchMOOze U.*

```
                    WTNVT: to host morgan.dnsi.com
   Session   Edit   Commands   Settings   Help
read news
It's the latest issue of the schMOOze U. Gazette, dated Sun Dec 11, 1994. To
 read it, type NEWS.

SchMOOze Housing - Jul 26 (Posted by Roadkill)

  If you would like housing, please send mail to Roadkill and he will set you
up with a room in the dorm.

Mud Clients - Aug 21 (Posted by Spaz)

A variety of mud clients are now available (in source and binary form for some
systems) via anonymous ftp to this system (morgan.dnsi.com or ftp.dnsi.com).

SchMOOzeLibrary - Oct 19 (Posted by Spaz)
    A new room has been added to the West Wing of the library, the Stacks.
Due to a SchMOOzeMOO funding crisis, there is only one volume available
currently (and that one volume has only one chapter). Hopefully more will be
added soon. Check it out.

Changes - Nov 29 (Posted by Spaz)
    There have been changes in several features that should be announced.
@move has been changed so you can only move your own objects, not yourself.
Whisper has been changed so that if your .show_whisper property is set

                                                        13:32:19
```

to a beginning class to get their feet on the ground at the U. The class-room description is shown in Figure 15.12.

FIGURE 15.12

The beginner's class-room at SchMOOze U.

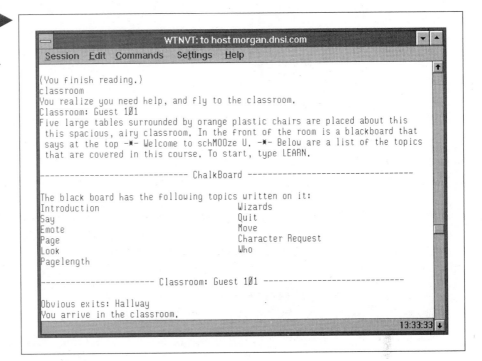

```
┌──────────────────────────────────────────────────────────────────┐
│ □                   WTNVT: to host morgan.dnsi.com            ▼ ▲  │
│  Session  Edit  Commands  Settings  Help                         ↑│
│(You finish reading.)                                              │
│classroom                                                         │
│You realize you need help, and fly to the classroom.             │
│Classroom: Guest 101                                             │
│Five large tables surrounded by orange plastic chairs are placed about this│
│ this spacious, airy classroom. In the front of the room is a blackboard that│
│ says at the top -*- Welcome to schMOOze U. -*- Below are a list of the topics│
│ that are covered in this course. To start, type LEARN.          │
│                                                                  │
│----------------------------- ChalkBoard -------------------------│
│                                                                  │
│The black board has the following topics written on it:          │
│Introduction                        Wizards                       │
│Say                                 Quit                          │
│Emote                               Move                          │
│Page                                Character Request             │
│Look                                Who                           │
│Pagelength                                                        │
│----------------------- Classroom: Guest 101 --------------------│
│                                                                  │
│Obvious exits: Hallway                                           │
│You arrive in the classroom.                                     │
│                                                     13:33:33 ↓  │
└──────────────────────────────────────────────────────────────────┘
```

▶▶ *Talking about MUDs in Newsgroups*

People talk about almost everything else in Usenet newsgroups, so it's not surprising that there are several newsgroups associated with MUDs. You can check out:

rec.games.mud.admin   Postings pertaining to the administrative side of MUDs.

rec.games.mud.announce   Moderated group, for announcements of MUDs opening, closing, moving, partying, and so on.

rec.games.mud.diku   Postings pertaining to DikuMUDs.

`rec.games.mud.lp`   Postings pertaining to LPMUDs.

`rec.games.mud.misc`   Miscellaneous postings.

`rec.games.mud.tiny`   Postings pertaining to the Tiny family of MUDs.

As always, post your news appropriately. If you want to post something to Usenet, please do it in the group where it best belongs—no posts about TinyMUSH in the Diku group, no questions about an LPMUD in the Tiny group, and so on.

▶▶ MUD Lore

The MUD Frequently Asked Questions list, compiled by Jennifer Smith, gives not only a lot of useful basic information, but also a vivid sense of what it's like to interact with MUDs (and MUDders). Following are some extracts, including a glossary.

▶ How Do I Start My Own MUD?

First, you need to pick server software. You'll have to figure out how to compile it and get it running, and you'll need to know how to keep it running, which usually involves some programming skills, generally in C, and a good deal of time. Of course, you also need to be well versed in the ways and commands of that particular MUD server, and you'll probably need help running the place from a few of your friends.

Don't forget that you'll have to have a computer system to run it on, and the resources with which to run it. Most MUDs use anywhere from 5 to 90 megabytes of disk space, and memory usage can be anything from 1 to 35 megabytes. A good rule of thumb is to first ask around for specifics on that server; average MUDs need around 25 megabytes of disk space for everything, and about 10 megabytes of memory, although the exact numbers vary widely.

If you don't *explicitly own* the machine you're thinking about right now, you had better get the permission of the machine owner before you bring up a MUD on his computer. MUDs are not extremely processing-consumptive, but they do use up some computing power. You wouldn't want people plugging in their appliances into the outlets of your home without your permission or knowledge, would you?

▶ Glossary

Here are some of the most important definitions from the FAQ list.

bot A *bot* is a computer program that logs into a MUD and pretends to be a human being. Some of them, like Julia, are pretty clever—legend has it that Julia's fooled people into believing that she's human. Others have less functionality.

clueless newbie A *newbie* is someone who has only recently begun to participate in some kind of activity. When we're born, we're all life newbies until we get experience under our belts (or diapers, whatever). You're a clueless newbie until you've got the hang of MUDding, basically.

cyborg A *cyborg* is defined as "part man, part machine." In the MUD world, this means that your client is doing some of the work for you. For instance, you can set up many clients to automatically greet anyone entering the room. You can also set up clients to respond to certain phrases (or 'triggers'). Of course, this can have disastrous consequences. If Player_A sets his client up to say Hi every time Player_B says Hi, and Player_B does likewise, their clients will frantically scream Hi at each other over and over until they manage to escape. Needless to say, runaway automation is very heavily frowned upon by anyone who sees it. If you program your client to do anything special, first make sure that it cannot go berserk and overload the MUD.

dino A *dino* is someone who has been around for a very long time (cf. 'dinosaur'). These people tend to reminisce nostalgically about dead or nonexistent MUDs that were especially fun or interesting.

furry A *furry* is an anthropomorphic intelligent animal. If you've ever seen Zoobilee Zoo on The Learning Channel, you know what I mean. Furries are not unique to MUDdom—they originated in comics, and can usually be found at comic or animation conventions and the like. Generally, any MUD character that has fur and is cute is deemed a furry. Most furries hang out on FurryMUCK, naturally.

Living Out Your
Fantasies: MUDs

▶ ▶

ch.

15

HAVEN On many TinyMUDs, there are several "flags" associated with each room. The HAVEN flag is probably the most famous one. In rooms where the HAVEN flag is set, no character may kill another. (See "player killing" below.)

log Certain client programs allow *logs* to be kept off the screen. A time-worn and somewhat unfriendly trick is to entice someone into having TinySex with you, log the proceedings, and post them to rec.games.mud—and have a good laugh at the other person's expense. Logs are useful for recording interesting or useful information or conversations, as well.

Maving Mav is a famous TinyMUDder who sometimes accidentally left a colon on the front of a whisper, thus directing private messages to the whole room. The meaning of the verb has changed to include making any say/whisper/page/pose typing confusion.

net lag The Internet (the network which connects your computer to mine) is made up of thousands of interconnected networks. Between your computer and the computer that houses the MUD, there may be up to 30 gateways and links connecting them over serial lines, high-speed modems, leased lines, satellite uplinks, etc. If one of these gateways or lines crashes, is suddenly overloaded, or gets routing confused, you may notice a long period of lag time between your input and the MUD's reception of that input. Computers that are (logistically) nearer to the computer running the MUD are less susceptible to net lag. Another source of lag is if the computer which hosts the MUD is overloaded. When net lag happens, it is best to just patiently wait for it to pass.

player killing Can you kill (permanently) another player's persona? The answer to this question varies widely. On most combat-oriented MUDs, such as LPMUD and Diku, player killing is taken quite seriously. On others, it's encouraged. On most TinyMUDs, as there is little or no combat system, player killing is sometimes employed as a means of showing irritation at another player, or merely to show emphasis of something said (usually, it means "and I really mean it!"). It's best to find out the rules of the MUD you're on, and play by them.

spam Spamming, derived from a famous Monty Python sketch, is the flooding of appropriate media with information (such as repeated very long 'say' commands). Unintentional spamming, such as what happens when you walk away from your computer screen for a few minutes, then return to find several screenfuls of text waiting to scroll by, is just a source of irritation. Intentional spamming, such as when you repeat very long 'say' commands many times, or quote /usr/dict/words at someone, is usually frowned on, and can get you in trouble with the MUD administration.

TinySex TinySex is the act of performing MUD actions to imitate having sex with another character, usually consensually, sometimes with one hand on the keyboard, sometimes with two. Basically, it's speed-writing interactive erotica. Realize that the other party is not obligated to be anything like he/she says, and in fact may be playing a joke on you (see *log, above*).

Wizard or God Gods are the people who own the database, the administrators. In most MUDs, wizards are barely distinguishable from gods—they're just barely one step down from the God of the MUD. An LPMUD wizard is a player who has 'won' the game, and is now able to create new sections of the game. Wizards are very powerful, but they don't have the right to do whatever they want to you; they must still follow their own set of rules, or face the wrath of the gods. Gods can do whatever they want to whomever they want whenever they want—it's their MUD. If you don't like how a god acts or lets his wizards act toward the players, your best recourse is to simply stop playing that MUD, and play another.

A more appropriate name for wizards would probably be 'janitor', since they tend to have to put up with responsibilities and difficulties (without pay) that nobody else would be expected to handle. Remember, they're human beings on the other side of the wire. Respect them for their generosity.

▶▶ *Time Spent, or Time Wasted?*

College officials and K–12 educators have stated publicly in some areas that MUDs, like other computer games, are a waste of time. Certainly those folks who've learned to do programming and database design in order to create their own MUDs would disagree. Most regular visitors to MUDs would agree that they are, like many other forms of netsurfing, highly addictive. Jennifer Smith says in the MUD FAQ: "The jury is still out on whether MUDding is 'just a game' or 'an extension of real life with game-like qualities...' You shouldn't do anything that you wouldn't do in real life, even if the world is a fantasy world. The important thing to remember is that it's the fantasy world of possibly hundreds of people, and not just yours in particular. There's a human being on the other side of each and every wire! Always remember that you may meet these other people some day, and they may break your nose. People who treat others badly gradually build up bad reputations and eventually receive the NO FUN Stamp of Disapproval."

▶▶ *Finding a MUD*

In Appendix D we give a partial list of MUDs, from the list posted to the various newsgroups associated with MUDs. Most are available via Telnet, but many are becoming available with WWW. This list is the most authoritative list of MUDs available; it may not contain every MUD (not all are publicly advertised), and some MUDs may be unavailable from time to time. However, this list should provide you with a solid entrance into the many worlds available via MUDs.

Becoming an
Information Provider

PART TWO

► ► CHAPTER 16

Should My Organization Be "On" the Net?

▶ ▶ *In* Part I, we talked about how individuals can use the Internet to find information and exchange ideas. Now we're going to turn our attention to businesses, government agencies, and other organizations. This chapter is addressed to those of you—managers, executives, and administrators—who must decide whether to connect your organization to the Net.

You've heard all the hype about fast communication, easy access to information, hidden treasures on the Net. You've also heard about the horror stories: crackers breaking into company data, employees storing pornography on accounting machines, and so on. How do you balance the potential for good against the headaches?

Certainly, getting an Internet connection, either by buying host accounts or biting the bullet and getting your whole company wired up, is an expensive proposition. You need to invest that money wisely.

And, once you've gotten connected, how do you make smart business decisions about that asset: who will use it, how will it be supported, and how will it enhance your service to your clients or customers?

Let's walk through these issues one by one.

▶▶ *What Are the Benefits?*

There is one most important question that a planner needs to be able to answer when considering an Internet connection—What do you want to accomplish?

- You want to communicate, internally and externally, more efficiently.

- You want to access resources quickly and for the least possible cost.

- You want to find up-to-date information on your product's marketplace—for example, what your competition is doing, what your customers want, and the business and government environment.

- You want to deliver information and support to your clients in the most cost effective, quickest, and most efficient manner.

As a business or governmental agency, presumably you want the same things anyone wants from a potential information and communications service. Let's look at an Internet connection the same way you look at any other corporate investment decision. You want to use your investment wisely:

- to reduce unnecessary expenditures.

- to improve the productivity of your staff.

- to improve relations with your customers (including funding agencies and boards of directors).

- to improve the speed and accuracy of your agency's communications.

Assuredly these are laudable goals. Now let's see how the Internet can help your organization meet them.

▶ *Reduce Unnecessary Expenditures*

Joel Maloff (maloff@aol.com) of The Maloff Company, a telecommunications consulting firm based in Dexter, MI, cites a study stating that more than 35 percent of most business long distance costs are for sending faxes. So, let's compare the cost of an e-mail message to that of a fax.

If the fax were a formal one, it would cost about the same as a business letter to produce. The outright and hidden costs of business letters are very high:

- The time of your professional and clerical staff to compose it.

- The time to enter it.

- The time to proofread and correct it.

- The time to print it out, copy it, and file it (using paper, disk files, or both).
- The amortized costs of the computer used for word processing.
- The cost of the paper you print it on.
- The cost of delivering it, using either US Mail or a courier service.

These are the production costs, and they can really add up! With a fax, the only difference is that for the delivery expense, you replace the postage or express courier charges with those of the telephone line toll charges and the amortized cost of the facsimile machine itself.

How could the Internet improve the cost picture? Look at these savings:

- No printing or stationery costs.
- Fax delivery long distance charges should be compared to the amortized or direct costs of the e-mail transmission over the Internet, that is, the telephone and networking costs.
- Reduced clerical costs: most professionals compose and correct their own e-mail correspondence, but clerical staff is often used to print and transmit faxes.
- The costs for filing and saving what was written would be incurred as part of the e-mail costs.

In addition, if an e-mail system already exists for internal or departmental use, the composition, proofreading, and storage costs could be amortized over a larger body of work.

We're sure that you can see how such calculations go. In order to present a well-documented case, of course, you need to be able to identify all the cost components of how you are doing things now and compare them with how you might do things with an Internet connection.

How about comparing delivery, though? Because we are more familiar with faxes, we tend to trust them more: common wisdom says they are more reliable, and you're using telephone lines in each case. Let's compare the typical e-mail delivery to a fax delivery.

Faxes can fail to go through because:

1. The phone line is busy on either end.

My Organization "On" the Net?

ch. **16**

2. The receiving fax had no paper.

3. The receiving fax misprinted the message and the message needed to be resent.

Lots of things can go wrong with faxes. E-mail generally has these advantages:

1. It transmits faster: most e-mail messages travel at line speeds of at least 14.4 kbps, and many go at the T1 rate or higher.

2. It monitors itself if it needs to be retransmitted.

3. It doesn't end up on the floor or in the wrong person's mailbox for days.

Can facsimiles be better than e-mail? Realistically, there are only two points where faxes would provide improved communication. The first is if the sending or receiving e-mail system is not capable of handling image files and images are needed in the communication. The second is if the person or organization you want to send e-mail to doesn't have e-mail.

M A S T E R   W O R D S

Of course, just to really confuse things, there are a couple of facsimile-transmission-over-the-Internet experiments that combine the two methods quite nicely. You can compose an e-mail message and send it through a gateway process to a fax machine in several locations. There are volunteer organizations who are running the necessary software and hardware to make it all work. For more information, send e-mail to tpc-faq@town.hall.org.

Phone Bill Blues

Let's suppose you have an office in England and an office in Atlanta. Your sales people talk regularly to coordinate shipments: the ten members of your staff may make five or more long-distance phone calls, lasting 20 minutes or more, to London a day. Your long-distance charges alone will be over $3000 a month, according to a cost estimate by a Southern Bell sales representative.

With Internet host accounts, your charges for those ten people, and all the e-mail traffic they send back and forth, would (in general) be less than $750 per month, computed on an average cost of $50 to $75 per person per month quoted by four Internet service providers.

With a direct link into your company LANs in both sites, after startup costs your phone bill for the phone line that links you into the Internet would be less than $1500, and *all the other advantages of the Internet come with it.*

One-Stop Shopping

If your organization is using information from several different dial-up information providers like Dialog or Dow/Jones, you might be able to consolidate your dial-up services in one Internet provider. This would allow you to concentrate your energy on interacting with the data and not with the method of acquiring the data. You would use your Internet connection (dial or dedicated) to reach the Internet itself. Then you would Telnet to the desired information services. Note that your contractual relationship with these services remains. You will still need to pay for the services that you use. There is nothing about the data access using the Internet that changes your relationship with the information provider.

Destroy Fewer Trees

Using e-mail instead of a photocopier to pass along announcements, memos, company-wide policies, and the whole range of items to be communicated can save thousands of dollars a year in paper, toner, maintenance, and replacement costs, not to mention the administrative staff time involved. No one has to stand at the photocopier, sort, or deliver the papers, either.

▶ Improve the Productivity of Your Staff

Faster access to information about new products and techniques can make a big difference in applying new methods for improving anyone's professional activities. News from professional colleagues can travel the Internet much faster than via the conventional methods of letters and papers given at conferences. And the news can get to more people at the same time.

Let's take two relatively recent examples from the scientific community: Do you remember the cold fusion experiments? A scientist believed that he had found a safe and sane method of producing nuclear energy. A great flurry of activity hit the Internet and many scientists around the world were discussing and criticizing the experiment upon whose results the assertion rested. Because of the quick release of the experimental methodology and experimental data, other scientists were able to point out the fatal flaw that made the experiment valueless.

During July 1994, the eyes and telescopes of the earth's astronomers were turned to the planet Jupiter to observe the pieces of the comet Shoemaker-Levy 9 strike the planet. Interest in the telescopic images photographed from the Hubble Telescope was so great among the Internet community at large that the common sites for astronomical images were swamped with requests. And those requests were from the amateur community!

▶ ▶MASTER WORDS

Want to see pictures from the impact? Using a Web client, open

`http://navigator.jpl.nasa.gov/s19.s19.html.`

The professional astronomers had set up private mailing lists that cited specific observations from each observatory. As the world turned in its diurnal rotation, different observatories would have views in turn. Some had views obstructed by cloud layers. Others had quite clear views. As each group in turn recorded its successes and failures and shared them with their colleagues, the groups that followed in the viewing pattern were able to modify the settings of their observations. One scientist remarked that without these communications, their observatory would have completely missed the excitement; they had been looking in the wrong part of the light spectrum. Information from another observatory allowed them time to change their settings before Jupiter rose in their night sky.

What about Regular Folk?

Yes, you say, but these people are scientists. They are used to collaborative efforts. That's how they work even without something like the Internet. Quite so. Let's think about how other people can become more productive doing research on the Net. Let's say a spreadsheet program is malfunctioning in your environment. Your network administrator sends an e-mail describing the problem to the customer support people for that product. They return a message saying that they know about the bug and have placed a patch (or fix) for it on their FTP server. Your administrator can then go and get the new program code, install the fix, and have your spreadsheet users up and running quite quickly.

Here's another type of research: Let's say that you are interested in determining the appropriate standards for a potential development project your company is preparing for possible purchase by a government agency. You can go to a library, look up the citations for the documents containing those standards, and then write the agency to ask for a copy of the relevant documents. Or you can use the Internet to connect with The Document Center (`http://www.service.com/doccenter`) and contract with them to supply you with the relevant documents much more quickly.

Or suppose you want to see whether the name of the product you're going to market clashes with other products. One naming service has published a Web page (illustrated in Figure 16.1) that lets you check out recent trademarks and product names.

Document sharing and collaborative work are enhanced by the Internet. For example, if you already have an internal e-mail system, you probably know that a document can be electronically circulated among your staff for comments much more easily than if the author had to print, photocopy, and distribute it by hand. An Internet connection lets you take the process a step further and circulate documents outside your organization. The author can put it in an FTP archive, Web page, or Gopher server, and then send an e-mail to the appropriate people telling them where to find it and what sort of feedback he needs.

FIGURE 16.1 ▶

The naming service Web page.

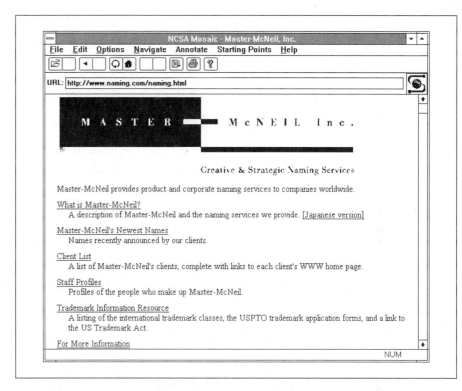

▶▶**WARNING**

Access to e-mail doesn't make people read and return documents faster if they are prone to leave them on their desk and forget them. You may still have to nag people to read and comment on documents, even with e-mail and document sharing. But at least it's easier to nag!

Quantity and Quality Time

Say a customer sends in a critical problem report via e-mail at 6 PM one evening. One of your staff checks her mail from home, and is able to set a fix for the client in motion over the network, including having a report back in the client's mailbox the next morning, and a shipping order cut to go out as soon as the courier service can get there in the morning.

One major Chicago newspaper discovered in the early 1990s that when they allowed their staffers to call in from home, the number of column inches produced increased by 16% over the next four months.

And, a side benefit to having Net access, particularly if your staffers can access your system from home, is that they can work from home even during domestic crises like chicken pox, broken cars, and visiting mothers-in-law.

Interoperability

It's a common problem: Let's say your accounting department bought their computer equipment from IBM, and your sales department bought theirs from Apple. They can't easily share documents, e-mail, or files.

Access to the Internet can provide you the ability to share these items between and among different e-mail systems. Your accounting department can send spreadsheet files via e-mail or transfer them using FTP to your sales department. Using interoperability software or hardware, you can link those departments and cut down on duplication of effort.

▶ Improve Relations with Your Customers

What's the most difficult thing to do well in business? We think it's providing enough information to keep your customer's happy.

Providing Information to Your Customer

As most of us know, getting and providing technical support for computer software and hardware can be a frustrating process for all concerned. If you've been on the consumer end, you've probably spent a lot of time listening to annoying elevator music, waiting for someone to field your call (or staring at your screen, waiting for an e-mail response).

Frequently the information that you needed is a simple fact, or something that should be in the company's literature. Internet information publishing provides a way to get that information into your customer's hands with fewer phone calls and happier customers.

Please note that this concept is not original: many, many technology companies provide customer communications using Internet publishing mechanisms. Offices of the United States federal government, like the Census Bureau, for example, have also been publishing information via the Internet for some time. More and more local and state offices are doing so, too.

Sometimes the information is relatively simple: agendas of meetings that are required by law to be published before the meeting happens; hours and telephone numbers of city offices, and so on. Sometimes the information provided is more complex: information about how to file an application for a specific type of permit, or even the application it-self. If the computer system checks the data as you enter it, you can file a complete and accurate form without traveling to the permit office. Everybody wins: you don't have to go to the permit office, the permit people have fewer walk-in applicants to interrupt their work flow, and the application itself is more complete the first time it is turned in.

▶ *Improve the Speed and Accuracy of Your Communications*

The permit application is a good example for this theme, too. If the ap-plication form is available on-line, the agency has, in effect, provided the necessary information immediately.

Or let's say that you suddenly have a job open in your organization. What could be quicker than to have your human resources agent post that job description to an appropriate newsgroup or job bulletin board where people who have the skills you need might see it? If you also sug-gest that qualified applicants e-mail their materials to you, you may have a pool of qualified applicants very quickly from a very broad base of potential candidates. You'll be able to respond to them with your questions via e-mail or the telephone that very day.

▶ ▶ N O T E

> **Recently, a call went out for proposals for multimedia projects for educators. Within two days, over 900 completed proposals were submitted—via e-mail. And when the organization asked for resumes for a coordinator for the project, close to 500 resumes flooded into their mailbox in just a few hours.**

This actually happened for Pat. Cygnus Support posted a job opening to the Net early one morning. Pat was living in Michigan, looking for opportunities in California. By 11:30 Michigan time (within an hour of the posting), Pat had e-mailed her resume and faxed some additional materials to Cygnus. By 2 PM Michigan time, she had a confirmed interview. All this was done by telephone and e-mail. (By the way, she got the job.)

 ▶ ▶**W A R N I N G**

If you're going to post a job announcement to the Net, make sure you've informed the people in your organization who might be affected by it. You don't want the job posting to reach the internal audience via an outside third party. If this happens, your quick, accurate communication can turn the affected department into a shambles even quicker than you will receive appropriate responses.

▶▶ *How Can We Use It?*

Back in Chapter 2 you saw a chart (Table 2.1) outlining different types of communications and mapping Internet applications and tools to those types. Now that you've had a closer look at those tools, let's go through those communication types and see how you can use the Internet to achieve certain types of communications that are appropriate and necessary for business and government organizations.

▶ *Interactive/Simultaneous Communications*

Interactive and simultaneous uses of the Internet are not as common as the asynchronous communications. For many users, one of the most convenient features of the Internet is that communication *doesn't* have to be simultaneous—you can send e-mail for someone to read at their convenience, you can download a file at midnight, or you can communicate with someone in a different time zone. Interactive communications have the same limitations as do telephone conversations: they are costly and they require people to be in a specific place at a specific time. If someone in California wishes to communicate with someone in France, for example, they have a lot of arranging to do ahead of time. Nonetheless, there are some valuable ways that businesses and other organizations can use the Internet's interactive/simultaneous tools.

Talk

Talk, discussed in Chapter 14, is the Internet tool to use for *Type I* Private, individual-to-individual communications that may be authoritative. It is best for the type of message that need never be saved: "Please bring home some milk, dear" is an important (and probably authoritative) message, but it need not be saved for posterity. Don't use Talk for anything that needs to be kept for organizational records.

Why not use the phone? It can be less expensive to use Talk than to use the telephone. Telephone calls from business telephones are expensive.

Figure 16.2 shows a Talk session in progress.

FIGURE 16.2

A Talk session in operation.

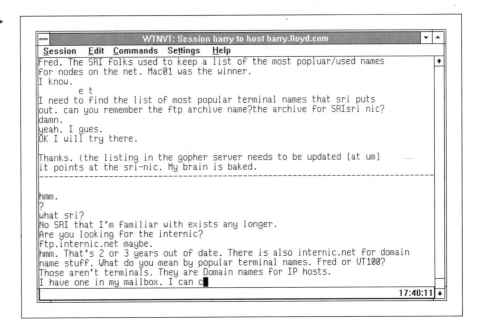

IRC and MUDs

These are the Internet tools to use for *Type II* Public, many-contributors-to-many-recipients, non-authoritative communications. IRC is discussed in Chapter 14 and MUDs are discussed in Chapter 15. While it's true that many MUDs specialize in slaying dragons and wielding swords, the idea of a shared world or environment can have more serious applications. Training is a good example of this. You need to train a group of people; they should be working interactively (research has shown that people learn more effectively if they are actively engaged in the process); and someone (the trainer) needs to manage their communication and the environment in which they're working. What to do? Have a multiuser shared environment designed to handle your training case. Instead of dragons and swords, you have your specific business case included: your products, competitor's tactics, and so on. You can then provide the training environment to many people, geographically dispersed or not, at the same time, keeping participants on the topics to be discussed and learned. The dragons you slay could be those of your competition.

IRC on internal networks has been used by several computer hardware development companies for conversation among geographically widespread engineers and programmers. It's the equivalent of a meeting without the travel time. Participants preferred IRC over a telephone conference call. You can always tell who was talking in IRC because each comment is labeled with the name of the "talker," no one was ever "inaudible," and participants had easy access to online information.

Audio/Video Conferencing

Audio/Video conferencing on the Internet isn't quite ready for "prime time" at this writing. When it is, it will be Type III communication—public, many-contributors-to-many-recipients communication which may be authoritative. As the technology improves, it may be possible to use the Internet to deploy this type of service in a relatively low-cost manner to anywhere that can be reached by the Internet. The advantages are obvious: being able to televise a complicated or unusual medical procedure would be a wonderful way to reach medical professionals who would like to have their skills kept up-to-date. Travel to meetings is expensive, yet the benefit of hearing from and seeing colleagues in similar positions in other organizations is again well-documented. Much that is useful comes from the interchange of information and ideas among colleagues. As the technology becomes less expensive and more widely deployed, the communication itself will become less formal. It will be easier to use, and more people will know how to use it and have access to it. When that happens, you will get the Internet equivalent of the gossip in the hallways at conferences; and everybody knows that that's where the *real* action is, anyway.

Broadcast Messages on Systems and Networks

These are not very exciting, but they represent the Type I*V* communications: they are public, published contributions to many recipients, and they are authoritative. When you are logged into a host system, and a message warning you about possible system instability is transmitted, you do believe it and act accordingly. This type of message is completely irrelevant to you if you are not connected to that system at that time.

One building facilities manager uses broadcast messages over the various networks in the building to send notices of impending fire drills, cars with lights on, and other time-critical information. This was the fastest way to reach most of the people in the many different companies housed in the building.

▶ Non-Simultaneous Communications

Asynchronous communication is where the Internet excels. The sender and the recipient need not be connected at the same time, and they may not even know one another. In particular, to distribute a published work on the Internet you don't need to know someone's address. The recipient comes to find the information. It's the best kind of direct mail advertising or announcing: the people who are interested read your material; the people who aren't interested don't read it. And you haven't wasted any material resources to provide the information to your audience.

E-Mail

E-mail (discussed in Chapter 8) remains the most used feature on the Internet. It's Type I communication: private, individual-to-individual, and possibly authoritative. In this category you find the responses to questions about your products: what does it do? where can I obtain it? what does it cost? what are the terms and conditions for a customer to use it? These questions can be directed to a specific person to answer, or to a specific mailbox (like Support or Accounting). You can designate a person to answer or have a programmed answer (prepared e-mail auto-responses) and then forward it to a specific person or group for action.

Figure 16.3 shows a typical customer request for information.

▶ ▶ **MASTER WORDS**

The most common address for folks to try if they don't know how to reach you is info@*youraddress* **(for example,** info@lloyd.com**). If you place an autoresponse at this address, people can get a summary of your services without someone having to answer all the e-mail personally—another savings in staff time.**

FIGURE 16.3 ▶

A typical customer inquiry via e-mail.

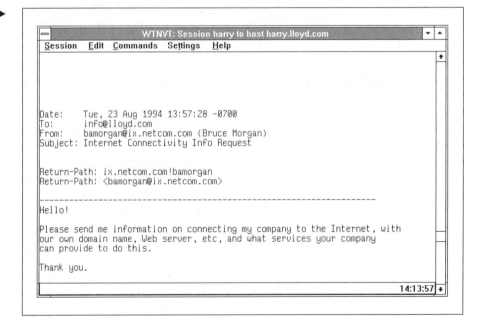

```
Date:    Tue, 23 Aug 1994 13:57:28 -0700
To:      info@lloyd.com
From:    bamorgan@ix.netcom.com (Bruce Morgan)
Subject: Internet Connectivity Info Request

Return-Path: ix.netcom.com!bamorgan
Return-Path: <bamorgan@ix.netcom.com>

------------------------------------------------------------------
Hello!

Please send me information on connecting my company to the Internet, with
our own domain name, Web server, etc, and what services your company
can provide to do this.

Thank you.
```

SETTING UP A FINGER INFORMATION FILE

You can easily set up information files which your clients and others can access using the Finger utility. (These instructions are for those on standard UNIX systems. If you're on another operating system, consult with your systems administrator to work out the exact details: the general principles hold.)

You (or your systems administrator) should set up a user named "sales" or "info" or any other name you want people to be able to access information from.

Then, on this user's account, create a ".plan" file with the information you want to distribute.

In this file, which should be no more than 24 lines long (if you want it to display as one screenful of information), you can put relevant and interesting information about your company. Remember to include access information, so that neophyte Net users can figure out how to reach you.

A sample file for sales@widget.com might look like this:

```
        Thanks for contacting The Widget Company!

You surprised us!


We knew our new model 27 automated Widgetwasher was a good
product, but you have been ordering them in unanticipated
quantities! As a result, deliveries are running
approximately 10 days behind. We are currently filling
orders placed by January 12, 1995.

We have added additional shifts to our manufacturing plant
to catch up with the demand. We expect to be back on top
of
our normal 2-day order turnaround by February 15, 1995.
```

> Our new Web pages now contain full-color images of our
> 1995 catalogue. Point your Web browser at http://www.wid-
> get.com/ to see it. Or, call 1-800-WIDGETS to get a free
> copy sent to you via regular mail.

Make sure permissions for this file are set correctly so that others
may write to it without having to sign on as user sales, so that you
can quickly and easily edit the information and keep it up to date.

You will also need to make sure that your systems administrator
has set up the *finger demon* correctly so that .plan files on your
system can be shown to those outside your local network. Be sure
to warn company staff before you enable this feature, if it's currently disabled.

FTP

Making files available for transfer via FTP (discussed in Chapter 8) is
another form of nonsimultaneous communication. The files you "put
up" can be something relatively simple like a list of telephone numbers
for various functions in your organization, or a list that describes the
products offered.

▶ ▶ **MASTER WORDS**

**Not everyone has PostScript or other specialized
software designed to view new formats that aren't
widely used yet. Luckily, it is possible to distribute
information with attached readers so that the people
"picking up" the information have the ability to
read/view it, but doing so makes the operation more
complex for the information consumer. Unless you can
provide self-extracting files, which more-or-less set
themselves up for your intended audience, you will
need to leave instructions that sometimes folks have
trouble following. Once you are at that point, it's time
to open a technical support department.**

Figure 16.4 shows the Apple Events directory from ftp.apple.com, selected using Netcom's NetCruiser FTP program.

FIGURE 16.4

Retrieving FTP files.

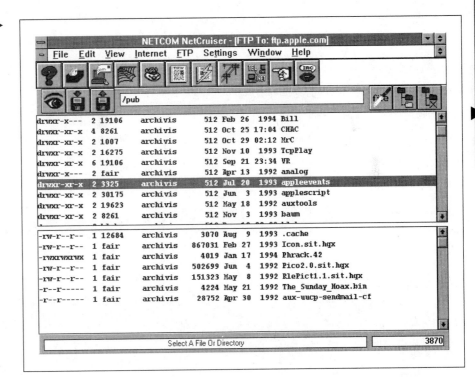

Finger

Another way of making information about your organization available to anyone who wants it is to place it in a file accessible by Finger, discussed in Chapter 9. This type of communication is suitable for relatively simple information, such as hours of operation or simple product literature.

Figure 16.5 shows the information that Cygnus Support makes available via Finger.

FIGURE 16.5 ▶

Response from fingering info@cygnus.com.

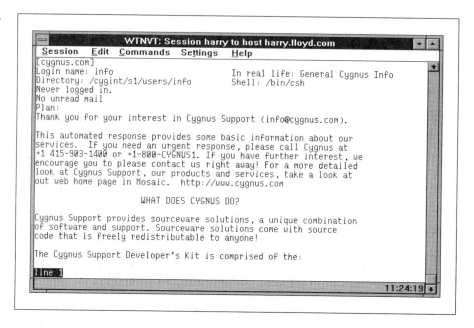

AUTORESPONSE FILES IN E-MAIL

One of the best uses of e-mail technology is to send an automated responses back to people who send messages to your company. A quick acknowledgment of e-mail, just as with regular mail, satisfies the customer that her message has actually been received and is in the pipeline. It also gives you two benefits: you can send them more information about your company, and you can give your staff some breathing room to answer the mail at a more convenient moment, sure that the client has received an acknowledgment of the original mail.

Setting up your e-mail to send an autoresponse is fairly easy on typical UNIX systems, using the capabilities of the *alias database*. Here's how it works:

Usually, sales or info is the alias for a group of folks who handle such mail. You can add a command to the alias database entry which says to the e-mail system, "Deliver this message to these folks, but also send a copy to this UNIX program." The program, called a *script file*, will use the email system to reply with a prepared file, sent to the sender of the original email.

Usually, the alias database has permissions set so that only the systems administrator can modify it, and setting up the script file is something best left to either that person or someone else who is UNIX literate. But you, or your marketing people, can (and should) write the response itself. It can look something like this, the response sent when someone sends e-mail to info@widget.com:

```
Thanks for contacting The Widget Company!

We have received your email message, and it has been
passed on to our Sales staff. We usually answer email
within two days during the business week, and sometimes
during the weekends, as well!

The Widget Company is the leading manufacturer of Widgets
and Widget support and upkeep equipment. In business
since 1867, we pride ourselves on the quality not only of
our Widgets, but on the service you, our customers, get
when you become a member of the Widget family.

If you are contacting us about an order for our new model
27 automated Widgetwasher, we need to ask your patience.
We knew this was a good product,but you have been order-
ing them in unanticipated quantities! As a result, deliv-
eries are running approximately 10 days behind. We are
currently filling orders placed by January 12, 1995.

We have added additional shifts to our manufacturing
plant to catch up with the demand. We expect to be back
on top of our normal 2-day order turnaround by February
15, 1995.

Our new Web pages now contain full-color images of our
1995 catalogue. Point  your Web browser at http://www.wid-
get.com/ to see it. Or, call 1-800-WIDGETS to get a free
copy sent to you via regular mail.
```

> ```
> Again, thanks for contacting the Widget Company. Our
> Sales staff will respond in detail to your email in the
> next day or two.
> ```
>
> **Make sure the file for this autoresponse is in a directory where your sales staff can easily edit and update it, so that information stays current. You'll probably want to make sure its permissions are set so that only the folks you want to edit the file have access to it; otherwise, you might send out something surprising!**

Usenet

Still another Internet tool for making your information available to people, no matter what time of day they want it, is Usenet. As discussed in Chapter 12, Usenet newsgroups may be either moderated or unmoderated.

Unmoderated Mailing Lists and Usenet Newsgroups These are examples of Type II communications—public, many-contributors-to-many-recipients, and non-authoritative. For our purposes there are no real differences between newsgroups and mailing lists in this context. In the appropriate newsgroups and mailing lists you can announce enhancements to your product lines, ask for help, find people who might like to work for you, and so on. They are the Internet's equivalent of the grocery store bulletin board; and as with most public bulletin boards, there is likely to be more information and data than you will want to know about. If you want to reach people in the insurance industry in Omaha, Nebraska, you will post in a different place than if you want to reach people in aircraft jet maintenance in Orlando, Florida. These lists and newsgroups can be good places for you to get information, too, of course. The unmoderated nature of these media make them non-authoritative, but after "lurking" for awhile you will know some of the "Net-personalities" of that particular Net arena and decide whether you believe what they say.

Figure 16.6 shows a newsgroup discussion about medical imaging.

FIGURE 16.6

A newsgroup discussion about medical imaging.

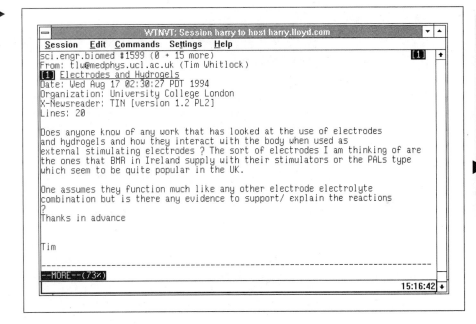

Another excellent way to use the News software is to set up in-house newsgroups, which can only be read by your staff. This lets you have good discussions taking advantage of the information sorting available with news, and still keep your conversations private. Figure 16.7 shows an example.

Moderated Mailing Lists and Usenet Newsgroups These tools are more difficult to use as communications media than the unrestricted groups. These *Type III* Public, many-contributors-to-many-recipients may be authoritative. Their authority depends directly upon their charter and the trustworthiness of the moderator. If the moderator is devoted to the charter of the group, everything posted to the list or group will meet the "contract." Less literal moderators may actually provide a better arena in which to hold discussions because articles or e-mail messages that are slightly off-topic might be interesting to the group as a whole and improve the value of the group.

Judicious moderators will usually let such topics be introduced in order to not appear dictatorial or have the group be too rigid. Generally, we believe the free flow of information and data will produce better results. The only place where this is not appropriate is the *. announce newsgroups. These groups are strictly moderated to include appropriate

FIGURE 16.7 ▶

An in-house newsgroup menu.

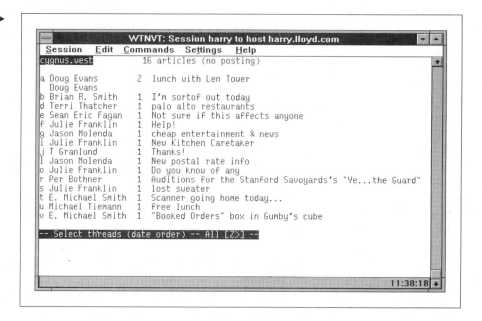

announcements only. This ensures that the readers will know exactly what to expect from the articles posted to these groups. These groups are used (usually) to announce meetings of interest to the readers. If the group is ba.announce, for example, the announcements are restricted to concerts, readings, meetings of general interest to the people living in the San Francisco Bay Area. If the mailing list is PACS-L (illustrated in Figure 16.8), which discusses issues related to public access in libraries, the announcements and discussion will range slightly wider since there are many issues related to the public access of information. The readers of the list discuss copyright law, and networking CD-ROMs on LANs, and conferences of interest to people who work in information provision, libraries, the development of library systems, and so on. The wide range of material discussed contributes to the value of the list.

Internet Publications

Internet Publications are the final type of communication we will discuss. These are *Type IV*: public, one-source-to-many-recipients, and authoritative. They are Web pages, Gopher documents, corporate/organizational files placed for FTP and Finger, and searchable databases made available to Internet users. The products or services might be

FIGURE 16.8 ▶

A PACS-L mailing.

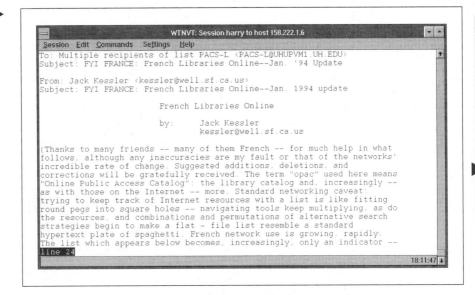

made available without charge or they might be available by purchasing access to the product or service. The resource listings we provide in the chapters on government, business, and education and general resources discuss many of these publications in detail. Look at them to get ideas on how you can publish your information on the Net.

How you choose to use the Internet as a publishing mechanism again depends on the results you want to achieve.

Web Pages As discussed in Chapter 11, using Web pages allows you to display color graphics, animation, and sound as well as explanatory text. As such, Web pages are more like brochures than anything you can produce using other Internet tools. You can present materials about your organization's products and services in an attractive and easy-to-use manner that can be read by anyone with access to a Web browser client program. Not all clients have the ability to see all the features, but as long as the Web page designer keeps the different clients in mind, the information can be conveyed well for any possible information consumer. Figure 16.9 shows the Web page for a bookstore.

Gopher Gopher, discussed in Chapter 11, allows quick and concise displays of hierarchical information. Its strength lies in the ability of associated services like Veronica and Jughead to build information menus

FIGURE 16.9 ▶

A bookstore "home page" on the Web.

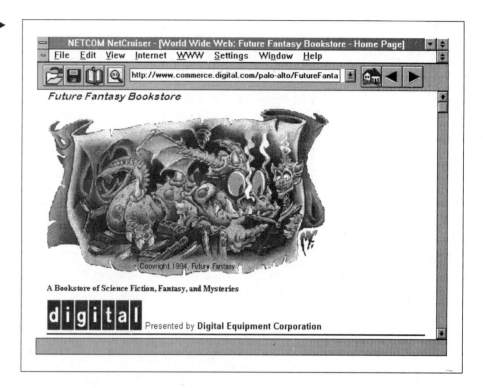

from all of gopherspace. Unfortunately, that's also its weakness for the information publisher. Because people can jump to your carefully de-signed menu item from anywhere, they may not see where it fits in the larger context of your menu hierarchy. This can make delivery of a total impression slightly more difficult.

Figure 16.10 shows the Gopher menu provided by MSEN, a Michigan Internet service provider. Notice that the menu items include both in-troductory material and product choices.

▶▶ Many Tools Make Light Work

As you've just seen, the Internet's tools can be used in virtually limit-less ways to find information for your organization, to make informa-tion about it available to the public, and to share information within your organization. The possibilities are limited only by your imagina-tion. Of course, to make the most effective use of these tools, you'll

FIGURE 16.10 ▶

The MSEN Gopher server.

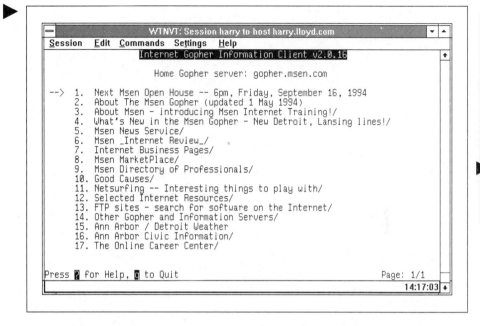

```
┌─────────────────────────────────────────────────────────────┐
│ ─        WTNVT: Session harry to host harry.lloyd.com      ▼ ▲│
│ Session  Edit  Commands  Settings  Help                       │
│           Internet Gopher Information Client v2.0.16         ↑│
│                                                               │
│              Home Gopher server: gopher.msen.com              │
│                                                               │
│  -->  1.  Next Msen Open House -- 6pm, Friday, September 16, 1994│
│       2.  About The Msen Gopher (updated 1 May 1994)          │
│       3.  About Msen - introducing Msen Internet Training!/   │
│       4.  What's New in the Msen Gopher - New Detroit, Lansing lines!/│
│       5.  Msen News Service/                                  │
│       6.  Msen _Internet Review_/                             │
│       7.  Internet Business Pages/                            │
│       8.  Msen MarketPlace/                                   │
│       9.  Msen Directory of Professionals/                    │
│       10. Good Causes/                                        │
│       11. Netsurfing -- Interesting things to play with/      │
│       12. Selected Internet Resources/                        │
│       13. FTP sites - search for software on the Internet/    │
│       14. Other Gopher and Information Servers/               │
│       15. Ann Arbor / Detroit Weather                         │
│       16. Ann Arbor Civic Information/                         │
│       17. The Online Career Center/                           │
│                                                               │
│ Press ? for Help, q to Quit                        Page: 1/1  │
│                                                     14:17:03 ↓│
└─────────────────────────────────────────────────────────────┘
```

need a good systems administrator (and possibly an Internet consultant) who can set up your system so that anyone inside or outside your organization can easily find the information they need.

▶▶ *How Should We Use It?*

By this question we mean not "which applications should we use to accomplish our goals" but "what conduct is acceptable?" The Internet is a strange part of cyberspace. Historically, it has developed through the academic and research community, and appears to be "free" to many students, faculty, and staff; and because of this, Internet users have been profoundly ambivalent about commercial activities on the Net. On one hand, Internet users—like everyone else—want to find out about products and services of interest to them; on the other hand, they want to preserve a medium of communication that is not dominated by commercial interests.

The easiest way to discuss this love-hate relationship is through anecdotes and examples. The clearest of these come from the Usenet newsgroups, where (at this writing) product advertisements are mostly not

INTERNETWORKING CONSULTANTS

▶

Selecting a consultant should be the same sort of process as selecting an employee. You'll need to work well with your consultant, being able to communicate your needs. The consultant should give you options about how to use internetworking to meet your needs.

You can probably find knowledgeable people among your personal community to help you. Maybe someone will help you for little or no money or will barter their services for yours. When you make this kind of arrangement, make sure that both parties understand the terms of the arrangement so there are no hard feelings later. Professional consultants will provide contracts and expected due dates. These may be better suited to your needs. In any case, always ask for and check the references of any consultant.

There are many people and organizations that can provide consulting for you and your organization in making your information available over the Internet. We have no special way to identify all of them. A number of consultants have registered with the CommerceNet registry of consultants. CommerceNet is supplying the directory space and makes quite clear that the list is made of those consultants who listed themselves. CommerceNet is not in a position to recommend specific consultants. The CommerceNet directory is available on the Web, at

```
http://www.commerce.net/directories/consultants/consult-
ants.html
```

Here are a few people and firms that we know will do a good job for you.

This short list is a completely biased one, made up of people we know and like to work with. It's by no means complete. Browse their Web pages or contact them to see if you can find a consultant that you will feel comfortable working with.

Consultants (listed alphabetically):

Bunyip Information Systems	`http://services.bunyip.com`
Ecommerce	`http://www.ecommerce.com`
John Mayes & Associates	`http://www.jma.com`
Lloyd Internetworking	`http://www.lloyd.com`
Liberty Hill Cyberwerks	`http://www.cyberwerks.com`
MSEN	`http://www.msen.com`
RealTech	`http://www.realtech.com`
Dave Taylor	`mailto://taylor@netcom.com`

welcome. We emphasize the word *mostly,* because there are places where this intention is ignored continually by the posters and the readers.

▶ Personal Classifieds or Yard Sales

The `misc.forsale` newsgroup is one where the fine distinctions seem clearer to the person who has been reading the newsgroup for awhile than to the person who has only recently come to the Internet. It's intended to be used by individuals occasionally selling items they don't need anymore, not by ongoing retail businesses. Netcom receives several complaints a week about postings to the group that are not considered appropriate, because of the sensitivity to commercial versus noncommercial use.

`Misc.forsale` is a widely dispersed garage sale. This means that while some people do occasionally post commercial advertisements for large numbers of hard disk drives for specific types of computers, the average seller has one piece of equipment or a book or a musical instrument that is no longer needed and is going to be turned into cash. The owner posts an article to `misc.forsale` and perhaps also the local supermarket bulletin board and maybe has a "real" garage sale rather than a virtual one. The user who wants to buy uses e-mail to negotiate a price, delivery method, and form of payment. When the price is agreed upon, a check is sent (usually) and the merchandise is shipped to the purchaser. Most people who purchase products this way are pleased that they have acquired something they wanted for not too much work and not too much expense—as in real garage sales, the prices charged in `misc.forsale` are much less than the retail price for the equivalent new product.

For example, Glee was pleased to find a set of German language lessons with both the manual and two CDs when she wanted to acquire some German quickly prior to a trip to Germany. The product description and price were posted. She sent an e-mail message indicating interest. The seller replied with a postal address. She sent a check. He sent the materials. Both parties were happy: the seller got rid of the materials and received money; Glee got the materials for a fair (that is, below retail) price.

 ▶ ▶**M A S T E R   W O R D S**

> **There are occasions when you send the check and the seller does not provide your product or service. You do have a few recourses should that happen. The one most frequently used is to post far and wide about the person who cheated. Be sure to read the FAQ called "HOW TO POST/BUY/SELL on MISC.FORSALE." before you participate.**

▶ New Product Announcements

Announcements offering information about a new product or service are generally tolerated (if not welcomed) in the Usenet newsgroups as long as two basic conditions are met:

1. The announcement is posted to a group that actually discusses something related to the product or service, and

2. The material posted is simply an announcement, not an advertisement.

The second condition is somewhat subjective—"beauty in the eye of the beholder." In the Internet environment, an announcement is regarded as "too much marketing fluff" if it contains a large number of adjectives and adverbs designed to enhance the nouns. The more adjectives, the more complaints that will be received by your Internet access provider about your posting. Most providers will discuss the complaints they receive with you, so you will know about them.

▶ Bad Karma on the Net

The most famous recent case of inappropriate posting to the newsgroups is that of the so-called "Green Card Lawyers." A husband-and-wife law firm posted a message to thousands of newsgroups offering their services in immigration information to foreign nationals residing in the United States. The posting was blatantly commercial. It was posted to practically every newsgroup that is widely distributed throughout the United States. It was read by many people who were really angry about the misuse of the newsgroups.

The angry readers "mail-bombed" the original poster with nasty e-mail messages. So many messages were received that the mail server for their Internet provider was overwhelmed and was taken out of service. Posting to a large number of groups like this is clearly done on purpose. A person might choose to do it once and be surprised about the vehemence of the reaction to the posting. After seeing that reaction, most posters begin to understand that posting to inappropriate newsgroups is not appreciated.

The first problem with this posting was not its content: it was that it was scattered indiscriminately across every newsgroup, including many where it was clearly not in line with the charter of the group. This is the first thing that made newsgroup readers angry.

Then they got angrier: the posters said they were not sorry for posting to inappropriate groups and that they intended to do it again. Furthermore, the posters stated their intention of opening an advertising business that would repeat their actions and said that they would be happy to do it again on behalf of other people, if they were paid a fee, since there was no law forbidding this activity.

At this point, Netcom (one of the providers with whom the poster had an account) decided to terminate the account. Another provider, PSI, worked out an agreement with the posters that was intended to keep them from continuing the behavior. Many articles were written and posted to mailing lists and newsgroups throughout the Internet and in print media as well.

In our opinion there were several things that made people feel so strongly about this case. One was the attitude of the posters. They seemed to take pride in throwing the culture of the Internet community back in our faces. Anytime one's culture is directly attacked, the reaction is loud and fast—reprisal! Also, the posters seem to believe that because a thing is not illegal, it is okay to do.

Many things in our culture are not illegal but they are taboo. Let's consider the example of changing clothes in the laundromat: not in the restroom, but out next to the dryer. Not only would most of us not do it, we probably wouldn't sell tickets to see others doing it, or charge money to sell the tickets for others.

The "Green Card Lawyers" not only put up their ads in the wrong place, they claimed that they were going to start selling tickets to others to do the same thing.

It seems that the posters were more interested in challenging the culture, the non-existent law, and the remediation process than they were in enlarging their business. They do claim, however, that the advertisement was quite successful.

Their example sparked a few more forays into posting indiscriminately to large numbers of newsgroups. One clever wordsmith declared that his posting was not against netiquette and therefore appropriate because he was giving away a product in a contest. No doubt this explanation would have sounded better to his access provider had he done a better job of matching the product one could win in the contest to the newsgroups to which he posted the contest advertisement. But he didn't, lots of people complained to his access provider, and he became another person with whom the Usenet posting rules were discussed in great detail.

The bottom line here is that you can't get your message out on the Net by ignoring the culture. If your postings are complained about to your service provider, your provider may well refuse you access.

▶ *Ethics and Legalities*

The central point of doing business in cyberspace is the same as doing business in physical space. If you represent yourself, your company, and your product or service well to the people who will be interested in knowing about it; provide the service or product ethically—good value at a fair price, for example—chances are you will do reasonably well. (Unless you have a product or service that no one wants, of course.) Conducting such a business requires knowledge of your market or audience, the applicable laws, and the ethics involved in your communities (the physical/cultural one in real space and the one in cyberspace).

▶ *Legal Issues*

If something is illegal, it is illegal. It remains illegal in cyberspace. Being on a network does not change the action. If you do, or are suspected of doing, something that is illegal—selling child pornography, for example—your access provider probably will cooperate with the appropriate governmental bodies to capture you and put you away.

Geographic boundaries may not protect you. In late 1994, bulletin board owners in Milpitas, California, were convicted by a Tennessee court for distributing obscene materials. *Under the laws of Tennessee*, the material was obscene by Tennessee community standards. A Tennessee user had dialed into the bulletin board in California. The Tennessee prosecutors successfully argued that this brought the California computer system and its owners into Tennessee's jurisdiction.

You should remember that special laws concerning business in cyberspace aren't there yet. Most law in the United States is based upon case law—that is, precedent cases. There aren't a lot of precedents in this area yet. And once the data or information crosses an International border, whatever laws there are become different.

The laws concerning computer crime and networking are changing as we write. Neither of us are qualified to give you legal advice. If you need legal assistance, talk to an attorney.

International Issues

There aren't a lot of global laws. There are some treaties and international agreements, but they are not always signed by all relevant governments.

One of the most interesting assumptions that most Americans make is that their right to free speech is guaranteed. Making some reference to that right is actually guaranteed to cause a lot of amused comments from people from other countries who contribute to the Internet's mailing lists and newsgroups.

Trademarks If you decide to operate a service on the Internet, you will lose the rights to the name of your service once any part of it crosses an international border, if you don't trademark the name in all the appropriate countries. To do that for the ten largest countries in terms of available Internet access in 1994 has been estimated to cost about $300,000. This puts that action outside the reach of most start-up companies.

Export Restrictions Certain kinds of products, notably security software with encryption, cannot legally be exported to some countries. Current government regulation takes the stance that if you have a public FTP archive with a restricted product available in it, you are *de facto* exporting it to restricted countries. This regulation and its interpretation are being argued hotly, but the law could conceivably apply to other things, such as catalog images in Web pages (some countries restrict images of naked or semi-naked people, birth control information, and so on), game or software demos, and the like.

▶ ▶ **MASTER WORDS**

For more information about export restrictions and the principles behind these restrictions, please see John Gillmore's writings in the Electronic Frontier Foundation archive available at `gopher.eff.org` **or look for discussions in the** `comp.protocols.kerberos` **newsgroup.**

▶▶ *Management Issues*

We've talked about things you can do with the Internet to either consume or provide information that will be to your advantage as a governmental organization or a business. There are some lessons to be learned from the access providers, too. These things involve policies for internal use, resource management, and security.

▶ *Developing Appropriate Use Policies*

Early use of the Internet in the research and education community sparked the development of Appropriate Use policies. This term is used to describe what sort of information is allowed to be carried on a network. The policy was developed to do two things: protect the government funding agency from being accused of providing subsidies to commercial services, and to provide a clear description of appropriate traffic so that inappropriate traffic could be kept off the network.

All network developers should have some sort of appropriate use policy. If the purpose of your network is to carry messages regarding work from one employee to another, say so. That way, when you find someone playing Doom on your network, or running an archive of pictures or sounds on the disk drives that are owned by your organization, you have a clear statement of why you are going to stop that action. Appropriate use policies don't need to be complex or difficult to understand. In fact, they will be best if they aren't. A good collection of policies can be found at `http://www.eff.org`, sponsored by The Electronic Frontier Foundation. This group was founded to address the complex issues of the rights provided by the United States Constitution in the global information economy.

Chapter 18 is a complete discussion of appropriate use policies, and we include there some sample policies. In this section we summarize the most important issues.

Clear Guidelines for Employees

One thing you will need to make clear to your employees is what you *will* allow them to do with their accounts.

Many of your employees will be interested in mailing lists that are not work-related. Will you allow them to read those lists on your organization's time? Will you allow them to read those lists using your organization's equipment? On their own time? Perhaps you will let them read things of personal interest during their lunch hours or coffee breaks (much as you allow reading a novel or magazine during breaks). Will you instead suggest that these people get personal accounts with an Internet Access provider?

▶ ▶**MASTER WORDS**

> **You probably already have policies concerning the use of company computers, printers, fax machines, photocopiers, and telephones. Coordinate your new Internet policies with the ones you already have.**

Can your employees FTP personal material to their work machines, and then print it off on your printers? Will you let them put personal material up to be collected via FTP or other means?

Are your employees allowed to post to non-work-related newsgroups, such as misc.kids, or rec.arts.startrek, from a user ID that points to your company? If they do post, do they need to put a disclaimer on the posting? (Something like: "This posting does not represent the policies of Automation International, or their affiliates.")

Will you let your staff put up personal Web pages, containing pointers to organizations they are affiliated with? Or to put up an organizational resource using your machines?

Some Internet service providers do their *pro bono* work by serving the Web pages of nonprofit organizations (for instance, see the pages at http://www.intac.com:/PubService/Service.html). Many university sites provide Web space to their students, faculty, and staff. Because of issues of academic freedom, the Web spaces are not usually moderated. Organizational policies concerning personal use vary as widely as the organizations themselves. Cygnus Software is very different from the United States Department of Defense.

Another issue to consider is use of the company *connection* to contact other machines. For example, Pat's contract with Cygnus requires that she not work on this book over their Internet connection. Her contract says that anything she creates on Cygnus equipment must be shared with Cygnus: the management has taken that to mean the wires that make up the Internet connection, as well. So Pat does not Telnet home to work on her home computer from a work machine, even during non-working hours.

(Cygnus participates in the GNU software distribution license. That is, they believe that you should give freely of your artistic creations, including software, without restriction. This book, along with other items Pat has written, would have fallen under that agreement.)

Many employees these days consider free (unrestricted) network access to be one of the perks of working for a company with Internet access. Obviously, you need to take that into consideration when you make your policies (just as you consider use of the phone and photocopy machine). Be sure to spell out your policies clearly so that everyone knows what to expect. If you are not yet connected, take the opportunity to develop your policies before your connection is installed. Then you can talk about the policies during training. If you are already connected, make certain your policies are covered during new employee orientation.

Appropriate Use Policies and Employee Privacy Rights

As a manager or as an employee, you should be familiar with the laws in your state regarding computers and employee privacy; and managers should formulate and implement your appropriate use policies accordingly. Recent cases have tended toward the point of view that *unless you tell them otherwise,* from the beginning of their employment or from the beginning of the time computer access is given to them, your employees have what is called a "reasonable expectation of privacy" concerning their computer transactions.

This means that unless you tell *every* employee when they join the company about your Appropriate Use policies, they have the right to expect that their e-mail is private. If it is your company or organization's policy that no private e-mail transactions should take place on the system, then you need to make sure that policy is well explained and broadly available.

Most employees assume that no one will go snooping in their computer files—the same assumption they make about their desk drawers. Unless you make it clear that you regularly check personal files (and, for that matter, desk drawers and lockers), your employees are considered by law to reasonably expect that their file space, unless they permit it to be readable by others, is safe from snooping.

> **N O T E**
>
> **If your organization does not have a policy in place regarding appropriate Internet use, and there is a conflict with an employee over it, mediation agencies, union management, and courts tend to look at your other policies for guidance in computer issues. Therefore, if you allow people to have private materials (books, letters, and so on) in their desks or lockers, the courts are likely to generalize that policy to include computer files. It's important to consider your policies and put them in place as soon as you put in the phone line that links you to the Internet.**

How Many Years of E-Mail Do You Have?

Archiving of system files is another issue related to privacy and employee rights. Some systems administrators make routine backups of their system every night (this is, actually, a Good Thing!), but those backups include the e-mail that is on the system, either incoming or in mailboxes, at the time.

Some backups are stored for years—one university recently announced that it had file backups for the past 25 years in their archives.

The problem for you, as a manager, is one of privacy and archives. Suppose you suspect an employee of giving away trade secrets. Should you ask the systems administrator to search all the file backups looking through all this person's e-mail? Or suppose an employee leaves the organization. What happens to all his electronic archive files? Can you just randomly search through them, or do you need to have a good reason?

Again, look to your policies on paper and other resources to give you guidance, as well as checking with the computer crime bureau in your state.

▶ *Resource Management and Planning for Growth*

Resource management, like the other topics we've discussed in this chapter, has two faces; your organization may be accessing the Internet both as a consumer and as a provider.

Use, Like Work, Grows to Fill the Resources Allotted

On the consumer side are those folks who are using your computing resources. For each and every person for whom you are managing Internet access, you need to maintain a data pipe wide enough to provide access to the kinds of services that person will need to carry out his or her responsibilities effectively.

Some of your people will need very little: access to their e-mail messages will do it. These folks will not stress your resources at all. Other people, like marketing research staff, or library staff, or legal representatives, people who gather information as part of their daily tasks, will stress your resources. These people will need full Internet access to use the navigation programs, to transfer large sets of statistical data from repositories, to use search engines like WAIS to find particular cases or citations in registers and court opinions. They will need fast IP-based or direct connections, rather than slower host-dial pipes. How do you figure out what you need?

Make a census of your employees to see how many of each type of consumer you have; this will help you plan. Make certain that you allow room for growth. Initially, people don't believe they will use the network for much of anything, but their use grows, sometimes exponentially. Measuring your network usage will allow you to (maybe) keep one step ahead of the growth curve.

Don't Outgrow Your Resource

If you are an information provider, you need to try to estimate the size and type of your audience. If you are providing statistical data, for example, and the data will be desired by many, many people, you will need a larger computer to use as a server than if you are simply providing a small number of e-mail messages as automatic bounce-backs to marketing inquiries.

Providing FTP directories is not difficult, and the people requirements for maintaining them are pretty low; however, transferring large files by FTP requires more network bandwith than delivery by Gopher or a short menu. You will need to plan not only for a fast network connection, but a computer with more memory and a faster CPU. If you need to restrict access, you can set up systems that refuse more than a set number of connections at one time. Limiting the number of simultaneous connections and being aware of the resources taken by the delivery method you have implemented will give you a controlled environment. You will need to keep track of the connections that you refuse, however, so that you can choose to expand the possible number of connections at an appropriate time for your organization.

This has necessarily been a general discussion of resource management issues. To plan specifically for your network resources now and in the future, you will spend your investment dollars wisely by either hiring a qualified full-time employee or contracting with an Internet consulting firm.

▶ Security

There are two kinds of security related to your Internet installation: protecting your organization from outsiders and protecting it from insiders.

Smart Defense

In a way, defending yourself from outsiders is easier. Sensitive data about your organization should be kept off the server that is connected to the Internet. The Internet is a very open environment. The most frequently used operating systems in the Internet are variations of UNIX, which is (from a security perspective) a very open system. If you want something to be private, the Internet is not a good place for it *at this time*.

There is a lot of very interesting work being done on data encryption technologies, on private keys, on trusted signatures, on access authorizations. These technologies will become more mature and more trusted in the next several years.

This does not mean that you can't be on the Internet if you have private data. It means *that* data shouldn't be connected to the Internet. Many installations use a firewall to protect their internal networks from unwanted intrusions. Firewalls are so named because they protect what is behind them from being burned, just like steel firewalls in your offices protect your file cabinets from being burned in a fire.

Usually, access through firewalls is limited to e-mail because a computer—the firewall machine—can act as a gateway between the internal and external networks. A well-known example of such an installation is the firewall that protects International Business Machines (IBM). IBM has one of the largest internal networks in the world (it's hard to know who exactly has the largest, because those statistics are proprietary). It is possible to send e-mail into the IBM internal network and to send e-mail out of the IBM internal network. But there are very, very few places where any IBM servers are actually connected to the Internet itself. And most IBM employees who use the Internet have personal accounts outside the IBM systems in order to do so.

Trouble from Within

The largest danger to any internal network and server system comes from the people who have access to it internally. Even if the people aren't malicious, they can cause havoc. Many really bright computer users (called hackers in some circles) feel that anything they can explore or do they should be allowed to do. If they make a mistake—even an innocent error—you can have real problems.

What kind of steps should you take? To start with, access to system-privileged accounts should be severely restricted. All changes should be logged. Careful backups of the systems should be taken and at least one cycle of backup tape stored off-site. Care should always be taken in training people about security concerns. This means teaching all your staff how to protect their own data, as well as making sure your systems administrators are trustworthy.

Getting Help with Security

It's better to build security in from the ground up. When planning your installation, you might want to have a security audit done. Many Internet consulting firms will check your installations for possible security gaps, which you can then plug yourself or hire them to fix. The goal is to find the gaps so that you can plug them before information about your organization leaks out all over the world.

Much more information about security can be found in RFC 1244, the Site Security Handbook by Paul Holbrook and Joyce K. Reynolds. An additional site for information about security is the COAST Security Archive at Purdue University in Indiana. In early August 1994, the FTP archive at that site was announced. It contains software, standards, tools, and other material dealing with everything from access control and authentication, to security tools and social impacts. The FTP site is `coast.cs.purdue.edu`. Information about the archive can be found in the /pub/aux directory. There are several mailing lists that discuss security issues. One of the better ones is `firewalls@greatcircle.com`. To sign up for this list, send to `firewalls-request@greatcircle.com`.

One of your best resources for system security is a savvy and ethical systems administrator. This person is worth her (or his) weight in gold. Don't skimp on the salary for this person when you are installing a network for your company that costs—and can save—you thousands of dollars a year.

▶▶ Training

Once you decide to get an Internet connection, how do you teach your staff to make the best use of it?

Perhaps you have an employee (the one who talked you into taking this leap) who can do beginning seminars and training. Peer-to-peer training is very powerful, and you'll be amazed at the number of folk on your staff who pop up with Internet knowledge.

Alternately, you can hire a consulting firm to come and do training. Sometimes this training is included along with the price of your connection from your Internet provider. Certainly they are the place to start when looking for a consulting firm to do training.

In general, you need to make sure your employees know the following when they finish their beginning course in NetSurfing:

- What the Internet is and why you are connected to it.
- What benefits they, and their clients or customers, will get from this connection.

- How to use the network clients you have installed: e-mail at least, and whatever others you plan to use.

- How to connect to the Net from their workstations.

- How to explore the Net to learn more.

- What your policies are concerning Net use and access.

- Whom to call for help.

▶▶ *Conclusion: The Picture Is Pretty Bright*

Because there are so many serious issues to consider when starting to do business on the Net, it can sound very daunting. Luckily, many other folks have taken this step before you, and resources for business and governmental use are springing up all over the Net. In Chapter 21, we present an annotated list of these resources, how to reach them, and what they can do for you.

In addition, you'll find that your customers and staff in general get pretty excited about using the Net. Perhaps e-mail will be the trigger, or using the Web (a lot of novices get hooked on the Net by using the Web). Once they do, you'll find that they are thinking up new and better ways to use the Net to help your business or organization.

▶ ▶ **CHAPTER 17**

The K–12 Internet Presence

► ► *The* Internet is an unparalleled resource for education. (Unparalleled aside from the teachers and students, that is!) Connectivity gives a school access to curriculum development tools, graphics, teaching associations, support groups, and even Net pen-pals for the students. The K–12 (Kindergarten to 12th grade) presence on the Net is perhaps one of the fastest growing. Ten years ago, we began to see the first library catalogs online. Teachers began talking to one another over the Net via e-mail and mailing lists. At conferences, teachers who had Net connections through local colleges, bulletin boards, or other sources would huddle together to try and figure out how to use this resource. Then schools began to get grants for inter- and intra-school networks. But it wasn't until the late 1980s that colleges and universities, in partnership with schools, businesses, and network-savvy parents, began to get the schools linked to the greater Internet.

In this chapter (along with the resource lists in Chapters 22 and 23 and the technical guidelines in Appendix E), the K–12 educator and student will find ways to enrich their classrooms by using the resources of the network. They will also find ways to share their knowledge with other students and teachers. Parents interested in bringing the Internet to local schools will find valuable source materials here, too.

 ► ►**MASTER WORDS**

The Internet was once a treasure trove for computer enthusiasts only, but today's Internet has resources for science, math, art, music, writing; you name it, and you can find it online. And thanks to the modern browser tools for the Web and for Gophers, today's Internet resources are available to even the most computer-shy.

▶▶ *Benefits and Consequences of Being Networked*

Just as with any other organization, being linked to the Internet gets you immediate access to a vast pool of resources. K–12 schools are the fastest growing new category of connected organizations. More and more organizations, connectivity providers, and other networked entities are recognizing that the K–12 crowd are a growing audience, and are providing more and more Web pages, Gopher servers, and other online resources for educators. To cope with this wealth of material, folks looking for K–12 resources need to be particularly savvy about using all the tools to find their specialty resources.

Additionally, more and more of you are talking to each other. Starting with the FidoNet-based K12Net project some years ago, teachers have taken to the nets to talk to each other in droves. Not only are teachers talking, but students are conversing, using IRC, doing collective projects, and so on.

Schools have particular problems associated with being connected, as do other public entities that have general access to the Net. Much of the material on the Net may not be appropriate for children to see or participate in. Parents have concerns about reading material, news groups with inappropriate images and material, games versus education, and so on. In some ways, for teachers, access to the Internet is just another ball in the juggling act they have always performed.

Schools can also find a ready-made audience for information they can provide, however. Some of those folks and some of their interests include:

- Everyone:
    1. Homework assignments
    2. Conference schedules
    3. School year schedule (including vacations, sports, meetings, etc.)
    4. Menus
    5. Policy information

The K–12
Internet Presence

▶ ▶

ch.
17

6. District election information

7. Class and bell schedules

8. E-mail to teachers, administrators, school board, each other, etc.

9. Bus Schedules

10. District contact information

11. Staff information (perhaps pictures!)

12. Newsletters

- Parents:

  1. Registration information

  2. PTA and other organizational information

- Students:

  1. Test results (password guarded, of course)

  2. Library research materials

  3. Social resources (IRCs, MUDs, mailing lists, newsgroups)

- Teachers:

  1. Sub lists

  2. New policy information

  3. Job postings

  4. Curriculum resources

  5. Staff conferencing and information sharing

- School boards and district officials:

  1. Student databases

  2. Meetings schedules and agendas

  3. Funding and other election materials

The potential list goes on and on. Schools could begin to reach out to their districts in ways that would allow for faster updating of information, more ecologically sound distribution, and technical training and literacy for students.

MASTER WORDS

Want to make sure folks begin to use the electronic resource instead of more traditional ways of distributing information? Distribute some interesting pieces of information *only* via e-mail or other distribution on the Net. Give your potential audience a chance to join you online.

▶▶ *Special Educational Advantages*

Schools, particularly K–12 public institutions, are very well placed to take advantage of networking. Here are some reasons:

- Schools hold our future in the form of our children. Parents, employers, and other groups are interested in seeing that schools get access to resources which help increase our future national productivity.

- Much of the legislation for networking infrastructure in the United States has special sections for making sure the K–12 education system is included in the connection strategies.

- Corporations are interested in getting into partnerships with K–12 schools in order to take advantage of tax and public relation benefits for such partnerships.

- School-related vendors (such as publishers of textbooks, curriculum materials, and so on) are putting special education resources on the Net to attract business from school districts.

- Because schools are not required to link to commercial providers, they can take advantage of government-subsidized network infrastructure.

- Some telephone service providers have funded special programs to connect K–12 schools to the Internet. Contact your providers to see if they have such a program.

- Granting agencies such as the National Science Foundation have grant competitions for K–12 networking projects.

**The K–12
Internet Presence**

▶ ▶
ch.
17

- Higher education institutions, particularly those which run mid-level or regional networks, have both a mission-related objective to connect K–12 institutions and a financial objective. (Hooking up schools can bring in grants and other funding, which benefits their entire infrastructure.)

►► *Strategies for Getting Funding*

Networks do cost money. In order to be connected, you will need to find the resources to fund equipment, design expertise, and ongoing staffing. No individual can do it alone; cooperation is essential. How will you—parents, teachers, administrators—achieve it?

► *Step One: Find Out What You Can Do with a Network*

The first thing you need to do in order to start building a people-network to support a school networking strategy is find out what you can do with it. Reading this book will help. Visit, write, or otherwise contact any of the school districts we mention (or that you know about from other sources) to find out how they are using the network. Call meetings of parents to find out what they want to do, and want the schools to do for their children. Contact your state Board of Education to see what the computing resources are at the state level. Most states have a commission or task-force working on this very problem (and it never hurts to get your input in as early in the game as possible).

Student and Classroom Examples

Here are some examples of projects undertaken by schools and collections of schools, to help you think about what you might do with a school network or network access. (Many of these examples came from the EDUCOM study on K–12 Networking, which was partially funded by IBM. Others came from Gleason Sackman's Net-Happenings news group, the K12-NET project, the NCSA and CERN education pages, and from the MichNet K–12 project. Some projects are described in the participants' own words; other descriptions are from published accounts.) You can find further examples, such as the New South Polar Times electronic newsletter, described in Chapters 22 and 23.

Learning through Collaborative Visualization (CoVis) Traditionally, K–12 science education has consisted of teaching well-established facts. This approach bears little or no resemblance to the question-centered, collaborative practice of real scientists. Through the use of advanced technologies, the CoVis Project is attempting to transform science learning to better resemble the authentic practice of science.

In the first-ever educational use of wideband ISDN networks, CoVis (sponsored by Northwestern University) enables high school students to join with other students at remote locations in collaborative work groups. Also through these networks, students communicate with university researchers and other scientific experts.

Participating students study atmospheric and environmental sciences— including topics in meteorology and climatology—through project-based activities. Using state-of-the-art scientific visualization software, specially modified to be appropriate to a learning environment, students have access to the same research tools and data sets used by leading-edge scientists in the field.

The CoVis Project provides students with a "collaboratory" workbench that includes desktop video teleconferencing; shared software environments for remote, real-time collaboration; access to the resources of the Internet; a "Software/Collaboratory" notebook (a multimedia scientist's notebook); and "CoVis Software" (scientific visualization software). In addition to providing new technology, the project is working closely with teachers at the participating schools to develop new curricula and new pedagogical approaches that take advantage of project-based science learning.

Figure 17.1 shows the home Web page for the CoVis project (http://www.covis.nwu.edu/).

Walpole, Massachusetts Here's how Bruce Goldberg, in his article "Restructuring and Technology: Part One" (*Radius*, October/November, 1988) described one of the earliest Internet classroom projects:

"Why are there fewer pets in a certain small Louisiana town than there are in Walpole, Massachusetts? Mrs. Griffith's fourth grade class sits in deep thought. They had already gathered the data, talked about classifying it, and through their telecommunications network, compared the findings with their Louisiana counterparts.

The K-12 Internet Presence

ch.
17

FIGURE 17.1 ►

The Collaborative
Vision Project Home
page.

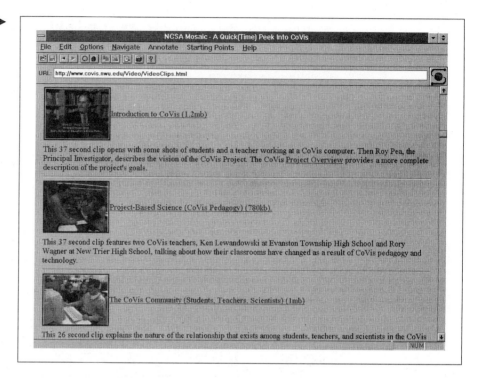

"Hands soon shot up. One thinks the difference has to do with climate. Another that parental attitudes are more restrictive. Still another thinks the Louisiana town might be poorer. 'I know,' shouts Joshua, a student classified as learning-disabled. 'I bet it has nothing at all to do with that stuff. I bet that school is in a place where there's government housing, and that the kids can't have any pets.'

"Mrs. Griffith and the rest of the class seem stunned. Not only had no one thought of this as a possible (and plausible) explanation, but no one had expected Joshua to think of it.

"The students got busy. At Joshua's lead, they contacted their Louisiana counterparts, and much to everyone's amazement, discovered that Joshua had been right. The Louisiana town does have a large proportion of its population housed in government housing, and yes, there are very explicit restrictions against owning pets.

"No one looks at Joshua the same way anymore. Especially Joshua. Buoyed by his success, he begins assuming a more assertive role in his small team."

Lincoln, Nebraska Kids in the Lincoln, Nebraska School District set up the Kids' Travel Agency as part of a summer school project. Using CMS School-Net, they sent a survey only to kids, requesting information such as their favorite restaurants, motels, and historical attractions. Several classes from San Diego, California, responded. These students were excited by the idea of being able to tell 'land-bound' students about Sea World, the Pacific Ocean, and Disneyland. The Lincoln students eagerly read, edited, and processed the data, then developed information packets from a kid's perspective for each area surveyed.

Lansing, Michigan The students at Grand River Elementary were the first K–12 school on the Web. The fifth graders in Brad Marshall's class have been building the Web server, and also reading and replying to e-mail sent to them from folks who had read the Web information. You can access the server by opening the URL http://web.cal.msu.edu/JSRI/GR/grintro.html with a Web browser. Figure 17.2 shows an explanation, written by the students, of how they managed e-mail for all the fifth graders. The students also calculated the usage statistics for their Web server, and their statistics are displayed in Figure 17.3.

FIGURE 17.2

How the students do e-mail.

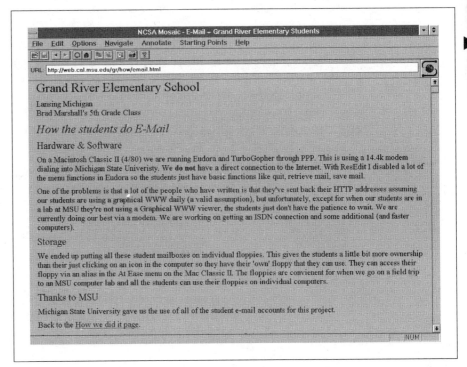

FIGURE 17.3 ►

Usage statistics for the Grand River Web server.

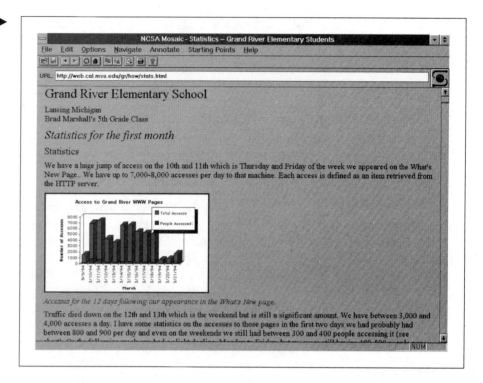

Binghamton, New York The Electronic Field Trip (described in the US Congressional Office of Technology Assessment report *Linking for Learning: A New Course for Education, November, 1989)* is an inexpensive way to put students in isolated areas in contact with professionals in a variety of fields. Field trips included "visits" to the local mayor, social activists, steel mill workers, international students in Australia, Alaska, and England, and musicians.

One electronic field trip was scheduled with a rock musician. Only those students interested enough to do background research were allowed to participate. The school's music teacher, telecommunications coordinator, and librarian guided the research. After two weeks of preparation, an enthusiastic audience of eight students, a mix of aspiring musicians, college-bound students, and kids with no stated future plans, communicated for over an hour.

Afterward, the students proudly talked about the project. One commented, "We would like to talk to another musician who has not made it big and compare the interviews." Another student regretted the lack of reporting from the local paper: "If this had been a local football game, they would have given it two columns of reporting."

The students' hard work paid off in many ways. They learned how to organize their thoughts on paper and on their feet, how to work together as a team, and how to plan; and they learned more about a career to which some of them aspire.

By the end of 1994, over 800 students have participated in electronic field trips.

Hillside Elementary, Cottage Grove, Minnesota Students at Hillside Elementary School in Cottage Grove, Minnesota are creating many pages of information on their World Wide Web server (`http://hillside.coled.umn.edu/`), a joint project with the University of Minnesota College of Education. Their goal is "to incorporate use of the resources on the Internet into the curriculum of elementary school students and to have students participate in creating resources that are on the Internet."

The 1994 school year Web contains, among other projects, Hillside Web Happenings, Mrs. Collins Sixth Grade Home Pages, The Buzz Rod Story, Career Interviews, Book Reviews, and general school information: Parent Teacher Association, School Calendar, and the School Newspaper. Hillside's award winning projects from 1993–94 are also available online.

Dublin, Ireland As an extracurricular activity, students in the Dalkey School Project in the suburbs of Dublin, Ireland, found pen-pals in the United States and Canada. Initially, the objectives were to share student writing and learn a little more about other cultures. This pen-pal project has opened up a new world to these students.

From the KidSPHERE distribution list (`kidsphere@vms.cis.pitt.edu`), contacts were made with other children from several locations in the United States, including Aurora, Colorado; Charlottesville, Virginia; Franklinville, New York; and Tallahassee, Florida; and from British Columbia, Canada. Students' tele-letters often contained information about themselves, their families, schools, and neighborhoods.

The students have begun to understand the nature and operation of the network, and have become very interested in people in distant places and how they live, primarily because they have been able to make friends so easily over the network. The students' keyboarding, editing, and word-processing skills have also improved.

Bosnia-Croatia Student E-Mail Exchange   Prompted by a letter from a Bosnian student, teachers and students in Minnesota and elsewhere have begun exchanging letters with Bosnian and Croatian students. For more information, point your Web browser at the URL `gopher://informs.k12.mn.us:70/00/best-K12/bosnia`. Figure 17.4 shows a letter from a Bosnian girl to her American Net pal.

Toronto, Canada   "What a wonderful learning experience it has been. It has given me a new perspective on learning and learning how to learn. With other writers of the world, we have all responded and contributed to one another. I see this as something that has changed my life. Education shouldn't always be within classroom walls."

This is what one 12th grade student (quoted in *DISTED Electronic Journal*. March 1990) wrote about her English class after telecommunications technology projects had been introduced into the curriculum.

FIGURE 17.4

Letter from a Bosnian student.

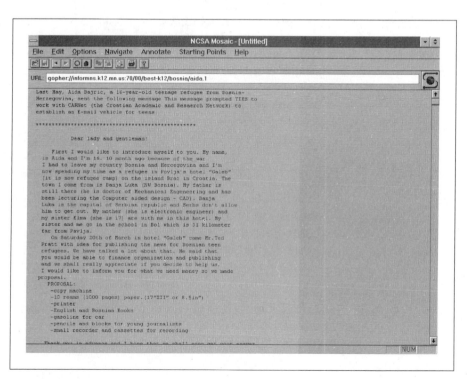

Students, teachers, and writers throughout Canada, the United States, and the world correspond, and the students' work is critiqued by the professionals. The "Writers in Electronic Residence" program of the Riverdale Collegiate Institute in Toronto is supported by the College of Education at Simon Fraser University, and forms the basis of these language-based studies.

Students' works, primarily poetry and short fiction, are posted in electronic conference areas established for their use. The students are in control of the media before them, and they use those media to broaden their classroom experiences. The "Electro-Poets" project involved a class in Toronto, one in British Columbia, and a poet also in British Columbia. During this four-month project, over 200 pages of original writing and comments were generated by the students. They readily accepted the telecommunications activities as part of their daily classroom activity. Another project, "New-Voices," involved a poet, a science-fiction writer, and a short-fiction author, and schools in Ontario and British Columbia. A third project, "Wired Writer," connects ten schools and one author from a past project.

These language-based telecommunications projects have inspired students to develop language appropriate to the activity, and they offer direct and personal access to computer activities that are relevant today. These telecommunications projects increased the students' access to the world and, as a result, bring to the classroom experiences that meet and enhance existing curricular needs.

The Armadillo Gopher A service of Rice University and the Houston area schools, the Armadillo Gopher has many area school projects and resources listed. One is a collection of familiar folk tales told by area students and their families. The Armadillo Gopher is available at the URL `gopher://chico.rice.edu:1170/11/`. Figure 17.5 shows the tale "If You Give a Rattler a Rifle" from the collection.

Roxboro, North Carolina A Global Grocery List has been posted on FrEdMail's IDEAS bulletin board by the Person County Schools in North Carolina. Students ask for the local price in local currency of specific quantities of 14 items. To date, students from Michigan, Illinois, California, North Carolina, and England have responded.

The K-12
Internet Presence

ch.
17

FIGURE 17.5 ▶

A student's folk tale from the Armadillo Gopher.

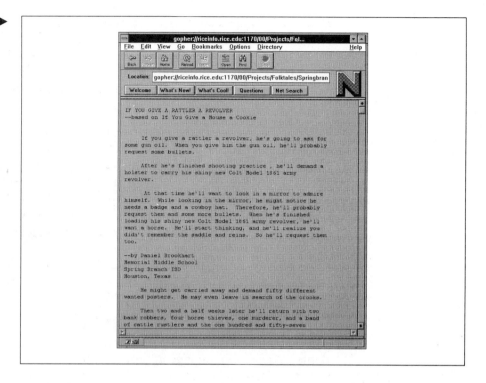

The Person County School students expect to use the data in other classroom projects including math, social studies, and science to study economics in the marketplace. Data are periodically compiled and posted to the IDEAS bulletin board for other classes who may wish to access the information.

FrEdMail (Free Education Mail) was founded by Al Rodgers to connect students and teachers, originally via modem-to-modem connections. Later, the project was helped onto the Internet by CERFNet, a regional mid-level network located in southern California. Mr. Rodgers's ideas for simple, shared projects "connected" many students throughout the United States and led to further projects like the Global Schoolhouse Project, funded by the National Science Foundation and many other sponsors (described in Chapter 23 and located on the Web at `http://k12.cnidr.org`).

Alconbury, England Peanut Butter and JAM—food for thought. JAM (Junior Atlantic Monthly) is one of several online projects of the Department of Defense Dependents Schools (DoDDS) Stars and Stripes

Bulletin Board System at Alconbury Elementary School. JAM, a student-generated magazine, contains classroom work from students in grades 4–6. A special K–3 section, called Peanut Butter, is being planned.

The magazine includes all types of creative writing, including short stories, poetry, essays, and interviews. A schedule of topics for each issue is posted on the bulletin board, as JAM hopes to integrate with current classroom curriculum. Submissions are uploaded to a special area on the bulletin board and editing is performed by editorial groups, located at various schools, as part of their language arts curriculum. Rejected articles are returned to the author with comments or explanations. Final works are uploaded to the bulletin board for publication and distribution.

Tallahassee, Florida Learning-disabled students at Rickards High School now have a bulletin board message area they can call their own. Knowing the educational value of being able to communicate with others around the world, the Leon County Schools in Tallahassee, Florida, established an electronic bulletin board at Rickards High School, available to those in the Tallahassee area with a computer and a modem. (For information on getting an account, contact the school at 904-488-1783.)

Initially, communication in the Special Students message area is limited to other Rickards High School students, as an intermediate step for those overwhelmed by the variety of message areas. Reading and writing skills are reinforced as messages are exchanged. Deaf and blind students have joined the fun through the use of adaptive devices on their computers.

When these students are ready to advance, they may join several projects which were developed for the bulletin board, including Alien Visit—where a teacher, parent, or other adult logs on and poses as an alien, asking questions on various topics; writing their own surveys and collecting data; writing and reading messages in foreign languages; establishing a county-wide magazine by and for students about their school's activities; and the online serial novel—where one class composes a section and posts it on the bulletin board for another class to continue.

Barriers of academic ability have broken down and a challenging and motivating curriculum has been provided for students, thanks to the foresight of the administrators in the Leon County School System.

Ralph Bunche Elementary School Ralph Bunche School, in New York City's Harlem, which houses third through sixth graders, has exceptional access to computers and other high-technology equipment. Figure 17.6 shows how one student describes the school.

One unusual project on the Bunche Web server (gopher://ralph-bunche.rbs.edu:70/11/Student_Work) combines pictures and stories. Students write stories about pictures and then post them on the server. Figure 17.7 shows one picture and the story it inspired. (This story demonstrates one of the "hidden" capabilities of the Net—helping to make the "haves," who have traditionally been the majority of Net users, aware of the realities of life for disadvantaged people.)

Ann Arbor, Michigan Motivating students is often a concern for teachers at the K–12 level. So, you can imagine the satisfaction it gives a high school teacher when students ask to give up their own lunch periods to go online or inquire about what they can read over the summer to increase their knowledge about international politics.

These exciting things are happening with students involved in Interactive Communications & Simulations (ICS), a program linking students around the world in an interactive, collaborative learning environment. In partnership with the University of Michigan, which provides the conferencing software, high schools and middle schools all over the United States are expanding their classrooms to include students of different cultures and backgrounds.

ICS has two types of programs, Communications Exercises (Earth Odysseys and International Poetry Guild) and Simulation Exercises (Environmental Decisions, Arab-Israeli Conflict, and United States Constitution). In Earth Odysseys students travel vicariously by conversing, via networked computers, with travelers on unusual expeditions. The Simulations Exercises involve role-playing, where the students act as real-life characters such as prominent world leaders.

For information, contact ICS by e-mail at info@ics.soc.umich.edu, or by phone at 313-763-6716.

Global Education: New Zealand and Colorado In the K12-NET newsgroup k12.ed.science, an enthusiastic student from New Zealand described his attempt to study the effect of the earth's rotation on the way toilets flush. His conclusion, that water drains clockwise in the

FIGURE 17.6 ▶

Renso Vasquez describes the Ralph Bunche School.

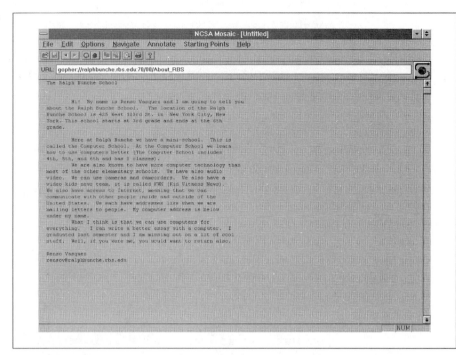

FIGURE 17.7 ▶

"The Three Girls Who Went into the Danger Park," a story from Ralph Bunche School.

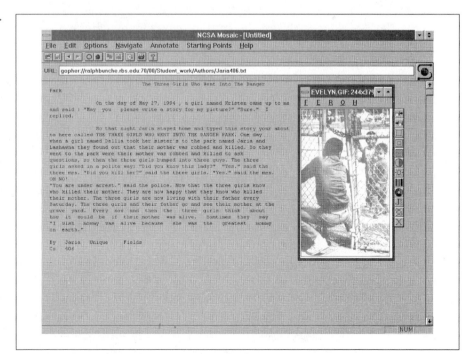

southern hemisphere, and counter-clockwise in the northern hemisphere, received a very detailed response from a correspondent at the University of Colorado in Boulder, who described the relevant scientific principle (the Coriolis force) in detail, and told him how to set up a scientifically verifiable experiment.

Physics Challenge High school physics students in Oregon, California, Maryland, and Nova Scotia attempted to replicate Eratosthenes' experiment to measure the size of the earth by measuring the length of a shadow cast by a stick at "true" noon on three successive Mondays in October 1991, posting their data, and performing the necessary calculations in the "Physics Challenge" IRC channel. Their calculations were accurate to within 7%. Their reports were posted on the `k12.ed.science` newsgroup.

Global Warming Study Students at all levels on K12-NET have participated in the "CO2 Challenge" project to reduce carbon dioxide in the environment. Led by Marshall Gilmore of Earth Kids Net, students have tackled the issue of global warming with "Quick Facts" questions and answers as well as a number of environmental projects. More recently, students have been participating in the "Global Environmental Watch." The Global Village News project solicits local news items from the student participants, and expects them to analyze the feature stories for local and regional differences in news reporting.

Special Needs A handicapped K12-NET system operator in the United Kingdom led a discussion of problems faced by those with special needs, and an important conclusion emerged from this topic— telecommunications networks are significant equalizers because the participants are evaluated by their contributions rather than their appearance, race, or ethnic background. It is this aspect of networking which offers the most significant opportunity to effect social change. Students who telecommunicate with their fellow students around the world are less likely to accept the stereotypes fostered by their communities and governments. Differences in the age of participants are similarly diffused in an environment which applauds eloquence and depth of expression. Teachers in rural schools can expand their gifted students' horizons by giving them access to K12Net and appropriate peers to stimulate their intellectual and artistic creativity.

Other Schools on the Net

There are literally hundreds of other K–12 projects on the Net. Three good resources for your own exploration are:

- *The Best of K12 on the Net,* sponsored by the University of Illinois at Champaign-Urbana (http://www.ncsa.uiuc.edu/Edu/MSTE/K12.html).

- *Janice's Outpost,* sponsored by CNIDR (http://k12.cnidr.org/janice_K12/k12menu.html), shown in Figure 17.8.

- Gleason Sackman's *K–12 Hotlist* (http://toons.cc.ndsu.no-dak.edu/~sackmann/k12.html), sponsored by North Dakota State University.

Special Education Collections

Many organizations now have special Web pages and other Internet resources for educators, providing links to education resources. Some of

FIGURE 17.8 ▶

Janice's Outpost at CNIDR.

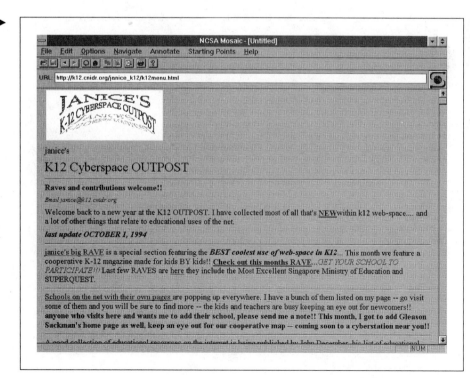

the best are listed here to help you discover more resources for educators and students.

NASA Education Resources NASA provides, as part of the High Performance Computing initiatives, a vast number of resources for teachers, including curriculum modules, access to databases and indices, and papers and other articles to help teachers better educate their students with the help of the Internet. Figure 17.9 shows the list of school and community resources available through the NASA server (`http://www.nasa.gov/HPCC/K12/edures.html`).

BBN Education Pages Bolt, Beranek, and Newman (BBN), one of the oldest network information providers (they began providing user information in the days of the ARPANET) has a special education server, located at `gopher://copernicus.bbn.com`.

Netcom Netcom provides a growing number of links to education resources through their education Web page (`http://www.netcom.com/netcom/educ.html`).

FIGURE 17.9 ▶

NASA's list of school and community networking resources.

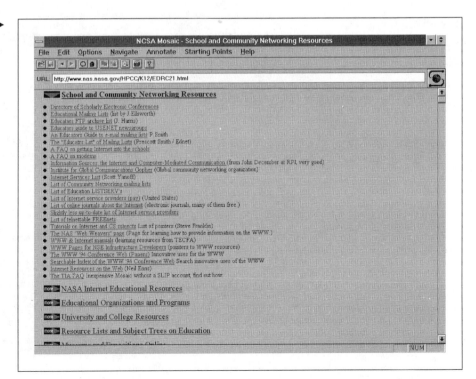

Merit Network Merit/MichNet provides resources for educators and a number of case studies of K–12 experiences using networking technology (`http://www.merit.edu`).

K12 Best From Minnesota comes a selected and varied listing of K–12 resources on the Internet, for both students and teachers (`gopher://informns.k12.mn.us:70/11/best-k12`). Figure 17.10 shows the first of many pages of directory listings of K12 resources.

Learning Resource Project University of Illinois at Champaign-Urbana (UIUC) has collected a tremendous number of invaluable resources for educators. Check out the server at `http://www.ed.uiuc.edu/`. Figure 17.11 shows the main index for the project.

The Computing Teacher *Computing Teacher* magazine has been providing expertise and education for teachers struggling to use new technology in their classrooms for several years now. Judi Harris, whose articles have helped teachers learn to mine the Internet, has now provided some of those articles online via the UIUC server. You can find out

FIGURE 17.10

K12 on the Net.

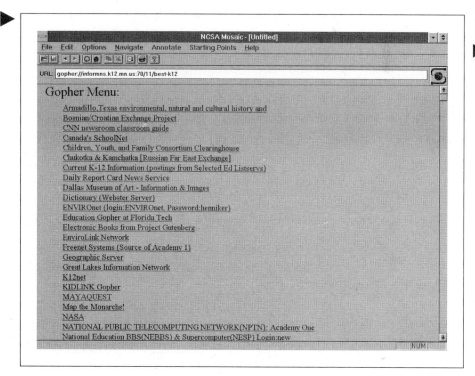

FIGURE 17.11 ►

*Learning Resource
Project at UIUC.*

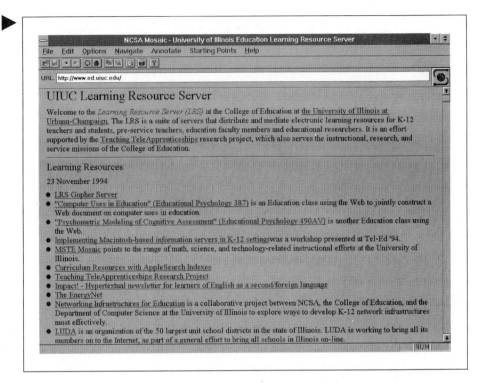

more about *Computing Teacher* by calling 800-336-5191, or via e-mail at `iste@oregon.uoregon.edu`. Harris's articles are available online at `http://www.uiuc.edu/Mining/overview.html`.

Web66 Web66 is a ground-breaking project sponsored as part of the Hillsdale, MN, computing project described earlier, to assist teachers in creating their own network resources. Just as Route 66 helped shape the development of the United States, Web66 wants to help shape the Internet to come. Figure 17.12 shows the Web66 home page.

SuperQuest for Teachers SuperQuest helps teachers sharpen their Internet skills and learn to translate those skills into the classroom to enrich their resources. The Web server for SuperQuest is available through the UIUC server, at `http://www.ncsa.uiuc.edu/Edu/Super-Quest/sqt/index.html`. Figure 17.13 shows the SuperQuest introductory page.

FIGURE 17.12 ▶

Web66 leads the way across the information highway.

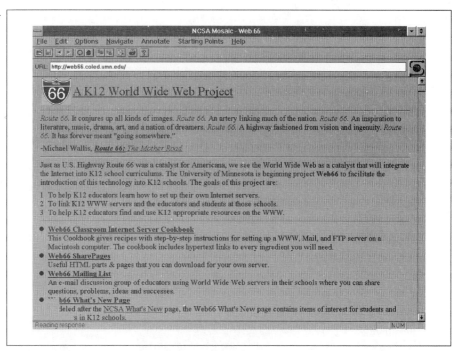

FIGURE 17.13 ▶

The SuperQuest Home page.

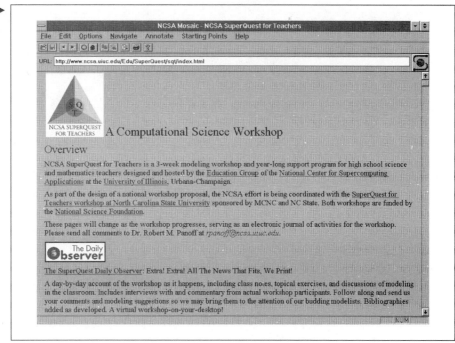

National Center for Research on Evaluations, Standards, and Student Testing As the name implies, this resource helps teachers better understand the ways they can evaluate their students, and it helps them understand testing and evaluation instruments as well. This server has the latest in research papers and guidelines. You can see it at gopher://cse.ucla.edu, and the introductory page appears in Figure 17.14.

New York State Education Department Gopher Server Looking for curriculum information in the arts, humanities, sciences, math, social studies? Looking for information on the newest standards for teaching students with disabilities? The New York State Education Gopher has unparalleled resources for teachers. The server is available at gopher://unix5.nysed.gov/, and Figure 17.15 shows the description of the purpose of the service.

FIGURE 17.14 ▶

National Center for Research on Evaluations main index.

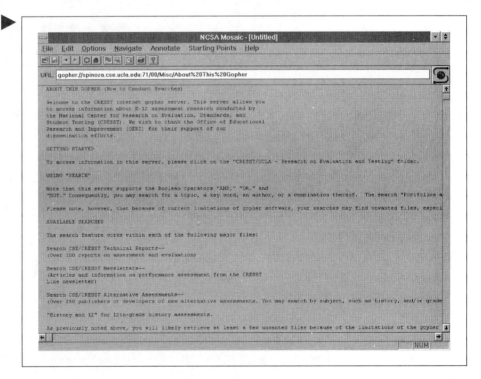

FIGURE 17.15 ▶

The description of the NYSED Gopher.

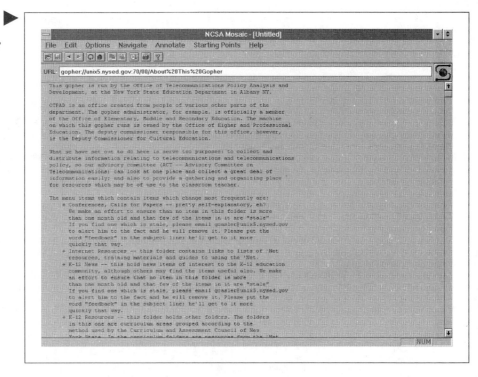

▶ *Step Two: Convince Others*

Many network consulting firms and network providers say that the impetus for getting a school connected comes from two main sources: a teacher or group of teachers who have decided that they want their school on the Net; or a school district that has come to the same conclusion. Obviously, it's easy for one teacher or one parent or one school board member to have an individual connection to the Net. The harder part is convincing others, especially those with money in their pockets, to help fund a network connection.

Once you've found out all the cool things that can be done with the Net, think about some projects that could be done in your area, particularly those which address visible issues in your community. Gather about you some like-minded folks. Schedule a series of discussions about the potential for network connection. You will need to make formal presentations to local boards and chambers of commerce, one-on-one sessions with local leaders and money folk. Talk to the PTA. Invite guest speakers, particularly teachers and administrators who have successfully integrated networking into their schools, to come and speak to your teachers' unions, training seminars or inservices, and so on.

▶ ▶ **M A S T E R   W O R D S**

> **If you can arrange to get continuing education credit for these workshops, so much the better. Your audience of teachers and administrators will jump.**

▶ *Step Three: Pull Together a Proposal*

Once it looks as though you are developing momentum, get a group together to write a formal proposal for a networking strategy in your school, town, district or unified district—whatever size seems right to your planning group. Contact your regional network providers; the phone company; LAN software and hardware vendors; corporate partners. The bigger the coalition backing the proposal, the better your chances of success.

Really successful proposals vary from district to district. We can only give you general guidelines on what's likely to be successful; you'll need to create your own with your specialized knowledge about your community.

You're more likely to succeed if your proposal:

- Has technical input—someone or some group who really know what they're talking about.

- Has a staged implementation plan that will allow spending to happen over a series of years rather than in a lump sum.

- Includes funding proposals that are researched and realistic. Partnerships, donations, and matching programs that have buy-in are all better than bake-sales or airy guesses.

- Includes a grant opportunity or other funding model from outside sources (but don't forget to talk about what to do when the grant runs out).

- Has references to successful programs modeled similarly to yours.

- Is timed so that it can be considered carefully. This means you need to get someone on your team who understands the proposal and budgeting cycle in your community or district.

- Builds on computer infrastructure that is already in place or in the pipeline.

- Can be included in a scheduled renovation, remodeling, or new building project rather than requiring extensive physical plant modifications. New phone systems or switches, cable installations, or new buildings are good opportunities to get a computer network in place.

Good politics say that after your proposal is prepared but before it is formally submitted is the time to start garnering wider support for it. Hold focus groups, public meetings, and coffees to talk to parents, businesses, and other taxpayer groups. Present your "draft" proposal, and see how it flies. If it meets with a storm of protest, the time may not be right for a formal proposal. Rework it until it seems to meet the needs of your community.

When your proposal has a head of steam and people are excited about it, get their support for the formal approval process. Start a mailing list: notify people about public hearings, votes, and so on. Invite people to come and speak in favor of the proposal at citizen's comment sessions, and encourage them to write to whoever is making the decision.

If you are working on a millage proposal (that is, one involving a tax increase), once your ideas get acceptance at the school board level, you become partners with them in the campaign for public acceptance. Get your mailing list together, and get those folks out to help campaign for the proposal.

From this point on, turning your proposal into reality is an exercise in local politics in your area. Find a savvy local person who knows this process, and recruit them to help get your school network in place.

▶▶ *Funding Models*

There are many models for funding school projects. We list three of the most common—you may find that a different model works best, or a blend of these three.

▶ *District Budgets and Millage Elections*

Getting the taxpayers to foot the bill is perhaps one of the hardest ways to fund a networking strategy, but it can be one of the more reliable. Convincing your district that networking is a serious objective, and getting a networking strategy in place so that it shows up on the budget, can only happen successfully when coalitions of parents, teachers, students, local government, and local business have been formed.

▶ *Partnerships*

Partnerships with computer software or equipment manufacturers or vendors are a fun way to get at least part of your network together. Usually such partnerships involve some outlay on the school's part, with a large donation of time and materials from the donor. Sometimes that donation comes with expertise in setting up the network; sometimes it doesn't. If you get a partnership going, make sure you also recruit a network designer or consultant to work with your school to make sure that what you get really solves your problems.

Potential partners might include:

- Network software vendors and manufacturers (Novell, Banyan, and so on)
- Regional network providers
- Telephone companies
- Cable companies
- Power utilities
- Hardware vendors (both the local computing stores and the big guys)
- Big local employers
- Chambers of Commerce

One good source for potential partnership information is a local regional or commercial network provider. Usually they are well-informed about initiatives from the government, vendors, and other sources. They can help leverage an expressed interest into a coalition or partnership.

Remember that you'll need ongoing funding once the network gets built to help maintain and upgrade the network.

▶ *Parent or Teacher-Driven Fund-Raisers (Private Donation)*

These campaigns are the easiest to propose, and the hardest to make fund a computing initiative for the long term. Since computing initiatives can cost well into the tens of thousands for start-up, and have on-going maintenance costs that include staff payrolls and equipment upgrades, this is an uphill fight unless you have a district populated with deep pockets.

But raising your own seed money, matching funds, or start-up funds can be an important part of a larger funding initiative.

Obviously, selling candy bars is not likely to fund a computer lab unless your kids are really good salespeople. But some other ideas, garnered from anecdotes from successful initiatives, include:

- Scrip sales
- "Worker" services (watch child labor laws!) where residents can contract for lawn work, housework, and other services on a regular or one-shot basis
- Grocery-store campaigns (people buy a tag or card for a donation, which the store passes along to the school)
- Series of yard sales, auctions, book sales, and raffles.

▶▶ *Technical Planning*

Appendix E presents an excellent paper, by Joan Gargano and David Wasley of the ISN Working Group, on planning your school network. It covers hardware, wiring, software, and suggested protocols. We recommend you study it carefully as you work out your proposal for your school network.

▶▶ *Plan before the Equipment Goes In*

When you get your plans for the physical network together (or perhaps while the funding drive is ongoing), you should also be planning for the management and policy issues for your network. Things you need to consider include:

- How will you deal with your employees?
- What policies do you want to set in place concerning who can get access to your network?
- How will you deal with student access to the Net?
- How will you accomplish training of staff and students?
- Who will manage your resource?

▶▶ *Schools Are Also Businesses*

If you are hoping to get your school on the network, you should realize that your school is also a business—you have a budget, and customers to serve, and you need to get the best possible advice about getting connected to the network.

If you have not already read the chapters on getting connected (Chapter 4) and businesses on the Net (Chapter 16), you should do so. There we talk about your options for connections, legal aspects of being on the Net, staffing, finding someone to help you design your Net, and so on.

One advantage that schools have over other businesses, however, is that you have a community of parents who want to see the best for their children. School districts can frequently find parents (or parents with connections) who have expertise in networking, computing strategies, electrical wiring and contracting, and many of the other skills you will need on hand to plan and execute your network. Even if you can't get the work done completely free, you can often get volunteer assistance in all phases of network planning, implementation, and ongoing management and maintenance.

You will also need to look at the realities of having your employees have Net access. All the same policy dilemmas that other businesses and organizations have to resolve need to be resolved for employees of schools, as well. Chapter 18 discusses "appropriate use" policies in detail.

If you currently have policies for your employees concerning use of school resources for private use, look to them for guidance for your electronic appropriate use policies as well. In addition, the Electronic Freedom Foundation is an excellent resource for education policies. In their FTP archives (`ftp.eff.org`) they have a wide collection of education policies and critiques on those policies, as well as recent legislation and other decisions and criteria that may help determine your policies.

▶ *Policies for Students as Well as Staff*

In general, the more you can treat your students, parents, and staff similarly in access policies, the easier to administer and less subject to challenge your policies will be. As general policy, computer media should be treated the same as other media. In K–12 settings, teachers and administrators should have the same privacy rights to their computer files as they have to their paper files. Policies for searches of student's computer files should be similar to those for searches of student's lockers. Outside computer material should be selected in the same way as library materials. Students should have exactly the same freedom of expression in computer media as they have in paper media.

▶ ▶**MASTER WORDS**

An excellent source of K12 appropriate use policies is Rice University's education Gopher. Using a Gopher client, go to `riceinfo.rice.edu`**; using a Web browser open the URL** `gopher://riceinfo.rice.edu:1170/11/ More/Acceptable`**.**

▶ ▶MASTER WORDS

If you are writing new staff policies to deal with the electronic age, be sure to include your staff in the writing process. You'll get better compliance if you have staff input from the beginning.

THE BREVARD COUNTY, FLORIDA, ACCEPTABLE USE POLICY

Here is the text of the Brevard County, Florida, policy on access and use of the network. It's a fairly typical policy, and covers a number of important issues. We include it (and similar policies) as examples to help you create your own policies.

APPLICATION FOR ACCOUNT

DIRECTIONS: Copy the following for use in applying for an account for your students. Edit the areas marked Name Name High School (NNHS) to reflect the name of your own school. Change each of the (NNHS) to reflect your school. Be sure that everybody who signs the contract has read the application and understands the terms.

Send a copy of both signed forms to:

Kevin Barry
Florida Institute of Technology
Academic & Research Computing Services
150 University Boulevard
Melbourne, FL 32901-6988

The user account will be assigned after the application forms are received.

APPLICATION FOR ACCOUNT AND TERMS AND CONDITIONS FOR USE OF INTERNET

Please read the following carefully before signing this document. This is a legally binding document.

Internet access is now available to students and teachers in the Brevard County School District. The access is being offered as part of a collaborative research project involving Name Name High School (NNHS), Florida Institute of Technology, and the US Department of Education. We are very pleased to bring this access to Brevard County and believe the Internet offers vast, diverse and unique resources to both students and teachers. Our goal in providing this service to teachers and students is to promote educational excellence in the Brevard County Schools by facilitating resource sharing, innovation and communication.

The Internet is an electronic highway connecting thousands of computers all over the world and millions of individual subscribers. Students and teachers have access to

1. electronic mail communication with people all over the world;

2. information and news from NASA as well as the opportunity to correspond with the scientists at NASA and other research institutions;

3. public domain and shareware of all types;

4. discussion groups on a plethora of topics ranging from Chinese culture to the environment to music to politics;

5. access to many University Library Catalogs, the Library of Congress, CARL and ERIC.

With access to computers and people all over the world also comes the availability of material that may not be considered to be of educational value in the context of the school setting. (NNHS) and Florida Institute of Technology have taken available precautions to restrict access to controversial materials. However, on a global network it is impossible to control all materials and an industrious user may discover controversial information. We [(NNHS) and Florida Institute of Technology] firmly believe that the valuable information and interaction available on this worldwide network far outweighs the possibility that users may procure material that is not consistent with the educational goals of this Project.

Internet access is coordinated through a complex association of government agencies, and regional and state networks. In addition, the smooth operation of the network relies upon the proper conduct of the end users who must adhere to strict guidelines. These guidelines are provided here so that you are aware of the responsibilities you are about to acquire. In general this requires efficient, ethical and legal utilization of the network resources. If a (NNHS) user violates any of these provisions, his or her account will be terminated and future access could possibly be denied. The signature(s) at the end of this document is (are) legally binding and indicates the party (parties) who signed has (have) read the terms and conditions carefully and understand(s) their significance.

Internet—Terms and Conditions

1. *Acceptable Use*—The purpose of NSFNET, which is the backbone network to the Internet, is to support research and education in and among academic institutions in the US by providing access to unique resources and the opportunity for collaborative work. The use of your account must be in support of education and research and consistent with the educational objectives of the Brevard County School District. Use of other organization's network or computing resources must comply with the rules appropriate for that network. Transmission of any material in violation of any US or state regulation is prohibited. This includes, but is not limited to: copyrighted material, threatening or obscene material, or material protected by trade secret. Use for commercial activities by for-profit institutions is generally not acceptable. Use for product advertisement or political lobbying is also prohibited.

2. *Privileges*—The use of Internet is a privilege, not a right, and inappropriate use will result in a cancellation of those privileges. (Each student who receives an account will be part of a discussion with a (NNHS) faculty member pertaining to the proper use of the network.) The system administrators will deem what is inappropriate use and their decision is final. Also, the system administrators may close an account at any time as required. The administration, faculty, and staff of (NNHS) may request the system administrator to deny, revoke, or suspend specific user accounts.

3. *Netiquette*—You are expected to abide by the generally accepted rules of network etiquette. These include (but are not limited to) the following:

a. Be polite. Do not get abusive in your messages to others.

b. Use appropriate language. Do not swear, use vulgarities or any other inappropriate language. Illegal activities are strictly forbidden.

c. Do not reveal your personal address or phone numbers of students or colleagues.

d. Note that electronic mail (e-mail) is not guaranteed to be private. People who operate the system do have access to all mail. Messages relating to or in support of illegal activities may be reported to the authorities.

e. Do not use the network in such a way that you would disrupt the use of the network by other users.

f. All communications and information accessible via the network should be assumed to be private property.

4. NNHS and Florida Institute of Technology make no warranties of any kind, whether expressed or implied, for the service they are providing. NNHS and Florida Institute of Technology will not be responsible for any damages you suffer. This includes loss of data resulting from delays, nondeliveries, misdeliveries, or service interruptions caused by it's own negligence or your errors or omissions. Use of any information obtained via NNHS or Florida Institute of Technology is at your own risk. NNHS and Florida Institute of Technology specifically deny any responsibility for the accuracy or quality of information obtained through its services.

5. *Security*—Security on any computer system is a high priority, especially when the system involves many users. If you feel you can identify a security problem on Internet, you must notify a system administrator or e-mail barry@sci-ed.fit.edu. Do not demonstrate the problem to other users. Do not use another individual's account without written permission from that individual. Attempts to log in to Internet as a system administrator will result in cancellation of user privileges. Any user identified as a security risk or having a history of problems with other computer systems may be denied access to Internet.

6. *Vandalism*—Vandalism will result in cancellation of privileges. Vandalism is defined as any malicious attempt to harm or destroy data of another user, Internet, or any of the above listed agencies or other networks that are connected to the NSFNET Internet backbone. This includes, but is not limited to, the uploading or creation of computer viruses.

7. *Updating Your User Information*—Internet may occasionally require new registration and account information from you to continue the service. You must notify Internet of any changes in your account information (address, etc). Currently, there are no user fees for this service.

8. *Exception of Terms and Condition*—All terms and conditions as stated in this document are applicable to the Brevard County School District, the Florida Institute of Technology, in addition to NSFNET. These terms and conditions reflect the entire agreement of the parties and supersedes all prior oral or written agreements and understandings of the parties. These terms and conditions shall be governed and interpreted in accordance with the laws of the State of Florida, and the United States of America.

I understand and will abide by the above Terms and Conditions for Internet. I further understand that any violation of the regulations above is unethical and may constitute a criminal offense. Should I commit any violation, my access privileges may be revoked, and school disciplinary action and/or appropriate legal action may be taken.

User Signature:_____ Date: ___/ ___/ ___

****

PARENT OR GUARDIAN (If you are under the age of 18 a parent or guardian must also read and sign this agreement.)

As the parent or guardian of this student I have read the Terms and Conditions for Internet access. I understand that this access is designed for educational purposes and (NNHS) and Florida Institute of Technology have taken available precautions to eliminate controversial material. However, I also recognize it is impossible for (NNHS) and Florida Institute of Technology to restrict access to all controversial materials and I will not hold them responsible for materials acquired on the network. Further, I accept full responsibility for supervision if and when my child's use is not in a school setting. I hereby give permission to issue an account for my child and certify that the information contained on this form is correct.

Parent or Guardian (please print):

_____

Signature: _____ Date: ___/___/___

★★

SPONSORING TEACHER (Must be signed if the applicant is a student). I have read the Terms and Conditions and agree to promote this agreement with the student. Because the student may use the network for individual work or in the context of another class, I cannot be held responsible for the student use of the network. As the sponsoring teacher I do agree to instruct the student on acceptable use of the network and proper network etiquette.

Teacher's Name (please print): _____

Teacher's Signature: _____ Date: ___/ ___/ ___

****

APPLICATION PORTION OF DOCUMENT

User's Full Name (please print): _____

Home Address: _____

Home Phone: _____ Work Phone: _____

I am a.....

____ (NNHS) student and will graduate in _____.

____ (NNHS) teacher, teaching _____ in grade_____.

_____ (NNHS) staff working as a _____

_____ Brevard County School District community member.

When your account is established you will be notified of your logon name and user password. Thank you for your interest and support of this exciting new resource in the Brevard County Schools.

▶▶ *Who Should Get Access?*

You will notice in the Brevard County policy that local members of the community can apply for access to the network. Other schools have allowed access to members of other schools, alumni of the school, local government members, senior citizens, and other special groups.

You may or may not want to allow access by persons not related to the school. Advantages include:

- You may be able to charge for such access, helping to fund school-related computing projects.

- You gain support in the community for your computer and networking projects, particularly when the community becomes dependent on your project for their access.

- Your students will gain a wider experience of the world by exchanging views and information with other members of the local community.

- Your students gain credibility with the members of the local community by their responsible and appropriate use of computing resources.

- Students and community members can exchange expertise.

However, there can be disadvantages, as well:

- Your students are bound by codes of behavior and at least minimal habit to follow the guidelines set down by the school authorities. Outsiders may not have such restrictions.

- It is harder ethically (because of First Amendment issues) to monitor non-school-related users for inappropriate use, including the storage of pirated software, inappropriate materials, and other problematic items.

- It is even harder to prevent outsiders from sharing these materials with your students once they are stored on your own system.

- If you allow general access by the community, you will need to allocate technical, administrative, and clerical resources to manage the accounts.

You will need to make your own decisions about allowing outsiders access to your system. One strategy is to get the system up and running first, and then allow access slowly, if at all. This lets you get some experience under your belt before opening this new can of worms.

▶ *Bill of Rights for Students and Institutions in Cyberspace*

One item that might help when thinking about appropriate use for students and staff alike is the *Bill of Rights and Responsibilities for the Electronic Community of Learners.* The Bill was begun as part of EDU-COM's Educational Uses of Information Technology program. EDU-COM is a consortium of around 600 colleges and universities focusing on the use of computers and telecommunications. EDUCOM leaders worked with leaders from the American Association for Higher Education (AAHE) in order to reach out to educational leaders across campus and in school districts.

The exciting thing about the *Bill of Rights* is that it covers all aspects of good policy-making for educational institutions: personal responsibility, security, institutional responsibility, training, and legal issues.

BILL OF RIGHTS AND RESPONSIBILITIES FOR THE ELECTRONIC COMMUNITY OF LEARNERS

PREAMBLE

In order to protect the rights and recognize the responsibilities of individuals and institutions, we, the members of the educational community, propose this Bill of Rights and Responsibilities for the Electronic Community of Learners. These principles are based on a recognition that the electronic community is a complex subsystem of the educational community founded on the values espoused by that community. As new technology modifies the system and further empowers individuals, new values and responsibilities will change this culture. As technology assumes an integral role in education and lifelong learning, technological empowerment of individuals and organizations becomes a requirement and right for students, faculty, staff, and institutions, bringing with it new levels of responsibility that individuals and institutions have to themselves and to other members of the educational community.

ARTICLE I: INDIVIDUAL RIGHTS

The original Bill of Rights explicitly recognized that all individuals have certain fundamental rights as members of the national community. In the same way, the citizens of the electronic community of learners have fundamental rights that empower them.

Section 1.

A citizen's access to computing and information resources shall not be denied or removed without just cause.

Section 2.

The right to access includes the right to appropriate training and tools required to effect access.

Section 3.

All citizens shall have the right to be informed about personal information that is being and has been collected about them, and have the right to review and correct that information. Personal information about a citizen shall not be used for other than the expressed purpose of its collection without the explicit permission of that citizen.

Section 4.

The constitutional concept of freedom of speech applies to citizens of electronic communities.

Section 5.

All citizens of the electronic community of learners have ownership rights over their own intellectual works.

ARTICLE II: INDIVIDUAL RESPONSIBILITIES

Just as certain rights are given to each citizen of the electronic community of learners, each citizen is held accountable for his or her actions. The interplay of rights and responsibilities within each individual and within the community engenders the trust and intellectual freedom that form the heart of our society. This trust and freedom are grounded on each person's developing the skills necessary to be an active and contributing citizen of the electronic community. These skills include an awareness and knowledge about information technology and the uses of information and an understanding of the roles in the electronic community of learners.

Section 1.

It shall be each citizen's personal responsibility to actively pursue needed resources: to recognize when information is needed, and to be able to find, evaluate, and effectively use information.

Section 2.

It shall be each citizen's personal responsibility to recognize (attribute) and honor the intellectual property of others.

Section 3.

Since the electronic community of learners is based upon the integrity and authenticity of information, it shall be each citizen's personal responsibility to be aware of the potential for and possible effects of manipulating electronic information: to understand the fungible nature of electronic information; and to verify the integrity and authenticity, and assure the security of information that he or she compiles or uses.

Section 4.

Each citizen, as a member of the electronic community of learners, is responsible to all other citizens in that community: to respect and value the rights of privacy for all; to recognize and respect the diversity of the population and opinion in the community; to behave ethically; and to comply with legal restrictions regarding the use of information resources.

Section 5.

Each citizen, as a member of the electronic community of learners, is responsible to the community as a whole to understand what information technology resources are available, to recognize that the members of the community share them, and to refrain from acts that waste resources or prevent others from using them.

ARTICLE III: RIGHTS OF EDUCATIONAL INSTITUTIONS

Educational institutions have legal standing similar to that of individuals. Our society depends upon educational institutions to educate our citizens and advance the development of knowledge. However, in order to survive, educational institutions must attract financial and human resources. Therefore, society must grant these institutions the rights to the electronic resources and information necessary to accomplish their goals.

Section 1.

The access of an educational institution to computing and information resources shall not be denied or removed without just cause.

Section 2.

Educational institutions in the electronic community of learners have ownership rights over the intellectual works they create.

Section 3.

Each educational institution has the authority to allocate resources in accordance with its unique institutional mission.

ARTICLE IV: INSTITUTIONAL RESPONSIBILITIES

Just as certain rights are assured to educational institutions in the electronic community of learners, so too each is held accountable for the appropriate exercise of those rights to foster the values of society and to carry out each institution's mission. This interplay of rights and responsibilities within the community fosters the creation and maintenance of an environment wherein trust and intellectual freedom are the foundation for individual and institutional growth and success.

Section 1.

The institutional members of the electronic community of learners have a responsibility to provide all members of their community with legally acquired computer resources (hardware, software, networks, databases, etc.) in all instances where access to or use of the resources is an integral part of active participation in the electronic community of learners.

Section 2.

Institutions have a responsibility to develop, implement, and maintain security procedures to insure the integrity of individual and institutional files.

Section 3.

The institution shall treat electronically stored information as confidential. The institution shall treat all personal files as confidential, examining or disclosing the contents only when authorized by the owner of the information, approved by the appropriate institutional official, or required by local, state or federal law.

> *Section 4.*
>
> **Institutions in the electronic community of learners shall train and support faculty, staff, and students to effectively use information technology. Training includes skills to use the resources, to be aware of the existence of data repositories and techniques for using them, and to understand the ethical and legal uses of the resources.**
>
> **August 1993**

▶▶ *The Lady or the Tiger: Dealing with Student Access Problems*

Welcome to the nightmare:

- *"Cool, man! Did you see the naked pictures Tom has?"*
- *"Joey's passing out copies of a really hot story he found on the computer."*
- *"Suzy programmed the Macintosh so it says 'F**K Me' when you turn it on."*
- *"I was mudding and someone tried to get me to tell him where I lived, and told me he was masturbating while he typed."*

The issue of access to age-appropriate material and contact with potentially abusive people is not limited to electronic media. Librarians, school security specialists, and every parent has faced these issues. They become more volatile when the computer networks are involved, perhaps because of the vast availability of materials of all kinds, the difficulty in monitoring and controlling appropriate access and contact, the general uncertainty and computer-phobia of the uninformed citizen, the tendency of the press to blow any network-related incident out of proportion, and the personal liberty and censorship issues involved.

Carl M. Kadie, attorney for the Electronic Freedom Foundation, has said this about access policies:

"If you fear that students will access material on the Net that you would rather they not, you have two practical choices:

• Try to set up your system so they can only access material you approve of. (This is analogous to keeping them on the school grounds.)

• Warn parents that the school has no control on what is available on the Net (This is analogous to having the parents sign releases for field trips.)

A high school has no legal (or moral) way to stop a Net site, say, at U. of Houston or 'U. of Finland' from making age-inappropriate material available to all. (This is analogous to not being able to make the U. of Houston library remove Playboy for fear that high schoolers might access it.)"

Donald Perkins, who set up the Armadillo Gopher system we cited earlier, says:

"I think the main problem will be how to use the Net with kids appropriately and let parents know that the Net is being used by the kids and that some sort of monitoring and discussion of the appropriate use of this resource must occur. And here I am puzzled and a bit concerned, because we live in a litigious society. And often excuses are sought for not moving into new realms."

► Is Censorship Possible in the Networks?

Parents and politicians, when asked about this problem, sometimes say, "Just don't let children get to the bad stuff." Accustomed to technological wizardry, they expect that restricting access to the Internet ought to be as simple as guarding the money in a bank or locking the final exams away. But reading any newspaper will tell you that even these security precautions can be circumvented. Can the Internet be censored?

Howard Rheingold, author of *The Virtual Community*, said in the *San Francisco Examiner*, (April 6, 1994):

"It's not hard to imagine Jesse Helms standing before the US Senate, holding up an X-rated image downloaded from the Internet, raging indignantly about 'public funds for porno highways.'

As the public begins to realize that communications technology is exposing them to an unlimited array of words and images, including some they might find thoroughly repulsive, the clamor for censorship and government regulation of the electronic highway is sure to begin.

But it would be a mistake to let traffic cops start pulling people over on the highway.

Yes, we have to think about ways of protecting our children and our society from the easy availability of every kind of abhorrent information imaginable. But the 'censor the Net' approach is not just morally misguided. It's becoming technically impossible. As Net pioneer John Gilmore is often quoted: 'The Net interprets censorship as damage and routes around it.'

The Net's technological foundation was built to withstand nuclear attack. The RAND Corporation designed the network to be a thoroughly decentralized command-and-control and communications system, one that would be less vulnerable to intercontinental missiles than a system commanded by a centralized headquarters."

Let's suppose that your school decides not to provide the `alt.sex` news hierarchy in your news service, to prevent your middle-school students from reading the potentially offensive materials on that group. Will that keep the students from reading them? Probably not—they could use the Veronica search engine to find the locations where the groups are archived and read the stories over a Gopher server.

What should you do? What kind of policies and procedures can you put in place to keep students, parents, and school personnel happy?

*The K–12
Internet Presence*

ch.
17

▶ *Discussion, Argument, and Consensus*

The best way to come up with a comprehensive policy that stands some chance of being acceptable to everyone is to get input on the policy from all the affected parties. Get a committee together that includes students, parents, local clergy, school board administrators, legal experts, teachers, and so on.

One excellent technique to help hammer out a good policy is to get everyone grounded in the same information. You might pass out articles and relevant policies, and have people report on each article or policy at your meetings, explaining the issues covered and the solutions discussed. As you do this, the members of your committee will (we hope!) start to discuss how they feel about the issues, how it affects your local situation, and other important concepts.

You'll undoubtedly have heated meetings. With luck, your committee will be committed enough to the needs of the community and to the process itself to be able to get through the tough times. Listen carefully to each other and to the underlying beliefs and needs that cause the hot words.

Make sure someone writes down anything that sounds like consensus or strong agreement on general principles. When you're done talking about the articles and background information, you should have a good list of principles to start forging into a policy.

Once it's drafted, send it out for comment as widely as you can. Unfortunately, some of your squeakiest wheels won't respond now: they'll holler when they find their child downloading pictures from *Wicked Lady* to Dad's work machine. But you'll be on higher moral ground if you can prove you have community support for the policy you've developed.

Obviously, no policy is going to satisfy everyone. The religious fundamentalists and the Libertarians can't agree on most other issues in your community, and you're unlikely to get them both to be satisfied with any policy which is agreeable to the middle ground. But if you can keep 90% happy, you'll have done well.

Remember to keep one guiding principle in mind: Treat computer media the same way you do other media. Do you have a policy on plagiarism? Are *Catcher in the Rye*, *Huckleberry Finn*, *Little Black Sambo*, and *Sons and Lovers* in your school library? What do you do when Nazi or other hate literature appears on campus? Do you restrict the rights of student editors of the campus newspaper concerning newspaper content?

▶ Responsibility and Agreements

Every user of your system, from the kindergartners learning their ABC's to the secretary in the School Board office, must be aware of the rules and responsibilities before they use the network. Anyone who can't be made to understand the limits under which they must operate should not use your computing resources, including the network. Make your users sign an application that includes the appropriate use policy, and make sure the student's parents sign it, too (the Brevard County, Florida, document presented earlier is a good example of such a combined policy/application).

Experienced principals say that making sure the parents understand the basic ground rules, and that they are aware of the potential (limited or otherwise) for encountering difficult materials and situations, is critical to the success of any policy. Not only will the parents be your allies when and if an infraction or incident occurs, but by requiring them to sign the application as well as the student, you make them equally responsible for enforcing the policy.

You know best how to enforce the policy for your community: remember the principle we discussed above, and treat infractions of the computing policy the same way you do infractions of other rules. But do enforce it. If you don't, the students won't respect it (and you may be legally liable for other problems).

▶ *Protecting Children by Educating Them*

Unfortunately, it's not always a nice world, even in cyberspace. Students may well encounter nasty e-mail, harassing or abusive adults, even truly sick individuals on the Net. Parents should have the right, and the ability, to control the massive information-flow into the home, to exclude things they don't want their children to see. But sooner or later, most children will be exposed to everything parents have shielded them from, and then all they will have left to deal with these shocking sights and sounds is the moral fiber that both parents and teachers have helped them cultivate. The rules for protecting them in cyberspace are similar to those you have taught them about existing in the physical world:

- You don't have to answer e-mail from anyone unless you know them.

- If anybody asks whether you are home alone, or says anything that makes you feel funny about answering, then just don't answer until you speak to a trusted adult.

- Be politely but firmly skeptical about anything you see or hear on the Net.

- Don't be afraid to reject anything—images, sounds, or text communications—that repels or frightens you.

- Develop and respect your own sense of your personal boundaries. You have a right to defend those boundaries physically and socially.

- People sometimes lie: they aren't always who they present themselves to be in e-mail, news, and other contexts.

- Predators exist. You don't have to be a victim.

- Keep personal information private.

- Confide in a parent, teacher, or other trusted adult if something doesn't seem right.

▶ Damage Control

What do you—teachers, administrators, parents—do if an incident occurs?

Virginia Rezmierski, who wrote the article in Appendix F about Internet censorship and college students, has handled many incidents at the University of Michigan with tact and good sense. We feel that some of the principles she uses in handling problems are worthy of wide distribution.

- Be sure your system is as secure as possible.

- Handle problems promptly. Don't let little problems grow into big ones.

- Handle problems privately. Respect the privacy of both the perpetrator and (if there is one) the victim.

- Handle problems appropriately according to your established procedures. Minor infractions should have minimal repercussions, major ones greater repercussions.

- Make sure that the solution you choose allows the student to learn and grow as much as possible within the context of the problem itself.

There are some things you cannot allow on your system: child pornography and pirated software, for example, can create a liability for you as the system owner. You will, of course, have made that clear in your policy and in your training for users, and you will need to remove any such material from your system promptly. (Some experts advise saving it to tape if evidence in any legal action becomes necessary.)

If necessary, call in the computer crime experts with your local or state law enforcement agencies for assistance.

FURTHER RESOURCES FOR K–12 POLICIES

The Electronic Frontier Foundation maintains the Computers and Academic Freedom Archive, including documents related to K–12 education, in its pub/academic directory. Carl Kadie of the EFF provides an annotated list of these resources, including complete instructions for downloading them. This list is available at `ftp.eff.org (/pub/CAF)`, `gopher.eff.org`, **and** `http:/www.eff.org/CAF/cafhome.html`.

▶▶ *Training*

Training for users will include not only how to find and use the Internet, but ethical and social policy information as well. A good basic curriculum would include all the topics included in this book, as well as a good grounding in the local policies for your school network and regional network provider.

There are many training service companies for educators today: your regional provider will be able to point you to training providers in your area. Additionally, look for training services that offer continuing education credits for training sessions, so that teachers will be able to continue to accrue these important points as well as become more Internet-literate. Continuing education credits are an added incentive for attending training courses.

You will most likely want to designate one or more teachers per site to have more extensive training in network topics, so that they can become trainers and troubleshooters for others at your school, and assist in designing curriculum modules for your students.

▶▶ *Maintaining the Network*

You will be best served by hiring at least one staff person to exclusively manage and maintain your system. Attempting to add system maintenance and management to the tasks already assigned to teaching or administrative staff is likely to result in less efficiency in both areas.

Some schools have had good success using high school and older middle-school students to help manage their networks and computer resources. The kids are excited about the project, usually very skilled, and in many instances this privilege can be used as extra credit or as a reward for exceptional leadership or scholarship.

Other resources for network management are parents, college interns, local network consultants, or the computing specialists for your district.

▶▶ *Order out of Chaos*

As in the rest of the networked world, the rise of K–12 networking started slowly. Ten years ago navigating the Internet was a trip for the most intrepid: both the tools and the technology required patience and specialized expertise, and the rewards for the K–12 teacher were slight. Today, with the advent of the two great user-friendly tools, the World Wide Web and Gopher servers, teachers are taking firm hold of this resource and using it to enrich their classrooms. We can expect to see more resources, more aids for classroom development and distance learning, and even more fun things to do as we move into the 21st Century.

▶ ▶ **CHAPTER 18**

Rules, Policies, and Other Mutual Agreements

▶ ▶ **A** *policy* is a course of action designed to both influence and determine decisions and actions. According to the American Heritage dictionary, both *policy* and *police* are derived from the Greek word *polis* or city. This makes sense, doesn't it? What we are talking about is our own behavior in the larger Internet community.

In this chapter we'll consider why formal Acceptable Use Policies (AUPs) are necessary, whom they serve, and what kinds of activities they should cover. At the end of the chapter, you'll find two examples of complete Acceptable Use Policies. The first is from the University of Michigan, and the second is from the commercial Internet service provider Netcom.

Before we begin, a few general words of advice:

> **Keep Your Goals Clear** In order for your policy to address all the relevant issues effectively, you need to be clear about what you are trying to do:
>
> - Are you trying to protect yourself from legal action?
> - Are you trying to protect your organization's resources from being misused?
> - Are you trying to stretch limited resources and not let any one person or activity grab more than a "fair share" of them?
> - Are you trying to protect your staff from harassment by others?
>
> In most cases the answer will be "all of the above." You'll be able to write much better policies if you define your goals first.
>
> **Ask Your Lawyers** While you are developing your policies, make sure your lawyers check them for legality and validity, particularly with regard to copyright issues and employee rights. The authors of this book aren't lawyers. Don't just follow our

advice: get some good advice from people who know the law, human resources policies, and how your company policies can make best use of both.

Make Your AUP Accessible   Make sure you tell your user community what the policies are: keep them where they can be referred to.

▶▶ *Why Do We Need Policies?*

Formal policies make some people quite uncomfortable and strike others as overkill. Others, of course, think there ought to be more rules, particularly rules that inhibit actions those people don't like.

In the Internet community, rules and laws are generally regarded with trepidation. After all, people have been getting by with pretty few rules and not too much trouble on the Internet for some time now. You'll often hear Internet users say something like this:

"Why should we need to include rules—Isn't that an invasion of privacy? Or at least against the kind of academic freedom that a lot of people on the Internet enjoy? What about just depending on people to be responsible— shouldn't that be enough? Besides, the Internet is a free-wheeling place and if someone from your organization steps out of line, no doubt they will be flamed, chagrined, and enlightened; and they won't make that particular mistake again. That's the Internet way."

Most of us would like to live in the kind of world where "net-police" aren't needed and the only rule would be "do unto others as you would have them do unto you." Unfortunately, we don't live in such a world. For example, what if one of your employees posts a copyrighted, unreleased version of some software where others can retrieve it? What if that retrieval space is on one of your computers? This is clearly a violation of someone's copyright. What are you, the manager of this space, going to do? Do you want to figure out your position on intellectual property only when you get a threatening letter or phone call from the copyright holder's lawyer? The alternative is better: get your ducks all in line *before* it happens, so that you know exactly what to do next.

What's a good yardstick to tell if you need policies? If there is more than one of you on your staff, you probably need policies. And even if you are a one person business or organization, we'd argue that you should have some clear delineation between resources for your personal use and those for use in the name of your organization or company. Policies, particularly written policies, can help you allocate resources and expenses for tax purposes, for example. There's nothing quite like the idea of an IRS audit to make us all think we should be better about our policies and our record-keeping.

Policies are similar to contracts in that they protect all the parties involved, not just the owners. Well-written policies will help people to understand the possible results of their actions. They might prevent the thoughtless act by someone that can hurt themselves or others. Well-written policies explain what *can* happen and then what *will* happen if the policy is not followed. This gives all parties the opportunity to understand each other's positions. And finally, well-written policies outline a process of appeal that allows the person who committed the violation of the policy a chance to explain his/her actions. Well-written policies should provide for due process—not just summary judgments.

For example, even though some tech-support people and moderators joke about shooting users in the kneecaps for posting inappropriate articles to scores of newsgroups, in fact the Netcom process for Usenet abuse is to warn the user via e-mail that a complaint was received and explain the policy. At this point most people say "oh, I didn't understand, I'm sorry" or something similar. The persistent abusers are warned again. If they continue, Netcom places their accounts on hold until they are talked to in person. If at this point, they promise to "be good," Netcom releases the hold. It's only after several (and continued), deliberate actions on the part of the user to ignore the policy that Netcom actually closes an account. This policy can be a pain for the enforcers as well as for the people who have to read the inappropriate articles and then complain to Netcom. But it does allow the abuser plenty of chances to change behavior. Since changed behavior is the desired outcome, Netcom finds that this policy usually works. And just as a service like Netcom wants to hold onto its customers, your organization presumably wants to hold onto its employees.

▶▶ Who Is Served by an AUP?

If you are an employer or provider of network services, policies best serve you and your users by being explicit, clear-cut, fair, and well advertised. We recommend that you avoid using "Guidelines," which are statements of reasonable and prudent behavior for the users and the organization; they state your intent but do not, usually, describe actions and consequences. Good policies, for the most part, detail the expected behavior and the consequences of undesirable behavior.

As a user, you are best served by reading and understanding the Appropriate Use Policies of your network provider and any network segments your traffic crosses. We believe that you shouldn't sign up with a network provider if you do not intend to abide by their policies: there are many providers available, some with more lenient policies and some with more restrictive policies. You should ask for the policies which affect you and be certain you can abide by them before you sign on the dotted line. If your network provider (or your employer, for that matter) is reluctant to show you copies of policies before you sign up, you should take care in your dealings with them.

▶▶ *What Should Your Policy Cover?*

Here are some of the topics you'll want to think about in formulating your Acceptable Use Policy. We say *think about* because every Internet site is different. Except for a really obvious policy like "no illegal stuff on our computers," there probably isn't an item on this list for which every site will have the same policy.

▶ *Actions by Individuals*

First, let's talk about policies concerning the things individual people do: e-mail, chat programs (like Talk), IRC, and FTP storage.

Personal Messages

Are your employees allowed to send and receive personal messages at an e-mail address at your organization's Internet site? If so, can the employees read personal messages when they arrive (most Internet e-mail is delivered continually, not in a batch at a specific time) or need the mail wait until lunch or break-time or after work? If they may not receive e-mail, can you effectively police this? As parents who are quite experienced in children sneaking things by us, we'd recommend against making an unenforceable policy.

Talk, IRC, MUDs?

Will you be running a Talk program? An Internet Relay Chat server? Will you allow connections to an IRC server during work hours from your equipment? Will you be running a multiuser program like a MUD to deliver training and information about your organization? If you answer "yes" to any of these questions, you'll need to state your position about their use for personal message traffic. We've noted in Chapter 14 that Talk can be really convenient to check in with one's spouse, roommates, and so on. It's much quicker than a telephone call.

What's Your Telephone Policy?

Your organization's policy about personal use of e-mail and Talk facilities should be derived from its policies on personal telephone use, although the two may not be exactly the same. Many organizations state that a few personal calls from time to time are fine, especially when there are family emergencies. However, personal long distance calls are expected to be paid for. Usually this is a cost-of-resource issue—the organization doesn't want to incur expensive long distance telephone bills unnecessarily. Interestingly enough, the Internet can shine here because the rates for Internet traffic are not usually based upon number of packets nor the distance the packets travel, so the motivation to forbid long-distance traffic isn't there.

To think about how your employee's e-mail and other personal message traffic can affect your organization you need to consider the resources they are using: intellectual effort, time, and network bandwidth. You probably should be most concerned about the time and intellectual effort employees might spend on personal communications.

I Spy or Reasonable Caution?

When creating policies concerning employee use of your systems, you must clearly address the privacy of employee e-mail and stored files. It's really important that everyone is clear on this one. Internet e-mail can inadvertently be read by someone not intended to see it for a number of reasons that have nothing to do with monitoring employee actions: for example, when someone prints out a message at a public printer.

We generally recommend that no one say anything in electronic mail that they wouldn't want to share with their mothers, but we *all* break that rule from time to time. Neither author would complain about our supervisors in a private message, for example. But if you do complain about someone and the e-mail gets forwarded to the person about whom you were complaining because you didn't think about what you were doing, you'll be embarrassed. Being embarrassed can be difficult, but it is not at all the same thing as having your e-mail monitored and your thoughts reported.

Your employees deserve to know if you are going to be monitoring their e-mail, just as they should know if you are monitoring their telephone calls. Sometimes it may be appropriate to monitor mail (when you are training people to answer e-mail for the organization, for example). If you are doing that, tell the people involved. Otherwise, people really do believe their e-mail conversations are private. No doubt this assumption has something to do with the fact that we interact only with a computer keyboard and screen. After all, there's no other person involved. It's unfair to let your employees continue to have this impression if you intend to monitor their mail.

We can think of one exception to this "rule." If you have a case where you are cooperating with a law enforcement agency, you should, of course, under the advice of your attorneys and within the bounds of the law, follow their instructions on whether or not to let people know they are being monitored.

For much more complete discussion of issues surrounding privacy and electronic messages, see the Electronic Frontier Foundation archives (available via the World Wide Web at www.eff.org, via Gopher at gopher.eff.org, and via FTP at ftp.eff.org). EFF staff members analyze and write extensively on issues of freedom and privacy in cyberspace. Their archives contain these writings as well as a complete copy of the Electronic Communications Privacy Act (ECPA) of 1986, and an extensive collection of terms and conditions-of-use statements and critiques of those statements. EFF and Computer Professionals for Social Responsibility (CPSR) are excellent sources for information about privacy issues.

Reading Newsgroups or Mailing Lists That Aren't Work-Related

Newsgroup reading can use a lot of time, too. Trade magazines are common in many fields now—magazines devoted to specific types of computing, for example, or to a specific type of medicine. Reading newsgroups or mailing lists that are related to the thrust of your organization is like reading these trade magazines. However, reading newsgroups or mailing lists that aren't directly related to work is more akin to reading magazines for pleasure. Some people like to read scientific journals for pleasure. Others like to read magazines devoted to the entertainment industry. If your organization is devoted to neither of these topics, reading either *Science* or *People* is probably something that shouldn't be done on your organization's time. If you agree, you will most likely want to say that reading `rec.art.books` or `rec.sport.soccer` or even `alt.adjective.noun.verb.verb.verb`, while interesting and certainly not evil, is something best not done during working hours.

Another area of concern involves the content of files—graphic images—that can be found on newsgroups such as `alt.sex.binaries` and others. These images may be offensive to people who have not initiated the download or display. In certain cases, using some of these graphic images as screen backgrounds or causing them to be printed to public printers has been deemed to be sexual harassment. We'd recommend that you state very clearly any policies you have about this type of material.

Game Playing on Your Organization's Time or Equipment

Unless you are in the business of designing, implementing, and/or testing games, it is hard to make a case for allowing employees to play games on your time or using your equipment. You could, of course, state that if the equipment is not needed for work-related activities during nonworking hours, and its use will not endanger the equipment itself, then using the equipment for playing games is permitted.

Non-Organization Business on Your Organization's Time or Equipment

Should employees be allowed to use your Internet connection, and company time, to do work for some other organization they're affiliated with? Given our strong stand on games, you may wonder why we even ask you to think about this topic. The answer doesn't seem quite as clear-cut to us. What will your policy be on using your organization's connection to find information for a nonprofit organization for which your company provides volunteers? What if it's the United Way and your company provides a lot of volunteers and donations? What if it is for an organization that is teaching literacy and/or language to some of your employees? What if the effort is in the name of a school that your organization has "adopted?" What if it's for a school attended by the children of some of your employees? Or a church, mosque, or synagogue attended by some of your employees? These are uses that you might well choose to allow.

No matter what your policy is on these issues, you should explicitly spell it out in your employee handbook. It should be in the same area as your policy about using company resources (even during the employee's nonwork hours) to run a for-profit business or to support political campaigns. This policy should parallel similar policies about use of the organization's libraries, copy machines, and the like.

Reasonable Care in Retrieving, Downloading, and Installing Documents or Programs

Throughout this book we've talked about the Internet as a place where you can find wonderful software and documents that will help you with research, provide new insights into recent discoveries, and give you useful tools to help you manage your software archive. By acquiring these materials, employees can certainly benefit your organization. Unfortunately, there are also some risks involved. Some files are illegally made available for downloading. You need to be careful about copyright and licensing issues just as with software you buy on a diskette. Moreover, some files may have viruses.

When you evolve your policies to cover these issues, think about the next four considerations in your discussions and writing sessions.

Where Is the Information From? Don't believe everything you can retrieve on the Internet just because it is on the Internet. Use the same criteria you would for other published materials. If the information or software comes from a recognized and announced archive site, it's more likely to be authoritative than if it comes from a file belonging to someone you (or your contacts) have never heard of. Do notice that we said "recognized and announced." Many individuals—Scott Yanoff and John December are two of the best-known examples—have given a lot to the Internet in their efforts to gather and make available information, and their work is indeed authoritative.

Run Virus Checkers If you download files, make sure that you run virus checkers on them. Make sure that this is not only a paper policy, but one that actually is implemented. If you buy software from other sources, run virus checkers on that software, too.

Understand and Enforce Copyright and Licenses Copyright is another issue that must be addressed for all information and software in your organization, but the availability of materials for downloading from the Internet makes it especially important to include in your Appropriate Use Policy. We suggest designating someone to serve as the "responsible party" for software. (In a large organization, you may need to assign this responsibility to one person in each department or division.) This person would be responsible for knowing what software is on each computer in your organization and for making sure that all the copyright and licenses for each piece of software are in order, that your organization can account for each installation, and that there is adequate documentation of the appropriate licensing kept for each copy of the software. It is easier to manage this if your policy also says that no software that is not owned by or licensed to the organization can be placed on organization systems or networks. This means that employees should not place their personal software on your systems. If an employee needs a specific piece of software to perform a task, the organization should purchase the software if it's going to be placed on one of your systems.

We have heard of disgruntled former employees "blowing the whistle" on organizations that weren't careful about their software licenses. The Software Publishers Association will visit and ask for an audit. You wouldn't want to fail such an audit.

Shareware is a special case of licensing. Usually you can download the software from a recognized archive. The terms and conditions suggest that you evaluate the software. If you continue to use it, you are asked to pay a fee. The fees are quite small and it might be tempting to disregard them. Don't. The entire concept of shareware depends on people paying their fair share. The developers don't get rich but are compensated somewhat for their work. It's a nice exchange.

Is the Information or Program Work-Related? If an employee downloads something from the Internet that isn't work-related, we'd recommend you not let it stay on your systems. One approach might be to let people download material, put it on diskette, and take the diskette to other some other machine (not at work) to run. In this case, you've provided the Internet connection that made the download possible. Again, explicit mention of your policy is best.

Consuming Bandwidth Resources

So far we've talked about how an individual's activities on the Internet can consume resources such as time and put the organization at risk of legal violations and "viral infections." It's also possible for one person's use of the Internet to impede the work of others. For example, if your connection to the Internet is low-bandwidth and is shared by many, someone transferring large quantities of information will prevent others from transferring information themselves. (As discussed in Chapter 4, *bandwidth* is a measure of the capacity of your physical connection— the telephone wires, satellite links, and so on—to carry information. You can think of the bandwidth available to you as a pipeline of a fixed size.)

You can expect that people will find more and more uses for Internet usage as time goes on. There'll be more organizations with whom you work that will get connected, and you will want to exchange messages with them. You'll want to look at more information from other people's information servers. You'll want to put more information on your servers, and more people will want to view that information.

With your own usage expected to grow, you will want to save some room for growth, even if it seems that you've obtained a connection with plenty of room for growth. This means that you will need to develop policies about how the bandwidth is used. Image and sound data files can carry much useful information, but they are also large files and therefore consume more bandwidth than, say, text files. As in a water pipeline, if the pipeline is busy, you can't pour more down it.

Viewing those large radar/weather map images or viewing the beautiful Impressionistic paintings displayed at the Louvre Museum in Paris is very enjoyable and fun. It's educational. It's impressive. It's probably not work-related.

Official Voice or Personal Voice?

One of the common practices in the Internet is to apply a "signature" of three or four lines to a posting to a public e-mail list or to a newsgroup. The signature is a text file that's appended to every message sent from a particular account. In its purpose, it resembles the way you sign a letter. If the account from which you are sending the posting or article is an organizational one, it is considered good netiquette to identify the organization. You might include an e-mail address where you can be reached and in some cases you might want to include a telephone number or postal address.

A good candidate for a policy about posting to public e-mail lists or Usenet newsgroups by your employees or from accounts within your organization is a statement about what to include in the signature file. If the posting is not "official" and the signature file includes some information identifying the signer as being part of your organization, you should have the signer include a disclaimer. Conversely, if the posting is "official," that information should be included in the signature, too. Make sure that everyone who will be posting knows your e-mail software's method for creating a signature.

Multiple Mailing Lists

A final shared-resource issue is mailing lists. If your mail machines handle and distribute a large number of mailing lists, you will affect the performance of your systems. Your list server takes a single piece of e-mail and mails it to the entire list. As long as the lists are in support of the organization's goals, no one should complain too much. However, if you allow other unofficial mailing lists to be managed by your mailing list handler, you may run into more difficult conflicts among the users who wish to share the same resource.

▶ Actions by or for the Organization

We've spent a lot of time trying to demonstrate how an organization can have an "Internet presence" to provide information about itself, and to shape an image for Internet citizens to see. Once you've made the commitment to do that, it's pretty important to make sure that the image you present is the one you intend. This means you need clear policies about who can post the official positions for the organization. You'll need your own terms and conditions of use for the information prepared, owned, and shared by the organization.

Who Can Post Official Company Material?

An effective method for many organizations is the check-off process. This means that for *anything* that goes into accessible cyberspace in the name of your organization, you should have a responsible person or persons review the posted material for spelling, avoiding offensive language, or whatever is important for your organization. These folks should agree to both the information content and the appropriateness of its placement. It's never a good idea to "surprise" the officers of your organization with a wonderful new feature that has to be retracted with much embarrassment and hard feelings by all.

While you are designing the check-off process, try to keep it simple. If you involve too many people or departments you lose the ability to get information out immediately—one of the real benefits of information dissemination over the Internet.

Disclaimers, We All Hate Them

In our litigious society disclaimers have become one of those "facts of life." You should include a disclaimer in the Web page, the Gopher space, the FTP directory, and in any other Internet-accessible resource stating the terms and conditions for the use of information owned or provided by your organization. You need something that states that you can't be held responsible if people use the information and they are harmed by it. Again, to have the type of disclaimer that best protects you, it is essential to consult with attorneys that represent your organization and are knowledgeable about your circumstances.

Do develop a set of terms and conditions and policies about use. We've included two general ones at the end of the chapter as examples. They contrast nicely because they are for totally different internetworked communities: a university and a commercial service provider. The one for the University of Michigan addresses the issues of shared resources from a sense of community and individual responsibility angle. The one from Netcom is very different. It tries to explicitly outline the contractual responsibility between the two parties: Netcom and the user. Both have paragraphs and ideas that we believe are well stated. If you are developing policies for a small business, you will probably want to state your policies in terms more like the Netcom policy. You have some sort of contractual or similar relationship with both your customers or clients and your employees. You'll want to spell out the responsibilities each has and brings. If you are a not-for-profit or community

Rules, Policies, and Agreements

ch.
18

organization, you may want to develop your policies more like the ones from the University of Michigan. You will be talking about shared responsibilities and shared (and probably limited) resources. Again, starting from a statement of your own goals will help you determine which type of policies are best for you.

▶▶ What Goes into a Policy, Anyway?

Policies don't need to be complicated. They really only must contain a statement about the desired (or conversely, the undesired) behavior and what consequences may be suffered if the policy is not followed. Each policy should contain the following sections.

▶ I. Background

This section might be necessary if you think that the audience might not understand why a policy on Internet use is necessary. Here you can explain what problems the policy is intended to address. You'll be the best judge of when you need this section and when you don't, because you know your audience best. The desired outcome is that you don't have to explain the policy in the heat of some moment. All who read it should understand what the policy addresses.

▶ II. The Policy Itself

Be sure and relate the policy stated here to other policies for your organization. Everyone potentially affected by the policy needs to understand where this one fits among all the possible policies of the organization.

Make sure that the policy is clearly stated and that the consequences of not following the policy are outlined. Include any appeal processes. Action and consequences are the heart of good policy development. If you are clear about what should be done and what will happen if it isn't, not only will you usually get the desired behavior, but you will also save yourself a lot of grief when someone doesn't choose to follow the policies.

Coordinate your Internet policy with other policies. If, for example, you have a policy about written memos, any policy about e-mail should relate to that policy as well as to any policies about other electronic information delivery or use of electronic resources, and so on. Include those other policies in the electronic one, or incorporate the electronic policy into the other policies. When you have policies that are hard to find, people trip over them (that is, they find out about them only when they have inadvertently broken a rule) and they are resentful.

Glee notes that the Standard Practice Guide, the large collection of policies made available to managers at the University of Michigan, helped her transition into management in that environment. It covered everything from the organization of the University itself (it's always a puzzle to figure out how the administrative part of a large institution is shaped), to the sick-leave policies, to the policies about use of computing resources. It's presented in a large binder, organized chronologically within a relatively wide organizational scheme. It has an index as well as a table of contents to let you find things quickly. The guide is kept available in all departments and it's easy to find and refer to when you have a question. We recommend similar access to policy information.

▶ *III. Policy Interpretations*

In this section go the hypothetical examples that you may want to add to your policy to demonstrate what you mean. If you decide to include this section in your policy, make sure that your examples are clear and understandable. It won't help at all if you make things "muddier" with your interpretative examples.

State here exactly what you want people to do or not to do. We believe that stating policies positively is better from a motivational viewpoint.

This section is where you should list the variations you can think of. If you give examples, make sure it's clear that they *are* examples. If you don't do this, you will end up with a "letter of the law" person who will try the old "But the policy doesn't say I can't do… <fill in some closely related thing that is almost but not quite what you said>" ploy. This section is a good place for a "standard disclaimer" that says that you are covering typical cases, not exhaustively listing all possible types of similar behavior.

▶ IV. Procedures

The final section should state exactly what steps will be taken if the policy is invoked. This section should include a chronology of expected actions.

Netcom's Usenet newsgroup abuse policy, for example, states that there is a set of steps that are to be taken and lists the order in which they are to be done. If the steps are followed in the proper order, *and* the abuser does not comply with the request to stop, Netcom will terminate the account. While this isn't pleasant for anyone involved, it is clear what will happen.

▶

POLICY: PROPER USE OF INFORMATION RESOURCES, INFORMATION TECHNOLOGY, AND NETWORKS AT THE UNIVERSITY OF MICHIGAN

May 26, 1990 (Policy Date)

It is the policy of the University to maintain access for its community to local, national and international sources of information and to provide an atmosphere that encourages access to knowledge and sharing of information.

It is the policy of the University that information resources will be used by members of its community with respect for the public trust through which they have been provided and in accordance with policy and regulations established from time to time by the University and its operating units.

In accordance with the above policies, the University works to create an intellectual environment in which students, staff, and faculty may feel free to create and to collaborate with colleagues both at the University of Michigan and at other institutions, without fear that the products of their intellectual efforts will be violated by misrepresentation, tampering, destruction and/or theft.

Access to the information resource infrastructure both within the University and beyond the campus, sharing of information, and security of the intellectual products of the community, all require that each and every user accept responsibility to protect the rights of the community. Any member of the University community who, without authorization, accesses, uses, destroys, alters, dismantles or disfigures the University information technologies, properties or facilities, including those owned by third parties, thereby threatens the atmosphere of increased access and sharing of information, threatens the security within which members of the community may create intellectual products and maintain records, and in light of the University's policy in this area, has engaged in unethical and unacceptable conduct. Access to the networks and to the information technology environment at the University of Michigan is a privilege and must be treated as such by all users of these systems. To ensure the existence of this information resource environment, members of the University community will take actions, in concert with State and Federal agencies and other interested parties, to identify and to set up technical and procedural mechanisms to make the information technology environment at the University of Michigan and its internal and external networks resistant to disruption.

In the final analysis, the health and well-being of this resource is the responsibility of its users who must all guard against abuses which disrupt and/or threaten the long-term viability of the systems at the University of Michigan and those beyond the University. The University requires that members of its community act in accordance with these responsibilities, this policy, relevant laws and contractual obligations, and the highest standard of ethics.

Rules, Policies, and Agreements

ch.

18

Though not exhaustive, the following material defines the University's position regarding several general issues in this area.*

The University characterizes as unethical and unacceptable, and just cause for taking disciplinary action up to and including non-reappointment, discharge, dismissal, and/or legal action, any activity through which an individual:

> (a) violates such matters as University or third party copyright or patent protection and authorizations, as well as license agreements and other contracts,

> (b) interferes with the intended use of the information resources,

> (c) seeks to gain or gains unauthorized access to information resources.

> (d) without authorization, destroys, alters, dismantles, disfigures, prevents rightful access to or otherwise interferes with the integrity of computer-based information and/or information resources,

> (e) without authorization invades the privacy of individuals or entities that are creators, authors, users, or subjects of the information resources.

This policy is applicable to any member of the University community, whether at the University or elsewhere, and refers to all information resources whether individually controlled, or shared, stand-alone or networked. Individual units within the University may define "conditions of use" for facilities under their control. These statements must be consistent with this overall policy but may provide additional detail, guidelines and/or restrictions. Where such "conditions of use" exist, enforcement mechanisms defined therein shall apply. Where no enforcement mechanism exists, the enforcement mechanism defined in the ITD Conditions of Use statement shall prevail.

Disciplinary action, if any, for faculty and staff shall be consistent with the University Standard Practice Guides and the Bylaws of the Regents of the University. Where use of external networks is involved, policies governing such use also are applicable and must be adhered to.

---

*Information resources in this document are meant to include any information in electronic or audiovisual format or any hardware or software that make possible the storage and use of such information. As examples, included in this definition are electronic mail, local databases, externally accessed databases, CD-ROM, motion picture film, recorded magnetic media, photographs, and digitized information such as the content of MIRLYN.

NETCOM ON-LINE COMMUNICATION SERVICES, INC. TERMS AND CONDITIONS FOR HOST DIAL-UP SERVICES

This agreement represents the complete agreement and understanding between Netcom On-Line Communication Services, Inc., (hereinafter called Netcom) and the account holder and supersedes any other written or oral agreement. Upon notice published on-line via Netcom Services, Netcom may modify these terms and conditions, amplify them, and/or modify the prices, as well as discontinue or change the services offered.

If you do not agree to these terms and conditions, please notify our accounting department at (800) 353-6600 so we may initiate a closure of your account and a refund of your initial set-up fee.

Rules, Policies, and Agreements

ch. **18**

1.0 Provision of services

1.1 Netcom will provide services on its host computing systems to individual account holders in exchange for payment of fees and compliance with the terms and conditions of this document.

1.2 Netcom Services are defined as the use by the account holder of computing, telecommunications, software, and information services provided by Netcom On-Line Communications Services. These services also include the provision of access to computing, telecommunications, software, and information services provided by others via the Global Internet.

1.3 Netcom Services include access to the complete USENET discussion groups (newsgroups). Some of the discussions contain language or pictures about subjects intended for Adult audiences. Account holders less than 18 years old must have a parent or legal guardian agree to these conditions to indicate acceptance and knowledge of this.

1.4 Netcom will publish a notice of fee increases 30 days before such increases take effect.

2.0 Use of Material

2.1 Public Domain materials (e.g., images, text, and programs) may be downloaded or uploaded using Netcom services. Account holders may also re-distribute materials in the public domain. The account holder assumes all risks regarding the determination of whether the material is in the public domain.

2.2 As provided by United States federal law and by International treaties, copyrighted materials (e.g., images, text, and programs) may not be uploaded using Netcom services without the permission of the copyright holder. Copyrighted materials may be downloaded for personal use. Except as expressly permitted, materials under copyright may not be distributed to others. Copyrighted material may not be changed nor can the author attribution notices nor the copyright notices be modified.

2.3 Note that some materials available on the global Internet are called "SHAREWARE." These materials may be downloaded and used, but they are copyrighted materials. The copyright holder usually gives permission to use the materials for examination. If you choose to continue using the materials, the copyright holder requests that you register your usage and may ask that you pay a license fee.

3.0 Use of Services

3.1 Netcom Host Dial-up accounts are for individual users and the account holder therefore agrees not to share the password of the account. The account holder acknowledges that Netcom will terminate the account without notice if the account holder does not comply.

3.2 The account holder agrees to maintain a secure password to the account. Secure passwords are those that are between 6 and 8 characters long, contain upper and lower case letters, and numbers or other characters, and can not be found in direct or reverse order in a dictionary, without regard to the language of the dictionary.

3.3 The account holder agrees not to use any process, program, or tool via Netcom services for guessing the passwords of account holders on Netcom or other systems. The account holder agrees not to use Netcom services to make unauthorized attempts to access the systems and networks of others.

3.4 The account holder agrees to use the services provided by Netcom as permitted by applicable local, state, and federal laws. The account holder agrees, therefore, not to use these services to conduct any business or activity or solicit the performance of any activity that is prohibited by law.

3.5 The account holder acknowledges that Netcom is a commercial entity and that Netcom is a member of the Commercial Internet eXchange (CIX). Netcom and connecting CIX networks may be used by account holders to conduct legal businesses. These businesses should, however, not impinge upon the use of Netcom services by other account holders. Netcom services should not be used to send unsolicited advertising or promotional materials to other network users. Electronic mail and appropriate USENET newsgroups may be used in the conduct of legitimate businesses.

4.0 Indemnification

4.1 The account holder acknowledges that Netcom makes an honest effort to keep the information available on Netcom's systems accurate. However, Netcom can make no warranty of any kind, either expressed or implied, regarding the quality, accuracy, or validity for the data and/or information available. Use of information obtained from or through Netcom is at the risk of the account holder.

4.2 The account holder also acknowledges that the information available through the interconnecting networks may not be accurate. Netcom has no ability or authority over the material. Netcom can make no warranty of any kind, either expressed or implied, regarding the quality, accuracy, or validity of the data and/or information residing on or passing through these networks. Use of information obtained from or through Netcom services is at the risk of the account holder.

4.3 The account holder agrees to indemnify and hold Netcom harmless from any claims, including attorney's fees, resulting from the account holder receiving Netcom services which cause direct or indirect damage to another party.

5.0 Payment of fees and penalties

5.1 The Netcom accounting cycle begins on the 15th of each month. Charges for new accounts are prorated. Charges for terminating accounts are not prorated.

5.2 Service payments will be submitted in advance of receiving services.

5.3 Payment is due upon receipt of our invoice.

5.4 Delinquent accounts are those that remain unpaid at the beginning of the next accounting cycle.

5.5 Accounts that are delinquent by two accounting cycles are put on "accounting hold" and may not be used. Accounts that are unpaid for three accounting cycles automatically have their files archived. Accounts that are unpaid for four accounting cycles have their files purged. Netcom accounts continue to accrue charges while they are on hold.

5.6 There is a service reconnection charge equal to one half the currently charged set-up fee to remove accounts from accounting hold status.

5.7 The account holder acknowledges responsibility for the account until payment in full is made.

5.8 There is a $15.00 service charge for each returned check.

6.0 Account Cancellations

6.1 Cancellation requests for Netcom accounts must be received in writing via e-mail, fax, or postal service at Netcom's main office. Such requests must be received by the 5 PM Pacific time on the 1st of the month in order to be processed by the beginning of the next accounting cycle.

6.2 All Netcom accounts must be paid in full before the transaction will be considered complete.

7.0 Abuse of Services

7.1 Any use of Netcom system resources that disrupts the normal use of the system for other Netcom customers is considered to be abuse of system resources and is grounds for administrative intervention. Some examples of system abuse include spawning dozens of processes, consuming excessive amounts of memory or CPU for long periods of time, and staying attached to modems while not really "active" on the line.

7.2 Depending on the nature and the severity of the abuse, the user may receive an E-mail warning or have their account suspended by Netcom Technical Support. If the misuse is unintentional, the suspension may be rescinded following discussion with Netcom Technical Support. If the misuse is intentional, the suspension may be rescinded at the discretion of the Operations Manager, and may require the payment of a service reconnection charge. Occasionally, unintentional misuse is misclassified as intentional misuse. Customers who believe their activity has been misclassified may appeal to the Operations Manager.

7.3 Violations of any of the Netcom conditions of use are unethical and may be criminal offenses. You are expected to report to Netcom any information you may have concerning instances in which the conditions of use have been or are being violated. When Netcom becomes aware of possible violations, we will initiate an investigation. At the same time, in order to prevent further possible unauthorized activity, Netcom may suspend access to services to the individual account in question. Confirmation of violations may result in cancellation of the individual account and/or criminal prosecution. The account suspension may be rescinded at the discretion of the Operations Manager, following payment of a reconnection charge.

These terms are also available on-line as ~ftp/pub/ne/netcom/terms, or via anonymous FTP in the /pub/netcom directory.

► ► **CHAPTER 19**

Building the Resource

***B**ecause* you are reading this chapter, you must have decided that you have information you want to share. Next you need to determine the best design for your networked information system—what tools might work best for you and how to present information using them. In this chapter we discuss three relatively simple ways to provide information via the Internet—FTP, Gopher, and WWW. These methods are not mutually exclusive. You can choose to use one, two, or all three of them at the same time.

This chapter is intended more for the designer of the information structure than for the information systems administrator who will construct the technical configuration for the information server. We do include notes about how to locate, install, and use specific server and client programs. These notes are sufficient to get a systems administrator started with these programs. More information about the server programs will be found at the Internet site that provides those programs. For example, John Franks of Northwestern University provides a server program called GN, which is capable of presenting information to both http and Gopher clients. The complete documentation for the server is located at the same address on the Internet as the server code itself. When you are ready to begin detailed implementation planning, you should read the documentation provided.

▶▶ *Let Client/Server Be Your Servant*

FTP, Gopher, and the Web all use the client/server computing model, which (as you learned in Chapter 1) divides the various tasks between two pieces of software—a client program and a server program. In making your information available for access by one of these tools, you are designing your information server. It will "serve" (or send) your information over the Internet to anyone who has a client program that can request it (and who also has appropriate permissions, of course). In theory, this means that to get the servers working, you don't really have to worry about all the commands, programs, computers, and connections the user will rely on to seek and display the information. That is taken care of by the client software.

Practically, however, you should test your information presentation with as many different clients as you can. Not all clients are created equally. You may find that your presentation works really well in Lynx, but not in Cello (even though both are WWW clients). Then you will need to change your presentation until it looks fine using both clients.

▶ ▶ *The Systems Development Process*

Designers of information systems have models that help them design and implement systems. These models are sets of steps that help to prevent some (but not all) mistakes in building information systems. The specifications and the steps we list don't need to take a long time to produce, nor do they need to be very formal in all cases. But if you take the time to do a bit of planning, we believe you will save time in the long run—you won't need to "re"-implement because someone didn't like what you produced. We like the development model that has these phases:

- **Functional Specifications**—A written plan that outlines what information you are trying to convey and to which intended audience. A good place to begin is an inventory of the information you want to dispense. The types (and forms) of your information may dictate what tools you will want to use. For instance, if the majority of information you have to present is in the form of graphical images, or if your information includes sound files, you probably will want to use the Web. If the information you have doesn't include graphical images, you may want to add images to your information. Again, you'll need to think about who your audience may be and how best to reach them. If you expect that your audience will not be able to use Web browsers but will have access to an FTP client, you will want to provide an FTP server instead of a Web server. The information gathering and analysis that you will do for a functional specification will help you decide what tools will best suit your needs. If you have any constraints (for example, what kind of a computer you must use, or when the project should be complete), they should be included explicitly in your plan. It is also a good idea to include a section which describes any assumptions you are making. If you expressly share your assumptions you may be able to prevent later misunderstandings. When everyone who has a "stake" in the system has agreed to your description, you'll have "buy in" for your project.

- **Detailed Specifications**—This is the stage where you expand on your functional specification to describe what server software you have chosen and exactly how the information you are serving will be updated. The analysis that leads to writing these specifications is the important step. The specifications themselves are simply the documentation of your decisions.

- **Implementation**—You may not believe this now, but this is the easy part. In this step you obtain the server software and documentation, install it on your chosen server hardware, configure the software and hardware to work properly in your environment. You obtain copies of the information you are going to present and store it on the server. Of course, "you" here can mean one person or a team of people working together. Implementation should include trying out all the client software you can to make certain that your information is presented well in as many different clients as possible.

- **Testing**—In this phase, the specifications are compared to the system as implemented. When the system and the specifications don't match, you'll need someone to decide which gets changed. Sometimes the specifications need to be changed because of something you learned in implementation. In other cases, the implementors erred and the system will need to be changed.

- **Deployment**—Announce your service. Accept congratulations. Prepare your plan for periodic review of your information service, because the systems development process is a continuing one.

► Design Considerations

Presenting information via FTP, Gopher, and/or WWW is relatively easy for those with a little technical skill. This ease of implementation has both its good points and its bad points. Ease of implementation enables your organization to make information available quickly, for instance. However, because many organizations don't yet know about or have firm policies about Internet information and presentation (and because a person with technical skills rather than presentation skills may have done the implementation), not all information presentations are well designed. Here we've tried to list some things to keep in mind while designing and implementing your own information exposition so that your ideas can be conveyed.

Keep Your Information Presentation Simple and Clean In any design, the space left between and among the words and images helps the reader/viewer to "receive" the messages much easier.

For an FTP space this means grouping similar files together within a single directory. Collect similar directories together to provide an "Information Tree" that your viewer can follow. Provide an INDEX or README file at each level of your information to describe the contents of each directory. Provide a "terms and conditions statement" that informs your viewers of their responsibilities as well as yours.

For a linking Gopher menu (one that leads to other menus as opposed to one that is a document or downloadable image file) this means keeping your Gopher menu titles short but descriptive. For most Gopher menus, keep the number of items on the menu to 15 or fewer so that the viewer can reasonably choose an appropriate item. Figure 19.1 shows the top-level menu for the Netcom Gopher server. You can see that it is easy to choose among these menu items.

If you are linking to an item not on your own server, include in your menu item an indicator that tells the viewer this. A parenthetical statement of source (for example, "from Notre Dame") is fine. The wonderful Internet Assistance section of the University of California at Irvine's PEG (Peripatetic, Eclectic Gopher) Gopher breaks the "don't put too many items on the menu" rule very successfully (see Figure 19.2). Cal Boyer has built a valuable entry point to many information sources about the Internet. When you are building a comprehensive resource you won't necessarily want to divide your information into smaller sections, making deeper information trees. Note that Boyer does indicate in his menu titles when the information is from another location.

For a linking Web page (one that leads to other pages as opposed to one that is a document or downloadable image file) this means including plenty of "white space" around your information.

FIGURE 19.1 ▶

The top-level menu for the Netcom Gopher server.

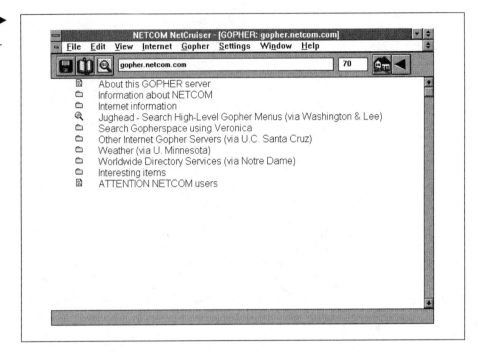

FIGURE 19.2 ▶

The Internet Assistance section of the PEG Gopher.

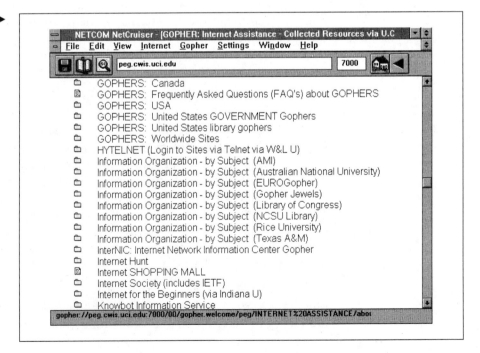

Allow for Users Who Cannot View Graphics Remember that many people (at least for the next several years) are looking at your design with computers that may not be able to display graphics. Use the graphics to illustrate, not necessarily to inform—or make parallel implementations for those with graphics and those without.

Allow for the User's Choice of Fonts Remember that you can't count on everyone choosing the same default fonts for the headings and text in their Web browser. Don't count on the particular look of a font. If the font choice is very important to you, make the font part of a displayable graphic image, rather than part of the text.

M A S T E R   W O R D S

> To make a displayable graphic of your text, use a drawing or publishing program. Enter the text in the work area, use the tools of the program to select the appropriate font, font size, and any emphasis characteristics like bold or italics. Make the complete image the appropriate size and shape for your Web page. Save your image in GIF or JPG format. Transfer your image to a computer and directory that can be accessed by your http daemon program. Then include a link to the image (and any alternate text for nongraphical browsers) in your hypertext document.

Test, Test, and Test Again Test your design and implementation on all the clients and platforms that you know about. Of course, not every designer and implementor has access to several kinds of Internet accounts or different computer systems (like both a Macintosh and a DOS computer) or to different types of Web browsers or Gopher clients. First, test using all the ways you can. Then do the next thing, ask your friends to help. You can also ask people who are on a mailing list or newsgroup in which you participate to test for you and report back. This kind of "early release" testing is the best way to get good feedback from people who have different types of connections. Many of your fellow Internauts will be happy to help you.

Ask a Person Unfamiliar with Your Product, Service, or Organization to "Test Drive" Your Information If it isn't clear to a newcomer why something is there, take it out. This type of testing can be done by people anywhere on the Internet, but you might want to be in the same room with your early testers so that you see and hear their first reactions. Make sure any questions your tester might have about your organization, products, or services are clearly answered. And remember to listen to their comments. Their reactions should cause you to modify your design and/or implementation before you release them to the world at large.

Think about the Next Generation of Information Dispensers As object-oriented systems become more prevalent and allow specific players/viewers to be shipped with the data and information, there will be more rather than fewer things to think about when you design for the user. Will what you are designing now lead to an improved design in the future?

▶ A Design Rule

You have probably noticed that we don't usually state our ideas in terms of rules. Partly that's because we believe in people choosing their own rules (at least for rules of reference) and partly it's because we both like (and approve of) lots of options for people. There is one rule that you must follow, however. *Don't put anything up on your information server that you don't have permission to distribute.* This means any information whose copyright you or your organization does not own should not be distributed via your information service. There is no difference between an FTP space, a Gopher server, or a Web page and any other publishing mechanism in the eyes of the law. Stealing someone's intellectual property (whether it is a graphic image, a sound file, a document, or a software program) is against United States law. You can be prosecuted.

In the United States, you also may not distribute child pornography (via electronic or any other means). Other jurisdictions may have other laws that can apply to what is and is not legal to distribute.

United States laws with regard to electronic information are not extensive yet. There is much work to be done. Fortunately, with the help of the publishing mechanism of the Internet itself, you can (and should) keep up by watching and reading the materials stored at the Electronic Frontier Foundation (`http://www.eff.org`). As more agencies of government (United States and others) come online, there will be more attention given to laws about what is and is not legal to distribute.

▶ Who Is (or Should Be) Your Audience?

As we've noted before, the people who use and cruise the Internet are quite varied. They could be geographically located in any place in the world where one can obtain telephone service. They could speak or read almost any language (although today there are more connections in English-speaking countries). They could be any age (elementary school children to respected elders). They could have any kind of equipment from very old 1200 baud modems and green-on-black screens to many-colored displays directly attached to a very high speed connection. You will need to decide whether you are going to try to reach *all* the users on the Internet as your audience, or to target a specific subset. As you work on your information presentation, you will want to keep your audience in mind.

Figure 19.3 shows the Index Web page from the webbed version of Ed Krol's book, *The Whole Internet Catalog*. This page is designed so that all the information is equally available to anyone regardless of the type of terminal and Web browser.

As a contrast, let's look at the home page for the online magazine *HotWired*. Here the designers have chosen to target their audience to those with faster connections and with good graphical browsers. Figure 19.4 illustrates the kind of presentation that is possible if you target the higher-end audience. Although there is an alternate textual interface, this site is not really designed for use without a graphical browser. The folks at *HotWired* believe that more and more people will get better and better connections to the Internet and they design for the audience they want to have. These are the two extremes; you'll want to figure out where your server should fit on the scale of what is possible.

▶ Choosing and Connecting Your Server

Once you have delineated the information you wish to serve and the audience you wish to reach, you will have a preliminary idea of the type of server software you will wish to operate. The other important factor

FIGURE 19.3 ▶

The index Web page from The Whole Internet Catalog.

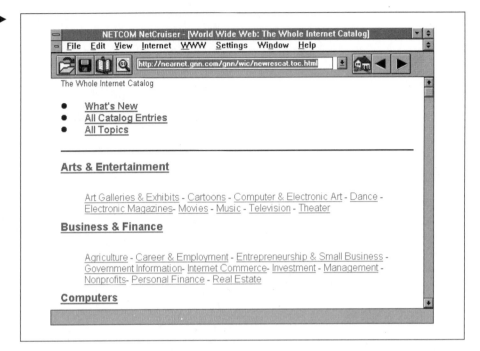

FIGURE 19.4 ▶

The Web home page for the online magazine HotWired.

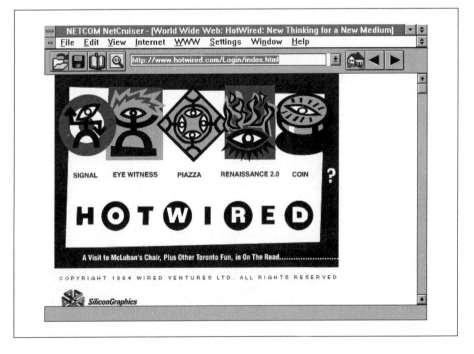

in a good information service on the Internet is the speed and connectivity of the server hardware itself. If you have the ability to specify new hardware and Internet connections, you will want to try to get a high-bandwidth connection and you will want to run a fast computer. (This is the same as you want to do as an Internet information consumer.) The processor speed and connection bandwidth will affect how quickly users can access your information and how many can access it simultaneously.

Must You Use UNIX?

Many of the Internet tools are written in UNIX. UNIX is a complex and rich environment, and most UNIX implementations include native TCP/IP implementations; this makes it relatively easy for programs written for one implementation to be moved (or "ported") from one UNIX environment to another. These facts explain why there are so many server programs written for the UNIX environment. Because many of the tools were written as part of grants where the funding was public funds, and because of the cooperative nature of the Internet, many of these server programs are in the public domain and easily accessible for you to use on your own computer. If your site already has expertise running a UNIX environment, a UNIX information server is probably the best choice. Such server environments typically come with an FTP daemon that can be configured to serve information. The http and Gopher daemons can be obtained from the Internet and configured to serve information. Then you are ready to begin structuring your information as you designed.

M A S T E R   W O R D S

Daemons **are the programs that listen for requests coming in to a server from the Internet. They are usually started when your computer is turned on. When a request arrives, the daemon "reads" the request and acts on it. For example, if an anonymous FTP request comes in, the daemon connects the request to the "anonymous" account, making the directory tree (all the information that the account is permitted to view, write, or execute) available to the connected user.**

Even if your site does not have experience running a UNIX environment, you may still want to use a UNIX server because of the availability of specific tools. There are an increasing number of relatively inexpensive UNIX servers ($10,000 to $15,000 or so, including both the hardware and the software) that can provide a base system from which to grow. When you are evaluating server packages, make certain to include configuration and management software so that you can effectively manage your server.

It is possible to run Web and Gopher servers on higher-end Macintosh and PC platforms. These platforms are suitable for schools and non-profit organizations that do not expect a lot of network traffic. One of the resources we list, the Prince Edward Island Crafts Council, uses (at the end of 1994) a pretty small server. If you connect to that resource (http://www.crafts-council.pe.ca), you can see the results. On a PC you can choose from among several operating environments, such as Microsoft Windows, Microsoft Windows NT, or a few UNIX implementations.

The speed of your operating environment is not the only consideration. You'll want to connect your server to as fast a network connection as you can reasonably afford. The lowest-speed connection from which you can provide information is a dedicated 14.4 Kbps connection. With the compression algorithms that are built into these modems, you can achieve higher transfer rates. Compression will be used if both your modem and the modem used by your Internet service provider can use the same transfer protocols, and so this is not something you would have to think about after making sure that you and your provider "speak" the same protocols. 28.8 Kbps modems are becoming more common. Again, with compression, these can transmit at higher speeds. Some Internet service providers can connect you using ISDN connections. This technology makes it possible to move multiple data streams through a conventional telephone line. ISDN is considerably faster than a 14.4 or 28.8 modem, but it requires synchronous communications processing that can be expensive to add to a computer (for both ends of the connection).

Without going to ISDN, the next level, 56 Kbps, provides a significant jump in speed (and cost). Here you will need a router (a special-purpose computer that moves packets off of and on to the Internet from your site) and special purpose connection equipment called CSUs/DSUs. The equipment is more expensive as is the price your Internet service provider will charge you. At the end of 1994, Internet Distribution Services had one of their servers connected at this speed. Go to Internet Distribution Services (`http://www.service.com`) to see this type of link.

Finally, if you will want to provide a large number of big graphics files, a lot of sound files, and/or a lot of motion picture files (look at the server from MCA—`http://www.mca.com`), you'll want to have a server connected at T-1. Figure 19.5 shows the top of the MCA Web page.

M A S T E R   W O R D S

Remember that the connection of your server to the Internet is only one part of the service equation: the connection of your potential customers is an important part of their perception of your service.

FIGURE 19.5

The beginning of MCA's Web page.

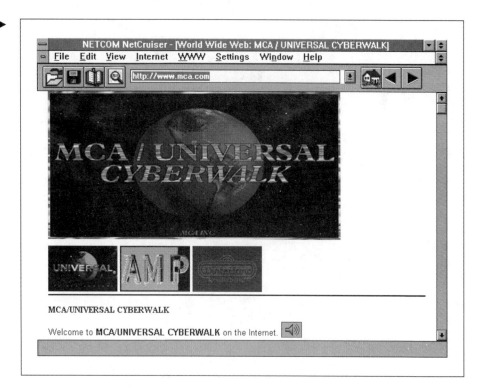

Now that we've covered some of the criteria for good design and service, you should be ready to think about which kind of presentation will work best for your information.

▸▸ *Providing Information via FTP*

FTP is the most basic form of Net communication. People have been using it for years to move data, images, and information between specific points. FTP's strength is the efficient transfer of data between two connected computers. In Chapter 8 you learned how to find and retrieve files from FTP servers that others have provided. Here we discuss how to set up your own FTP server. If you'd like more information about the underlying FTP protocol itself, you'll find it in RFC959. Figure 19.6 shows the Web version of RFC959 as done by Tim Berners-Lee, the "father" of the World Wide Web.

FIGURE 19.6 ▸

RFC959 as it appears on the Web.

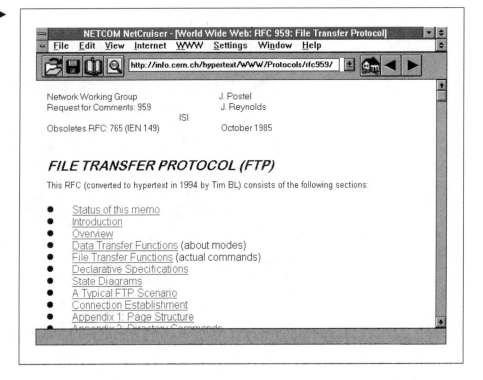

▶ *What You'll Need*

In order to create your own FTP server (or "FTP space"), you will need, in addition to a computer capable of running FTP and connected to the Internet, the following:

- Information you want to provide. The design work of an FTP space is organizing the information in some reasonable manner (similar files in the same directory, for example). Of course, "reasonable" is in the eye of the beholder. It's a good idea to show your design schema to someone else before you implement it. Testing your design this way can save you time and effort if your design isn't clear to someone else.

- A plan for security. File permissions must be established to restrict users to read from or write to specific files within specific directories.

- The authority to set up a user account (usually either "anonymous" or "FTP") using standard procedures for setting up a new user. This authority resides with a systems administrator for your system.

- The authority to create directories within the appropriate user account. If you have the password for the account you can do this.

- The FTP daemon (ftpd) should be started each time the system is started. You should be able to find more information about ftpd on your system by entering the command man ftpd at the command prompt.

The following additional items are also valuable:

- README or Index files in each directory to tell your users what they can expect to find in your FTP space. An index usually contains the name of each file in the directory and a short description of the contents of the file.

- Terms-and-conditions statements. Your organization's legal staff might require you to add such statements. Or maybe you'll want to add copyright and service mark information for your organization's products and services. Figure 19.7 shows an example of such a terms-and-conditions statement. Here Netcom reminds the user that the FTP archive is provided as a service to Netcom

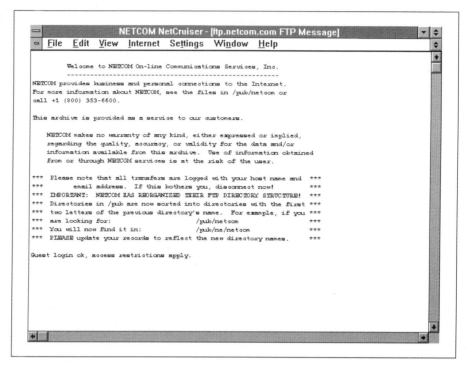

customers and that all risks are borne by the user. There is also a warning that access to the Netcom FTP archive is logged.

- You can choose to "log" or record the address of each user who accesses your FTP space. Logging is a good idea. With logging you can have some idea who has been visiting. Furthermore, you can run statistical processing programs on the logged information. These programs can give you an idea of the type of user by domain, or the times of day when your FTP space is the busiest, and the like. Reviewing the logs can help you improve your service.

 ▶▶ **M A S T E R W O R D S**

The FTP application in the Chameleon Sampler on Companion Disk 2 can function as a server as well as a client. See Appendix H for details.

► *Anonymous FTP*

Recall from Chapter 8 that with FTP you can make your files accessible to anyone who has an Internet connection, or you can restrict access so that specific login names are required. The first option is known as anonymous FTP (because anyone can log in using the account anonymous), and it's the method used by most organizations that publish files to be copied by FTP.

The strength of anonymous FTP lies not only in the fact that every user has access to the files you've chosen to make available in this way, but also in the fact that the informed Internet user can guess to look for such access given the name any particular domain.

Remember the Domain Naming System we talked about in Chapter 3? You can use that system to set up an address for your site that anyone who's interested can easily find. For example, suppose a Macintosh user wants to see what information (and perhaps software enhancements) Apple Computer provides for anonymous FTP. She could reasonably guess that the domain name would be `apple.com`, and attach to `ftp.apple.com`.

If your site already has a domain name, you should have the computer (or host) for your FTP space configured with the name `ftp.your.domain`. If you don't have a domain name yet, you'll need to work with your Internet Service provider to have one assigned and registered. This is usually part of connecting your server or network to the Internet. After your domain name is assigned, you should have the host computer configured with the name `ftp.your.domain`.

Helping Users Find Your Files

Once users have found your FTP site, they also need to find specific files within your directory structure. You can make that task easier for them by following a few simple conventions. The first convention is to place the available files in a directory named /pub. This name usually denotes that the directory is public. Members of the public may only be able to read files in the directory, not write to them, but anyone who can access the computer system using the account anonymous can read from the directory.

If the files you're making available are executable programs, it's conventional to group them into subdirectories by platform or operating system. put your Macintosh programs in a directory named /mac; your DOS programs in /msdos, /pcdos, /dos, or /pc; and your Windows (version 3 or later) in /win3. Similarly, your UNIX software might go into directories named, for example, /sun or /bsd; or you might place them all in a directory named /bin. A directory named /doc is a good place to put documentation.

Within each directory, it's a good idea to place a text file called something like 00index or 00README or README or Index to describe the contents of the directory. (The zeroes at the beginning of the file name cause the item to appear first in an alphabetical directory listing.)

Besides listing and describing available files, your README files should describe the terms and conditions of use for the available files. Both items should carry the date they were last changed. This helps the user determine whether the information is current.

In very active FTP spaces, some publishers also make available a file that describes any recent changes to the FTP space—additions, enhancements, deletions, and so on. Figure 19.8 shows the README

FIGURE 19.8 ▶

The README file from Oakland University's Oak archive.

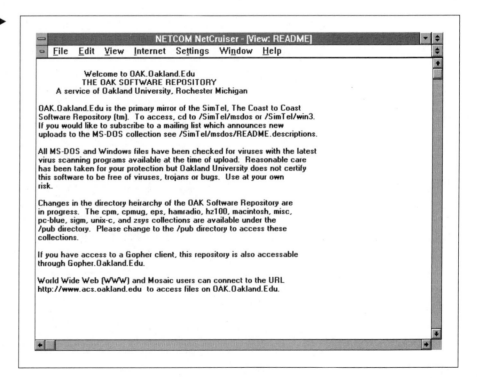

```
                      NETCOM NetCruiser - [View: README]
  File   Edit   View   Internet   Settings   Window   Help

              Welcome to OAK.Oakland.Edu
              THE OAK SOFTWARE REPOSITORY
        A service of Oakland University, Rochester Michigan

  OAK.Oakland.Edu is the primary mirror of the SimTel, The Coast to Coast
  Software Repository (tm).  To access, cd to /SimTel/msdos or /SimTel/win3.
  If you would like to subscribe to a mailing list which announces new
  uploads to the MS-DOS collection see /SimTel/msdos/README.descriptions.

  All MS-DOS and Windows files have been checked for viruses with the latest
  virus scanning programs available at the time of upload.  Reasonable care
  has been taken for your protection but Oakland University does not certify
  this software to be free of viruses, trojans or bugs.  Use at your own
  risk.

  Changes in the directory heirarchy of the OAK Software Repository are
  in progress.  The cpm, cpmug, eps, hamradio, hz100, macintosh, misc,
  pc-blue, sigm, unix-c, and zsys collections are available under the
  /pub directory.  Please change to the /pub directory to access these
  collections.

  If you have access to a Gopher client, this repository is also accessable
  through Gopher.Oakland.Edu.

  World Wide Web (WWW) and Mosaic users can connect to the URL
  http://www.acs.oakland.edu  to access files on OAK.Oakland.Edu.
```

file from the Oakland University Oak archive. Usually README files are text files that can be displayed easily. Sometimes the more complex files are arranged in reverse chronological order. That is, there will be a heading at the top of the file with the date of the last changes to the directory. Following the date will be a short paragraph describing the changes. Then there is a line with the date of the previous change followed by its descriptive paragraph, and so on. Each time there is a change, the maintainer inserts a date and descriptive paragraph at the top of the file. Such a file provides the user with a brief history of the development of the space—a very nice feature indeed.

An anonymous FTP space can be a convenient place for people to leave files for your organization, too. For example, suppose your business is having some work done by an outside consultant. If that consultant is connected to the Internet, drafts of the consultant's work or reports might be left in your FTP directory for review. This is both quicker and less expensive than using a courier service.

If you expect that people will be leaving documents, information, or programs on your computer, for simple security you should set up a separate directory (usually called /incoming) for them to use. That way, you can set the permissions on the files that you want people to transfer to read-only. The directory where you want people to leave things for you must have its permissions set to write. Otherwise the person who is trying to store a file on your computer will have that transmission refused. Usually, you won't want people to have write access to your complete FTP space. Including an /incoming directory and designating it as the only directory within the anonymous account to have write access will take care of that problem.

Security for Incoming Files

You should be aware of a potential misuse of /incoming FTP directories—as a "drop point" for software pirates. In 1994, someone left 60 MB of copyrighted software in an /incoming directory of one of the more popular archives on the Internet. The software pirate then "announced" the action to many by telling people about the directory, and these people told others. The software was distributed throughout the Internet.

There is a program available for UNIX systems at the archive at Washington University in St. Louis (wuarchive.wustl.edu) that offers a solution. It sets up a process so that materials dropped into /incoming by an anonymous user will have the permissions set to another account resident on that computer system. This will stop someone from using your anonymous FTP space as a transshipment point for files. There may be similar programs for non-UNIX systems, or you may wish to have something similar written for your system.

Who's Playing in Your Space?

Many FTP daemons offer the ability to log transactions. This is a very nice feature if you want to track access to your FTP space. You can either write a small program to process the log and produce reports that tell you what files are more popular, or you can search for such a program on the Internet. This is the kind of feedback that you don't often get from making material available.

If you are going to log transactions, it is usually good netiquette to tell people so. You can put this announcement in the README file you have placed in your directory for people to read.

Again, Washington University in St. Louis (`wuarchive.wustl.edu`) has some very good logging software for keeping track of who's been connecting to your FTP server and taking and leaving materials. The directory wuarchive-ftpd has the entire `wuarchive` FTP server and associated software available for downloading.

▶ Dos and Don'ts for Providing Anonymous FTP

- Do make an index file (and keep it up to date).
- Do make any terms and conditions clear.
- Do structure the directories so that people can find things—keep related things together and name them clearly.
- Do make a special directory for people to leave files for you.
- Do use archive management software that changes permissions on incoming files so that no one can use it as a transfer point for stolen software. This protects you.
- Don't forget to keep copies of your information in some other electronic form (on another disk, on a tape, on diskette, etc.) in case your disk fails.

▶▶ *Providing Information via Gopher*

The best reasons to publish your information via Gopher are its ease of use, its ease of implementation, and the near ubiquity of simple clients. Pretty much anyone who is connected to the Internet has access to a simple Gopher client.

Gopher is extremely popular. There are thousands of servers around the globe. If you add one, you'll be part of an interconnected network of *information*, not just a network of computers. The servers (assuming you choose to announce your Gopher server to the world for other Gophers to link to) can provide access to vast quantities of information in a simple-to-learn format. And you can use it to connect to other services through several "gateway" Gophers or links—Telnet or e-mail or telephone directories. Also, of course, it's fun.

▶ *If It's So Easy*...

Why doesn't everyone use it? Well, some people don't like the fact that all the servers are connected to one another in such an unstructured way. They find this especially confusing because the design of the menus makes Gopher appear structured. Also, there really isn't a good way of conveying enough information in a menu item. The indexing is a little wacky (there is no good way to eliminate duplicate entries, for example) and the presentation of the search results as a menu with little or no hint as to where the menu item resides can be really confusing.

▶ *What You'll Need*

In order to create your own Gopher server (or "gopherhole"), you need the following:

- Gopher server software that will work in your computing environment or the ability to add information to a Gopher server being managed by someone else. Suitable Gopher servers can be found from the University of Minnesota team (`boombox.micro.umn.edu`) or the GN server from John Frank at Northwestern University (`ftp.acns.nwu.edu/pub/gn`). The examples in this section were taken from the GN server.

- Files of text, images, or information that you want to serve. The best design document for a Gopher server is an outline (Gopher is hierarchical, so an outline best mirrors the organization of your Gopher server) organized in some reasonable manner (similar files on the same menu, for example).

- File permissions established to allow users to read from specific files within specific directories pointed to by the menu structure. If you neglect to make the files readable, people will be able to select the menu item but not to see the item.

You'll also find the following items valuable:

- README or Index files in each directory. A good place for these is usually at the top of the menu for that directory.

- A link from the top-level menu to a gopherspace search server (Veronica) so your clients can find materials that are not on your server.

- Terms-and-conditions statements. Your organization's legal staff might require you to add such statements. Or maybe you'll want to add copyright and service mark information for your organization's products and services.

- A facility that allows your user to search either the directory contents or the file contents of the information contained within your Gopher server.

- Logging and statistical processing of the logs so you have some idea who has been visiting.

- Copies of the public domain and commercial Gopher clients for as many of the computing platforms as possible, so that you'll be able to test your design and implementation. At least obtain the major ones for the most common platforms: Macintosh, DOS, and UNIX systems.

▶ Getting and Installing the GN Server

Rather than taking the time and space to rewrite the excellent documentation that accompanies John Frank's GN Gopher, we'll just point you to the code and the documentation and give you enough to get started. You can use your Web browser or your Gopher client to read the documentation or to download the software. The URL is `http://hopf.math.nwu.edu` or `gopher://hopf.math.nwu.edu`. Or you can use anonymous FTP to connect to `ftp.acns.nwu.edu`. In the pub/gn directory you will find the latest copy of the GN code in a ".tar.gz" file. Transfer the file using binary mode. Uncompress the code, configure the server as specified in the documentation, compile it, and install it. After you have installed the server, you will need to add GN to your `inetd` configuration tables. (Inetd is the process that controls a lot of the UNIX networking processes.) Then, you are ready to create the data directories and put the information into them.

▶ A Few Implementation Details

While the focus of this chapter is on information presentation design, it is helpful to know a few things about implementation details because they may affect what you are able to do as well as how it is done. (If the next few paragraphs of information are more than you want to know about implementing Gopher menus, please feel free to skip this part and go on to more design issues.)

Gopher clients read and act on two kinds of files that they obtain from a Gopher server as a result of a Gopher request: the file that builds and displays the Gopher menu (the links file) and the file that transmits the information that the viewer wants, no matter what format (image or text, for instance) in which the information is (the item itself). The links file is read by the client program and used to display the menu for the user. When a particular item is selected, the Gopher client uses the data stored with the menu name in the links file to construct the next Gopher request. If the item requested is another menu, another links file is fetched and another Gopher menu is constructed and displayed. If the item requested is the last point on the information tree, the item is fetched and displayed or stored.

You make a links file on your server for each menu that you want to present. A links file is made by processing a file that contains lines of text with specific "command" words that tell your Gopher server what to do with the information stored on that line. Figure 19.1, earlier in this chapter, shows the relatively simple top-level menu that makes the `gopher.netcom.com` Gopher. The links file was built from command word data fed to a program called *mkcache*. mkcache creates the links file that the server returns as a Gopher request result. Compare the menu presented to the file that produced it, and you can see what we mean.

▶ BEHIND THE NETCOM GOPHER MENU

```
# This is the top level menu for the NETCOM gopher
# Comments are in italics.
Name=About this GOPHER server
Path=0/about.server
Type=0
# This section provides a pointer to a file within the
# same directory which holds the links file.

Name=Information about NETCOM
Path=1s/guest
Type=1
# This section provides a pointer to another directory on
# the same computer system as this links file.

Name=Internet information
Path=1s/internet-info
Type=1
# This section provides a pointer to another directory on
# the same computer as this links file.

Name=Jughead - Search High-Level Gopher Menus (via
Washington & Lee)
Path=
Type=7
Host=liberty.uc.wlu.edu
Port=3002
# This section provides a pointer to a search service on
# another computer system.

Name=Search Gopherspace using Veronica
Path=1/veronica
Type=1
Host=veronica.scs.unr.edu
Port=70
# This section provides a pointer menu which points to
# to a search service on another computer system.

Name=Other Internet Gopher Servers (via U.C. Santa Cruz)
Path=1/The World/Other Internet Gopher Servers
Host=scilibx.ucsc.edu
Port=70
```

```
# This section provides a pointer to a menu on another
# computer system.

Name=Weather (via U. Minnesota)
Path=1/Weather
Host=ashpool.micro.umn.edu
Port=70
# This section provides a pointer to a menu on another
# computer system.

Name=Worldwide Directory Services (via Notre Dame)
Path=1/Non-Notre Dame Information Sources/Phone Books--
Other Institutions
Host=gopher.nd.edu
port=70
# This section provides a pointer to a menu on another
# computer system.

Name=Interesting items
Path=1/interesting-items
Type=1
# This section provides a pointer to a menu on the same
# computer system as this links file.

Name=ATTENTION NETCOM users
Path=0/netcom.notice
Type=0
# This section provides a pointer to a file in the same
# directory as this links file.
```

Giving the User Choices The top-level menu in the Netcom Gopher offers the user a small number of items that can be easily read. The choices that are presented are sufficiently different that the user can quickly decide what path is appropriate for the task at hand.

If the user chooses the first or last item, a text file is presented. That file is stored in the current directory. The name of the file appears in the Path= statement.

If the second, third, or ninth choice is selected, Gopher presents another menu, stored in the directory referenced by the path statement. Gopher changes its pointers to the new directory, and displays the file named Menu in that new directory. The menu file will appear similar to this one, except, of course, that it will point to other files and links.

If the fourth, fifth, sixth, seventh, or eighth choice is selected, the server connects to the host listed in the `Host=` statement and presents the menu item listed in the `Path=` statement. Notice that you can specify more than one level of menu from the linked Gopher. Each slash (/) in the path statement represents a level in the linked menu. For example, the statement

```
Path=1/The World/Other Internet Gopher Servers
```

presents the menu (type=1) linked by the "The World" menu and within that menu the Other Internet Gopher Servers menu from the host `scilibx.ucsc.edu`. When the user selects Other Internet Gopher Servers from the Netcom Gopher menu, the next menu that is presented comes from the University of California, Santa Cruz (UCSC) server. Specifically, it comes from the The World selection in that server's top-level menu and then from the Other Internet... selection within the next menu. This way you can link material to your Gopher that your clients might find very useful, no matter what menu level the material may have in some other Gopher.

The Structure of a Gopher Menu Entry

From the example, you can see that entries in a Gopher menu file have a common structure:

- Comments can be liberally sprinkled throughout the menu. If you add them, someone coming along after you may be able to understand what you intended. You identify a comment by putting a "#" in the first character of the field.

- Each menu item has a `Name=` statement. The words following the equal sign will be displayed on the screen for the user to select.

- Each menu item has a `Path=` statement. This statement contains the type of the data, followed by a slash (/) character and then the pathname for linked entry. The path may include multiple levels of a Gopher directory hierarchy, if the pointer is to a linked Gopher.

That's all you really need, if all the items you are going to link are stored on the same computer with your server. However, if you are linking in menus from Gopher servers on other computers, you will need

Type=, Host=, and Port= fields. These fields tell your server what remote computer (the "host") to connect to; what TCP/IP "port" to connect to, and what information it must ask for when it gets the connection to the remote computer.

One of the Gopher information types is "menu." This tells the server that the information that will be displayed is another list of links that the user may choose. When the host statement is not present, the menu will be found in the path specified on the current host. This is how you link in menus that are lower in your hierarchy of design.

Build Your Next-Level Menus

Once you have coded your top-level menu, you know exactly how to code the rest of your information. Simply follow the design that you outlined, making sure that you store your menu, image, and data files in the appropriate directory for your menu in order to link them in. Then you just repeat the process until you're done.

GOPHER FILE TYPES

Gopher servers can serve a number of different kinds of file types. To do this successfully, the server must have information about what kind of file any particular file is—so that the user's client will not try to send an ASCII text file through a graphical viewer, for example. Or so it won't try to send a search through a sound file. Here are the file types that you'll need to know to set up your menus so that Gopher can process them as you intended:

0   Plain or html text. The server will transmit the contents of the file as it is stored. The client will display it. If the file type has a Z appended to it, it is compressed (type=0Z). The Gopher server will automatically uncompress it before handing it to a client.

1　The menu. This type defines the contents as a set of links to other files. The server transmits it as text. The client presents it as the next set of choices for the user.

2　A link to the CSO telephone book servers: Gopher passes this on to the CSO servers. The server transmits it as stored. The data is only a URL.

3　An error message from the server.

4　Binary files processed by the Macintosh Binhex program. Transmitted as text files.

5　DOS .exe files. Binary files.

6　Uuencoded files. Transmitted as text files.

7　A menu that invokes special processing within the server—for example, searches of the Gopher menus.

8　A link to the Telnet protocol: Gopher passes this on to Telnet. Not all clients implement this link.

9　Binary files. If the file type has a Z appended to it, it is compressed (type=9Z). The Gopher server will automatically uncomprcss it before handing it to a client.

I　Binary image files. If the file type has a Z appended to it, it is compressed (type=IZ). The Gopher server will automatically uncompress it before handing it to a client.

s　Binary sound files. If the file type has a Z appended to it, it is compressed (type=sZ). The Gopher server will automatically uncompress it before handing it to a client.

▶ *Public vs. Private Gopher Holes*

If you want to limit access to your information to specific people or groups of people, you may do so. The GN Gopher is very flexible and you can set your server up to allow the "world" into much of your Gopher and yet allow a restricted set of domains or addresses to access material intended only for that group. This feature allows you to present both private and public information from the same Gopher.

▶ *Peering into Gopherspace*

There are several Gopher design techniques that you can use to help your users find things within your gopherspace.

The first and simplest is to include a file within each directory that lists what the user can expect to find linked to each menu item. The hardest thing about this technique is to remember to change the text when you change the menus. One way to leave yourself a reminder is to use the comment field within the menu. Include a comment that says

```
# Description of menu items—remember to update!
```

or something similar.

The second method is to provide a search capability. Searching in Gopher causes the servers to build a new menu display, with any file that contains the search term listed as an entry. With the GN server, there are two methods you can use to do this.

The Simple Search

The first is a simple search that works really well if you keep the number of files to less than 100 or so and the files are not very large. To build the simple search mechanism, you add two menu entries to your Gopher menu. The first entry tells the server that you are providing searching:

```
Path=1s/directory path and file name
```

Adding the "s" to the type code gives the server permission to run searches on the files in the named directory.

Then you add another menu entry:

```
Path=7g/directory path and file name
```

This tells the server that the directory may be searched with an UNIX "grep-like" search. The "7" tells the server "search." The "g" tells the server "grep-like." Grep is the "regular expression" search, which is rather complicated and really beyond the scope of this book. Generally, simple requests—for example, using a single word or word part as a search argument—will return results that are useful.

Indexing with WAIS

For larger collections of directories and files, you'll want to investigate using WAIS indexing for your server. GN has special methods of providing WAIS indexing. For example, it can provide you with a "Search all the menus" item for your server. Because the server builds special files called ".cache" in each directory, you can use these files as searchable data. You just add a menu item with a search type and a special path type that tells the server to search the cache file.

▶ Providing Efficient Service

If you have really large files, you may want to store them in compressed format. The servers are capable of keeping documents in compressed format and uncompressing them only when it is time to transfer them to a client process. To do that you need only compress the files that you want to serve, and add a pointer to the decompression program that you'd like to use in the configuration file set up when you install your Gopher server. When you set up your menu, add a letter "Z" to the path type field to tell the server that the named file is compressed and instruct the server to uncompress it when required.

You can even give your users a choice with compressed files—just put in two menu items for the same file, one with the "Z" added to the path type and one without it. The user who chose the second option would have the compressed file moved to his/her computer system and would uncompress it at that site. People might want to do this if the files are particularly large. Obviously, larger files take longer to transfer than smaller files, and sometimes time connected to the network is of more concern than work performed on the local computer. In any case, uncompression/expansion is done only once. If you choose to do this, you'll want to add information somewhere about what compression program you used. Remember, compression programs are not all compatible with each other; one program may not be able to expand another program's output.

▶ *Think about the User's Needs*

When you design your Gopher menus, think about the information
needs of the users who will most often access it. The Netcom Gopher,
for example, serves (usually) as an entry point into the larger Internet
gopherspace. The UCSC Gopher, by contrast, is serving information
about its locality, and it's a focal point for a very specific geographical
and institutional location. Its top-level menus are designed to serve the
students, faculty, and staff of the University of California, Santa Cruz.
These are of lesser interest to subscribers to Netcom, so the links are
best made directly to the lower level to be useful for most Netcom users.

▶ *Check the Links*

Once you have constructed your Gopher, you'll need to test it. Make
sure that each and every link works—that is, that it jumps to the server
you intended and to the file or menu you intended. You'll also need to
make sure that you do a "link" audit periodically. Gophers move their
holes. Files move from Gopher to Gopher. Servers shut down, or move
domains, or...

Over time you'll want to modify the links to point to new and interesting places to visit, to improve the information you provide about your
organization, or to remove links to places that disappeared from
cyberspace.

▶ *Dos and Don'ts for Gopherhole Diggers*

- Do make an outline. Since Gopher uses hierarchies, outlines are a
  most effective design tool.

- Do make sure your file permissions are set properly so that they
  can be read by the intended readers and not written to by people
  who shouldn't be writing to them.

- Don't put too many items on a single menu. Make the hierarchies
  deeper if you can, instead. This makes choosing among the items
  on the list easier for the user.

- Do make explicit the difference between links to data on your
  server and to data elsewhere on the Net. You need to make it clear

that you aren't responsible for all the information accessible through your server.

- Do put in a disclaimer that holds your organization harmless from incorrect information received via your server.

- Do point to the gateway servers if your system doesn't provide complete access to all the services available on the Internet. You can let people use WAIS, X.500 directories, time-of-day around the world, and so on from within your Gopher server.

- Don't point to FTP access if your system also provides FTP. Using Gopher to serve FTP files is not a good use of resources. Direct use of FTP is much more efficient.

- Do check your Gopher links to see if they still point to what you thought. A good program to do this is go4check, a Perl utility that will help automate your link audit.

- Do review your text files every four or five weeks. Periodic checking prevents possible embarrassment.

- Do spell-check your menus.

- Do have someone other than the person who designed it look at the menu structure. Maybe it only makes sense to the designer.

- Don't forget to keep copies of your link files and data on another disk, a tape, or diskette, in case your disk fails.

- Don't install your server or the files (images or information) that you want to serve on an account that is owned by a person. If you do, you will need to find that person each time you want to enhance your server. Make the "owner" of the directories an account named for the function (for example, you might name the account "gophermaster" or "support").

- Do read the documentation provided by the server software's authors. It contains valuable information that will improve your ability to do a good design and provide a good service.

▶ ▶ *Providing Information via the World Wide Web*

The Web may be the most popular technology since the Swiss Army knife. And it is being used for just about as many things as that little knife with all the built-in clippers, screwdrivers, and so on.

We think the reason for the popularity is that the Web best combines all the things we like about slick magazines with the ability to jump around from page to page with little effort. It's pretty; it's useful; it's amusing. How can you miss?

People respond to Web pages in much the same way as they respond to magazines. Web page designers need to consider their audiences much more than the designer of a Gopher menu or an FTP space. For example, compare the pages shown in Figures 19.9 and 19.10. The Web page for Hewlett Packard, the computer and instrument manufacturing company (http://www.hp.com), says something totally different than the Web page for the Rolling Stones (http://stones.com). Clearly

FIGURE 19.9 ▶

The Web page for Hewlett Packard.

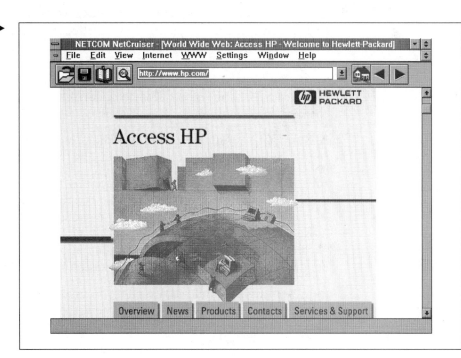

FIGURE 19.10 ▶

The Web page for the Rolling Stones.

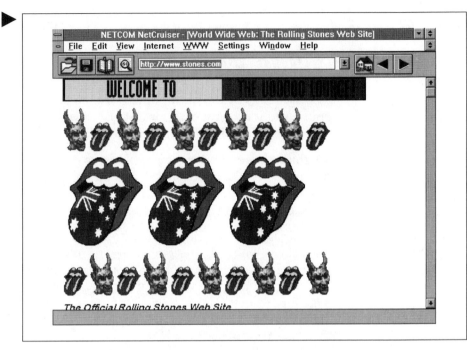

these services are aimed at different audiences—or the same audience at different times. Both pages are very effective. They convey image, attitude, information, and provoke specific behavior in response to that image, attitude, and information. Even if the same person who would buy a Voodoo Lounge Tour T-shirt might also purchase a piece of equipment from HP, they would not do so for the same reasons; so the presentation for each is entirely appropriate.

A Web "page" is actually a multimedia presentation. It can include sound and images and motion pictures as well as text.

An effective presentation should have something in it that will capture the attention of the visual learner, the aural learner, *and* the kinesthetic learner—those who learn by seeing, those who learn by listening, and those who learn by doing and touching. World Wide Web is the first application that allows the Internet information service implementor to do all of those things in the same environment.

In presenting information, we all try to give our audience a clear understanding of what we want them to know, to feel, and to do with the information we have conveyed. Using text, images, and sometimes sound in a Web page, we can do that and have our message delivered quickly down the hall, across the street, or across several time zones, to people who ask to see it. This makes the Web a presentation builder's dream tool.

▶ *What You'll Need*

To create your own information Web, you'll need all of the following:

- An http server. If you are going to run your own system, suitable server programs can be found at both the NCSA (ftp.ncsa.uiuc.edu) and CERN (info.cern.ch) public domain sites.

- Information you want to serve organized in some reasonable manner. If you want to display existing text files, you should add HTML coding which will allow the http clients to display the text properly. Images need to be stored in .gif, .jpeg (.jpg), or .mpeg (.mpg) format. Sound files need to be in .au format.

- File permissions must be established to restrict users to read from or write to specific files within specific directories. If you plan on having users enter data into fill-the-blank forms, you'll need to set up data space to receive the information they enter. If you don't plan on that, you can restrict the directories which contain your information to read-only for all but the account that is allowed to add, change, or remove information for your organization.

You may also want to include or have available these items:

- Graphical images like the symbol that represents your organization, or some image that highlights the topics covered on the page.

- Terms and conditions and/or disclaimer statements. Your organization's legal staff might require you to add such statements. Or maybe you'll want to add copyright and service mark information for your organization's products and services.

- A link from the top-level menu to a Web space search server so your clients can find materials that are not on your server.

- Logging and statistical processing of the logs so you have some idea who has been visiting.

- For testing your pages, you'll need access to the public domain and commercial Web browser clients for as many of the computing platforms as possible. At least obtain the major ones for the most common platforms: Macintosh, DOS, and UNIX systems.

▶ Dos and Don'ts for Web Spinners

- Do try to make your page visually interesting—remember your audience! Use the facilities within HTML to provide a visually pleasing as well as useful page. Provide plenty of white space, for example. Use spacing to make the anchor links obvious. Provide visual cues like horizontal bars to separate different types of information on the same Web page.

- Don't try to put too much on one page. Some clients don't handle scrolling around in a large page very well. If you must put a very large batch of text on one page, put in within-page index links, so that the user can jump to a specific part of the page.

- When you do include graphics, remember that really large graphics take a long time to transmit, and many graphical clients allow you to turn off the automatic display of "in-line" graphics (those designed to be displayed immediately on the page rather than to be fetched and displayed by themselves). If they have to wait a long time, people may choose not to view your graphics. Design your in-line images so that they are informative and attractive but are respectful of people's time and patience. You want most people to view the images, not to turn them off because they are a pain to wait for.

- Don't use too many images, either. Fetching each image requires a separate action across the network. If you use too many, users will either turn off automatic image display or halt displaying your page before it is finished being fetched. Neither action will achieve what you wanted when you designed the page.

- Do include descriptive paragraphs that accompany each linked "anchor" on your page.

- Do include a judicious mix of things to do, things to see, and things to know in your own information as well as in the information that you link in from other points around the Web.

- Do include an address block at the end of your page. This section should include the e-mail address to which page visitors should send their questions. It can also include the date the page was last changed. This is a nice way to tell people how current the information on the page is.

- Do put in a disclaimer that does not hold your organization responsible for incorrect information received via your server. Everyone needs to understand that not all of the information to which your Web page points is under your control. One suggestion from Tim Berners-Lee, the original WWW developer, is to put your disclaimer on a page which is pointed to by an anchor in the address block.

- Do point to the gateway servers if your system doesn't provide complete access to all the Internet services. You can let people use WAIS, X.500 directories, time-of-day around the world, and so on from within your Web page.

- Do make sure your file permissions are set properly so that they can be read by the intended readers and not written to by people who shouldn't be writing to them.

- Do check your Web links to see if they still point to what you thought.

- Do review your pages every four or five weeks. Periodic checking prevents possible embarrassment.

- Do spell-check your pages, even the headings! And especially check the words in your images. Reversed signs or misspellings, particularly in things like the name of your organization, will be quite embarrassing.

- Do have someone other than the person who designed it look at the page. Maybe it only makes sense to the designer.

Code by Example

Figure 19.11 shows the Netcom home page, a very simple Web page that includes links to other Web pages. The accompanying listing shows the HTML code that produced the page. Looking at the code, you can see the elements needed to produce a simple, yet informative set of links.

FIGURE 19.11 ▶

Netcom's home Web page.

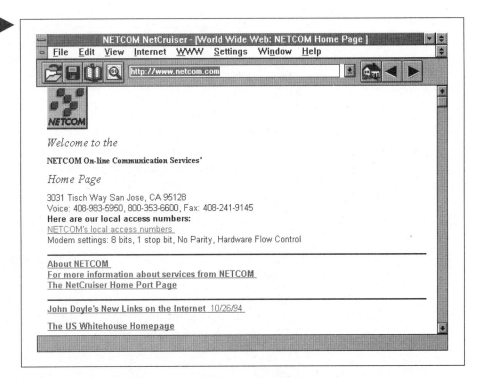

THE ANNOTATED CODE UNDERLYING THE NETCOM WEB PAGE

▶ Annotations appear in *italic* type. Note that the line breaks in this HTML code are here only for ease of maintenance. It is not necessary to insert blank lines where they are here, nor is it necessary to begin new parts of the HTML code with a new line.

```
<title> NETCOM Home Page </title>
```

The <Title> block (which is what the pair of identifiers <title> and </title> are called) gives the name of the page as it will be displayed in the title bar shown by graphical Web browsers. This is the bar across the top of the screen.

```
<A NAME="top"></A>
```

The <A> block tells the client that the item which follows is an "anchor." Anchors are the identifiers that specify the location to which the user can jump or upon which the user will "land."
The Name anchor provides a destination label. Destination labels are used to provide a "landing spot" for a jump within the same page or for a jump to a specific point on the page from another page.

```
<IMG SRC="http://www.netcom.com/netcom/netcom.gif"
alt="The NETCOM Logo"
align=top>
```

The IMG (for image) identifier contains source (SRC), alternative text (alt), and alignment directives (align). Taken together, this block of instructions gives the URL for the image, the text to display when the user decides not to (or cannot) display graphical images, and the alignment of any subsequent text. Note that the angle brackets enclose all three elements.

```
<H3><I>Welcome to the</I></H3>
```

<H3> is a Header block that means "display the enclosed text in Header Type 3 font."
<I> means "display the enclosed text in Italics." Note that you must "close" the Italics directive before you close the Header 3 directive.

```
<H2> NETCOM On-line Communication Services' </H2>
```

<H2> is a header block that means "display the enclosed text in Header type 2 font."

```
<H3><I> Home Page </I></H3>
3031 Tisch Way  San Jose, CA  95128 <BR>
```

The <BR> directive means "break the line here."

```
Voice: 408-983-5950,   800-353-6600,  Fax: 408-241-9145
<BR>
```

```
<B>Here are our local access numbers:</B> <BR>
```

The *<B> directive means "display the enclosed text in boldface."*

```
<A HREF="http://www.netcom.com/netcom/numbers.html">
NETCOM's local access numbers </A>
```

The HREF directive defines the location of the page (here a URL for a page that will be fetched and displayed) to which the user will jump if this anchor is selected. The HREF anchor statement includes two parts: the anchor itself and the element to be displayed on the screen. Here the display anchor is text, but it can be an image.
```
<BR>
```

```
Modem settings: 8 bits, 1 stop bit, No Parity, Hardware
Flow  Control <BR>
<HR>
```

The <HR> directive means "insert a horizontal rule."

```
<A HREF=#ABOUT><b>About NETCOM</b> </A>
```

This anchor block contains a jump to a destination label on this page. The reference is preceded by the # symbol. The anchor's text is displayed in boldface because there is a block of <B>—"make this bold"—directives.

```
<BR>
<A HREF="ftp://ftp.netcom.com/pub/ne/netcom/netcom_info">
<b>For more information about services from NETCOM</b>
</A>
<BR>
<A HREF="http://www.netcom.com/netcom/cruiser.html">
<b>The NetCruiser Home Port Page</b></a><br>
<HR>
<A HREF="http://www.netcom.com/net-
com/new941026.html"><b>John Doyle's New Links on the In-
ternet </b> 10/26/94 </A> <P>
```

The <P> directive means that the paragraph ends here. A paragraph usually causes a blank line to be inserted before the next paragraph. The <br> directive does not *include a blank line. Again, note the explicit use of the bold font.*

```
<A HREF="http://www.whitehouse.gov"><b>The US Whitehouse
Homepage</b></a><p>
<a HREF="http://www.netcom.com/netcom/fav.html"><b>Favor-
ite Internet Destinations </b> </A>
These sites were nominated by members of the NETCOM User
Community. <P>
```

Note that in the URL here, the fully qualified name is used. It is not necessary to use the full name in the URL if the page to which you are jumping is in the same direc- tory or located on the same host computer. We recommend full names for clarity. It makes it easier for you to maintain (change or update) your Web page if you can see the complete link information.

```
<A HREF="ftp://ftp.netcom.com/pub/sp/spea-
cock/html/nuglops_info.html"> <b>Information for NETCOM
host dial users from a group of NETCOM Users </b> </A>
Here you will find information about programs and scripts
for NETCOM's host dial systems written and made available
by this group of NETCOM's users. <P>
<A HREF="http://www.netcom.com/netcom/assist.html"><b>In-
ternet Assistance and Information </b> </A>
Here you will find links to subject guides, a Web Index,
and the Virtual Reference Desk, as well as to information
about the World Wide Web itself. <P>
<A HREF="http://www.netcom.com/netcom/wac-
cess.html"><b>Web Access to other Internet services </b>
</A>
Here you will find links to other Internet services like
a list of ftp sites, and some service gateways. <P>

<A href= "http://wings.buffalo.edu/contest/"> <b>1994
Best of the Web </B> </A> Results from The 1994 Best of
the Web awards, voted on by the Web user community and
presented at the 1994 WWW Conference in Geneva, May
1994.<P>

<A NAME="ABOUT"><H3>About NETCOM </H3></A>
```

Here the named label is just before a header directive. When the user jumps from the anchor above to this point, the heading will be displayed on the top line of the screen.

NETCOM On-line Communication Services, Inc is the nation's leading commercial Internet Service provider. NETCOM provides local access points in many of the major metropolitan areas in the United States. The services provided include News Feeds, E-mail, and Domain Service, file transfers, and access to the global Internet including locating and downloading files and remote login access to other computer systems. <P>

This is the first full text paragraph on this page. The only coding needed is the <P> directive to signal the end of the paragraph.

NETCOM provides high-speed network connections to individual and business customers as well as its host dial service. NETCOM is entering its 6th year as a reliable service provider of quality products and services. Our customers include defense contractors, chip manufacturers, oil companies, investment brokerage services, and thousands of individuals. NETCOM has proven to be a communication leader in delivering high quality and reliable connectivity around the clock, 7 days a week and 52 weeks a year. <P>

NETCOM owns, operates, and maintains a high speed digital network that provides a full range of local-call services to over 200 cities in the USA. Our nationwide network can be used to inter-connect branch offices, to provide local calling for telecomputing, and to establish on-demand Internet connections for USENET, E-mail, and personal dial-up service. <P>
<ADDRESS> NETCOM Home Page / NETCOM / glee@netcom.com </ADDRESS>

The Address block generally includes at least the e-mail address of the person who wrote the page or to whom inquiries should be sent. Sometimes the address will be

```
"webmaster" or "webspinner" at some domain. There is a
paragraph after the address block.

<A HREF="#top"> Go to top of page </A>

This last anchor, to the destination named at the begin-
ning of the page, will take the user quickly to the top
of the page. This is a nice thing to do for people who
don't have scroll bars at the edge of their screen or Web
browsers with the ability to scroll up and down.
If the page is not the entry point for your organiza-
tion's Web presence, you will want to add anchors to your
home page here. Anchors that jump to other specific pages
might be included at this point, too. Some designers in-
clude several common anchors at the bottom of each page
in their Web. This makes it easy for people to navigate
within your pages and gives a common design theme for the
pages as well.
```

The HTML code includes an opening image, a title statement, a third-level heading, and jumps to several linked pages. The links include jumps to other pages in the Netcom Web, with short paragraphs describing why people might want to look at these pages. At the bottom of the page there are several paragraphs of text, an address block, and a jump back to the top of the page.

This page does not include examples of all the things you can do with a Web page, of course. It leaves out structured and unstructured and/or bulleted lists. It leaves out connections via other protocols than http and FTP. Remember that Web browsing clients can use the Gopher protocol, too. And many Web clients can use the netnews (Usenet), mailto, and Telnet protocols, as well as process input from the user by using forms. If you use forms, you will need underlying programs to process the input in addition to the HTML code that provides the input areas on the displayed page.

You can adapt this code to reflect your organization's needs. If you do, be sure to follow the "Web etiquette" hints shown in Figure 19.12, by the CERN WWW project team (`http://info.cern.ch/hypertext/WWW/ Provider/etiquette.html`), and read the other Web pages that you can

FIGURE 19.12 ▶

Web etiquette hints
from CERN.

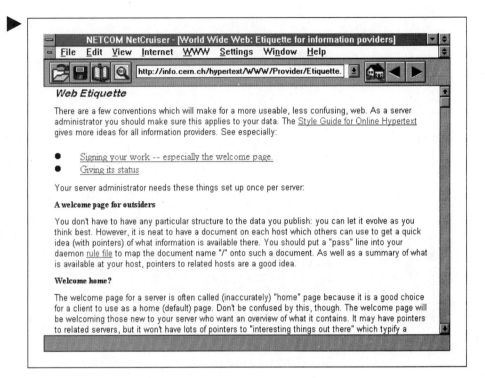

find by taking a jump to the Web developer's page maintained by Barry R. Greene (`http://oneworld.wa.com/htmldev/devpage/dev-page.html`). Then you'll soon be spinning Web pages with the rest of us.

▶▶ *Opening the Door to the World*

Whether you're working with FTP, Gopher, or the Web, once you've got your server running, and your data formatted and ready, you need to let people on the Internet know you are receiving requests.

If your server contains data of particular interest to a specific community of users, be sure to announce it to any mailing lists or newsgroups that specialize in that subject.

Send an announcement of your new server to the `net-happen-ings@is.internic.net` mailing list maintained by Gleason Sackman.

▶ *Announcing Your New FTP Site*

For new FTP sites, if you wish your files to be included in the Archie indexes, you'll need to send e-mail to `archie-admin@bunyip.com`. You should include the fully qualified domain name of your FTP server and the root directory from which you are making information available. For example, Netcom might send this message:

```
Files for indexing will be found in the /pub directory of
ftp.netcom.com.
```

▶ *Announcing Your New Gopher Server*

For new Gophers, you need to:

1. send e-mail to `gopher@boombox.micro.umn.edu` with the following items in the body of the message:

   - The name of your server.
   - The host name on which the server is running.
   - The port number (70 is assumed).
   - The administrative contact.
   - a selector string (to be used in other people's Gopher menus to point to your server).

2. Send an announcement to the `comp.infosystems.announce` newsgroup.

If you do not announce your server, people will still be able to access it directly by giving the appropriate server name. However, other Gopher server designers won't necessarily know about your server and won't be able to point their servers to yours. Also, the Gopher indexing services only gather data from those servers that are announced via the "mother" Gopher at the University of Minnesota. Clearly, there are real disadvantages to going it alone.

▶ *Announcing Your Web Server*

To announce your new Web server to the rest of the Internet, you need to:

1. Register with CERN the following information:

- The title under which you wish your service to be referenced.
- The location—country, state.
- A summary (2–3 lines) of what your server provides.
- The URL of the entry point you would like. (Include the relevant port number if you are using another port. Port 70 is the common port for Gopher, port 80 is the common port for http, and port 21 is the common port for FTP.)
- If the information is officially mandated and representative of your organization, you could say so.

2. Send e-mail to `whats-new@ncsa.uiuc.edu`. These folks like the e-mail to be in HTML format so they can just drop your announcement into the "what's new" page.

3. Send an announcement to the `comp.infosystems.announce` newsgroup.

▶▶ *What Next? Feedback from the Community*

Well, you won't get to sit back and admire your work for very long. Get ready for visitors!

If you put an e-mail address on your Web or Gopher server, make sure it is working because the traffic will rise dramatically from the first day. You'll need to prepare procedures for answering the mail, for reviewing what's on your server, and for adding new things to your server. You'll get lots of comments for improving your services. Some you'll like and want to implement. Some will be from people who were pleased to receive your information. It's really nice to get those!

Don't forget to watch the logs of traffic. You can look at them to see which pages and menus are being used the most. You may want to re-arrange your pages and menus based on how others actually use them.

Internet Resources

PART THREE

## CHAPTER 20

General Resources for Internet Masters

► ► **Y**ou'll remember we said at the beginning of the book that there were too many fun things going on with the Net for any one person to be able to know and use all of them. But here are some useful, interesting, or just plain fun things that we think everyone ought to know about.

Many of our favorite resources have been documented in the chapters devoted to individual Internet tools. We have tried not to duplicate those references here.

Be sure to check the other "Resources" chapters as well as this one; our categories necessarily overlap a little, and you may find items of interest in those chapters, too.

► ► General Resources

We'll start with some useful items of general interest.

► Alex: A Catalog of Electronic Texts on the Internet

Alex uses Gopher to find and retrieve the full text of over 700 texts on the Internet taken from Project Gutenberg, Wiretap, the On-line Book Initiative, Eris at Virginia Tech, the English server at Carnegie-Mellon University, and the online portion of the Oxford Text Archive. Users can search by author and title.

Gopher: gopher.rsl.ox.uk (the World/Gopherspace/Alex)

▶ *Voice of America News*

Despite the end of the cold war, the Voice of America still broadcasts its news services all over the world. This is one of the few free daily news services on the Internet and offers much more in-depth reporting than the headline services by USA Today and others. The main focus is on international news, and the sports reporting is mainly about soccer. The time lag is minimal—five minutes from when the report is released by VOA central—making this a very timely and useful resource. Figure 20.1 shows recent additions to the Gopher.

Gopher: `gopher.voa.gov`

FIGURE 20.1 ▶

Recent additions to the Voice of America Gopher, showing items available using FTP.

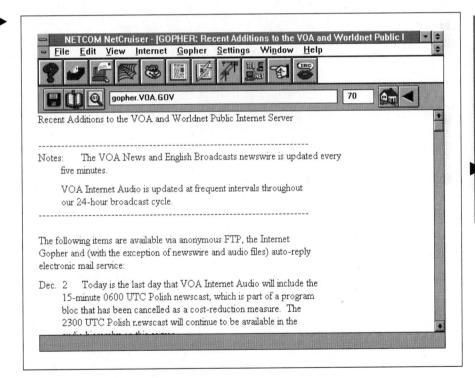

▶ *American Memory Project*

The American Memory Project, from the Library of Congress, contains over 4000 prints and photographs. Primary source materials and archival materials relating to American culture are available through the library's Web server. There are photographs from the Civil War (Figure 20.2), the American Farm Bureau, and Carl Van Vechten, photographer of American celebrities, artists, and literary figures. A manuscript section is underway, and a list of collections from the American Memory project that will be added in 1994–95 can be scanned. The Library of Congress' Web pages can be reached via

WWW: `http://lcweb.loc.gov`

FIGURE 20.2 ►

Selected photos are available from the American Memory Project Web pages.

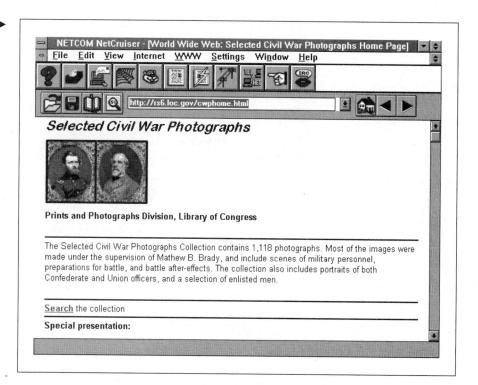

► *GoMLink*

An electronic public library from the University of Michigan Library. It's arranged by broad subject categories: business and economics; computers and technology; education; entertainment and recreation; environment; government and politics; health and nutrition; humanities; libraries and librarianship; Michigan; news services, newsletters and journals; a reference desk; science; social issues and social services; and the Internet and its other resources. This service is one of the best starting points for new Internet users and has subject collections in great depth for experienced users. One of the better reference desks on the Internet. A public client is available.

Gopher: `vienna.hh.lib.umich.edu`

▶ CARL

The Colorado Alliance of Research Libraries (CARL) offers much more than just an online library catalog of Colorado academic, public, and special libraries. The CARL UnCover document delivery service was recently opened to the public, offering over 4 million articles. Journal Graphics will mail or fax television news transcripts in their archives. You must have a credit card or deposit account with CARL. Telnet to `pac.carl.org` for more information. (The letters PAC stand for Public Access Catalog.) This address is also the entry point for accessing many of the library catalogs supported by CARL Systems.

▶ LC Marvel

The main Gopher server at the Library of Congress, LC Marvel, contains an enormous amount of information not only about the Library of Congress itself, but also about the US government. Library of Congress publications, the Center for the Book, Services to the Blind and Physically Handicapped, Reading Rooms, the American Folklife Center, the Asian Collection, Geography and Maps, and the On-line Business Center are only a few of the areas covered by this Gopher. Although it's sometimes hard to move through because of the incredible amount of information, this Gopher is worth delving into. A hierarchical menu tree file of what's available is helpful.

Gopher: `marvel.loc.gov`

▶ Crafts Information Service

The "Crafts Information Service" project, illustrated in Figure 20.3, was started to help crafts producers on Prince Edward Island, Canada, find sources for the raw materials, tools, equipment and services they need to produce. Prince Edward Island is located far from major sources of supply, and finding out simply "who sells what" is a major impediment to islanders; the "Crafts Information Service" serves to help solve this problem by having available a comprehensive body of information on sources of supply. The Crafts Information Service currently has information about some 5000 suppliers on file, with catalogs—indexed by product and service—for half of those. The extensive catalog indexing allows specific products and services to be easily searched for and listed.

Gopher: gopher.crafts-council.pe.ca

WWW: http://www.crafts-council.pe.ca/Welcome.html

FTP: gus.crafts-council.pe.ca

FIGURE 20.3 ▶

The Web page from the Prince Edward Island Crafts Council.

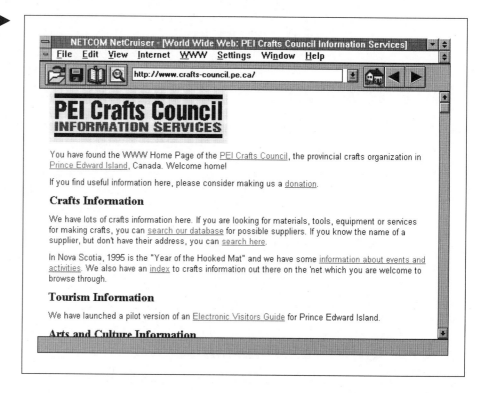

▶ Grant-Getter's Guide to the Internet

A Gopher resource that serves as a major entry point for grant-finding on the Internet. The Federal Register, FEDIX, MOLIS, Fedworld, and others can be accessed from this one site. The Guide itself is a nice bibliography of grant sources on the Internet.

Gopher: gopher.uidaho.edu

▶ 1990 Census Data

Census Data from the US government is of great importance to almost every business, institution, nonprofit and other organizations for planning and implementing new products, programs, services and marketing. Since much of the government's data is now being released in machine-readable format (and in some cases *only* in machine-readable format), and since that information is in the public domain, a number of depository libraries have found the Internet to be an ideal method of disseminating this data. Not all census data is available yet, but the University of Michigan, the University of Missouri, and Rice University have made available their respective state data and a good deal of national data as well. The University of Missouri's files are available in Lotus format.

University of Michigan:

 Gopher: gopher.lib.umich.edu

 FTP: una.hh.lib.umich.edu

University of Missouri:

 Gopher: gopher.bigcat.missouri.edu

Rice University:

 Gopher: gopher.riceinfo.rice.edu

The Census department itself has a Web site, illustrated in Figure 20.4:

WWW: http://www.census.gov

General
Resources

▶ ▶

ch.
20

FIGURE 20.4 ▶

The Web page from the United States Census Department.

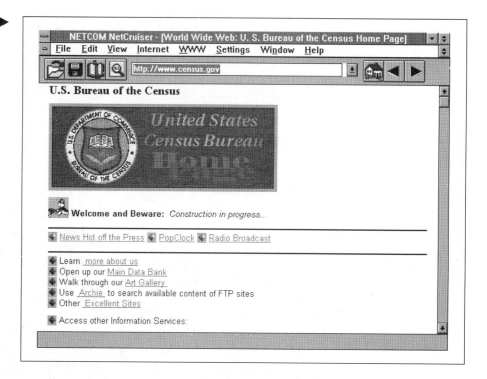

▶ *Rehabilitation Center*

The National Rehabilitation Information Center provides resources to disabled persons and their families via Gopher. Some of their full-text online materials include resources for stroke victims and their families, and resources for those who have suffered spinal cord injuries and brain trauma.

> **Gopher:** `val-dor.cc.buffalo.edu`

▶ *Community Idea Net*

A Gopher resource from Sunsite at the University of North Carolina that "disseminates ideas about making governments more effective." Descriptions of projects, contact persons, and information on teenagers, bugs, highways, budgets, immigrants, farming, graffiti and more.

> **Gopher:** `calypso-2.oit.unc.edu`; then choose Sunsite by Subject ➤ US and World Politics ➤ Community Idea Net from the menus.

▶▶ *E-Mail Mailing Lists*

Here are some mailing lists to join if you'd like announcements of new services to be delivered directly to your e-mail in-box.

▶ *Net-Happenings*

"The" list for users who want to know *everything* that's new on the Net and that's happening to the Net. List owner Gleason Sackman forwards thousands of bytes of information a day to keep up with the ever-changing Internet environment. This list has a digest option that will allow you to receive the postings in big gulps rather than dribs and drabs; but be warned, even in Digest form it generates a large amount of mail. This list is essential to Gopher or Web administrators and others who serve as the Internet expert for their community. To subscribe, send a subscription message to: majordomo@is.internic.net and include either **subscribe net-happenings** or **subscribe net-happenings-digest** in the body of your message, depending upon which you'd like to receive.

▶ *PACS-L*

A discussion focusing on computer systems that libraries make available to their patrons. You do not need to be a librarian to join the list. This is a great list for getting help with specific computer problems related to OPACs (On-line Public Access Catalogs), CD-ROMs, and databases. The discussion is library-oriented but may be of help to professionals in many other areas. To subscribe: listserv@uhupvm1.bitnet listserv@uhupvm1.uh.edu.

▶ *List-of-Lists*

The List-of-Lists (also known as the NISC List-of-Lists) is a good way to find a list for your own special interest. Special-interest-group mailing lists from both Bitnet and the Internet are listed, with updates available. You can FTP the list from ftp.nisc.sri.com and subscribe to the updates by sending e-mail to interest-groups-request@nisc.sri.com.

General Resources

▶ ▶
ch.
20

► GopherJewels

This mailing list sends out a small amount of daily traffic on interesting Gopher finds. Usually there are no more than five messages per day. This list is perfect for those who'd like to see what's good and new in gopherspace or who are maintaining a Gopher server that includes outside resources. To subscribe: `listproc@einet.net`.

► GopherJewels-Talk

Since the GopherJewels list is limited to postings about interesting Gopher sites, GopherJewels-Talk supplies a place for people to ask questions about Gopher or discuss issues. It's mainly for Internet neophytes who are looking for a friendly place to pose a Gopher question and not get flamed by the "experts." To subscribe, send a message to: `listproc@einet.net`.

► NEWNIR-L

Announcements of new Network Information Retrieval services and OPACs (On-line Public Access Catalogs) are made here and include WWW, Gopher or WAIS servers and CWISes. Another high-traffic list like Net-Happenings, but without the extra "information technology" postings. To subscribe: `listserv@itocsivm.bitnet` or `listserv%itocsivm.bitnet@icineca.cineca.it`.

► SIGLIST

The Dartmouth SIGLIST is a subject-organized list of both Internet and Bitnet discussion lists that is updated monthly. Various computer formats are available and most are searchable.

FTP: `dartcms1.dartmouth.edu` in directory SIGLISTS.

► New-List Mailing List

New-List is an announcement service for new mailing lists on the Internet and Bitnet. To subscribe: `listserv@ndsuvm1.nodak.edu`.

▶ *ASSESS List*

ASSESS—Assessment in Higher Education. Assessment methodology is not just relevant to higher education situations; it can also be transferred to other learning environments. Topics in the past have included teacher effectiveness, TQM (Total Quality Management), surveys, and portfolio assessment. Subscribe to: `listserv@ukcc.bitnet` or `listserv@ukcc.uky.edu`.

▶ *COM-PRIV*

A heavy-traffic list that discusses the commercialization/privatization of the Internet. This is a hot issue right now, with the big communications corporations wanting part of the pie and the "old culture" of the Internet wanting things to remain the same. A good place to find out who's doing what on which front. To subscribe, send e-mail to: `com-priv-request@psi.com`.

▶▶ *Newsgroups*

As discussed in Chapter 12, there are literally thousands of Usenet newsgroups. Here are a few of the most useful and interesting. (Thanks to Dave Taylor for the descriptions from his FAQ about social newsgroups.)

▶ *comp.infosystems.announce*

This is where new Internet services and tools are announced. Be sure to look later for corrections. Many service providers get excited and jump the gun, leaving out pertinent information.

▶ *comp.infosystems.gopher*

This newsgroup focuses mainly on the technology behind Gopher and announcements of new Gopher servers. However, there are better ways to find out about new Gopher servers if you aren't interested in the technological talk. (See GopherJewels and Net-Happenings under "Discussion Lists.")

General
Resources

▶▶

ch.
20

▶ *comp.infosystems.www.users*

This heavy-traffic group discusses ways to use the World Wide Web and new Web servers and services.

▶ *comp.society.privacy*

This group discusses privacy and networking subjects such as credit card information and bank accounts on the Internet, how to make an anonymous posting on the Internet, e-mail privacy cases, and phone taps.

▶ *soc.couples*

Being in a short- or long-term relationship offers much in the way of joy, pleasure, and emotional satisfaction, but it also offers the chance for major arguments and other problems. This is where you can talk about the relationship you're in with others who are also in relationships.

▶ *soc.feminism*

This is a moderated newsgroup for the discussion of feminist issues. Both men and women are encouraged to post to it, and discussion is not limited to the pro-feminist viewpoint. This group differs from soc.women (see below) in that moderation keeps out the flames and inappropriate cross-posts. In addition, there are subjects appropriate for soc.women but not soc.feminism (for example, the sporadic "where do I find comfortable shoes?" discussion that turns up in soc.women or discussions of women's health that aren't related to policy).

▶ *soc.men*

This group discusses similar issues to soc.women (see below), but from the male perspective. Topics include equal rights, child support, custody of children, relationships, and so on. In addition, there are often topics specific to men including shaving in the shower, post-workout skin care, and similar. Both men and women are active participants in this group. Figure 20.5 shows a sampling of recent topics.

FIGURE 20.5 ▶

*The newsgroup
soc.men.*

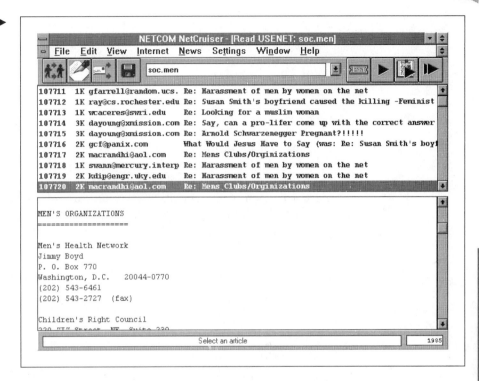

▶ soc.motss

While the Usenet community is pretty open-minded, many social
groups tend to be populated primarily by heterosexuals. Soc.motss
(Members of the Same Sex) is where people who are lesbian, gay, bisexual, or just interested and sympathetic can share conversation about
relationships, dating, travel, and the like. Discussion of the validity or
appropriateness of homosexuality is inappropriate, however, and will
not be appreciated.

▶ soc.singles

Of all the things that people seem to have in common, perhaps the
most common thread of all is the bouts of being single, and the hunt-
ing and searching for relationships that this implies. This group is a forum for all discussions even vaguely related to either being single or the
quest for a relationship. Indeed, it has been likened to an electronic

cocktail party, where people have known each other (electronically, usually) for years. There are also a number of people in relationships who share their thoughts, as well as a high level of aggression between some of the contributors.

▶ *soc.women*

Soc.women is an unmoderated group that discusses similar issues to soc.men, but from the female perspective. Topics include equal rights, child support, custody of children, relationships and so on. In addition, there are often topics specific to women including shaving legs, finding comfortable shoes, and so on. Both men and women are active participants in this group. Figure 20.6 shows a sampling of recent topics.

FIGURE 20.6 ▶

*The newsgroup
soc.women.*

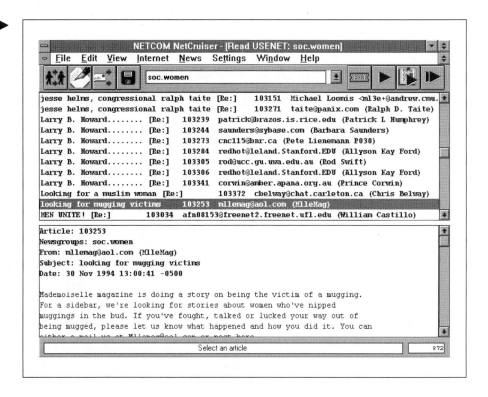

▶ *Support Groups*

In the `alt.support`, `misc.health`, and `alt.psychology` Usenet hierarchies, you'll find a variety of online support groups:

Depression and mood disorders:

`alt.support.depression`

Eating disorders (anorexia, bulimia, etc.):

`alt.support.eating-disord`

Learning disabilities (dyslexia, etc.):

`alt.support.learning-disab`

Stopping or quitting smoking:

`alt.support.stop-smoking`

Stuttering and other speaking difficulties:

`alt.support.stuttering`

Other support topics and questions:

`alt.support`

Diabetes, hypoglycemia:

`misc.health.diabetes`

General discussion of AIDS and HIV:

`misc.health.aids`

General help with psychological problems:

`alt.psychology.help`

▶▶ *Archives*

Archive is the general name given to any authoritative or at least well-maintained site that stores interesting articles, programs, or texts from newsgroups for long periods. Searching Internet archives can be as interesting as searching the archives at a major research library. These are sites you can "mine" for historical treasure—even though the history is relatively recent.

▶ CERT Security Archives

The Computer Emergency Response Team is the group responsible for tracking and fixing security problems on the Internet. When problems are reported to the group, it responds to the Internet community by issuing CERT Advisories that detail the problem and the solutions. Being able to access these advisories is important to any and all system administrators on the Internet.

> **Gopher:** `gopher.systems.cit.princeton.edu`; then choose Production ➤ workstations ➤ security ➤ cert from the menus.
>
> **FTP:** `cert.sei.cmu.edu`; then go to the pub/cert_advisories directory.

▶ Electronic Frontier Foundation

The Electronic Frontier Foundation (EFF) is an organization formed in 1990 to ensure that the First Amendment rights and the principles of the US Constitution are protected as we move into the new technologies. They also support people waging legal battles in this new area and offer materials to help support community building and equal access to electronic information. They maintain a large archive of documents related to legal cases in this area, news releases, articles of interest, recent and proposed legislation, materials for online activists, electronic publications, and information alerts. Figure 20.7 shows the EFF Web page.

> **Gopher:** `gopher.eff.org`
>
> **FTP:** `ftp.eff.org`
>
> **WWW:** `http://www.eff.org/`

▶ CICNet Journal Archive

The CIC universities (the Big Ten plus the University of Chicago and Notre Dame) oversee the CICNet Electronic Journal Archives, which contain back issues of all public-domain journals available on the Internet. CICNet is the regional education and research network in the

FIGURE 20.7

Web page for the Electronic Frontier Foundation.

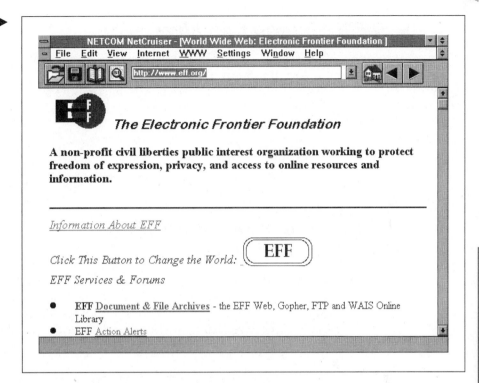

Great Lakes region of the United States. It is interesting among networks because it is an activity of the Committee on Institutional Cooperation (CIC), where the Universities have been working together for more than 30 years. In its About file, CIC notes that they focus on FTP site-available journals and are less aggressive about e-mail journals. The CICNet journal archive is an important resource as librarians and publishers struggle over the issue of maintaining records in an electronic environment. A Subject arrangement provides more access than the usual list of titles. Like the Research Libraries of its member institutions, CICNet and its Networked Information Resources Committee have developed collection policies for this archive.

Gopher: gopher.cic.net

WWW: www.cic.net

▶ *MERIT Internet Archives*

The MERIT Organization keeps archives for NSFnet (the US backbone to the Internet) statistics in its Gopher and FTP services. These statistics are especially useful for charting the growth of the backbone and of particular services on the backbone (for example, "last month WWW usage increased by 45%...").

> **Gopher:** `gopher.merit.edu`
>
> **FTP:** `nic.merit.edu`

▶ *MERIT/University of Michigan Software Archives*

A large body of public-domain, freeware, shareware and licensed software (the licensed software is *not* available by anonymous FTP) with Macintosh software by far the best represented. Atari, MS-DOS and Apple II files are also maintained to a lesser degree. This site is mirrored in many places around the world.

> **Gopher:** `gopher.archive.merit.edu` (Gopher access is lighter than FTP, so this may be your first choice).
>
> **FTP:** `mac.archive.umich.edu`; `msdos.archive.umich.edu`; `atari.archive.umich.edu`; and `apple2.archive.umich.edu`. Other US mirror sites: `wuarchive.wustl.edu` (mirrors); `grind.isca.uiowa.edu` (mac/umich); `archive.orst.edu` (pub/mirrors).

▶ *webNews*

With the overload of information about the exploding World Wide Web, this service is a welcome relief from searching through the `comp.infosystems.www` newsgroups, where the traffic can reach 300 messages per day. webNews is a Web- and Gopher-based archive of Usenet News articles that are about the World Wide Web. Announcements of new Web pages, software and other Web-related topics are covered here.

> **Gopher:** `twinbrook.cis.uab.edu`; then choose Internet Resource Discover ➤ webNews.

▶ *Archive Services*

Free archive space is available for those who wish to store electronic materials and have them available for anonymous FTP to anyone around the world. All types of materials are accepted, with the non-negotiable exception of pornographic images. Files are maintained in either plain ASCII text or PostScript and compressed with GNU Zip. All materials archived must be freely and legally available for distribution, and copyrighted materials must have permission from the copyright holder. Space is available as long as it lasts. Contact `ftp@etext.archive.umich.edu`.

▶ *Privacy Rights Clearinghouse*

A good collection of fact sheets, legislation, resources and press releases on issues relating to privacy. Some materials are available in both Spanish and English.

> **Gopher:** `gopher.acusd.edu`; then choose USD Campus-Wide Information System ➤ Privacy Rights Clearinghouse from the menus.

▶▶ *World Wide Web Pages*

Here are a few interesting starting points in the World Wide Web that we haven't mentioned elsewhere.

▶ *NCSA Mosaic Home Page*

The home of Mosaic, the University of Illinois at Champaign-Urbana's Supercomputing Center is "the" place to get information about the Mosaic client for the World Wide Web. Mosaic is only one of a handful of WWW clients and browsers, but it has made the greatest impact on the use of the Web. Their home page includes a Mosaic demo, What's New on the Web, Web security information, e-mail addresses for help with Mosaic, and connections to FTP sites for the various Mosaic clients available.

General Resources

ch.
20

WWW: `http://www.ncsa.uiuc.edu/SDG/Software/Mosaic/NCSA-MosaicHome.html`

▶ World Wide Web of Sports

"Spanning the globe to bring you a constant variety of sports information." This is a wonderful example of creative use of the Web. It has included video highlights of World Cup soccer (with only a one day lag time), schedules, video highlights from the previous day's major league baseball games, the Olympics, professional sports in the US and less media-covered sports such as rowing, speed skating, and rugby. You can customize this service for your own sports interests. A Best of the Web '94 winner.

WWW: `http://www.lcs.mit.edu/cgi-bin/sports/`

▶ Vatican Exhibit

The Vatican Exhibit offers a well-organized tour of the Vatican Library and some of its treasures in a mix of images and hypertext. Manuscripts and music can be enlarged into full-size images and even downloaded. Cited here mainly for its interesting use of mixed-media, this is definitely a spot to visit when taking a tour of the World Wide Web with a client such as Mosaic or Cello. It's not as interesting though, if you are limited to a VT100 or terminal browser.

WWW: `http://www.ncsa.uiuc.edu/SDG/Experimental/vatican.exhibit/Main_Hall.html`

▶ Internet Resources Meta-Index

A hypertext bibliography of tools for finding information on the Internet, such as the World Wide Web Worm, The Clearinghouse for Subject-Oriented Internet Resource Guides, The NCSA Mosaic What's New page, the Central Index of WWW servers at CERN and more. A good starting place for new Web users.

WWW: `http://www.ncsa.uiuc.edu/SDG/Software/Mosaic/MetaIndex.html`

▶ *CyberZine*

CyberZine describes itself as a paper version of the "Yellow Pages or TV Guide, a user-friendly guide to Cyberspace...." Besides supplying the subscriber with information about the Net, Sparky (the name of the company behind CyberZine) can provide you with a home page starting at $10.00 or a smaller advertisement for your service or business. How-to, Internet tools, electronic texts, home improvement, sports, travel, recreation, and AIDS are just some of the areas they cover. For $3 US or $5 overseas, CyberZine will be delivered to your postal address four times a year. Contact cyberzine@cyberzine.org or visit their WWW home page at http://cyberzine.org/.

▶ *Xerox Map Viewer*

The Xerox Palo Alto Research Center (PARC) is providing the PARC Web Map Viewer as an experiment in dynamic information retrieval. Maps of the world and the United States can be requested using a WWW client such as Mosaic. Embedded hypertext links allow you to pan, zoom or change the level of detail. Map data (all of which is public domain) is from the CIA World Data Bank II with higher-resolution US data provided by the USGS 1:2,000,000-Scale Digital Line Graph Data. Though not as sophisticated as using some of the commercially available Graphical Imaging System (GIS) software, this is an important move toward easy-to-use GIS on the Internet. A Best of the Web '94 winner for both Technical Merit and Best Use of Interaction. Figure 20.8 shows the opening Web page, and Figure 20.9 shows the view after clicking on a point in northern California.

WWW: http://pubweb.parc.xerox.com/map/

▶ *World Wide Web Worm*

What Archie and Veronica are respectively to FTP and Gopher, the WWWW is to the Web. The Worm will accept keyword searches and compare your search term to its index built by its "wander" through the Web, then return the results to you in hypertext form. Expect slowdowns since this is a very heavily used resource and one of only a handful like it. There has been a significant lag time from when the Worm was last run through the Web, though the opening page will tell you

FIGURE 20.8

The Globe via the PARC Web map viewer.

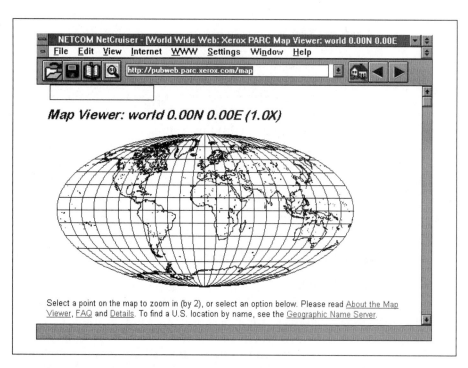

FIGURE 20.9 ►

Zooming in on northern California via the PARC Web map viewer.

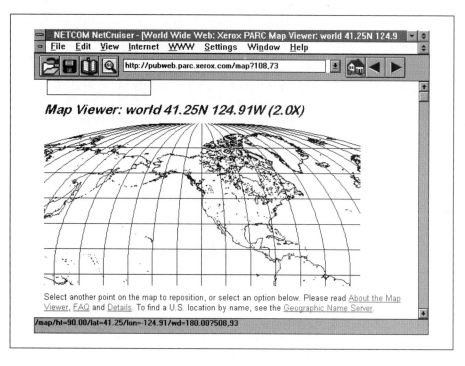

how recently that occurred. Note: WWWW searches require a browser that supports forms.

WWW: http://www.cs.colorado.edu/home/mcbryan/wwww.html

Another wonderful index can be found at

WWW: http://cui-www.unige.ch/W3catalog

▶ *Internet Shopping Network*

Better than the Home Shopping Channel on TV! The Internet Shopping Network (Figure 20.10) lets you choose from over 15,000 products and 800 vendors in full-graphic mode or text-only ("97% fat free"!). Power shopping lets you specify what you're looking for and in what price range. Membership fees allow you access to the full text of InfoWorld Magazine and some other perks.

WWW: http://shop.internet.net

FIGURE 20.10 ▶

Entry into the Internet Shopping Network.

▶ The Internet Shopping Mall

Also known as Dave Taylor's List of Commercial Internet Services. The author is the same Dave Taylor who wrote Elm and RAYS and *Teach Yourself Unix in a Week*. There are many ways to retrieve this list:

FTP: `ftp.netcom.com` in the `/pub/Gu/Guides` directory.

Gopher: `peg.cwis.uci.edu: 7000`; then choose The World ➤ Internet Assistance ➤ Internet Shopping Mall from the menus.

E-Mail Address: `taylor@netcom.com` (subject **send mall**).

▶ Shopping 2000

Many new virtual shopping malls being added to the World Wide Web; this one is notable because it has almost exact counterparts in your postal mail. This is a large collection of products and services offered from a single entry point. Here you will find mountain climbing equipment and sleeping bags, coffee, flowers, and records and CDs.

WWW: `http://www.shopping.com`

▶ Worldwide Classifieds

A part of the Internet Ad Emporium where individuals or organizations can place or read advertisements.

WWW: `http://mmink.cts.com/mmink/classifieds`

▶ The Vermont Teddy Bear Company

Yes, you can purchase teddy bears on the Web and do some window shopping!

WWW: `http://www.service.digital.com/tdb/vtdbear.html`

▶ DeLorme Mapping

CD-ROMs Street Atlas USA and Global Explorer are two popular mapping products from DeLorme. DeLorme offers test drives of some of their products at this Web server site. People who travel frequently and many companies and libraries use DeLorme's products.

> **WWW:** `http://www.delorme.com/`

▶▶ *Professional or Special Interest Groups (SIGs)*

Special Interest Groups and societies have long been a way to meet other people with similar interests and share resources. Here's a short list of those that might interest you in seeking more that you can contribute to as well as gain from your time on the Internet.

▶ *Internet Society (ISOC)*

The Internet Society is an international organization that seeks to facilitate the collaborative means by which the Internet is run. Thousands of organizations are part of the Internet, and those organizations are eligible to participate through an institutional membership. Individuals may also be members. A journal, an annual meeting, workshops, and symposia are sponsored by this group. In addition to the Web page shown in Figure 20.11:

> **WWW:** `fttp://www.isoc.org`

they also maintain an archive of materials relating to the Internet:

> **Gopher:** `ietf.cnri.reston.va.us`

Further information may be obtained by sending an e-mail request to `isoc@cnri.reston.va.us`. For membership information contact:

The Internet Society
1895 Preston White Drive, Suite 100
Reston, VA 22091

FIGURE 20.11 ►

The Internet Society Web page.

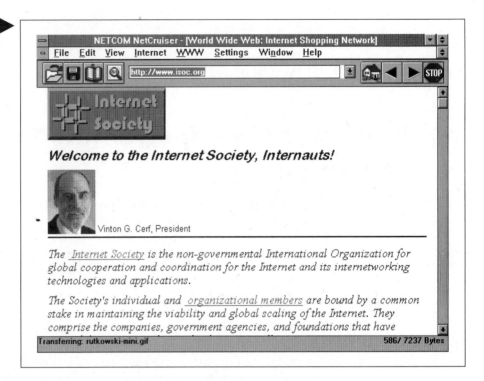

► Americans Communicating Electronically (ACE)

Membership of ACE is very broad and includes individuals and private and government organizations wishing to promote interaction between any and all information providing bodies. For information on how to join send an e-mail message to: info@ace.esusda.gov. To subscribe to the ACE almanac information service: almanac@ace.esusda.gov.

Gopher: ace.esusda.gov

► Electronic Frontier Foundation

Besides maintaining the vast archive of materials related to computing and civil liberties issues discussed earlier, the EFF allows individuals to join. For information contact: info@eff.org.

▶▶ *Other Goodies*

Finally, here are a few interesting items that didn't fit well into other categories. We hope you'll enjoy them.

▶ *Pizza on the Internet*

Only in California... can you order your pizza via the Internet. Pizza Hut has debuted PizzaNet, a way for hungry cybernauts to get their nutrition with one hand while surfing with the other! You need to be in the Santa Cruz area and have a WWW client to place an order.

WWW: `http://pizzahut.com`

We wonder if it gets cold over the Internet...

▶ *WWW Virtual Library*

A hypertext document links you to Internet collections of resources on various topics in WWW, Gopher and FTP. The list is not comprehensive, and is organized (we think) by keyword as opposed to a classification scheme of some type. Consider this a good place to start a research project. Alphabetical by keyword.

WWW: `http://info.cern.ch/hypertext/DataSources/bySubject/Overview.html`

▶ *Clearinghouse of Subject-Oriented Internet Guides*

The University of Michigan Library and the School of Information and Library Studies began the clearinghouse as a joint project to help make librarians and students more aware of the wealth of Internet resources for reference and collection development work. It now houses bibliographies of Internet sources from people all over the world and serves as the major site for Internet subject bibliographies. More are added regularly and most are updated by their authors at least annually.

> **Gopher:** gopher.lib.umich.edu; then choose What's New &
> Featured Resources ➤ Clearinghouse from the menus.
>
> **FTP:** una.hh.lib.umich.edu

▶ Pete's FTP List

Pete Russo's list of anonymous FTP sites on the Internet available as
an electronic list. To subscribe: ftp.list@launchpad.unc.edu (put
subscribe in the subject line).

▶ ARL Directory of Electronic Journals and Newsletters on the Internet

The fourth edition of a printed work begun by Michael Strangelove
and now produced by the Association of Research Libraries. For each
journal or newsletter you'll find a description of the item and subscription information.

> **Gopher:** arl.cni.org

▶ Direct from Pueblo

The US Consumer Information Center (you know, the one in Pueblo,
Colorado) is now online. Warning: this is a very congested service, and
it may not be up reliably on weekends.

> **BBS:** 202-208-7679
>
> **WWW:** http://www.gsa.gov
>
> **Gopher:** www.gsa.gov; then choose Gopher ➤ staff ➤ pa ➤ cic
> from the menus.

▶ Golfer's Paradise

The 19th Hole (a.k.a. "the Clubhouse") now offers the Rules of Golf
Online, which answers all of your questions about the rules; it also lets
you settle your score and tell a few tall tales in the Clubhouse after a
hard 18. The 19th Hole is a place for golfers to relax, share some stories and maybe even settle a bet or two (not that golfers bet!). Included

is Headlines! with info on the latest scores, tournaments, and local happenings. The 1994 Golf Digest Record Book is the place to find out how your favorite golfer did in 1993 or who won the British Open in 1863.

WWW: `http://dallas.nmhu.edu/golf/golf.htm`

▶ Comprehensive Disability Resource List

There is a short but comprehensive list of Internet resources on disabilities available from the Do-It program. For a copy FTP it from `hawking.u.washington.edu` or if you'd like a copy by e-mail, contact Dean Martineau: `deamar@u.washington.edu`.

## CHAPTER 21

Government and Business Resources

► ► ***T**his* listing of resources that are especially interesting for businesses is not exhaustive, but it does detail some of the best available. For each resource there is a description and an address where you can find it, whether by Gopher, the Web, or by using Telnet to connect to the service.

Many of the general resources listed in Chapter 20 are also pertinent to businesses.

► ► *General Resources*

Because the interests of business people are as far-ranging as the myriad businesses that can exist, this list of general resources is pretty far-ranging, too. We have included mostly United States government sources, because we do live in the United States. The US government, however, is by no means the only government providing information via the Internet, so we've included some pointers to government information outside the US. And no list of government resources would be complete without a note that you can send e-mail to the president and vice president of the United States quite simply. Their addresses are `president@whitehouse.gov` and `vice.president@whitehouse.gov`. Bob Rae, the premier of Ontario province in Canada, can also be reached via e-mail. His address is `premier@gov.on.ca`.

► *EDGAR Dissemination Project*

The EDGAR dissemination project makes available 1994 corporate filings with the US Securities and Exchange Commission. Indexes are listed by company name and are updated daily. Users should note that not all corporations' files are public. Moreover, this is an experimental service; and they change the formats without notice while they are trying to find the best way to present this data. This service is of particular interest to businesses and investors who used to pay big bucks to a big corporation to get copies of these reports.

Gopher: gopher.town.hall.org

FTP: FTP.town.hall.org

WWW: http://www.town.hall.org

The EDGAR project was an early success story of Ralph Nader's Taxpayer Asset Project (TAP). Jamie Love with TAP is an active advocate of each and every citizen having reasonable access to the information gathered in the name of the citizenry. You can find out more about the project at

WWW: http://cpsr.org/pub/taxpayer_assets

▶ *The White House*

The Executive Branch of the United States government now has an Internet entry point beginning at the White House. Figure 21.1 shows the picture index that you will see with a graphical Web browser. From here you can take a virtual tour of Washington, DC, see pictures of the "First Family," and move to other sources of federal information. Clicking on the portion of the picture (or choosing from the textual index) "the Executive Branch" will present you with choices for "the President's Cabinet" (Figure 21.2) and "the Independent Federal Agencies and Commissions" (Figure 21.3).

This entry point provides "one-stop" shopping for information from the top down. If you have trouble remembering which particular agency goes with which cabinet department, there is an index to federal sources of information that is available on the "Executive Branch" Web page. Or, from that same page, if you remember where the office is geographically, you can use a map of Washington, DC, to locate your information source.

WWW: http://www.whitehouse.gov

FIGURE 21.1 ▶

The Web page for the White House.

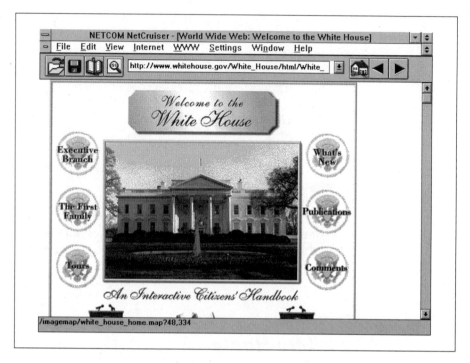

FIGURE 21.2 ▶

The Web page for the President's Cabinet.

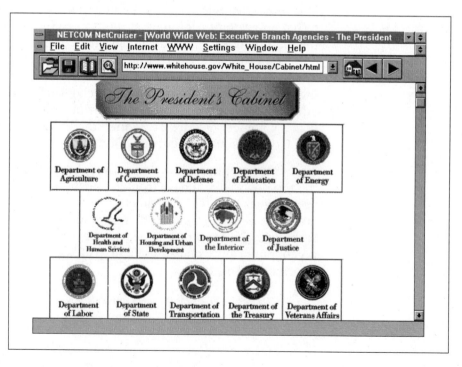

FIGURE 21.3 ▶

The Web page for Independent Federal Agencies and Commissions.

▶ *STAT-USA*

The Department of Commerce includes among its information providers the Economics and Statistics Administration. This service provides economic, business, and social/environmental information from more than fifty federal sources. This service was built around the popular National Trade Data Bank (NTDB). STAT-USA provides data using the Web, Gopher, and FTP. The access is free for most data. Some cost recovery fees are charged for more recent data being served by the Web. The STAT-USA FTP site shown in Figure 21.4 contains data for which there are no access charges.

Gopher: gopher.stat-usa.gov

FTP: ftp.stat-usa.gov

WWW: http://www.stat-usa.gov

Government and Business Resources

▶ ▶

ch.
21

FIGURE 21.4 ▶

The STAT-USA FTP Site.

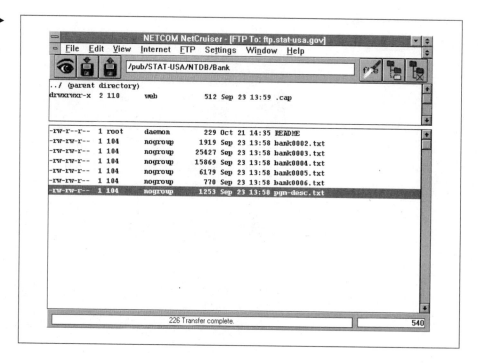

▶ SBA Online

The Small Business Administration provides another extremely useful federal information site. From their Web pages you can find information about, for example, financing businesses and about export arrangements. Figure 21.5 shows the graphical entry point to this information.

WWW: http://www.sbaonline.sba.gov

▶ Canadian Federal Government Open Government Pilot

The federal government of Canada is also sponsoring a project to make its information more widely available via the Internet. Because of the long distances and sparse population of Canada, they've chosen to distribute their information across the country by keeping copies of the information at "mirror sites." This allows Canadians (and other interested people, too, of course) reasonable access to the sites. Figure 21.6 shows a section of the entry Web page, with the bilingual entry points

FIGURE 21.5

The Web page for the Small Business Administration.

FIGURE 21.6

The Web page for Canada's Open Government Pilot.

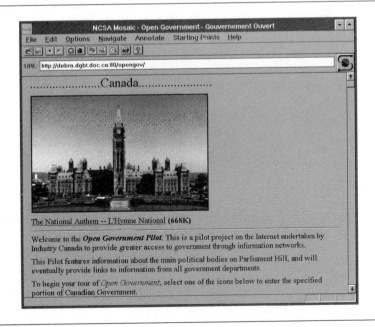

to the House of Commons and the Canadian Senate. From this page you can also find entries for the federal departments and agencies.

WWW: http://debra.dgbt.doc.ca/opengov

► *Her Majesty's Information*

It's not just North American countries that are making their national information available. Figure 21.7 shows an entry point for the United Kingdom. These pages are being developed by the Government Centre for Information Systems. It's the CCTA Government Information Service. They are responsible for stimulating and promoting effective use of Information Systems in support of efficient delivery of business objectives and improved quality of services by the public sector.

WWW: http://www.open.gov.uk/cctagis/central.htm

FIGURE 21.7 ►

The Web page for the UK's Government Centre for Information Systems.

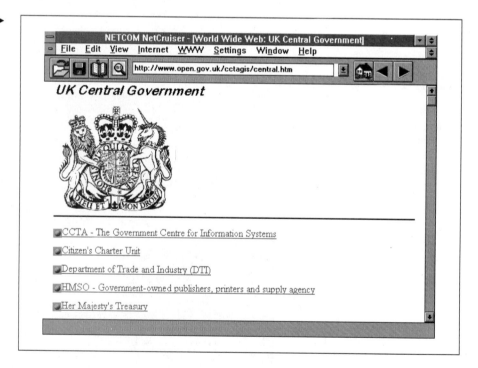

▶ *South Dakota*

Government information on the Internet isn't limited to that from national governments. South Dakota provides an entry point (shown in Figure 21.8) with its most famous landmark, Mount Rushmore, featured prominently. Click around the mountain for information about tourist locations, business opportunities, and education located within the boundaries of this Plains State.

WWW: http://www.state.sd.us

FIGURE 21.8 ▶

The Web page for the State of South Dakota.

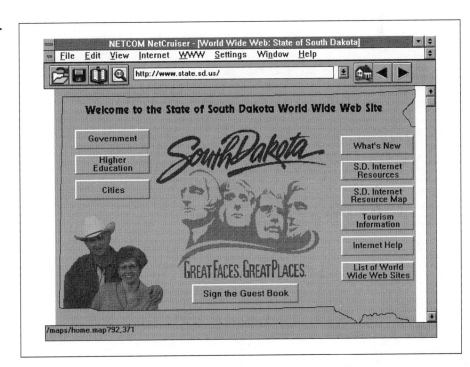

▶ *Fedworld*

Fedworld is a bulletin board system from the National Technical Information Service. Some of the $70 billion in scientific and technical research is represented here in the form of downloadable files or publications one can purchase from NTIS. Almost every scientific field you can think of has a research report here. The NTIS publications catalog can be downloaded here also, and online ordering is available.

Fedworld also offers a gateway to other federal services such as federal job openings.

Telnet: `fedworld.gov`

Log in as `new` if you haven't used the system before.

▶ *FEDIX and MOLIS*

The Federal Information Exchange provides online information on agency grants, scholarships, procurement notices and minority opportunities from the US federal government. MOLIS, which is a part of FEDIX, gives information about historically black colleges and universities and Hispanic-serving institutions and universities, including research centers, scholarships and fellowships, statistics, faculty profiles, and enrollment figures.

Telnet: `fedix.fie.com`

Gopher: `gopher.fie.com`

URL: `http://web.fie.com/`

▶ *US Department of Agriculture*

Export statistics and research reports on agricultural products, situation and outlook reports, and other information about agriculture in the United States is made available full-text from the USDA. Of particular importance to exporters and agribusiness:

Gopher: `gopher.esusda.gov`

▶ *Commerce Business Daily*

The US Department of Commerce's Commerce Business Daily is available on the Internet full-text (for a fee), and the government bids notices are provided here free. For a fee, CNS On-Line Systems and Softshare Government Information Systems will set up a company profile and automatically mail out articles that meet the profile. The CBD is updated every business day and offers keyword searching of the text.

For the free bids articles:

> **Gopher:** gopher.cscns.com

For more information about setting up a company profile:

> **E-Mail:** info@cscns.com

▶ *Economic Bulletin Board*

The US Department of Commerce's Bulletin Board comes in two versions on the Internet. The data provided by the Department of Commerce is from the horse's mouth, but the offerings are rather limited. The University of Michigan Library's Documents Center downloads all of the files from the EBB daily and makes it available on their Gopher. The EBB provides an incredible amount of data on economic indicators, business statistics, employment, industry statistics, and summary text files for the economic indicators. Also a good source for currency exchange information. Many of the files are in compressed format, and all but the text files are tabular. The help files are very well written and definitely needed for this source. You have to visit to see what's actually there because there's too much to list.

> **Gopher:** gopher.lib.umich.edu
>
> **FTP:** una.hh.lib.umich.edu (/bin)

▶ *EconData*

A huge number of economic time series—over two hundred thousand—are mounted by the University of Maryland and updated from the Economic Bulletin Board three to four days after they're released. You need to use the help files before downloading because the procedure gets complicated.

> **Gopher:** info.umd.edu
>
> **FTP:** info.umd.edu; then choose Educational_Resources ▶ Economic Data from the menus.

▶ *Economic Development Information Network*

An interactive service from the Pennsylvania State Data Center that allows the user to retrieve data for any state about business, capital resources, government, income, labor force, economic development, agriculture, and international trade. A nice feature is the Economic Development Directory, which allows the user to construct a search for an agency or organization.

> **Telnet:** psuvm.psu.edu, port 23 (this is a tn3270 site)
>
> **Gopher:** psuvm.psu.edu

▶ *Community Idea Net*

A Gopher resource from Sunsite at the University of North Carolina that "disseminates ideas about making governments more effective." Descriptions of projects, contact persons, and information on teenagers, insect pests, highways, budgets, immigrants, farming, graffiti and more.

> **Gopher:** calypso-2.oit.unc.edu; then choose Sunsite by Subject ➤ US and World Politics ➤ Community Idea Net from the menus.

▶ *Catalog of Federal Domestic Assistance*

Each year the federal government of the US issues a new edition of this guide to grants and monies available to states, groups, and individuals from most government agencies and projects. From food stamps to information technology to building projects, this searchable version of the CFDA is an important contribution to the Internet.

> **Gopher:** peg.cwis.uci.edu; then choose Politics & Government ➤ Catalog of Federal Domestic Assistance from the menus.

▶▶ *E-Mail Special Interest Lists*

Sometimes, rather than seeking information via your own actions, you'd like some person or organization to let you know when they are doing something you might find interesting. Special-purpose mailing lists serve that purpose. If you subscribe to one of these listed here, you'll receive messages in your e-mail. When you read them, you can forward them to other people (respecting the intellectual property rights of others, of course), save them for future reference, reply solely to the author, or take part in a list-wide discussion of the matter at hand by replying to the list. Mailing lists are a good way to discuss ideas with other people who have similar interests.

▶ *St. Petersburg Business News*

Not St. Petersburg, Florida, but Russia. Twice per week in English or daily in Russian, you can receive a digest of business news taken from St. Petersburg and Russian newspapers, television and radio, the mayor's office and other sources. Subscribers can also order information from the Mayor's office about laws, regulations and decrees and consultations with the staff of the St. Petersburg Business Agency on topics ranging from foreign investment to technology transfer. Economic outlooks, summaries and commentaries will also be distributed on an irregular basis. You can choose to receive the news via e-mail or fax. Subscription information is complicated by the language and delivery system choices, so it's best to check with the publisher by (traditional) mail:

> PAS Systems
> 1832 Bathhurst Street
> Toronto, Ontario, Canada M2P 3K7

▶ *The Internet Business Journal*

This e-mail journal is published monthly by Strangelove Press. Some of the material in the journal is available via Gopher, but the rest is strictly for subscribers only. Past issues have included a list of Internet consultants and trainers, software reviews, and services to networked businesses. For information about *The Internet Business Journal* contact the following:

> **Voice phone:** 613-565-0982
>
> **Fax:** 613-569-4433
>
> **Gopher:** `fonorola.net`
>
> **E-mail:** John Curtin (Subscription Manager) at `at380@freenet.carleton.ca`

▶▶ *Newsgroups*

Here are some of the more useful Usenet newsgroups for business users. In addition, you may want to subscribe to a service that includes the ClariNet news service, which has extensive business feeds.

ClariNet is a specific, commercial service that provides "real" news through the avenue of Usenet news feeds. Some Internet Service providers, like Netcom, for example, have arrangements with ClariNet to "feed" the ClariNet news to their subscribers. An easy way to find out if your provider does this is to look in your provider's list of active newsgroups for any group that begins with the letters "clari." Information about ClariNet itself is available via the Web.

> **WWW:** `http://www.clarinet.com`

▶ *alt.business*

This is one of the sections for business in Usenet, but generally it contains advertisements.

▶ *biz.books.technical*

This newsgroup announces new books that may be useful to business computer users.

▶ *biz.comp.services*

This newsgroup announces and discusses Internet services available to commercial businesses.

▶ *biz.software*

This newsgroup has lots of advertisements for business software but also is a place to ask about software before you invest.

▶ *biz.comp.hardware*

Mostly ads but some discussion of computer hardware suitable for business use.

▶ *biz.comp.services*

Advertisements for computer services of use to businesses.

▶ *biz.comp.software*

Sporadic questions surrounded mostly by advertisements for business software.

▶ *biz.general*

Anything goes on this business-oriented newsgroup as a topic of conversation or solicitation.

▶ *biz.job.offered*

Not comprehensive, but still a source worth checking out for computing jobs.

▶ *biz.misc*

Takes up where `biz.general` leaves off.

▶▶ *Professional or Special Interest Groups (SIGs)*

Among the many groups and organizations presenting information or a "presence" on the Internet are those organized around a specific theme. We've included some that you might be interested in here. Also, there are contact points for some organizations that aren't on the Internet but in which you may be interested anyway.

▶ *Center for Civic Networking*

CCN/CIVICNET is an organization devoted to helping shape policies for the emerging national information infrastructure and a national vision to include civic networking. For information contact:

E-Mail: Miles Fidelman (mfidelman@world.std.com)

The Center provides a Web page at:

WWW: http://www.civic.net:2401

▶ *Data Processing Management Association*

Founded in 1951 as the National Machine Accountants Association, this 24,000 member organization includes educators, managerial personnel, staff and individuals associated with the management of information resources. An online network, professional certifications and courses, research projects and on-site managerial seminars are available to members. Publications include a monthly newspaper called Inside DPMA. They also hold an annual International Computer Conference and Business Exposition. For membership information contact:

Suzanne Lattimore
505 Busse Hwy.
Park Ridge, IL 60068
Phone: 708-825-8124

▶ *International Association for Computer Information Systems*

The membership of IACIS consists of individuals and organizations of educators and computer professionals at all levels of educational institutions. Publications include a quarterly *Journal of Computer Information Systems* and a periodic newsletter. For membership information contact:

Dr. Susan Haugen
Dept. of Accountancy
University of Wisconsin—Eau Claire
Eau Claire, WI 54702
Phone: 715-836-2952

▶▶ *World Wide Web Pages*

Finally, we list some interesting starting points for you that haven't been mentioned elsewhere. These pages will connect you to even more interesting sites. Remember that the best place to get information about what's on the Web is the Web itself. So from pages like these, and others you may find that reflect your own interests, you can discover even more interesting information.

▶ *Commercial Use (of the Net) Strategies Home Page*

A copyrighted article by Andrew Dinsdale that provides information and advice for companies looking to use the Internet as an information, telecommunications, or marketing network. Topics covered include how to get connected, security concerns, impact on employees, government action on the national information infrastructure, and other issues of concern to businesses. Obviously of great use to businesses both large and small.

WWW: `http://pass.wayne.edu/business.html`

▶ *Direct Marketing World*

Mainsail Marketing Information, Inc. has made available this electronic directory of the direct marketing industry. They include industry professionals, mailing lists, information about direct marketing, jobs wanted, and jobs offered.

WWW: http://mainsail.com

▶ *The Company Corporation*

The Company Corporation is the largest on-line incorporation service in the world. Especially useful to small businesses thinking of incorporating.

WWW: http://incorporate.com/tcc/home.html

▶ *INFORUM*

The Center for Global Communications, a research institute at the University of Japan, has gathered together information from varying sources about Japan and mounted it on this WWW server. Their primary aim is to lessen the friction between Japan and its trading partners and offer more timely information from literature that is often difficult to locate outside Japan. This is an important resource for people doing business with Japan or seeking information about Japan.

WWW: http://www.glocom.ac.jp: 80/Inforum/

These Web pages are presented in either Japanese or English.

## CHAPTER 22

Resources for K–12 Education Information Providers

▶▶ **I**n this list we present some of the more helpful aids to kindergarten through 12th grade educators—and education—that are available on the Internet. As with all the lists presented in this book (because of the ever-changing nature of the Internet itself—so many new sites are coming on each week), the list can't be complete. When we started compiling this list, for example, we only knew about the Net presence of one of the United States Regional Educational Laboratories. Now several of them can be represented here. The Internet can provide access to resources that might not otherwise be readily accessible to you.

▶▶ General Internet Resources

Here are some general resources that are designed to provide curriculum assistance to teachers. Emphasis is placed on information about programs themselves and the hints and advice the researchers in the field have gathered.

▶ K–12 Library of Resources

Internet education resources are arranged in a meaningful manner for educators in this Gopher. Although most are accessible from other sites, this site from the New York State Education Department is by far one of the best collections of K–12 resources.

Gopher: `unix5.nysed.gov`

Figure 22.1 shows the top-level menu of this valuable Gopher.

FIGURE 22.1 ▶

The main menu of the New York State Education Department Gopher.

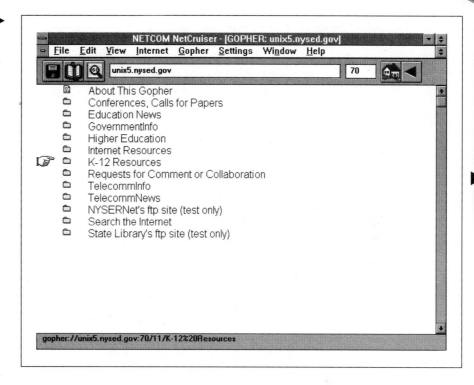

▶ *National Distance Learning Center (NDLC)*

The NDLC Gopher provides resources for both program providers and users of distance learning. Primary, secondary, adult and higher education are supported. The database is searchable by keyword.

Gopher: gopher.occ.uky.edu

Telnet: ndlc.occ.uky.edu

▶ *Centre for Women's Studies in Education*

This facility at the Ontario Institute for Studies in Education (OISE) provides descriptions of their projects, a gateway to other women's resources on the Internet, and a list of degrees and programs in women's studies.

Gopher: porpoise.oise.on.ca

▶ *National Center on Adult Literacy/Litnet*

This is the major center for information on literacy at the US and international levels. Research, the development of programs, curricula, and the use of new technologies are all areas that receive a good deal of attention. If you have a need in the area of literacy, the answer is likely to be here.

Gopher: muspin.gsfc.nasa.gov

▶ *National Consortium for Environmental Education and Training (NCEET)*

NCEET describes itself as a clearinghouse for environmental education (EE) information and aims its services at K–12 educators including teachers, curriculum planners, and information specialists. To reach this audience, it produces and gathers EE information in all formats and offers access to electronic resources through a Gopher, EE-Link, as well as a Web page.

WWW: http://www.nceet.snre.umich.edu

Figure 22.2 shows the Web page.

▶ *EE-Link*

The Environmental Education Gopher offers original materials for use in environmental education, a source for Internet resources, and full-text of print or other media materials (with permission) not accessible on the Internet. Classroom resources, grant information, literature, and a great deal more are gathered here in one place. This is definitely a first stop for anyone involved in environmental education.

Gopher: nceet.snre.umich.edu

▶ *Research for Better Schools*

Many programs, papers and resources for the improvement of both elementary and secondary schools are available here. There is also a nice

FIGURE 22.2 ▶

The National Consortium for Environmental Training and Education Web page.

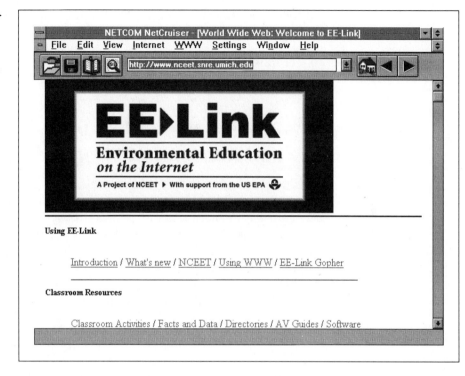

list of upcoming events for educators in K–12.

Gopher: gopher.rbs.org

▶ *United States Department of Education (USDE)*

This is a gold mine of information for educators, ranging from software programs to statistics, to research and school improvement programs. There are resources for all areas of education. The USDE provides connections to all of the ERIC Clearinghouses and has a Web site that includes a teacher's guide to the Department, a researcher's guide to the Department, and a valuable list of pointers to other educational sites on the Web. The full text of the 1994 edition of *Educational Programs That Work,* the National Diffusion Network's directory of programs and facilitators, is available through the US Department of Education's Gopher server.

Gopher: `gopher.ed.gov`

WWW: `http://www.ed.gov`

▶ *Clearinghouse for Networked Information Discovery and Retrieval (CNIDR)*

CNIDR is a cooperative effort between the National Science Foundation (NSF) and MCNC, Information Technologies Division. These folks gather information about network retrieval tools, and they share those tools and the technology widely. Part of their efforts include the continuing support of FreeWAIS, the public domain version of the WAIS software, and the Global Schoolhouse project. You'll find their list of educational Web sites on many Web pages dedicated to education. You can find out more about all their efforts on the Web itself:

WWW: `http://kudzu.cnidr.org`

▶ *Indiana Department of Education*

Along with information about the state's Department of Education, Indiana also offers a Professional Education Employee Referral Service (PEER). Job openings in Indiana, DOE openings, sample resumes, and resumes from licensed education professionals make this a nice one-stop-shopping resource for the state; it will also be useful to educators outside Indiana.

Gopher: `ideanet.doe.state.in.us`

Figure 22.3 shows the top of the CNIDR home page. Take the jump labeled "CNIDR Projects" to find out about specific projects like the Global Schoolhouse.

▶ *Michigan Department of Education*

The state of Michigan compiles statistics on every school in the state, including teacher/student ratio, teacher salaries, enrollment figures,

FIGURE 22.3 ▶

The beginning of the Clearinghouse for Networked Information Discovery and Retrieval home page.

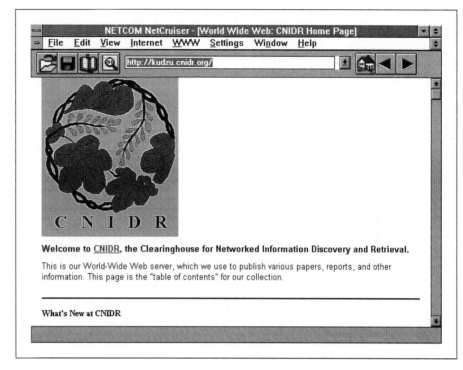

and scores on standardized tests. This resource also provides information about state grants to schools, school districts and teachers, and about classroom resources and educational technology.

    Gopher: `gopher.mde.stat.mi.us`

▶ *University of Minnesota's Web66 Project*

Here's how the Web66 project at the University of Minnesota describes itself in its home page:

"Just as US Highway Route 66 was a catalyst for Americana, we see the World Wide Web as a catalyst that will integrate the Internet into K–12 school curriculums. The University of Minnesota is beginning project Web66 to facilitate the introduction of this technology into K12 schools. The goals of this project are:

1. To help K–12 educators learn how to set up their own Internet servers.

2. To link K–12 WWW servers and the educators and students at those schools.

3. To help K–12 educators find and use K–12 appropriate resources on the World Wide Web."

WWW: http://web66.coled.umn.edu

▶ Missouri Department of Elementary and Secondary Education

This department of the State of Missouri is constructing an education support tool for Missouri students, teachers, parents, administrators, and others interested in improving educational effectiveness. This resource contains Missouri school laws and legislation, school rules and regulations, and facts about the public schools in Missouri.

Gopher: services.dese.state.mo.us

A similar effort for higher education in Missouri can be found at

Gopher: dp.mocbhe.gov

▶ Society for Technology and Teacher Education (STATE)

The Society for Technology And Teacher Education, the University of Virginia, and the University of Houston have established this site to explore ways in which the Internet could provide benefits to teacher education programs around the world.

WWW: http://curry.edschool.virginia.edu/teis/

Gopher: teach.virginia.edu

Figure 22.4 shows the Web page for the Teacher Education Internet Server (TEIS).

FIGURE 22.4

The Teacher Education Internet Server (TEIS) Web page.

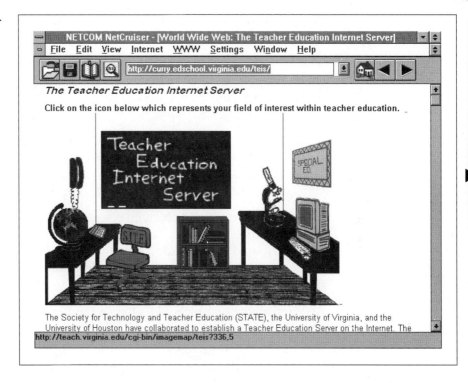

▶ *Texas Education Network (TENET)*

TENET Web's purpose is to enable educators and students to move information across the barriers of time and space and to explore an evolving technology that is breaking down the isolation of the classroom.

WWW: http://www.tenet.edu

▶ *North Dakota's SENDIT Project*

In North Dakota, K–12 educators and students have plugged into computer BBS-type networking that also gives them access to the Internet, thanks to SENDIT, a telecommunications network connected to the Internet via the North Dakota Higher Education Computer TCP/IP Network.

Developed by the North Dakota State University School of Education and Computer Center for use by school districts across the state of

North Dakota, SENDIT is funded by the Educational Telecommunications Council (ETC).

Through SENDIT, North Dakota students and teachers can exchange, share, search, and retrieve information. Currently, dial-up access can be from terminals or personal computers such as Apple IIe, IIGs, Mac, or PC, and a modem.

SENDIT offers access to over 70 forums that focus on specific topics of interest to its members. They include topics for both teachers and students such as: Junior Chat, Senior Chat, English, Mathematics, Educational Technology, TAG-L, EduTech, Kidsnet, and more.

SENDIT also offers K12Net, an educational BBS network consisting of more than 300 bulletin boards located in schools around the globe, and distributed via the FidoNet network. K12Net offers chat areas, curriculum areas, classroom project areas, and foreign language areas, to name but a few.

Another service that SENDIT offers is the Electronic Classroom, where SENDIT users have access to CNN Newsroom guide, Newsweek guide/quiz, discussion groups, historical documents, and the like.

For more information about SENDIT, contact Gleason Sackman:

> **E-mail Address:** sackman@sendit.nodak.edu

To try it yourself:

> **Telnet:** sendit.nodak.edu (134.129.105.1).

After you have connected, press Return until you see the prompt. Then log in as bbs and give the password sendit2me—this will give you a chance to "visit" parts of SENDIT or become a registered user.

▶ Gleason Sackmann's HotList of K–12 Schools

Gleason Sackmann is one of the great resources of the Internet. Besides being the moderator for the InterNIC-sponsored What's Happening list and newsgroup, he has built a wonderful Web site that links to all the K–12 schools that are currently on the Internet. New schools go up daily, so you'll want to visit often.

WWW: http://toons.cc.ndsu.nodak.edu/~sackmann/k12.html

▶ *Eisenhower National Clearinghouse for Mathematics and Science Education*

The Eisenhower Center provides K–12 teachers with a central source of information on science and mathematics curriculum materials. The United States Department of Education funds this site.

WWW: http://kepler.enc.org

Gopher: enc.org

▶ *International Society for Technology in Education (ISTE)*

This nonprofit professional organization is dedicated to improvement of education through computer-based technology. Hosted at the University of Oregon, ISTE compiles a useful list of conferences that emphasis computer-based technology in conjunction with education.

E-mail Address: iste@oregon.uoregon.edu

Gopher: iste.gopher.uoregon.edu

▶ *Deaf Education Resource Archive*

Information for teachers and parents from Kent State University. Information includes education resources, the Americans with Disabilities Act, exemplary programs, addresses and contacts and much more. A well-packed site.

Gopher: shiva.educ.kent.edu; then choose Education gophers ➤ Special Education ➤ Deaf Education from the menus.

► *Deaf Education Resources from Ontario Institute for Studies in Education*

This is another good resource on deaf education and does not duplicate the materials at Kent State's Deaf Education Resource Archive. Many text files cover the history of deaf education, social issues surrounding deafness, children's needs, American Sign Language, services to the deaf, legal issues, resources for educators, and other online resources.

Gopher: `porpoise.oise.on.ca`

► *National Center for Research on Teacher Learning*

This site at Michigan State University focuses on leadership for teacher learning. It contains issue papers, craft papers, conference reports, research reports and abstracts of their technical publications.

Gopher: `burrow.cl.msu.edu`; then choose Internet ➤ MSU ➤ NCRTL from the menus.

► *North Central Regional Education Laboratory (NCREL)*

NCREL provides papers and other resources on issues they consider critical to education in the North Central region, but certainly of interest to other areas of the United States as well. NCREL's programs include: Curriculum, Instruction & Assessment; Early Childhood and Family Education; Evaluation; Midwest Consortium for Mathematics and Science Education; Midwest Regional Center for Drug-Free Schools & Communities; Professional Development; Regional Policy Information Center; and Rural Education and Urban Education. Each program makes contributions to the site.

Gopher: `gopher.cic.net`; then choose CIC-Net Gophers ➤ NCREL Gopher/ from the menus.

Other regional educational laboratories also provide information on the Internet. The Northwest Regional Educational Laboratory (NWREL):

WWW: `http://www.nwrel.org`

Gopher: `gopher.nwrel.org`

The Farwest Regional Laboratory:

Gopher: `198.49.171.206`

▶ *CICNet Education Gopher*

CIC includes the Big Ten universities plus the University of Chicago and Notre Dame. They have banded together to share resources via CICNet. This is a very comprehensive collection of K–12 education sources on the Internet, originally created by Jeanne Baugh and now maintained by CICNet. Items tend to be arranged by type, which is helpful if you know what you're looking for; otherwise, you can use the Search This Gopher feature to find sites connected to a topic.

Gopher: `gopher.cic.net`; then choose CIC-Net Gophers ➤ K–12 Gopher from the menus.

▶ *Consortium for School Networking (CoSN)*

This is both a Gopher site with numerous K–12 resources and an organization that includes all types of groups and individuals willing to take on a leadership role for K–12 education. CoSN keeps up-to-date on issues surrounding the National Information Infrastructure and is helping to expand K–12 resources on the net. Membership information is available at the Gopher site. A World Wide Web site is growing.

WWW: `http://cosn.org`

Gopher: `cosn.org`

▶ EDNET Guide to Usenet Newsgroups

A large guide with brief descriptions of each group related to education including K–12, higher education, media centers and specialists, and many more.

FTP: nic.umass.edu and go to the pub/ednet directory

Gopher: gopher.lib.umich.edu; then choose What's New and Featured Resources ▶ Clearinghouse of Internet Subject-Oriented Guides from the menus.

▶ Child and Family Literature Reviews

Child and Family Literature Reviews from the University of Minnesota provides a full-text summary of research on topics about children, youth, and families. Though some are Minnesota-based, many have applications elsewhere. Some sample titles include: Community Culture in Rural Communities; Understanding Mentoring Relationships; Parental Attitudes Regarding Punishment as Discipline; and Secondary Level Nutrition Education.

Gopher: tinman.mes.umn.edu: 80

▶ Center for Talented Youth (CTY)

The Center for Talented Youth at Johns Hopkins University provides a resource for parents and educators of gifted children. Information is provided about CTY's acclaimed summer programs as well as resource materials for parents and teachers.

Gopher: jhuniverse.hcf.jhu.edu

▶ National Center for Education Statistics (NCES)

Statistics on education are maintained constantly but seem to take forever to get released. The National Center for Education Statistics (NCES) collects these statistics and makes them available through their Gopher (a branch of the US Department of Education Gopher). They also provide statistics and analyses from their own studies in elementary and secondary education, post-secondary education, assessment, vocational education, and libraries.

> **Gopher:** `gopher.ed.gov`; then choose Education Research, Improvement, and Statistics (OERI & NCES) from the menu.

▶ *Edupage (Electronic Journal)*

EDUCOM supplies this three-times-weekly electronic newsletter, which digests news about information technology. Some nice features are its list of stories at the beginning of the file and its easy-to-read style. Current issues and archives are available via Gopher.

> **Gopher:** `ivory.educom.edu`

▶ *Academy One*

This is the educational portion of the National Public Telecomputing Network, which began at the Cleveland Freenet. It's heavily used by teachers and students in the Cleveland area, and making a connection is often difficult.

> **Telnet:** `freenet-in-a.cwru.edu`, `freenet-in-b.cwru.edu`, and `freenet-in-c.cwru.edu`

▶ *AskERIC Virtual Library*

The Educational Resources Information Center (ERIC) has long been a provider of education-related resources. The ERIC indexes *Research in Education* and *Current Index to Journals in Education* have been standards in libraries for over thirty years. ERIC is federally funded by the US Department of Education and also supports the ERIC Clearinghouses, which provide varying levels of service to people in the field of education. The AskERIC Virtual Library has lesson plans, ERIC Digests (great short essays by professionals on "hot topics"), ERIC publications, reference tools, Internet guides and directories, government information, and archives for education-related discussion lists on

Usenet. Of special interest to educators and media specialists, it's also a great resource for parents.

Gopher: `ericir.syr.edu`

FTP: `ericir.syr.edu`

► *The Scholastic Internet Center*

Scholastic, Inc. has been a leading publisher in the field of education; most of us remember their paperback children's books, which we would purchase through our schools. The Scholastic Internet Center provides a catalog and ordering mechanism for those books plus hundreds of other educational books and materials listed in their Ultimate Education Store Directory. The Ultimate Learning Libraries provide curriculum-based lesson plans, activity guides, and research and resource materials. The full text of some materials are present on-line. Catalog entries for other sources are presented. They also offer electronic newsletters and the Scholastic Network, an interactive online service for students and teachers. Educators and parents should find this service useful.

Gopher: `gopher.scholastic.com`

WWW: `http://scholastic.com :2005`

Figure 22.5 shows the top of Scholastic's Web page. Notice that the second jump here takes you to "Press Return," an online magazine written by students.

► *Wilson Library Bulletin Online*

Excerpts from the *Wilson Library Bulletin* are now available on Gopher. The September 1994 issue has the Internet Cafe, an editorial, a table of contents and an index to the reviews.

Gopher: `gopher.wilson.com`

In GoMLink (`vienna.hh.lib.umich.edu`) it's available under Libraries and Librarianship/Journals.

FIGURE 22.5

The Web page for the Scholastic Internet Center.

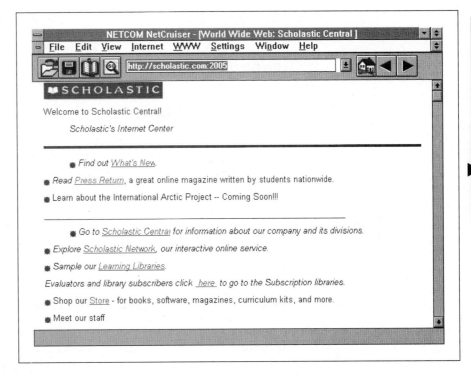

▶ *Academe This Week*

Academe This Week is an online portion of the *Chronicle of Higher Education*. You'll find job postings, a table of contents, events in academe, portions of the statistical almanac, best-selling books on college campuses, and more from this standard resource.

> **Gopher:** `chronicle.merit.edu`

▶ *Big Sky Telegraph*

The great state of Montana provides low-cost access to their version of a freenet, one that has already gathered quite a reputation in education circles. You can have twenty minutes of free time as a visitor, but only $50 a year makes you a subscriber. Many of the forums concern education, and there is one especially for rural education issues. There are lots of curriculum ideas, a list of teachers and resource persons, and on-line classes.

Telnet: `bigsky.bigsky.dillon.mt.us`

▶ NCSA's "Incomplete Guide"

Incomplete Guide to the Internet and Other Telecommunications Opportunities Especially for Teachers and Students, K–12, from the National Center for Supercomputing Applications, is a resource guide and manual for students and teachers at all levels of Internet use.

FTP: `zaphod.ncsa.uiuc.edu` or `ftp.ncsa.uiuc.edu`; then choose Education ➤ Education_Resources ➤ Incomplete_Guide from the menus.

▶ Grant-Getter's Guide to the Internet

A Gopher resource that serves as a major entry point for grant-finding on the Internet. The Federal Register, Fedix, Molis, Fedworld and others can be accessed from this one site. The Guide itself is a nice bibliography of grant sources on the Internet.

Gopher: `gopher.uidaho.edu`; then choose Science Research and Grant Information ➤ Grant Information.

Figure 22.6 shows the Gopher menu.

▶▶ E-Mail Special Interest Lists

If you subscribe to these lists, you'll be a part of the current discussions taking place on the Internet about education. Here's the place to begin your own contributions.

▶ KIDSPHERE

Teachers, parents, software and curriculum developers, and others interested in education meet to discuss K–12 issues on this list. New

FIGURE 22.6 ▶

The main Gopher menu for the Grant-Getter's Guide to the Internet.

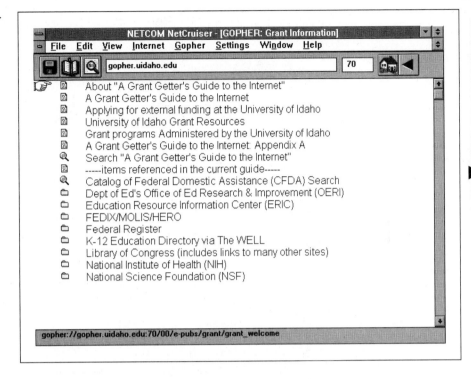

network services, emerging networks, computer interfaces for children's use, and national and international collaborative projects are just some of the topics discussed. To subscribe:

E-mail Address: kidsphere-request@vms.cis.pitt.edu

A spinoff list for children to use is called KIDS. To subscribe to KIDS:

E-mail Address: joinkids@vms.cis.pitt.edu.

▶ *Communet*

Communet is *the* list for community networking advocates and anyone interested in community building. (As discussed in Chapter 17, building a network of community support is an essential part of creating and implementing a school district's Internet presence.) This list is very active and you'll receive a lot of messages, but we think you'll find it worthwhile. To subscribe:

E-mail Address: `listserv@uvmvm.uvm.edu`.

► *Daily Report Card of National Education Goals Panel*

A good-sized daily electronic newsletter that analyzes education news in light of the goals set for US schools. Announcements of new services, innovative projects, and Washington news are some examples of topics covered. The newsletter tends to be technology-oriented. To subscribe to the digest version (a digest is sent once daily):

E-mail Address: `listserv@gwuvm.gwu.edu`. The body of the message should be: `subscribe edpol-d` *your name*.

► *ACADLIST*

ACADLIST is the 8th edition of Diane Kovacs's scholarly electronic conferences list. The entries are by academic subject area and make up eight separate text files. You can also download it as a two-file hypercard stack and a one-file MS Mac Word document.

FTP: `ksuvxa.kent.edu` in the directory \library.

► *M-Link Newsbytes*

A weekly electronic newsletter focusing on Internet resources of interest to libraries and librarians, but also to general users. Brief items on Internet resources and what can be found through them.

Gopher: `vienna.hh.lib.umich.edu`

To subscribe, send an e-mail request to `davidsen@umich.edu`.

▶ *Network News*

An online newsletter focusing on library and information resources on the Internet. Updates the information found in A Guide to Internet/Bitnet. To subscribe:

E-mail Address: `listserv@vm1.nodak.edu`

▶ *AAESA-L*

AAESA-L is an open, unmoderated discussion list on the topic of Educational Service Agencies (ESAs) throughout North America. Discussion topics include such items as ESA problems and their resolution, new ESA ventures, ESA resources, and ESA futures. AAESA-L is for all ESA staff, their member districts, and anyone interested in sharing their ideas and comments to ESAs; it's open to the world. To subscribe:

E-mail Address: `mailserv@admin.aces.k12.ct.us`

▶ *Other Lists*

ACSOFT-L	Discussion of educational software. **E-mail Address:** `listserv@ wustl.edu.`
ADLTED-L	Canada-based adult education list. **E-mail Address:** `listserv@ureginal.uregina.ca.`
AEDNET	Discussion of adult education. **E-mail Address:** `listserv@suvm.syr.edu.`
AI-ED	Artificial Intelligence in education. **E-mail Address:** `AI-ED-REQUEST@SUN.COM.`
ALTLEARN	Discussion of alternative approaches to learning. **E-mail Address:** `listserv@sjuvm.stjohns.edu.`
BGEDU-L	Educator's forum on reform. **E-mail Address:** `bgedu-l@ukcc.uky.edu.`
BIOPI-L	Biology and education. **E-mail Address:** `listserv@ksuvm.ksu.edu.`

CNEDUC-L	Computer networking in education. **E-mail Address:** `listserv@tamvm1.tamu.edu`.
COSNDISC	COSN discussion list. **E-mail Address:** `listproc@yukon.cren.org`.
CTI-L	Discussion of computers in teaching. **E-mail Address:** `listserv@irlearn.ucd.ie`.
CPI-L	List concerning the College Preparatory Initiative. **E-mail Address:** `listserv@cunyvm.bitnet`.
CURRICUL	Discussion of curriculum development. **E-mail Address:** `listserv@saturn.rowan.edu`.
DEOS-L	List of the American Center for the Study of Distance Education. **E-mail Address:** `listserv@psuvm.bitnet`.
DEOSNEWS	Distance Education On-line Symposium. **E-mail Address:** `listerv@psuvm.bitnet`.
DISTED	Discussion of distance education. **E-mail Address:** `listserv@uwavm.bitnet`.
ECENET	Early childhood education list. **E-mail Address:** `listserv@uiucvmd.bitnet`.
EDNET	Discussion of education and networking. **E-mail Address:** `listserv@nic.umass.edu`.
EDPOL	Education policy discussion. **E-mail Address:** `listproc@wais.com`.
EDPOLYAN	Educational policy analysis. **E-mail Address:** `listserv@asuvm.inre.asu.edu`.
EDPOLYAR	Educational policy analysis archive. **E-mail Address:** `listserv@asuvm.inre.asu.edu`.
EDSYLE	Discussion of educational styles. **E-mail Address:** `listserv@sjuvm.stjohns.edu`.
EDTECH	Education and technology list. **E-mail Address:** `listserv@msu.edu`.
EDUPAGE	EDUCOMs news update. **E-mail Address:** `edupage@educom.edu`.

ED2000-PILOT	Discussion of technological reform in education. **E-mail Address:** `mailbase@mailbase.ac.uk`.
EDUCAI-L	Discussion of artificial intelligence in education. **E-mail Address:** `listserv@wvnvm.wvnet.edu`.
ELED-L	Elementary Education list. **E-mail Address:** `listserv@ksuvm.bitnet`.
EUITLIST	Educational uses of information technology. **E-mail Address:** `euitlist@bitnic.educom.edu`.
HORIZONS	Adult Education journal. **E-mail Address:** `listserv@alpha.acast.nova.edu`.
ICU-L	Discussion of research on computers in education. **E-mail Address:** `listserv@ubvm.cc.buffalo.edu`.
IECC	International E-Mail Classroom Connection. Cultural exchange. **E-mail Address:** `iecc-request@stolaf.edu`.
INFED-L	Broad discussion of computers in the classroom. **E-mail Address:** `listserv@ccsun.unicamp.br`.
ITTE	Discussion on information technology and teacher education. **E-mail Address:** `listserv@deakin.oz.au`.
JEI-L	Discussion of technology (especially CD-ROM) in K–12. **E-mail Address:** `listserv@umdd.umd.edu`.
JTE-L	Journal of Technology in Education. **E-mail Address:** `listserv@vtvm1.cc.vt.edu`.
KIDCAFE	Kid's discussion group. **E-mail Address:** `listserv@vm1.nodak.edu`.
KIDS-ACT	Activity projects for kids. **E-mail Address:** `listserv@vm1.nodak.edu`.

K12ADMIN	Discussions concerning educational administration. **E-mail Address:** `listserv@suvm.syr.edu`.
LM_NET	Library media specialist information exchange. **E-mail Address:** `LM_NET@suvm.syr.edu`.
MEDIA-L	Discussion of media in education. **E-mail Address:** `listserv@bingvmb.cc.binghamton.edu`.
MMEDIA-L	Discussion of multimedia education. **E-mail Address:** `listserv@vmtecmex.bitnet`.
MSPROJ	Discussion of the Annenberg/CPB Math-Science Project. **E-mail Address:** `listserv@msu.bitnet`.
MULTI-L	Discussion of multilingual education. **E-mail Address:** `listserv@barilvm.bitnet`.
NCPRSE-L	Discussion of science education reform. **E-mail Address:** `listserv@ecuvm1.bitnet`.
NEWEDU-L	Discussion of new patterns in education. **E-mail Address:** `listserv@uhccvm.uhcc.hawaii.edu`.
NLA	National Literacy Advocacy list. **E-mail Address:** `majordomo@world.std.com`.
SCHOOL-L	Discussion of primary and secondary school issues. **E-mail Address:** `listserv@irlearn.ucd.ie`.
SIGTEL-L	Discussion of telecommunications in education. **E-mail Address:** `SIGTEL-L@unmvma.unm.edu`.
STLHE-L	Teaching and learning in higher ed list. **E-mail Address:** `listserv@unbvm1.csd.unb.ca`.
SUSIG	Discussion of math education. **E-mail Address:** `listserv@miamiu.bitnet`.

TEACHEFT	Discussion of teaching effectiveness. **E-mail Address:** `listserv@wcupa.edu`.
UKERA-L	Dialog on education reform policy making. Similar to BGEDU-L. **E-mail Address:** `UKERA-L@ukcc.uky.edu`.
VOCNET	Vocational Education discussion. **E-mail Address:** `listserv@cmsa.berkley.edu`.

▶▶ *Newsgroups*

Usenet newsgroups (discussed in Chapter 12) offer another way to participate in discussions of education. Some people prefer to use their news readers (the client software that presents the news on your computer) to help them organize their reading into specific topic lines. Using a news reader to pick and choose among the messages on a topic can be a handy way to browse through a lot of messages quickly. If the name of a newsgroup begins with the letters `bit.listserv`, it's a *gateway*, presenting the traffic on a mailing list copied into a newsgroup. You can choose which way you'd like to follow the discussion topics. Newsgroups that begin with `k12` have been sent through a gateway from FidoNet, which is a direct computer-to-computer network widely used in the teaching community. (Before access to the Internet became more widely available, teachers and educators used their computers to set up this network, where each computer owner would call another computer and pass on files and messages with specific FidoNet software. This cooperation is rather like the "telephone tree" that is used by parents to pass messages from a teacher to all the parents in a classroom, for example.)

▶ *alt.education.distance*

Distance learning is becoming a hot topic with the use of technologies like satellite downlinks and online courses. The `alt.education.distance` newsgroup has professionals and end users discussing new technologies, concerns and experiences.

▶ *bit.listserv.edpolyan*

A BITNET discussion list that allows discussion about education is-sues between professionals and students.

▶ *bit.listserv.edtech*

A moderated LISTSERV redistributed on Usenet for the discussion of educational technology.

▶ *comp.edu*

For teachers of computer science and those interested in computer literacy.

▶ *k12.ed.art*

A discussion group for K–12 art education.

▶ *k12.ed.comp.literacy*

A discussion group for K–12 computer literacy.

▶ *k12.ed.math*

A discussion group for K–12 mathematics education.

▶ *k12.ed.music*

A discussion group for K–12 music and performing arts education.

▶ *k12.ed.science*

A discussion group for K–12 science education.

▶ *k12.soc-studies*

A discussion group for K–12 social studies and history education.

▶ *k12.ed.special*

A discussion group for K–12 education of students with disabilities and special needs.

▶ *k12.ed.tag*

A discussion group for K–12 education of talented and gifted students.

▶ *k12.ed.tech*

A discussion group for K–12 industrial arts education.

▶ *k12.lang.art*

A discussion group for K–12 language arts education.

▶ ▶ *Professional or Special Interest Groups (SIGs)*

Again, we call to your attention some groups that provide special information or special emphasis on using internetworking. You may want to participate.

▶ *Center for Civic Networking*

CCN/CIVICNET is an organization devoted to helping shape policies for the emerging national information infrastructure and a national vision to include civic networking. For information contact Miles Fidelman:

E-mail Address: mfidelman@world.std.com

The Center's archives are part of the EFF archives:

FTP: ftp.eff.org (pub/Groups/CCN)

▶ *Association for Educational Communications and Technology (AECT)*

An international professional association dedicated to "the improvement of instruction through the utilization of media and technology." Publications and job announcements are just two of the resources in the AECT Gopher. Membership information is also available on the Gopher.

Gopher: `sunbird.usd.edu`

▶ *Special Interest Group for University and College Computing Services (SIGUUCS)*

A special interest group of the Association for Computing Machinery, SIGUCCS looks at all aspects of university and college computing from training to supercomputer sites. A quarterly newsletter and an annual conference are offered. Membership is for individuals. Contact: Russell S. Vaught, Center for Academic Computing, 229 Computer Bldg., University Park, PA 16802, 814-863-0421. Information about ACM and all its special interest groups can be found on the World Wide Web, too.

WWW: `http://www.acm.org`

▶ *Coalition for Networked Information (CNI)*

The Coalition for Networked Information is a joint project of the Association of Research Libraries (ARL), CAUSE, and EDUCOM. Their work "promotes the creation of and access to information resources in networked environments in order to enrich scholarship and to enhance intellectual productivity." Membership is limited to organizations and institutions; however, the CNI Gopher server is available to the public and includes a good deal of helpful information about the coalition, its members, and their work.

Gopher: `gopher.cni.org`

CNI also sponsors a number of mailing lists.

▶ *International Association for Computer Information Systems (IACIS)*

The membership of IACIS includes individuals and organizations of educators and computer professionals at all levels of educational institutions. Publications include a quarterly *Journal Of Computer Information Systems* and a periodic newsletter. For membership information contact: Dr. Susan Haugen, Dept. of Accountancy, University of Wisconsin—Eau Claire, Eau Claire, WI 54702, (715) 836-2952.

▶ *International Society for Technology in Education (ISTE)*

This organization is for individuals interested in using technology to improve education. ISTE promotes the use of standards and communication between international policy-formers and professionals. Publications include *Computing Teacher*, *Journal of Research on Computing in Education*, and *Update*. For membership information contact: Maia S. Howes, University of Oregon, 1787 Agate Street, Eugene, OR 97403, (503)346-4414.

> **E-mail Address:** iste@oregon.uoregon.edu
>
> **Gopher:** iste.gopher.uoregon.edu

▶ *Special Interest Group for Computer Science Education*

Another SIG of the Association for Computing Machinery. SIG CSE supports computer science educators at the secondary, associate, undergraduate and graduate degree levels. Publications include the *SIG-SCE Bulletin*, and SIG CSE holds an annual meeting and symposium. For membership information contact: Nell B. Dale, Computer Sciences Dept., University of Texas at Austin, Austin, TX 78712, (512)471-9539.

▶ NETCOM Education Resources

Netcom provides a link to some of the best education resources, archives, and information servers.

WWW: http://www.netcom.com/netcom/education.html

▶ San Francisco State University (SFSU) Department of Instructional Technologies WWW Server

The Department of Instructional Technologies at SFSU now has a World Wide Web server. You'll find information, educational tech resources, K–12 educator resources, and a great collection of links to job listings.

WWW: http://edu-52.sfsu.edu

Figure 22.7 shows this "friendly little pothole on the information superhighway."

▶ World Wide Web Virtual Library Education Page

Journals, lectures and tutorials, books, software, major education sites and networks, and specialized sources in education are hypertextually linked on this page. Though a large amount of data is linked, this list is a "good start."

WWW: http://life.anu.edu.au/education/library.html

▶ Whole Frog Project

Only it's not whole anymore after you go through this interactive dissection! The Lawrence Berkeley Laboratory Imaging and Distributing Computing Group has taken the basic junior-high science project high-tech. The dissection is performed at the major organ level, and views can be generated from many different angles. You have got to see this!

FIGURE 22.7

The SFSU Department of Instructional Technologies home Web page.

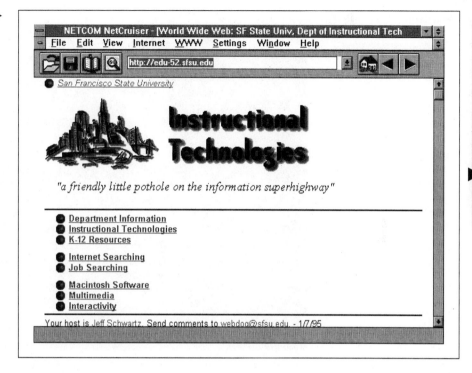

WWW: http://george.lbl.gov/ITG.hm.pg.docs/dissect/info.html

Figure 22.8 shows the frog's skeleton.

This project has been translated into Spanish, French, German, and Dutch by volunteer translators. If you can help by translating it into another language, the group would love to hear from you.

▶ *Learning Research and Development Center (LRDC)*

The LRDC at Pitt is a national center for education research. Descriptions of its projects, programs, scientists, departments and services are available on their Web page along with connections to other related Internet organizations and resources.

WWW: http://www.lrdc.pitt.edu

FIGURE 22.8 ▶

The Whole Frog Project.

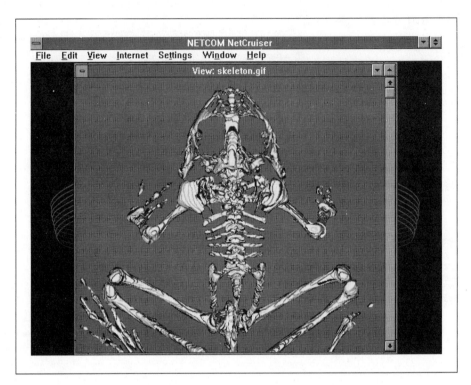

▶ ▶ CHAPTER **23**

Resources
for Kids

►► **T**his listing of resources that are especially interesting for kids is not exhaustive, but it does detail some of the best available. With each resource you'll see how to find it, whether by Gopher, the Web, or by Telnetting to the service. We have attempted to find educational and fun resources, as well as game archives of various sorts.

You will need to be the judge of the fitness of various resources for your child's emotional and educational needs. We have not included any material that we know to be especially violent or in other ways objectionable, but your family's values and needs may vary.

Many of the general resources listed in Chapter 20 are also interesting for kids. We've also included some resources that are interesting to people who are interested in kids.

►► *Educational Projects and Resources*

More and more people are moving more and more items of interest to kids to the Internet. This is for the same reason that other information providers are adding resources to the Internet: the Net provides a quick, efficient, and sometimes colorful and graphically interesting way to share ideas. Some of the more interesting projects being added are intended to share human as well as intellectual resources—they are projects that "connect" scientists or mathematicians or artists with kids. Here are a few of those types of projects as well as others that we hope you'll find fun.

▶ CyberSpace Middle School

Middle school, yuck! Everybody knows middle school is the worst! Here's one you might want to go to—and go back to again and again. It includes student resources, interesting projects for teachers, and "Surf City," a great jumping off point to surf the World Wide Web.

WWW: `http://www.scri.fsu.edu/~dennisl/CMS.html`

Figure 23.1 shows the Web page.

FIGURE 23.1 ▶

The Web page for Cyberspace Middle School.

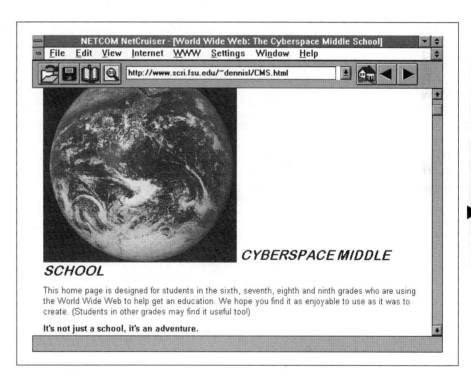

▶ Project JASON

Dr. Robert Ballard, the exploring scientist who led the expedition to investigate the *RMS Titanic,* leads another type of expeditionary force— that of students throughout North America, Bermuda, and Britain, on virtual voyages to remote parts of the world, which he calls Project JA-SON. The students are in their classrooms, helped by teachers who have been given lesson plans and curriculum targeted to these specific voyages. The students assist the scientists, who are actually present in the remote sites. The students can operate some of the equipment remotely and talk with the scientists who are doing the physical as well as intellectual work. You can visit past JASON expeditions and find out more about upcoming work on the Web.

WWW: http://seawifs.gsfc.nasa.gov/JASON/JASON.html

Figure 23.2 shows a part of the 1995 expeditionary description.

FIGURE 23.2 ►

The Web page for Project JASON.

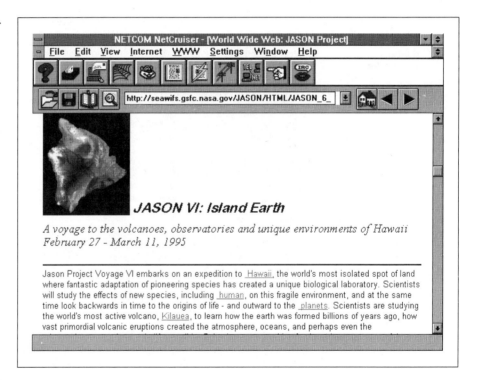

► *NASA's Picture Books*

Have you noticed how many of the addresses in this book show World Wide Web sites from NASA? NASA works hard to share its many resources with educators and students. It's the technology or knowledge transfer part of the High Performance Computing and Communications program (HPCC) that encourages these activities. Of course, the real reason we included these sites is that they are so well done and interesting. If you wanted to see them all gathered together you could start from the Web page shown in Figure 23.3, which is devoted to gathering education resources.

WWW: http://www.nasa.gov/HPCC/K12/edures.html

From here you can see lots of connecting points to many of NASA's own interesting sites as well as to other sites interesting to kids. See if you can find NASA's Electronic Picture Books. Some of them are called *Gems of Hubble, Images of Mars,* and *Endeavor Views the Earth.* These hyperbooks are available to download to a Macintosh computer where you can use the Hypercard program to show them. Or you can view them as a collection of snapshots across the Internet. If you'd like to add these books to your permanent collection, the Web pages also tell you where you can order CD-ROM copies.

FIGURE 23.3 ▶

The Web page for NASA's Electronic Picture Books.

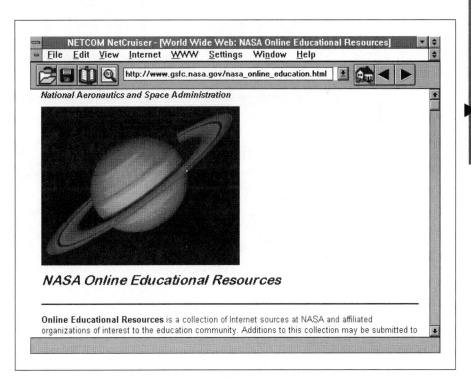

Resources for Kids

▶ ▶

ch. **23**

► *The New South Polar Times Project*

NASA shows us views of the earth which can include the South Pole from space. This project gives us a newsletter from the Amundsen-Scott South Pole Station itself. Lt. Tom Jacobs writes a biweekly newsletter named after the first newsletter to be written at the South Pole. And Deakin University in Australia houses the newsletter on the project's Web pages. You can read the latest version as well as find out more about the South Pole and things like blizzards via the Web.

WWW: http://www.deakin.edu.au/edu/MSEE/GENII/NSPT/
NSPThomePage.html

► *Explorer*

Tired of trekking around the world in the cold? Or flying about the earth in a space shuttle? How about exploring mathematics? The University of Kansas contributes a site that develops and dispenses mathematics teaching programs. Figure 23.4 shows an example from one of

FIGURE 23.4 ►

Explorer, from the University of Kansas.

these programs. To use them, you'll need a Macintosh computer running System 7.1 or later, MacTCP, and Clarisworks 2.0. The software is intended to be used in classrooms. Download the software via the Web.

WWW: http://unite.tisl.ukans.edu

▶ *Corporation for Public Broadcasting EdWeb*

Usually when you think of the Corporation for Public Broadcasting, you think of Bert and Ernie and Big Bird, or maybe *Mystery* or *Masterpiece Theatre*. Well, CPB is on the Internet, too. Andy Carvin of CPB has one of the more interesting sites under construction. It's call Ed-Web—The Online K-12 Resource Guide. At this writing late in 1994, the site is changing so fast it's difficult to describe all the interesting things that are happening there. You'll probably want to drop in here often.

WWW: http://198.187.60.80

▶ *Canada's SchoolNet*

Industry and Science Canada sponsors this Gopher, which provides students from preschool through grade 12 with fun and educational projects, ideas and network resources. A SchoolNet MOO and the full text of experiments and just plain fun things to do are here for non-Canadians, too. Point your Gopher client at: schoolnet.carleton.ca. Figure 23.5 shows the introduction to the MOO.

ch.
23

▶ *WhaleNet*

WhaleNet uses statistics gathered from whale watches to educate students. Students, teachers, and the Whale Conservation Institute collect and compile data on a BBS. Curricula and other classroom supports are available and described in the "about" files. Figure 23.6 shows information about participating in Whalenet, taken from the CICNet Gopher.

Gopher: gopher.cic.net; then choose the menu path Cicnet-Gophers ➤ K12-Gopher ➤ Classroom ➤ Whalenet.

FIGURE 23.5 ▶

The SchoolNet MOO.

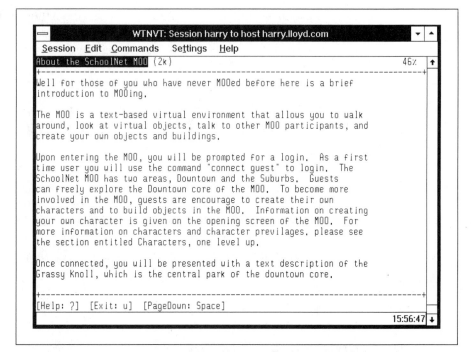

```
┌──────────────────────────────────────────────────────────────────────────┐
│ ▬             WTNVT: Session harry to host harry.lloyd.com           ▼  ▲  │
├──────────────────────────────────────────────────────────────────────────┤
│  Session   Edit  Commands    Settings    Help                             │
├──────────────────────────────────────────────────────────────────────────┤
│ About the SchoolNet MOO (2k)                                      46%  ↑  │
│ +------------------------------------------------------------------------+ │
│ Well for those of you who have never MOOed before here is a brief          │
│ introduction to MOOing.                                                    │
│                                                                            │
│ The MOO is a text-based virtual environment that allows you to walk        │
│ around, look at virtual objects, talk to other MOO participants, and       │
│ create your own objects and buildings.                                     │
│                                                                            │
│ Upon entering the MOO, you will be prompted for a login.  As a first       │
│ time user you will use the command "connect guest" to login.  The          │
│ SchoolNet MOO has two areas, Downtown and the Suburbs.  Guests             │
│ can freely explore the Downtown core of the MOO.  To become more           │
│ involved in the MOO, guests are encourage to create their own              │
│ characters and to build objects in the MOO.  Information on creating        │
│ your own character is given on the opening screen of the MOO.  For         │
│ more information on characters and character previlages, please see        │
│ the section entitled Characters, one level up.                            │
│                                                                            │
│ Once connected, you will be presented with a text description of the       │
│ Grassy Knoll, which is the central park of the downtown core.             │
│                                                                            │
│ +------------------------------------------------------------------------+ │
│ [Help: ?]  [Exit: u]  [PageDown: Space]                                    │
│                                                                  15:56:47 ↓ │
└──────────────────────────────────────────────────────────────────────────┘
```

FIGURE 23.6 ▶

Information about Whalenet, via Gopher.

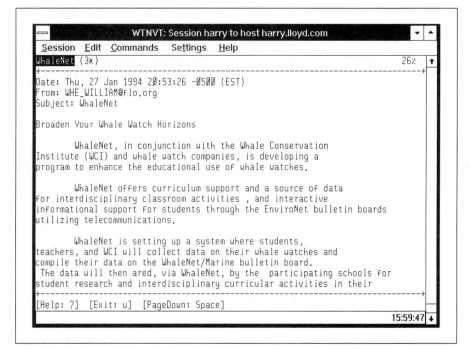

```
┌──────────────────────────────────────────────────────────────────────────┐
│ ▬             WTNVT: Session harry to host harry.lloyd.com           ▼  ▲  │
├──────────────────────────────────────────────────────────────────────────┤
│  Session   Edit  Commands    Settings    Help                             │
├──────────────────────────────────────────────────────────────────────────┤
│ WhaleNet (3k)                                                     26%  ↑  │
│ +------------------------------------------------------------------------+ │
│ Date: Thu, 27 Jan 1994 20:53:26 -0500 (EST)                               │
│ From: WHE_WILLIAM@flo.org                                                  │
│ Subject: WhaleNet                                                          │
│                                                                            │
│ Broaden Your Whale Watch Horizons                                         │
│                                                                            │
│       WhaleNet, in conjunction with the Whale Conservation                 │
│ Institute (WCI) and whale watch companies, is developing a                 │
│ program to enhance the educational use of whale watches.                   │
│                                                                            │
│       WhaleNet offers curriculum support and a source of data             │
│ for interdisciplinary classroom activities , and interactive              │
│ informational support for students through the EnviroNet bulletin boards  │
│ utilizing telecommunications.                                              │
│                                                                            │
│       WhaleNet is setting up a system where students,                      │
│ teachers, and WCI will collect data on their whale watches and            │
│ compile their data on the WhaleNet/Marine bulletin board.                 │
│  The data will then ared, via WhaleNet, by the  participating schools for  │
│ student research and interdisciplinary curricular activities in their     │
│ +------------------------------------------------------------------------+ │
│ [Help: ?]  [Exit: u]  [PageDown: Space]                                    │
│                                                                  15:59:47 ↓ │
└──────────────────────────────────────────────────────────────────────────┘
```

▶ *KNSO News Service*

This service from the Knoxville News-Sentinel reproduces news stories from the paper that are aimed at students of junior and senior high school age. Figure 23.7 shows a story about student dress codes.

Telnet: use.usit.net

Log in as knso with the password knso.

FIGURE 23.7 ▶

Student-oriented news story from KNSO.

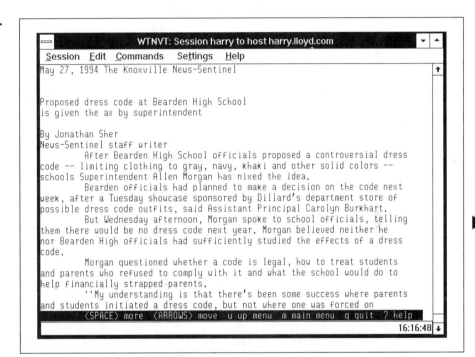

```
┌─────────────────────────────────────────────────────────────┐
│          WTNVT: Session harry to host harry.lloyd.com     ▼ ▲│
├─────────────────────────────────────────────────────────────┤
│ Session  Edit  Commands  Settings  Help                      │
│May 27, 1994 The Knoxville News-Sentinel                     ↑│
│                                                              │
│                                                              │
│Proposed dress code at Bearden High School                    │
│is given the ax by superintendent                             │
│                                                              │
│By Jonathan Sher                                              │
│News-Sentinel staff writer                                    │
│        After Bearden High School officials proposed a        │
│controversial dress code -- limiting clothing to gray, navy,  │
│khaki and other solid colors -- schools Superintendent Allen  │
│Morgan has nixed the idea.                                    │
│        Bearden officials had planned to make a decision on   │
│the code next week, after a Tuesday showcase sponsored by     │
│Dillard's department store of possible dress code outfits,    │
│said Assistant Principal Carolyn Burkhart.                    │
│        But Wednesday afternoon, Morgan spoke to school       │
│officials, telling them there would be no dress code next     │
│year. Morgan believed neither he nor Bearden High officials   │
│had sufficiently studied the effects of a dress code.         │
│        Morgan questioned whether a code is legal, how to     │
│treat students and parents who refused to comply with it and  │
│what the school would do to help financially strapped parents.│
│        ''My understanding is that there's been some success  │
│where parents and students initiated a dress code, but not    │
│where one was forced on                                       │
│    <SPACE> more  <ARROWS> move  u up menu  m main menu  q quit ? help │
│                                                   16:16:48  ↓│
└─────────────────────────────────────────────────────────────┘
```

Resources for Kids

▶ ▶
ch.
23

▶ *Global Student Newswire*

Student-written news stories from around the world are featured on this new World Wide Web server. Intended for high school through graduate levels, GSN works on the newswire model, where a subscriber to a newswire (like Associated Press, United Press International, or Reuters) receives articles distributed "on the wire" and can use them or not. The GSN home page is shown in Figure 23.8. You can reach this resource in either of two ways:

WWW: `http://www.jou.ufl.edu/forums/gsn.htm`

FTP: `132.236.225.25`; then choose pub ➤ gsn ➤ gsnfaq.txt.

FIGURE 23.8 ►

The Global Student Newswire home page.

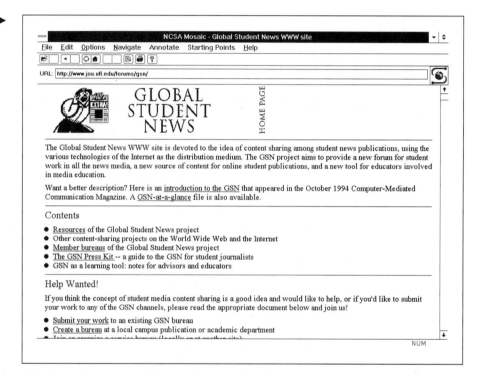

► *The Global Schoolhouse Project*

The National Science Foundation sponsors this project, which provides examples of student and teacher publishing on the Web. The Global Schoolhouse project features partner schools, profiles of student participants, and the like. The home page is featured in Figure 23.9. You can reach this project by both the Web and Gopher:

WWW: `http://k12.cnidr.org/gshwelcome.html`

Gopher: `gsh.cnidr.org`

FIGURE 23.9

The Global School-house home page.

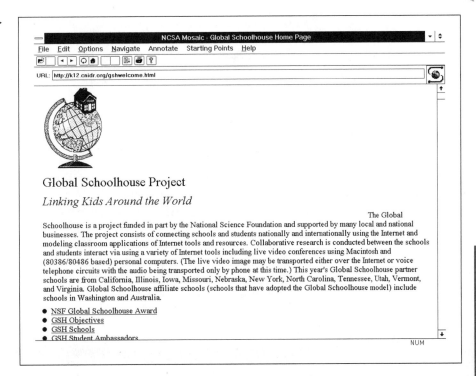

▶ *Ask Prof. Maths*

Mathematics students and teachers are encouraged to ask questions related to mathematics and math education, and the professor will send a response. Address queries to the e-mail address shown below and in the subject line indicate K–5 or 6–9 grade levels. State your question, some background to it, your name, grade level, your e-mail address and whether you're a teacher or a student. Archives can be found via FTP. The archive and the e-mail service are hosted at Saint Bonaventure University's Electronic Archives.

> **E-Mail Address:** maths@sbu.edu

> **FTP:** ftp.sbu.edu; then choose the pub/prof.maths directory.

▶ *Ask Mr. Science*

Like Prof. Maths, Mr. Science will take on any challenge a student can pose in any field of science. Answers are usually posted within

48 hours; please send no more than five at a time.

E-Mail Address: apscichs@radford.vak12ed.edu

Your questions will be answered courtesy of the Virginia Department of Education.

▶ *Weather Underground*

Interested in today's weather in your town? Information on hurricanes or earthquakes? Special classroom weather projects? The University of Michigan shares with you the National Weather Service's answers.

Telnet: madlab.sprl.umich.edu 3000

Follow the prompts. Figure 23.10 shows a special weather announcement about Hurricane Conrad.

FIGURE 23.10 ▶

A Special Weather Announcement for the Florida Keys.

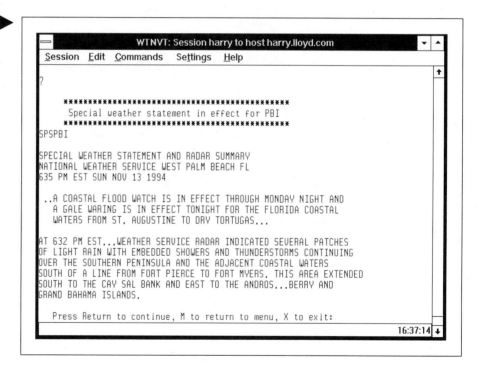

▶ Schmoozing on the Infobahn

Careful you don't get into a wreck! schMOOze University is an interactive place on the Internet where educators and students can meet to hold classes, chat, and schmooze. There are language games, a grammar maze, classrooms, a Usenet feed, and Gopher access. You don't need any special software to do this. Included for newcomers is a map of the virtual university, shown in Figure 23.11.

Telnet: morgan.dnsi.com port 8888

Type **CONNECT GUEST** at the prompt.

FIGURE 23.11 ▶

A Map of schMOOze University.

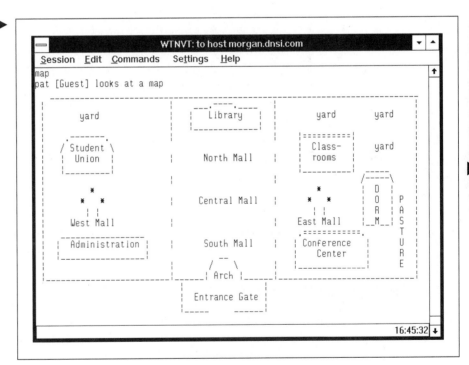

▶ Alex: A Catalog of Electronic Texts

Alex uses Gopher to find and retrieve the full text of over 700 texts on the Internet taken from Project Gutenberg, Wiretap, the Online Book Initiative, Eris at Virginia Tech, the English server at Carnegie-Mellon

University and the online portion of the Oxford Text Archive. Users can search by author and title. Figure 23.12 shows a browse for authors, in this case those with last names beginning with I.

> **Gopher:** gopher.ox.ac.uk; then choose the World ➤ Gopherspace ➤ Alex.

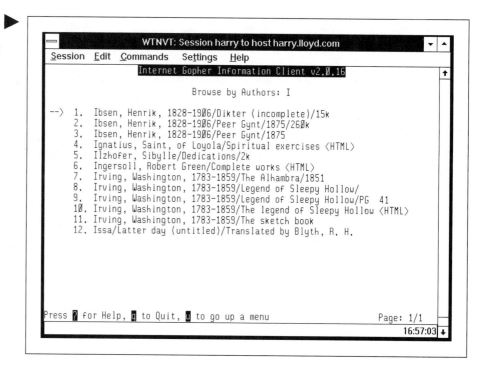

▶ New Scholastic Internet Center

Scholastic, Inc. has been a leading publisher in the field of education for decades; most of us remember their paperback children's books, which we would purchase through our schools. The Ultimate Learning Libraries provide curriculum-based lesson plans, activity guides, research and resource materials full text and online. Figure 23.13 shows calendar activities for students and teachers. They also offer electronic newsletters and the Scholastic Network, an interactive online service for students and teachers. Their Internet Center provides a catalog and ordering mechanism for those books plus hundreds of other educational books and materials listed in their Ultimate Education Store Directory. Figure 23.14 shows the Electronic Store directory page.

Gopher: `gopher.scholastic.com`

WWW: `http://scholastic.com :2005`

▶ *What Time Is It?*

The University of Melbourne's Local Times Around The World server will help you figure it out. What time is it in Turkey? Figure 23.15 shows.

Gopher: `gopher.austin.unimelb.edu.au`; then choose General Information ➤ Local Times

FIGURE 23.13 ▶

Calendar activities for June.

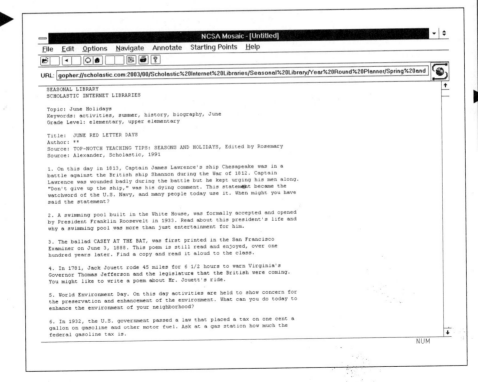

```
┌──────────────────────────────────────────────────────────────────────┐
│ ▬                     NCSA Mosaic - [Untitled]                  ▾  ⬍   │
│  File   Edit   Options   Navigate   Annotate   Starting Points   Help  │
│  [icons]                                                               │
│  URL: gopher://scholastic.com:2003/00/Scholastic%20Internet%20Libraries/Seasonal%20Library/Year%20Round%20Planner/Spring%20and │
│  SEASONAL LIBRARY                                                      │
│  SCHOLASTIC INTERNET LIBRARIES                                        │
│                                                                       │
│  Topic: June Holidays                                                 │
│  Keywords: activities, summer, history, biography, June               │
│  Grade Level: elementary, upper elementary                            │
│                                                                       │
│  Title:  JUNE RED LETTER DAYS                                         │
│  Author: **                                                           │
│  Source: TOP-NOTCH TEACHING TIPS: SEASONS AND HOLIDAYS, Edited by Rosemary │
│  Source: Alexander, Scholastic, 1991                                  │
│                                                                       │
│  1. On this day in 1813, Captain James Lawrence's ship Chesapeake was in a │
│  battle against the British ship Shannon during the War of 1812. Captain │
│  Lawrence was wounded badly during the battle but he kept urging his men along. │
│  "Don't give up the ship," was his dying comment. This statement became the │
│  watchword of the U.S. Navy, and many people today use it. When might you have │
│  said the statement?                                                  │
│                                                                       │
│  2. A swimming pool built in the White House, was formally accepted and opened │
│  by President Franklin Roosevelt in 1933. Read about this president's life and │
│  why a swimming pool was more than just entertainment for him.        │
│                                                                       │
│  3. The ballad CASEY AT THE BAT, was first printed in the San Francisco │
│  Examiner on June 3, 1888. This poem is still read and enjoyed, over one │
│  hundred years later. Find a copy and read it aloud to the class.     │
│                                                                       │
│  4. In 1781, Jack Jouett rode 45 miles for 6 1/2 hours to warn Virginia's │
│  Governor Thomas Jefferson and the legislature that the British were coming. │
│  You might like to write a poem about Mr. Jouett's ride.              │
│                                                                       │
│  5. World Environment Day. On this day activities are held to show concern for │
│  the preservation and enhancement of the environment. What can you do today to │
│  enhance the environment of your neighborhood?                        │
│                                                                       │
│  6. In 1932, the U.S. government passed a law that placed a tax on one cent a │
│  gallon on gasoline and other motor fuel. Ask at a gas station how much the │
│  federal gasoline tax is.                                            │
│                                                                 NUM   │
└──────────────────────────────────────────────────────────────────────┘
```

FIGURE 23.14 ▶

The Scholastic Store Directory.

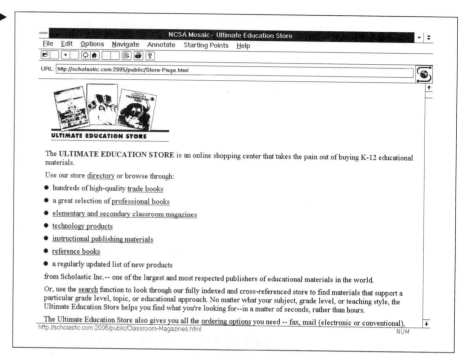

FIGURE 23.15 ▶

Local time in Turkey.

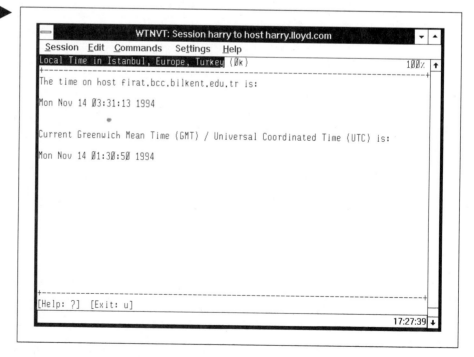

▶ The Alfred Wegener Institute for Polar and Marine Research

The AWI is a German national research center for polar and marine research, and as such has collected huge amounts of data related to Global Change research. Figure 23.16 shows information about the Neumeyer Antarctic Research Center.

WWW: http://www.awi-bremerhaven.de

Direct any problems, comments, or ideas to:

E-Mail Address: webmaster@awi-bremerhaven.de

FIGURE 23.16 ▶

The Neumeyer Antarctic Research Center, including diagram of the station.

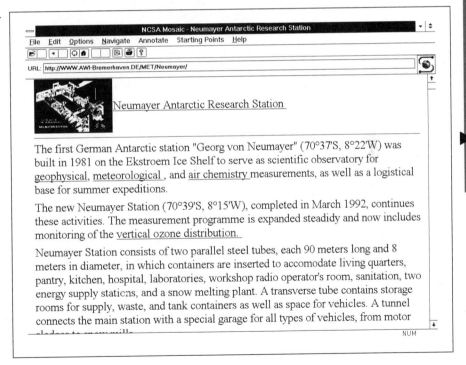

▶ iMpulse Magazine

A comprehensive journal of music news, reviews, information and opinion. It's delivered via Internet e-mail and published monthly. Recent topics have included Lollapalooza '94, the release of Boyz II Men's CD *II*, copyright issues on the Net, and Kaleidospace. To subscribe to iMpulse:

E-Mail Address: iMpulse@dsigroup.com

In the Subject line, type **SUBSCRIBE IMPULSE**.

▶ *Remote Tele-Excavation via the Web*

An interdisciplinary team at the University of Southern California is pleased to announce Mercury Site, a WWW server that allows users to tele-operate a robot arm over the Net. Users view the environment surrounding the arm via a sequence of live images taken by a CCD camera mounted on a commercial robot arm. The robot is positioned over a terrain filled with sand; a pneumatic system, also mounted on the robot, allows users to direct short bursts of compressed air into the sand at selected points. Thus users can "excavate" regions within the sand by positioning the arm, delivering a burst of air, and viewing the newly cleared region. Figure 23.17 shows instructions for new users of the excavation materials. To operate the robot you'll need a WWW client that handles forms. Have a blast:

WWW: http://www.usc.edu/dept/raiders/

▶ *AgriGator*

AgriGator is the Web server operated by the Institute of Food and Agricultural Sciences (IFAS) at the University of Florida (UF). In addition to providing information about UF, the IFAS, and different types of "Gators," it provides an extensive list of agricultural resources worldwide. Other topics are also available (biotechnology, space, weather, environment and the "funny farm") and new ones are still under development and will be added later. Come visit the AgriGator swamp as it is being built. Watch out for the Gators in Figure 23.18, the home page.

WWW: http://gnv.ifas.ufl.edu/www.agator_home.htm

FIGURE 23.17

Instructions for users at the Mercury excavation site.

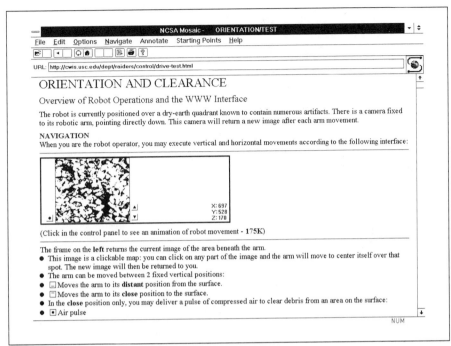

FIGURE 23.18

The AgriGator home page.

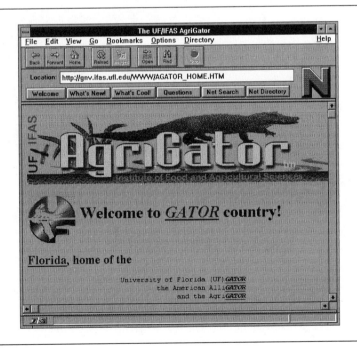

Resources
for Kids

ch.
23

▶ *Egyptian Items*

At the University of Memphis, the Institute of Egyptian Art and Archaeology operates a Web server that includes an exhibit of some of the Egyptian antiquities residing at the Institute and a short tour of Egypt. In Figure 23.19, you can see a perfectly preserved loaf of bread, and what it was used for other than eating.

WWW: `http://www.memst.edu/egypt/main.html`

FIGURE 23.19 ▶

The Institute of Egyptian Art and Archaeology Web server.

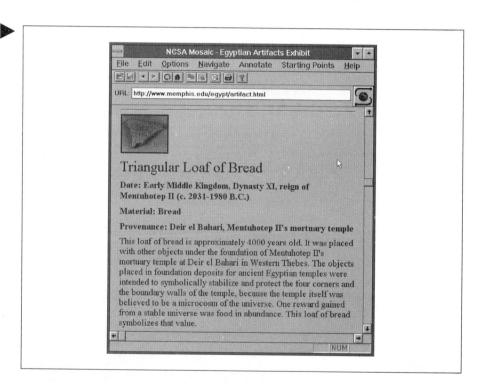

▶ *African Continent Disaster Material*

The recent civil war in Rwanda has forced hundreds of thousands of people into refugee camps in neighboring Burundi and Zaire. Over 26 megabytes of materials about this crisis are available on the Internet via the WWW or e-mail. Documents come from the VOA, CBC, DHA, UNICEF, UNHCR, WHO, ICRC, InterAction, VOICE, FFH, Amnesty International, HRW/Africa, USAID, OFDA and the White

House. President Bill Clinton's letter in response to e-mail generated on the site's E-Mail-the-President gateway is also online; its screen is shown in Figure 23.20.

WWW: `http://www.intac.com/PubService/rwanda/)`

This site is composed, developed, and maintained by volunteers as a public service by the people at Hungerweb hosted at Brown University (`http://ww.hunger.brown.edu`) and by INTAC, an Internet Service provider (`http://www.intac.com`).

FIGURE 23.20 ▶

Mail to the President about Rwanda.

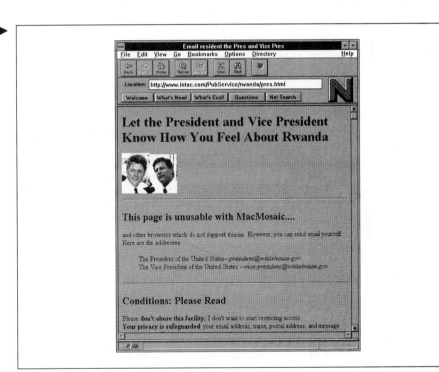

▶ *Aviation/Aerospace Newspaper*

The Avion Online is Embry-Riddle Aeronautical University's weekly college newspaper specializing in coverage of aerospace activity, such as the space shuttle, and aviation topics like the Lockheed/Martin merger.

Avion is the first Aviation/Aerospace newspaper to be available on the Internet, via the World Wide Web:

WWW: http://avion.db.erau.edu

▶ *Army Handbooks*

The US Army Area Handbooks provide a great deal of information about a country's culture, land, economy and people. They are often found missing from library shelves, but they are on the Internet. You'll find information about Egypt, China, and more. Figure 23.21 shows an excerpt from the guide on Somalia.

Gopher: UMSLVMA.UMSL.EDU; then choose Library ➤ Government Documents from the menus.

FIGURE 23.21 ▶

US Army Handbook on Somalia.

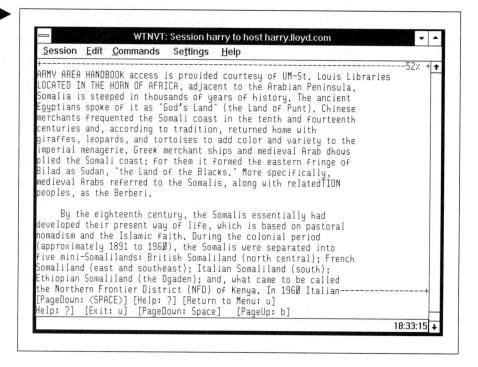

▶ Earthquake Info

Want to find out what was shaking in the night? Use Finger to get information about recent earthquake activity for different regions from the following sites.

The world: spyder@dmc.iris.washington.edu

The United States: quake@gldfs.cr.usgs.gov

Washington and Oregon: quake@geophys.washington.edu

Alaska: quake@fm.gi.alaska.edu

Southern California: quake@scec2.gps.caltech.edu

Eastern Missouri and Southern Illinois: quake@slueas.slu.edu

Nevada and eastern California: quake@seismo.unr.edu

Northern California: quake@andreas.wr.usgs.gov

Utah, Wyoming, and Montana: quake@eqinfo.seis.utah.edu

Hawaii: quake@tako.wr.usgs.gov

Figure 23.22 shows earthquake activity in eastern Missouri and Illinois.

▶ Magellan Images

The Jet Propulsion Laboratory provides an archive of images collected by the Magellan spacecraft, along with associated indexes and documentation.

FTP: wuarchive.wustl.edu

Log in as anonymous, use your e-mail address as the password, and then use cd to go to the graphics/magellan directory.

▶ NASA Network Information Center Gopher

This Gopher server provides one-stop access to resources at more than a dozen NASA information centers. Figure 23.23 shows a list of scientific resources available from NASA.

Resources
for Kids

ch.
23

FIGURE 23.22 ▶

*Output from
quake@slueas.slu.edu.*

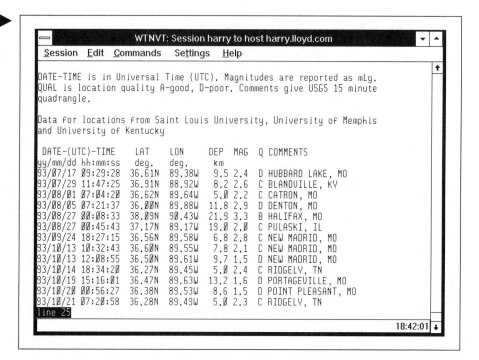

FIGURE 23.23 ▶

*Scientific resources
available from NASA,
via Gopher.*

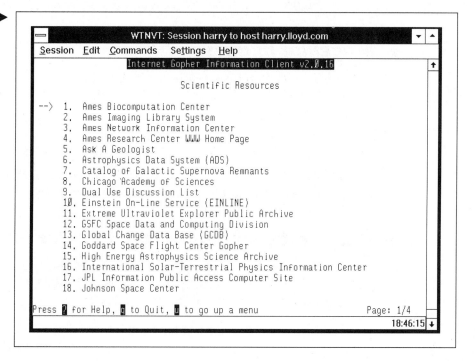

Gopher: naic.nasa.gov; then choose NASA Center NIC Information.

Telnet: naic.nasa.gov

Log in as naic, and choose NASA Center NIC Information.

▶ *Kidlink*

The Kidlink Gopher provides a large amount of information about the KIDS-*nn* (fill in a year) projects. Many of the things a kid can do via the Internet are accessible or described here. A rich resource for classroom teachers. Point your Gopher client to kids.ccit.duq.edu.

▶ *FYI on Questions and Answers: Answers to Commonly Asked "Primary and Secondary School Internet User" Questions (RFC 1578)*

This is an important FAQ for educators who are interested in finding Internet resources for their students and themselves. Available from the Directory and Database Services part of the InterNIC.

Gopher: ds.internic.net

WWW: http://ds.internic.net/rfc/rfc1578.txt/

▶ *CIA World Factbook*

The Central Intelligence Agency produces this annual report, providing information about the geography, people, government, economy, communications and defense of countries around the world.

Gopher: umslvma.umsl.edu; then choose this menu sequence:
The Library ➤ Government Information ➤ CIA World Factbook.

▶ *NCSU Library of Historical Documents*

Got a history term paper due? Too nasty out to go to the library? North Carolina University's Library of Historical documents provides the full text of dozens of historic government documents from the time of independence to the present day. It's available by three Gopher servers:

Gopher: `dewey.lib.ncsu.edu`; then choose ➤ NCSU's Library Without Walls ➤ Study Carrels ➤ History.

or

Gopher: `wiretap.spies.com`; then choose Government Docs ➤ US Historical Documents.

or

Gopher: `fatty.law.cornell.edu`; then choose Foreign and International Law.

▶▶ *Mailing Lists*

The resources we've listed so far fall generally into the category of things you need to seek out each time you want to use them. Another category of materials can be delivered to your e-mail box (your front door on the Internet). By subscribing to a mailing list, you can read materials on particular topics when you read your e-mail. And, unlike Gopher and Web information, you can contribute, too, by replying to the message.

▶ *Fish-Junior*

The Fish-Junior mailing list is a way for students to communicate with marine scientists. Students of all ages and all countries are welcome. To subscribe send a standard subscription message to:

E-Mail Address: `listserv@searn.sunet.se`

or to

E-Mail Address: `listserv@searn.bitnet`

Remember not to add a Subject line, and to enter

`subscribe fish-junior` *yourfirstname yourlastname*

in the body of your e-mail message.

▶ *KidCafe*

Children ages 10–15 from all over the world are invited to join this chat list and learn more about each other and their cultures. Adults may read but not post. Send a standard subscription message to:

E-Mail Address: `listserv@vm1.nodak.edu`

or

E-Mail Address: `listserv@ndsuvm1`

▶ *THIS JUST IN*

A tasty weekly collection of strange news from a California tech publisher. One issue told of a New Jersey man fined for "needlessly" killing an animal—a rat! Another story concerned a Venezuela teen who, needing a spot to relieve himself, somehow went into a lion's pen: "Perez struggled both to live and to get his pants up; a friend helped by hitting the lion with a brick. And that brick came from … where?" To subscribe, send e-mail to:

E-Mail Address: `listserv@netcom.com`

The Subject line should be `Ignored`; and the body of the message should read `Subscribe This-Just-In`.

▶▶ *MUDs (Interactive Player Games)*

There are many MUDs and other interactive player games available through the Internet. Some use a Web browser, some use Gopher, many have you Telnet to a specific site using a specific port number. Here are two of the good lists available using the Web.

Resources for Kids

▶ ▶
ch.
23

As part of the Virtual Library project to "catalog" the Web, there is a list maintained of games and recreation.

WWW: http://www.cis.ufl/.edu/~thoth/library/recreation.html

The Virtual Library itself is a distributed catalog project built and maintained by volunteers. You can find out more about it at

WWW: http://info.cern.ch/hypertext/DataSources/bySubject/Overview.html

Another good games list is part of the Yahoo environment at Stanford:

WWW: akebono.stanford.edu/Entertainment/Games

You will see a list of MUDs and other games. Middle-school play-testers suggest DIKU MUDs (shown in Figure 23.24), including Dragon's Fire (based on the Anne McCaffery's Pern series), TRON, Imperial, and End of the Line (EOTL). These MUDs do have mixed-age players.

FIGURE 23.24 ▶

A list of DIKU MUDs as reached from the starting points documents.

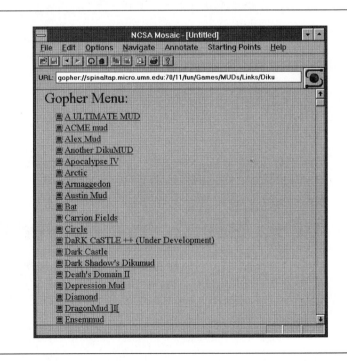

▶▶ *Newsgroups*

Newsgroups are something like mailing lists in that you have to subscribe to them and you may choose to participate in the discussions. But they're something like published information in Gopher or the World Wide Web, too, because they're broadcast to a lot of people around the world. One of the fun things to do in a newsgroup is to practice a language that you've been studying in school. You can find newsgroups where you can correspond (in public, of course) with students in Germany, for example. Try the `k12.lang.german` group. You'll meet some great people.

▶ *Chat/Discussion Newsgroups*

K–12 students and teachers can discuss topics of interest in the appropriate `k12.chat` newsgroups.

> Kindergarteners through fifth grade: `k12.chat.elementary`
>
> Sixth graders through eighth graders: `k12.chat.junior`
>
> Freshmen through seniors: `k12.chat.senior`
>
> Teachers at all levels: `k12.chat.teacher`

▶▶ *Other Interesting Things*

Here are a few more items of interest to kids, their parents, and their teachers.

▶ *Confidential Health Question Service*

Teenagers sometimes have sensitive health questions that they are afraid or unwilling to discuss with their parents (or with family physicians, school nurses, or other health providers who might contact their parents). The University of Michigan Health Service provides a way to ask such questions.

> **Telnet:** `hermes.merit.edu`

At the "Which Host?" prompt, enter **UM-UHS-INFO**, and follow the prompt to ask a confidential question. Give a secret code to get anonymous responses. Figure 23.25 shows the initial screen for the service.

FIGURE 23.25 ▶

The U-M Health Service server.

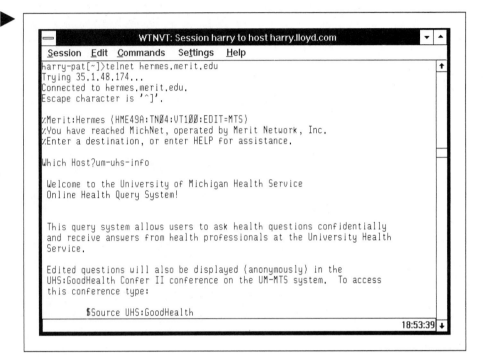

```
                    WTNVT: Session harry to host harry.lloyd.com          ▼ ▲
 Session  Edit  Commands   Settings   Help
harry-pat[~]>telnet hermes.merit.edu                                          ↑
Trying 35.1.48.174...
Connected to hermes.merit.edu.
Escape character is '^]'.

%Merit:Hermes (HME49A:TN04:VT100:EDIT=MTS)
%You have reached MichNet, operated by Merit Network, Inc.
%Enter a destination, or enter HELP for assistance.

Which Host?um-uhs-info

Welcome to the University of Michigan Health Service
Online Health Query System!


This query system allows users to ask health questions confidentially
and receive answers from health professionals at the University Health
Service.

Edited questions will also be displayed (anonymously) in the
UHS:GoodHealth Confer II conference on the UM-MTS system.  To access
this conference type:

        $Source UHS:GoodHealth
                                                                   18:53:39  ↓
```

▶ Personalized Children's Books

Make your child the star of his or her own story. Personalized children's books incorporate your child's name, age, city, and up to three friends' names in the text of the story. Currently there are five titles to choose from. Figure 23.26 shows general information about the books.

WWW: http://mmink.cts.com/mmink/dossiers/pi.html

▶ Cookie Servers

Cookie servers don't really serve cookies, of course. They are databases of funny quotes and sayings. The name comes from the idea of the "fortune" cookies that are served in Chinese restaurants in the United

FIGURE 23.26

Information about personalized books via the Web.

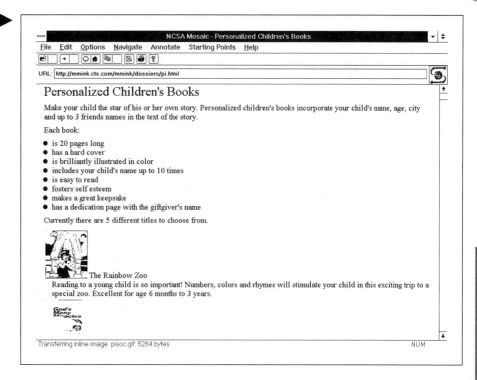

States. The sayings are a time-honored Internet tradition and you'll see .sig (e-mail signature) files with cookie sayings built into them. Each time you Telnet to a cookie server, the server sends back a different saying. Be sure and include the port numbers!

> **Telnet:** `astro.temple.edu` port 12345

or

> **Telnet:** `129.32.1.100`

or (for Star Trek quotes)

> **Telnet:** `149.132.2.11` port 10250

▶ *Fun Fingers*

With the Finger command, kids of all ages can find information that people have provided for fun (or their idea of fun, anyway), such as the status of drink and candy machines at various universities:

```
finger info or drink or graph@drink.csh.rit.edu
finger coke@cs.cmu.edu or finger coke@xcf.berkeley.edu
finger pepsi or cocacola@columbia.edu
finger coke@ucc.gu.uwa.edu.au
```

Weekly Trivia:

```
finger cyndiw@magnus1.com or cyndiw@198.242.50.4
```

▶ *Sports on the Web*

Sports lovers can cruise the Internet at length with a multitude of sports information services available. Figure 23.27 shows the Sports

FIGURE 23.27 ▶

The Sports Info server at MIT.

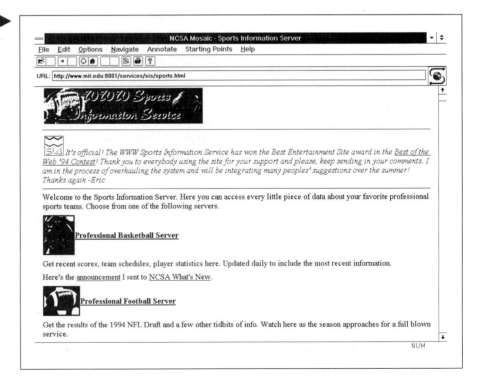

Information server at MIT, available via the Web at any of the following addresses:

```
http://tns-www.lcs.mit.edu/vs/vssportsbrowser.html
http://www.mit.edu:8001/services/sis/sports.html
http://sunsite.sut.ac.jp/gate/sports.html
http://sfgate.com/sports/
http://www.cs.fsu.edu/projects/group12/title.html
```

▶ Sports Schedules

Here are some fun servers at the University of Colorado. You use Telnet to connect to a specific port number and you can see information about the National Basketball Association, the National Hockey League, the National Football League, or Major League Baseball. This is handy if you want to plan an outing to a game on a specific day, for example. Once you are connected to the server with the specific information you need, you can enter a date, for example 1/19, and see the schedule for that day for that sport. If you pick a day that isn't within the "season" for the sport, the servers will tell you that, too. If you follow a specific team, you can enter a code for that team. Or if you want to know only about a specific division within the particular league, you can enter a code for that, too. And if you just press the ENTER key, the servers will display the games for "today". Enter "help" for a complete set of instructions as well as a list of all the teams and leagues for that sport.

Enter the command **quit** to exit the service.

> NBA: Telnet to `culine.colorado.edu`, port 859 or to the IP address 128.138.129.170, port 859.

> NHL: Telnet to `culine.colorado.edu`, port 860 or to the IP address `128.138.129.170`, port 860.

> Major League Baseball: Telnet to `culine.colorado.edu`, port 862, or to the IP address `128.138.129.170`, port 862.

> NFL: Telnet to `culine.colorado.edu`, port 863 or to the IP address `128.138.129.170`, port 863.

You can also Finger `copi@oddjob.uchicago.edu` for sports schedules.

► *Sports Reports*

Starwave has created a Web site called Satchel Sports that features continuously updated stories, scores, features, photos, and opinion columns about professional and college sports in the United States. The sports articles even carry a time stamp on them (this means the articles have the exact release time displayed), so you can make sure you are getting the latest information. You'll find it at:

WWW: `http://www.starwave.com/SatchelSports.html`

► *National Hockey League Info*

Extensive National Hockey League information is summarized on a new home page, including the latest NHL scores, the present league standings, team records against each other, the 1994 Stanley Cup Playoff matchups broken down game-by-game, and the leading scorers. Current information, in late 1994, was for the 1993–94 season. Plans are to keep the HTML files updated automatically with the use of two FORTRAN programs that take as their input game scores and the names of players who have registered goals or assists. In addition, you can also get the history of matchups in the Stanley Cup finals, and NHL awards like the Rookie of the Year Award or the Most Valuable Player Award. Figure 23.28 shows the NHL Home page.

WWW: `http://maxwell.uhh.hawaii.edu/hockey/hockey.html`

► *The Games Domain*

This Web server offers the largest collection of games-related connecting points on the Internet. This site contains over 140 links to various FAQs, walk-throughs, pointers to FTP sites, home pages, host sites for interactive environments, information documents, and much more! Figure 23.29 shows the result of a search for games related to music. There are also games reviews via the Web version of GameBytes magazine.

WWW: `http://wcl-rs.bham.ac.uk/GamesDomain.`

FIGURE 23.28

The National Hockey League home page.

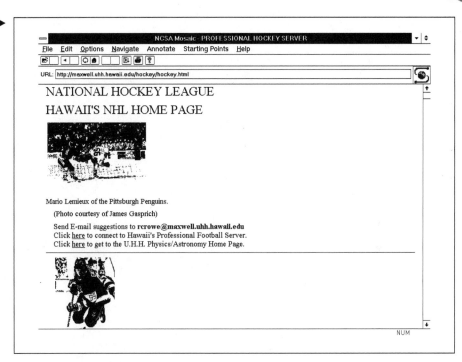

FIGURE 23.29

Results of a search for music games at the Games Domain.

An Internet
User's Glossary

PART FOUR

We've tried to include here every term that you might want to look up while reading this book. However, not all of the words in this glossary appear in the book. Some are included because you will come across them as you continue to explore the Internet; others are here because they're fun, and certainly one of the benefits of Internet communication is that it's fun.

Many of these definitions were derived from the User Glossary Working Group in the User Sources Area of the Internet Enginerring Task Force (IETF).

10Base-T A variant of the *Ethernet* networking standard that allows stations to be attached via *twisted pair* cable.

822 See *RFC 822*.

:-) This peculiar-looking symbol is one of the ways a person can portray emotions in the low-bandwidth medium of computer-mediated communication—by using "smiley faces." There are literally hundreds of such symbols. This particular example expresses "happiness". Don't see it? Tilt your head to the left 90 degrees. Smiles are also used to denote sarcasm. See also *Emoticon*. (Thanks to Brendan Kehoe.)

.plan A plan file on a UNIX system is one that can be read by users on- and off-system using the *Finger* program (if the systems administrator has set up the system to allow it). It has the filename extension .plan and usually contains some information you want people to know about you, such as name, preferred e-mail address, and business phone. Some plan files also include information about the user's interests. Some systems administrators do not permit remote fingering of .plan files for security or privacy reasons.

Acceptable Use Policy (AUP) Many networks, both the larger *transit* and regional networks as well as company networks and public BBSes, have policies that restrict the uses to which the network or computing facility may be put. A well-known example is NSFNET's AUP, which does not allow commercial use. Enforcement of AUPs varies with the network and systems administrator. See also *National Science Foundation*.

Access Control List (ACL) A list of services available on a network, each with a list of the hosts permitted to use the service. Many network security systems operate by allowing selective use of services. An Access Control List is the usual means by which access to services is permitted or denied.

acknowledgment (ACK) A response sent to confirm receipt of a message. See also *Negative Acknowledgment*.

AD See *Administrative Domain*.

address The unique identifier for a specific location on a network. There are three types of addresses in common use within the Internet. They are *e-mail address*; *IP*, internet or Internet address; and *hardware* or *MAC address*.

address mask A pattern of numbers used to identify which parts of an *IP address* correspond to the network, *subnet*, and *host* portions of the address. This mask is often referred to as the *subnet mask*.

Address Resolution Protocol (ARP) A method used to determine the low-level physical network hardware address that corresponds to the high-level *IP address* for a given *host*. It is defined in RFC 826. See also *proxy ARP*.

Administrative Domain (AD) A collection of hosts and routers, and the interconnecting network(s), managed by a single administrative authority. See also *domain*.

Advanced Research Projects Agency An agency of the US Department of Defense responsible for the development of new technology for use by the military. ARPA was responsible for funding much of the development of the Internet we know today, including the Berkeley version of UNIX and TCP/IP.

pt.
IV

Advanced Research Projects Agency Network (ARPANET) A network funded by ARPA (formerly DARPA). It served as the basis for early networking research in the 1960s, as well as the central *backbone* during the development of the Internet. The ARPANET's architecture consisted of individual *packet-switching* computers interconnected by leased lines.

agent In the *client-server computing* model, the part of the system that performs information preparation and exchange on behalf of a *client* or *server* application. For example, in some database searches, the agent lets you ask questions in a format that is comfortable to you, and reformats the question as a strictly defined search argument for the database.

alias A name, usually short and easy to remember, that is translated into another name, usually long and difficult to remember. In networking, aliases are frequently used to associate a service with a logical name, rather than with a particular computer or machine address. Aliases are also used to reroute mail and service requests from one computer to another; this allows the system or network management to change the computer providing the services when needed without affecting users, or to keep the underlying architecture hidden. Aliases are also used to indicate the service available from the host: for example, `www.weather.org`, `gopher.msu.edu`, or `ftp.netcom.com`. See also *mail alias*.

alias database The group of public aliases on an e-mail system. Aliases include group names, nicknames, and services, such as "sales" or "support," which allow mail to be redirected inside the e-mail system.

American National Standards Institute (ANSI) This organization is responsible for approving US standards in many areas, including computers and communications. Standards approved by this organization are often called ANSI standards (for example, ANSI C is the version of the C language approved by ANSI). ANSI is a member of ISO. See also *International Organization for Standardization*.

American Standard Code for Information Interchange (ASCII) A standard character-to-number encoding widely used in the computer industry. Plain text, Postscript files, and BinHex files are among the types of data transferred in ASCII format. Spreadsheets, compiled programs, and graphics are transferred across the net in *binary* format. In addition, the computer community has extended the ASCII character set to allow for the transmission of control and other characters within the data being transferred. This change allowed for high speed, "8-bit clean" data transmission, essential for the development of workstation TCP/IP applications. This lets users turn their home computers into Internet hosts. See also *EBCDIC*.

anonymous FTP Anonymous *FTP* allows a user to retrieve (and sometimes deposit) documents, files, programs, and other archived data from archives in the Internet without having to establish a user ID and password on the computer that contains the archive. Many, but not all, computers used as FTP *archive sites* allow anonymous access. By using the special user ID anonymous and the password guest you can have limited access to publicly accessible files on the remote system. Many systems now request the user's e-mail address as a password, in order to have better access tracking. See also *File Transfer Protocol*.

ANSI See *American National Standards Institute*.

API See *Application Program Interface*.

AppleTalk A networking protocol developed by Apple Computer, Inc. for communication between Apple products and other computers. AppleTalk runs on several kinds of network media and underlying protocols.

application A program that performs a function directly for a user. FTP, Mail and Telnet clients are examples of network applications. DOS, Windows, MacOS, and UNIX are examples of operating systems, on which applications run.

Application Program Interface (API) In general, a definition of all the functions that an operating system provides to application programs for performing tasks such as file management and displaying information on the screen, and of how the application should use those functions. In networking, an API also defines the method by which applications can take advantage of network features.

Archie A system to automatically gather, index and serve archive information on the Internet. The initial implementation of Archie provided an indexed directory of filenames from *anonymous FTP* archives on the

An Internet User's Glossary

pt.
IV

Internet. Later versions provide other collections of information. See also *archive site, Gopher, Prospero, Wide Area Information Servers.*

archive site A computer that provides access to a collection of files across the Internet. An *anonymous FTP* archive site, for example, provides access to this material via the FTP protocol. See also *Archie, Gopher, Prospero, Wide Area Information Servers.*

ARL See *Association of Research Libraries.*

ARP See *Address Resolution Protocol.*

ARPA See *Advanced Research Projects Agency.*

ARPANET See *Advanced Research Projects Agency Network.*

ASCII See *American Standard Code for Information Interchange.*

Association of Research Libraries (ARL) An association of research libraries within the United States. A research library is one whose collection is acquired primarily for academic research, rather than for general circulation—contrasted with a public library whose collection is acquired primarily for general circulation rather than for research. ARL has taken a leadership role in putting library resources on the Internet and making them widely available to the research community. The association has offices in Washington, DC, and represents the interests of academic research collections.

Asynchronous Transfer Mode (ATM) A method for the dynamic allocation of bandwidth using a fixed-size *packet* (called a cell). ATM is also known as "fast packet." ATM technology is an up-and-coming offering from many network providers.

at-sign (@) The at-sign (@) is the separator for most *e-mail addresses*; it separates the *user ID* from the *domain name* of the mail computer. See also *bang path, UUCP.*

ATM See *Asynchronous Transfer Mode.*

AUP See *Acceptable Use Policy.*

authentication The verification of the identity of a person or process. The most common authentication process most users experience is the login challenge, which requests a valid login ID and a password. PIN numbers, "carding," and the famous military checkpoint challenge "Friend or foe?" are all examples of authentication in everyday life. See also *authorization*.

authorization The granting of privilege based on identity. Authorization is a partner to authentication in computer networking, where your access to services is based on your identity, and an authentication procedure guarantees that you are who you say you are. See also *authentication, Kerberos, password*.

backbone The top level in a hierarchical network. *Stub networks* and *transit networks* that connect to the same backbone are guaranteed to be interconnected. Backbone networks usually run at a higher speed, and with a larger *bandwidth*, than the networks that branch off of them.

bandwidth Technically, the difference, in Hertz (Hz), between the highest and lowest frequencies of a transmission channel. However, as typically used, the amount of data that can be sent through a given communications circuit. People are now beginning to also consider the amount of information in human interactions, such as expressions (smiles, frowns) and other body language that cannot be sent over electronic channels such as e-mail and news, and describe electronic transactions as being "low in emotional bandwidth."

bang path From the UNIX jargon: a *bang* is an exclamation point (!). A series of computer names used to direct electronic mail from one user to another, typically by specifying an explicit UUCP path through which the mail is to be routed. UUCP mail pathways looks like this, with the user name last: andros!mailrus!jabberwock!cs-wisc!susan. See also *at-sign, e-mail address, mail path, splat, UNIX-to-UNIX CoPy (UUCP)*.

baseband A transmission medium through which digital signals are sent without complicated frequency shifting. In general, only one communication channel is available at any given time. *Ethernet* is an example of a baseband network. See also *broadband*.

BBS See *Bulletin Board System*.

BCNU Be Seein' You.

Berkeley Internet Name Domain (BIND) Implementation of a DNS server developed and distributed by the University of California at Berkeley. Many Internet hosts run BIND, and it is the ancestor of many commercial BIND implementations.

Berkeley Software Distribution (BSD) An implementation of the UNIX operating system and its utilities developed and distributed by the University of California at Berkeley. "BSD" is usually preceded by the version number of the distribution, for example, "4.3 BSD" is version 4.3 of the Berkeley UNIX distribution. Many Internet hosts run BSD software, and it is the ancestor of many commercial UNIX implementations.

binary "It's all ones and zeros." Computers store information in the form of on/off electrical impulses, which correspond to the binary (base 2) digits 0 and 1. Files can be transferred over the Internet in either binary or *ASCII* (text) format. A binary file is one that contains any nonprintable characters; such as compiled programs, graphics files, word-processing and spreadsheet files, audio files, and so on. See also *File Transfer Protocol.*

BIND See *Berkeley Internet Name Domain.*

Birds Of a Feather (BOF) A Birds Of a Feather (flocking together) is an informally structured, common-interest discussion group. It is formed, often *ad hoc,* to consider a specific issue and, therefore, has a narrow focus. *BOFs* are often held during long breaks or after the main sessions at computer and technology-related conferences; the term is spreading to more mainstream events.

bit *BI*nary digi*T*. A unit of data. There are eight bits in a byte. There are eight bits in one ASCII character. See also kilobit, megabit.

BITNET A largely academic computer network that provides interactive electronic mail, interactive conversation, and file transfer services, using a *store-and-forward* protocol, based on IBM Network Job Entry protocols. BITNET-II encapsulates the BITNET protocol within IP packets and depends on the Internet to route them. See also *spooling.*

BOF See *Birds Of a Feather.*

BOOTP The Bootstrap Protocol, described in RFCs 951 and 1084, is used for booting network nodes that do not have the boot instructions stored within the computer on a hard disk. See also *Reverse Address Resolution Protocol.*

bounce The return of a piece of mail because of an error in its delivery.

bounce-o-gram A message from an automated mailer telling you that mail has bounced.

bridge A device that forwards traffic between network segments. These segments would have a common network layer address. *Apple-Talk* networks and *Ethernet* networks sometimes use bridges. See also *gateway, router.*

broadband A transmission medium capable of supporting a wide range of frequencies. It can carry multiple signals by dividing the total capacity of the medium into multiple, independent bandwidth channels, where each channel operates only on a specific range of frequencies. Traditional cable television services operate on a broadband service. See also *baseband.*

broadcast A special type of *multicast packet* that all *nodes* on the network are always willing to receive.

broadcast storm An incorrect *packet broadcast* onto a network that causes multiple *hosts* to respond all at once, typically with equally incorrect packets; this causes the storm to grow exponentially. A broadcast storm can bring down a network in moments, usually from overloading of the *routers* and other packet handling equipment.

brouter A device that *bridges* some packets and *routes* other packets. The bridge/route decision is based on configuration information.

Browser *World-Wide Web* and *gopher* services are accessed using *client* software called browsers, because they let you drift from link to link without having to have a purposeful search. Browsers encourage discovery by serendipity, hence the name.

BSD See *Berkeley Software Distribution.*

BTW By The Way.

Bulletin Board System (BBS) A computer (with associated software), that typically provides electronic messaging services, archives of files, and any other services or activities of interest to the bulletin board system's operator. Although BBSes were traditionally the domain of hobbyists and accessible only by using a modem, an increasing number of BBSes are connected directly to the Internet, and many are currently operated by government, educational, and research institutions. See also *Electronic Mail, Internet, MUD, Usenet.*

Campus Wide Information System (CWIS) A CWIS makes information and services publicly available on campus via kiosks (information stations named for the familiar circular bulletin boards with posters stapled to them), and it makes interactive computing available via kiosks, interactive computing systems, and campus networks. They are usually found on college campuses, although some K-12 school systems are beginning to develop CWISes. Services routinely include directory information, calendars, bulletin boards, and databases.

CAUSE CAUSE is an association of administrative computing officers of institutions of higher education. CAUSE helps determine policy and availability of campus-based computer networks, as well as the major academic and research-based network infrastructure (such as the NSFNET backbone).

CCIRN See *Coordinating Committee for Intercontinental Research Networks.*

CCITT See *Comite Consultatif International de Telegraphique et Telephonique.*

CERT See *Computer Emergency Response Team.*

checksum A method of verifying the accuracy of transmitted data, a checksum is a computed value calculated from the contents of a packet. This value is sent along with the packet when it is transmitted. The receiving system computes a new checksum (using the same algorithm as the transmitting end used) based upon the received data and compares this value to the one sent with the packet. If the two values are the same, the receiver has a high degree of confidence that the data was received correctly.

CIDR   See *Classless Internet Domain Routing.*

circuit switching   A communications paradigm in which a dedicated communication path is established between two hosts, and on which all packets travel. The telephone system is an example of a circuit-switched network. See also *connection-oriented, connectionless, packet-switching.*

CIX   The Commercial Internet eXchange is an association of Internet providers in the United States. CIX members have agreed to carry the commercial traffic of each member network. The CIX was formed to provide routing for commercial Internet traffic during the time that the NSFNET AUP (Acceptable Use Policy) specifically forbade purely commercial traffic. For more information, see the CIX Gopher and Web servers at CIX.ORG.

Classless Internet Domain Routing (CIDR)   A routing protocol for working with multiple Class C addresses.

client   In *client-server computing,* the "front-end" program that the user runs to connect with, and request information from, the *server* program. For most of the common Internet tools, many different client programs are available, designed to work in DOS, Windows, Macintosh, and UNIX environments. See also *Archie, WAIS, www.*

client-server computing   The model or scheme underlying practically all programs running on the Internet (as well as other network and database software). In this design, the work of an application (such as *FTP* or *Gopher*) is divided up between two programs—the *client* (or front end) and the *server* (or back end). The client program handles the work of connecting to the server and requesting files or information, and the server handles the work of finding and "serving up" the information (or of providing some other service, such as directing print jobs to a printer). See also *Archie, client, ftp, gopher, server, Domain Name System, Network File System, WAIS, WWW.*

Coalition for Networked Information (CNI)   A consortium formed by the Association of Research Libraries, CAUSE, and EDUCOM to promote the creation of, and access to, information resources in

networked environments in order to enrich scholarship and enhance intellectual productivity. See also *ARL, CAUSE, EDUCOM.*

Coaxial Cable Also referred to as "coax," a transmission medium or cable in which one conductor completely surrounds the other. The outer layer is generally the ground. Coaxial cable does not give off an electric field and is not susceptible to fields from other sources, because the field stops at the outer conductor. Cable TV is transmitted over coaxial cable. See also *Ethernet.*

Comite Consultatif International de Telegraphique (CCITT) This organization is part of the United Nations International Telecommunications Union (ITU) and is responsible for making technical recommendations about telephone and data communications systems. Every four years CCITT holds plenary sessions where they adopt new standards; the most recent was in 1992.

Computer Emergency Response Team (CERT) The CERT was formed by DARPA in November 1988 in response to the needs exhibited during the Internet worm incident, where a program sent out on the Internet by a college student used security loopholes in networked computers to replicate itself, send itself on to other computers, and disable critical functions on the affected computers. The CERT charter is to work with the Internet community to facilitate its response to computer security events involving Internet hosts, to take proactive steps to raise the community's awareness of computer security issues, and to conduct research targeted at improving the security of existing systems. CERT products and services include 24-hour technical assistance for responding to computer security incidents, product vulnerability assistance, technical documents, and tutorials. In addition, the team maintains a number of mailing lists (including one for CERT Advisories), and provides an anonymous FTP server, at `cert.org`, where security-related documents and tools are archived. The CERT may be reached by e-mail at `cert@cert.org` and by telephone at +1-412-268-7090 (24-hour hotline). See also *Advanced Research Projects Agency, worm.*

congestion Congestion occurs when the load exceeds the capacity of a data communication path. You may be experiencing congestion when any of the following happens: you get a busy signal when you dial into a modem pool; the response from the server or host you are trying to reach is slow; you get an error message telling you that no ports are available for the service or host you want to use.

connection-oriented Describes a data communication method in which communication proceeds through three well-defined phases: connection establishment, data transfer, connection release. TCP is a connection-oriented protocol. See also *circuit switching, connectionless, packet-switching, Transmission Control Protocol.*

connectionless Describes a data communication method in which communication occurs between hosts with no previous setup. Packets between two hosts may take different routes, as each is independent of the other. See also *circuit switching, connection-oriented, packet switching.*

Coordinating Committee for Intercontinental Research Networks (CCIRN) A committee that includes the United States *Federal Networking Council* (FNC) and its counterparts in North America and Europe. Co-chaired by the executive directors of the FNC and the European Association of Research Networks (*RARE*), the CCIRN provides a forum for cooperative planning among the principal North American and European research networking bodies. These bodies are the principal planning and organizing bodies that plan the political and funding growth of the world-wide networks, as opposed to the IETF, which plans the technological growth.

core gateway Historically, one of a set of *gateways* (*routers*) operated by the Internet Network Operations Center at Bolt, Beranek and Newman (BBN). The core gateway system formed a central part of Internet routing in that all groups must advertise paths to their networks from a core gateway.

Corporation for Research and Educational Networking (CREN) This organization was formed in October 1989, when *BITNET* and CSNET (Computer + Science NETwork) were combined under one administrative authority. CSNET is no longer operational, but CREN still runs BITNET.

cracker An individual who attempts to access computer systems without authorization. These individuals are often malicious, as opposed to *hackers* (who see themselves as benevolent explorers), and have many means at their disposal for breaking into a system. See also *Computer Emergency Response Team, Trojan Horse, virus, worm*.

CREN See *Corporation for Research and Educational Networking*.

CSLIP Serial Line Internet Protocol with compressed headers. See also *Point-to-Point Protocol, Serial Line IP*.

CWIS See *Campus Wide Information System*.

Cyberspace *Cyber* comes from the 50s term *cybernetics*, which is used to describe the science of computers. *Space* harkens to the 60s terms "inner space," "head space," and so on. Cyberspace is a term coined by either computer hackers or science fiction writers (both claim credit) to describe the place you are when you are traversing the virtual geography of the Internet. The term first appeared in print in William Gibson's 1984 fantasy novel *Neuromancer* to describe the "world" of computers and the society that gathers around them.

Data Encryption Key (DEK) Used for the *encryption* of message text and for the computation of message integrity checks (signatures).

Data Encryption Standard (DES) A popular, standard *encryption* scheme.

datagram A self-contained, independent entity of data carrying sufficient information to be routed from the source to the destination computer without reliance on earlier exchanges between the source and destination computers and the transporting network. This entity has given rise to several joking and serious other sorts of communications: a bounce-o-gram, for example, is a message from an automated mailer telling you mail has bounced. A nastygram is an unpleasant message, usually e-mail but sometimes in news, which has unpleasant contents. See also *frame, packet*. [Term coined by J. Postel]

DCA See *Defense Information Systems Agency*.

DCE Data Circuit-terminating Equipment. See also *DTE*.

DCE See *Distributed Computing Environment*.

DDN See *Defense Data Network*.

DDN NIC See *Defense Data Network Network Information Center*.

DECnet A proprietary network protocol designed by Digital Equipment Corporation.

default route An entry in a *routing table*, used to direct packets addressed to networks not explicitly listed in the routing table. See also *static route*.

Defense Advanced Research Projects Agency (DARPA) See *Advanced Research Projects Agency*.

Defense Data Network (DDN) A global communications network serving the US Department of Defense and composed of the MIL-NET, other portions of the Internet, and the classified networks that are not part of the Internet. The DDN is used to connect military installations and is managed by the Defense Information Systems Agency. See also *Defense Information Systems Agency*.

Defense Data Network Network Information Center (DDN NIC) Often called "the NIC." The DDN NIC's primary responsibilities are assigning Internet network addresses and Autonomous System numbers, administering of the root domain, and providing information and support services to the DDN. It is also a primary repository for RFCs. See also *Internet Registry, Network Information Center, Request For Comments*.

Defense Information Systems Agency (DISA) Formerly called the Defense Communications Agency (DCA), this is the government agency responsible for managing the DDN portion of the Internet, including the MILNET. Currently, DISA administers the DDN, and supports the user assistance services of the DDN NIC. See also *Defense Data Network*.

DEK See *Data Encryption Key*.

DES See *Data Encryption Standard*.

dialup A temporary, as opposed to dedicated, connection between computers established over a standard phone line.

An Internet
User's Glossary

pt.
IV

Directory Access Protocol The *X.500* protocol used for communication between a *Directory User Agent* and a *Directory System Agent*.

Directory System Agent (DSA) The software that provides the *X.500* Directory Service for a portion of the directory information base. Generally, each DSA is responsible for the directory information for a single organization or organizational unit.

Directory User Agent (DUA) The software that accesses the *X.500* Directory Service on behalf of the directory user. The directory user may be a person or another software element.

DISA See *Defense Information Systems Agency.*

Distributed Computing Environment (DCE) In our current computing environment of heterogeneous computers, network architectures, and protocols, some standards had to be created for conventions to allow users of these varied computers to be able to function on remote systems. These standards define user interfaces, the way data will be formatted so that systems with differing internal structures will be able to process it, and other methods of interoperability. The goal is that the user will never have to know and negotiate the differences between systems. the DCE standards are promoted and controlled by the Open Software Foundation (OSF), a consortium led by Digital, IBM, and Hewlett Packard.

distributed database A collection of several different data repositories that looks like a single database to the user. A prime example in the Internet is the *Domain Name System.*

DIX Ethernet See *Ethernet.*

DNS See *Domain Name System*

DNS Server A computer that translates the *domain name* of another computer into an *IP address,* and vice versa, upon request. Most DNS servers maintain a large database of such correspondences, which is refreshed on a regular (at most daily) basis. Usually the request for translation comes from another computer, which needs the IP address for routing purposes.

domain A named collection of network *hosts*. Some important domains are: .COM (commercial), .EDU (educational), .NET (network operations), .GOV (US government), and .MIL (US military). Most countries also have individual domains; for example, .US (United States), .UK (United Kingdom), .AU (Australia). See also *Administrative Domain, Domain Name System.*

domain name The human-language name of a computer on the Internet, as opposed to its more computer-friendly numeric *IP address.* For example, `hermes.merit.edu` is a domain name or address, and `42.1.1.6` is an IP address.

Domain Name System (DNS) The set of conventions for naming *host* computers on the Internet and the directory service for looking up names. Each host name corresponds to an *IP address.* The DNS is defined in STD 13, RFCs 1034 and 1035. See also *Fully Qualified Domain Name.*

dot address (dotted decimal notation) Dot address refers to the common notation for IP addresses of the form A.B.C.D; where each letter represents, in decimal, one byte of a four-byte IP address. See also *IP address.*

DSA See *Directory System Agent.*

DTE Data Terminal Equipment. See also *DCE.*

DUA See *Directory User Agent.*

dynamic adaptive routing Automatic rerouting of traffic based on a sensing and analysis of current actual network conditions.

EARN See *European Academic and Research Network.*

EBCDIC See *Extended Binary Coded Decimal Interchange Code.*

Ebone A pan-European backbone service.

EFF See *Electronic Frontier Foundation.*

EGP See *Exterior Gateway Protocol.*

An Internet
User's Glossary

pt.
IV

Electronic Frontier Foundation (EFF)   A foundation established to address social and legal issues arising from the impact on society of the increasingly pervasive use of computers as a means of communication and information distribution. You can reach the EFF at info@eff.org. The EFF's anonymous FTP archive of user policies at schools and universities is particularly useful.

electronic mail (e-mail)   A system whereby a computer user can exchange messages with other computer users (or groups of users) via a communications network. Electronic mail is one of the most popular uses of the Internet.

e-mail   See *electronic mail.*

e-mail address   The domain-based or UUCP address that is used to send electronic mail to a specified destination. For example, one of the authors' addresses is pat@lloyd.com. See also *bang path, mail path, UNIX-to-UNIX CoPy.*

encapsulation   The technique used by layered protocols in which a *layer* adds header information to the protocol data unit (PDU) from the layer above. As an example, in Internet terminology, a packet would contain a header from the physical layer, followed by a header from the network layer (IP), followed by a header from the transport layer (TCP), followed by the application protocol data.

encryption   The manipulation of a *packet*'s data in order to prevent any but the intended recipient from reading that data. There are many types of data encryption, and they are the basis of network security. See also *Data Encryption Standard, Kerberos.*

Ethernet   A 10 Mbps standard for LANs, initially developed by Xerox, and later refined by Digital, Intel and Xerox (DIX). All hosts are connected to a coaxial cable, where they contend for network access using a Carrier Sense Multiple Access with Collision Detection (CSMA/CD) paradigm. See also *802.x, Local Area Network, token ring.*

Ethernet meltdown   An event that causes saturation, or near saturation, on an *Ethernet*. It usually results from illegal or misrouted *packets* and typically lasts only a short time. See also *broadcast storm.*

European Academic and Research Network (EARN) A network connecting European academic and research institutions with electronic mail and file transfer services using the *BITNET* protocol.

Extended Binary Coded Decimal Interchange Code (EBCDIC) A standard character-to-number encoding used primarily by IBM computer systems. Most Internet hosts USC ASCII encoding; however, you may encounter EBCDIC if you transfer data via tape or other physical media to or from a large IBM installation. Additionally, while most systems translate EBCDIC to ASCII during FTP or other electronic transmission, some older computers in non-US countries may still have files stored in EBCDIC. See also *ASCII*.

Exterior Gateway Protocol (EGP) A protocol that distributes routing information to the routers that connect autonomous systems. The term "gateway" is historical, as "router" is currently the preferred term. There is also a routing protocol called EGP defined in STD 18, RFC 904. See also *Interior Gateway Protocol*.

FARNET A non-profit corporation, established in 1987, whose mission is to advance the use of computer networks to improve research and education. You can reach FARNET at info@farnet.org.

FAQ Frequently Asked Question; that is, a document containing answers to a set of such questions. Many newsgroups put out these FAQ documents so that each new person does not ask the same questions; many computer product companies, as well as organizations that distribute information or do business over the Internet, have begun creating FAQs for their product, service, or information. Many FAQs are stored in an *anonymous FTP* archive, and many are broadcast across interested *mailing lists* at least once per month. See also *Flame*.

fast packet See *Asynchronous Transfer Mode*.

FDDI See *Fiber Distributed Data Interface*.

Federal Information Exchange (FIX) One of the connection points between the US governmental internets and the Internet. See also *CIX*.

Federal Networking Council (FNC) The coordinating group of representatives from those federal agencies involved in the development and use of federal networking, especially those networks using TCP/IP and the Internet. Current members include representatives from DOD, DOE, DARPA, NSF, NASA, and HHS. See also *Defense Advanced Research Projects Agency, National Science Foundation*.

Fiber Distributed Data Interface (FDDI) A high-speed (100 Mbps) LAN standard. The underlying medium is fiber optics. See also Local Area Network, token ring.

file transfer The copying of a file from one computer to another over a computer network. See also *File Transfer Protocol, Kermit*.

File Transfer Protocol (FTP) A protocol that allows a user on one host to access, and transfer files to and from, another host over a network. Also, FTP is usually the name of the program the user invokes to execute the protocol. It is defined in STD 9, RFC 959. See also *anonymous FTP, archive*.

Finger A program that displays information about a particular user, or all users, logged on the local system or on a remote system. It typically shows full name, last login time, idle time, terminal line, and terminal location (where applicable). It may also display any *.plan* and .project files left by the user.

FIX See *Federal Information Exchange*.

flame A strong opinion and/or criticism of something, usually in a deliberately insulting tone, in an electronic mail message or news posting. Flaming is frowned upon in polite Internet society. It is common to precede a flame with an indication of pending fire (such as "FLAME ON!"). "Flame Wars" occur when people start flaming other people for flaming when they shouldn't have. They can also start when a new reader in a *newsgroup* asks a question that older readers have answered many times, and that has been incorporated into a Frequently Asked Questions list. A warning to new users: some folk enjoy flame wars and deliberately try to provoke one. See also *Electronic Mail, FAQ, kill file*.

FNC See *Federal Networking Council*.

Forms-Capable Browser A *World Wide Web browser* that allows users to "fill in the blanks" in questionnaires and other user-response items.

Most *GUI* browsers are forms-capable, as are some of the line-mode browsers.

For Your Information (FYI) A subseries of RFCs that are not technical standards or descriptions of protocols. FYIs convey general information about topics related to TCP/IP or the Internet. See also *Request For Comments, STD.*

forwarding Passing mail from one mailbox to another, particularly when the user is not reading mail regularly on the first system. Some users with accounts on many computers prefer to read mail on one of them (for convenience, better user interface, cost, or other reasons), and so have all their mail forwarded to that account. Forwarding is also used to have mail come to a well-known public name (such as `info@host`, `postmaster@host`, or `help@host` without the need for a specific separate mailbox for that name. See also *alias.*

FQDN See *Fully Qualified Domain Name.*

fragment A piece of a packet. When a router is forwarding an IP packet to a network that has a maximum packet size smaller than the packet being forwarded, it is forced to break up that packet into multiple fragments. These fragments will be reassembled by the IP layer at the destination host. See also *packet.*

fragmentation The IP process in which a *packet* is broken into smaller pieces to fit the requirements of a physical network over which the packet must pass. See also *reassembly.*

frame A frame is an encapsulating *packet* that contains the header and trailer information required by the physical medium. That is, information or data packets are encapsulated to become frames. See also *datagram, encapsulation, packet.*

freenet Community-based bulletin board system with e-mail, information services, interactive communications, and conferencing. Freenets are funded and operated by individuals and volunteers—in one sense, like public television. They are part of the National Public Telecomputing Network (NPTN), an organization based in Cleveland, Ohio, devoted to making computer telecommunication and networking services as freely available as public libraries. See also *Bulletin Board System.*

FTP See *File Transfer Protocol.*

Fully Qualified Domain Name (FQDN) The FQDN is the full name of a *host* computer on the Internet, rather than just its host name. For example, xrayf is a host name and xrayf.ge.com is an FQDN. The host named xrayf is located within the institutional domain .ge (General Electric), which is within the top-level domain .com (commercial institutions). An FQDN corresponds to an *IP address*, but this correspondence is not fixed. If the service provided by xrayf is moved to a different computer, the administrator will be able to reassign the FQDN to the new computer's IP address. See also *host name, Domain Name System.*

FYI See *For Your Information.*

gated (Pronounced "gate-dee"); Gate-daemon. A program that supports multiple routing protocols and protocol families. It may be used for routing, and it makes an effective platform for routing protocol research. The software is freely available by anonymous FTP from gated.cornell.edu. See also *Exterior Gateway Protocol, routed.*

gateway The term "router" is now used in place of the original definition of "gateway." Currently, a gateway is a communications device/program that passes data between networks having similar functions but dissimilar implementations. This should not be confused with a protocol converter, which allows dissimilar protocols (for example, DECnet and AppleTalk) to pass data between them. See also *mail gateway, router, protocol converter.*

Gopher A menu-based program for retrieving information from resources across the Internet. Gopher uses a simple protocol that allows a single Gopher client to access information from any accessible Gopher server, providing the user with a single menu of information. Menu topics may lead to hierarchically organized subtopics. Depending on context, the term "gopherspace" refers either to the whole collection of documents available from gopher servers, or to what's available based on the menu selections you've already made. Public domain versions of the client and server are available. See also *Archie, archive site, Prospero, Wide Area Information Servers.*

Government OSI Profile (GOSIP) A subset of OSI standards specific to US Government procurements, designed to maximize interoperability in areas where plain OSI standards are ambiguous or allow excessive options. See also *Open Systems Interconnection*.

GUI (Graphical User Interface) A GUI is a software "front end" that lets the user use pictures and "point-and-click" technology to access the software application. Many modern Internet clients are based on GUI principles and technology. See also *browser, World-Wide Web, Gopher.*

hacker Among programmers, a person who delights in having an intimate understanding of the internal workings of a computer system or network. The term is often misused in a pejorative context, where *cracker* would be the correct term. Hackers take joy in accomplishing difficult tasks ("hacking out" a working program, for example) and learning more and more about networking and computer systems.

hardware address Particularly on AppleTalk and Ethernet networks, each computer has an address specific to the technology itself. These hardware addresses are mapped to the assigned *IP addresses*, and sometimes *domain addresses* as well.

header The portion of a *packet*, preceding the actual data, containing source and destination addresses, and error checking and other fields. A header is also the part of an *electronic mail* message that precedes the body of a message and contains, among other things, the message originator, date, and time.

heterogeneous network A network running multiple *network layer* protocols. See also *DECnet, IP, IPX, XNS.*

hierarchical routing The complex problem of *routing* on large networks can be simplified by reducing the size of the networks. This is accomplished by breaking a network into a hierarchy of networks, where each level is responsible for its own routing. The Internet has, basically, three levels: the backbones (such as the NSFNET or SPRINT backbones), the mid-level or *transit networks* (such as CICNet, PSINet, or SURANET), and the *stub networks* (such as The Little Garden Network Collective in San Francisco, or other small local networks). The backbones know how to route between the mid-levels, the mid-levels know how to route between the sites, and each site (being an *autonomous system*) knows how to route internally. See also *Exterior Gateway Protocol, Interior Gateway Protocol, stub network, transit network.*

High-Performance Computing and Communications (HPCC) High-performance computing encompasses advanced computing, communications, and information technologies, including scientific workstations, supercomputer systems, high speed networks, special purpose and experimental systems, the new generation of large scale parallel systems, and application and systems software with all components well integrated and linked over a high speed network. The HPCC Acts, legislation passed by the US Congress in the early 1990s (also known as the Dole bills), established national networking objectives for the United States. See also *NREN.*

High Performance Parallel Interface (HIPPI) An emerging ANSI standard that extends the computer bus over fairly short distances at speeds of 800 and 1600 Mbps. HIPPI is often used in a computer room to connect a supercomputer to routers, frame buffers, mass-storage peripherals, and other computers. This allows for faster transmission of data (or faster interactions in an interactive session like Telnet) between the computer and the network. See also *American National Standards Institute.*

HIPPI See *High Performance Parallel Interface.*

home page A home page is, in World Wide Web terms, the base page for an individual or organization. From this page there may be other pages of information or resources listed. The home page is generally what appears when you point a Web browser at http://www.*organization*/ (whatever address is signified by *organization*).

hop A term used in routing. A path to a destination on a network is a series of hops, through routers, away from the origin.

host A computer that allows users to communicate with other host computers on a network. Individual users communicate by using application programs, such as electronic mail, Telnet and FTP. In some contexts, and in some philosophies of the way the Internet should work, the host itself is less important than the servers which run on it. For example, Web and Gopher servers distribute data to users without requiring the user to know which host the server is located on. See also *server*.

host address See *internet address*.

host name The domain name given to a computer. For example, `nic.ddn.mil`, `eff.org`, and `terminator.um.cc.umich.edu` are all host names. The terms "host name" and "*Fully Qualified Domain Name*" are interchangeable in most contexts; host name is a more informal term.

host number See *host address, IP address*.

HPCC See *High Performance Computing and Communications*.

hub A device connected to several other devices. In ARCnet, a hub is used to connect several computers together. In a message-handling service, a hub is used for the transfer of messages across the network.

I-D See *Internet-Draft*.

IAB See *Internet Architecture Board*.

IANA See *Internet Assigned Numbers Authority*.

ICMP See *Internet Control Message Protocol*.

IEEE Institute of Electrical and Electronics Engineers. The IEEE is one of the bodies that create and distribute standards for network protocols, interoperability, and hardware compliance, all of which allow for smooth operation of networks. In addition, many computer professionals belong to the IEEE and subscribe to its standards of professional behavior and ethics.

IEN See *Internet Experiment Note*.

IESG See *Internet Engineering Steering Group*.

IETF See *Internet Engineering Task Force*.

IINREN See *Interagency Interim National Research and Education Network*.

An Internet
User's Glossary

pt.
IV

IGP See *Interior Gateway Protocol.*

IMHO In My Humble Opinion.

IMR See *Internet Monthly Report.*

Integrated Services Digital Network (ISDN) An emerging technology that is beginning to be offered by the telephone carriers of the world. ISDN combines voice and digital network services in a single medium, making it possible to offer customers digital data services as well as voice connections through a single "wire." The standards that define ISDN are specified by *CCITT*. If you are interested in finding out whether ISDN is available in your area, you may need to contact a local university or other large Internet site, or ask for the Data Marketing division at your local phone company. Many residential marketing customer agents at local phone companies are not fully briefed on ISDN.

Interagency Interim National Research and Education Network (IINREN) An evolving operating network system. Near term (through 1996) research and development activities will provide for the smooth evolution of this networking infrastructure into the future gigabit NREN.

Interior Gateway Protocol (IGP) A protocol that distributes routing information to the routers within an autonomous system. The term "gateway" is historical, as "router" is currently the preferred term. See also *Autonomous System, Exterior Gateway Protocol, Routing Information Protocol.*

Intermediate System (IS) An OSI system that performs *network layer forwarding.* It is analogous to an IP router. See also *Open Systems Interconnection.*

International Organization for Standardization (ISO) A voluntary, nontreaty organization founded in 1946, which is responsible for creating international standards in many areas, including computers and communications. Its members are the national standards organizations of the 89 member countries, including ANSI for the US. See also *American National Standards Institute, Open Systems Interconnection.*

internet A collection of networks interconnected with routers. "Small-i" internets are often used to refer to collections of LANs, metropolitan or campus networks, or other regional networks. See also *network*.

Internet The "Capital-I" Internet is the conglomeration of all the "small-i" *internets* connected together in the world. It is a three-level hierarchy composed of *backbone networks* (for example, NSFNET, MIL-NET), *mid-level networks* (ANSnet, CICNet, PSINet, NYSERNet), and *stub* networks. The Internet uses numerous protocols to ensure that all of its parts work together. See also *transit network, Internet Protocol, Corporation for Research and Educational Networks, National Science Foundation.*

internet address An IP address that uniquely identifies a node on an internet. An Internet address (capital "I") uniquely identifies a node on the Internet. See also *internet, Internet, IP address.*

Internet Architecture Board (IAB) The technical body that oversees the development of the Internet suite of protocols. It has two task forces: the IETF and the IRTF. "IAB" previously stood for Internet Activities Board. See also *Internet Engineering Task Force, Internet Research Task Force.*

Internet Assigned Numbers Authority (IANA) The central registry for various Internet protocol parameters, such as port, protocol and enterprise numbers, and options, codes and types. The currently assigned values are listed in the Assigned Numbers document (STD2). To request a number assignment, contact the IANA at iana@isi.edu. See also *assigned numbers, STD.*

Internet Control Message Protocol (ICMP) ICMP is an extension to the Internet Protocol. It allows for the generation of error messages, test packets and informational messages related to IP. It is defined in STD 5, RFC 792.

Internet-Draft (I-D) Internet-Drafts are working documents of the IETF, its Areas, and its Working Groups. As the name implies, Internet-Drafts are draft documents. They are valid for a maximum of six months and may be updated, replaced, or made obsolete by other documents at any time. Very often, I-Ds are precursors to RFCs. See also *Internet Engineering Task Force, Request For Comments.*

Internet Engineering Steering Group (IESG) The IESG is composed of the IETF Area Directors and the IETF Chair. It provides the first technical review of Internet standards and is responsible for day-to-day management of the IETF. See also *Internet Engineering Task Force.*

Internet Engineering Task Force (IETF) The IETF is a large, open community of network designers, operators, vendors, and researchers whose purpose is to coordinate the operation, management and evolution of the Internet, and to resolve short-range and mid-range protocol and architectural issues. It is a major source of proposals for protocol standards that are submitted to the IAB for final approval. The IETF meets three times a year and extensive minutes are included in the IETF Proceedings. To subscribe to the mailing list that carries IETF announcements, send e-mail to `ietf-announce-request@cnri.reston.va.us`. See also *Internet, Internet Architecture Board.*

Internet Monthly Report (IMR) Published monthly via e-mail, Internet Monthly Reports communicate to the Internet Research Group the accomplishments, milestones reached, or problems discovered by the participating organizations. To subscribe to the IMR, send e-mail to: `imr-request@isi.edu`.

internet number See *internet address.*

Internet Protocol (IP) The Internet Protocol, defined in STD 5, RFC 791, is the network layer for the TCP/IP Protocol Suite. It is a *connectionless*, best-effort *packet-switching* protocol. ("Best-effort" means that each packet is separately evaluated to find the best route available *at that moment* for sending the packet. Routes have formulas assigned to determine which is the most efficient for any given packet.)

Internet Registry (IR) The Internet Registry assigns *Internet Addresses,* registers unique *domain names,* keeps the main *whois* database, and performs other registry and organizational tasks to allow the smooth running of the Internet. See also *Autonomous System, network address, Defense Data Network, Internet Assigned Numbers Authority.*

Internet Relay Chat (IRC) A world-wide "party line" protocol that allows users to converse with each other in real time. IRC is structured as a network of servers, each of which accepts connections from client programs, one per user. Some schools and organizations have disabled IRC on their computers and networks because of congestion problems or organizational policies about appropriate use. IRC had world-wide notice during the Gulf War, when citizens on their computers in Tel Aviv during the bombing raids were describing the events as they happened over IRC to listeners around the world. See also *Talk*.

Internet Research Steering Group (IRSG) The "governing body" of the *Internet Research Task Force* (IRTF).

Internet Research Task Force (IRTF) The IRTF is chartered by the Internet Architecture Board (IAB) to consider long-term Internet issues from a theoretical point of view. It has Research Groups, similar to IETF Working Groups, which are each assigned to discuss different research topics. Multicast audio/video conferencing and privacy-enhanced mail are examples of technologies that have emerged from IRTF Research Groups. See also *Internet Architecture Board, Internet Engineering Task Force, Privacy Enhanced Mail*.

Internet Society (ISOC) The Internet Society is a nonprofit, professional membership organization that facilitates and supports the technical evolution of the Internet, stimulates interest in and educates the scientific and academic communities, industry and the public about the technology, uses and applications of the Internet, and promotes the development of new applications for the system. The Society provides a forum for discussion and collaboration in the operation and use of the global Internet infrastructure. The Internet Society publishes a quarterly newsletter, the *Internet Society News*, and holds an annual conference, INET. The development of Internet technical standards takes place under the auspices of the Internet Society with substantial support from the Corporation for National Research Initiatives under a cooperative agreement with the US Federal Government. [Source: V. Cerf]

Internetwork Packet eXchange (IPX) Novell's protocol used by NetWare. A *router* with IPX routing can interconnect LANs so that Novell NetWare clients and servers can communicate. See also *Local Area Network*.

internic.net This is the domain name of the Internet Services NIC, the granddaddy of all NICs. See also *Network Information Center.*

interoperability The ability of software and hardware from different vendors, and using different operating systems, to communicate meaningfully. Interoperability is a desirable feature when researching hardware and software to build or add onto an existing network. The goal of most Internet *standards* and *protocols* is the smooth interaction and transmission of data between *heterogeneous networks*, which we also call interoperability.

IP See *Internet Protocol.*

IP address The 32-bit address defined by the Internet Protocol in STD 5, RFC 791. It is usually represented in dotted decimal notation. For example, an IP address looks like this: 127.0.0.1, while a domain name looks like this: nic.cicnet.net. See also *domain address, dot address, internet address, Internet Protocol, network address, subnet address, host address.*

IP datagram See *datagram.*

IPX See *Internetwork Packet eXchange.*

IR See *Internet Registry.*

IRC See *Internet Relay Chat.*

IRSG See *Internet Research Steering Group.*

IRTF See *Internet Research Task Force.*

IS See *Intermediate System.*

ISDN See *Integrated Services Digital Network.*

ISO See *International Organization for Standardization.*

ISO Development Environment (ISODE) Pronounced eye-so-dee-eee. Software that allows OSI services to use a TCP/IP network. See also *Open Systems Interconnection, TCP/IP Protocol Suite.*

ISOC See *Internet Society.*

ISODE See *ISO Development Environment.*

KA9Q An implementation of TCP/IP and associated protocols for amateur packet radio systems. KA9Q is most popular with users of home computers: KA9Q implementations for computers rather than radios run on many varieties of computers (including Atari and Apple II) to allow them to function as standalone Internet-connected workstations. "KA9Q" is the Amateur Radio call sign of the original author, Phil Karns. See also *TCP/IP Protocol Suite.*

Kerberos Named after the three-headed watchdog of Hades in Greek and Roman mythology, Kerberos is a security system developed by MIT's Project Athena and others on the Net. It is based on symmetric key cryptography; you give your login and password to a trusted agent on your local computer, who authenticates your identity to the services you wish to use on another computer. See also *authentication, authorization, encryption, password.*

Kermit A popular file transfer protocol developed by Columbia University. Because Kermit runs in most operating environments, it provides an easy method of file transfer. Kermit is *not* the same as FTP. See also *File Transfer Protocol.*

kill file An automatically processed database of names, user IDs, topics, and so on, from whom or about which you do not wish to see e-mail or news postings. Kill files are useful to trim your information processing time down to something manageable, or to prevent you from seeing mail or postings from people who persist in behavior with which you do not agree. See also *Flame, news.*

kilobit One thousand bits. The kilobit is a convenient unit of data for talking about transmission speeds over computer networks. A 56-kilobit line, for example, can transmit 56,000 bits per second. A *T1* line, by comparison, can transmit 1,544,000 bits per second. Kilobits per second is abbreviated Kbps. See also *bit, byte, megabit.*

Knowbot An experimental directory service. See also *white pages, WHOIS, X.500.*

LAN See *Local Area Network.*

LATA Local Area Telephone Authority. Most states are divided into several LATAs. Knowing which LATA you are in will help you evaluate service offerings from your local "telco" and Internet providers, because phone lines that cross LATA boundaries are more expensive than those that do not.

layer Communication networks for computers may be organized as a set of more or less independent *protocols*, each in a different layer (also called "level"). The lowest layer governs direct host-to-host communication between the hardware at different hosts; the highest consists of user applications. Each layer builds on the layer beneath it. For each layer, programs at different hosts use protocols appropriate to the layer to communicate with each other. TCP/IP has five layers of protocols; OSI has seven. The advantage of using different layers of protocols is that the methods of passing information from one layer to another are specified clearly as part of the protocol suite, and changes within a protocol layer are prevented from affecting the other layers. This greatly simplifies the task of designing and maintaining communication programs. See also *Open Systems Interconnection, TCP/IP Protocol Suite.*

listserv An automated *mailing list* distribution system originally designed for the BITNET/EARN network. Listserv programs now also run on UNIX and other operating systems. See also *BITNET, European Academic Research Network.*

little-endian A format for storage or transmission of binary data in which the least significant byte (bit) comes first. See also *big-endian.*

LLC See *Logical Link Control.*

Local Area Network (LAN) A data network intended to serve an area of only a few square kilometers or less. LANs usually serve either a single building or a group of closely located buildings. Because the network is known to cover only a small area, optimizations can be made in the network signal protocols that permit data rates up to 100 Mbps. Popular LAN software includes Novell NetWare and Banyan Vines. See also *Ethernet, Fiber Distributed Data Interface, token ring, Wide Area Network.*

Lurking In a mailing list or Usenet newsgroup, listening without responding publicly. As the name implies, this activity is considered somewhat antisocial, but it allows beginners to get a feel for the flavor and response patterns of the participants of the group, and also lets them get up to speed on the history of the group. See also *Electronic Mail, FAQ, mailing list, Usenet.*

MAC See *Media Access Control.*

MAC address The *hardware address* of a device connected to a shared medium. See also *Media Access Control, Ethernet, token ring.*

mail alias A name for one computer which handles mail but which points to another computer. For example, `harold@saxon.org` may be a mail alias for `thane@danelaw.ac.uk`. The university system accepts mail addressed to `saxon.org` and routes it to the correct user mailbox. Mail aliases are used in many situations, including assistance when one computer is down and mail needs to be spooled at another computer or when a domain name has been registered but no computers or physical network yet exist that correspond to that domain name. See also *alias, forwarding.*

mail bridge A mail *gateway* that forwards *electronic mail* between two or more networks while ensuring that the messages it forwards meet certain administrative criteria. A mail bridge is simply a specialized form of mail gateway that enforces an administrative policy with regard to what mail it forwards. For example, SprintNet e-mail users cannot receive e-mail that originates from CompuServe.

mail exploder Part of an *electronic mail* delivery system that allows a message to be delivered to a list of addresses. Mail exploders are used to implement *mailing lists*. Users send messages to a single address, and the mail exploder takes care of delivery to the individual mailboxes in the list. Some systems administrators prefer to receive mailing list mail at a local exploder address on their system, and to have a local mailing list that users can subscribe to or from locally, rather than having each user subscribe to the various mailing lists separately. This helps control the amount of disk space used by copies of e-mail, and can also prevent problems that would occur if the user's ID changes locally or the account terminates on the host. See also *e-mail address.*

An Internet
User's Glossary

pt.
IV

mail gateway A computer that connects two or more electronic mail systems (possibly dissimilar) and transfers messages between them. Sometimes the mapping and translation can be quite complex, and it generally requires a *store-and-forward* scheme whereby the message is received from one system completely before it is transmitted to the next system, after suitable translations. Some mail gateways also have the capability to select which messages will be allowed through, either on political or technical grounds. See also *Electronic Mail, mail bridge*.

mail path A series of computer names used to direct electronic mail from one user to another. This system of e-mail addressing has been used primarily in UUCP networks, which are trying to eliminate its use altogether. See also *bang path, e-mail address, UNIX-to-UNIX CoPy*.

mail server A program that distributes files or information in response to requests sent via e-mail. Internet examples include Almanac and netlib. Mail servers have also been used in *BITNET* to provide FTP-like services. See also *BITNET, Electronic Mail, FTP*.

mailing list A list of e-mail addresses, used by a *mail exploder*, to forward messages to groups of people. Generally, a mailing list is used to discuss a particular set of topics. If a mailing list is moderated, messages sent to the list are actually sent to a *moderator* who determines whether to send the messages on to everyone else. Requests to subscribe to, or leave, a mailing list should ALWAYS be sent to the list's "-request" address (for example, `ietf-request@cnri.reston.va.us` for the IETF mailing list).

MAN See *Metropolitan Area Network*.

man pages Along with FAQs and RTFM, *man* pages (short for manual pages) are one of the single most useful online sources of information on UNIX systems. The complete documentation for many system utilities can be accessed through the man pages. To ask for help, type **man man.** This peculiar-looking command gives you instructions on using the *man* facility itself. See also *FAQ, RTFM*.

Martian A humorous term applied to packets that turn up unexpectedly on the wrong network because of incorrect routing entries. Also used as a name for a packet that has an altogether bogus (non-registered or ill-formed) internet address.

megabit One Million Bits. See also *bit, byte, kilobit, TI.*

Media Access Control (MAC) The lower portion of the datalink layer. The MAC differs for various physical media. See also *MAC Address, Ethernet, Logical Link Control, token ring.*

message switching See *packet-switching.*

Metropolitan Area Network (MAN) A data network intended to serve an area approximating that of a large city. Such networks are being implemented by innovative techniques, such as running fiber cables through subway tunnels. A popular example of a MAN is SMDS. See also *Local Area Network, Switched Multimegabit Data Service, Wide Area Network.*

MIB See *Management Information Base.*

mid-level network Mid-level networks (a.k.a. regionals) make up the second level of the Internet hierarchy. They are the *transit networks* that connect the *stub networks* to the *backbone* networks. NYSERNet, CERFNet, SESQUINET, and BARRNet are examples of mid-level networks.

MIME See *Multipurpose Internet Mail Extensions.*

mirror Just as a mirror reflects accurately the image portrayed in it, an "*FTP* archive mirror" contains all the contents of an original *archive* site (typically because the original site is heavily used). Mirror sites are updated on a regular basis to maintain congruency with the original site.

moderator(s) A person, or small group of people, who manage moderated mailing lists and newsgroups. Moderators are responsible for determining which submissions are passed on to the list or newsgroup. The message must meet the standards the group has established for itself for topicality, civility of speech, and noncommercial content. See also *Electronic Mail, mailing list, Usenet, Frequently Answered Questions.*

MOO MUD, object-oriented. A MUD that incorporates the ability to describe and manipulate objects in its command language. See *Multi-User Dungeon.*

An Internet
User's Glossary

pt.
IV

MUD   See *Multi-User Dungeon.*

multicast   A packet with a special destination address, which multiple nodes on the network may be willing to receive. See also *broadcast, broadcast storm, Ethernet meltdown.*

multihomed host   A host that has more than one connection to a network. The host may send and receive data over any of the links but will not route traffic for other nodes. See also *host, router.*

Multipurpose Internet Mail Extensions (MIME)   An extension to Internet e-mail that provides the ability to transfer nontextual data, such as graphics, audio, and fax. Most common e-mail clients, such as *Pine, mh,* and *Eudora* have at least simple Mime capabilities. It is defined in RFC 1341. See also *ascii, binary, Electronic Mail.*

Multi-User Dungeon (MUD)   Adventure or role-playing games or simulations (such as political campaigns, conferences, or creativity exercises) played on the Internet. Devotees call them "text-based virtual reality adventures." The games can feature fantasy combat, booby traps and magic. Players interact in real time and can change the "world" in the game as they play it. Most MUDs are based on the Telnet protocol. MUDs can be an excellent interaction and learning tool, as advanced "wizards" must learn to program the underlying structures in order to create their own realities, but the popularity of the game can cause resource problems for network administrators. See also *congestion, MOO, Telnet.*

MX Record   See *Mail Exchanger Record.*

NAK   See *Negative Acknowledgment.*

name resolution   The process of mapping a name into its corresponding *IP address.* See also: *Domain Name System.*

namespace   A commonly distributed set of names in which all names are unique.

nastygram   An unpleasant message, usually e-mail but sometimes in a *Usenet newsgroup.* Usually nastygrams come from a human being who is in a bad mood, but some folks refer to automated warning messages as nastygrams, as well.

National Institute of Standards and Technology (NIST) The United States governmental body that provides assistance in developing standards. Formerly the National Bureau of Standards.

National Research and Education Network (NREN) The NREN is the realization of an interconnected gigabit computer network devoted to High Performance Computing and Communications. See also *HPPC, IINREN*.

National Science Foundation (NSF) A US government agency whose purpose is to promote the advancement of science. NSF funds science researchers, scientific projects, and infrastructure to improve the quality of scientific research. The NSFNET, funded by NSF, has been an essential part of academic and research communications. It is a high speed "network of networks" that is hierarchical in nature. At the highest level, it is a backbone network. Attached to that are mid-level networks and attached to the mid-levels are campus and local networks. NSFNET also has connections out of the US to Canada, Mexico, Europe, and the Pacific Rim. The NSFNET is part of the Internet. The NSFNET is being converted to a new model of Network Access Points (NAPs) rather than a backbone.

Negative Acknowledgment (NAK) Response to receipt of a corrupted packet of information. See also *Acknowledgment*.

netiquette A pun on "etiquette" referring to proper behavior on a network. There currently is no "Emily Post" of the Internet. There is, however, Emily Postnews. Look for this `period posting` in the `answers` newsgroups.

Netnews See *Usenet*.

network A data communications system that interconnects several computer systems. A network may be composed of any combination of LANs, MANs or WANs. See also *Local Area Network, Metropolitan Area Network, Wide Area Network, internet*.

network address The network portion of an *IP address*. For a class A network, the network address is the first byte of the IP address. For a class B network, the network address is the first two bytes of the IP address. For a class C network, the network address is the first three bytes of the IP address. In each case, the remainder is the *host address*. In the Internet, assigned network addresses are globally unique. See also *subnet address, Internet Registry*.

Network File System (NFS) A protocol developed by Sun Microsystems, and defined in RFC 1094, which allows a computer system to access files over a network as if they were on its local disks. This protocol has been incorporated in products by more than two hundred companies, and is now a de facto Internet standard.

Network Information Center (NIC) An NIC provides information, assistance and services to network users. *The* Nic is the common name for the NIC run by Internet Services, Inc., the central clearinghouse for network addresses, maps, documentation, and so on. See also *Defense Data Network Network Information Center, Internet Registry, Network Operations Center*.

Network Information Services (NIS) A set of services, generally provided by a NIC, to assist users in using the network. See also *Network Information Center*.

Network Layer See *layer*.

Network News Transfer Protocol (NNTP) A protocol, defined in RFC 977, for the distribution, inquiry, retrieval, and posting of news articles. See also *Usenet*.

network node A machine, usually a computer, on the Internet. Routers, workstations, and modems are all nodes. Some nodes are at endpoints of a piece of the network, some are way stations or entry points.

network number See *IP address, network address*.

Network Operations Center (NOC) A location from which the operation of a network or internet is monitored. Additionally, this center usually serves as a clearinghouse for connectivity problems and efforts to resolve those problems. See also *Network Information Center*.

Network Time Protocol (NTP) A protocol that assures accurate local time-keeping with reference to radio and atomic clocks located on the Internet. This protocol is capable of synchronizing distributed clocks within milliseconds over long time periods. It is defined in STD 12, RFC 1119.

newsgroup A set of topically related articles distributed by the Usenet news mechanism. Newsgroup topics range from philosophy to health support groups to computer-intrinsics. There are over 9000 newsgroups world-wide, with over 6000 available to users in the United States. The term also refers to the group of people who read and respond to the above; sometimes these groups become friendly and close-knit as a result of their discussions.

NFS See *Network File System.*

NIC See *Network Information Center.*

NIS See *Network Information Services.*

NIST See *National Institute of Standards and Technology.*

NNTP See *Network News Transfer Protocol.*

NOC See *Network Operations Center.*

node An addressable device attached to a computer network. See also *host, router.*

NREN See *National Research and Education Network.*

NSF See *National Science Foundation.*

NSS See *Nodal Switching System.*

NTP See *Network Time Protocol.*

octet 8 bits. In networking, this term is sometimes used instead of "byte," because some systems have bytes that are not 8 bits long.

Open Systems Interconnection (OSI) A suite of *protocols*, designed by ISO committees, to be the international standard computer network architecture. See also *International Organization for Standardization*.

OSI See *Open Systems Interconnection*.

OSI Reference Model A seven-layer structure designed to describe computer network architectures and the way that data passes through them. The lowest levels handle the physical media and transmission characteristics of the network. The highest levels handle the user applications and data transmission. This model (sometimes referred to as the "seven-layer model") was developed by the ISO in 1978 to clearly define the interfaces in multivendor networks, and to provide users of those networks with conceptual guidelines in the construction of such networks. See also *International Organization for Standardization*.

packet The unit of data sent across a network. "Packet" is a generic term used to describe a unit of data at all levels of the protocol stack, but it is most correctly used to describe application data units. Users of commercial networks should be careful to determine whether their pricing model includes a cost-per-packet; some do, and large file transfers, because of the number of packets involved, should be done at the least expensive (and least congested) time. See also *datagram, frame*.

Packet INternet Groper (PING) A program used to test whether a destination can be reached, by sending it an ICMP echo request and waiting for a reply. The term is used as a verb: "Ping host X to see if it is up!" Early tricksters on the ARPANET used to try to crash network gateways by overwhelming them with automated pinging; repeated pinging is also used as a test of network robustness today. See also *Internet Control Message Protocol*.

Packet Switch Node (PSN) A dedicated computer whose purpose is to accept, route, and forward *packets* in a packet-switched network. See also *packet switching, router*.

packet switching A communications paradigm in which *packets* (messages) are individually routed between *hosts*, with no previously established communication path. See also *circuit switching, connection-oriented, connectionless*.

password A secret key that you have chosen (or that is assigned to you by a systems administrator or key distribution program) and that you type every time you log into your system or services. Along with your valid login ID, this constitutes the two parts of your *authentication* process on most systems. See also *Authorization*.

PD Public Domain.

PDU See *Protocol Data Unit*.

PEM See *Privacy Enhanced Mail*.

periodic posting An article posted to a *Usenet viewsgroup*.

PING See *Packet INternet Groper*.

Point Of Presence (POP) A site where there exists a collection of telecommunications equipment, usually digital leased lines and multi-protocol routers. Many network providers have modem pools in areas where they have POPs. Sometimes network providers have their equipment co-located with telephone company POPs.

Point-to-Point Protocol (PPP) The Point-to-Point Protocol, defined in RFC 1171, provides a method for transmitting packets over serial point-to-point links. PPP, like SLIP, allows dial-up users to connect their home computers to the Internet as peer hosts. See also *Serial Line IP*.

POP See *Post Office Protocol* and *Point Of Presence*.

port Although your computer has a physical port into which you plug things, in TCP/IP ports are also values defined in the protocol. For example, most computers that accept Telnet sessions create a port "23" to accept Telnet transmissions. When a packet comes in with the Telnet request, it will carry a request for port 23. Each application has a unique port number associated with it. See also *Transmission Control Protocol, User Datagram Protocol*.

Post Office Protocol (POP) A protocol designed to allow single-user hosts to read mail from a server. There are three versions: POP, POP2, and POP3. Later versions are NOT compatible with earlier versions. See also *Electronic Mail*.

Postal Telegraph and Telephone (PTT) Outside the USA, PTT refers to a telephone service provider (usually a monopoly) in a particular country.

postmaster The person responsible for taking care of e-mail problems, answering queries about users, and other related work at an e-mail server site. By agreement between sites, codified in the RFCs for e-mail, any site that has e-mail connectivity must have a human being who answers mail addressed to postmaster@host. Many postmasters are also handling security questions and systems ethics questions. See also *Electronic Mail*.

PPP See *Point-to-Point Protocol*.

Privacy Enhanced Mail (PEM) Internet e-mail that provides confidentiality, *authentication* and message integrity using various *encryption* methods. See also *electronic mail*.

Prospero A distributed file system that provides the user with the ability to create multiple views of a single collection of files distributed across the Internet. Prospero provides a file naming system, and file access is provided by existing access methods (for example, anonymous FTP and NFS). The Prospero protocol is also used for communication between clients and servers in the Archie system. See also *anonymous FTP, Archie, archive site, Gopher, Network File System, Wide Area Information Servers*.

protocol A formal description of message formats and the rules two or more computers must follow to exchange those messages. Protocols can describe low-level details of computer-to-computer interfaces (for example, the order in which the bits from a byte are set across a wire), or high-level exchanges between application programs (for example, the way in which two programs transfer a file across the Internet).

protocol converter A device or program that translates between different *protocols* that serve similar functions (for example, between TCP and TP4).

Protocol Data Unit (PDU) What international standards committees call a *packet*.

protocol stack A layered set of *protocols* that work together to provide a set of network functions. Most Internet networks use a TCP/IP stack. See also *layer*.

proxy ARP The technique in which one computer, usually a router, answers ARP requests intended for another computer. By "faking" its identity, the router accepts responsibility for routing packets to the "real" destination. Proxy ARP allows a site to use a single IP address with two physical networks. Subnetting would normally be a better solution. See also *Address Resolution Protocol*.

PSN See *Packet Switch Node*.

PTT See *Postal, Telegraph and Telephone*.

queue A backup of packets awaiting processing. See also *spool*.

RARE See *Reseaux Associes pour la Recherche Européenne*.

RARP See *Reverse Address Resolution Protocol*.

RBOC Regional Bell Operating Company.

RCP See *remote copy program*.

reassembly The IP process in which a previously fragmented packet is reassembled before being passed to the transport layer. See also *fragmentation*.

regional See *mid-level network*.

remote copy (rcp) An early Berkeley protocol that allows transfer of files over the network. RCP requires an *access control list* to enable the protocol to know which computers can be accessed. FTP is a more modern file transfer protocol. Most older *Kerberos* implementations use rcp and *rlogin* rather than *FTP* and *Telnet*.

An Internet
User's Glossary

pt.
IV

remote login (rlogin) Operating on a remote computer over a computer network, as though locally attached. rlogin is an early Berkeley protocol, like rcp. It is used in some security programs (such as *Kerberos*); security precautions must be taken to prevent unauthorized use of the system via rlogin. See also *rcp*, *Telnet*.

Remote Procedure Call (RPC) An easy and popular paradigm for implementing the *client-server* model of distributed computing. *rcp* and *rlogin* use remote procedure calls. In general, a request is sent to a remote system to execute a designated procedure, using arguments supplied, and the result returned to the caller. There are many variations and subtleties in various implementations, resulting in a variety of different (incompatible) RPC protocols. Most modern Internet clients, such as Gopher and Web, use TCP/IP instead.

repeater A device that propagates electrical signals from one cable to another. See also *bridge, gateway, router.*

Request For Comments (RFC) The document series, begun in 1969, that describes the Internet suite of protocols and related experiments. The name comes from bureaucrat-speak (as do its government procurement cousins RFQ (Request For Quote) and RFP (Request For Purchase). Not all (in fact very few) RFCs describe Internet standards, but all Internet standards are written up as RFCs. The RFC series of documents is unusual in that the proposed protocols are forwarded by the Internet research and development community, acting on their own behalf, as opposed to the formally reviewed and standardized protocols that are promoted by organizations such as CCITT and ANSI. See also *For Your Information, STD.*

Reseaux Associes pour la Recherche Européenne (RARE) European association of research networks.

Reseaux IP Européenne (RIPE) A collaboration between European networks that use the *TCP/IP* protocol suite.

Reverse Address Resolution Protocol (RARP) A protocol, defined in RFC 903, that provides the reverse function of ARP. RARP maps a hardware (MAC) address to an internet address. It is used primarily by diskless nodes when they first initialize to find their internet address. See also *Address Resolution Protocol, BOOTP, internet address.*

RFC See *Request For Comments.*

RFC 822 The Internet standard format for *electronic mail* message *headers.*

RIP See *Routing Information Protocol.*

RIPE See *Reseaux IP Européenne.*

Round-Trip Time (RTT) A measure of the current delay on a network. It measures the time it takes a packet or other bit of information to reach the destination and the acknowledgment to return to the sender.

route The path that network traffic takes from its source to its destination. Also, a possible path from a given host to another host or destination.

routed Pronounced "route-dee." Route daemon. A program that runs under 4.2BSD/4.3BSD UNIX systems (and derived operating systems) to propagate routes among computers on a local area network, using the RIP protocol. See also *gated.*

router A device that forwards traffic between networks, using information from the *network layer* and from routing tables. Some routers are "dedicated," meaning that they do nothing but shuffle traffic; some are used for other purposes, including file storage. See also *bridge, gateway.*

routing The process of selecting the correct interface and next *hop* for a packet being forwarded. See also *router, Exterior Gateway Protocol, Interior Gateway Protocol.*

routing domain A set of *routers* exchanging routing information within an *administrative domain.*

routing table A table or database of routing paths and decision variables that allows a *router* to send packets on to the correct destination. Routing tables are maintained both by humans and computers.

RPC See *Remote Procedure Call.*

RTFM Read the "Fine" Manual. An acronym used to admonish neophyte users of a computer system to consult published sources of information first, before requesting the attention of someone whose time (or patience) may be limited. The popularity of this idiom can be considered a measure of the Internet's explosive growth.

RTT See *Round-Trip Time*.

Serial Line IP (SLIP) A protocol used to run IP over serial lines, such as telephone circuits or RS-232 cables, interconnecting two systems. SLIP is defined in RFC 1055. SLIP, along with *PPP,* is one of two popular protocols which allow home computer users to connect their computers to the Internet as peer hosts. SLIP and PPP encapsulate TCP/IP packets for transmission over phone lines.

server In *client-server computing,* the "back-end" program from which a *client* program requests information or other resources. The server handles the work of locating and extracting the information. The term is also often used to refer to the computer running a server program, particularly if it is used only for that purpose (as, for example, a "print server" in a LAN). The various Internet *addresses* cited throughout this book as sources of information or files are the locations of computers running server programs for *applications* such as *FTP* or *Gopher*. See also *client, Domain Name System, Network File System*.

Shareware Shareware is software whose creator or author stores it on the network for access by anyone to try out. Once you decide you want to continue using the software, it is ethically correct to pay the shareware fee. Once you do, you will receive any updates to the software and/or manuals.

SIG Special Interest Group.

signature The three- or four-line message at the bottom of an e-mail message or a Usenet article that identifies the sender. Large signatures (over five lines) are generally frowned upon. These files usually have the filename extension .sig or .signature. With many news readers and some e-mail clients this file is automatically appended to the sender's messages or postings. See also *Electronic mail, Usenet*.

Simple Mail Transfer Protocol (SMTP) A protocol, defined in STD 10, RFC 821, used to transfer electronic mail between computers. It is a server-to-server protocol, so other protocols are used to access the messages. See also *Electronic Mail, Post Office Protocol, RFC 822.*

Simple Network Management Protocol (SNMP) The Internet standard protocol, defined in STD 15, RFC 1157, developed to manage nodes on an IP network. It is currently possible to manage wiring hubs, computers, multiple CD management hardware (called jukeboxes), etc. See also *Management Information Base.*

SLIP See *Serial Line IP.*

SMDS See *Switched Multimegabit Data Service.*

SMI See *Structure of Management Information.*

SMTP See *Simple Mail Transfer Protocol.*

SNA See *Systems Network Architecture.*

snail mail A pejorative term referring to the Postal Service to contrast with *e-mail.* Sometimes people use the term "earth mail" instead.

SNMP See *Simple Network Management Protocol.*

splat A colloquial name for the asterisk (*), which is used in UNIX and DOS file names as a wild-card, that can be read out quickly over the phone or shouted across an office without fear of misunderstanding.

spool, spooling A *spool* is a storage area where e-mail, print jobs, and some other service requests are stored up until they can be sent on to their destinations. *Spooling* is the act of storing up such messages or jobs. Items may be spooled for any of several reasons: most commonly if the destination *host* is down or for some reason not accepting transmissions, or (particularly in print jobs) the receiving printer has not finished printing a job or jobs ahead of the spooled job. *BITNET* traffic is often spooled if the next node on the line cannot accept it for any reason. For a long time, the story goes, disruptions in the phone lines between France and Israel because of the Gulf Wars made it faster for the French to send a tape with BITNET messages stored on them to Israel for redistribution than to wait for the phone lines to stay stable long enough to transmit all the messages spooled up and waiting. See also *queue*.

static route, static routing A table or database of destinations and pathways used to route packets to the correct destination. These tables are not dynamically updated by other computers in response to changing network operating conditions. For example, they cannot be automatically updated if a network portion goes down or if the router they want to send to is not functioning. As such, they are prone to problems if the network changes or is not functioning correctly. See also *routing, routing table*.

STD A subseries of RFCs that specify Internet standards. The official list of Internet standards is in STD 1. See also *For Your Information, Request For Comments*.

Store-and-Forward A method of transmitting data where all the information is transmitted from one computer to another before any information is passed along to the next host in line. Packet transmission methods ship each packet as it comes along, choosing the best path for each individual packet, rather than using a fixed routing and time for an entire set of data. See also *BITNET*.

stream-oriented Describes a type of transport service that allows its client to send data in a continuous stream. The transport service will guarantee that all data will be delivered to the other end in the same order as sent and without duplicates. See also *Transmission Control Protocol*.

Structure of Management Information (SMI) The rules used to define the objects that can be accessed via a network management protocol. This protocol is defined in STD 16, RFC 1155. See also *Management Information Base*.

stub network A stub network only carries packets to and from local hosts. Even if it has paths to more than one other network, it does not carry traffic for other networks. See also *backbone, transit network*.

subnet A portion of a network (which may be physically independent from the rest of the network) that shares a network address with other portions of the network and is distinguished by a *subnet address*. A subnet is to a network what a network is to an internet. See also *internet, network*.

subnet address The subnet portion of an IP address. In a subnetted network, the host portion of an IP address is split into a subnet portion and a host portion using an address (subnet) mask. See also *address mask, IP address, network address, host address*.

subnet mask See *address mask*.

subnet number See *subnet address*.

Switched Multimegabit Data Service (SMDS) An emerging high-speed *datagram*-based public data network service developed by Bellcore and expected to be widely used by telephone companies as the basis for their data networks. See also *ISDN, Metropolitan Area Network*.

Systems Network Architecture (SNA) A proprietary networking architecture used by IBM and IBM-compatible mainframe computers.

T1 An AT&T term for a digital carrier facility used to transmit a signal at 1.544 megabits per second. The fiber links between many network nodes run at T1 speed; in some areas, you can get T1 service into your local home or office.

T3 A term for a digital carrier facility used to transmit a signal at 44.746 megabits per second. The NSFNET backbone fiber runs at T3 speed.

TAC See *Terminal Access Controller (TAC)*.

Talk A protocol that allows two people on remote computers to communicate in a real-time fashion. See also *Internet Relay Chat*.

TCP See *Transmission Control Protocol*.

TCP/IP Protocol Suite Transmission Control Protocol over Internet Protocol. This is a common shorthand that refers to the suite of transport and application protocols that runs over the Internet. TCP/IP is the set of rules which makes the whole shebang run smoothly. See also *IP, ICMP, TCP, UDP, FTP, Telnet, SMTP, SNMP*.

TELENET A public packet-switched network using the CCITT X.25 protocols. It should not be confused with telnet. In the United States the network is called SprintNet. Telenet/SprintNet has recently entered the IP networking market, and is beginning to offer IP dialup and direct connections.

Telnet Telnet is the Internet standard protocol for remote terminal connection service. It is defined in STD 8, RFC 854 and extended with options by many other RFCs. See also *rlogin*.

Terminal Access Controller (TAC) A device that connects terminals to the Internet, usually using dialup modem connections and the TACACS protocol.

terminal emulator A program that allows a computer to emulate a particular type of terminal, in order to communicate with a remote host computer that is programmed to work with terminals of that type.

terminal server A device that connects many terminals to a LAN through one network connection. A terminal server can also connect many network users to its asynchronous ports for dial-out capabilities and printer access. See also *Local Area Network*.

Three Letter Acronym (TLA) A tribute to the use of acronyms in the computer field.

TIA Thanks In Advance.

TimeTo Live (TTL) A field in the IP header that indicates how long the packet should be allowed to survive before being discarded. It is primarily used as a hop count. TTL also gives DNS servers an indication of how recent and therefore reliable the information they receive about other hosts is. See also *Internet Protocol*.

TLA See *Three Letter Acronym*.

TN3270 A variant of the Telnet program that allows one to attach to IBM mainframes and use the mainframe as if you were using 3270 or similar terminal. IBM 3270 terminals (and *terminal emulators*) are noted for having full-screen displays, instead of line-oriented displays, and frequently have fixed fields or cells in the display where information can be entered and updated. Several popular library catalog interfaces work best with TN3270 emulators.

token ring A token ring is a type of LAN with nodes wired into a ring. Each node constantly passes a control message (token) on to the next; whichever node has the token can send a message. Often, the term "Token Ring" is used to refer specifically to the IEEE 802.5 token ring standard, which is the most common type of token ring. See also *Local Area Network*.

topology A network topology shows the computers and the links between them. A network layer must stay abreast of the current network topology to be able to route packets to their final destination.

transceiver Transmitter-receiver. The physical device that connects a host interface to a local area network, such as *Ethernet*. Ethernet transceivers contain electronics that apply signals to the cable and sense collisions between packets and other conditions on the circuit.

transit network A transit network passes traffic between networks in addition to carrying traffic for its own hosts. It must have paths to at least two other networks. See also *AUPs, backbone, stub network*.

Transmission Control Protocol (TCP) An Internet Standard transport layer protocol defined in STD 7, RFC 793. It is *connection-oriented* and *stream-oriented*, as opposed to UDP. See also *connection-oriented, layer, stream-oriented, User Datagram Protocol*.

Trojan Horse A computer program that carries within itself a means to allow the creator of the program access to the system using it. See also *virus, worm*.

TTFN Ta-Ta For Now.

TTL See *Time to Live*.

tunnelling Tunnelling refers to *encapsulation* of protocol A within protocol B, such that B treats A, and its data, as if it were its own. Tunnelling is used to get data between *administrative domains* that use a protocol not supported by the Internet, and to make pseudo-connections in connectionless protocol systems like the Internet. For example, recent experiments in AppleTalk tunnelling have allowed users on one university campus to access services on another campus directly from their own Macs, with the services showing up in the pull-down menus, and being accessed as transparently as local services. See also *protocol*.

twisted pair A type of cable in which pairs of conductors are twisted together to produce certain electrical properties. Most recently, *Ethernet* run over twisted-pair wiring has proved an inexpensive method to wire up schools, campuses, and other clustered buildings.

UDP See *User Datagram Protocol*.

Universal Time Coordinated (UTC) Greenwich Mean Time.

UNIX-to-UNIX CoPy (UUCP) Initially, a program run under the UNIX operating system that allowed one UNIX system to send files to another UNIX system via dial-up phone lines. Today, the term is more commonly used to describe the large international network that uses the UUCP protocol to pass news and electronic mail. See also *Electronic Mail, Usenet*.

urban legend A story, which may have started with a grain of truth, that has been embroidered and retold until it has passed into the realm of myth. Urban legends never die, they just end up on the Internet! Some legends that periodically make their rounds include "The Infamous Modem Tax," "Craig Shergold/Brain Tumor/Get Well Cards," and "The $250 Cookie Recipe." There are also urban legends about computer systems and networks themselves.

Usenet A collection of thousands of topically named newsgroups, the computers that run the protocols, and the people who read and submit Usenet news. Not all Internet hosts subscribe to Usenet and not all Usenet hosts are on the Internet. See also *Network News Transfer Protocol, UNIX-to-UNIX CoPy*.

user ID An account name or login name.

UTC See *Universal Time Coordinated*.

UUCP See *UNIX-to-UNIX CoPy*.

virtual circuit A network service that provides connection-oriented service regardless of the underlying network structure. See also *connection-oriented.*

virus A program that replicates itself on computer systems by incorporating itself into other programs that are shared among computer systems. See also *Trojan Horse, worm.*

W3 See *World Wide Web.*

WAIS See *Wide Area Information Servers.*

WAN See *Wide Area Network.*

Web page Using a *World Wide Web browser,* you can access "pages" of information placed on the network for your perusal by other people, companies, and organization. A page may include graphics, text, sounds, and movies.

white pages The Internet supports several databases that contain basic information about users, such as e-mail addresses, telephone numbers, and postal addresses. These databases can be searched to get information about particular individuals. Because they serve a function akin to the telephone book, these databases are often referred to as "white pages." See also *WHOIS, X.500.*

WHOIS An Internet program that allows users to query a database of people and other Internet entities, such as domains, networks, and hosts, kept at the NIC. The information for people shows a person's company name, address, phone number and e-mail address. See also *white pages, X.500.*

Wide Area Information Servers (WAIS) A distributed information service that offers simple natural-language input, indexed searching for fast retrieval, and a "relevance feedback" mechanism that allows the results of initial searches to influence future searches. Public domain implementations are available. See also *Archie, Gopher, Prospero.*

Wide Area Network (WAN) A network, usually constructed with serial lines, that covers a large geographic area. See also *Local Area Network, Metropolitan Area Network.*

World Wide Web (WWW or W3) A hypertext-based, distributed information system created by researchers at CERN in Switzerland. Users may create, edit or browse hypertext documents. The clients and servers are freely available from info.cern.ch.

worm A computer program that replicates itself and is self-propagating. Worms, as opposed to viruses, are meant to spawn in network environments. The Internet worm of November 1988 is perhaps the most famous; it successfully propagated itself on over 6000 systems across the Internet. See also *Trojan Horse, virus.*

WRT With Respect To, With Regard To.

WWW See *World Wide Web.*

WYSIWYG What You See is What You Get

Xerox Network System (XNS) A network developed by Xerox corporation. Implementations exist for 4.3BSD-derived systems, as well as the Xerox Star computers.

Yellow Pages (YP) A service, available from Sun Microsystems, used by UNIX administrators to manage databases distributed across a network.

zone A logical group of network devices. Zones have differing meanings in differing environments: a "zone" in AppleTalk may not be the same group of network devices described by a systems administrator when discussing a "DNS Zone Transfer."

zone transfer The exchange of a block of addresses and corresponding domain names between authoritative Domain Name Servers.

Hobbes' Internet Timeline v1.3

▶ ▶ by Robert Hobbes Zakon

hobbes@hobbes.mitre.org

(used with Permission)

Hobbes' Internet Timeline Copyright ©1993–4 by Robert H Zakon.

Permission is granted for use of this document in whole or in part for noncommercial purposes as long as appropriate credit is given to the author/maintainer. For commercial uses, please contact the author first.

Contributors to Hobbes' Internet Timeline have their initials next to the contributed items in the form (:zzz:) and are:

amk: Alex McKenzie (mckenzie@bbn.com)

esr: Eric S. Raymond (esr@locke.ccil.org)

glg: Gail L. Grant (grant@pa.dec.com)

jg1: Jim Gaynor (gaynor@agvax.ag.ohio.state.edu)

mpc: Mellisa P. Chase (pc@mitre.org)

sc1: Susan Calcari (susanc@is.internic.net)

sk2: Stan Kulikowski (stankuli@uwf.bitnet)

vgc: Vinton Cerf (vcerf@isoc.org)

Comments/corrections should be sent to hobbes@hobbes.mitre.org.

1957 USSR launches Sputnik, first artificial earth satellite. In response, US forms the Advanced Research Projects Agency (ARPA) within the Department of Defense (DOD) to establish US lead in science and technology applicable to the military (:amk:).

1962 Paul Baran, RAND: "On Distributed Communications Networks"—Packet-switching networks; no single outage point.

1967 ACM Symposium on Operating Principles—Plan presented for a packet-switching network.

1968 Network presentation to the Advanced Research Projects Agency (ARPA).

1969 ARPANET commissioned by DOD for research into networking. First node at UCLA and soon after at Stanford Research Institute (SRI), University of California at Santa Barbara, and University of Utah.

   Use of Information Message Processors (IMP) [Honeywell 516 minicomputer with 12K of memory] developed by Bolt Beranek and Newman, Inc. (BBN).

   First Request for Comment (RFC): "Host Software" by Steve Crocker.

1970 ALOHAnet developed by Norman Abrahamson, University of Hawaii (:sk2:).

   ARPANET hosts start using Network Control Protocol (NCP).

1971 15 nodes (23 hosts): UCLA, SRI, UCSB, University of Utah, BBN, MIT, RAND, SDC, Harvard, Lincoln Lab, Stanford, UIU(C), CWRU, CMU, NASA/Ames.

1972 International Conference on Computer Communications with demonstration of ARPANET between 40 machines organized by Bob Kahn.

   InterNetworking Working Group (INWG) created to address need for establishing agreed upon protocols. Chairman: Vinton Cerf.

   Ray Tomlinson of BBN invents e-mail program to send messages across a distributed network (:amk:).

1973   First international connections to the ARPANET: England and Norway.

Bob Metcalfe's Harvard Ph.D. thesis outlines idea for Ethernet (:amk:).

1974   Vint Cerf and Bob Kahn publish "A Protocol for Packet Network Internetworking," which specified in detail the design of a Transmission Control Program (TCP) (:amk:).

BBN opens Telenet, commercial version of ARPANET (:sk2:).

1975   Operational management of Internet transferred to DCA (now DISA).

"Jargon File", by Raphael Finkel at SAIL, first released (:esr:).

1970s   Store and Forward Networks—Used electronic mail technology and extended it to conferencing.

1976   UUCP (Unix-to-Unix CoPy) developed at AT&T Bell Labs and distributed with UNIX one year later.

1977   THEORYNET created at University of Wisconsin, providing electronic mail to over 100 researchers in computer science (using UUCP).

1979   Meeting between University of Wisconsin, DARPA, NSF, and computer scientists from many universities to establish a Computer Science Department research computer network.

USENET established using UUCP between Duke and UNC by Tom Truscott and Steve Bellovin.

1981   BITNET, the "Because It's Time NETwork":

- Started as a cooperative network at the City University of New York.
- Provides electronic mail and listserv servers to distribute information.
- Unlike USENET, where client software is needed, electronic mail is the only tool necessary.

CSNET (Computer Science NETwork) built by UCAR and BBN through seed money granted by NSF to provide networking services (especially e-mail) to university scientists with no access to AR-PANET. CSNET later becomes known as the Computer and Science Network (:amk:).

Minitel (Teletel) is deployed across France by French Telecom.

1982 INWG establishes the Transmission Control Protocol (TCP) and Internet Protocol (IP), as the protocol suite, commonly known as TCP/IP, for ARPANET:

- This leads to one of the first definition of an "internet" as a connected set of networks, specifically those using TCP/IP, and "Internet" as connected TCP/IP internets.
- DOD declares TCP/IP suite to be standard for DOD (:vgc:).

EUnet (European UNIX Network) is created by EUUG to provide e-mail and USENET services (:glg:).

1983 Name server developed at University of Wisconsin, no longer requiring users to know the exact path to other systems.

Switch from NCP to TCP/IP (1 January).

CSNET/ARPANET gateway put in place.

ARPANET split into ARPANET and MILNET; the latter became integrated with the Defense Data Network, created the previous year.

Desktop workstations come into being, many with Berkeley UNIX (which includes IP networking software).

Need shifts from having a single, large time-sharing computer connected to Internet per site, to connection of an entire local network.

Berkeley releases 4.2BSD incorporating TCP/IP (:mpc:).

EARN (European Academic and Research Network) established. Very similar to the way BITNET works.

FidoNet developed by Tom Jennings.

1984 Domain Name System (DNS) introduced.

Number of hosts breaks 1000.

JUNET (Japan Unix Network) established using UUCP.

JANET (Joint Academic Network) established in the UK using the Coloured Book protocols.

1986   NSFNET created (backbone speed of 56Kbps):

- NSF establishes five supercomputing centers to provide high-computing power for all (JVNC@Princeton, PSC@Pittsburgh, SDSC@UCSD, NCSA@UIUC, Theory Center@Cornell).
- ARPANET bureaucracy keeps it from being used to inter-connect centers, and NSFNET comes into being with the aid of NASA and DOE.
- This allows an explosion of connections, especially from universities.

Cleveland Freenet (start of NPTN) comes on-line (:sk2:).

Network News Transfer Protocol (NNTP), designed to enhance Usenet news performance over TCP/IP.

Mail Exchanger (MX) records developed by Craig Partridge, allowing non-IP network hosts to have domain addresses.

1987   NSF signs a cooperative agreement to manage the NSFNET backbone with Merit Network, Inc. (IBM and MCI involvement was through an agreement with Merit). Merit, IBM, and MCI later found ANS.

UUNET is founded with Usenix funds to provide commercial UUCP and Usenet access.

1000th RFC: "Request For Comments reference guide."

Number of hosts breaks 10,000.

Number of BITNET hosts breaks 1000.

1988   Internet worm burrows through the Net.

1989   Number of hosts breaks 100,000.

NSFNET backbone upgraded to T1 (1.544Mbps).

RIPE (Reseaux IP Europeens) formed (by European service providers) to ensure the necessary administrative and technical coordination to allow the operation of the pan-European IP Network (:glg:).

First relay between a commercial electronic mail carrier (CompuServe) and the Internet through Ohio State University (:jg1:).

1990 ARPANET ceases to exist.

Second relay between a commercial electronic mail carrier (MCI Mail) and the Internet through the Corporation for the National Research Initiative (CNRI).

Electronic Frontier Foundation is founded by Mitch Kapor.

1991 Commercial Internet eXchange (CIX) Association, Inc. formed by General Atomics (CERFnet), Performance Systems International, Inc. (PSInet), and UUNET Technologies, Inc. (AlterNet) (:glg:).

WAIS released by Thinking Machines Corporation.

Gopher released by University of Minnesota.

US High Performance Computing Act (Gore 1) establishes the National Research and Education Network (NREN).

1992 Internet Society is chartered.

World-Wide Web released by CERN.

Number of hosts breaks 1,000,000.

NSFNET backbone upgraded to T3 (44.736Mbps).

First MBONE audio multicast (March) and video multicast (November).

1993 InterNIC created by NSF to provide specific Internet services (:sc1:):

- directory and database services (AT&T)
- registration services (Network Solutions Inc.)
- information services (General Atomics/CERFnet)

US White House comes on-line:

- President Bill Clinton: `president@whitehouse.gov`
- Vice-President Al Gore: `vice-president@whitehouse.gov`
- First Lady Hillary Clinton: `root@whitehouse.gov` (-:rhz:-)

Internet Talk Radio begins broadcasting (:sk2:).

United Nations and World Bank come on-line (:vgc:).

US National Information Infrastructure Act.

Businesses and media really take notice of the Internet.

Mosaic takes the Internet by storm; WWW proliferates at a 341,634% annual growth rate of service traffic. Gopher's growth is 997%.

1994   Communities begin to be wired up directly to the Internet.

US Senate and House provide information servers.

First flower shop taking orders via the Internet.

Shopping malls arrive on the Internet.

Mass marketing finds its way to the Internet with mass e-mailings.

Worms of a new kind find their way around the Net—WWW Worms (W4), joined by Spiders, Wanderers, Crawlers, and Snakes.

"A Day in the Life of the Internet" begs to be published (:rhz:).

B

User Guidelines:
Two Views

▶▶ This appendix presents two documents that offer different but overlapping guidelines for "behaving yourself" on the Internet—using shared resources responsibly, avoiding harassment by others, and generally staying out of trouble. The first, by Arlene H. Rinaldi of Florida Atlantic University (`rinaldi@acc.fau.edu`), is addressed to users in an academic setting; the second, by Hilary Gardner (`calliope@well.sf.ca.us`), is addressed to all new users learning their way around the Internet.

▶▶ *The Net: User Guidelines and Netiquette*

By: Arlene H. Rinaldi

Academic/Institutional Support Services

Florida Atlantic University

May, 1993

▶ *Preface*

The formulation of this guide was motivated by a need to develop guidelines for all Internet protocols to ensure that users at Florida Atlantic University realize the Internet capabilities as a resource available, with the provision that they are responsible in how they access or transmit information through the Internet (the Net).

It is assumed that the reader has some familiarity with the terms and protocols that are referenced in this document.

Permission to duplicate or distribute this document is granted with the provision that the document remains intact.

For additions, comments, suggestions and requests for revisions, please send e-mail to rinaldi@acc.fau.edu.

▶ *Acknowledgments*

Much of this guide was developed from comments and suggestions from NETTRAIN@UBVM (formally NET-TRAIN) LISTSERV subscribers and from several sources available on the Net:

- A special acknowledgment to Wes Morgan, University of Kentucky Engineering Computing Center, for his advice and recommendations.

- Paul F. Lambert, Bentley College; Philip M. Howard, Saint Mary's University; Gordon Swan, Florida Atlantic University; Pauline Kartrude, Florida Atlantic University; Beth Taney, Penn State; Debbie Shaffer, Penn State and USDA-CIT; Henry DeVries, Cornell; Jim Milles, SLU Law Library; Martin Raish, State University of New York at Binghamton; Steve Cisler, Apple Corporation; Tom Zillner, Wisconsin Interlibrary Services; Tom Goodrich, Stanford University; Jim Gerland, State University of NY at Buffalo; Ros Leibensperger, Cornell; Paul White, Northern Michigan University; Marilyn S. Webb, Penn State; Judith Hopkins, State University of NY at Buffalo; Ros McCarthy.

User Guidelines: Two Views

▶ ▶
ap.
B

▶ *Introduction*

It is essential for each user on the network to recognize his/her responsibility in having access to vast services, sites, systems and people. The user is ultimately responsible for his/her actions in accessing network services.

The "Internet," or "the Net," is not a single network; rather, it is a group of thousands of individual networks which have chosen to allow traffic to pass among them. The traffic sent out to the Internet may actually traverse several different networks before it reaches its destination. Therefore, users involved in this internetworking must be aware of the load placed on other participating networks.

As a user of the network, you may be allowed to access other networks (and/or the computer systems attached to those networks). Each network or system has its own set of policies and procedures. Actions that are routinely allowed on one network/system may be controlled, or even forbidden, on other networks. It is the user's responsibility to abide by the policies and procedures of these other networks/systems. Remember, the fact that a user *can* perform a particular action does not imply that they *should* take that action.

The use of the network is a privilege, not a right, which may temporarily be revoked at any time for abusive conduct. Such conduct would include the placing of unlawful information on a system, the use of abusive or otherwise objectionable language in either public or private messages, the sending of messages that are likely to result in the loss of recipients' work or systems, the sending of "chain letters," or "broadcast" messages to lists or individuals, and any other types of use that would cause congestion of the networks or otherwise interfere with the work of others. Permanent revocations can result from disciplinary actions taken by a panel judiciary board called upon to investigate network abuses.

▶ Electronic Mail and Files—User Responsibility

The content and maintenance of a user's electronic mailbox is the user's responsibility:

- Check e-mail daily and remain within your limited disk quota.

- Delete unwanted messages immediately since they take up disk storage.

- Keep messages remaining in your electronic mailbox to a minimum.

- Mail messages can be downloaded or extracted to files and then to disks for future reference.

- Never assume that your e-mail can be read by no one except yourself; others may be able to read or access your mail. Never send or keep anything that you would not mind seeing on the evening news.

The content and maintenance of a user's disk storage area is the user's responsibility:

- Keep files to a minimum. Files should be downloaded to your personal computer's hard drive or to disks.

- Routinely and frequently virus-scan your system, especially when receiving or downloading files from other systems, to prevent the spread of a virus.

- Your files may be accessible by persons with system privileges, so do not maintain anything private in your disk storage area.

▶ *Telnet Protocol*

- Many Telnet-accessible services have documentation files available online (or via FTP). Download and review instructions locally as opposed to tying up ports trying to figure out the system.

- Be courteous to other users wishing to seek information or the institution might revoke Telnet access; remain on the system only long enough to get your information, then exit off of the system.

- Screen-captured data or information should be downloaded to your personal computer's hard disk or to disks.

▶ *Anonymous FTP—File Transfer Protocol*

- Users should respond to the PASSWORD prompt with their e-mail address, so if that site chooses, it can track the level of FTP usage. If your e-mail address causes an error, enter GUEST for the next PASSWORD prompt.

- When possible, limit downloads, especially large downloads (1 Meg+), to times after normal business hours locally and for the remote FTP host; preferably late in the evening.

- Adhere to time restrictions as requested by archive sites. Think in terms of the current time at the site that's being visited, not of local time.

- Copy downloaded files to your personal computer hard drive or disks to remain within disk quota.

- When possible, inquiries to Archie should be in mail form.

User Guidelines:
Two Views

ap.
B

- It's the user's responsibility, when downloading programs, to check for copyright or licensing agreements. If the program is beneficial to your use, pay any author's registration fee. If there is any doubt, don't copy it; there have been many occasions on which copyrighted software has found its way into FTP archives. Support for any downloaded programs should be requested from the originator of the application. Remove unwanted programs from your systems.

▶ *Electronic Communications (E-Mail, LISTSERV Groups, Mailing Lists, and Usenet)*

- Keep paragraphs and messages short and to the point.

- Focus on one subject per message.

- Be professional and careful what you say about others. E-mail is easily forwarded.

- Cite all quotes, references and sources.

- Limit line length and avoid control characters.

- Follow chain-of-command procedures for corresponding with superiors. For example, don't send a complaint via e-mail directly to the "top" just because you can.

- Don't use the academic networks for commercial or proprietary work.

- Include your signature at the bottom of e-mail messages. Your signature footer should include your name, position, affiliation and Internet and/or BITNET addresses and should not exceed more than four lines. Optional information could include your address and phone number.

- Capitalize words only to highlight an important point or to distinguish a title or heading. *Asterisks* surrounding a word also can be used to make a stronger point.

- Use discretion when forwarding mail to group addresses or distribution lists. It's preferable to reference the source of a document and provide instructions on how to obtain a copy.

- It is considered extremely rude to forward personal e-mail to mailing lists or Usenet without the original author's permission.

- Be careful when using sarcasm and humor. Without face-to-face communications your joke may be viewed as criticism.

- Respect copyright and license agreements.

- When quoting another person, edit out whatever isn't directly applicable to reply. Including the entire article will annoy those reading it.

- Abbreviate when possible. Examples:

  - IMHO = in my humble/honest opinion
  - FYI = for your information
  - BTW = by the way
  - Flame = antagonistic criticism
  - :-) = happy face for humor

▶ *LISTSERV and Mailing List Discussion Groups*

Some mailing lists have low rates of traffic; others can flood your mailbox with several hundred mail messages per day. Numerous incoming messages from various listservers or mailing lists by multiple users requires extensive system processing, which can tie up valuable resources. Subscription to Interest Groups or Discussion Lists should be kept to a minimum and should not exceed what your disk quota can handle, or you for that matter.

- Keep your questions and comments relevant to the focus of the discussion group.

- Resist the temptation to "flame" others on the list. Remember that these discussions are "public" and meant for constructive exchanges. Treat the others on the list as you would want them to treat you.

- When posting a question to the discussion group, request that responses be directed to you personally. Post a summary or answer to your question to the group.

- When replying to a message posted to a discussion group, check the address to be certain it's going to the intended location (person or group).

- When signing up for a group, save your subscription confirmation letter for reference.

- When going away for more than a week, unsubscribe or suspend mail from any mailing lists or LISTSERV services.

- If you can respond to someone else's question, do so through e-mail. Twenty people answering the same question on a large list can fill your mailbox (and those of everyone else on the list) quickly.

- Use your own personal e-mail account; don't subscribe using a shared office account.

- Occasionally, subscribers to the list who are not familiar with proper netiquette will submit requests to SUBSCRIBE or UNSUBSCRIBE directly to the list itself. Be tolerant of this activity, and possibly provide some useful advice as opposed to being critical.

- Other people on the list are not interested in your desire to be added or deleted. Any requests regarding administrative tasks such as being added or removed from a list should be made to the appropriate area, not the list itself. Mail for these types of requests should be sent to the following, respectively:

LISTSERV GROUPS	LISTSERV@*host*
MAILING LISTS	*listname*-REQUEST@*host* or *listname*-OWNER@*host*

For either Mailing Lists or LISTSERV groups, to subscribe or unsubscribe, in the body of the message include:

SUBSCRIBE *listname yourfirstname yourlastname*

(to be added to the subscription), or

UNSUBSCRIBE *listname*

(to be removed from the subscription).

▶ *The Ten Commandments for Computer Ethics*

From the Computer Ethics Institute:

1. Thou shalt not use a computer to harm other people.
2. Thou shalt not interfere with other people's computer work.
3. Thou shalt not snoop around in other people's files.
4. Thou shalt not use a computer to steal.
5. Thou shalt not use a computer to bear false witness.
6. Thou shalt not use or copy software for which you have not paid.
7. Thou shalt not use other people's computer resources without authorization.
8. Thou shalt not appropriate other people's intellectual output.
9. Thou shalt think about the social consequences of the program you write.
10. Thou shalt use a computer in ways that show consideration and respect.

▶ *Bibliography*

Kehoe, Brendan P. *A Beginner's Guide to the Internet: Zen and the Art of the Internet*, First Edition, January 1992. [Published on the Internet.]

Shapiro, Norman, et al. *Towards an Ethics and Etiquette for Electronic Mail*, Santa Monica, CA: Rand Corporation (publication R-3283-NSF/RC), 1985.

Von Rospach, Chuq. *A Primer on How to Work With the USENET Community*

Horton, Mark, Spafford, Gene. *Rules of conduct on Usenet.*

A Guide to Electronic Communication & Network Etiquette, revised and submitted by Joan Gargano, edited by Ivars Balkits, Computing Services, University of California Davis.

User Guidelines:
Two Views

ap.
B

Heartland Free-Net Registered User Guidelines, Bradley University, Peoria, IL.

Terms and Conditions of Membership and Affiliation, CREN Information Center, October 25, 1990

Electronic Mail and Networks: New Tools for Institutional Research and Planning. by Dan Updegrove, John Muffo and Jack Dunn, University of Pennsylvania.

Exploring Internet Training Series, Module 1—"Exploring Internet: Using your Computer to Communicate", by Deborah Shaffer, ES-USDA, CIT and Pennsylvania State University, Henry DeVries; Extension Electronic Technology Group, Cornell University; Gregory Parham, ES-USDA, CIT.

Exploring Internet Training Series, Module 2—"Mail-based Information Delivery: Almanac and Listservs" by Deborah Shaffer, ES-USDA, CIT and Pennsylvania State University; Henry DeVries, Extension Electronic Technology Group, Cornell University; Gregory Parham, ES-USDA,CIT.

►► *General Hints for the New Online User*

by Hilary Gardner

The benefits of being online far outweigh the risks, but being aware of the risks, the tools, and the support available better prepares the newcomer for the adventure.

► *Understand the Impediments to Perceived Safety*

1. That system footprints or tracks may be read to see:

   - when and where your logins occurred
   - when and what commands you've executed
   - even information deleted that may be retrieved from backups

2. That your account is only as secure as its password.

3. That sysops or root-holders (those with unlimited system permission):

   - may read mail, files, or directories without leaving footprints
   - may undelete files you've erased
   - may release your files, etc., under warrant.

4. That default file protection may not be secure for newly created files.

5. That mail:

   - may be compromised by each forwarding site
   - if it bounces may appear in entirety to the postmaster
   - is owned by *both* the sender and the receiver.

6. That identifying biographies may be system-searched or remotely fingered.

7. That other users' identities:

   - may not be what they appear.
   - may be falsely registered.
   - may have had their own account compromised.

▶ Be Aware of the Social Dangers Possible Online

- Harassment, or frequent or unsolicited messages from another user, occasionally sent randomly to women's IDs.
- Stalking, or being watched or followed online, occasionally coupled with physical confrontation.
- Flaming, or emotional verbal attacks.
- Addiction, or the need for support/feedback available online outweighing a reasonable budget of time or money.

ap.
B

▶ Know How to Protect Yourself (Privacy Begins at Home)

1. Protect your password:

- Choose a strong password (a combination of upper- and lowercase characters, and not a name or a dictionary word).
- Do not leave your terminal logged in unattended.
- Do not let anyone watch you log in.
- Log out cleanly.

2. Protect your files:

- Know the default (permissions) for newly created files.
- Occasionally monitor your files.

3. Protect your information:

- Never send compromising information (your phone number, password, address, or vacation dates) by *chat, sends, mail,* or in your *bio.*
- See if encryption is available, if necessary.

▶ See What Education/Communication Means Are Available

- Join a support group like the Santa Monica PEN's PEN Femmes, or the online groups BAWiT or SYSTERS.
- Attend seminars, classes, or study groups.
- Make use of private, special interest forums online.
- Use peer pressure in public online to settle disputes.
- Answer harassment and inappropriate behavior directly and unambiguously, and then post for comment and discussion.
- Advocate for grievance procedures, tolerance guidelines and the discouragement of false or anonymous user registrations.

- Do not submit to unreasonable pressure.
- Speak up for what you want.

Please distribute this advice wherever appropriate, and please contact me with any questions, comments, or suggestions.

User Guidelines:
Two Views

ap.
B

APPENDIX C

Internet Standards for Business Users

▶ ▶ by Daniel P. Dern

© Copyright 1994 Daniel P. Dern

From "The Internet Business Handbook," ed/auth. Daniel P. Dern, Prentice-Hall, 1995, by permission of the author.

This appendix summarizes major Internet protocol standards (and a few other items that seemed to belong) that relate to networking, applications, and use of Internet facilities which any organization making use of the Internet should be aware of.

(Note: This material was reviewed by members of the Internet Engineering Steering Group—and many Internet developers helped suggest/cull what information belonged in a summary such as this—but there is no guarantee as to the accuracy or currency of the information in this document.)

How much of this do you need to know? Answer: The degree of in-depth familiarity you will need depends on the nature of your activities and the manner in which your organization provisions its Internet service.

In many cases, you will only need to know enough to be able to recognize key terms and numbers for purposes of discussion, such as referencing a standard as a selection criterion, e.g., "Does your e-mail gateway support RFC 822 format?"

▶▶ *Naming and IDs for Internet Standards*

Most Internet efforts are defined in documents called RFCs (Requests for Comments). RFCs are created by members of the Internet community—developers, users, etc. The nature of RFCs ranges widely, from protocol definitions through informational documents, glossaries, history, and humor.

RFCs are identified by a number, e.g., RFC 1541, and a text name, e.g., Dynamic Host Configuration Protocol.

Standards-related RFCs also have an STD number, e.g. STD 01; introductory overview RFCs also have FYI numbers, e.g., FYI 01. STD numbers don't change, but the RFC associated with it may; this assures that the STD always refers to the most recent RFC.

Bear in mind that not all RFCs are "standards track"—if the RFC a vendor claims to follow is Informational, for example, it doesn't mean any other vendors will also follow it.

The STATE of a standards-track-oriented RFC is either PROPOSED, DRAFT, or Internet Standard (Full). Each standard also has a REQUIREMENTS Level, such as Required, Recommended, Elective, Limited Use, and Not Recommended. "Internet-drafts" reflect in-progress activity by Internet Engineering Task Force groups and individuals; as such, they are subject to change or deletion and therefore are not for longer-term citation.

▶▶ *To Get Current Status and More Info about RFCs*

You can get a current "snapshot" of what's happening by retrieving and reading STD 1, "Internet Official Protocol standards." STD 1 is a quarterly-updated RFC index containing citations for all RFCs, including Status; more information can be found in the similarly updated "Standards Track RFCs Eligible for Advancement," "IAB Standards Index," and "IESG Protocol Tracking Report" documents.

For more information on RFCs, see RFC 1310 "The Internet Standards Process"; also see draft-iab-standards-processv2-02.txt in the Internet Drafts directory of `ds.internic.net` and other Internet document repositories. For more information on the IETF, see FYI 17, "The Tao of the IETF: A Guide for New Attendees of the IETF" and FYI 18, "Internet Users' Glossary." (It's worth reading FYI 17 in any case.)

In any case, your best source of up-to-date information about these Internet standards, the standards themselves, and RFCs in general, is via the Internet itself (e-mail, anonymous FTP, Gopher, WorldWideWeb), hardcopy, and CD-ROM. (See below.)

►► *RFCs*

► *Network, Transport and Routing*

NAME: TCP/IP

Brief Description: The Transmission Control Protocol/Internetworking Protocol (TCP/IP) suite is the general protocol suite of the Internet, encompassing protocols for network activities such as datagram delivery and acknowledgement, and protocols for user activity such as remote login (Telnet) and file transfer (FTP). A given implementation of TCP/IP typically contains a dozen or more protocols and facilities essential to the use of TCP/IP applications in a TCP/IP environment.

Status: Full.

Primary Relevant Documents: The Host Requirements Specifications Documents, RFC 1122 (Communications) and 1123 (Applications). These documents are intended to serve as the official specification for users and vendors of how TCP/IP protocol specs are to be applied in computers used on the Internet, to help ensure that they do the proper tasks and interoperate (work with each other).

The book *TCP/IP* by Douglas Comer is considered a definitive technical text on TCP/IP.

Name: IP (Internetworking Protocol)

Brief description: The network layer protocol of TCP/IP, IP provides the functions needed "to deliver a 'package of bits' (Internet datagram) from source to destination over an interconnected system of networks" (e.g., the Internet).

Status: Full.

Primary relevant document(s): RFC 791 "Internet Protocol"; also see RFCs 919, 922, 950, 1122

NAME: TCP (Transmission Control Protocol)

Brief Description: One of the Internet's two predominant transport layer protocols, TCP provides a reliable connection-oriented, byte stream service.

Status: Full.

Primary Relevant Document(s): RFC 793; also RFCs 1122, 1323

NAME: User Datagram Protocol (UDP)

Brief Description: A simple, datagram-oriented transport layer protocol—sends and receives datagrams for Internet applications; service is defined as "unreliable."

Status: Full.

Primary Relevant Documents: RFC 768, 1122

NAME: Internet Control Message Protocol (ICMP)

Brief Description: ICMP is used by the IP layer in hosts and routers (and by applications such as ping) to exchange error messages and other information.

Status: Full.

Primary Relevant Document(s): RFC 792, 1122

NAME: Internet Group Multicast Protocol (IGMP)

Brief Description: Host functions for multicasting applications such as audio, video and shared-document real-time teleconferencing over the Internet and other IP environments; also involves the Real Time Protocol (RTP).

Application and other related protocols under development include the Internet Whiteboard (WB), Visual Audio Tool (VAT), Network Video (NV), Resource Reservation Setup Protocol (RSVP), Multimedia Multiparty Session Control (MMUSIC), and INRIA Videoconferencing System (IVS).

Primary Relevant Document(s): RFC 1112.

NAMES: RIP, OSPF, IS-IS, BGP Network Routing Protocols

Brief Description: There are a variety of routing protocols and schemes in use within the Internet today, notably RIP (Routing Information Protocol), OSPF (the Open Shortest-Path First protocol for TCP/IP), IS-IS (Intermediate System to Intermediate System), and BGP (Border Gateway Protocol) for use between separate Autonomous Systems.

Having some understanding of the Internet's decentralized routing environment is essential, especially if you're coming from a traditional point-to-point private-line network, or going to a frame-relay backbone.

Status:

RIP v1: FULL

RIP v2: PROPOSED

OSPF: Version 1 FULL, Version 2 Draft

BGP version 3: Draft

BGP version 4: Submitted for Proposal

Primary relevant document(s):

> RIP: RFCs 1058, 1388
>
> SPF: RFC 1248, 1249, 1349
>
> Dual IS-IS: 1195
>
> BGP3: RFC 1267
>
> BGP4: RFC 1467

NAME: PPP, SLIP Serial Line Protocols

Brief Description: Serial line protocols provide packetizing services, to enable network communication over phone lines (versus LANs, etc). The Point-to-Point Protocol (PPP) and its predecessor Serial Line Internetworking Protocol (SLIP) are used by routers to communicate over telephone lines; PPP (and SLIP) enable a user's personal computer to establish a network connection (multiple sessions, running TCP/IP applications) over a phone line, versus asynchronous terminal emulation. There are also serial protocols to support X Windows over serial lines.

Status:

> PPP: Draft
>
> SLIP: FULL

Primary Relevant Document(s):

> PPP: RFC 1570, 1331, 1332
>
> SLIP: RFC 1055

▶ Network Management

NAME: Simple Network Management Protocol (SNMP)

Brief Description: The SNMP provides a framework for monitoring and control of network and computing devices over a TCP/IP network, including of non-TCP/IP devices.

Status:

SNMP version 1: FULL

SNMP version 2: Proposed/In process

Primary Relevant Document(s): RFCs 1098, 1157

▶ Network Services

NAME: Domain Name System (DNS)

Brief Description: DNS provides a way to map an Internet-wide structure of unique alphanumeric names (e.g., is.internic.net) for computer hosts against TCP/IP numeric host addresses and the methods by which these "names" can be managed and mapped to identifiers.

Status: FULL

Primary Relevant Document(s): RFC 1034, 1035, 1123

NAME: Network Time Protocol (NTP)

Brief Description: NTP provides a way to define time within the Internet's distributed environment, for timestamping, synchronizing and sequencing events.

Status: FULL

Primary Relevant Document(s): RFC 1119

▶ Electronic Mail

NAME: RFC 822 MAIL

Brief Description:

The format of Internet electronic mail message headers and content is defined by RFC 822; if your site's e-mail systems or gateways can't "speak RFC 822" you won't be able to swap Internet e-mail. RFC-compliant mail systems and/or gateways are available for most leading environments. (Be sure they work reliably.)

Status: FULL

Primary Document(s): RFC 822

NAME: Multipurpose Internet Mail Extensions (MIME)

Brief Description: The MIME standard specifies extensions to RFC 822 message body formats to include "multimedia" and other binary data—such as word processing documents, PostScript, graphic, binary files, video, fax, and voice messages—as attachments to Internet e-mail messages. MIME also specifies how to encode binary data into 7-bit form using ASCII characters, and convert it back at the other end. MIME avoids the problems traditionally associated with e-mail "protocol converter" gateways such as loss of data; MIME is being used for multimedia mail and EDI applications.

The HARPOON extension (Proposed Status) uses MIME to provide interworking between the 1984 and 1988 X.400 specifications, enabling 1988 X.400 body parts that can't be represented in 1984 X.400 to be encapsulated as MIME objects, which can then be received by 1984 X.400 systems.

Status: DRAFT.

Primary Relevant Document(s):

MIME: RFC 1563; also 1522, 1521

HARPOON: RFCs RFC 1494, 1495, 1496 (**Status**: Proposed)

NAME(S): Simple Mail Transfer Protocol (STMP)

Brief Description: STMP defines how systems will exchange RFC 822-formatted messages over IP.

Status: FULL

Primary Relevant Document(s):

STMP: RFC 821, 1425

Message formats: RFC 822

X.400/SMTP Gateway Tutorial: RFC 1506

Gatewaying between RFC822 and X.400(88): RFC 1327 (**Status**: Proposed Standard), 1506 (Tutorial on RFC 1327)

NAME: Post Office Protocol(s) versions 2 and 3

Brief Description: The Post Office Protocols (POP2, POP3) define how systems may act as "post offices" for users' messages, queuing them until the user retrieves them with a client program (e.g., Eudora, ZMail), and letting the POP2/POP3 mail client upload messages for delivery.

Status: POP3, Draft.

Primary Relevant Document(s): RFC1460.

NAME: Interactive Mail Access Protocol (IMAP)

Brief Description: IMAP will let PC users browse and read their email on remote mail servers without, unlike POP2/POP3, having to transfer and be responsible for storage of read/stored messages.

Status: Experimental.

Primary Relevant Document(s): RFC 1176

▶ Usenet News, a.k.a. "NetNews"

NAME: Network News Transport Protocol (NNTP)

Brief Description: NNTP defines how Usenet News articles are propagated across the Internet (i.e., over IP connections) and over dial-up UUCP connections. The Usenet currently comprises over 7,000 Newsgroups with daily traffic averaging 100 Mbytes (however, business sites may not need to receive more than a fraction of the "full feed").

Status: Full.

Primary Relevant Document(s): RFC 977

▶ *Tools*

NAME: Telnet (remote login) Protocol

Brief Description: The Telnet protocol defines how remote-login terminal-emulation sessions may be established between IP hosts. Protocols supporting 3270 emulation are also available.

Status: Full.

Primary Relevant Document(s): RFCs 854, 855, 1123

NAME: File Transfer Protocol (FTP)

Brief Description: The File Transfer Protocol (implemented as the File Transfer Program, also known as FTP) defines how IP-connected hosts may transfer ASCII and BINARY files and perform related activities (e.g., obtaining directory listings). "Anonymous-FTP" is a mechanism to provide shareable access to files, e.g., group projects, publicly accessible archives.

Status: Full.

Primary Relevant Document(s): RFC 959

NAME: Finger, WHOIS

Brief Description: The Finger and WHOIS protocols support local and remote look-up of user-related information which may include data in user-created files (.signature, .plan, .project) and system information about the user.

Status: Draft

Primary Relevant Document: Finger: RFC 1288

NAME: Gopher, WorldWideWeb, WAIS, Archie, etc.

Brief Description: These (and other) Network Information Discovery Resource (NIDR) tools provide a variety of indexing, searching, browsing, access and retrieval facilities for Internet-based ASCII and multimedia information, and other resources and services. They have become de facto standard protocols and tools for Internet navigation and information-mounting, but are not, as yet, standards themselves.

Status: Widely deployed—millions and millions served!

Primary Relevant Document(s): FAQs and related documents.

NAME: MOSAIC, CELLO, LYNX, TurboGopher, etc.

Brief Description: These and other "Internet front ends" help provide single-program point-and-click access to Internet resources and services. ASCII and color bitmapped GUI clients are available for popular user computing platforms. (Dial-up users may find transfer rates useful only for ASCII text.)

Status: Widely deployed.

Primary Relevant Document(s): FAQs and other documents.

NAME: Universal Resource Names (URNs)

Brief Description: URNs are location-independent "persistent" names for resources on the Internet; just as, say, domain names provide a stable ID for objects whose numeric IP address may change, URNs will provide stable pointers to files, archives and other Internet information resources.

Status: Under development.

► Security

NAME: Privacy Enhanced Mail (PEM)

Brief Description: PEM offers author/message authentication and privacy for end-to-end transmission of electronic mail, by using a combination of RSA public-key and DES private key encryption technologies.

Status: Proposed standard

Primary Relevant Document(s): RFCs 1319, 1321, 1421-1424. For more on Internet security, see the Site Security Handbook (RFC 1244) and the various books on the subject.

►► *For More Information*

For additional information regarding RFCs and Internet standards, read the following documents:

- Request for Comments on Request for Comments [RFC1111]
- F.Y.I. on F.Y.I: Introduction to the F.Y.I notes [RFC1150]
- Introduction to the STD Notes [RFC1311]
- Guidelines to Authors of Internet Drafts [GAID]
- The Internet Activities Board [RFC1160]
- The Internet Standards Process [RFC1310]
- IAB Official Protocol Standards [STD1]

► *To Obtain Copies...*

To obtain copies of RFCs, Internet-Drafts and other Internet standard information, you can use any of the following methods.

On-line via the Internet

1. Via e-mail, send a message to any of the following

- info@internic.net or mailserv@ds.internic.net
- rfc-info@isi.edu, message body:

  ```
  help: help
  help: manual
  help: ways_to_get_rfcs
  ```

- mailserv@rs.internic.net with message SUBJECT of help or rfc index.

2. Via Gopher or anonymous FTP:

```
ds.internic.net
isoc.org
nic.near.net
```

(or do a VERONICA/archie search for "RFCs").

Hard Copy (Which May Go Out of Date!)

Order from InterNIC Information Services, $.05/page + S&H, minimum $10. **Phone orders**: Call 1-800-444-4345 and choose the option "Information Services." **Fax orders** (using InterNIC order form or authorized purchase orders): 1-619-455-4640. **Mail:** InterNIC, P.O. Box 85608, San Diego, CA

CD-ROM

Collections of RFCs are available from several CD-ROM publishers, including:

- Walnut Creek CD-ROM
- SRI International

Doran's MUDlist

▶ ▶ The following list of MUDs (see Chapter 15) is maintained by Andy Wozniak, who can be reached at awozniak@geordi.calpoly.edu for further information about the list. (The list is named historically after its originator, but is maintained by Wozniak.) The list is also posted periodically to the Usenet newsgroup rec.games.mud.announce and list is also available on the World Wide Web at

http://www.cm.cf.ac.uk/user/Andrew.Wilson/MUDlist/

For more information about MUDs or MUDding, read the biweekly Frequently Asked Questions sheet posted to rec.games.mud.announce and available via anonymous FTP from

ftp.math.okstate.edu:/pub/muds/misc/mud-faq

TYPE <unknown> (2)

Name: CyberEden
Domain: rivendel.slip.umd.edu
IP: 128.8.11.201
Port: 5000

Name: Starwars
Domain: starwars.wis.com
IP: 199.3.240.54
Port: 4402

TYPE aber (15)

Name: AbermuckI
Domain: fert2.fe.psu.edu
IP: 146.186.62.132
Port: 6969

Name: DIRT
Domain: alkymene.uio.no
IP: 129.240.21.60
Port: 6715

Name: BabeMUD
Domain: teaching4.physics.ox.ac.uk
IP: 163.1.245.204
Port: 4001

Name: DragonMud
Domain: fermina.Informatik.rwth-aachen.de
IP: 137.226.224.20
Port: 6715

Name: EclipseMUD
Domain: mud.bsd.uchicago.edu
IP: 128.135.90.79
Port: 6715

Name: Infinity
Domain: sirius.nmt.edu
IP: 129.138.2.119
Port: 6715

Name: Kender'sKove
Domain: harvey.esu.edu
IP: 192.148.218.99
Port: 6715

Name: Mustang
Domain: mustang.us.dell.com
IP: 143.166.224.42
Port: 9173

Name: NorthernLights
Domain: harlie.ludd.luth.se
IP: 130.240.16.29
Port: 6715

Name: SilverMUD
Domain: dante.exide.com
IP: 198.85.1.1
Port: 6715

Name: SleeplessNights
Domain: cs3.brookes.ac.uk
IP: 161.73.1.2
Port: 6789

Name: Terradome
Domain: cmssrv-gw.brookes.ac.uk
IP: 161.73.101.20
Port: 8888

Name: TyrannII
Domain: muselab-gw.runet.edu or
muselab.ac.runet.edu
IP: 137.45.128.10 or 137.45.33.100
Port: 6715

Name: Whirlwind
Domain: bubba.ucc.okstate.edu
IP: 139.78.201.76
Port: 6715

TYPE almost IRC (1)

Name: OlohofBbs
Domain: morra.et.tudelft.nl
IP: 130.161.144.100
Port: 2993

TYPE bsx(1)

Name: Regenesis
Domain: birka.lysator.liu.se
IP: 130.236.254.159
Port: 7475

TYPE circle(2)

Name: HexOnyx
Domain: marble.bu.edu
IP: 128.197.10.75
Port: 7777

Name: VirtualWorldofMagma
Domain: magma.leg.ufrj.br
IP: 146.164.53.33
Port: 4000

TYPE cold (1)

Name: TheColdDark
Domain: recumbent.declab.usu.edu
IP: 129.123.1.36
Port: 6666

TYPE darkmud (1)

Name: Midian][
Domain: pandora.mit.csu.edu.au
IP: 137.166.16.2
Port: 3333

TYPE dgd(5)

Name: AlbionMud
Domain: veda.is
IP: 193.4.230.1
Port: 4000

Name: PaderMUD
Domain: mud.uni-paderborn.de
IP: 131.234.12.13
Port: 3000

Name: GodsHome
Domain: godshome.solace.mh.se
IP: 193.10.118.131
Port: 3000

Name: Pattern
Domain: Theepsilon.me.chalmers.se
IP: 129.16.50.30
Port: 6047

Name: IgorMUD
Domain: ny.mtek.chalmers.se
IP: 129.16.60.9
Port: 1701

TYPEdiku (70)

Name: <unknown>
Domain: abjs01.aberdeen.geo-quest.slb.com
IP: 134.32.86.21
Port: 6969

Name: ACMEmud
Domain: mud.cc.geneseo.edu
IP: 137.238.1.14
Port: 9000

Name: AbsolutMUDb
Domain: 3740.student.cwru.edu
IP: 29.22.248.252
Port: 4000

Name: AbyssII
Domain: helpmac.its.mcw.edu
IP: 141.106.64.52
Port: 8888

Name: Albanian
Domain: fred.indstate.edu
IP: 139.102.12.14
Port: 2150

Name: AlexMUD
Domain: marcel.stacken.kth.se
IP: 130.237.234.17
Port: 4000

Name: ApocalypseIV
Domain: peabrain.humgen.upenn.edu or sapphire.geo.wvu.edu
IP: 128.91.3.204 or 157.182.168.20
Port: 4000

Name: Arctic
Domain: hobbes.linfield.edu
IP: 192.147.171.2
Port: 2700

Name: AustinMud
Domain: aufs.imv.aau.dk
IP: 129.142.28.2
Port: 4000

Name: Chaos
Domain: chaos.bga.com
IP: 198.3.118.12
Port: 4000

Name: CopperIII
Domain: scooter.denver.colorado.edu
IP: 132.194.30.9
Port: 4000

Name: DarkCastlemud
Domain: jive.rahul.net
IP: 192.160.13.4
Port: 6666

Name: Death'sDomain
Domain: wizard.ece.miami.edu
IP: 192.88.124.22
Port: 9000

Name: DikuMudII
Domain: marcel.stacken.kth.se
IP: 130.237.234.17
Port: 4242

Name: DragonMud
Domain: eve.assumption.edu
IP: 192.80.61.5

Port: 5000

Name: Empire
Domain: einstein.physics.drexel.edu
IP: 129.25.1.120
Port: 4000

Name: EnsemMud
Domain: didon.enserb.u-bordeaux.fr
IP: 147.210.18.16
Port: 000

Name: FieryMud
Domain: fiery.eushc.org
IP: 163.246.5.109
Port: 4000

Name: ForbiddenLand
Domain: squeen.mcs.drexel.edu
IP: 129.25.7.100
Port: 4000

Name: Formosa
Domain: db88.ee.ncu.edu.tw
IP: 140.115.70.88
Port: 4000

Name: FuskerMud
Domain: wombat.nexagen.com
IP: 192.153.215.103
Port: 4000

Name: G.O.D.MUD
Domain: cyberspace.com
IP: 199.2.48.11
Port: 4000

Name: Ghostwheel
Domain: cyberspace.com
IP: 199.2.48.11
Port: 4000

Name: GrimneMUD
Domain: gytje.pvv.unit.no
IP: 129.241.36.226
Port: 4000

Name: HOLOmud
Domain: um.ics.missouri.edu
IP: 128.206.187.188
Port: 7777

Name: Harz-Site-Diku
Domain: majestix.rz.tu-clausthal.de
IP: 139.174.2.24
Port: 4000

Name: HerculesMUD
Domain: sunshine.eushc.org
IP: 163.246.32.110
Port: 3000

Name: Imperial
Domain: supergirl.cs.hut.fi
IP: 130.233.40.52
Port: 6969

Name: KAOSHQ
Domain: sg25.aud.temple.edu
IP: 129.32.66.7
Port: 4000

Name: KallistiMud
Domain: jadzia.csos.orst.edu
IP: 128.193.40.23
Port: 4000

Name: Land,The
Domain: nora.gih.no
IP: 128.39.140.150
Port: 4000

Name: LastOutpost
Domain: kimiyo.summer.hawaii.edu
IP: 128.171.137.195
Port: 4000

Name: Legend
Domain: stimpy.washcoll.edu
IP: 192.146.226.4
Port: 4000

Name: Legend
Domain: thumper.cc.utexas.edu
IP: 128.83.135.23
Port: 4000

Name: LegendoftheWind
Domain: sccsun44.csie.nctu.edu.tw
IP: 140.113.17.168
Port: 4040

Name: MUME
Domain: lbdsun4.epfl.ch
IP: 128.178.77.5
Port: 4242

Name: Mayhem
Domain: thrash.isca.uiowa.edu
IP: 128.255.200.25
Port: 1234

Name: MeatMUD
Domain: sneezy.cc.utexas.edu
IP: 128.83.135.8
Port: 2800

Name: MedieviaCyberspace
Domain: bigboy.cis.temple.edu
IP: 129.32.32.98
Port: 4000

Name: MooseHeadMud
Domain: mud.eskimo.com
IP: 162.148.13.44
Port: 4000

Name: Mozart
Domain: kitten.mcs.com
IP: 192.160.127.90
Port: 4500

Name: MudWithNoName
Domain: ronin.bchs.uh.edu
IP: 129.7.2.127
Port: 5000

Name: MuddePathetique
Domain: `flysex.berkeley.edu`
IP: `128.32.128.36`
Port: 2999

Name: NaVie
Domain: `mud.cs.odu.edu`
IP: `128.82.6.145`
Port: 4000

Name: NexusMUD
Domain: `didec3.epfl.ch`
IP: `128.178.164.5`
Port: 4000

Name: NorthernCrossroad
Domain: `sugsparc13.eecg.toronto.edu`
IP: `128.100.13.63`
Port: 9000

Name: OpalMUD
Domain: `opal.cs.virginia.edu`
IP: `128.143.60.14`
Port: 4000

Name: PKmud
Domain: `kennedy.ecn.uoknor.edu`
IP: `129.15.24.14`
Port: 5000

Name: PerilousRealms
Domain: `PR.mese.com`
IP: `155.229.1.4`
Port: 23

Name: Phantazm
Domain: `fpa.com`
IP: `198.242.217.1`
Port: 4000

Name: RealmofMagic
Domain: `p107.informatik.uni-bre-men.de`
IP: `134.102.216.8`
Port: 4000

Name: RealmsofDarkShadows
Domain: `jericho.connected.com`
IP: `162.148.251.252`
Port: 2550

Name: RenegadeOutpost
Domain: `daisy.cc.utexas.edu`
IP: `128.83.135.15`
Port: 9999

Name: Rip'sQuest
Domain: `kennedy.ecn.uoknor.edu`
IP: `129.15.24.14`
Port: 5500

Name: RockyMud
Domain: `hermes.dna.mci.com`
IP: `166.41.48.146`
Port: 4000

Name: Shadowdale
Domain: `dale.hsc.unt.edu`
IP: `129.120.107.70`
Port: 7777

Name: SiliconReal
Domain: mssampan.ee.fit.edu
IP: 163.118.30.9
Port: 4000

Name: SillyMUD
Domain: stone.cis.ufl.edu
IP: 128.227.100.197
Port: 4000

Name: StrangeMUD
Domain: sleepy.cc.utexas.edu
IP: 128.83.135.5
Port: 9332

Name: StrikeNet
Domain: falcon.depaul.edu
IP: 140.192.1.7
Port: 4000

Name: TemporaryMUD
Domain: cc.joensuu.fi
IP: 128.214.14.12
Port: 4000

Name: TheCrystalShard
Domain: metten.cs.csbsju.edu
IP: 152.65.167.11
Port: 9000

Name: TheFinalLevel
Domain: huey.ee.cua.edu
IP: 136.242.140.31
Port: 7777

Name: TheGlassDragon
Domain: surf.tstc.edu
IP: 161.109.32.2
Port: 4000

Name: ThunderDome
Domain: tdome.montana.com
IP: 199.2.139.3
Port: 5555

Name: WISNEYWORLD
Domain: levant.cs.ohiou.edu
IP: 132.235.1.100
Port: 5000

Name: Wayne'sWorld
Domain: drake.eushc.org
IP: 163.246.32.100
Port: 9000

Name: WizzyMudII
Domain: euston.city.ac.uk
IP: 138.40.41.1
Port: 1992

Name: WorldsofCarnage
Domain: orcrist.digital.ufl.edu
IP: 128.227.133.214
Port: 4000

TYPE: dum (3)

Name: CanDUM
Domain: `itrchq.itrc.on.ca`
IP: `128.100.3.100`
Port: 2001

Name: FranDUMII
Domain: `mousson.enst.fr`
IP: `137.194.160.48`
Port: 2001

Name: DUMII
Domain: `elektra.ling.umu.se`
IP: `130.239.24.66`
Port: 2001

TYPE: lp (135)

Name: 3-Kingdoms
Domain: `marble.bu.edu`
IP: `128.197.10.75`
Port: 5000

Name: AncientAnguish
Domain: `end2.bedrock.com`
IP: `131.158.153.39`
Port: 2222

Name: 5thDimension
Domain: `gauss.ifm.liu.se`
IP: `130.236.50.9`
Port: 3000

Name: Asteroth(LPSwat)
Domain: `aviator.cc.iastate.edu`
IP: `129.186.140.6`
Port: 2020

Name: Actuator
Domain: `actlab.rtf.utexas.edu`
IP: `128.83.194.11`
Port: 4000

Name: Aurora
Domain: `aurora.etsiig.uniovi.es`
IP: `156.35.41.20`
Port: 3000

Name: AlexMUD
Domain: `mud.stacken.kth.se`
IP: `130.237.234.17`
Port: 4000

Name: BatMUD
Domain: `bat.cs.hut.fi`
IP: `130.233.40.180`
Port: 23

Name: AncientAnguish
Domain: `dancer.ethz.ch`
IP: `129.132.57.66`
Port: 2222

Name: BatMUD
Domain: `palikka.jyu.fi`
IP: `130.234.40.3`
Port: 2001

Name: Callandor
Domain: warns.et.tudelft.nl
IP: 130.161.147.41
Port: 5317

Name: Castalia
Domain: miucs1.miu.edu
IP: 192.103.45.2
Port: 4444

Name: Chatter
Domain: hawking.u.washington.edu
IP: 140.142.58.99
Port: 6000

Name: Conservatorium
Domain: crs.cl.msu.edu
IP: 35.8.1.10
Port: 6000

Name: Coupworld
Domain: honey.st-and.ac.uk
IP: 138.251.33.32
Port: 7425

Name: CrossedSwords
Domain: shsibm.shh.fi
IP: 128.214.44.251
Port: 3000

Name: DarkSaga
Domain: cobber.cord.edu
IP: 138.129.1.32
Port: 5555

Name: DarkWind
Domain: darkwind.i-link.com
IP: 198.67.37.33
Port: 3000

Name: DarkerRealms
Domain: worf.tamu.edu
IP: 128.194.116.25
Port: 2000

Name: Dartmud
Domain: fermat.dartmouth.edu
IP: 129.170.28.31
Port: 2525

Name: DeeperTrouble
Domain: alk.iesd.auc.dk
IP: 130.225.48.46
Port: 4242

Name: Dirtymud
Domain: bsu-cs.bsu.edu
IP: 47.226.112.101
Port: 5454

Name: Discworld
Domain: cix.compulink.co.uk
IP: 192.188.69.2
Port: 4242

Name: Dragon'sDen
Domain: hellfire.dusers.drexel.edu
or oyster01.mcs.drexel.edu
IP: 129.25.56.246 or 129.25.7.111
Port: 2222

Name: DragonFire
Domain: typo.umsl.edu
IP: 134.124.42.197
Port: 3000

Name: DreamShadow
Domain: jericho.connected.com
IP: 162.148.251.252
Port: 3333

Name: Dshores
Domain: kcbbs.gen.nz
IP: 202.14.102.1
Port: 6000

Name: EasternStoris
Domain: cisppc2.cis.nctu.edu.tw
IP: 140.113.204.42
Port: 8000

Name: ElementsofParadox
Domain: elof.acc.iit.edu
IP: 192.41.245.90
Port: 6996

Name: EndOfTheLine
Domain: aus.stanford.EDU
IP: 36.21.0.99
Port: 2010

Name: Enigma
Domain: kcbbs.gen.nz
IP: 202.14.102.1
Port: 6000

Name: Etheria
Domain: csgi60.leeds.ac.uk
IP: 129.11.144.190
Port: 7777

Name: EverDark
Domain: atomic.com
IP: 198.64.6.24
Port: 3000

Name: Evolution
Domain: popgen.biology.umt.edu
IP: 150.131.50.1
Port: 4445

Name: FarSide or Farside
Domain: photobooks.gatech.edu or quark.gmi.edu
IP: 128.61.44.21 or 192.138.137.39
Port: 2500

Name: FirstLight
Domain: gold.t-informatik.ba-stuttgart.de
IP: 141.31.1.16
Port: 3000

Name: GateWay
Domain: idiot.alfred.edu
IP: 149.84.4.1
Port: 6969

Name: Genesis
Domain: hamal2.cs.chalmers.se
IP: 129.16.226.142
Port: 3011

Name: Genocide
Domain: `pip.shsu.edu`
IP: `192.92.115.10`
Port: 2222

Name: Gilgamesh
Domain: `shiner.st.usm.edu`
IP: `131.95.115.131`
Port: 3742

Name: HallofFame
Domain: `marvin.df.lth.se`
IP: `130.235.88.94`
Port: 2000

Name: HariMUD
Domain: `tc0.chem.tue.nl`
IP: `131.155.94.3`
Port: 6997

Name: Haven
Domain: `idrz07.ethz.ch`
IP: `129.132.76.8`
Port: 1999

Name: Highlands
Domain: `highlands.lp.mud.org`
IP: `132.241.4.202`
Port: 2000

Name: HolyMission
Domain: `alijku05.edvz.uni-linz.ac.at`
IP: `140.78.3.1`
Port: 2001

Name: Igor
Domain: `ny.mtek.chalmers.se`
IP: `129.16.60.9`
Port: 1701

Name: Imperial2
Domain: `hp.ecs.rpi.edu`
IP: `128.113.5.43`
Port: 3141

Name: Infinity
Domain: `olympus.ccs.neu.edu`
IP: `129.10.111.80`
Port: 3000

Name: IvoryTower
Domain: `marvin.macc.wisc.edu`
IP: `144.92.30.207`
Port: 2000

Name: Kingdoms
Domain: `gwaihir.dd.chalmers.se`
IP: `129.16.117.21`
Port: 1812

Name: Kingdoms
Domain: `kili.dd.chalmers.se`
IP: `129.16.117.17`
Port: 1812

Name: KoBra or Kobra
Domain: `duteca4.et.tudelft.nl` or
`kobra.et.tudelft.nl`
IP: `130.161.144.22` or `130.161.144.236`
Port: 8888

Name: LOSTMud
Domain: louie.cc.utexas.edu
IP: 128.83.135.4
Port: 6666

Name: LochNess
Domain: indigo.imp.ch
IP: 157.161.1.12
Port: 2222

Name: LooneyMud
Domain: looney.cp.tn.tudelft.nl
IP: 192.31.126.102
Port: 8888

Name: LostSouls
Domain: ronin.bchs.uh.edu
IP: 129.7.2.127
Port: 3000

Name: LustyMud
Domain: lusty.tamu.edu
IP: 128.194.9.199
Port: 2000

Name: MarchesofAntan
Domain: checfs2.ucsd.edu or
chem.ucsd.edu
IP: 132.239.68.9 or 32.239.68.1
Port: 3000

Name: Mathmud
Domain: medusa.math.fu-berlin.de
IP: 130.133.4.4
Port: 3000

Name: MidnightSun
Domain: holly.ludd.luth.se
IP: 130.240.16.23
Port: 3000

Name: Moonstar
Domain: pulsar.hsc.edu
IP: 192.135.84.5
Port: 4321

Name: Muddog
Domain: catalyst.math.ufl.edu
IP: 128.227.168.38
Port: 2000

Name: Muddywaters
Domain: hot.caltech.edu
IP: 131.215.9.49
Port: 3000

Name: Mythos
Domain: mann.uni-koblenz.de
IP: 141.26.4.41
Port: 3000

Name: NANVAENT, Nanvaent, or
NANVAENT3
Domain: corrour.cc.strath.ac.uk
IP: 130.159.220.8
Port: 3000

Name: Nameless
Domain: complex.is
IP: 193.4.210.1
Port: 2000

Name: NannyMUD
Domain: `birka.lysator.liu.se`
IP: `130.236.254.159`
Port: 2000

Name: NightFall
Domain: `nova.tat.physik.uni-`
`tuebingen.de`
IP: `134.2.62.161`
Port: 4242

Name: Nightmare
Domain: `nightmare.connected.com`
IP: `162.148.251.220`
Port: 4000

Name: Nirvana and Nirvana4 or Nir-vanaIV
Domain: `elof.acc.iit.edu`
IP: `192.41.245.90`
Port: 3500

Name: Nuclearwar
Domain: `melba.astrakan.hgs.se` or
`pyrus.astrakan.hgs.se`
IP: `130.238.206.12` or `130.238.206.11`
Port: 23

Name: Onyx
Domain: `onyx.cs.iastate.edu`
IP: `129.186.3.56`
Port: 3456

Name: Overdrive
Domain: `castor.acs.oakland.edu`
IP: `141.210.10.109`
Port: 5195

Name: Paradox
Domain: `adl.uncc.edu`
IP: `152.15.15.181`
Port: 0478

Name: Phoenix
Domain: `albert.bu.edu`
IP: `128.197.74.10`
Port: 3500

Name: PixieMud
Domain: `elof.acc.iit.edu`
IP: `192.41.245.90`
Port: 6969

Name: Pixilated
Domain: `elof.acc.iit.edu`
IP: `192.41.245.90`
Port: 6996

Name: PrimeTime
Domain: `prime.mdata.fi`
IP: `192.98.43.2`
Port: 3000

Name: Prydein
Domain: `spock.austin.apple.com`
IP: `17.127.4.14`
Port: 4567

Name: Psycho-thriller
Domain: `atlantis.edu`
IP: `192.67.238.48`
Port: 3000

Name: Pyromud
Domain: elektra.cc.edu
IP: 140.104.1.100
Port: 2222

Name: QUOVADIS
Domain: nemesis.imp.ch
IP: 157.161.1.10
Port: 2345

Name: Ragnarok
Domain: ragnarok.teleport.com
IP: 192.108.254.22
Port: 2222

Name: RealmsofChaos
Domain: xmission.com
IP: 198.60.22.2
Port: 3456

Name: RealmsofTabor
Domain: penguin.tamucc.edu
IP: 165.95.7.123
Port: 9999

Name: RealmsoftheDragon
Domain: cw-u04.umd.umich.edu
IP: 141.215.69.7
Port: 3000

Name: Realmsmud
Domain: donal.dorsai.org
IP: 198.3.127.6
Port: 1501

Name: Regenesis
Domain: regenesis.lysator.liu.se
IP: 130.236.254.159
Port: 7475

Name: Regular
Domain: rzc8.rz.uni-regensburg.de
IP: 132.199.30.8
Port: 3000

Name: RevengeoftheEndoftheLine
Domain: aus.stanford.edu
IP: 36.21.0.99
Port: 2010

Name: Rhovania
Domain: tghost.neosoft.com
IP: 198.64.6.21
Port: 4000

Name: STYX
Domain: dreamtime.nmsu.edu
IP: 128.123.8.116
Port: 3000

Name: Shadowriver
Domain: eskinews.eskimo.com
IP: 162.148.13.31
Port: 5000

Name: ShatteredWorl
Domain: dip1.cs.monash.edu.au
IP: 130.194.64.102
Port: 2666

Name: Sojourn
Domain: sojourn.cem.msu.edu
IP: 35.8.25.23
Port: 9999

Name: SplitSecond
Domain: lestat.shv.hb.se
IP: 130.241.246.10
Port: 3000

Name: Starmud
Domain: krynn.solace.mh.se
IP: 193.10.106.2
Port: 7373

Name: StickMUD
Domain: kalikka.jyu.fi , or lance-lot.cc.jyu.fi, or stickmud.jyu.fi
IP: 130.234.40.2 or 130.234.40.4
Port: 7680

Name: SvenskMUD
Domain: bodil.lysator.liu.se
IP: 130.236.254.152
Port: 2043 or 2046

Name: T'Mud or T'mud
Domain: wave.st.usm.edu
IP: 131.95.119.2
Port: 2222

Name: TAPPMud
Domain: surprise.pro.ufz.de
IP: 141.65.31.2
Port: 6510

Name: TMI-2
Domain: kendall.ccs.neu.edu
IP: 129.10.114.86
Port: 5555

Name: TheHolyMission
Domain: alijku03.edvz.uni-linz.ac.at
IP: 140.78.3.30
Port: 4242

Name: TheLandsofTabor
Domain: penguin.tamucc.edu
IP: 165.95.7.123
Port: 9999

Name: TheRoundTable
Domain: darasia.chem.wfu.edu
IP: 152.17.20.15
Port: 2222

Name: Timewarp
Domain: quark.gmi.edu
IP: 192.138.137.39
Port: 5150

Name: Tron
Domain: polaris.king.ac.uk
IP: 141.241.84.65
Port: 000 or 4000

Name: TubMUD
Domain: morgen.cs.tu-berlin.de
IP: 130.149.19.20
Port: 7680

Name: Ultimate
Domain: rkw-risc.cs.up.ac.za
IP: 137.215.18.10
Port: 1984

Name: Valhalla
Domain: valhalla.com
IP: 192.187.153.1
Port: 2444

Name: VikingMUD
Domain: sid.dsl.unit.no
IP: 129.241.36.75
Port: 2001

Name: Windy
Domain: bitsy.apana.org.au or
eppie.apana.org.au
IP: 203.2.134.3
Port: 2000

TYPE: lp-german (2)

Name: MorgenGrauen
Domain: PASCAL.UNI-MUENSTER.DE
IP: 28.176.121.56
Port: 711

TYPE mare (1)

Name: WindsMare
Domain: cyberion.bbn.com
IP: 128.89.2.139
Port: 7348

TYPE merc(11)

Name: ConchMud
Domain: aann.tyrell.net
IP: 198.175.8.3
Port: 4000

Name: Wonderland
Domain: gorina3.hsr.no
IP: 152.94.1.43
Port: 3287

Name: WorldofMizar
Domain: delial.docs.uu.se
IP: 130.238.8.40
Port: 9000

Name: Zebedee
Domain: rszircon.swan.ac.uk
IP: 137.44.102.2
Port: 7000

Name: flame
Domain: marlin.ucc.gu.uwa.edu.au
IP: 130.95.100.4
Port: 4242

Name: UNITOPIA
Domain: helpdesk.rus.uni-stuttgart.de
IP: 129.69.221.120
Port: 3333

Name: Farside
Domain: farside.atinc.com
IP: 198.138.35.199
Port: 3000

Name: HiddenWorlds
Domain: cns.cscns.com
IP: 192.156.196.1
Port: 4000

Name: Highlands
Domain: jedi.cis.temple.edu
IP: 129.32.32.70
Port: 9001

Name: LegendsofWind
Domain: sccsun44.csie.nctu.edu.tw
IP: 140.113.17.168
Port: 4040

Name: LostRealms
Domain: iguana.ucs.uoknor.edu
IP: 129.15.10.23
Port: 4000

Name: MadROM
Domain: dogbert.ugcs.caltech.edu
IP: 131.215.133.151
Port: 1536

Name: Medievia
Domain: bigboy.cis.temple.edu
IP: 129.32.32.98
Port: 4000

Name: MurkyMUD
Domain: matad.athena.livjm.ac.uk
IP: 150.204.38.33
Port: 4567

Name: StackMUD
Domain: marcel.stacken.kth.se
IP: 130.237.234.17
Port: 8000

Name: StickintheMUD
Domain: ugsparc11.eecg.utoronto.ca
IP: 128.100.13.61
Port: 9000

TYPE moo (11)

Name: DiversityUniversity
Domain: erau.db.erau.edu
IP: 155.31.1.1
Port: 8888

Name: Dragonsfire
Domain: moo.eskimo.com
IP: 162.148.13.31
Port: 7777

Name: FinalFrontiers
Domain: moougly.microserve.net
IP: 192.204.120.2
Port: 2499

Name: Ghostwhee
Domain: lmooghostwheel.bga.com
IP: 198.3.118.4
Port: 6969

Name: Harper'sTale
Domain: moonetman.widener.edu
IP: 147.31.1.51
Port: 8888

Name: MuMOO
Domain: chestnut.enmu.edu
IP: 192.94.216.74
Port: 7777

Name: LambdaMOO
Domain: lambda.xerox.com
IP: 192.216.54.2
Port: 8888

Name: StarTrekMOO
Domain: gibeah.connected.com
IP: 162.148.251.253
Port: 7777

Name: MOOsaico
Domain: mes05.di.uminho.ptu or
moo.di.uminho.pt
IP: 193.136.20.104 or 193.136.20.102
Port: 7777

Name: ZenMOO
Domain: cheshire.oxy.edu
IP: 134.69.1.253
Port: 7777

TYPE muck (17)

Name: #AfterFive
Domain: moe.coe.uga.edu
IP: 128.192.22.3
Port: 9999

Name: DivinationWeb
Domain: bill.math.uconn.edu
IP: 137.99.17.5
Port: 9393

Name: AfterFive
Domain: pa.itd.com
IP: 128.160.24.249
Port: 9999

Name: FurToonia
Domain: seagull.rtd.com
IP: 198.102.68.2
Port: 8888

Name: AnimeMUCK
Domain: tcp.com
IP: 128.95.44.29
Port: 2035

Name: FurryMUCK
Domain: sncils.snc.edu
IP: 138.74.0.10
Port: 8888

Name: CaveMUCK
Domain: tcp.com
IP: 128.95.44.29
Port: 2283

Name: HoloMuck
Domain: collatz.mcrcim.mcgill.edu or
lightning.mcrcim.mcgill.edu
IP: 132.206.78.1 or 132.206.4.25
Port: 5757

Name: KoogMUCK
Domain: `ghostrider.journalism.indiana.edu`
IP: `129.79.115.146`
Port: 4201

Name: NAILS
Domain: `flounder.rutgers.edu`
IP: `128.6.128.5`
Port: 5150

Name: NonSenseMUCK
Domain: `rigel.dsif.fee.unicamp.br`
IP: `143.106.8.131`
Port: 4201

Name: Quartz
Domain: `quartz.rutgers.edu`
IP: `128.6.60.6`
Port: 9999

Name: QuartzParadise
Domain: `quartz.rutgers.edu`
IP: `128.6.60.6`
Port: 9999

Name: RealmsMUCK
Domain: `tcp.com`
IP: `128.95.44.29`
Port: 7765

Name: TapestriesMUCK
Domain: `tcp.com`
IP: `128.95.44.29`
Port: 2069

Name: WizMUCK
Domain: `alf.zfn.uni-bremen.de`
IP: `134.102.20.22`
Port: 9999

TYPE mudwho (3)

Name: DarkestDomain
Domain: `spew.ecst.csuchico.edu`
IP: `132.241.7.8`
Port: 2028

Name: Nova
Domain: `nova.tat.physik.uni-tuebingen.de`
IP: `134.2.62.161`
Port: 6889

Name: okwho
Domain: `riemann.math.okstate.edu`
IP: `139.78.1.15`
Port: 6889

TYPE mug (1)

Name: UglyMug
Domain: wyrm.cs.man.ac.uk
IP: 192.150.182.3
Port: 6239

TYPEmuse(12)

Name: BTech
Domain: mccool.cbi.msstate.edu
IP: 130.18.104.2
Port: 3056

Name: Rhostshyl
Domain: rhostshyl.cit.cornell.edu
IP: 128.253.180.15
Port: 4201

Name: BTech3056
Domain: btech.netaxs.com
IP: 192.204.4.38
Port: 3056

Name: TOSTrek
Domain: musesiher.stanford.edu
IP: 36.109.0.64
Port: 1701

Name: BattleTech
Domain: step.polymtl.ca
IP: 132.207.7.32
Port: 3026

Name: TimeMuse
Domain: murren.ai.mit.edu
IP: 18.43.0.179
Port: 4201

Name: Fantasia
Domain: betz.biostr.washington.edu
IP: 128.95.44.22
Port: 4201

Name: TrekMUSE or TrekMuse
Domain: laurel.cnidr.org
IP: 128.109.179.14
Port: 1701

Name: MicroMUSE
Domain: chezmoto.ai.mit.edu
IP: 18.43.0.102
Port: 4201

Name: VegaMuseII
Domain: planck.sos.clarkson.edu
IP: 128.153.32.14
Port: 2095

Name: OceanaMUSE
Domain: k12.cnidr.org
IP: 128.109.179.45
Port: 4201

TYPE mush (48)

Name: AmalgamMUSH
Domain: comtch.iea.com
IP: 198.17.249.2
Port: 2010

Name: Amarynth
Domain: pharos.acusd.edu
IP: 192.55.87.201
Port: 9999

Name: ApexMUD
Domain: apex.ccs.yorku.ca
IP: 130.63.237.12
Port: 4201

Name: ApexMUSH
Domain: apex.ccs.yorku.ca
IP: 130.63.237.12
Port: 4201

Name: Asgard
Domain: d.speech.cs.cmu.edu
IP: 128.2.250.118
Port: 5565

Name: CitadelMUSH
Domain: ccnet.com
IP: 192.215.96.2
Port: 6250

Name: CityofDarkness
Domain: melandra.cs.man.ac.uk
IP: 130.88.240.110
Port: 2000

Name: Conspiracy!
Domain: almond.enmu.edu
IP: 192.94.216.77
Port: 1066

Name: CrystalMUSH
Domain: moink.nmsu.edu
IP: 128.123.8.115
Port: 6886

Name: Cybermush
Domain: tlaloc.cms.dmu.ac.uk
IP: 146.227.102.4
Port: 6250

Name: DAMNED
Domain: Thejanus.library.cmu.edu
IP: 128.2.21.7
Port: 6250

Name: DeepSeas
Domain: a.cs.okstate.edu
IP: 139.78.9.1
Port: 6250

Name: DragonDawn
Domain: cashew.enmu.edu
IP: 192.94.216.78
Port: 2222

Name: Dragonlance
Domain: yacht.slip.andrew.cmu.edu
IP: 128.2.116.75
Port: 6250

Name: Dune
Domain: mellers1.psych.berkeley.edu
IP: 128.32.243.78
Port: 4201

Name: EleniumMUSH
Domain: clayton.ru.ac.za
IP: 146.231.128.89
Port: 4201

Name: Fast-JackMUSH
Domain: ganymede.ics.uci.edu
IP: 128.195.10.9
Port: 5150

Name: Garou
Domain: party.apple.com
IP: 130.43.2.10
Port: 7000

Name: GlobalMUSH
Domain: lancelot.cif.rochester.edu
IP: 128.151.220.22
Port: 201

Name: HemlockMUSH
Domain: pelyco.soar.gsia.cmu.edu
IP: 128.2.18.7
Port: 1973

Name: ImagECastle or ImageCastle
Domain: fogey.stanford.edu
IP: 36.22.0.31
Port: 4201

Name: Incarnations
Domain: gart.sonoma.edu
IP: 130.157.2.34
Port: 4201

Name: LegionMUSH
Domain: a.cs.okstate.edu
IP: 139.78.9.1
Port: 2996

Name: Masquerade
Domain: phobos.unm.edu
IP: 129.24.8.3
Port: 4444

Name: NarniaMush
Domain: argo.unm.edu
IP: 129.24.9.24
Port: 6250

Name: NeverEndingStory or
TheNeverendingStory
Domain: jove.cs.pdx.edu
IP: 131.252.21.12
Port: 9999

Name: PernMUSH
Domain: cesium.clock.org
IP: 130.43.2.43
Port: 4201

Name: PrairieMUSH
Domain: firefly.prairienet.org
IP: 192.17.3.3
Port: 4201

Name: ShadowrunMUSH
Domain: yacht.slip.andrew.cmu.edu
IP: 128.2.116.75
Port: 4201

Name: Shards
Domain: vesta.unm.edu
IP: 129.24.120.253
Port: 7777

Name: SouCon
Domain: beechnut.enmu.edu
IP: 192.94.216.86
Port: 4201

Name: SpaceMadness
Domain: a.cs.okstate.edu
IP: 139.78.9.1
Port: 6250

Name: SpatialWastes
Domain: chestnut.enmu.edu
IP: 192.94.216.74
Port: 2001

Name: StarWarsMUSH
Domain: techno.stanford.edu
IP: 36.73.0.71
Port: 4402

Name: StarWars
Domain: starwars.wis.com
IP: 199.3.240.54
Port: 4402

Name: SwordsMUSH
Domain: world.std.com
IP: 192.74.137.5
Port: 4201

Name: TelaMagica
Domain: wizards.com
IP: 198.151.161.6
Port: 6250

Name: TheAwakening
Domain: cestus.gb.nrao.edu
IP: 192.33.116.67
Port: 999

Name: TinyCWRU
Domain: caisr2.caisr.cwru.edu
IP: 129.22.24.22
Port: 4201

Name: TinyTim
Domain: myelin.uchc.edu
IP: 155.37.1.251
Port: 5440

Name: TolkienMUSH
Domain: ghost.cse.nau.edu
IP: 134.114.64.6
Port: 1892

Name: TooMUSH]I[
Domain: lodestar.gb.nrao.edu
IP: 192.33.116.108
Port: 7070

Name: TrippyMush
Domain: `newton.sos.clarkson.edu`
IP: `128.153.32.6`
Port: 7567

Name: TwoMoonsmush
Domain: `lupine.org`
IP: `198.4.75.40`
Port: 4201

Name: X-men
Domain: `lupine.org`
IP: `198.4.75.40`
Port: 1994

Name: Xmush
Domain: `xmen.lupine.org`
IP: `198.4.75.40`
Port: 1994

TYPE oxmud (2)

Name: Island
Domain: `teaching4.physics.ox.ac.uk`
IP: `163.1.245.204`
Port: 2092

Name: Island
Domain: `teaching4.physics.ox.ac.uk`
IP: `163.1.245.204`
Port: 2093

TYPE talker (10)

Name: Addicted
Domain: `sun1.gwent.ac.uk`
IP: `193.63.82.1`
Port: 6666

Name: DS9
Domain: `rivendel.slip.umd.edu`
IP: `128.8.11.201`
Port: 3000

Name: Dragon'sLair
Domain: `rivendel.slip.umd.edu`
IP: `128.8.11.201`
Port: 7777

Name: Foothills
Domain: `marble.bu.edu`
IP: `128.197.10.75`
Port: 2010

Name: GammaQuadrant
Domain: `rivendel.slip.umd.edu`
IP: `128.8.11.201`
Port: 6000

Name: JurassicPark
Domain: `squid.code3.com`
IP: `143.122.16.85`
Port: 4782

Name: SomeWhereElse
Domain: `atalanta.pcs.cnu.edu` or
`kehleyr.phys.ttu.edu`
IP: `137.155.2.21` or `129.118.41.9`
Port: 2010

Name: Surfers
Domain: muscle.rai.kcl.ac.uk
IP: 137.73.16.2
Port: 3232

Name: TheChattingZone
Domain: zeus.sc.plym.ac.uk
IP: 141.163.11.1
Port: 8342

TYPE teeny (3)

Name: (EVIL!)Mud
Domain: cyber1.gate.net
IP: 198.80.2.35
Port: 4201

Name: ApexMUD
Domain: apex.yorku.ca
IP: 130.63.237.12
Port: 4201

Name: (EVIL!)Mud
Domain: intac.com
IP: 198.6.114.2
Port: 4201

TYPE tiny(3)

Name: ApexMUD
Domain: pex.ccs.yorku.ca
IP: 130.63.237.12
Port: 4201

Name: PRISM
Domain: lister.cc.ic.ac.uk
IP: 129.31.80.167
Port: 4201

Name: DragonMUD
Domain: satan.ucsd.edu
IP: 132.239.1.7
Port: 4201

TYPE uber (1)

Name: TheLandofDrogon
Domain: drogon.meiko.com
IP: 192.131.107.11
Port: 6123

TYPE uri (3)

Name: DarkestDomain
Domain: spew.ecst.csuchico.edu
IP: 132.241.7.8
Port: 2030 or 2040

Name: MulberryMud
Domain: spew.ecst.csuchico.edu
IP: 132.241.7.8
Port: 2032

Name: TheRealmofDoth
Domain: spew.ecst.csuchico.edu
IP: 132.241.7.8
Port: 2042

TYPE yamud (1)

Name: GoolandIII
Domain: payday.etdesg.trw.com
IP: 129.193.42.226
Port: 6715

K–12 Internetworking Guidelines

► ► This excellent guide to K–12 Internet connections is an informational memo (RFC 1709) from the Network Working Group of the Internet Engineering Task Force. We include it here as a supplement to Chapter 17's discussion of K–12 educational uses of the Internet.

► ► *Authors*

ISN Working Group

Internet Draft November 1994

Joan Gargano
University of California, Davis

David Wasley
University of California, Berkeley

► ► *Status of This Memo*

This memo provides technical guidance to the K–12 educational community on school networking and connections to the Internet. Distribution of this memo is unlimited.

► ► *I. Introduction*

Many organizations concerned with K–12 educational issues and the planning for the use of technology recognize the value of data communications throughout the educational system. State-sponsored documents such as the California Department of Education's "Strategic Plan for Information Technology" recommend the planning of voice, video, and data networks to support learning and educational administration, but they do not provide specific technical direction.

The institutions that built the Internet and connected early in its development are early adopters of technology, with technical staff dedicated to the planning for and implementation of leading-edge technology. The K–12 community traditionally has not had this level of staffing available for telecommunications planning. This document is intended to bridge that gap and provides a recommended technical direction, an introduction to the role the Internet now plays in K–12 education, and technical guidelines for building a campus data communications infrastructure that provides internetworking services and connections to the Internet.

For a more general introduction to the Internet and its applications and uses, the reader is referred to any of the references listed in the following RFCs:

- 1392 "Internet Users' Glossary" (also FYI 18)
- 1432 "Recent Internet Books"
- 1462 "What is the Internet" (also FYI 20)
- 1463 "Introducing the Internet—A Short Bibliograpy of Introductory Internetworking Readings for the Network Novice" (also FYI 19)

▶▶ *II. Rationale for the Use of Internet Protocols*

In 1993, the Bank Street College of Education conducted a survey of 550 educators who are actively involved in using telecommunications.[1] The survey looked at a wide variety of ways telecommunications technology is used in K–12 education. Their findings on Internet usage are summarized below.

"Slightly less than half of these educators have access to the Internet, which is supplied most frequently by a university computer or educational service."

"Internet services are used almost twice as often for professional activities as for student learning activities."

"Sending e-mail is the most common use of the Internet, followed by accessing news and bulletin boards and gaining access to remote computers."

The following chart shows the percentage of respondents that use each network application to support professional and student activities.

Applications	Professional Activities	Student Activities
Electronic mail	91	79
News or bulletin board	63	50
Remote access to other computers	48	32
Database access	36	31
File transfer	34	19

The value of the Internet and its explosive growth are a direct result of the computer communications technology used on the network. The same network design principles and computer communications protocols (TCP/IP) used on the Internet can be used within a school district to build campuswide networks. This is standard practice within higher education, and increasingly in K–12 schools as well. The benefits of the TCP/IP protocols are listed below.

- **Ubiquity:** TCP/IP is available on most, if not all, of the computing platforms likely to be important for instructional or administrative purposes. TCP/IP is available for the IBM compatible personal computers (PCs) running DOS or Windows and all versions of the Apple Macintosh. TCP/IP is standard on all UNIX-based systems and workstations and most mainframe computers.

- **Applications:** TCP/IP supports many applications including, but not limited to, electronic mail, file transfer, interactive remote host access, database access, file sharing and access to networked information resources. Programming and development expertise is available from a wide variety of sources.

- **Flexibility:** TCP/IP is flexible, and new data transport requirements can be incorporated easily. It can accommodate educational and administrative applications equally well so that one set of network cabling and one communications system may be used in both the classroom and the office.

- **Simplicity:** TCP/IP is simple enough to run on low-end computing platforms such as the Apple MacIntosh and PCs while still providing efficient support for large minicomputer and mainframe computing platforms. TCP/IP benefits from over twenty years of refinement that has resulted in a large and technically sophisticated environment.

- **Capacity:** TCP/IP supports local area network and wide area network services within the entire range of network data rates available today, from dial-up modem speeds to gigabit-speed experimental networks. Communications can occur reliably among machines across this entire range of speeds.

- **Coexistence:** TCP/IP can coexist successfully with other networking architectures. It is likely that offices and classrooms that already have networks may be using something other than TCP/IP. Networks of Apple Macintosh computers will probably be using AppleTalk; networks of PCs may be using any of the common network operating systems such as Novell Netware or LANManager. Mainframe computers may be using IBM's System Network Architecture (SNA). None of these proprietary protocols provides broad connectivity on a global scale. Recognizing this, network technology vendors now provide many means for building networks in which all of these protocols can coexist.

- **Multimedia:** TCP/IP networks can support voice, graphics and video as part of teleconferencing and multimedia applications.

- **Compatibility:** All of the major universities, as well as thousands of commercial and governmental organizations, use TCP/IP for their primary communications services. Commercial networks such as CompuServe and America Online are also connected to the Internet. Many state Departments of Education have sponsored statewide initiatives to connect schools to the Internet, and many K–12 school districts have connected based upon local needs.

- **NREN:** The High Performance Computing Act of 1991 and the Information Infrastructure and Technology Act of 1992 provide

K–12 Guidelines

▶ ▶

ap.
E

the foundation for building the national telecommunications infrastructure in support of education and research. The National Research and Education Network (NREN) will be based upon Internet technology.

The benefits of internetworking technology have been demonstrated through twenty years of use by thousands of organizations. This same experience also provides tested technical models for network design that can be adapted to K–12 campus-wide networking in schools of all sizes and technical development.

▶▶ III. A Technical Model for School Networks

The vision of a modern communications network serving all primary and secondary schools has been articulated and discussed in many forums. Many schools and a few school districts have implemented ad hoc network systems in response to their own perception of the importance of this resource. This section of the ISN RFC presents a standard network implementation model to assist county offices of education and school districts in their planning so that all such implementations will be compatible with each other and with national networking plans intended to enrich K–12 education.

The future goal of "an integrated voice, data, and video network extending to every classroom" is exciting, but so far from what exists today that the investment in time and dollars required to realize such a goal will be greater than most districts can muster in the near term. We suggest that a great deal can be done immediately, with relatively few dollars, to provide modern communications systems in and between all schools around the nation.

Our present goal is to define a highly functional, homogeneous, and well supported network system that could interconnect all K–12 schools and district, county, and statewide offices and that will enable teachers and administrators to begin to use new communications tools and network-based information resources. It takes considerable time to adapt curricula and other programs to take full advantage of new technology. Through the use of standard models for implementation of current network technologies, schools can begin this process now.

Many states have already developed communications services for their schools. A notable example is Texas, which provides terminal access to central information resources from every classroom over a statewide network. Modem-accessible systems are available in many states that serve to encourage teachers to become familiar with network resources and capabilities. Although modem-access may be the only practical option today in some areas, it always will be limited in functionality and/or capacity. In anticipation of emerging and future bandwidth-intensive information resource applications and the functionality that they will require, we believe it is essential to provide direct network access to the National Research and Education Network (NREN) Internet[2] from computers in every classroom.

The Internet communication protocols, commonly known as "TCP/IP," are the "glue" that will allow all computers to communicate. As noted above, software that implements Internet protocols is available for all modern computers. These protocols support a very wide variety of applications, from electronic messaging to client/server data access. The use of Internet protocols will ensure that all networked computers will have direct access to the vast range of existing information and education resources on the Internet, as well as to the emerging National Information Infrastructure.

▶ Approach

The implementation we suggest would use current proven and cost effective technology and would be expandable and upgradable to newer technology with minimum additional investment. This approach requires careful, modular design to meet the following criteria:

1. Any physical infrastructure development should be general and flexible enough to be reused as technology improves. For example, a school office might have a simple terminal today that could be wired to a network adapter serving the school building. Later a Macintosh, DOS, or Windows-based PC might replace the terminal, and the type of connection to the network would change accordingly. However, the wiring between the office and the network "hub" site could remain the same if it is designed properly to begin with. This is an important consideration since wiring typically

represents 20 to 40 percent of the cost of individual network hookups.

2. Existing computers and terminals in schools and district offices should be integrated as much as possible into the communication system. This installed base represents a large investment, albeit in many cases a somewhat dated set of equipment. Wholesale replacement of that base would be a large additional burden on funding resources. A consequence of the above is that the user interface and the services available will vary depending on the type of equipment used to access the network. For example, DOS PCs, Macintosh computers, or UNIX workstations would be connected directly to Local Area Networks (LANs) and would be provided with communications software to support a broad set of functions, many of which will have graphical user interfaces and will make use of client/server technology. Apple II computers, "dumb" terminals, or other such devices could be connected to intelligent network hubs that would allow access to network server computers or information resources, but almost certainly will not support the full range of functionality provided by a direct network connection. In the short term, this is a limitation that we must accept.

3. Network servers will be located where they can be managed and supported, and they must also provide access paths with adequate bandwidth. A system of hierarchical servers should be created in larger school districts, with automatic transfer of common information from a central system to the secondary systems each night, or at appropriate intervals. Local servers will allow each school to provide on-line information particular to its programs and community. This model optimizes use of network bandwidth as well.

4. School interconnect topologies (links) must be both cost effective and manageable. Communication between schools, district offices, county offices of education, and the State Department of Education must be reliable and of sufficient capacity to support the primary applications as well as allow development of new applications.

Capacity is measured both by total data traffic volume and by response time when information is requested over the network. Reliability is measured by the percentage of time that the network is able to transport data. Reliability should be well over 99.7%. Capacity should be such that no more than 10% of the communications bandwidth is used during a typical work day. This is intended to leave adequate capacity for good response time to short-term communication demands.

Many schools already have some form of communications infrastructure in place. In some cases this infrastructure can be adapted to newer technologies; in other cases it may have to be replaced over time. These issues are explored further following presentation of the basic model that serves as a guideline for future communications system development.

▶ *Implementation Model*

There is no one "blueprint" for a network that will drop into every school. Each school will have particular physical constraints, functional needs, an existing technology base, funding constraints, and opportunities for collaboration with vendors and support groups in its area. What is presented here is a set of general guidelines that can be followed in the planning of a school network implementation.

The strategic decision to use Internet protocols in developing school networks provides the opportunity to avoid the major expense of building new statewide backbone infrastructures in the near term. Interconnection of schools, districts, county offices of education and the State Department of Education can be accomplished by acquiring Internet connection service from any of the existing Internet service providers in the state[3]. It is critical that Internet connection service meet criteria for reliability and capacity but connection to any Internet service provider will provide communication capability to all other Internet subscribers within the state, the nation, and the world.

Internet technology is designed to allow very flexible intersite topologies, but a hierarchical topology is the simplest to engineer. Generally this will mean hierarchical connection of school facilities to district offices, in many cases further aggregated at county offices, and finally a link to an Internet service provider. Coordination of circuit services and a single point of connection to an Internet service provider serves both to minimize overall costs and increase opportunities to make use of newer technologies.

The basic school network implementation model is quite simple: create a local area network (LAN) within each school building or cluster of buildings, provide at least one network server for that LAN, interconnect that LAN with the local school district offices where a similar LAN should be installed and where centrally managed information resources should exist, and connect the district offices to the nearest Internet service provider, possibly through the county office of education.

Primary technical support for network monitoring and problem resolution, and for managing network resource servers, should come from the district or county offices initially to avoid unnecessary duplication at the local level. As expertise is developed at the local level, more of the responsibility for daily operation and problem resolution can be assumed by individual schools.

It is impossible to cover all conceivable scenarios for implementation of this model in specific schools. However, it is possible to state general principles that should be followed in designing school network implementations. The discussion below is organized into sections corresponding to the basic model summarized in the previous paragraph. It includes a description of the general principles that are important to each level of the implementation.

Step 1: School Local Area Network Implementation

A "school" is used here to mean a building or cluster of buildings that are managed as a unit and typically are on contiguous, district-owned property. Implementation of a LAN in this setting will involve installation of a cabling system to distribute the network throughout the structure(s), installation of premise wiring to support connections of computers and terminals to the network distribution system, installation of one or more network server machines in a central location[4], and provision of a network router and telecommunications circuit or radio link to connect that school to the district offices.

The most common LAN technologies in use today are Ethernet and LocalTalk[5]. Both are quite inexpensive and easy to install and maintain. Ethernet is adaptable to most modern computers and is built-in to high performance workstations such as Sun, Hewlett-Packard, SGI, or Digital Equipment Corporation computers. LocalTalk is built-in to all Macintosh computers and is adaptable to DOS PC computers as well. Ethernet is roughly 20 to 40 times faster than LocalTalk. Therefore, Ethernet is recommended for all computer connections, when possible, and for the school LAN "backbone" or network distribution system.

1.1 Network Adapters and Software Individual computers will require network or communications adapters and appropriate software. Table E.1 gives basic recommendations for the computers most commonly found in schools. Basic communications software is available in the public domain for many personal computers at no cost. More sophisticated software is being developed by a number of vendors for applications such as electronic mail, distance learning, and multimedia database access. For example, the California Technology Project is developing very easy-to-use software for Macintosh and DOS or Windows PC computers that will enable access to a wide variety of information resources and services. Schools should look at all the available software

▶ **TABLE E.1:** *Network Adapters and Software for Typical Computers*

EQUIPMENT TYPE	NETWORK ADAPTER	COMMUNICATION SOFTWARE
Simple terminal	"Network Access Server" located centrally.	Built-in to the network access server.
Apple II, Amiga, Tandy, Commodore, older IBM PCs, etc.	Serial asynchronous port that will allow connection to the above.	Serial communications software that emulates a simple terminal.
Newer IBM PCs	Ethernet adapter card with "10-base-T" port. "Thin-net" port may be used in lab clusters.	TCP/IP "TSR" software, for example "FTP Software" package. Additional software for special applications.
Older Apple Macintosh computers	PhoneNet adapter (external) and shared LocalTalk to ethernet router, for example the Shiva FastPath.	MacTCP or equivalent plus "telnet" and "ftp". For example, NCSA Telnet. Additional software for special applications, e.g. "electronic mail client."
Newer Apple	May use same as the Macintosh computers above. For higher performance, use an Ethernet adapter card with "10-base-T" port. "Thin-net" port may be used in lab clusters.	Same as the above.
UNIX workstations	Ethernet adapter card, if not already built in.	Typically comes with the basic system. Additional software may be needed for special applications.

K–12 Guidelines

ap.
E

and base choices on required functionality and support costs as well as acquisition costs. In locations where computers will be purchased, the choice of computer type should be driven by the availability of software for the particular application(s) to be supported. Almost all modern computers can be attached to the type of network described in this document.

1.2 Premise Wiring A major component of the implementation will be installation of cabling to connect individual computers or clusters of computers to the LAN. The recommended topology is a "star" where each computer is wired directly to a "hub site" within the building, as shown in Figures E.1 and E.2. A cluster of computers, typically found in a teaching lab or library, may be interconnected within the room where they are installed, and the cluster connected to the hub site with a single cable, as shown in Figures E.3 and E.4.

FIGURE E.1 ▶

Individual Ethernet connection to the network.

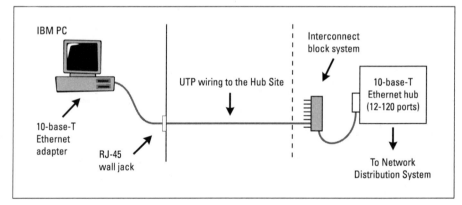

FIGURE E.2 ▶

LocalTalk connection to the network.

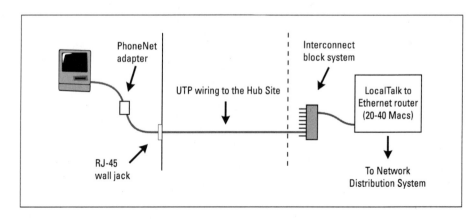

FIGURE E.3 ▶

A cluster of computers connected to the network.

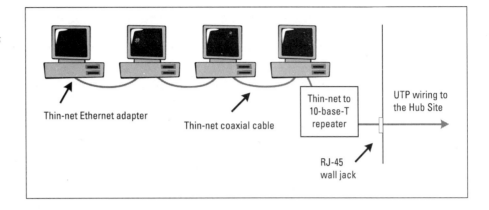

FIGURE E.4 ▶

A Macintosh cluster connection to the network.

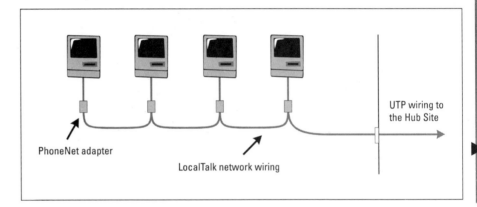

The recommended premise wiring is "unshielded twisted pair" (UTP) wire that meets the Electronic Industries Association (EIA) category 5 standards for high-speed data communication service[6]. While 2-pair cable may be adequate for most purposes, industry standards recommend installation of 4-pair cable. The difference in cost is minimal, so we recommend installation of the latter. One end of each cable terminates in a category 5 RJ-45 jack[7] located near the computer. The other end terminates on a standard "110 distribution block"[8] at the hub site utility closet. A labeling scheme must be chosen and strictly adhered to so that cables can be identified at both ends later, as needed.

In most cases, the hub site utility closet will be shared with telephone services. It is essential that a separate wall area be set aside within the closet for data service interconnections. Typically there will be a "field" of interconnect blocks for termination of all premise wires, another field for termination of trunk cables (used for low-speed data terminals), and a third field for hub equipment ports. Interconnections between premise wiring blocks and hub or trunk blocks are installed as needed in order to provide the appropriate service to each location where communication service is required.

Installation of wiring in a building typically is performed by a qualified data wiring contractor. This is a critical aspect of the program and must be planned and installed professionally with both current and future requirements in mind[9]. To be prepared for future distribution of video signals, school network planners should consider installation of RG-59 coaxial cable to those locations where video may be required at the same time that the UTP premise wiring is being installed. The co-axial cable would terminate on an "F" connector mounted on a wall plate in the classroom, and would be left unterminated in the utility closet. Future technologies may support video signals over other media, so the installation of RG-59 cable should be limited to near term potential requirements.

It will be cost effective to install premise wiring to as many locations as might ever serve a computer. This will include administrative offices as well as classrooms, laboratories as well as libraries. In high density locations such as offices, consideration should be given to installation of two UTP cables to each outlet location in order to provide the potential for several computers or workstations. Terminating both cables on the same wall plate will add little to the overall wiring project costs and will add greatly to the flexibility of the system. Premise wiring that is not to be used initially will not be connected to any electronics in the hub site.

Hub sites should be utility closets or other protected, unoccupied areas. Hub sites can be created by construction of small closets or cabinets in low-use areas. A hub site must be located within 300 feet of any connection. Typically, multiple hub sites are required in large or multistory buildings.

1.3 Network Distribution System All hub sites within a school must be interconnected to complete the school LAN. The design of this network distribution system will depend greatly on the physical layout of the school buildings. We assume that Ethernet technology will be used since higher speed technology is still quite expensive.

If all hub sites are within 300 cable feet of a central location, then 10-base-T wiring can be used from a central hub to connect each hub site, as shown in Figure E.5. If longer distances are required, specific design of the "backbone" network distribution system will depend on the layout of the buildings to be served. Either thin-net or standard thick Ethernet can be used. Fiber optic cable can be used if distance requires it and funding permits[10]. With proper design as many as 250 computers can be connected to a single Ethernet segment. Most often the practical maximum number will be much lower than this, because of the amount of data sent onto the network by each computer. For planning purposes, one can assume 100–125 computers per segment. Beyond that size the network must be subdivided using "subnetworks." Design of a such a system is not difficult, but is beyond the scope of this document.

The network distribution system cabling should include unshielded multipair trunk cabling as well as Ethernet trunk cabling. The multipair trunk cable will be needed to connect terminals or older computers emulating terminals to a central "network access server" (NAS). A typical NAS can serve from 8 to 128 such connections. It is most cost-effective to provide one per LAN, if needed. The NAS connects directly to the Ethernet LAN.

FIGURE E.5 ▶

A complete small school LAN.

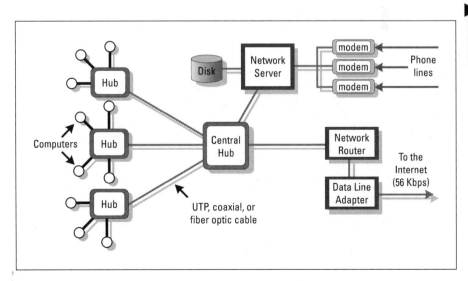

1.4 Local Network Server It is highly recommended that each school install a "network server" to support local storage of commonly used information, software, electronic mail, and other functions that may require high-speed communication to the user's computer. Since the connection to the outside network will be much slower than the school LAN, it will be most efficient to access information locally. In particular, software that is to be shared among the school's computers must be stored locally since it would be very tedious to transfer it across the slower external link. The network server will be connected directly to the Ethernet network.

The location of the server should be chosen carefully to ensure its protection from abuse and environmental damage. Traditionally the school library is the focus of information gathering and storage activities, and many school libraries have clusters of computers or terminals already installed. The library would be a very logical place to locate the network server computer. The Network Router (see below) might also be located there if a suitable utility space is not available.

The network server will be a small but powerful computer with a large amount of disk storage capacity, typically 1–4 gigabytes. It will run software capable of supporting access by a large number of users simultaneously. It could also support dial-in access from teachers' or students' homes using standard inexpensive modems[11]. If more than a few modems are to be installed, an NAS might prove more cost-effective. If dial-in access is to be provided to more than a few school sites within a district, a single central modem pool maintainted at the district offices will be the most cost-effective.

1.5 External Connection A single communication circuit will connect the school LAN to the local school district offices. In the school, there will be a Network Router attached between the LAN and this circuit. On the LAN side, the connection will be a typical Ethernet cable. On the external side, the connection will depend on the type of communication circuit used, as discussed in step 2 below.

Step 2: Interconnection of Schools with District Offices

All schools within a district should be connected individually to the network router at the school district offices. This "star topology" will be much easier to manage and the capacity of each schools connection can be increased appropriately as needs change. Several standard communication circuit services may be used to effect this connection. The least expensive for situations where only limited use is needed will be dial-up using high speed modems. However, this type of connection is not recommended for serious usage, because of its very limited capacity. Also, since most schools receive telephone service under business tariffs, usage will be measured and the cost will be dependent on how long the connection is maintained. This will be true in general for other "switched services" as well, such as "switched-56" and ISDN. Dedicated (permanently installed) communications circuits are strongly recommended since they will allow unattended access to and from the school network at all hours. This will be particularly important if information files are to be downloaded during the night to local network servers or teachers and students are to access the school's information resources from home.

Table E.2 shows the most common options for dedicated circuit services. Costs are indicated in relative terms since they vary greatly by location and as tariffs are modified. The exact costs must be determined by contacting local communications service providers. Total cost must take into account the equipment needed at each location as well.

Frame Relay communication services are becoming available in many areas. Frame Relay is a shared, packet-based data transport service. A school site would contract for Frame Relay service as part of a larger service group that includes the school district office and may include the Internet service provider. All members of that group would share

TABLE E.2: *External Connection Communications Options*

TYPE OF CIRCUIT	DATA RATE	RELATIVE COST
Voice grade leased telephone line	20 kilobits per sec (Kbps)	modest[12]
ADN-56	56 Kbps	high
ISDN, where available	64 or 128 Kbps	modest[13]
Low power radio	64 to 256 Kbps	high startup cost
Frame Relay	56 Kbps to 1.5 Mbps	modest to high
DS1	1.5 megabits per sec	very high

the communications capacity. The advantage of this service is that only one end of the circuit needs to be ordered (each member orders a connection to the common service) and the capacity offered to each member can be upgraded independently. Also, in many areas the cost of Frame Relay service is not dependent on distance to the service provider which will make service to rural schools much less expensive than equivalent services. Overall system costs will be minimized since the central router at the district office will need fewer connections.

If Frame Relay is chosen, the overall service group must be carefully engineered. For example, since all schools would share the connection to the district office (and possibly to the Internet service provider), that must be a high capacity connection. For the initial design, the aggregate capacity of all school links should not exceed the capacity into the district office (or the Internet service provider) by more than a factor of 3, or there may be noticeable congestion and variability in response times across the system. There are many other factors that must be considered as well, such as the virtual connection topology and how best to connect to an Internet service provider. Therefore, it is recommended that an experienced network engineer be utilized to develop an operational plan for Frame Relay if it is chosen as the school interconnection service.

Future options for interconnecting schools and district offices will include[14]:

- Community Access Television (CATV) cable systems offering either shared or dedicated bidirectional data communication services

- Metropolitan area fiber optic communications service providers

- Switched Multi-megabit Digital Service (SMDS) providing data transport service at speeds up to 34 megabits per second

- Asynchronous Transfer Mode (ATM) connection services supporting voice, data, and video communications at speeds into the gigabit-per-second range

The costs for the last three options are unknown at this time, but may be generally higher than those indicated in Table E.2. The cost for the CATV option may be negotiable as part of the local CATV contract with the community.

As demands for network speed develop due to heavy use of multimedia or other bandwidth intensive application, higher speed communications circuits can replace the initial circuits with minimal change in the equipment or LAN. This gives great flexibility in tailoring service to funding levels and application needs.

Step 3: School District Office LAN and Support Systems

The School District offices should form the focal point for interconnection of all schools in the district. Within the District offices, network operations can be monitored and problem resolution managed. One or more network servers can provide essential network support as well as central archiving of common information and software.

A critical role of the district office will be to manage Internet "Domain Name System" (DNS)[15] service for the districts schools. DNS is required of all Internet networks. It defines the basic network-level identity of each computer, workstation, server, and active network component. This function is described more fully below under Network Management and Operational Monitoring. The district offices should be wired in a manner similar to a typical school, as shown above. This will allow teachers, superintendents, and principals to communicate and share information easily. In addition, an NAS connected to a central pool of modems could provide dial-in access to the district network.

Step 4: Interconnection of the School District with the Internet

Connection of the entire school district to the Internet will take place through the district office interconnect site, as shown in Figure E.6. This hierarchical model can be extended another level to interconnection of the school district offices through the county office of education facilities. Many administrative information resources could be located at the county level, and there might be cost savings if the entire county connects to an Internet service provider through a single point. The bandwidth required for this single connection, however, will be much greater than that required for each school district since traffic will be aggregated.

This hierarchical topology also provides a logical model for network support and information resource management. The school district or

Interconnection of schools to the Internet through local School District Offices

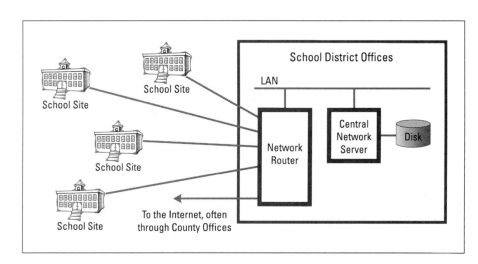

county offices can provide continuous monitoring of the network and provide high-level technical expertise for problem resolution, relieving the individual schools of this burden. Interactions with communications circuit providers and Internet service providers will be more effective if handled through a central "trouble desk." Similarly, it is highly desirable that network users have a single, well known point of contact in case of problems or questions.

Internet service should be acquired from the most cost effective, reliable Internet service provider. Circuit services can be similar to those shown in Table E.2 above. The higher speed services should be considered if traffic demands increase and funding permits. Circuit costs usually will be lowest when connecting to the provider with the nearest "point of presence" (POP), but newer technologies such as Frame Relay and SMDS[16] make circuit costs less dependent on distance. The Internet connection will require a high-quality router that can be configured to interact correctly with the service provider's routers. In most cases, this can be the same router used to support the local school connections.

▶ Integration of Existing School Networks

Many schools have developed LAN systems in support of particular classroom activities or administrative functions. In some cases the technologies used are not those recommended for new installations. If these older LAN systems are capable of transporting Internet protocols they may be integrated into a new LAN system and replaced later as funding permits.

For example, IEEE 802.5 Token Ring is often used to interconnect DOS PC-type computers and IBM minicomputer servers. Token Ring networks can transport Internet protocols, and software is available for DOS computers to support basic Internet functions. Many Internet routers support optional Token Ring adapters. This is the recommended way that existing Token Ring LANs can be integrated into a wider school LAN system in order to extend Internet information resources to those PC users.

Another example is a Novell NetWare system using Ethernet as a LAN. The Ethernet LAN, if implemented well, is perfectly capable of transporting Internet protocols as well as Novell protocols, simultaneously. Each PC or Macintosh can be given software that will allow both Novell and Internet services to be used as needed. This coexistence is important so that, for example, a person using a PC that depends on the Novell server for disk file space can transfer a large file from a remote Internet server to the PC's pseudo-disk. It also permits each user to run client software such as Eudora (electronic mail), Gopher (information services), and Mosaic (World Wide Web information services) which require direct Internet access. To integrate the Novell Ethernet LAN into the wider school LAN system a simple Ethernet repeater can be used in a manner similar to Figure E.3 above.

An alternative to supporting both protocols that is sometimes suggested in cases such as the one cited above in which a network server already exists is to use the server as a "network application gateway." This approach is strongly discouraged. It is essential that each computer and workstation support Internet protocol data communication directly so that modern client/server applications can be supported where the server or servers may be located anywhere on the Internet. The "gateway" approach severely restricts the workstations' potential ability to access multimedia and other important information resources.

Some technologies, such as "arcnet," may not be capable of supporting Internet protocols but may offer "terminal emulation" shared access to something like a "modem pool." The modem adapter might be rewired to connect to ports on a network access server instead. This would provide simple access to information resources for the arcnet users.

K–12 Guidelines

▶ ▶

ap.
E

In any case, older LAN technologies should *not* be expanded and should be phased out as funding permits. It is critical that there be a relatively homogeneous installed base of technology in order that new applications of information resources can be provided to the entire school community.

▶ Network Management and Operational Monitoring

All networks require some level of network management in order to ensure reliable service. Monitoring of the health of the network can help identify problems before they become detrimental to network users. It also can help predict trends in traffic patterns and volume.

Internet technology network management consists primarily of determining the proper routing parameters for optimal and reliable network operation, assignment of network Internet Protocol (IP) addresses and maintenance of a network-accessible database of node names corresponding to each address[17], and monitoring the daily operation of the network. These functions typically are performed by the staff of a Network Operations Center (NOC).

▶ Domain Name System

The Internet Domain Name System (DNS) is the mechanism for documenting and distributing information about the name and address of each computer attached to the network (network nodes). The DNS service is provided by software that runs on the main network server. It uses a database that is created and maintained by the NOC staff.

An Internet address is the numerical identifier for a node and it must be unique among all nodes associated with the network. Furthermore, if the network is to be part of the global Internet, all addresses must be legitimate within the worldwide Internet system.

Associated with each numerical address can be one or more "node names." Although computers have no difficulty using numerical addresses, it is often easier for computer users to remember and use the node names rather than the numerical addresses. In particular, electronic mail addresses use node names. DNS node names are hierarchical and by appropriately using this hierarchy "subdomains" can be assigned to each school site or district office. In this way, naming can be structured to be flexible as well as meaningful in the context of the whole organization.

A plan for the assignment of IP network addresses and node names should be developed early in the planning for the network installation. Initially, the database serving the DNS should reside on the "district server" so that there is one site at which all assignments are officially registered. As the network grows and expertise is developed, secondary DNS service can be run on the servers at larger school sites.

The main DNS server for the district should be located as close to the Internet connection (topologically) as possible. This proximity is to help ensure that network problems within the district network will have minimal impact on access to the server. This design is illustrated in Figure E.1, where the district server is on an Ethernet connected directly to the main distribution router.

Associated with the assignment of node names and addresses should be a database of specific information about the computers connected to the network. When trying to resolve problems or answer user questions, it is very important to know where the computers and other nodes are located, what type of computer and software are in use, and what type of network connection is installed. With proper software this database can be used to extract the DNS database discussed above.

▶ *Network Monitoring*

Internet network monitoring serves three primary purposes:

1. Constant observation of the "health" of the network, network components, and external network connectivity. Standard Simple Network Management Protocol (SNMP) support is built into most active components today. Even network servers and workstations can be monitored in this way. Operations staff can be provided with network monitoring stations that will display alerts immediately upon detecting a wide variety of problems or anomalies.

2. Collection of statistics on the performance of the network and patterns of traffic in order to identify needed enhancements or re-engineering. Using the same SNMP capabilities mentioned above,

K–12 Guidelines

▶ ▶

ap.

E

data on packet forwarding and total traffic volume can be collected and used to generate periodic reports on network utilization.

3. More rapid problem resolution. When problems do occur, SNMP tools can help to pinpoint the source of the problem(s). Such problems include transient routing anomalies, DNS query failures, or even attempts at breaking into network accessible host computers.

Since network management and monitoring is a technically demanding task and requires special equipment and software, it should be a centralized function in the initial design of school network systems, as discussed above.

The model for school network implementation described above is based on broad experience with this technology in higher education and administrative environments. Many schools have already installed networks very similar to this model. We believe that it is a practical first step towards bringing a powerful resource to bear for enriching all of the nations school programs.

None of the suggestions above preclude or postpone in any way future development of an integrated voice, data, and video network for the nation's schools. Use of existing Internet carriers does not in any way preclude future development of a separate "backbone" for the K–12 community if such a "backbone" is determined to be cost effective or required for enhanced functionality. Rather, the infrastructure recommended above can be the foundation at the local level in preparation for future high capacity networks.

▶▶ IV. Network Support

The installation of a campus-wide network or Internet connectivity will also require a commitment to ongoing network support and its related resource requirements. There are two major areas of network support, network operations and user services. These support functions are usually performed through the establishment of a Network Operations Center (NOC) and Network Information Center (NIC); however, both functions can be performed by the same individual or groups of individuals.

▶ *Network Operations Center (NOC)*

The Network Operations Center (NOC) oversees the performance of the physical network and some of its software support systems. The staff may install networks, configure network devices and provide configurations for computers attached to an organization-wide network. Real-time monitoring of the network can be performed using the Simple Network Management Protocol and many vendors produce monitoring systems that graphically display network performance, log events and usage, and produce trouble tickets. The use of this type of network monitoring allows NOC staff to quickly detect problems and greatly reduces the personnel required to perform this function. Routine monitoring of the network can help to anticipate problems before they develop and lead to reconfigurations and upgrades as indicated. If problems do arise, NOC personnel may go on-site to troubleshoot a problem and repair it. If the problem is not local, NOC personnel will work with school district, county or regional network technical staff to resolve the problem.

NOC personnel also assign addresses to network computers and devices and maintain the Domain Name service (DNS) for their organization. Domain Name service is a machine registry service that runs on a network server and enables access to machines by easy-to-remember names, rather than a network number. DNS is required for any organization connected to the Internet and critical to the establishment of an electronic mail system.

It is most cost-effective to have the Network Operation Center serve an entire organization or region. In order to ensure timely service all the way out to the most remote LAN, it is recommended that an organization assign local area network administration duties to on-site personnel to interact with NOC staff and assist with the maintenance of the network. In the case of a school district, administrative support staff, teachers, librarians or school-based technical staff can each take responsibility for a LAN or group of LANs. If a problem arises, it can be reported to the LAN administrator. The LAN administrator can determine if the problem is local or remote and if NOC staff need to be notified. If so, the LAN administrator acts as the single point of contact for the NOC to provide a good communications channel for information and ensure efficient coordination of problem resolution. This method of delegating responsibility provides for a high level of service for each LAN and optimally uses the time of NOC staff to provide economies of scale.

▶ Network Information Center (NIC)

The Network Information Center (NIC) provides information and support services to facilitate the use of the network. The NIC often provides a help-desk service to answer questions about use of the network, references to useful resources and training in new tools or applications. The NIC may also provide services such as an online directory of network users and their electronic mail addresses, bulletin board services of information and notices about the network and online training materials. These NIC services could be provided on a school district or county level. Most of the information would not be site specific and can be delivered electronically using electronic mail, electronic conferencing, online bulletin boards or other document delivery mechanisms. These types of services may be well suited for a school or school district librarian.

Other types of support services may be performed by NIC personnel such as maintenance of the electronic mail system or postmaster duties, coordination of an online bulletin board or campus-wide information system (CWIS) and management of an online conferencing system. These duties are more technical in nature and will require technical staff to maintain them.

▶ Postmaster

Every organization which uses electronic mail should have an electronic mail postmaster and a mailbox, Named postmaster, for the receipt of messages regarding use of the electronic mail system, mail problems, and general inquiries about reaching people within the organization. The postmaster is responsible for reading postmaster mail and responding to inquiries. These duties can be performed by non-technical staff with forwarding of messages to the appropriate technical support person as required.

► *CWIS Administrator*

Campus-wide information systems or bulletin boards are one of the most useful applications on the network. These systems allow people to share timely notices, documents and other resources with large groups of people. These systems typically provide a hierarchical or tree-like structure of menus that lead to online documents or other services. Common types of information include deadline notices, grant announcements, training schedules, lists of available resources such as videos in a library or reference materials.

Information need not be stored all in one location. Figure E.7 shows a set of distributed servers. These servers can receive new information automatically from a central server and can also contain information generated locally that may pertain only to the local school. Users of the information need not know where the information is stored: the information access software will present choices on an integrated menu.

A CWIS or bulletin board must have an administrator or sponsor to oversee the design and maintenance of the system so that it is easy to navigate and find information, provides a professional presentation of

FIGURE E.7 ►

Distributed Network Information Servers

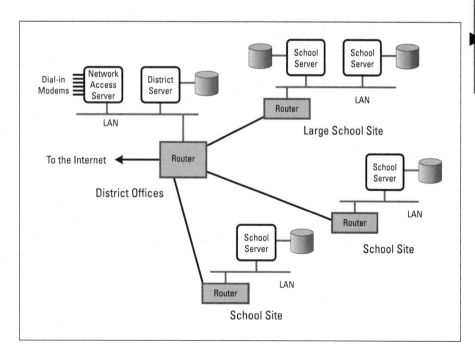

information, and ensures that information remains timely and relevant. This function can be performed by NIC staff or trained librarians or administrative staff as appropriate.

▶ *Management of Online Conferences*

Online conferences provide a way for groups of people to share information, discuss ideas, and pose questions. Conferences usually are set up to serve the needs of a group of people sharing a common interest. For example, an online conference might be established for teachers to discuss a new science teaching framework or a teacher may establish a conference for the discussion of the Civil War as part of an American History class. Some conferences are ongoing and may exist for years. Others are short-term and may exist for only one semester. Conferences may be created using the electronic mail system or a facility called Usenet News.

Online conferencing systems require a server computer on the network that collects messages posted to a conference and distributes them when requested. Usually these systems are managed by a systems administrator and someone must configure the system to establish and delete groups upon request. Other management duties include scheduling the deletion of old messages and archiving especially valuable conversations. Typically these duties are performed by a systems administrator or technical staff.

▶ *Staffing Considerations*

The duties described above do not necessarily require hiring new staff and they may be shared by people already within an organization. Small schools or districts may rely on County Office of Education Information Systems staff to perform all functions. Larger schools or districts may have staff to take on any combination of duties and rely on the County Office of Education for others. Access to the network and the use of electronic communications allows people throughout the organization to perform these functions remotely. The assignment of responsibility for any of these duties is flexible and should be approached with the goal of providing the highest quality of service in the most cost effective and workable manner.

►► *V. References*

Margaret Honey, Andres Henriquez, "Telecommunications and K–12 Educators: Findings from a National Survey," Bank Street College of Education, New York, NY, 1993.

Susan Estrada, *Connecting to the Internet*, OReilly & Associates, Inc. (ISBN 1-56592-061-9)

Carole Teach, editor. "Building the Future: K–12 Network Technology Planning Guide," California Department of Education, Research, Evaluation & Technology Division, 1994.

►► *VI. Special Thanks*

Special thanks to Brian Lloyd of Lloyd Internetworking, Inc. for his contributions to this document. Brian was one of the contributors to the California Department of Education "K–12 Network Technology Planning Guide," which served as the motivation for writing most of this document. Brian contributed significantly to Section II, "Rationale for the Use of Internet Protocols" and thoroughly reviewed Section III, "A Technical Model for School Networks," providing valuable feedback.

►► *VII. Security Considerations*

Security issues are not discussed in this memo.

►► *VIII. Notes*

[1] Margaret Honey and Andres Henriquez, "Telecommunications and K–12 Educators: Findings from a National Survey," Bank Street College of Education, New York, NY, 1993.

[2] The Internet is a "network of networks" that interconnects institutions of higher education, research labs, government agencies, and a rapidly growing number of technology and information vendors.

K–12 Guidelines

►►
ap.
E

[3] *Connecting to the Internet*, Susan Estrada, OReilly & Inc. (ISBN 1-56592-061-9) lists Internet service providers in California and the nation.

[4] Other protocols, such as AppleTalk or Novell's IPX, may be supported on a school's local area network (LAN) as needed for local function such as printer sharing or local resource servers.

[5] IEEE 802.5 Token Ring is not recommended for new installations. It is more expensive and it is not available for as wide a range of computers.

[6] See EIA/TIA-568 "Commercial Building Telecommunications Wiring Standard."

[7] A standard RJ45 jack can be used for Ethernet or lower speeds if initial cost is a major factor. Such jacks can be replaced with category 5 versions later as needed.

[8] In older sites, M66 distribution blocks may already be installed. These can be used for the time being but will not support newer higher speed technologies.

[9] See "Virtual Schoolhouse—A Report to the Legislature on Distribution Infrastructures for Advanced Technologies in the Construction of New Schools, K through 12" (Department of General Services, State of California, Feb 1993) for example conduit and utility closet plans.

[10] If fiber-optic cable is installed, consideration should be given to including both multimode fiber for current and future data requirements and single-mode fiber for video and future very-high-speed data systems.

[11] Access control with user authentication is essential if dial-in service is to be provided.

[12] Measured service charges must be taken into account.

[13] At this time, most ISDN tariffs include message unit charges which can make the use of ISDN prohibitively expensive for full-time connectivity.

[14] Many more options will become available as new technologies come to market.

[15] See RFCs 1034 and 1035 for the full explanation of DNS.

[16] At this time, SMDS services are not widely available.

[17] See RFC 1480 for a discussion of Internet naming conventions for school networks.

▶▶ *IX. Authors' Addresses*

Joan C. Gargano
Information Technology
Distributed Computing Analysis and Support
University of California
Davis, CA 95616
E-Mail: jcgargano@ucdavis.edu

David L. Wasley
Data Communication & Network Services
Information Systems and Technology
University of California
Berkeley, CA 94720
E-Mail: dlw@berkeley.edu

► ► APPENDIX **F**

Seeing through the Smoke and Haze

►► Virginia E. Rezmierski, Ph.D.
1132 Argus Building
535 West William Street,
University of Michigan,
Ann Arbor, MI 48106

E-Mail Address: Virginia_Rezmierski@um.cc.umich.edu

[Note: Dr. Rezmierski has stated that this is not a position paper for K–12 administrators. The issues facing college campuses are clearly different because of the age of the students and the history of academic freedom and responsibility on college and university campuses in the United States. McG.&C.]

►► *Introduction*

As rapidly as the technology is changing, college and university administrators are being faced with ethical and values issues regarding the use of information technology on their campuses. In many cases when a behavioral incident happens involving the technology, the administrator is pressed to respond—to react—even before they have had sufficient opportunity to understand the competing values and issues at hand. In some cases the issues are so fraught with emotion that not only does the urgency for a response cause stress, but the smoke of anger and the haze of disbelief over the incident cause stress as well. Electronic access to pornography on the networks and from other sources on campuses is one such issue for some administrators. It is important in this, as in other ethical and values laden issues, to carefully remove the smoke and haze and to think the issues through before responding.

This paper addresses the issues pertaining to electronic access to potentially offensive material and pornography on campuses. It provides one proactive course of action thought to empower both those individuals on campuses who wish to access the materials and those who do not.

►► *Access to Information*

The electronic availability of information has increased exponentially in the last ten years. Of course this includes information containing all types of content. It includes information in a variety of written, graphic, audio, and animated forms as well. University and college faculty, staff, and students are increasingly able to access materials, from a variety of sources, that would be considered offensive to some others on the campus. Most prominent among the electronic sources of potentially offensive materials are the news groups and electronic bulletin boards that are available through the Internet.

The information that might fall into this category covers, as you would expect, the full spectrum. It is possible to access a range of information, from written material with minor sexual innuendo and pictures or drawings of partially or fully nude figures to explicitly written descriptions of sexual acts, descriptions of violent sexual torture, and color graphics of acts of bestiality, bondage, and child pornography. Not only is it possible to access this material but it is also possible to send the material with great speed to one or hundreds of others, to send the material to a common printer where others are retrieving their work, to place the material in accounts that others are required to access for class work, and so on.

►► *Difficult Issues and Balances*

University and college administrators are faced with difficult decisions in regards to this issue and the related behaviors of some of the members of their community. Balances must be reached; balances between community values, existing laws and protections, and the sensitivies of members of the community need to be found. Policies and guidelines can be useful in clarifying community values and guiding responses. In regards to policy making in this area however, as one Stanford administrator expressed it, "There is no clear winning position on this set of issues."

▶▶ *Values Continuum*

Some portion of each campus community will feel strongly that no access to this material should be allowed on the campus. They feel that, in its existence, it is an act of violence against a group of individuals—women. They advocate that no university resources should be expended to facilitate in any way, access, transport, or storage of this material. And they maintain that not to restrict this material is to minimize or ignore the rights of an entire segment of the community. Conversely, some portion of each campus community will feel strongly that access to information of all types is critical to academic freedom. For this group, the material is a form of expression and not an act in and of itself. They argue that it is the university's appropriate role to facilitate access to information and not to predetermine by content the usefulness of any information for the purposes of its community. For this segment of the community, any act of screening, restriction, or selection is a critically dangerous step towards loss of liberty. Admittedly, these are the more purely extreme positions. However, these positions and the many variations in between are found on most university and college campuses. The topic stimulates high emotions and heated discussions.

One might ask, "If there is no political win in this arena, is there a reason to engage this set of issues or should administrators wait until the courts have produced more clarity in this area or until there is an explicit complaint or suit?" There are important reasons to address these issues—reasons that are integrally related to the missions of institutions of higher education. On an issue such as this, where the values of different segments of the community seem to be at such extreme odds, there is a need to foster social cognitive development, social thinking, and to encourage the sharing of points of view. There is a need to increase the valuing of diversity in the college community, a community that will become increasingly diverse over time and that will live within an increasingly diverse nation. And there is a need to promote the development of conflict management skills around issues such as this, issues that stimulate conflict and reduce reasoned discourse.

Ernest Boyer is eloquent in his writing about university and college life. Three of the principles he identifies for campus educational purposefulness are directly related to why this issue needs to be engaged. He writes:

"A college or university is an open community, a place where freedom of expression is uncompromisingly protected and where civility is powerfully affirmed."

"A college or university is a just community, a place where the sacredness of each person is honored and where diversity is aggressively pursued"

and,

"A college or university is a disciplined community, a place where individuals accept their obligations to the group and where well-defined governance procedures guide behavior for the common good."

A look now at the balances and decisions that must be made will illustrate the complexity of the issues.

▶▶ *Art vs. Pornography*

Many individuals, as they begin to discuss the issue of electronic access to potentially offensive material, try immediately to discern whether the material is art or pornography. It is probably impossible to make this determination and therefore this is probably not the place to begin discussions. The judgment will vary with each piece of material, with each viewer, and perhaps for a given viewer, will vary at different times. Other than where specific legal interpretations exist, e.g., child pornography which is determined to be illegal, the judgments vary by community and cannot be generalized. While for some of the material there would readily be an agreement on a campus that the material is pornographic and offensive, the community would quickly split on the question of whether it threatens and intimidates as an act or whether it constitutes artistic expression. Rather than expending community energy trying to make these determinations, questions about access appear to be more critical.

▶▶ *Institutional Provision of Service*

To analyze these questions it is important to separate the issue of a university or college providing access to a service from the issue of an individual accessing certain material. The first question to be asked is, "Should the university or college provide access to the news groups in general and to the Internet?" As a service provider, if access is provided to the news service, most likely it is provided to all of the groups within the news service. Likewise, if access is provided to the networks, it is to the service in its entirety. The value of the overall service is the determinant for whether the service is provided. A decision about access to a part, e.g., the bulletin boards that exist on the networks, is subordinate to the decision to provide access to the service in general.

It is possible to apply a selection criteria in order to allow only certain portions of the news service to be received. By doing so, however, an institution moves away from the question of whether to provide the service to the question of whether to allow individuals to access certain material. This very important distinction gets blurred in discussion of this issue. It gets blurred because issues of service provision become mixed with issues of institutional vs. individual power.

Some administrators have tried to address the second question indirectly. They argue that while in the case of Usenet News, for example, they provide access to the service, but they do not provide access to those pieces of the service that are storage-space–intensive, e.g., the graphics. The argument falls apart when it becomes clear that some graphics are provided as part of the service but not those that are pornographic in content. In reality, a content judgment has determined service, mixing again the issues of service provision and institutional vs. individual power.

Many institutions, like the University of Michigan, provide extensive access to the Internet and to News services, generally to anything on those services for which there is a request. The decision to do this is based on the recognition that a diverse community of scholars requires a diverse set of information sources and contents and that for a service provider to make the determination based on anything other than expressed demand would be inappropriate.

▶▶ *Institutional vs. Individual Power: Access to Information*

Having determined that providing access to the service is valuable to a university or college community, the issue of power between institutions and individuals can be addressed with more clarity. Does a university or college have a role in determining whether individuals should access certain material? In addressing this question it is helpful to restrict our focus, for the moment, to one individual accessing material for his/her own personal use. (The ramifications of a broader, multi-person focus will be considered in later sections of this paper.)

It needs to be recognized that a university or college essentially has no control in this regard. Once the decision has been made to provide individuals access to the networks and to information services, and once the decision has been made to allow members of a community to use information technology to interact with, store, and potentially transport information of all types, the options and possibilities are nearly endless. Individuals no longer need to go to specifically designated locations—adult book stores—to obtain pornographic materials. Such materials are available on the networks, on bulletin boards, from other users, and from servers where other students, faculty and/or staff may be storing the information. It can be scanned from hard copy and photographs or integrated with material from movies and videos.

One might ask, "Should individuals be allowed to use university property to access, store and transport this material? Can we establish the fact that such property is to be used only for the business of the university, the teaching, learning, research, administrative, and service behaviors of the members?" While the answers to these questions may help to shape a community response, they do not provide reason for assertion of institutional power over the individual in the form of censorship.

Universities, if it is consistent with their values, need to make a strong and frequently heard statement about appropriate and intended use of information technology resources on the campuses. Perhaps these resources are clearly provided only for, or primarily for, the purposes of teaching, learning, research, administration, and service. At the author's institution, the University of Michigan, the word "primarily" needs to be emphasized. Resources have been provided to enable the community to communicate, socialize, and exchange points of view

Clarifying Issues

▶▶
ap.
F

electronically, as well as to specifically participate in class-related learning and teaching. However, even with emphasis on the primary missions of the institution, one must ask, "What is learning and how might this material fit into that process? What is research and how might this material fit into that process? What is teaching and how might this material fit into that process? Who can determine this for another? And, how would the institution go about identifying the moments when the question should be asked?"

Without access to this material, those who most oppose it cannot know what exists and cannot speak out against it. John Stuart Mill wrote:

"If all mankind minus one, were of one opinion and only one person were of the contrary opinion, mankind would be no more justified in silencing that one person, than he, if he had the power, would be justified in silencing mankind... The peculiar evil of silencing the expression of an opinion is, that it is robbing the human race; posterity as well as the existing generation; those who dissent from the opinion, still more than those who hold it; If the opinion is right, they are deprived of the opportunity of exchanging error for truth; if wrong, they lose, what is almost as great a benefit, the clearer perception and livelier expression of truth, produced by its collision with error."

Without access, the researchers cannot study the effects of its existence.

Dan M. Lacy wrote:

"The goal of freedom in information and communication is a double one, with its two aspects inseparably complementary: for all who wish to speak or write to be free to do so, and for all who wish to hear or read them to have that opportunity."

Without discussions about these differing positions, members of the community cannot begin to understand the effects of this material on each other. In a previous paper, I wrote:

"I have discovered that there is a war going on within me around this topic. My body and feelings scream out for censorship and even violence against the creators of some of the material—reactions that are quite foreign to my usual manner of doing business. My mind reasons and rallies energy to maintain reasoned discourse about liberty, about freedoms, about fairness and about balance of power."

Many administrators would argue that most of the access to this material is not for assignments, research, or explicit teaching duties. To claim to be able to determine which is which, however, or to say that teaching and learning are not happening, would be foolish. The important Liberty and First Amendment Rights must take precedence in this question. They demand that the power to decide whether to access this material remain in the hands of the individuals, where decisions about the value of the information and the purposes for which it is to be used can best be made. They demand a position against censorship.

▶▶ *Ensuring Empowerment to All: Institutional Responsibility*

Having made this critical decision to protect against censorship for the individual, to empower individuals to make their own choices about accessing information, and to restrain institutional power, it is now important to widen our focus from one individual accessing the material for their own personal use in order to examine the interaction between individuals. What are the effects of one person's access to potentially offensive material on another who wishes not to access or to be exposed to the material?

Changing focus in this way, from the question of whether an individual at a university or college should be able to access potentially offensive material to a focus on rights within a two- or multiperson interaction, moves decisions from the arena of First Amendment constitutional rights to the arena of community sensitivities, standards, civilities and the specific protections that are provided under derivative constitutional law. Many universities have taken a position to protect freedom of speech and press. However, the grayer areas ahead, in this more extended focus, require that a balance be achieved between freedom of speech and freedom from harassment and intimidation.

▶▶ *Individual Access: Unconscious Intrusion*

It has been argued that individuals within a university community must be empowered to select what they need to access for their learning, teaching, research, and personal purposes. Further, it has been argued that the choice about what to access and how to use the information should best be left to the individual without institutional censorship (albeit with strong standards for using resources primarily for the purposes for which they were provided where those have been specified). Are there interpersonal conditions that must be considered if universities and colleges are to achieve the educational purposefulness about which Boyer writes? What are the limits to this individual empowerment? Are there boundaries between individuals that must be observed? Does one empowered individual who chooses to access information that may be considered offensive and even threatening by another have the right to access it in a way that crosses beyond his/her own personal space and boundaries?

The questions of interpersonal boundaries and information access are central to decisions regarding all types of potentially offensive material, not just that which is considered pornographic. These questions are complicated by the different forms in which information may be delivered. Some information will exist in graphic form, some in text only. Some information will contain, or primarily consist of, sound. If material that is accessed by one individual contains audible sound, for example, are there reasons to restrict access in a shared worksite where others, who may not wish to access or be exposed to the material, also work? e.g., a public computing site? A recent incident at one university will illustrate the issue.

A student, bored with his current assignments, recently developed a method for loading a sound segment onto machines in a public computing site. He placed the faked orgasm sound segment from the movie *When Harry Met Sally* onto all of the machines. When any other user turned on a machine, the entire sound segment played without the user having a method for disengaging the sequence until the segment was completed.

For information contained in the form of sound, the potential disturbance can be readily recognized. Administrators may decide that sound is intrusive to the personal work space of others and therefore should be restricted regardless of content.

Visual images or printed content may be harder to understand in terms of interpersonal space, however. Is a visual image, accessed by one individual, intrusive to the personal work space of others and therefore to be restricted, particularly if the content is offensive? University and college communities will need to contemplate the scope and importance of an individual's work space. Within a public computing site for instance, does such individual space comprise the workstation, desk, and chair, or does it include all of the workstations, desks, and chairs within the viewing range of the individual? What can we say to individuals who access offensive messages or visual images of any type about intrusion into the space of the others who are working within those shared resources? Does a university or college have any responsibility in this regard?

▶▶ *The Opportunity*

Universities and colleges have an opportunity to lead through an educational effort, not to censor, but to proactively encourage individuals to think about the needs, rights and values of others. Other options such as to restrict a person's access to potentially offensive material to only certain machines within a public site, or to require only nonpublic access for material that might be considered offensive, move the community unnecessarily and dangerously toward censorship. Instead, encouraging and empowering individuals to interact, to ask each other to be considerate of their reactions to offensive material, to ask them to CONSIDER a more private and less intrusive site for accessing it, is to encourage community sensitivity and social thinking.

For an institution to proactively anticipate such situations because they will happen and are already happening is to make a topic that can be divisive a topic that can lead to community growth. To provide discussions and education about empowerment and about the rights of all individuals, those who wish or need to access such material and those who do not, does not cross the line to censorship, but instead purposefully crosses a line towards community consciousness raising and responsiveness. Experience with this approach at two universities has found that the majority of those who engage in unconscious intrusion into another's space respond positively to such suggestions and learn from the encounter.

At one university, students working in a multiple window environment on powerful public site workstations were accustomed to displaying a variety of material beside their text documents, while they worked. On several machines, students had one of their available windows displaying, at one minute intervals, pictures of nude women in various provocative poses. While the student typed a paper, he was "entertained" by the changing photos. Women at that university, a significant minority of the campus population, found that working in the public sites was often uncomfortable and felt intrusive. They found it difficult to work next to public stations where such multiple window displays were active. They questioned their rights to a work and learning environment free from such stress and embarrassment. When the male students were asked to consider accessing that material from a more private space, the vast majority of them agreed to do so, expressing regret for their unconscious insensitivity.

▶▶ *Individual Access and Purposeful Intrusion*

Within each community, however, there are those who access material that may be offensive to others and then purposefully send or otherwise deliver the material to another person. Should we consider all such purposeful acts as harassment? The answer has to be "no," because what is offensive to one may not be offensive to another. Some will appreciate, enjoy, or find useful, the delivery of the material.

There are increasing numbers of incidents on university and college campuses involving individuals who, after exercising their right to access material that they themselves do not find offensive, purposefully use it to intrude on the work or private space of another individual. They send it to the machine of an unsuspecting user, place it into the files of an unsuspecting group, or send it to a public printer that is used by an unsuspecting group. These acts are generally designed for "comic or shock value." Sometimes, they are designed to target, threaten, intimidate, and/or harass another person. In these cases the empowered individual anticipates that the recipient will find the material offensive, yet purposefully intrudes.

At one university, a student sent a racist message in broad print to a public printer and waited for the reactions which she received. At another, a student sent a file of pornographic images to a class account that a group of students were required to access for their daily assignment. At another college, a young student, though asked to stop sending electronic mail to an unwilling recipient, continued to send daily solicitations for homosexual sex, including in them increasingly intimidating descriptions of the acts to be committed and the violence that would be included.

Should a university or college administrator intervene in these interpersonal conflicts? Should a university take a position regarding the kind of work and study environment it provides on its campus? Is there a critical educational and disciplinary process that should be followed if we are to achieve the sensitive educationally purposeful community of reasoned discourse about which Boyer writes?

It would be difficult to view even a sampling of the pornography that exists on the networks, in the selected newsgroups, or in some of the files collected by individuals on the campuses, as benign artistic expressions. Few women could view the bestial reduction of females in pornographic pictures involving animals and not feel hurt or frightened—hurt for the women who participated in the making of the pictures, frightened that the possibility even exists that someone could place them in such a situation against their will or for monetary gain. Few women could see the repeated emphasis placed on dominance and power in pornography and not rage at the possibilities of such dominance. Few could recognize the themes of violence or, minimally, the symbolized hurtful sexual entry into all orifices, and not quiver with fear that such acts might be possible or cry for those for whom such acts have occurred in real life. To suggest that being forced to view these pictures unwittingly or unwillingly is anything but an act of intimidation and violence is to be so involved in the power struggle for rights as to be blinded by the obvious.

This is not about an individual's right to access material. It is about an individual's rights to choose NOT to access or be exposed to the material. This is about a small number of individuals intentionally intruding into the private, personal, work and psychological space of other people—to assert their power at the expense of another's, in the name of rights.

Clarifying Issues

ap.
F

▶▶ Conclusions

The university's proactive role begins through education and awareness when an individual's access to potentially offensive materials results in unintentional intrusion for another. Its role in discipline and intervention increases significantly when acts of purposeful intrusion and harassment occur. To ignore or take lightly such acts is to enable the disintegration of a community, to allow hostilities and misunderstandings to increase, and to allow the disempowering of some individuals within the community as an expense for the empowering of others.

This is a topic that may not have a political win within it, but which has a tremendous learning-teaching win for institutions of higher education. This is a learning moment. If we are to achieve Boyer's notions of an open, just, and disciplined community where freedom of expression and civility are affirmed, where persons are honored and valued, and where individuals will discipline themselves for the sake of others, "electronic access to potentially offensive material" is a topic to be engaged. This is a topic around which learning and teaching can be built. This is an opportunity to empower all individuals.

▶▶ Endnotes

1. Boyer, Ernest L. 1990. *Campus Life: In Search of Community,* The Carnegie Foundation for the Advancement of Teaching, Princeton, New Jersey, p.17.

2. Ibid, p. 25.

3. Ibid, p. 37.

4. Mill, John S., 1859. in *Civil Liberties,* Syracuse University Press, Syracuse, New York. p. 24, 25.

5. Lacy, Dan M.,1986. *Freedom and Equality of Access to Information: A Report to the American Library Association, Commission on Freedom and Equality of Access to Information,* American Library Association, Chicago. p. 3.

6. Rezmierski, V. "No Ostriches, Only Eagles: It's Time to Speak," paper presented to Women's Studies, the University of Michigan, Ann Arbor, MI, 1994.

Day-Month-Year format. Times are expressed in GMT + or − several hours; for example, +1 means the site's local time is one hour later than Greenwich Mean Time, and −5 means it's five hours earlier. Some sites listed request that you use them during off-peak (1800–0600 or 6 PM–6 AM local time) hours. Please respect these restrictions.

You can obtain a complete, updated version of this list in any of the following ways:

- Send an e-mail message to `mail-server@rtfm.mit.edu` with no subject and these lines in the body:

```
send usenet/news.answers/ftp-list/faq
send usenet/news.answers/ftp-list/sitelist/part1
send usenet/news.answers/ftp-list/sitelist/part2
send usenet/news.answers/ftp-list/sitelist/part3
send usenet/news.answers/ftp-list/sitelist/part4
send usenet/news.answers/ftp-list/sitelist/part5
send usenet/news.answers/ftp-list/sitelist/part6
send usenet/news.answers/ftp-list/sitelist/part7
send usenet/news.answers/ftp-list/sitelist/part8
send usenet/news.answers/ftp-list/sitelist/part9
send usenet/news.answers/ftp-list/sitelist/part10
send usenet/news.answers/ftp-list/sitelist/part11
send usenet/news.answers/ftp-list/sitelist/part12
send usenet/news.answers/ftp-list/sitelist/part13
```

- FTP to `rtfm.mit.edu` and get all the files from the /pub/usenet/new.answers/ftp-list/sitelist directory for the sitelist and /pub/usenet/news.answers/ftp-list/faq for the FAQ List (ASCII files).

- FTP to `garbo.uwasa.fi` and get the file /pc/doc-net/ftp-list.zip (PKZip 2.x archive: PKUnzip 2.x or Unzip 5.x or higher needed).

- FTP to `oak.oakland.edu` and get the file /SimTel/msdos/info/ftp-list.zip (PKZip 2.x archive: PKUnzip 2.x or Unzip 5.x or higher needed).

- FTP to `ftp.edu.tw` and get the file in the format you want from the `/documents/networking/guides/ftp-list` directory. Several formats are available, including a .Z and .gz version of the FAQ and site list.

Don't forget to set the transfer mode to 'binary' or 'image' type before transferring the .ZIP, .Z or .gz version of the file!

Site: allspice.lcs.mit.edu

Country: USA

GMT: –5

Organization: Massachusetts Institute of Technology Laboratory of Computer Sciences; Cambridge, Massachusetts

System: UNIX

Files: CMU-PCIP; dartnet; disktab; ecma-desd; mcode; netsim; PCMAIL; SNMP; SNPP; white-pages; WP

Site: american.megatrends.com

Country: USA

Organization: American Megatrends Inc.

System: UNIX

Comment: Read the files INDEX.DOS and INDEX.UNIX.

Files: chipset guides; EISA LAN; EISA VGA; general utilities; LAN SCSI; motherboard specific; PC defender; PCMCIA LAN; press releases; SCSI; tech tips; VLB SVGA

Site: archive.umich.edu

Country: USA

GMT: –5

Organization: University of Michigan; Ann Arbor, Michigan

System: UNIX (OS: several depending on machine)

Comment: Weekends: 60 connections, weekdays, 11 PM 'til 4 AM (EST): 60, weekdays, 6 PM 'til 11 PM and 4 AM 'til 6 AM (EST): 30, weekdays, 6 AM 'til 11 PM and 4 AM 'til 6 AM: 10 connections; daily mirrors: ftp.wustl.edu (/systems/{apple2,mac,atari,ibmpc,next}/umich.edu), ftp.doc.ic.ac.uk (/packages/mac/umich), archie.au (/micros/mac/umich); connecting to mirror.archive.umich.edu will automatically connect you to one of the above mirrors.

Files: Apple2; Apollo; Atari; Celia; economics; Internet; linguistics; Mac; MS-DOS; newton; NeXT; OS/2; physics

Site: `archie.au`

Country: Australia

GMT: +10

Administrative Address: `ftp@archie.au` (Craig Warren)

Organization: Australian Academic and Research Network (AARNet), Melbourne

System: UNIX

Comment: This archive is primarily intended for Australian users and consists mostly of mirrors of international sites to reduce the load on the Australian link. A note on the archive: due to disk space limitations, the mirrors of Amiga, Mac, and graphics are only shadowing files created in the last 365 days; complaints about this to `ccw@archie.au` please.

Files: AARNet; alex; archie; mirrors: 4.4BSD, ACS, Amiga, CIAC, FreeBSD, GNU, gopher, graphics, Kermit, Linux, Mac, micros, MicroSoft, NCSA, packet-drivers, RFCs, security, Simtel Software Repository mirror (/micros/pc/oak), `garbo.uwasa.fi` (/micros/pc/garbo), talk-radio, UNIX, Usenet, WAIS, wu-ftpd; NetWorkShop; projects; Weather; X11

Site: `archive.afit.af.mil`

Country: USA

GMT: −5

Administrative Address: `archivist@afit.af.mil`

Organization: US Air Force—Air Force Institute of Technology; Wright-Patterson AFB, Ohio

System: UNIX

Comment: Archives from `blackbird.afit.af.mil`.

Files: 386BSD; AFFORMS; ANNS; blackbird; bp; drawland; ghostdos; GNU; mpc; MS-DOS; Neural graphics; news; OARNet maps; RFCs; Satellite software, documents, elements; simnet; sound; space; sweep; tech-reports; virus research; wavelets; xntp

Site: archive.cis.ohio-state.edu

Country: USA

GMT: –6

Organization: Ohio State University; Columbus, Ohio

System: UNIX

Comment: Index in files-modified-last-week.Z.

Files: algebra; analyrim; att7300; bibliographies; byacc; cast; chameleon; cleanup; clp; communication; comp.sources.{3b1, misc, unix}; compress; condela; condor; console-server; cops; CTEXT; deliver; drafts; dspl; elm; firearms; fsuucp; ftpdu; GNU; GNU-mpw; GNUdu; hci; hcibib; holthouse; i386; ibm-pc; ICCCM; ICS; idea; ien; imap; internet-drafts; Interviews; isode; ispell; kbridge; kgen; Linux; lpf; m3; Mac-Unix; mgr; mitscheme; name-server; NCSA; netinfo; neuroprose; NeWS; NeXt; nfswatch; nntp; nntp-readers; ntp; oraperl; ozTeX; papers; paranoia; patch; pathalias; pbmplus; pcomm; pcroute; pcrrn; perl; PEX; picasso; plan9; plot2ps; policy-docs; popl; postgres; postscript; PPP; Proxyarp; rastps; rcs; regionals; RFCs; RN; rpc; rsrg; rx7club; sac2; sbprolog; sdbm; security; sendmail; siggraph92; slipware; smail; stat; stdwin; style-files; style-guide; sun-src; sysgen; talkradio; taylor-uucp; tcl; tcsh; tech-report; tensor; TeX; tiff; tknews; tn3270; toolset; top; traceroute; uemacs; Usenix; W3browser; WWW; X11R5; xcomm; XDCMP; XLFD; XTEST; XVIEW; Xo; ziggy; zoo

Site: archive.epas.utoronto.ca

Country: Canada

GMT: –5

Organization: University of Toronto; Toronto, Ontario

System: UNIX (386)

Comment: Mirrored on several sites.

Files: Gravis Ultrasound Soundcard (GUS) files

Site: `archive.nevada.edu`

Country: USA

GMT: –7

Organization: University of Nevada at Las Vegas; Las Vegas, Nevada

Comment: Problem: I/O error on network device.

Files: US Constitution & supporting docs; religious texts; Bible; lds texts

Site: `archive.orst.edu`

Country: USA

GMT: –8

Administrative Address: `archivist@archive.orst.edu` (Kean Stump)

Organization: Oregon State University; Corvallis, Oregon

System: UNIX (SunOS, Sun 6/690)

Comment: Open 24 hours; max. 500 users

Files: astro-data; comm; doc; gaming; lang; mirrors: `ucs.orst.edu`, Simtel Software Repository (pub/mirrors/oak.oakland.edu/simtel20/ msdos); network; news; noc; OSU-gopher; packages; publishers; security; skunk-works; SNMP; Sun; systems; Usenet; WAIS

Site: `asuvax.eas.asu.edu`

Country: USA

GMT: –7

Organization: Arizona State University; Tempe, Arizona

System: UNIX (Ultrix 4.1)

Files: Fidonet node list

Site: asylum.sf.ca.us

Country: USA

GMT: −8

Organization: Private system; San Francisco, California

System: UNIX

Files: best.of.internet; cerebus; clover; exile; fsb; ftpd; GOLD; gub; klf; langz; leadheads; mind-l; netspace; ping; politics; privacy; void; wintalk; ztt

Site: atitech.ca

Country: Canada

GMT: −5

Organization: ATI

System: UNIX

Files: ATI product (videocard) drivers, info, utilities (AVIs, images, OS/2, Windows)

Site: audrey.levels.unisa.edu.au

Country: Australia

GMT: +9

Administrative Address: ftp@audrey.levels.unisa.edu.au

Organization: University of South Australia, Signal Processing Research Institute, Digital Communications Group

Comment: Open 24 hours.

Files: lemacs; space flight info (manifests, launch times, etc.); satellite modems; speech; Twin Peaks (TV series) info

Site: `avahi.inria.fr`

Country: France

GMT: +1

Organization: INRIA

System: NEWS-OS 4.0c

Comment: more files in /pub

Files: Amiga; COSE; egeria; Free Compilers List; gipe; gopath; gwm; IBM PC; ISM; K-Edit; Klone; Koalabus; Meta-X; pixmap; TCL; videoconference; wtk; xmh; xpm; xfedor; xtrek

Site: `barnacle.erc.clarkson.edu`

Country: USA

GMT: –5

Administrative Address: `root@grape.ecs.clarkson.edu` (Brad Clements)

Organization: Clarkson University; Potsdam, New York

System: UNIX

Comment: Good source of packet drivers for using TCP/IP software on DOS machines. Some files have moved here from `grape.ecs.clarkson.edu`.

Files: packet drivers; MS-DOS, Opus BBS; MSDOS; graphics; Freemacs; `comp.binaries.ibm.pc`

Site: `biochemistry.cwru.edu`

Country: USA

GMT: –5

Administrative Address: `ftpserv@biochemistry.cwru.edu`

Organization: Case Western Reserve University; Cleveland, Ohio

System: MS-DOS (PC)

Comment: Transfers are logged; anonymous logins restricted to between 17:00–09:00 local time on weekdays (no restrictions on weekends); FTP inactivity timeout set to 5 minutes; Gopher available.

Files: MS-DOS; MS-Windows QVT/NET software; NOS; pdbview; psaam; SLIP; Slipper; Trumpet (DOS/Winsock); WinTCP

Site: biomol.univ-lyon1.fr

Country: France

GMT: +1

Organization: Université de Lyon (University of Lyon); Lyon, France

System: UNIX (SunOS 4.1)

Comment: Only online source of this biomolecular research database.

Files: ACNUC nucleic acid sequences database

Site: bobcat.bbn.com

Country: USA

GMT: –5

Organization: Bolt, Beranek & Newman; Cambridge, Massachusetts

System: MS-DOS (PC running KA9Q)

Files: beatles; KA9Q; kerm311; music; utils; video

Site: boombox.micro.umn.edu

Country: USA

GMT: –6

Organization: University of Minnesota

Comment: Main source of Gopher materials.

Files: Gopher (origin); Minuet; networking material; POPmail

Site: `boulder.colorado.edu`

Country: USA

GMT: −7

Organization: University of Colorado at Boulder; Boulder, Colorado

System: UNIX

Comment: Boulder-transmogrified FTP server; previous writable /tmp dir is gone due to uploads of pirated software.

Files: 3b1; addhost; aliases; bsdi; dod; enya; localization; scholar-line; sendmail; Varsity; Sun progs; tv+movies

Site: `brimbank.apana.org.au`

Country: Australia

GMT: +10

Administrative Address: `nick@brimbank.apana.org.au` (Nick Langmaid)

System: Windows NT (PC)

Files: antivirus; APANA; encoders; images; UUPC; Waffle; Windows (games, mail, NT, utilities, winsock)

Site: `byrd.mu.wvnet.edu`

Country: USA

GMT: −5

Organization: Marshall University; Huntington, West Virginia

System: UNIX

Comment: Directory: /pub/history/military/NATO; mirrored on `sunsite.unc.edu`.

Files: aircraft-related files; ejvc; ejvdeds; estepp; history; merton; NATO documents; Novell; vleadr; yeager

Site: cathouse.org

Country: USA

GMT: –6

Administrative Address: jrh@cathouse.org

System: NeXT (NeXT 1.0)

Comment: One of the largest humor sites.

Files: humor: animals, ascii, authors, better, Bob Christ, British humour: Black Adder, bottom, Fawlty Towers, Mr. Bean, Monty Python, Red Dwarf, Young Ones, Beyond the Fringe, Biographies, Britcomedy digest, Fry and Laurie, Peter Cook and Dudley Moore, Rowan Atkinson; computer, death, flying, geography, jobs, misc, Murphy's Laws, politically correct, quotes, religion, school, sex, simon (bofh, the bucket stories and more), sports, standup, synonyms, test, true (animals, awards, death, hospitals, kids, misc, police, politics, sex, tabloid, transportation), women; lyrics (lots of song lyrics); movies (database, tools, scripts); Rush Limbaugh transcripts; television: Beavis and Butthead, Black Adder, bottom, cheers, David Letterman, Fawlty Towers, Married with Children, misc American, misc. British, Muppets, Red Dwarf, Saturday Night Live, SeaQuest DSV (guides, synopses), Seinfeld, The Simpsons, Young Ones; urban legends: afu-faq, shergoldian, awards, minutes, people (Vicki Robinson, Kibo, Joel Furr), smileys, snide, animals, Loch Ness, books, Blue Star Tattoos, Craig Shergold, pull tabs, snuff films, electric chair, lights out, disney, drugs, cocaine money, food, gifs, language, etymology, legal, medical, shakespeare, movies, net.legends, products, science, sex, songs, tv, cpt.pugwash

Site: caticsuf.csufresno.edu

Country: USA

GMT: –8

Administrative Address: steve@caticsuf.cati.csufresno.edu (Steve Mitchell)

Organization: California State University at Fresno—California Agricultural Technology Institute (CATI), Advanced Technology Information Network; Fresno, California

System: UNIX

Comment: Major source of dairy economic information; paintball information. Currently unrestricted access. Accesses are logged.

Files: Dairy market reports; California irrigation information; Paintball archives; rec.sport.paintball article archive

Site: ccphys.nsu.nsk.su

Country: Russia

GMT: +6

Administrative Address: mbo@ccphys.nsu.nsk.su (Konstantin Yu. Boyandin)

Organization: Novosibirsk State University, Ad Initio Design group (AIDg); Novosibirsk, Russia

System: Netware 3.11 (PC fileserver)

Comment: Default directory: /PRIVATE/FTPSITE; available all day.

Files: AD&D; adventure games; D&D; DDL; games; MUD; RPG; SSG; strategic/ economic/role-playing engines and description languages to develop several types of software; wargames

Site: cecelia.media.mit.edu

Country: USA

GMT: –5

Organization: Massachusetts Institute of Technology Media Lab; Cambridge, Massachusetts

System: UNIX (Ultrix 4.1)

Comment: Some loose files in /pub.

Files: ACT; art-of-ai; beerud; boccibob; Csound; framer; machine-rhythm; mas602; mood; mt; narrative-intelligence-archive; reverb; schubert; slobores; subg

Site: `cell-relay.indiana.edu`

Country: USA

GMT: −5

Administrative Address: `cell-relay-request@indiana.edu`

Organization: University of Indiana University Computing Services (UCS); Bloomington, Indiana

System: UNIX (SunOS 4.1, Sun SPARCstation2, 64Mb RAM, 2Gb disk; connected through Ethernet->FDDI->T1->Internet)

Comment: Also available through Gopher; please try that first.

Files: Information concerning cell-relay technologies (e.g. ATM, DQDB, SONET), research, FAQs, conferences, workshops, bibliographies, vendor addresses, product descriptions, standards documents and the archives (searchable via Gopher) for the following mailing lists and newsgroups: `comp.dcom.cell-relay`, IP over ATM, Routing over Large Clouds (ROLC), VINCE (Q.93B signalling software)

Site: `celtic.stanford.edu`

Country: USA

GMT: −8

Administrative Address: `ceolas@celtic.stanford.edu` (Gerard Manning)

Organization: Stanford University CEOLAS; Menlo Park, California

Other Access: none

System: UNIX (Irix, Iris Indigo)

Comment: No restricted hours; submits should be accompanied by note to the admin; comments welcome.

Files: Anything related to celtic music. Currently has artist biogs, discographies, tour schedules, lists of radio shows, music sessions, festivals, publications. Associated with `rec.music.celtic` and IRTRAD-L listserv.

Site: `cert.org`

Country: USA

GMT: –5

Organization: Carnegie-Mellon University Software Engineering Institute (SEI), Computer Emergency Response Team (CERT); Pittsburgh, Pennsylvania

System: UNIX

Comment: Official CERT server.

Files: CERT information and files; COPS; FIRST; network tools; NIST; ssphgw; Virus-L/comp.virus archives;

Site: `chara.gsu.edu`

Country: USA

GMT: –5

Organization: Georgia State University Astronomy Dept.; Atlanta, Georgia

System: UNIX

Files: Array (chapters of the proposal of the Center for High Angular Resolution Astronomy to construct a large interferometric telescope facility); BeNews; BrightStars; Gies; Saguaro Astronomy club papers (postscript); Speckle; Zeus

Site: `coast.cs.purdue.edu`

Country: USA

GMT: –5

Administrative Address: `security-archive@cs.purdue.edu`

Organization: Purdue University Computer Science Dept., Computer Operations, Audit and Security Technology (COAST) archive; West-Lafayette, Indiana

System: UNIX

Comment: User activity is logged and may be monitored; disclaimer and export control notice; if you are not familiar with the structure of the archive, please read the information in /pub/aux first. The archive currently contains software, standards, tools, and other material in the following areas: access control, artificial life, authentication, criminal investigation, cryptography, e-mail privacy enhancement, firewalls, formal methods, general guidelines, genetic algorithms, incident response, institutional policies, intrusion detection, law & ethics, malware (viruses, worms, etc), network security, password systems, policies, privacy, risk assessment, security related equipment, security tools, social impacts, software forensics, software maintenance, standards, technical tips, the computer underground.

Files: alert (CERT, CIAC, DEC, HP, Mac, NIST, NeXT, SERT, SGI, Solbourne, Sun); COAST info; dict (several dictionaries mirrored from ftp.funet.fi and ftp.netsys.com); doc (documents relating to computer security and security tools); mirrors (numerous sites with security info are mirrored here); news+lists (several mirrored magazines and mailing list archives); patches; Purdue info; response teams; tools

Site: col.hp.com

Country: USA

GMT: –7

Organization: Hewlett-Packard—Colorado

Files: NOS; utilities archives

Site: convex.com

Country: USA

GMT: –6

Organization: Convex Computer

System: UNIX

Files: avs; bsdi; doc; iserv; news; Perl sources and examples; pexic quarterly; qualix; smail; tac patches; taylor uucp; unitree

Site: `crimelab.com`

Country: USA

GMT: –6

Organization: Crimelab

System: UNIX

Comment: Some files are mirrored on `ftp.sterling.com`; FTP sessions logged and monitored.

Files: bugtraq; security; skey

Site: `crl.dec.com`

Country: USA

GMT: –5

Organization: Digital Equipment Corp—Massachusetts

Files: binaries; DEC; neural nets; news; sources; TinyMud; X11

Site: `cs.bu.edu`

Country: USA

GMT: –5

Organization: Boston University; Boston, Massachusetts

System: UNIX (SunOS 4.1)

Files: alpert; amass; bestravos; CN; Conquer, XConquer (Roguelike game); hedaya; IEEE-RTTC; IRC clients; listserv; lnd; marvit; pbe; PC; shaban; tech-reports; unproto

Site: `cs.indiana.edu`

Country: USA

GMT: –5

Administrative Address: `ftp@cs.indiana.edu`

Organization: Indiana University Computer Science Dept.; Bloomington, Indiana

Other Access: `mailserv@cs.indiana.edu`: the word `help` should be in the body.

System: UNIX

Comment: Open 24 hours.

Files: aikido; CIC; conacyt mailing list archive; elisp; Faces (sources and bitmaps); lics; Linux; LISTING; logic; Mosis; MS-DOS; RW5; s88; sage; Scheme source and material; sigma; source for Webster dictionary servers; stiquito; tech-reports; University computer science tech reports; Usenet oracle; vsh

Site: `cs.oswego.edu`

Country: USA

GMT: –5

Administrative Address: `tymann@cs.oswego.edu`

Organization: State University of New York at Oswego; Oswego, New York

Comment: Successor of `moxie.oswego.edu`; transfers are logged.

Files: Material related to the Soviet coup.

Site: `cs.rutgers.edu`

Country: USA

GMT: –5

Organization: Rutgers University; Piscataway, New Jersey

System: UNIX

Comment: loose files in /pub and / directories; WWW home pages.

Files: borgida; colloquia; Ethernet-codes; hyperplane animator; IETF; interest groups; Internet Drafts; Internet Resource Guide;

Interop; Linux; NCSA Telnet for Mac and MSDOS; Linux material; networking info; RFCs; RUNET docs (Rutgers info); `soc.religion.christian`; suns-at-home; tech-reports; trec2; venugopa

Site: `cs.ucsd.edu`

Country: USA

GMT: –8

Administrative Address: `software@cs.ucsd.edu`

Organization: University of California at San Diego Computer Science & Engineering Dept.; San Diego, California,

System: UNIX

Comment: tar and (un)compress on the fly

Files: admissions; aikido; corpus_data; csegsa; csl; cslcalendar; CTF; framemaker; funrun; GAbench; GAucsd; Gemini; Infoscope; Lee; Mac; multimedia; prep-p; q-System; Sun; tech-reports; theory; zsh

Site: `cs.utah.edu`

Country: USA

GMT: –7

Organization: University of Utah; Salt Lake City, Utah

System: UNIX

Files: Amiga; DES; Forth; grad_info; graphics; Lyon-Lamb; netinfo; neural nets; news service archive; PAF; range-database; Reverse Engineering; robot-prototyping; rose; router; sobh; stc-report; SUNcrash; Stagecraft; tech-reports; Utah raster; Worm Tour

Site: `cs.utexas.edu`

Country: USA

GMT: –6

Organization: University of Texas at Austin Computer Science Dept.; Austin, Texas

System: UNIX

Files: Academic info; avi; brewery; courses; csc94; FIG; genesis; ham-radio; INN; neural-nets; ops5; porter; predator; QSIM; tech-reports

Site: csd4.csd.uwm.edu

Country: USA

GMT: –6

Administrative Address: help@csd4.csd.uwm.edu

Organization: University of Wisconsin at Milwaukee; Milwau-kee, Wisconsin

System: UNIX (Ultrix 4.1)

Files: agesa; aragorn; Behavior Analysis; bri; carinhas; chinese; Custard Workshop files; DirDir; laptop; high-audio; Internetwork Mail Guide; Milwaukee; Optimus; Palmtop; Internet Services; kyol-art; Mac; MS-DOS; pink; Portables; Psion; Psychology; Satel-lite; sstor; sumit; UNIX; Wingspread; wraith

Site: csli.stanford.edu

Country: USA

GMT: –8

Organization: Stanford University Center for the Study of Language and Information (CSLI); Menlo Park, California

System: UNIX (SunOS 4.1)

Comment: Please avoid using during local business hours (8 AM to 5 PM Pacific); transfers are logged with host name and e-mail address.

Files: Archimedes; bibliography; ChineseTalk; Gandalf; linguis-tics; MacCup; PrePrints; prosit; publications; shreview; TeX

Site: csrc.ncsl.nist.gov

Country: USA

GMT: –5

Administrative Address: `root@csrc.ncsl.nist.gov`

Organization: National Institute for Standards and Technology, Computer Security (NCSL); Gaithersburg, Maryland

System: UNIX

Files: computer-security related alerts, articles and other information; FIRST; NISTbulletin; NISTgen; NISTir; NISTnews; NISTpubs; Posix; privacy; risk forum; secalert; secnews; secpolicy; secpubs; training; virinfo; virreviews; virus-l; warning

Site: `darwin.cc.nd.edu`

Country: USA

GMT: –8

Organization: Notre Dame University; Notre Dame, Indiana

System: UNIX

Files: comics; gopher; NAFTA; NeXT; PC; Soviet archive; UNIX

Site: `debra.dbgt.doc.ca`

Country: Canada

GMT: –5

Organization: The Communications Research Centre and the Canadian Broadcasting Corporation.

Other Access: `http://debra.dbgt.doc.ca/cbc/cbc.html`; Gopher: `debra.dbgt.doc.ca`

System: UNIX

Comment: CBC Radio Trial; WWW access using the NCSA Mosaic client is preferred.

Files: Canadian Broadcasting Corporation (CBC) radio programs stored as 8-bit, 8KHz .AU files; chat; IRC; dvi; freenet; ISC; opengov; sox sound conversion tool for .AU to .VOC, .WAV conversion for PC use; usenet-survey

Site: dell1.us.dell.com

Country: USA

Organization: Dell Computer Corporation

System: UNIX

Files: Dell product info, drivers etc.

Site: delcano.mit.edu

Country: USA

GMT: –5

Administrative Address: pds-request@space.mit.edu

Organization: Massachusetts Institute of Technology Center for Space Research; Cambridge, Massachusetts

Other Access: E-mail to pds-listserv@space.mit.edu, with Subject or text line of help

System: UNIX

Comment: Use 6 PM – 8 AM please.

Files: NASA Planetary Data Systems Microwave Subnode; Planetary Radar and Radio data, mostly Venus data from Pioneer 12, Venera 15/16, and Magellan missions (/mgn, /pub, /pv, /venera)

Site: elbereth.rutgers.edu

Country: USA

GMT: –5

Organization: Rutgers University; Piscataway, New Jersey

Comment: Directory: sfl, get the 00Index file.

Files: SF-lovers archive; lots of text files about tv series; program guides; text files on a number of subjects; FAQs related to SF (Bladerunner); info on SF awards and writers (Hugo Awards, Adams, Asimov, and more)

Site: emx.utexas.edu

Country: USA

GMT: –6

Organization: University of Texas at Austin Computing Center; Austin, Texas

System: UNIX

Files: abwcism; ajit; docs; gatekeeper; images; kermit; lyon; math-lib; maziar; meav350; music; netinfo; npasswd; phantasia; srips; ta-jima book; TeX; TeXsis; thenet; VMS software

Site: epona.physics.ucg.ie

Country: Ireland

GMT: 0

System: UNIX

Files: 386BSD; astro; audio; cad; cd-index; dsp; earthsci; elec-tronics; FAQs; fax; fits; games; GCC; GNU; gps; graphics; HPUX; ix86ux; Linux; Mac; MS-DOS; net; numerical; nuts; oreilly; PGP; physics; pic; redo; space; transputer; UCG; UnixUG; util; VMS; wbase20; Wine; WWW; X11; xgames

Site: esusda.gov

Country: USA

GMT: –5

Organization: Extension Service US Dept. of Agriculture (ESUSDA), National Agriculture Library

System: UNIX

Comment: Also available through Gopher.

Files: ace; directions; disasters; education; feds; internet; POW; us-policy; water

Site: etlport.etl.go.jp

Country: Japan

GMT: +10

System: UNIX

Files: 386BSD; akcl; alex; arts; barr-wells; benchmark; Canna22; ccipr; cmucl; datacube; eus; GNU; gs; handa; hence; hol; hp-archive; HPFF; hterm; IBM-PC; images; ina; inaz; INN; IV3.1; j3100; jTeX; junet-guide; jvi; kterm; kuniyosh; Larch; laura; Linux; Lisp; lotos; magna; mh; mime; monsanto-nqs; mule; nemacs; neuro-intro; nevprop; NNTP; NeXT; OhShow; p4; pam; pclu; poi; prolog; pvm; realtime; RFCs; robotics; sc22wg13; seimitu; sendmail; shidara; sml; SNSS; SWoPP; Sun-patches; taniyama; tcl; TeX; Uranus; VHDL; vin; wadalib-font; X11; xf2.2; xfig2.8; XFree86-2.0; xnetlib; zsh

Site: eugene.gal.utexas.edu

Country: USA

GMT: –6

Administrative Address: perry@eugene.gal.utexas.edu (John Perry)

Organization: University of Texas at Galveston Medical Branch; Galveston, Texas

System: UNIX

Files: anti-virus utilities, mirror of Simtel's pub/msdos/virus directory

Site: explorer.arc.nasa.gov

Country: USA

GMT: –8

Administrative Address: yee@atlas.arc.nasa.gov (Peter Yee)

Organization: NASA—Ames Research Center; Mountain View, California

System: UNIX

Comment: A CD-ROM farm with 84 NASA image and data discs on-line, /cdrom; also files from the `ames.arc.nasa.gov` site, /pub/SPACE directory.

Files: Images and data mostly of Jet Propulsion Laboratory space probes Viking, Voyager, Magellan, etc.

Site: `explorer.dgtp.toronto.edu`

Country: Canada

GMT: –5

Organization: University of Toronto; Toronto, Ontario

System: UNIX

Comment: Several personal pub directories under /pub.

Files: alex; depth; Half-QWERTY; Macsockets; marking; nastos; nms; radek; SGI; siggraph; stampaper; telepresence; thesis; timelines

Site: `first.org`

Country: USA

GMT: –5

Organization: FIRST (National Computer Security Center NCSC); Fort Meade, Maryland

Files: FIRST/CERT advisories; security-related material

Site: `flinux.tu-graz.ac.at`

Country: Austria

GMT: +1

Administrative Address: `ftpadmin@flinux.tu-graz.ac.at`

Organization: Technischer Universitaet Graz (Graz Institute of Technology); Graz, Austria

System: UNIX

Files: Doom; graphics (33, 3D, boris, BSD, fantasy, fenn, hajime, mpg, series); Linux (Debian, handbuch, Linus, lst, network, slacksrc, slackware, source, sunsite); MS-DOS (archiver, ATI, djgpp, info, network, Novell, romulus, turbo_C, turbo_pascal, TurboVision, Ultrasound, virus, XWindows, zip); MUD; Qdeck; Wine

Site: flop.informatik.tu-muenchen.de

Country: Germany

GMT: +1

Administrative Address: brychcy@informatik.tu-muenchen.de

Organization: Technische Universitaet Muenchen (Munich University of Technology) Computer Science Dept., TIGKI; Munich, Germany

System: UNIX

Files: Alpha; Atari; bib; dfgsa; emsy; EmTeX; fki; gik; i386; ispell; lispprk; Mac; Minix; Neres; Nethack; Scheme; Simgen; stol; Sunpatches; talks; tcl; TeX; theory; tptp-library; X11

Site: fpspux.fapesp.br

Country: Brazil

GMT: −3

Administrative Address: root@fpspux.fapesp.br

Organization: FAPE Sao Paolo; Sao Paolo, Brazil

System: UNIX (DEC Station 3100)

Comment: 600Mb disk space; directory list in /pub3/fpspux_fapesp_br/ls-lR; max. 100 users; FSP server available.

Files: CCITT; docs; graphics; listserv; maps; mirror.inpe; NCSA; packing; PC; RFCs; security; standards; Sun; TCP/IP; UNIX; UnixTeX; Usenet; viewers; X11

Site: freebie.engin.umich.edu

Country: USA

GMT: −5

Administrative Address: ftp_support@mingin.engin.umich.edu

Organization: University of Michigan Computer-Aided Engineering Network; Ann Arbor, Michigan

System: UNIX (Ultrix 4.2)

Comment: mingin and knob2 are different machines but show the same dir.

Files: Apollo; babysit; EMSA+MAS; InterViews; IRC; kperl; mail; Mac; Maple; Mice; MSA+MAS; netuse; Newsletter; Nihongo; stoprobs; Sun; technotes; uniqname; urt; usenet; vsh

Site: ftp.3com.com

Country: USA

GMT: –8

Administrative Address: ftp@3com.com

Organization: 3COM

System: UNIX

Comment: directories: adapters, cs-utils, internet-drafts, netinfo, pub, tech-tips, Orange-Book, rfc, ql-archive, 3com-mibs

Files: 3COM technical tips, network info & drivers for 3COM network cards MIB info; AppleTalk IETF; communication server utilities; elisp; email; gas-coff; GNU; ids; internet-drafts (mirror); ispell; lpf (mirror); mib (mirror); MS-DOS; NCSU; network info (mirror of NIC templates); Orange Book (Trusted Computer System, Evaluation Criteria); Perl 3.0/4.0; Posix; Quantum Leap (TV show on NBC) archive; rbcs1; RFCs (mirror); security; sesame_project; snt; Solaris 2.0; Sun-dist; TeX; viewer; X11R5

Site: ftp.acns.nwu.edu

Country: USA

GMT: –6

Organization: Northwestern University; Evanston, Illinois

System: UNIX (SunOS 4.1)

Files: acns-jobs; acoustic guitar; afcm; `bbs.lists`; comm-studies; crowded-house; DalMOO; dicty; disinfectant; firstclass; flatfield; gabriel; gn; gowebtools; hispanic.studies; jlnstuff; law-and-politics; listserv; ltp; MDM-II; MS-DOS; murmur; named; newswatcher; NUPOP (POP3 daemon for MS-DOS); p-speaking; PC Route; ph; poppassd; recguns; sound-patterns; Sun-dist; superscript; tilt; wavefront; wif; xpres; zen

Site: `ftp.adobe.com`

Country: USA

GMT: –8

Administrative Address: `archive-keepers@mv.us.adobe.com`

Organization: Adobe Systems Inc.

Other Access: E-mail to `ps-file-server@adobe.com`

System: UNIX

Comment: Font and Postscript information and fixes; read-only server; enter a valid e-mail address or you will be denied future access.

Files: Adobe info, patches, programs, textfiles, updates; AFM files; developer support

Site: `ftp.ai.mit.edu`

Country: USA

GMT: –5

Organization: Massachusetts Institute of Technology AI Lab; Cambridge, Massachusetts

System: UNIX

Comment: Refers to `publications.ai.mit.edu` for publications; several user pub directories under /pub.

Files: 6.824; AI material; cube-lovers; GA; hebrew; Iterate; j-machine; jupiter; lemacs; lisp3; lptrs; mobile-dist-telecomp; pdp8-lovers archive; pinouts; poker; rbl-94 archive; refer-to-bibtex; sanger (figures, papers); scheme-libraries; screamer; screen; series; square-dancing; surf-hippo; tbs; TS; vis; x3j13

Site: ftp.anu.edu.au

Country: Australia

GMT: +10

Organization: Australian National University

System: UNIX (SunOS 4.1)

Files: AARNet; cscdocs; gs; icons; library; micro; modem software; NCSA; patches; pictures; RFCs; security; Solaris; Sun-fixes; technegas; UNIX PC

Site: ftp.apple.com

Country: USA

GMT: –8

Organization: Apple Computer

Comment: Please use during non-business hours; refuses access to any host whose IP address does not reverse into a hostname.

Files: Apple (Mac, II, IIgs) product info, software, developer support

Site: ftp.austria.eu.net

Country: Austria

GMT: +1

Administrative Address: help@austria.eu.net

Organization: EUnet; Austria, Vienna

System: UNIX

Files: books; EUnet; GNU; info; Mac; Mail; modem; MS-Access; network; news; NeXT; PC; security; support; util; vendor; wais; WWW; X11

Site: ftp.barrnet.net

Country: USA

GMT: –8

Organization: BARRnet; San Francisco, California

System: UNIX

Comment: Transfers are logged; access allowed all day.

Files: BARRNet; BSDI; CERT; imr; lists; mbone; Mosaic; netin-tro; nets; news; nsfnet-nren-nii; OSI; ref; RFCs; security; src; templates; Usenet; WAIS

Site: ftp.bbcnc.org.uk

Country: UK

GMT: 0

Organization: British Broadcasting Corporation (BBC) Networking Club

Other Access: WWW: //www.bbcnc.org.uk

System: UNIX

Files: BBCNC; membership; WWW

Site: ftp.belnet.be

Country: Belgium

GMT: +1

Administrative Address: ftpmaint@belnet.be

Organization: BelNet; Antwerpen, Belgium

System: UNIX

Files: Belnet; DNS; docs (FAQs, misc, RFCs, RIPE); GNU; infosystems (archie, gopher, misc, news, www); mail; networking (management, PC internet kit, winsock); OS (Linux); RUCA; security; X11R6

Site: ftp.bilkent.edu.tr

Country: Turkey

GMT: +2

Administrative Address: akgul@bilkent.edu.tr (Mustafa Akgul)

Organization: Bilkent University Computer Center; Ankara, Turkey

Other Access: Gopher: gopher.bilkent.edu.tr; WWW: www.bilkent.edu.tr; mail: bilkent-server@bilkent.edu.tr; FTP: ftp.bilkent.edu.tr

System: UNIX

Comment: tar and compress on the fly; use aliases to change directories: quote site alias for a list; Gopher: gopher.bilkent.tr; Notifier can be used as mail-server, read /pub/INFO/Netinfo; successor of firat.bcc.bilkent.edu.tr [considered obsolete, still allows anonymous ftp and has a Photos directory that might be interesting].

Files: Amiga; benchmark; GIF; humor; IEOR; INFO; Linux; Mac; Machine learning; Math; meetings; Neural; PC; Reports; TeX; UNIX; Utils

Site: ftp.bio.indiana.edu

Country: USA

GMT: −5

Administrative Address: archive@bio.indiana.edu

Organization: Indiana University Biology Dept.; Bloomington, Indiana

System: UNIX (SunOS 4.1)

Comment: Directory: /util/wais; see Archive.Doc for details.

Files: IUBIO archive: biology software and data; WAIS-related files

Site: ftp.biostr.washington.edu

Country: USA

GMT: −8

Administrative Address: jsp@glia.biostr.washington.edu

Organization: University of Washington; Seattle, Washington

System: UNIX

Files: browser; digital anatomist; Mac; MIDI; mri; muckdocs; muq; Queensryche; qwestdocs; slisp; tech; tinyfugue; xlisp

Site: `ftp.bouw.tno.nl`

Country: Netherlands

GMT: +1

Administrative Address: `Johan.Taal@bouw.tno.nl`

Organization: The Netherlands Organization For Applied Scientific Research (TNO), Building and Construction Research; Rijswijk, Netherlands

System: UNIX

Comment: Please use local servers first; most of our material is mirrored; open 24 hours; big downloads between 18:00 and 07:00 local time please; Gopher via `ftp.bouw.tno.nl`, port 70; 2.2GB.

Files: Windows utilties; Novell; Pmail (ENG + DUTCH version); Graphic images; TNO Company information; a lot of PD PCware; Security docs; div. MAILserver software; FTP daemons; network tools; SUN-fixes; CERT docs; UNIX utilities; infosystems: WAIS, GOPHER, WWW, ALEX, anonymous FTP servers, ARCHIE; MAC material; GNU; RIPE docs; PostScript material; packet drivers; BBS software and other material

Site: `ftp.bme.hu`

Country: Hungary

GMT: +1

Organization: Technical University of Budapest Centre of Information Systems; Budapest, Hungary

System: UNIX

Files: atm; emulators; games; Linux; MS-DOS; MS-Windows3; Novell; UNIX; VMS

Site: ftp.brad.ac.uk

Country: UK

GMT: 0

Organization: University of Bradford; Bradford, England

System: UNIX

Comment: Directories: /pub/mods, /incoming/mods, /pub/misc/graphics; Transfer type set to BINARY; Bradford users read README.bradford; major source of sound and graphics files.

Files: AU sound files; graphics (GIF, JPG); Married With Childen program guide; mods; MS-DOS

Site: ftp.brown.edu

Country: USA

Organization: Brown University; Providence, Rhode Island

Files: Eudora X (Usenet Newsreader); POP3 client for UNIX (popper)

Site: ftp.bsdi.com

Country: USA

GMT: –8

Administrative Address: archive@bsdi.com

Other Access: WWW: www.bsdi.com.

Organization: Berkeley Software Design Inc.

System: UNIX

Comment: *The* source of BSDI info; transfers are logged.

Files: BSDI: info, patches, support; contrib: admin, applications, database, games, GNU, info, infosystems, kernel, languages, lib, mail, mailing.list, networking, news, sound, TeX, utilities, X11, yuval

Site: `ftp.cac.psu.edu`

Country: USA

GMT: –5

Administrative Address: `ftp@ftp.cac.psu.edu`.

Organization: Pennsylvania State University; Philadelphia, Pennsylvania

System: UNIX

Comment: Directory: /pub/dos/info/tcpip.packages.

Files: access; ANSI REXX; courses; docs; folk music; genealogy; gopher; gymn; humanities; internexus; jbe; Mac; MS-DOS; NIC: OS/2; Shoemaker-Levy 9 (SL9) info/images; tv-networks; UNIX; VM

Site: `ftp.cac.washington.edu`

Country: USA

GMT: –8

Organization: University of Washington—Computing and Communications; Seattle, Washington

System: UNIX

Comment: Read the README.FIRST file.

Files: bind; Clearinghouse of Subject Oriented Internet Resources; Easymail irdp (router-discovery); MailManager; IMAP2, POP23 for NeXT and UNIX client and server programs; kermit; MS-DOS; NCSA; netinfo; noc-tools; Pine; sendmail; sun-fix; utils; willow; winsock; X

Site: `ftp.can.nl`

Country: Netherlands

GMT: +1

Organization: Computer Algebra Nederland; Amsterdam, Netherlands

System: UNIX

Files: akcl; aldes; alpi-cocoa; arith; bignum; CA-meetings; Cal-ICo; cc4; GB-Linz; GB-POSSO; chevie; dsl; felix; form; form1; gap; HISC; info; jacal; kan; KANT; kcl; kent; macaulay; Maple; mas; mathematica; MuPAD; pari-gp; reduce-netlib; saclib; simath; symbmath; symmetrica; weyl

Site: `ftp.cc.columbia.edu`

Country: USA

GMT: –5

Administrative Address: `ftp-bugs@columbia.edu`

Organization: Columbia University; New York, New York

System: UNIX

Comment: One of the successors of `columbia.edu/ftp.colum-bia.edu`; all transfers and connections are logged; username `ftp` possible instead of `anonymous` (no quotes); all transfers and connections are logged; public file transfer point: /pub/ftp.

Files: mm (Mail Manager); ccmd (C-language interactive command-parsing package); bibliographic items; bootp (RFC1395 UNIX bootp server); dj (automatic backup of network to jukebox); Kermit; misc; patch (Larry Wall's PATCH program); packet-drivers (the Crynwyr nee Clarkson packet driver collection); PC fonts (from Yossi Gil); VMS-make (new MAKE for (Open-)VMS VAX and AXP); vms-libcmu (Berkeley sockets library for CMU/Tek VMS TCP/IP)

Site: `ftp.cc.gatech.edu`

Country: USA

GMT: –5

Organization: Georgia Tech Computing Center; Atlanta, Georgia

System: UNIX (SunOS 4.1)

Files: adr; AI; AIX; Amiga; architecture; bodhi; coc; coc_graduate_info; cogsci94; database; dbpvm; gvu; IBM; ibm-understand; ims1000; Mac; menu; music; NeXT; pat; sounds; tech-reports; TimeWarp; UIST; UIST94; UNIX

Site: `ftp.cc.monash.edu.au`

Country: Australia

GMT: +10

Administrative Address: `steve@cc.monash.edu.au` (Steve Balogh: Windows, Vietnam etc.), `jwb@capek.rdt.monash.edu.au` (Prof. Jim Breen: Nihongo)

Organization: Monash University—Clayton Campus Computing Center; Melbourne

System: UNIX

Comment: Directories: pub/win3, pub/nihongo, pub/vietnam, pub/wwdj, pub/vi.

Files: graphics.formats; hlst; Mac; MS-Windows 3.x and MS-Windows NT (mirrors `ftp.cica.indiana.edu`); MS-Windows/DOS Developers Journal sources; Nihongo (Japanese); palmtop; PC; Vi editor; Vietnamese language and culture; wddj; womcs; WordPerfect

Site: `ftp.cc.ruu.nl`

Country: Netherlands

GMT: +1

Organization: Rijks Universiteit Utrecht (Utrecht University) Computing Center; Utrecht

System: UNIX

Comment: Extremely useful benchmark files, major source of Macintosh, MS-DOS TCP/IP applications; mirror for NCSA TCP/IP applications.

Files: Benchmarks; campus-online; cap; CERT-UU; DNS; gopher; Mac; Mail; MS-DOS; NCSA; Netinfo; PC Raster; Sun; UNIX; WWW; X; X500

Site: `ftp.cc.tut.fi`

Country: Finland

GMT: +2

Organization: Tampere University of Technology Computing Center; Tampere, Finland

System: UNIX

Comment: also available through Gopher (`gopher.cc.tut.fi`)

Files: ATM; gopher (Mac, PC, Unix client); PC SLIP (executable and info); Sol2-patches; x500

Site: `ftp.cc.uch.gr`

Country: Greece

GMT: +2

Administrative Address: `stefan@cc.uch.gr` (Stefanos Pihas)

Organization: University of Crete Computing Center; Heraklion, Crete

System: UNIX

Comment: Descriptive ls-format.

Files: computer: DECUS, games, graphics, Mac, misc, MS-DOS, network, packages, UNIX; hobby: music, lyrics, sports; local material; scientific: ai, audio, chem, clinchem, computer, geo, graphics, library, math, medical, misc, molbio, neural, papers, parallel, physics, psychology, simulation, systems

Site: `ftp.cc.umanitoba.ca`

Country: Canada

GMT: –6

Organization: University of Manitoba; Winnipeg, Manitoba

System: UNIX

Comment: No Poland information is stored here.

Files: astro-ccd; astro-courses; buhr; dallas; Doom; e-journal; fordemo; frontier; GUS digest; icpsr; LaTeX; Mac; Mac develop; MIDI; mods; Oedipus; OS/2 beta/fixes; pam; PC; PiHKAL; Pink

Floyd; psgendb; pspice; rahardj; rcj; rec.travel Info Library; Ren & Stimpy; renegade; SLS; StarTrek; Sun-fixes; ttn; vega; Wolf 3D; XV 3.00a

Site: `ftp.cc.utexas.edu`

Country: USA

GMT: −6

Organization: University of Texas at Austin Computation Center Archive; Austin, Texas

System: UNIX

Comment: Access allowed all day, but preferred outside of 6 AM–6 PM CST; transfers are logged.

Files: AI_ATTIC; amadeus; anime; cypherpunks; databaselib; delta-clipper; doc; genetic-programming; graphics: GIF, JPG; lewo; lips; mathlib; microlib; statlib; plant-resources-center; real-time; skywatch; snakes; sourdough; statgopher; tatp; texsis; txunion; ut-facts; ut-images; ytalk

Site: `ftp.cco.caltech.edu`

Country: USA

GMT: −8

Organization: California Institute of Technology; Pasadena, California

System: UNIX (SunOS 4.1)

Comment: Successor of `tybalt.caltech.edu` and `punisher.cco.caltech.edu`; directories: pub/heathh, pub/humor; excellent source of Mathematica information, large humor repository, Disney graphics and information.

Files: adnd; Apple2; Aquaria; calmsa; card; ccf; cetf; disney; dissertations; docs; graphics; GraphWidget; heathh; humor; jokes; IBM PC; mathematica; nyet; plays; reefkeepers; SB programming material; sol-drivers; Solaris; specs; Sun; surfing; txt; UA; willow; X; X11; xyplex

Site: `ftp.ccs.carleton.ca`

Country: Canada

GMT: –5

Organization: Carleton University Computing Services (Computer CenterS); Ottawa, Ontario

System: UNIX (SunOS 4.1)

Comment: SchoolNet K–12 information repository; source information for beginning a freenet.

Files: aucc; banyan; bootp; civeng; dkbtrace; fedelect; freenet; gopher; math; novell; parasol; pov-ray; schoolnet; security; sendmail; smallktalk; stats.can; vipcu; workbench; wpl

Site: `ftp.cd.chalmers.se`

Country: Sweden

GMT: +1

Comment: Successor of `alcazar.cd.chalmers.se`.

Files: MUD (LPMUD) related files; NetBSD; Netrek; ZyXel

Site: `ftp.cdrom.com`

Country: USA

GMT: –8

Administrative Address: `ftp-admin@ftp.cdrom.com` (general questions or comments), `ftp-bugs@ftp.cdrom.com` (bug reports or problems)

Organization: Walnut Creek CD-ROM; Walnut Creek, California

System: UNIX

Comment: Successor of `cdrom.com`; OS/2 users use `ftp-os2.cdrom.com` because `ftp-os2.cdrom.com` might start to point to another machine sometime; most of these archives are available on CD-ROM as well; major archive of games; major US mirror for garbo.

ap.
G

Files: ADA; Aminet; CD-ROM related material; FreeBSD; games; Gutenberg (mirror of `etext.archive.umich.edu`); Linux; MS-Windows (mirror of `ftp.cica.indiana.edu`); OS/2 programs and mirror of `ftp-os2.nmsu.edu` (hobbes); `garbo.uwasa.fi` mirror (/pub/garbo); Perl; XFree86 (mirror of `ftp.xfree86.org`)

Site: `ftp.census.gov`

Country: USA

GMT: −5

Administrative Address: `gatekeeper@census.gov`

Organization: United States Bureau of the Census; Bowie, Maryland

Other Access: `www.census.gov`; `gopher.census.gov`.

System: UNIX

Files: census info

Site: `ftp.cic.net`

Country: USA

GMT: −5

Administrative Address: `ftp@cic.net`

Organization: CICNet Inc.; Ann Arbor, Michigan

System: UNIX (SunOS 4.1.3, SPARCstation 10/30)

Comment: Journals are in /pub/nircomm/gopher/e-serials.

Files: Nearly 600 different electronic journals

Site: `ftp.cica.indiana.edu`

Country: USA

GMT: −5

Administrative Address: `ftp-admin@cica.indiana.edu` (Michael Regoli)

Organization: Indiana University Center for Innovative Computing Applications (CICA); Bloomington, Indiana

System: UNIX

Comment: The major MS Windows archive; open 24 hours.

Files: UNIX; MSDOS; NeXT updates; MS Windows 3.x archive (is mirrored around the world, so use those mirrors!)

Site: ftp.cis.ksu.edu

Country: USA

GMT: –6

Administrative Address: ftp@cis.ksu.edu

Organization: Kansas State University Dept. of Computing & Information Sciences (CIS); Manhattan, Kansas

Other Access: E-mail to mailserver@cis.ksu.edu

System: UNIX

Comment: Open 24 hours; 10 maximum connections; directory: /pub/Games

Files: alt.startrek.creative; Angband; CIS; Empire; Frame User network files; FUN; Linux; mirrors; Moria; Netrek; NetBSD; PC games; pictures; projects; Sparcsounds; tech-reports; vtmovies

Site: ftp.cis.nctu.edu.tw

Country: Taiwan

GMT: +10

Administrative Address: gis83504@cis.nctu.edu.tw

Organization: National Chiao Tung University Computer and Information Sciences Dept.; Hsin Chu, Taiwan

System: UNIX

Comment: Directories: /pub/msdos, /pub/win3; support keyword file searching; when files are updated, you can be mailed a notice (check 00README.FUN).

Files: 0packet (several packages); 3D-Object; ASCII-art; CIS (local info); Chinese; Documents (information on different packages, formats (graphics and sound), Chinese UNIX Guide, RFCs, security); Games; Languages (Perl, TCL); MIDI; Mac; MS-DOS (antivirus, arcers, chinese, diskutils, docs, graphics, info, network, sysinfo, utility; MS-Windows; Packages; Pictures; Vendors (JPSoft: 4DOS, 4OS2, 4NT, 4TeX); X11

Site: `ftp.cis.ufl.edu`

Country: USA

GMT: –5

Administrative Address: `consult@cis.ufl.edu`

Organization: University of Florida Dept. of Computer & Information Sciences (CIS); Gainesville, Florida

System: UNIX

Comment: Successor of `bikini.cis.ufl.edu`; directory: /pub/thoth.

Files: boomerang; `comp.simulation`; docs; fed; fishwick; fract; games; gopher; IA; IBM RT BSD patches; IBM RS6000 fixes; Motif; MS-DOS; Netrek for several systems in /pub/thoth/paradise; NTU; pc-conference; pcph; perl; ph; sag; simdigest; smalltalk; smg; spp; succeed; Sun-patches; UF-wormark; UF Multi; UF thesis; UMF pack; xmpeg; xph

Site: `ftp.clarinet.com`

Country: USA

GMT: –8

Organization: ClariNet Communications Corp.

System: UNIX

Files: clarinet info (price info, Internet World, jokebooks, newsbytes, techwire, trnhelp); help (bbs, bbsadmin, bizarro, dilbert, graphics, newusers, tech, worldviews); SF anthology; sources (abe, arbit, dynafeed, nc, netrtf)

Site: ftp.clarkson.edu

Country: USA

GMT: –5

Administrative Address: root@omnigate.clarkson.edu

Organization: Clarkson University; Potsdam, New York

System: UNIX

Comment: Some files moved to barnacle.erc.clarkson.edu; limit of 20 users.

Files: Annotated C++; aviator; broken connections; C++; comp.graphics; CUTCP; docs; encoders; FSF; gsstools; IETF; ISETL; KA9Q; marquis; MS-DOS, NCSA 2.2 TN; net; Novell; Opus BBS; packet drivers; scheme; SimTel CD-ROM; TCL; TeX; UUPC

Site: ftp.cnam.fr

Country: France

GMT: +1

Administrative Address: ftp-admin@cnam.fr

Organization: Conservatoire National des Arts et Metiers (National Conservatory of Arts and Professions, CNAM); Paris

Other Access: www.cnam.fr, web.cnam.fr

System: UNIX

Comment: Uploads to /incoming.

Files: ABU (French texts); Ada; Amiga; Astro (pictures); Atari; Boizumault (sources for the interpretation of Prolog); camlada (teaching excercises in CAML and ADA); CNAM (local literature); CNU (administrative material); Fractals (pictures); Gutenberg; Modulog; Network; RFCs; VMS

Site: ftp.cni.org

Country: USA

GMT: –5

Organization: Coalition for Networked Information

Other Access: Gopher: `gopher.cni.org`;WWW: `www.cni.org/home.html`

System: UNIX

Comment: Telnet: `a.cni.org` (login: brsuser).

Files: ARL; CNIl Current cites; docs: CIMI, compriv, digitlibs, gils, Hugo Nebula, npr, oclc, scita; forums; FYI; LITA; MARBI; net-guides; NII; RFCs; other files in /pub/software

Site: `ftp.cnidr.org`

Organization: CNIDR

System: NeXT (NEXT 1.0)

Comment: Directory: /pub/NIDR.tools.

Files: CNIDR info; K12; Mud; NIDR tools; WAIS sources (freeWAIS)

Site: `ftp.cpsc.ucalgary.ca`

Country: Canada

GMT: –7

Organization: University of Calgary

System: UNIX

Comment: Successor of `cpsc.ucalgary.ca`.

Files: arithmetic coding; astels; blob; brg; charity; CSCW bibliography; Gesture paper; Gnosis; GNU; Graduate Handbook; handwriting recognition; images; KAW94; KSI; papers; RFCs; Sisyphus; Text Compression Corpus; The Reactive Keyboard; Xinterface

Site: `ftp.cpsr.org`

Country: USA

GMT: –8

Organization: Computer Professionals for Social Responsibility

System: UNIX

Other Access: `gopher.cpsr.org`, `wais.cpsr.org`

Files: cong-reform; cpsr; CuD archives; cypherpunks; netinfo; nii; njohnson; nl-kr; sunnyside; taxpayer_assets

Site: `ftp.creaf.com`

Country: USA

GMT: −8

Administrative Address: `ftpadmin@creative.creaf.com`

Organization: Creative Labs; Santa Clara, California

System: UNIX

Comment: *The* source of Soundblaster information; unfortunately, a limited host (max. 8 users), so be patient.

Files: SoundBlaster-related files (patches, press releases, utils for all platforms)

Site: `ftp.crs4.it`

Country: Italy

GMT: +1

Administrative Address: `ftp@crs4.it`

Organization: Centro di Ricerca, Sviluppo e Studi Superiori (Centre for Advanced Studies, Research and Development) Sardegna; Sardinia

Other Access: `www.crs4.it`

System: UNIX

Comment: Dedicated to the MPEG compression standard; read 00README for info.

Files: MPEG files, programs, utilities

Site: `ftp.cs.buffalo.edu`

Country: USA

GMT: −5

Organization: State University of New York at Buffalo; Buffalo, New York

System: UNIX (SunOS 4.1)

Files: 386BSD; caving; chorus-reports; Emacs; GNU; graphics; ham-radio; Linux; Mac; Mule; PC; `rec.radio.amateur`; RFCs; sigart; sneps; Solaris 2.0 docs; sound files; TCP; tech-reports; worm; WWW

Site: `ftp.cs.colorado.edu`

Country: USA

GMT: −7

Administrative Address: `trouble@cs.colorado.edu`

Organization: University of Colorado at Boulder Computer Science Dept.; Boulder, Colorado

System: UNIX (Sun)

Comment: Also available through WAIS; all transfers are logged.

Files: energy shootout; Esperanto; faces; Ghostscript; HPSC; Netfind sources; standards; tech-reports; Texas92; Vis

Site: `ftp.cs.cuhk.hk`

Country: Hong Kong

GMT: +9

Administrative Address: `ftp@cs.cuhk.hk`

Organization: Chinese University of Hong Kong Computer Science Dept.

System: UNIX

Comment: Available through `www.cuhk.hk`: University info, Housing Design Project, CSC publications, photos of the campus and Hong Kong; compress and tar on the fly.

Files: CICA; EC; FreeBSD; GNU; graphics; Linux; MS-DOS (EmTeX); neuro; SimTel; Slackware; SLS; TCL; tech-reports; X11R6; X-contrib

Site: `ftp.cs.pdx.edu`

Country: USA

GMT: –8

Administrative Address: `ftp-admin@cs.pdx.edu`

Organization: Portland State University Computer Science Dept.; Portland, Oregon

System: UNIX

Comment: Max. 30 users; successor of `potemkin.cs.pdx.edu`.

Files: aber (MUD); blackadder; csqr; Dylan; Elvis; flamingos; frp; games; GNU; Ileaf; League for programming freedom; LPMUD; music; Parker Lewis archive; people; perl; politics; Pratchett; RFCs; Sun-patches; utek; yama

Site: `ftp.cs.toronto.edu`

Country: Canada

GMT: –5

Organization: University of Toronto; Toronto, Ontario

System: UNIX

Files: ailist; CA domain reg. forms; C-News; cogrob; combin; coopis; darwin; dgp; dkbs; dt; dvix; emv; ftpd; Jove; mirror of `nic.ddn.mil`; molbio; NeXT; pathalias; PC; reports; scheme; SGI; sigview; SunOS SLIP; sun-spots; S/SL; TeX; tff; tron; UofT BIND; usenet; VIS; X11R4; X11R5 xerion; zen; zmailer

Site: `ftp.cs.ualberta.ca`

Country: Canada

GMT: –7

Organization: University of Alberta Computer Science Dept.; Edmonton, Alberta

System: UNIX

Files: AI-GI-VI94; ARnet; cssa; dbms; DCE12; Enterprise; exodus; geompack; gno; gradinfo; graphics; Internship; kube; Mizar; Mizar-MSE; narrow; oolog; rasit; robotics; scsiping; smillie; spreadsheet; tartar; tech-reports; theorist;

Site: `ftp.cs.ubc.ca`

Country: Canada

GMT: –8

Administrative Address: `ftp-admin@cs.ubc.ca`

Organization: University of Britsh Columbia Computer Science Dept.; Vancouver, British Columbia

System: UNIX

Comment: Directories: /pub/pickup/spline, /pub/local/src/snacc; the file 'arrangement' contains an index of the directories; problems with mirror1 and mirror3 directories.

Files: archive (mirrors): Apollo, doc (RFCs), GNU, Mac, Sun, UNIX; ca-domain; cdnnet; cicsr; example images and data files; graphics bibliography in BiBTeX format; images; mirrors: Linux (`tsx-11.mit.edu`, nightly), NeXT (`sonata.cc.purdue.edu`, nightly), djgpp (`ftp.clarkson.edu`, nightly), GNU (`prep.ai.mit.edu`, nightly), Mach (`mach.cs.cmu.edu`, weekly), export.lcs.mit.edu (X-contrib, nightly), 386BSD (mirrored ag-ate.berkeley.edu, weekly), EFF (`ftp.eff.org`, nightly), BSD-sources (`ftp.uu.net`, weekly), canarie (`unbmvs1.csd.unb.ca`, daily), EmTeX (`ftp.cs.ruu.nl`, weekly), IETF (`ftp.wustl.edu`, daily), internet drafts (`ftp.wustl.edu`, daily), MS-DOS (`ftp.wustl.edu`, daily), ndtl (`hsdndev.harvard.edu`, daily), RFCs (`venera.isi.edu`, daily), SNMP-MIBs (`ftp.3com.com` and `venera.isi.edu`, daily); PCpickup; raster; Raven; security; snacc; Sunfixes; Tourism in British Columbia (Hypercard stack); UBC crest bitmaps; UBC CS tech-reports; UBC UNIX Users Group; vista (software for computer vision research); X11R6

Site: `ftp.cs.widener.edu`

Country: USA

GMT: –5

Administrative Address: `ftp-manager@cs.widener.edu`

Organization: Widener University; Chester, Pennsylvania

System: UNIX (SunOS 4.1)

Comment: directory: pub/zen

Files: Simpsons archive, nixpub listing, Archie clients (home of Kehoe's C client); Zen and the Art of the Internet

Site: `ftp.cs.wisc.edu`

Country: USA

GMT: –6

Administrative Address: `ftp@cs.wisc.edu`

Organization: University of Wisconsin Computer Science Dept.; Madison, Wisconsin

System: UNIX

Comment: Directories: /exodus, /pub/ultimate; server can (de)compress, tar files and directories; RoadMap contains list of directories; Problem: I/O error on network device.

Files: AIX; CDIFF; computer-vision; condor; connectivity table; coral; cpo dataset; Exodus; ghost; HP; larry; lists; machine learning; markhill; networks; novell; par-distr-sys; spim; spimsal; tech-reports; TeX; TeX for Tom; Ultimate Frisbee files; UW; warts; wisc; wwt; X; xunet

Site: `ftp.cs.wits.ac.za`

Country: South Africa

GMT: 0

Organization: University of Witwatersrand Computer Science Dept.; Witwatersrand, South Africa

System: UNIX

Comment: Descriptive ls/dir command, very nice.

Files: FAQs (Africa, Wine); general (distributions, thesis, tech-reports); images (gif, jpg, mpeg, obj for X3D); Linux (games, info, packages, raytracing, sound, utils, X11); MS-DOS (arcers, comm, games, mouse, network, proglang, utils, virus, windows); MS-Windows, MS-Windows NT (compress, graphics); UNIX (applications, audio, benchmark, bin, games, graphics, lang, network, postscript, research, sgb, shells, Sun, SGI, TeX, utils)

Site: `ftp.csd.uch.gr`

Country: Greece

GMT: +2

Administrative Address: `postmaster@csd.uch.gr`

Organization: University of Crete Computer Science Department; Heraklion, Crete

System: UNIX (SunOS 4.1)

Comment: Max. 5 foreign users; read /README for special features; max. allocated bandwidth varies.

Files: abacus; antivirus; archie; compressors; CSD: papers, tech-reports; GNU; Greek fonts—printing/editing sw; graphics; images; locally developed material, IRC; Linux; Mac; Mach; network; NeWS; NFS; papers; Parix; postgres; postscript; posybl; RFCs; Sun; UNIX; UNIX-benchmarks; vi-stuff; TeX; WWW; X11

Site: `ftp.cu.nih.gov`

Country: USA

GMT: −5

Organization: US National Institute of Health

Files: US Government info files

Site: `ftp.cuhk.hk`

Country: Hong Kong

GMT: +9

Administrative Address: ftp-admin@ftp.cuhk.hk

Organization: Chinese University of Hong Kong, CSC

System: UNIX

Comment: available through www.cuhk.hk: University info, Housing Design Project, CSC publications, photos of the campus and Hong Kong; compress and tar on the fly; max. 60 users.

Files: chinese newchars; cuhk; doc; events; gopher; Mac; mov; msc; info; netinfo; news; packetdrivers; PC; ph; pictures; POP; proceedings; RFCs; Sun-fixes; UNIX; viz; WAIS; WWW

Site: ftp.cwru.edu

Country: USA

GMT: –5

Organization: Case Western Reserve University; Cleveland, Ohio

System: UNIX

Files: US Supreme Court rulings

Site: ftp.cyf-kr.edu.pl

Country: Poland

GMT: +1

Administrative Address: yskarock@cyf-kr.edu.pl
(Piotr Karocki)

Organization: CYFRONET Academic Computer Center; Cracow, Poland

System: UNIX (Convex C120)

Comment: Max. 50 users; some directories mounted from other machines.

Files: agh (mounted, including GIFs in /agh/reserve/gifs); Cyfronet (local info); ecuc94 (European Convex Users Conference); ifuj (mounted); lfs (mounted); mirrors: AMI info (american.mega-trends.com), Comm programs (boombox.micro.umn.edu:/pub/pc),

GNU, JPG viewers (`ftp.portal.com`), MS-DOS (`oak.oakland.edu` via `ftp.switch.ch`), MS-Windows (`ftp.cica.indiana.edu:/pub/win3` via `ftp.switch.ch`), NCSA Telnet (`ftp.ncsa.uiuc.edu:/PC/Tel-net`), RFCs, UNIX-arcers (`garbo.uwasa.fi:/unix/arcers`), X11R5, X contrib (`ftp.x.org:/contrib`); netinfo (mostly out-dated); TeXmex; UNIX

Site: `ftp.dartmouth.edu`

Country: USA

GMT: –5

Administrative Address: `ftp@ftp.dartmouth.edu`, `postmaster@darthmouth.edu`

Organization: Dartmouth College; Hanover, New Hampshire

Other Access: `ftpmail@ftp.dartmouth.edu`

System: UNIX

Comment: Host name and user ID are logged for transfers.

Files: ATT6300+; Dante; Dartmouth material (rn; mail; etc.); Exceptions; GNUplot; Hyperbooks; ICMA library; LLTI-IALL; Mac; security; SOP

Site: `ftp.dcs.gla.ac.uk`

Country: UK

GMT: 0

Administrative Address: `support@dcs.gla.ac.uk`

Organization: University of Glasgow Computer Science Dept.; Glasgow, Scotland

System: UNIX

Other Access: `gopher.dcs.gla.ac.uk` and `www.dcs.gla.ac.uk`.

Comment: Access is allowed all day.

Files: actress; Ansible; Avalanche; BCS; fide; flare; gist; glasgow-fp; haskell; hug94; iii; imis; Linux; Mac; merill; mail; NASA; news; pj-lester book; recipes; src; SF archives; theory; triangle; types

Site: `ftp.demon.co.uk`

Country: UK

GMT: 0

Administrative Address: `amn@ubik.demon.co.uk` (Anthony M. Naggs, antivirus section)

Organization: Demon Internet

System: UNIX

Comment: Directory: /ibmpc; has a mail server: `mxserver@ubik.demon.co.uk` for the antivirus section.

Files: 4.3BSD; ACCU (/pub/cug); Amiga; Antivirus (comprehensive across all platforms); Archimedes; Atari; books; commercial demos; CP/M; CUG; Dialup IP, PGP and Usenet software; doc; games; GNU; ham-radio; KA9Q; images; Mac; mail; MS-DOS (Simtel 20); news; NetBSD (mirror of sun-lamp.cs.berkeley.edu); NeXt; NT; OS/2; perl; PGP; pick; PPP; roundhill; SCO; SLIP; Sun; trumphurst; UNIX; Xenix; XWindows; XFree86 (mirror from `ftp.xfree86.org`)

Site: `ftp.diku.dk`

Country: Denmark

GMT: +1

Administrative Address: `ftpadm@ftp.diku.dk`

Organization: University of Copenhagen Computer Science Dept.; Copenhagen

System: UNIX

Comment: Open 24 hours; please restrict transfers of large amounts of data to outside normal working hours, i.e. before 9 AM and after 5 PM MET; several archives moved to `ftp.denet.dk`.

Files: DIKU; elisp-archive; GNU; HP UX patches; Linux; MIB; Mirrors of the guitar archive; networking; news.answers; programming languages; Sun fixes

Site: `ftp.doc.ic.ac.uk`

Country: UK

GMT: 0

Administrative Address: `wizards@doc.ic.ac.uk`

Organization: Imperial College of Science, Technology and Medicine, Dept. of Computing, SunSITE Northern Europe; London

Other Access: `ftpmail@doc.ic.ac.uk`

System: UNIX (Solaris 2.3, SparcServer 1000, 6 CPUs, 30Gb diskspace)

Comment: Max. 300 users; extra features include: ls -sf:package (searches for 'package').

Files: Aminet; biology; faces; geology; GNU; IAFA-SITEINFO; info; literary; media; mirrors: MS-DOS programs from the Simtel Software Repository (/pub/packages/simtel20), MS-DOS games from `ftp.uml.edu` (/computing/systems/ibmpc/msdos-games/Games), MS-Windows from `ftp.cica.indiana.edu`; politics; RFCs; Sun; TeX from `ftp.tex.ac.uk`; UKUUG; UNIX; Usenet; weather

Site: `ftp.earn.net`

Country: France

GMT: +1

Administrative Address: `ftpadmin@earn.net`

Organization: European Academic Research Network (EARN)

Other Access: `gopher.earn.net`; gophermail through `gopher@earn.net` (send mail with `help` for instructions)

System: UNIX

Comment: Server can compress and tar.

Files: cnre; docs; earnest; general EARN info; gophermail; listserv archives; nethelp; networking info; networking services; nsc; tools

Site: `ftp.edu.tw`

Country: Taiwan

GMT: +8

Administrative Address: `ftp-adm@nctuccca.edu.tw` (ftp administration), `hch@nctuccca.edu.tw` (Chih-Hsien Huang), `james@nctuccca.edu.tw` (James Huang), `postmaster@nctuc-cca.edu.tw` (system administration),

Organization: Campus Computer Communication Association, National Chiao Tung University

Other Access: `ftpmail@ftp.edu.tw` (local archive only)

System: UNIX (SunOS 4.1.3, Sun SPARC 10 Model 51)

Comment: Mirrors of over 100 sites; largest site in Asia; 13GB used; overseas users welcome; max. 200 users; server supports on-the-fly g(un)zip; FSP available via port 21; Author FTP accounts available.

Files: Aminet; BSD; Chinese Apps; Computing Languages; E-Text; ftp-list (documents/networking/guides/ftp-list); Images; GNU; Linux; MaasInfo files (documents/Internet/Maasinfo); Mac; mirrors: `garbo.uwasa.fi` (/PC/garbo), `ftp.uml.edu` (/Ulowell/msdos), `ftp.cica.indiana.edu`, Simtel Software Repository (/pub/mirrors/msdos); MS-DOS; MS-Windows; NCSA Apps; NCTU; Netlib; Next; OS/2; Packages; Sound; Statlib; UNIX; Usenet; Vendorware; VLSI; X-Windows; XFree86 (mirror from `ftp.xfree86.org`)

Site: `ftp.ee.lbl.gov`

Country: USA

GMT: −8

Organization: Lawrence Berkeley Laboratory; Berkeley, California

Files: graphics related files and programs; pbmplus; Rayshade data files

Site: ftp.ee.und.ac.za

Country: South Africa

GMT: 0

Administrative Address: ftp@ftp.ee.und.ac.za

Organization: University of Natal at Durban Electrical Engineering Dept.; Durban, South Africa

System: UNIX

Comment: Transfers are logged; descriptive ls/dir command.

Files: Alternet SA; archiving; bible; crypto; docs; f2c; Internet info (drafts, netinfo, RFCs); ioccc (International Obfuscated C Code Competition); mail; MS-DOS (mostly networking related); Novell; optics; Plan9 man; security; superconductivity; TeX; time; UniNet ZA; UNIX; usenet news; WAIS

Site: ftp.eff.org

Country: USA

GMT: –5

Organization: Electronic Frontier Foundation (EFF)

System: UNIX

Files: Computer Underground Digest (CuD) archives; EFF-related materials; Internet resource guide; network info

Site: ftp.elka.pw.edu.pl

Country: Poland

GMT: +1

Organization: Technical University of Warsaw Electrical Engineering Dept.; Warsaw

System: UNIX (System V Release 4.0)

Files: docs; DOS (clipper, doc, dos_unix, dpmi, gnu, gopher, graph, gs, html, ka91, novell, pcbridge, pcroute, pegasus, perl, pkt, tcp, telnet.win, TeX, waterloo, windows, wintcp, xapeal); ELKA;

FAQs; IAPW; ISO; RFCs; UNIX (database, DTP, GNU, gopher, graphics, Ks, Linux, mail, network, news, programming, publishing, shells, TeX, WWW, X11R5

Site: `ftp.elvis.msk.su`

Country: Russia

GMT: +2

Administrative Address: `ftpman@elvis.msk.su`

Organization: ELVIS+, Co.

Other Access: `mailserv@elvis.msk.su`; `ftpmail@elvis.msk.su` (send `help`)

Files: apple; books; databases; dos; editirs; FAQ; faxgate; FreeBSD; galaxy; games; gnu; graphics; images; infosystems; multimedia; network; news; relcom; rfc; security; sun; unix; usenet; vendors; windows; X11

Site: `ftp.estec.esa.nl`

Country: The Netherlands

GMT: 0

Organization: European Space Agency (ESA); Noordwijk, Netherlands

System: UNIX

Files: CODE; csds; ers; esbtc; ESIS (European Science Information System) data files including current ESA science program project files (CLUSTER, ISO, POEM etc); gp; network files and ESA administrative documents; ntp; opex; piers; poem; public relations documents + PC/MAC files; soho; TOPSIM; TST; WDP; wm; xe; ypa

Site: `ftp.etext.org`

Country: USA

GMT: −5

Administrative Address: `ftp@etext.org`, `ftp@etext.archive.umich.edu`

Organization: Private site.

Other Access: `gopher.etext.org`, `www.etext.org`

System: UNIX (SunOS 4.1.3, SPARCstation IPX)

Comment: Alternative politics, zines, fiction, poetry; 32Mb RAM; 1.5GB disk.

Files: Text files and electronic journals: Computer Underground Digest (CuD) archives, other zines (electronic magazines)

Site: `ftp.eu.net`

Country: Netherlands

GMT: +1

Administrative Address: `ftp@eu.net`, `info-admin@eu.net`

Organization: EUNet European Backbone; Amsterdam

Comment: Successor of `mcsun.eu.net` as central European archive; the file FULLINDEX contains a listing of all files.

Files: GNU; graphics; mail; misc network; znews; programming; ripe; text proc utils; UUmap; windows; security; eurographics; bootstrap; some archives of Usenet groups

Site: `ftp.eunet.cz`

Country: Czech Republic

GMT: +1

Administrative Address: `archive-admin@eunet.cz`

Organization: EUNet Czechoslavakia (CZ)

System: UNIX

Comment: Transfers are logged; max. 10 users.

Files: Big Dummy's Guide to the Internet; cdrom; CERT; GNU; Guidebooks; Kermit; MERIT; network; NIC; Novell; RIPE; security; SURANet info; Telnet; Web/WWW; Winsock; X11

Site: `ftp.eunet.sk`

Country: Slovakia

GMT: +1

Administrative Address: `info@slovakia.eu.net`

Organization: EUNet Slovakia (SK), Bratislava

System: UNIX

Comment: Access is logged; max. 256 users; also available through Gopher, WWW and FSP (2001); over 700MB of software.

Files: CD-ROM (NLUUG CD-ROM: best public SW); EUNet SK; Internet Talk Radio; Slackware; X11R6

Site: `ftp.fct.unl.pt`

Country: Portugal

GMT: 0

Administrative Address: `admin@fct.unl.pt`

System: UNIX

Comment: Server supports compression on the fly.

Files: adm; AIX; Atari; DEC; di; docs; eps; FCT; FCT airphotos; games; GNU; humor; languages; Linux; lpnmr; Mac; MS-DOS; MS-Windows; mw; net; news; NeXT; packages; people; Portugal; px; research; sys; tao-pub; TeX; util; weather; X; zen-pub

Site: `ftp.fedworld.gov`

Country: USA

GMT: −5

Administrative Address: `kroyer@fedworld.gov`

Organization: FedWorld

System: PC fileserver (Novell Netware)

Comment: Access is read-only; in MAIN you will find the file ALLFILES; ⋆.LST files give info about directories; max. 20 minutes; also through BBS at 703-321-8020 (USA).

Files: a-dr-cmt; cals; cim; comments; commerce; ctn; d-rule; healthact; healthrpt; jobs; media; nafta; nii; npr; ntis; ota-pres; p-dr-cmt; patent; results; ruleinfo; s-cmts; s-draft; sat-images; sca; teltrend; whitehouse

Site: `ftp.fee.vutbr.cz`

Country: Czech Republic

GMT: +1

Administrative Address: `FTP-ADM@fee.vutbr.cz`

Organization: Technical University of Brno Faculty of Electrical Engineering and Computer Science; Brno, Czech Republic

System: UNIX

Comment: Max. 10 users; several mirrors: `garbo.uwasa.fi`, Simtel Software Repository (temporarily removed) and others.

Files: bible; books; docs; GNU; Hyper-G; languages; MS-DOS (Borland, Buttonware, games, Garbo, McAfee, Novell, Pmail, Qdeck, Share, Simtel, TCP/IP); networking (mirror from `ftp.uu.net/networking`: AppleTalk, applic, archival, athena, cisco, fax, gopher, ident, info-service, IP, isis, Lynx, mail, news, OSI, RPC, serial, terms, UUCP, uumap, wais, WWW, x25); sources; systems (FreeBSD, Linux, mach, NetBSD, SCO, Unixware); usenet (`comp.sources.(d,games,misc, postscript,unix,x)`); X; X11; X11R5; X11R6; XFree86 (mirror from `ftp.xfree86.org`)

Site: `ftp.fenk.wau.nl`

Country: Netherlands

GMT: +1

Administrative Address: `service@fenk.wau.nl`

Organization: Landbouw Universiteit Wageningen (Wageningen Agricultural University) Physical & Colloid Chemistry Dept.; Wageningen, Netherlands

System: UNIX

Comment: Transfers are logged; Gopher: `ftp.fenk.wau.nl`; max. 60 users.

Files: International Association of Colloid and Interface (IACI) scientists info; mirrors: `info-mac.stanford.edu`, jagubox (Mac); Linux (Slackware); Molecular Modelling progs bases on the Scheutjens-Fleer theory; pceudora; popper; Simula/simed; Sun-fixes; verman

Site: `ftp.fh-wolfenbuettel.de`

Country: Germany

GMT: +1

Administrative Address: `ftp-admin@fh-wolfenbuettel.de`

Organization: Fachhochschule Wolfenbuettel (Wolfenbuettel Polytechnical Institute); Wolfenbuettel, Germany

System: UNIX

Files: alliance; archiver; Atari; audio; doc (Filter, Lyrics, O'Reilly, Posix, SCSI); games; gametool; ghostscript; graphics; Khoros; in-fosys; languages; Linux (Linus, Slackware, SLS, sunsite.unc.edu, tsx-11.mit.edu); LPMUD; lyrics; magazine; MS-DOS; nethack; Netrek; network; Oberon; parallel; shells; Simulation; Sun; TeX; Terminal; TinyMUD; tools; UNIX (games, PVM); WWW-FHWF; X11 (contrib, misc and more misc)

Site: `ftp.fie.com`

Country: USA

GMT: −5

Organization: Federal Information Exchange, Inc.

Other Access: `www.fie.com`

System: UNIX

Comment: Also accessible through Telnet to the same system; index in FILE.LIST; subdirectories per agency; probably also accessible through the WWW.

Files: AFR; AGR; DOE; FAA; MIN; MOLIS; NAS; ONR

Site: ftp.ftp.com

Country: USA

GMT: –5

Organization: FTP Software

System: UNIX

Comment: Official source of FTP software (DOS/Windows TCP/IP utilities).

Files: FTP info & apps; FTPNUZ (/support/pubdom); packet drivers; UNIX software; other network related programs

Site: ftp.fu-berlin.de

Country: Germany

GMT: +1

Administrative Address: ftp-adm@fu-berlin.de

Organization: Freie Universitaet Berlin (Free University of Berlin); Berlin, Germany

System: UNIX (IRIX 5.2)

Comment: Open 24 hours; max. 300 users; supports on-the-fly (de)compression, g(un)zipping, and tarring of directories.

Files: Amiga; Atari; Deutsche Anonyme FTP-Server List; Documents: FAQs, FYI, RFCs, etc.; ftp-sites; GATeway Orientierungs Ratgeber (gator); maps; MS-DOS: 4DOS, Telix, kermit, graphics, GNUish, mags, networks, emTeX; Official FTP

Site: ftp.funet.fi

Country: Finland

GMT: +2

Administrative Address: problems@ftp.funet.fi, msdos-adm@nic.funet.fi, msdos1@nic.funet.fi (Petri Hartoma)

Organization: Finland Academic & Research Network (FUNET) NIC; Espoo, Finland

System: UNIX

Comment: Transfers are logged with host name and whatever you entered for password; max. 100 users; retrieval of top-level README possible before logon; read README.FILETYPES for information on the different file types.

Files: Amiga; Astro; Atari; cae; CBM; cryptography; Computer Underground Digest (CuD) archives; csc; culture; docs; dx; FUNET; GNU; graphics; ham-radio; IRC clients, GIFs of IRC and Relay people: pub/pics/gif/pics/people/misc; kermit; languages; lyhty; Mac; Mach; microprocs; Minix; MS-DOS; netinfo; networking; NeXT; OS/2; pictures; sci; security docs and apps; Simtel20 mirror (/pub/msdos/SimTel-mirror); Sony NeWS OS software; sounds; sports; standards; Tao; UNIX; VM; VMS; Windows NT; X11; XFree86 (mirror from ftp.xfree86.org under consideration)

Site: ftp.germany.eu.net

Country: Germany

GMT: +1

Administrative Address: archive-admin@germany.eu.net (Ingo Dressler), osadm@ftp.germany.eu.net (Holger Muenx, MS-DOS section)

Organization: German EUnet backbone; Dortmund, Germany

Other Access: archive-server@germany.eu.net, mail-server@germany.eu.net

System: UNIX

Comment: Open 24 hours; Gopher access: gopher.germany.eu.net 70; 7Gb; WWW access: http:www.germany.eu.net 80; FSP access via port 2001; directories: /pub, /shop (commercial software and data), /itr (Internet Talk Radio: for EUnet customers only).

Files: 386BSD; Amiga; archiver; Atari; benchmark; CT-Magazin; GNU; IX-Magazin; Linux; mail; Motif; MS-DOS; Network docs; news; newsarchive; OS/2; programming; RFCs; RIPE; sources and binaries for various systems; X11R5 (official server)

Site: ftp.gsfc.nasa.gov

Country: USA

GMT: –5

Administrative Address: postmaster@gsfc.nasa.gov

Organization: NASA—Goddard Space Flight Center, Network Support Group for Large Systems of the Center-wide Networking Environment; Greenbelt, Maryland

System: UNIX

Comment: United States Government computer system: Un-authorized access to this system is a FEDERAL OFFENSE; there are no comet pictures here; files from toybox in directory TOY-BOX, from gsfc in GSFC; dftsrv.gsfc.nasa.gov is obsolete.

Files: ALEX; ccb; cne; email-info; help-files; images; info-servers; internet; IP; Mac; MacSecure anti-virus pkg; mail; nameserver; se-curity; Sun: dist, fixes, misc; tools; Ultrix; UNIX; VMS; X

Site: ftp.halcyon.com

Country: USA

GMT: –8

Administrative Address: ralphs@halcyon.com (Ralph Simms)

Organization: Northwest NEXUS Inc.; Bellevue, Washington

Other Access: E-mail to archive-server@halcyon.com, in text of message put help; FSP; anonymous UUCP through remote.hal-cyon.com.

System: UNIX

Comment: Specializing in Waffle, Off-line mail/news-readers etc.; read 00-README.

Files: activism; `alt.missing-kids.gifs`; batpower; Computer Underground Digest (CuD) archives; esdl; Eudora; faf; Fidonet; FWDP; Go; II; ITR; jargon; mirrors (etext: `mrcnext.cso.uiuc.edu`, Linux); North West Nexus; Pink Floyd; Raosoft; recipes; RKBA; seabird; SLIP; Supra; Tidbits; tiskwin; Waffle; wuarchive

Site: `ftp.health.org`

Country: USA

System: UNIX (Linux)

Files: DOS, MAC, UNIX and WP text files relating to all kinds of health issues (alcoholism, child abuse, drugs, etc.)

Site: `ftp.ibp.fr`

Country: France

GMT: +1

Administrative Address: `ftp@ftp.ibp.fr`

Organization: University Pierre et Marie Curie—MASI Lab., Paris, Centre National de la Recherche Scientifique (National Center for Scientific Research, CNRS), Institut Blaise Pascal (Blaise Pascal Institute, IBP)

System: UNIX

Comment: Max. 100 users; index files new-last-month, new-this-week; transfers are logged.

Files: Annex; AppleTalk; CERT; distributed_systems; docs; emacs; faces; FreeBSD; gnat; GNU; IBP info; IFIP; iman; Linux; Mac; Mach; meteo; MS-DOS; NetBSD; parallel; RFCs; sfca95; Sun; tcl; TeX; UNIX; vsta; Windows3; WWW

Site: `ftp.iclnet.org`

Country: USA

GMT: −8

Administrative Address: `root@iclnet93.iclnet.org`

Organization: Institute for Christian Leadership

System: UNIX

Files: astronomy; bench; calculators; cccoalition; cdrom; cisco; clm; cygnus; database; docs; facdialogue; games; GNU; graphics; InterVarsity; mail; math; multimedia; music; network; news; NeWS; postscript; programming; rainet; resources; RFCs; security; shells; simulation; Solaris; Sun; SunOS-patches; sysadmin; text; UCB; X11; XView

Site: ftp.ics.uci.edu

Country: USA

GMT: −8

Organization: University of California at Irvine Information & Computer Science Dept. (ICI); Irvine, California

System: UNIX

Comment: Directory: /mrose/isode-snmpV2; server can tar and (de)compress; transfers are logged.

Files: anime; answer-garden; arcadia; atm; cadlab; cheers; classweb-code; comp.protocols.{iso,x400}; cyberspace; dbox; dos-virus; GNU; heimdahl; honig; ibl; ifip; internet; isode-snmpV2; Mac; machine-learning; mentoring-workshop; mh; ml-list; perfect hash function gen.; Protoize/Unprotoize; rec.games.frp; RFCs; soc.feminism; Sun; sureality; taketani; tcas; TeX; Think C; UNIX; usenet; volper-katz; Web-to-C; wang

Site: ftp.iglou.com

Country: USA

GMT: −5

Administrative Address: postmaster@iglou.com

Organization: IgLou Internet Services

System: UNIX

Comment: The major repository of Shoemaker-Levy 9 images in comet/images; DOOM patches; modem information.

Files: FAQs; IgLou info; Linux; Mac; mirrors: Doom: `infant2.`
`sphs.indiana.edu`, MS-DOS games: `ftp.uml.edu`, MS-Windows:
`ftp.cica.indiana.edu`; modem; Shoemaker-Levy 9 (SL9)
images; slip; Uninet

Site: `ftp.iitb.ernet.in`

Country: India

GMT: +5:30

Administrative Address: `postmaster@iitb.ernet.in`,
`vijay@iitb.ernet.in` (Vijay Talati)

Organization: Indian Institute of Technology (IIT)—Bombay

Other Access: `ftpmail@iitb.ernet.in` (Indian sites only)

System: UNIX (SunOs 4.1.1)

Comment: Would be too slow for users outside India.

Files: FAQs; imaging software; networking; Public domain material of interest to IITs and other Indian sites; RFCs; UNIX;
X11R6; xutils

Site: `ftp.informatik.rwth-aachen.de`

Country: Germany

GMT: +1

Administrative Address: `ftpadm@informatik.rwth-aachen.de`

Organization: RWTH Aachen Rechnersbetrieb Informatik
(Computer Science Dept. Computer Center), Aachen

System: UNIX

Comment: Open 24 hours.

Files: Amiga; Atari; Bible; GNU; graphics; GRAS
(/pub/unix/GRAS); mail+news; MS-DOS; RFCs; Simtel mirror
(/pub/simtel: archives, Info-MAC, misc, MS-DOS, UNIX-C,
PC-blue, CP/M from another campus host (`reze-2.rz.rwth-`
`aachen.de`); programming; PROGRES Sun 4 (/pub/unix/PRO-
GRES); sounds; TeX; UNIX; X11

Site: `ftp.informatik.uni-rostock.de`

Country: Germany

GMT: +1

Administrative Address: `ftpadm@informatik.uni-rostock.de`

Organization: Universitaet Rostock (Rostock University), Rostock

System: UNIX

Comment: Restrict working day access outside 08:00–16:00 local time; uploads to incoming/; several new-{month} index files.

Files: Amiga; antivirus; compiler; database; doc; GNU; graphics; knowledge; Linux; magazine; Maple; MS-DOS games, patches etc.; MUD-related files (Galaxy client); network; OS/2; PC; RFCs; simulation; text; UNIX; utils; Windows; X11

Site: `ftp.intel.com`

Country: USA

GMT: −6

Organization: Intel Corp.

System: UNIX

Files: benchmarks; dmtf; EtherExpress; i960; Intel Architecture Labs (IAL); ipg; isv; landesk; mcs51; mcs96; neural; papers; pld_fpga; rmx; support; tis; x86

Site: `ftp.internic.net`

Country: USA

Administrative Address: `admin@internic.net`, `info@internic.net`

Organization: Internet NIC—Directory and Database Services by AT&T and the NSF

Comment: Open 24 hours; lengthy disclaimer by AT&T.

Files: IETF; IESG; Internet-drafts; RFC; InterNIC info; resource databases (plus files from ftp.nisc.sri.com)

Site: `ftp.irisa.fr`

Country: France

GMT: +1

Administrative Address: `ftpmaint@irisa.fr`

Organization: Institute de Recherche en Informatique et Systemes Aleatoires (IRISA, INRIA/CNRS, Universite de Rennes I/Insa de Rennes); Rennes, Brittany

System: UNIX

Comment: Open 24 hours; disclaimer.

Files: AFUU-BPL; bench; C++; com; compress; docs; Frame-Maker; games; GNUplot; graphics; m-emac; micro-spell; mirrors; mp; mtools; Postscript; Sather; siames; tcsh; tech-reports; VT100; X11

Site: `ftp.jvnc.net`

Country: USA

GMT: –5

Administrative Address: `root@nisc.jvnc.net,`
`root@r2d2.jvnc.net`

Organization: John von Neumann Network Information Center; Princeton, New Jersey

System: UNIX

Comment: Directory: /jvncnet-packages/nocol.

Files: beta; dialin-tiger; docs; JvNC Net info; k12; Mac; mail-list; Meaddata; Meckler; megabytes; MS-DOS; network info; NO-COL (NOC On Line); packages; RFCs; site-reps; traffic-reports; UNIX

Site: ftp.kcl.ac.uk

Country: UK

GMT: 0

Organization: King's College, London, Computer Center

System: VAX/VMS running MadGoat/OpenVMS

Comment: default directory: ANONYMOUS_ROOT:[000000]

Files: alarm; archie; bison; boss; bulletin; cmu-tcpip; cproto; date-book; deliver; dism32; dumper32; dx; elvis; emacs; etek; ether-mon; fdvd; fidogate; fileutils; finger; flex; flist; fts; games; gas; gawk; gifsixel; GNU; GNUchess; GNUplot; gopher; hassle; hpgl2ps; hytelnet; irc; iupop; jed; juicer; kermit; laser; ldb; lex; lynx; lzw; madgoat; make; mftu; micro-support; mosaic; mpeg; mx; name-router; nanny; news; nsquery; patch_diff; pbmplus; pcx; perf_meter; perl; pgp; psutils; que_mon; rcs; rz/sz; scanuaf; sed; setpql; sixel_print; spell; sunclock; swim; swing; tcl; tcsh; tex-lsedit; tscon; twm; vaxtrek; vds; vi; vitpu; vmstpc; vms_share; vnews; watcher; X11; XDVI; XFIG; XFORECAST; XSCOPE; XSHARE; XTERM; XV; XVIEWGL; XWINDOWS; YACC; zen-ternet; zip/unzip; zmodem; zoo

Site: ftp.law.cornell.edu

Country: USA

GMT: –5

Administrative Address: ftpmaster@ftp.law.cornell.edu

Organization: Cornell University Law School, Legal Informa-tion Institute (LII); Ithaca, New York

System: UNIX

Comment: Directory: /pub/LII/Cello, pub/LII/Directory, pub/Internet.

Files: Cello (WWW client for MS-Windows); CILP; Folio Views version of Legal Academia; humor; Internet; Jim Milles Internet Training files; listservs; TRI

Site: `ftp.luth.se`

Country: Sweden

GMT: +1

Administrative Address: `ftp@ludd.luth.se`

Organization: University of Lulee; Lulee, Sweden

System: UNIX

Comment: Top archive of Europe; use `dir` or `ls -Fl` for faster directory listing; read README and README.uploads; transfers are logged.

Files: 386bsd; infosystems; Amiga (Aminet); FAQs; Linux; mods; OS/2; songs (from `ftp.sdsu.edu`); X11; X11-contrib

Site: `ftp.lysator.liu.se`

Country: Sweden

GMT: +1

Administrative Address: `ftp@lysator.liu.se`

Organization: Linkoping University, Lysator ACS; Linkoping, Sweden

Other Access: `ftpserv@lysator.liu.se` with `help` in the body

System: UNIX

Comment: Server has special file access features: see /README.

Files: abc1600; Amiga; Apollo; archivers; asl; aviation; Blake 7; comics; comm; daemons; doc; dynix; emacs; emulators; europa; faces; games; gardening; geography; GNU; gopher; hp28; hp48; ident; IRC; kiwi; languages; libraries; Linux; LPF; LPMUD; Lysator; LysKOM; magick; mail; marine mammals; mgr; mods; MS-DOS; net; news; NYS; PC Eudora; pdp10; Postgres; Prime/PRIMOS; religion; rmt; rom; runeberg; science fiction; sgml; shell; solutions; Sun; Sunview; SvenskMUD; texts; Windows NT; WWW; X11

Site: `ftp.marist.edu`

Country: USA

Organization: Marist College; Poughkeepsie, NY

System: MUSIC/SP

Comment: No password needed.

Files: authors; Bush; Clinton; Gutenberg; Netmonth; Perot; REPUB-L; SAS-L; VM-UTIL

Site: `ftp.math.okstate.edu`

Country: USA

GMT: –6

Organization: Oklahoma State University

Files: MUDS: clients, FAQ etc.

Site: `ftp.math.uni-hamburg.de`

Country: Germany

GMT: +1

Administrative Address: `ftpadm@math.uni-hamburg.de`

Organization: University of Hamburg Math Dept.; Hamburg, Germany

System: UNIX (AIX 3.2, IBM RS6000)

Comment: Directories: /pub/chess, /pub/misc/tolkien and sub-directories, /pub/pc/game_solutions; uploads to /pub/incoming; server can (un)compress and tar on the fly; transfers are logged; max. 10 users.

Files: graph chess (daily mirror of `chess.uoknor.edu`); MS-DOS game solutions; Tolkien JPG graphics files, FAQs etc.; UNIX material (Linux)

Site: `ftp.mcs.com`

Country: USA

GMT: –6

Administrative Address: postmaster@mcs.com [unless otherwise posted in specific directories]

Organization: MCSnet; Chicago, Illinois

System: UNIX

Comment: transfers are logged

Files: acmesoft; copyright; Mac: Packet, Packrat utils; MCSnet info; MS-Windows Winsock archive; user sponsored ftp-directories in /mcsnet.users: falcon/add (Att'n Deficit Disorder mirror for the CompuServe ADD forum libraries, falcon/addult.news (ADDult News Online magazine archive site), jorn/ascii-art (mirror of ASCII art archives)

Site: ftp.michnet.net

Country: USA

GMT: –5

Organization: MERIT/NSF; Ann Arbor, Michigan

System: UNIX (SunOS 4.1)

Files: Acceptable Use Policies; cise; conference proceedings; docs; IETF; Internet Info; Internet-drafts; internet-monthly report; Introducing the Internet; maps; Merit's Internet Cruise; Michnet info; newsletters; NFSNET Link Letter, statistics, maps; NREN info; OMB; resources; RFCs; statistics; working groups; X11R6

Site: ftp.microsoft.com

Country: USA

GMT: –8

Administrative Address: csftpad@microsoft.com, each area has a contact alias

Organization: Microsoft Corp., Internet Support Server

System: MS-Windows NT (PC)

Comment: Free updates to Microsoft utilities; directories: Advsys, DESKAPPS, DEVCAST, DEVTOOLS, MSDN, MSFT, Softlib; DOS 6.2 is NO LONGER AVAILABLE because of a legal conflict between MS and Stac.

Files: Microsoft utilities and updates: Developer Relations Group, Lan Manager, Windows NT, MS Mail, SQL Server

Site: ftp.mii.lu.lv

Country: Latvia

GMT: +2

System: UNIX (Ultrix 4.1)

Files: GNU; graphics; Internet; Latvian; Mac; MS-DOS; Mosaic; OS/2; UNIX

Site: ftp.morningstar.com

Country: USA

GMT: –5

Organization: Morningstar Technologies, Morningstar support server

System: UNIX

Comment: Source for Morningstar PPP software for DOS and Macintosh machines.

Files: PPP; SCO UNIX tools

Site: ftp.mpgn.com

Country: USA

GMT: –5

Organization: Multi-Player Games Network

System: UNIX

Comment: Fantasy gaming portion is sometimes unavailable.

Files: gaming (ADND, fantasy, Hero, HomeBrew, Traveller, utilities, Warhammer); MPG-Net (DrakVision, EmpireBuilder, MarketGarden, StarCruiser)

Site: ftp.msen.com

Country: USA

GMT: –5

Administrative Address: ftp-service@msen.com

Organization: MSEN; Ann Arbor, Michigan

System: UNIX

Comment: excellent Gopher at gopher.msen.com.

Files: ann-arbor; comp.newprod archive; docs; emv; Gopher; internet-review; MIME; Msen; newsletters; packages; systems; time; vendor (Crynwr); WAIS

Site: ftp.ncsa.uiuc.edu

Country: USA

GMT: –6

Administrative Address: stgadmin@ncsa.uiuc.edu, softdev@ncsa.uiuc.edu (NCSA tools), archive-manager@ncsa.uiuc.edu (for the archive server)

Organization: University of Illinois at Urbana/Champaign; Urbana, Illinois

Other Access: E-mail to archive-server@ncsa.uiuc.edu

System: UNIX

Comment: HyperFTP users: use a '-' as the first character of your password; Delphi users: enclose case-sensitive directory and filenames in "".

Files: DEC_ALPHA; DTM; Docs; education; Global Models; HDF (Hierarchical Data File system); LCA; Mac; misc (scientific and file) formats; Mosaic; NCSA (Telnet/FTP programs); PC; SGI; samples; sc22wg5; survey; UNIX; VR; Web (WWW); x3j3

Site: `ftp.near.net`

Country: USA

GMT: –5

Administrative Address: `nearnet-eng@nic.near.net`

Organization: New England Academic Regional Network NIC (service offering of BBN Technology Services Inc., a whole subsidiary of Bolt, Beranek and Newman Inc.)

System: UNIX

Comment: The NEARNET FTP archive; successor of `nic.near.net`; several files/ directories limited to NEARnet hosts only.

Files: CERFnet; Commerce Business Daily (in /cbd); docs; forms; Gopher; image; Internet Talk Radio (in /talk-radio); internet-drafts; internet-information; K12; mail-archives; maps; NEARNet info; NeTraMet; nosupport directory; RFCs; seminars; ucp

Site: `ftp.nec.com`

Country: USA

GMT: –6

Administrative Address: `cornell@syl.cl.nec.com` (Cornell Kinderknecht)

Organization: NEC System Labs Inc. C&C Software Technology Center (CSTC); Irving/Dallas, Texas

System: UNIX

Comment: CSTC release of SOCKS is in /pub/security/ socks.cstc; get a copy of the README file in the top directory.

Files: ecpa; ftp-list (old); japan; Linux; mail; misc; modems; multimedia; news; OSI; PC misc; PC net; products; RFCs; security; sendmail; slip; Sun-fixes; TCL-TK; UNIX; WWW; Weath; X-misc

Site: `ftp.nectec.or.th`

Country: Thailand

GMT: +7

Administrative Address: `trin@nwg.nectec.or.th` (Trin Tantsetthi)

Organization: National Electronic and Computer Technology Center (NECTEC), Ministry of Science, Technology and Environment, Bangkok

System: UNIX

Files: Dharma Electronic File Archive (from `ftp.netcom.com`, buddhism); GNU (mirror from `prep.ai.mit.edu`); Internet drafts; Linux (mirror from `tsx-11.mit.edu`); Microsoft docs (mirror of `ftp.microsoft.com`); MS-DOS games (mirror from `ftp.uml.edu`); MS-Windows 3 (mirror from `ftp.cica.indiana.edu`); Simtel Software Repository mirror (/pub/mirrors/msdos); Thai/Lao MS-DOS software (/pub/pc); Thailand info (/pub/info); Thai daily news (/pub/news); UNIX PD; XFree86 (mirror from `ftp.xfree86.org`)

Site: `ftp.netcom.com`

Country: USA

GMT: −8

Organization: Netcom On-Line Communications Services Inc., San Jose, California

System: UNIX

Comment: Use only `ftp.netcom.com`.

Files: computer game development material; several informational files in /pub directory: every user has his/her own /pub directory directories are further divided by the first two letters of user ID—e.g., files in the /netcom directory will be found in the /pub/ne/netcom directory; Netcom info; aamram; AB1264; Acme; activis; alumlist; ASCUS; billa (Space/Astro related GIFs, e.g. Shoemaker-Levy 9 (SL9), HST GIFs) and SL9 sitelist; boutell (FAQ); bradleym (40Hex, IRC, KOH, NuKE); gamedir; GNO; GTU; Guides; imagecft; info-deli; Iris; Isis; kaminski; KBBS (/pub/ tc/smith); lotus-cars; ltubbs (Enigma archive: DiskExpress

(/pub/ tc/smith); lotus-cars; ltubbs (Enigma archive: DiskExpress (DXP), Finfo, PMatno, VX-REXX runtime (VROBJ)); metal; micromed; microspc; Militia; mnemonic; mushroom; Nascent (Linux CD); net app; netcom; netmail; newmedia; notgnu; Nutec; OPN; pearl-jam; PineSoft; PPS-info; Seti; Silk; Simpsons (/pub/ ca /calliope); skylines; softhelp; surfgear; Tetra-Soft; thinknet; Trek; tweek (FAQ); urimud; US Network; UUCP; VE3SUN; veritools; vidgames; WD6CMU; Weitek; X3H6; Yggdrasil (Linux CD); Zytek

Site: `ftp.netlib.org`

Country: USA

GMT: –5

Organization: University of Tennessee Computer Science Dept.; Knoxville, Tennessee

System: UNIX

Comment: Also through Gopher and WWW.

Files: aicm; alliant; amos; ampl; anl-reports; Apollo; att.com; benchmark; bib; bihar; blas; bmp; C; C++; cephes; chammp; cheney-kincaid; clapack; confdb; conformal; contin; crc; crpc; ddsv; domino; eispack; elefunt; errata; f2c; fdlibm; fftpack; fishpack; fitpack; floppy; fmm; fn; Fortran; Fortran-M; fp; gcv; genome; gmat; go; graphics; harwell; hence; hompack; hpf; hypercube; IEEEcss; ijsa; image; imsl; itpack; keyword; kincaid-cheney; la-net; lanczos; lanz; lapack; laso; libs; linalg; linpack; list; listL; lp; machines; magic; maspar; master; microscope; minpack; misc; mpi; na-digest; nac.no; nag; napack; netlib; news; newtoms; nse; numeralgo; ode; odepack; odrpack; opt; p4; papers; paragraph; parallel; paranoia; parkbench; parmacs; pascal; patents; pbwg; pchip; pdes; performance; picl; pltmg; poly2; polyhedra; polyhedron; popi; port; Posix; pppack; presto; problem-set; pu; pvm; pvm3; quadpack; random; reqlog; research; rkpack; scalapack; sched; scilib; seispack; sequent; sfmm; shpcc94; slap; slatec; sminpack; sort-pascal; sparse; sparse-blas; sparspak; specfun; spin; sscpack; statistics; stoeplitz; stringsearch; svdpack; templates; tennessee; toeplitz; toms; treegr; typesetting; uncon; UTK; vanhuffel; vfftpack; vfftpk; vfnlib; voronoi; whois; xmagic; xnetlib; xnl4; xnlindex; y12m

Site: ftp.netmanage.com

Country: USA

GMT: –8

Organization: NetManage; Cupertino, California

System: UNIX

Files: bootp; pc nfsd; snmp; vb; Win snmp; WinSock

Site: ftp.netsys.com

Country: USA

GMT: –8

Administrative Address: len@netsys.com (Len Rose)

Organization: Netsys Inc.

System: UNIX

Comment: Weather images moved to westsat.com.

Files: 40Hex magazine archives; aleph1; freedom; getsat; irc; lan-wan; mtrek; NetSys info; Novell; patches; Phrack magazine archives; pictures; quake; satellite; smc; smh; Sun; tklgifs; trinity; worldlists

Site: ftp.nis.garr.it

Country: Italy

GMT: +1

Administrative Address: staff@nis.garr.it

Organization: Harmonisation Group for Research Networks, Network Information Service (NIS)

System: UNIX

Files: GARR info; Gopher; MBONE; mirrors; Perl; pictures; sendmail; service providers; SunOS; traceroute; WAIS; X500

Site: ftp.noao.edu

Site: ftp.noao.edu

Country: USA

GMT: −7

Administrative Address: grandi@noao.edu

Organization: National Optical Astronomy Observatories (NOAO)

System: UNIX

Files: aladdin; some astronomical catalogs; fts; gong; Gemini project info; kpno; kpvt; IRAF archive; NOAO; nso; preprints; Solar Data; SN 1987 Spectral Atlas Files; starform_project; TeX; utils; Weather Satellite Pictures; wiyn

Site: ftp.nosc.mil

Country: USA

GMT: −8

Organization: NOSC; San Diego, California

System: UNIX

Files: aburto; ads; avp; benchmarks; BSD; ccmail; cds; clarkson; dct (doc, src); dis; gimber; GAP; GAPFS; GNU; HAC; HACK; HGI; HIIP; IBM; Internet info (articles); kwriter; MUC; modbot; mosaic; music_banjo; network info; nfasdict; nsap; pat; PC NFS; pegasus; pgc; pktmux; plant19; powerr; powers; Processing Graph Method; radio communications; radio propagation; scales; SCAPS; secure 4.3; security; sepo; sbookla; srf-guam; STA files; Sun-fixes; tac4; telerobotics; techdoc; trumpet; wmail; vocar

Site: ftp.novell.com

Country: USA

GMT: −7

Administrative Address: ftp@novell.com, webmaster@novell.com (WWW)

Organization: Novell, Inc.; Provo, Utah

System: UNIX

Comment: Publicly available portions of the Netwire forum; access to Novell's Online services is available through: FTP: `ftp.novell.com`, Gopher: `gopher.novell.com`, World Wide Web: `www.novell.com`; transfers are logged.

Files: Novell utilities, patches, fixes, information etc.: Netwire, Unixware; WWW

Site: `ftp.novell.de`

Country: Germany

GMT: +1

Administrative Address: `ease-adm@novell.de`

Organization: Novell Germany—Novell's Easy Access System Europe (EASE); Dusseldorf, Germany

Comment: Also available via Gopher and WWW (`http://www.novell.de/index.html`).

Files: doc; Linux; Mosaic; netwire; Novell utilities, patches, fixes, information, on-line technical support database etc.; OS/2; sjf-lwp; UNIX; Unixware; Windows 3

Site: `ftp.nus.sg`

Country: Singapore

GMT: +8

Organization: National University of Singapore

System: UNIX

Comment: Read ARCHIVES.TXT for info on which mirrors are maintained.

Files: bio; docs; du.info; infoserver; infosystems; Mac; misc; multimedia; NT; NUS; OOT; Opensys; PC; UNIX; Windows; Winsock (Sunsite)

Site: ftp.oar.net

Country: USA

GMT: –6

Organization: Ohio Academic Research Network (OARNet)

System: UNIX (SunOS 4.1)

Comment: Gopher: gopher.oar.net.

Files: dialup; DNS; docs; FYI; GEI; hocking; IETF-drafts; imr; mibs; news; noc-training; OARnet info; occ; opstat; RFCs; saturn; sci.military; security; sendmail; US.domain; vendors

Site: ftp.parc.xerox.com

Country: USA

GMT: –8

Organization: Xerox—Palo Alto Research Center (PARC); Palo Alto, California

System: UNIX

Files: MOO (MUD) clients

Site: ftp.pasteur.fr

Country: France

GMT: +1

Administrative Address: netmaster@pasteur.fr

System: UNIX

Comment: Max. 200 users allowed.

Files: 4.3BSD; Empire; FAQ; games; gensoft; GNU; Go; gopher; Logo; Mac; MycDB; network; news; PC; Perl; PolyDoc; resig; RFCs; security; sendmail; SimpleTimes; systems; TeX; X11R5

Site: ftp.portal.com

Country: USA

GMT: –8

Administrative Address: cs@portal.com

Organization: Portal Communications; Cupertino, California

System: UNIX

Comment: Several public directories of Portal users under /pub.

Files: artnet; bookware; fineline; function; netpower; portal-info; puzzle; relevant; roadkill; unix-sig; zone

Site: ftp.psg.com

Country: USA

GMT: –8

Organization: RAINet/PSG, Oregon/Washington

System: UNIX

Files: bbslists; CIX; docs; Eiffel; Elvis; FIDONet; GNU; Intel; Internet; IP-for-PC; K12; lists; Mac; Modula-2; MS-DOS; nets; Oberon; Pascal; Python; RAINet; SCSI (Adaptec); unced; UNIX; UUCP-for-PC

Site: ftp.psi.com

Country: USA

GMT: –5

Organization: Performance Systems International; Herndon, Virginia

System: UNIX (SunOS 4.1)

Files: archive; dns; doc; gopsi; ien; ietf; info; irg; isode; maps; net-info; newsletter; pilot; press releases; psilink; psisnmp; radio; RFCs; sendmail; snmp; snmpstats; src; srmftp; Sun; Usenet; uuftp; waan; WP

Site: ftp.psychologie.uni-freiburg.de

Country: Germany

GMT: +1

Administrative Address: ftp@psychologie.uni-freiburg.de, stumpf@psychologie.uni-freiburg.de (Michael Stumpf)

Organization: Universitaet Freiburg (University of Freiburg) Psychology Dept.; Freiberg, Germany

System: UNIX (SunOS 4.1)

Comment: Open 24 hours.

Files: Research-related information—documents and software (psychology, cognitive psychology, cognitive science, artificial intelligence); Sun-related software, patches, and documents

Site: ftp.qdeck.com

Country: USA

GMT: –8

Administrative Address: support@qdeck.com (Thomas Bortels and others)

Organization: Quarterdeck Office Systems, Santa Monica, California

System: UNIX

Comment: Quarterdeck memory manager software utilities, patches, technical notes; sound files. Directory: /pub.

Files: audio; Internet Talk Radio; Quarterdeck product information, utilities, patches, fixes: DV, DV_QEMM FAQ, memory, Qemm, technotes

Site: ftp.quote.com

Country: USA

GMT: –8

Administrative Address: support@quote.com (bug reports), staff@quote.com (suggestions)

Organization: QuoteCom financial data archives, Reno, Nevada

Other Access: www.quote.com

System: UNIX

Comment: Additional info in /pub/info; index in INDEX; greater access when you register through `services@quote.com`.

Files: bulletins; bwire; hoover; library; newsletters; programs; spguide; symbols; usenet

Site: `ftp.ripe.net`

Country: Netherlands

GMT: +1

Administrative Address: `ncc@ripe.net`

Organization: Reseaux IP Europeennes (European IP Research, RIPE), Network Coordination Centre (NCC); Amsterdam

System: UNIX

Comment: Max. 25 users; transactions are logged.

Files: cidr; EARN; EBONE; FYI; IAB; IESG; IETF; Internet-drafts; Internet Society (ISOC); ISO3166-codes; NSF; pride; RARE; RFCs; RIPE; tools

Site: `ftp.seds.lpl.arizona.edu`

Country: USA

GMT: −7

Administrative Address: `chrisl@lpl.arizona.edu`
(Chris Lewicki)

Organization: University of Arizona, Students for the Exploration and Development of Space (SEDS); Tucson, Arizona

Other Access: `ftpmail@seds.lpl.arizona.edu`

System: UNIX (SunOS, SparcServer 10)

Comment: Open 24 hours; max. 50 users; server can uncompress; also available through Gopher; transfers are logged.

Files: anim; astro; clementine; dosdirs; FAQs; images (Apollo, asteroid, ccd, charts, clementine, comets, dcx, deepspace, earth, eclipse, HST, Hubble, jpeg, Jupiter, launcher, logos, Mars, Mercury, misc, Moon, Neptune, observatories, Pluto, rme, Saturn, scans, shuttle, space, spacestation, spacecolony, spacecraft, stsci, Sun, supercomputing, supernova, Uranus, Venus, WFPC2); info; sat; SEDS; Shoemaker-Levy 9 (SL9) images; software (Amiga, Atari, CP/M, general, HP48, instruments, Mac, NeWS, NeXT, obsdbase, obsprog, OS/2, PC, Space, Spacelink, text, UNIX, VMS); spacecraft

Site: `ftp.sei.cmu.edu`

Country: USA

GMT: –5

Administrative Address: `postmaster@sei.cmu.edu`

Organization: Carnegie-Mellon University, Software Engineering Institute (SEI); Pittsburgh, Pennsylvania

System: UNIX

Comment: Directory: /pub/serpent; server can (de)compress and tar files and directories; max. 20 users.

Files: ACVC; aim; cmm; design-for-reuse; docs; domain-analysis; education; gateway 2000; Ingres; Mac; network; onetime; pager; Posix; pp; psfig; rek; rest; RMA-Validation tests; rtsia; secmm; Serpent; spice; struct_model; wsett_94; x3j21; xmh

Site: `ftp.senate.gov`

Country: USA

GMT: –5

Administrative Address: `ftpadmin@scc.senate.gov`

Organization: United States Senate, Office of the U.S. Senate Sergeant at Arms and the Senate Committee on Rules and Administration; Washington D.C.

System: UNIX

Comment: No files can be uploaded; US Senate info in directory 'general', specific senators' directories by two-letter state abbreviation.

Files: US Senate info: committee, general, member

Site: ftp.spc.edu

Country: USA

Organization: St. Peter's College; Jersey City, New Jersey

GMT: –5

Administrative Address: terry@spcvxa.spc.edu (Terry Kennedy), goathunter@wku.edu (Hunter Goatley)

System: VAX/VMS running Multinet

Comment: Read 0-README.1ST for information; partial mirror on ftp.switch.ch in pub/vms/spc; Macro-32 directory is mirrored at ftp.technion.ac.il in directory pub/unsupported/vms/macro-32; default directory: USER1:[ANONYMOUS].

Files: BBOARD; BOC-L; COOKIE; DECUS-archives; DECUS UUCP; Dr. Who; finger; humor; I-Finger; K11; listserv; macro32; madison; mailutils; mop-server; msfinger; mudbug; MultiNet; MX; NEWSRDR; PAVMS; pendor; posix; rstscle; tools; UCX; UNIX; Usenet; video

Site: ftp.spry.com

Country: USA

Organization: SPRY, Inc.; Seattle, Washington

System: UNIX (SunOS 4.1)

Files: docs; internet-drafts; Mac; MS-DOS; MS-Windows; RFCs; talk-radio; UNIX; vendor

Site: ftp.sri.ucl.ac.be

Country: Belgium

GMT: +1

Administrative Address: Kuypers@sri.ucl.ac.be (Jean-Pierre Kuypers)

Organization: Universite Catholique de Louvain (Catholic University of Louvain) Service des Reseaux d'Information (SRI); Louvain-la-Neuve, Belgium

System: UNIX (SunOS 4.1.1)

Comment: French versions of Macintosh network software, as Anarchie, Eudora, Fetch, FTPd, Gopher Surfer, lpr, MacPPP, MacTCP Switcher, MacTCP Watcher, NCSA Telnet, NewsWatcher, TurboGopher.

Files: Anarchie; CricketGraph; Eudora; FTPd; Fetch; Gopher; ISO.8859-1; Mac.lpr.lpd; MacPPP; MacTCP-Switcher; MacTCP-Watcher; MacTCP; Minuet; NCSA_Telnet; NewsWatcher; poppassd; popperQC; tn3270

Site: ftp.stack.urc.tue.nl

Country: Netherlands

GMT: +1

Administrative Address: ftp@ftp.stack.urc.tue.nl (or ftp@stack.urc.tue.nl)

Organization: Technische Universiteit Eindhoven (Eindhoven University of Technology), MCGV Stack; Eindhoven, Netherlands

System: UNIX

Comment: stack-ftp archives; open 24 hours; 1.8Gb; has an FSP

Other Access: ftp.stack.urc.tue.nl port 21; transfers are logged.

Files: Amiga; EmTeX; esix; Esperanto; FSP; Linux; meteosat; Minix; MS-DOS; news; NeXT; NetBSD; PC netware; PC NFS; SimTel mirror; sounds; System V 386; Winsock; ZyXel

Site: ftp.std.com

Country: USA

GMT: –5

Organization: Software Tool and Die—The World Public Access UNIX; Boston, Massachusetts

System: UNIX

Comment: files from `world.std.com`

Files: activist forum; alt.religion.kibology; amo; Apropos; arj; arj2; AW; astronomy; Atari; b100demo; bball; bbedit; bcs; bitnet addresses; bmug; boston rsi; catnip; cenvi; clipart; cmellow; consultants; dance; dj500; DSPdev; epimbe; fbpro; fix; fontutil; freelance; fullview; funne-archive; genesoft; GNU; graph; ham-radio; idg2; IMA; info-futures; ipv7; IsetlSymdiff; Kluwer; lawyer; Lexicor; liant; lingua; majordomo; MenuDropper; MetaCard; mmodel; NE; obi; OBS; onset; QLS; Quantum; patents; periodicals; python; ra; radio; RAT-archive; renascence; Rgirls; sable; sabre; ScreenSaverKit; SShare; Softpro; sold; talk.bizarre; TECO; Termcomp; Tierra; toolbox; tv-networks; ultracom; vendors; winmag; World info; WWW; Xtty

Site: `ftp.stolaf.edu`

Country: USA

GMT: –6

Administrative Address: `ftp@stolaf.edu` (Craig Rice)

Organization: St. Olaf College; Northfield, Minnesota

System: UNIX

Comment: Do not abuse the world-writable FTP dirs. We regularly scan the area for bogus files and will remove anything that doesn't belong here.

Files: acts; Amiga; anylchem experiments; Budapest; diffEQ; IECC (Intercultural Email Classroom Connections); Indian Music; Kierkegaard; lacnet; Linux-doc; Macpsych mailing list and software archive; mn-math; MuTeX and MusicTeX mailing list and software archive; newlist; NeXT managers mailing list and software archive; oscar (Omni Cultural Academic Resource); OZ; perseus; PEW; Plan9; proksch; quanstro; sca; sci; snap; stat-ed; steen; Tamil; tchechon; teach; trainset; travel-advisories (U.S. State Dept.); UltraStor boot; xcp (Cross Cultural Psychology)

Site: `ftp.sun.ac.za`

Country: South Africa

GMT: +2

Administrative Address: `ftp@ftp.sun.ac.za` (Pieter Immelman)

Organization: University of Stellenbosch, Cape Town

System: UNIX

Comment: 1.9GB, biggest site in Africa; descriptive ls/dir command.

Files: 386BSD; daily weather image; FreeBSD; Games hacks; GNU; Linux; MS-DOS; mirrors: Simtel Software Repository, `ftp.uml.edu` (/pub/msdos/uml); NETBSD; Oberon; OS/2; packages (archie, describe, elm, emtex, fsp, ftpmail, irc, listproc, mirror, musictex, ntp, procmail, smail, tex, texshell, tin, wu-ftpd, xarchie; RFCs; South Africa; Stellenbosch; UNIX; X11

Site: `ftp.sunet.se`

Country: Sweden

GMT: +1

Administrative Address: `archive@ftp.sunet.se`

Organization: Swedish University Network (SUNET) NIC

System: UNIX

Comment: Directory /pub/pc/windows/mirror-cica; max. 150 users; Open 24 hours; server can (de)compress, g(un)zip, tar files and directories; read README files for access methods, compression methods, uploads etc.; access available through Gopher and FSP.

Files: Alex; conferencing; docs; etext; global-net; GNU; Gopher; graphics; information systems; Internet documents; Internet drafts; lang; library; Mac; MIME; molbio; movies; multimedia; music; network; Network User Guides; news; NIDR tools; NT; PC; pictures; Science; security; text-processing; tv+movies; UNIX; Usenet; vendor; Wais; whois; WWW; X11; X500

Site: ftp.tamu.edu

Country: USA

GMT: –6

Administrative Address: root@tamsun.tamu.edu

Organization: Texas A&M University; Computing Services Center; College Station, Texas

System: UNIX

Comment: access is logged

Files: comet; compression; docs; gopher; herps; images; Info Magic CD; Mac; network; newsgroups; OS/2; PC-SIG; ph; RFCs; security; soc.penpals; Sun-fix; SunOS4; SunOS5; Suntools; tamsun config; terms; TeXrox; UNIX-helpdesk; Uts4; web; win3; winsock; X; xyplex

Site: ftp.think.com

Country: USA

GMT: –5

Organization: Thinking Machines Corporation; Cambridge, Massachusetts

System: UNIX (SunOS 4.1)

Comment: Directory: /wais.

Files: adoption; Alife III shirt; animal-rights; aviation; caia-93; carpal; cellular-automata; cm; cmost; cvs; dgg; disinfectant; GNUs; gurps; HPFF; jpeg; libernet; moose; Oh No More Lemmings Demo (Mac); pc532; radio; space-comp-std; Sse; Think; UUCP; Waco; WAIS related files; WX (weather); xpbiff

Site: ftp.ucdavis.edu

Country: USA

GMT: –8

Organization: University of California at Davis; Davis, California

System: UNIX (SunOS 4.1)

Comment: Some loose files in /pub.

Files: bitsites; cpumeter; dialppp; domain-info; Eclipse; econet; Hitchhikers Guide to the Internet; INET93; inet-drafts; Internet Resource Guide; JIS; Kanji; lacnet; listoflists; Mac; MS-DOS (old archivers); PC lisp; peacenet; popmail; RFCs; sendmail; slnet; UCD info; UNIX; USGS; VMS

Site: `ftp.udel.edu`

Country: USA

GMT: −5

Administrative Address: `staff@louie.udel.edu`

Organization: University of Delaware, EE & CIS Dept.; Newark, Delaware

System: UNIX

Comment: Try to avoid our busy hours: 10:00–18:00 weekdays. User ID `ftp` can be used instead of anonymous; file transfers are logged with your host name and e-mail address.

Files: Amiga; arrk, arrl_7 papers; BBS; Beavis and Butthead; grope; highball; hu; info-minix; Internet; KA9Q; maps; midi; misc; mmdf; music; nbstime; nsfnet; ntp; packet drivers; PC NFS; portal; RFCs; rose; stdwin; supermodels; thebox; udelnet; USA

Site: `ftp.uni-kl.de`

Country: Germany

GMT: +1

Administrative Address: `ftpadm@uni-kl.de`

Organization: Universitaet Kaiserslautern (University of Kaiserslautern); Kaiserslautern, Germany

System: UNIX

Comment: Transfers are logged; put uploads in the appropriate incoming directory with descriptive filename and e-mail the admin.

Files: Acorn; Amiga; AMInet; amoeba; Apple II; Astro; Atari; Athena; bio; BSD-sources; docs; EMBL; FUN; game-solutions; GNU; gopher; graphics; ham-radio; helios; humor; Info-Mac (`sumex-aim.stanford.edu`); info KL; informatik; Internet; IRC; ISIS; languages; Linux; lists; Mac; Mach3; Minix; MS-DOS; net-infas; netlib; NeXT; Novell; panda; Pegasus; RFCs; sat.met; security; Sun; TCP/IP; tech-reports; TeX; Transputer; UNIX; vektorproz; vendor; X11R5, directories: /incoming/acorn: Upload directory, /pub/acorn; also other directories for: amiga, apple2, atari, bio(logy), game-solutions, informatik, linux, mac, novell, pc, sun-patches and unix

Site: `ftp.uni-lj.si`

Country: Slovenia

GMT: +1

Organization: University of Ljubljana; Ljubljana, Slovenia

System: VAX/VMS running Multinet

Comment: Default directory SOFT$:[ANONYMOUS].

Files: Astro; PC-SOFT (ANU docs, en, gen, GIF, gopher, graphics, Linux, Mac, mgs, NCSA, OS/2, OS/2 beta, PC, riva, SCO, sesam, systems, TeX, text, Ultrasound, usenet news, ZyXel); Vlado; VMS (numerous files)

Site: `ftp.univie.ac.at`

Country: Austria

GMT: +1

Administrative Address: `manager@ftp.univie.ac.at`

Organization: Universitaet Wien (University of Vienna); Vienna

System: UNIX (AIX 3.2.5, IBM RS/6000-340)

Comment: Max. 50 users; maintainers per directory: e.g. maintainer of the HP/UX directory: `hpux-adm@ftp.univie.ac.at`.

Files: Austria; docs; GNU; Mac; netinfo (aconet, docs, EARN, Europanet, FYI, IEN, IETF, infos, internet-drafts, ISO, networking, RFCs, zone-info); Novell; OS/2 (hobbes, servicepack-gr);

packages (compression, GNU, grass, khoros, lapack, mathematica, network, oberon, octave, TeX, X11); PC; security; systems (HP/UX, Linux, Mac, MS-DOS, Novell, OS/2, Solaris, UNIX, Windows3); TeX; UniVie

Site: `ftp.unm.edu`

Country: USA

GMT: –7

Organization: University of New Mexico; Albuquerque, New Mexico

System: UNIX (Ultrix 4.3, DECStation 5000/120)

Comment: Successor of `ariel.unm.edu`, `unma.unm.edu` (now obsolete).

Files: BSDI-386; docs; icb; internet; library; Mac; NAFTA; PC; University networking ethics documents; UNIX; Usenet

Site: `ftp.urz.uni-heidelberg.de`

Country: Germany

GMT: +1

Administrative Address: `ftp-admin@ftp.urz.uni-heidelberg.de`

Organization: Universitaet Heidelberg (University of Heidelberg) Computer Center; Heidelberg, Germany

System: UNIX

Comment: Server is capable of (un)compressing files on the fly.

Files: AIX RS/6000; Amiga; BSD-sources; div-sources; fonts; games (mirrored on `ftp.fht-mannheim.de`); games solutions; GNU; gopher; graphics; Heidelberg info; Linux; MS-DOS (archivers, astronomy, comm, demos, educ, educgames, graphics, libs, music, Novell, physics, SCSI, sounds, utilities, virus, windows3, X11); NCSA; net; OS/2; SAS; Simtel Software Repository (mirror of oak.oakland.edu); Sun-dist; UNIX; X11; xed

Site: `ftp.usask.ca`

Country: Canada

GMT: −6

Organization: University of Saskatchewan; Saskatoon, Saskatchewan

System: UNIX

Comment: Directory: /pub/hytelnet; max. 10 users.

Files: Amiga; crash; cwi; dcs-docs; dec-fixes; Gutenburg project; Hytelnet (Hypertext list of Telnet sites); incometax; Library of Congress rule interpretations; Literature works of many kinds; Mac; MS-DOS; MS-Windows; MS-Windows NT; netinfo; ntp; selected SunOS patches; OS/2; U of S logo; U of S recommended e-mail software; vendor directories; weather

Site: `ftp.uu.net`

Country: USA

GMT: −5

Organization: UUNET Technologies; Falls Church, Virginia

System: UNIX

Comment: Directories: /archiving, /doc, /graphics, /pub, /published, /systems, /vendor; transfers are logged; open 24 hours.

Files: AI; Athena; BSD-sources; C-utils; cake; calc; CLIM; comp.sources: 3b1, amiga, games, misc, reviewed, unix, x; comp.std.unix; database; economics; editors; faces (Usenix); franzinc; FTPNUZ (/support/pubdom); games; GNU; government; graphics; Internet docs; ioccc; languages; library; linguistics; Mach; mail; math; mtools; music; news; networking galore; nutshell; opinions; physics; printers; prob-tracking; prob-libs; SCO; security; shells; Simtel Software Repository mirror (/systems/ibmpc/msdos/simtel20); Sun-fixes; sysadm; UNIX Today; UNIX World; UUmap; UUnet info; vendor; window-sys; X

Site: `ftp.uv.es`

Country: Spain

GMT: +1

Administrative Address: ftpadmin@power.vi.uv.es

Organization: Universitat de Valencia (University of Valencia); Valencia, Spain

System: UNIX

Files: biology; Linux; Mac; medicin; meteo; MS-DOS; MVS; satellites; UNIX; VM; workshops

Site: ftp.uwp.edu

Country: USA

GMT: −6

Administrative Address: ftp@ftp.uwp.edu, ftp@cs.uwp.edu

Organization: University of Wisconsin—Parkside; Kenosha, Wisconsin

System: UNIX

Other Access: gopher.uwp.edu

Comment: Open 24 hours; limits users (80 off-campus users during business hours, 150 users all other times)

Files: Music-related files: lyrics, pictures, discographies, many music mailing lists and press kits; Official ID software games distribution; several site mirrors; ftp-list; Tin; programs for SB, ProAudio etc.; mirror of ftp.uml.edu (/pub/msdos/games/ulowell): MS-DOS games and wasp.eng.ufl.edu (/pub/msdos/demos): MS-DOS demos

Site: ftp.vslib.cz

Country: Czech Republic

GMT: +1

Administrative Address: ftpadm@vslib.cz

Organization: Liberec University of Technology; Liberec, Czech Republic

System: UNIX

Other Access: Gopher: gopher.vslib.cz

Comment: Transfers are logged.

Files: CESNet; graphics; info; Liane; Liberec; Mac; McAfee (anti-virus); mirrors; MS-DOS; MS-Windows; network; news.answers; Pegasus; Sun; TeX; texts; UNIX; weather

Site: ftp.wais.com

Country: USA

Administrative Address: ftpmaster@wais.com.

Organization: WAIS

System: UNIX

Comment: Directory: /pub.

Files: WAIS-related files, clients, servers, etc.

Site: ftp.whitehouse.gov

Country: USA

GMT: –5

Organization: White House, Washington D.C.

System: UNIX

Comment: Look at the 'dirmap' files and read NEW-THISWEEK and NEW-TODAY.

Files: political science; White House announcements

Site: ftp.whnet.com

Country: USA

GMT: –8

Organization: WH Networks, Mountain View, California

System: UNIX

Comment: Get the file /pub/BLURB to get subscription info about this system; transfers are logged with your user name and/or e-mail address; user public directories in /pub.

Files: anarch; aradmin; artemis; asher; babba; bats; bhc; bromgrev; brywanw; conquest; canwise; dhesi; envisions; grafpoint; juxta; lp; lumina; medianet; online access; rocknet; waffle; wolfgang (modem related material: FAQs, docs, etc.); xalt

Site: ftp.win.tue.nl

Country: Netherlands

GMT: +1

Administrative Address: ftp@win.tue.nl

Organization: Technische Universiteit Eindhoven (Eindhoven University of Technology) Math & Computer Science Dept.; Eindhoven, Netherlands

System: UNIX

Comment: Archie compliant; Gopher: ftp.win.tue.nl, port 70; WWW: www.win.tue.nl, port 80; WAIS: news.answers only through the Gopher server; 450-500MB; big downloads outside working hours please; transfers are logged.

Files: BSD net-1, net-2, network-tape, sources; compression; conferencing; databases; doc; editors; games; GNU; hypernews; infosystems; languages; Linux; Mac; mail; math.prog.construction; Minix; misc; MS-DOS; networking; news; programming; psf; religion; security tools (TCP wrapper); Sun; Sun-fixes; Sys V X86; tech-reports; TeX; textproc; UNIX; usenet; windowsys; X11R5; X11R4_386; XFree86

Site: ftp.wri.com

Country: USA

GMT: –5

Administrative Address: ms-admin@wri.com (MathSource Administrator)

Organization: WRI

System: UNIX

Comment: MathSource, the electronic resource for Mathematica materials; transfers are logged; items are numbered, see /pub/Numbered/Items.

Files: Everything you always wanted to find for Mathematica but were afraid to look for.

Site: ftp.x.org

Country: USA

GMT: –5

Administrative Address: ftp@x.org

Organization: Massachusetts Institute of Technology, Cambridge, Massachusetts, Laboratory of Computer Sciences/X Consortium

Other Access: www.x.org

System: UNIX

Comment: Successor of x.org and expo.lcs.mit.edu; transfers are logged; server can (de)compress, g(un)zip and tar on the fly; activity is logged.

Files: CLX and CLUE; digest; GNU; gwm; portable bitmaps; X (lots of it: X11R4, X11R5, X11R6 official site)

Site: ftp.xfree86.org

Country: USA

GMT: –5

Administrative Address: xf86admin@xfree86.org

Organization: X Consortium, XFree86 Project

System: UNIX

Comment: Server can tar, compress and gzip; check mirrors to optimze network (xfree86.cdrom.com, ref.tfs.com, ftp.ias-tate.edu, tsx-11.mit.edu, sunsite.unc.edu, x.phys-ics.su.oz.au, ftp.fee.vutbr.cz, ftp.uni-mannheim.de,

ftp.uni-stuttgart.de, orgchem.weizmann.ac.il, ftp.unipi.it,
ftp.iij.ad.jp, nova.pvv.unit.no, sprocket.ict.pwr.wroc.pl,
ftp.nectec.or.th, ftp.demon.co.uk, ftp.edu.tw).

Files: XFree 86 offical site

Site: galaxy.uci.agh.edu.pl

Country: Poland

GMT: +1

Administrative Address: js@galaxy.uci.agh.edu.pl

Organization: Akademia Gorniczo-Hutnicza; Krakow, Poland

System: UNIX

Comment: Polish text; some CD-ROMs mounted (Simtel).

Files: archiving; BSD; docs; e-press; GIFs (lots, including Tolkien
and fine-art, partly mirror of ftp.funet.fi); GNU; Linux; MS-
DOS; network; Novell; papers; pigulki; security; TeX; UNIX-
professionals; X11R5

Site: garbo.uwasa.fi

Country: Finland

GMT: +2

Administrative Address: ts@uwasa.fi (Timo Salmi: MS-DOS,
Publicity), ajh@uwasa.fi (Ari Hovila: Garbo sysadmin, Freeport
BBS, MS-DOS, MS-Windows), te@uwasa.fi (Tuomas Eerola:
Mac), hh@chyde.uwasa.fi (Hannu Hirvonen: postmaster, UNIX,
VMS)

Organization: University of Vaasa

System: UNIX

Comment: One of the major shareware archives; overseas users,
use local mirrors; max. 100 users; read /pc/UPLOAD.INF before
uploading: .zip files only and e-mail to the appropriate address:
mac-up@uwasa.fi, pc-up@uwasa.fi, ql-up@uwasa.fi, unix-
up@uwasa.fi, win-up@uwasa.fi; actions are logged; use valid
e-mail addresses!

Files: ftp-list; Mac; MODERxx.ZIP; MS-DOS; MS-Windows 3; QL (Sinclair); sounds; TS-progs; UNIX; Turbo Pascal; UNIX; VMS

Site: gatekeeper.dec.com

Country: USA

GMT: −8

Administrative Address: gw-archives@pa.dec.com

Organization: Digital Equipment Corp—Palo Alto; Palo Alto, California

Other Access: ftpmail@decwrl.dec.com

System: UNIX (4.3BSD)

Comment: Major mirror of CICA archive (major source of MSWindows utilities and shareware); open 24 hours; a nice motd (message of the day) with Export Control Codes; some extended commands (discussed in motd).

Files: Alpha; Athena; BSD (386BSd and NetBSD, used to mirror agate.berkeley.edu); case; CICA (ftp.cica.indiana.edu) mirror; comm; conferences; database; DEC; Digital; docs; editors; forums; games; GNU; graphics; Larry Wall material; Mach; mail; maps; micro; misc; multimedia; net; news; NIST; plan; published; recipes; sf; Standards; sysadm; text; UCB; Usenet; Usenix; VMS; X11; X11-contrib

Site: genbank.bio.net

Country: USA

GMT: −8

Comment: Sometimes congested.

Files: National Repository for Gene Sequence Data.

Site: geom.umn.edu

Country: USA

GMT: −6

Administrative Address: ftp@geom.umn.edu

Organization: University of Minnesota Geometry Center

System: UNIX

Comment: Successor of poincare.geom.umn.edu; send mail to register@geom.umn.edu to let us know you use the software.

Files: Differential Geometry Material: Geomview (pub/software/geomview), Surface Evolver (pub/software/evolver), SnapPea (pub/software/snappea); images

Site: george.lbl.gov

Country: USA

GMT: –8

Organization: Lawrence Berkeley Laboratory; Berkeley, California

System: UNIX (SunOS 4.1)

Files: BAGigabit; ccs-ecl; Collab; Healthcare; ISS; LBL-UCB; mjj; Whole Frog

Site: girch1.hsch.utexas.edu

Country: USA

GMT: –6

Organization: University of Texas at Austin; Austin, Texas

Files: Physiological research info and programs.

Site: grivel.une.edu.au

Country: Australia

GMT: +10

Administrative Address: gordon@grivel.une.edu.au

Organization: University of New England at Armidale; Armidale, New South Wales

Files: Amateur Radio Topics

Site: handicap.afd.olivetti.com

Country: USA

GMT: –5

Administrative Address: wtm@bunker.afd.olivetti.com
(Bill McGarry)

Other Access: gopher.afd.olivetti.com

Organization: Olivetti; Shelton, Connecticut

System: UNIX

Comment: Large archive of software that enables handicapped
individuals to use personal computers.

Files: Handicap-related software and info.

Site: helix.nih.gov

Country: USA

GMT: –5

Organization: US National Institute of Health; Bethesda,
Maryland

System: UNIX

Files: chp; demacs; f2c; infosystems; kermit; lib; lpd; mail;
mhservicespa; moosejaw; ncidata; nihdir; pcoff; printgl; pub: breg-
man, decio, fusion, parker_data, pdq, ruy; training

Site: hmcvax.claremont.edu

Country: USA

GMT: –8

Organization: Claremont College; Claremont, California

System: VAX/VMS running Multinet

Comment: Only complete source of Cyrillic fonts outside Russia.

Files: cyrillic fonts

Site: hobbes.nmsu.edu

Country: USA

GMT: –7

Organization: New Mexico State University Computer Science Dept.; Las Cruces, New Mexico

System: UNIX

Comment: Most OS/2 files have now been moved to ftp-os2.nmsu.edu and are being replaced by MultiMedia files.

Files: Hobbes OS/2 archive (mirrored around the world); WAV, MID files; MultiMedia archive.

Site: hq.demos.su

Country: Russia

GMT: +2

Administrative Address: bad@demos.su

Organization: DEMOS

Other Access: ftpmail@hq.demos.su; ms@demos.su (send help)

Files: Music; NET; News; RFC; arcers; astrology; books; databases; demo; demos; esperanto; hosts; languages; mac; maps; math; msdos; servers; unix

Site: husky1.stmarys.ca

Country: Canada

GMT: –5

Organization: St. Mary's College

Comment: Default directory: SYS$DISK2:[ANONYMOUS].

Files: Amiga; docs; Earth Centered Universe (Windows planetarium); Mac; MS-Windows; PC; Sun; UNIX; VMS

Site: iamftp.unibe.ch

Country: Switzerland

GMT: +1

Administrative Address: horn@iam.unibe.ch (Heike Horn)

Organization: University of Berne Computer Science and Applied Math Dept.; Berne, Switzerland

System: UNIX (Sun)

Comment: Everything is logged; server can tar and (de)compress.

Files: C++; comm; databases; emacs; exptrees; FAQ; forte94; ftp-list (old); GNU; games; graphics; IAM; images; languages; lgtlib; mail-lists; Mathematica; MPATH; multimedia; network; Otter; PC; Postscript; Profile; Range Images; sound; Suntools; Systemtools; tech-reports; Tex; text-processing; Usenet; X11

Site: iicm.tu-graz.ac.at

Country: Austria

GMT: +1

Administrative Address: ktrummer@iicm.tu-graz.ac.at

Organization: Technischer Universitaet Graz (Graz Institute of Technology); Graz, Austria

System: UNIX

Comment: Home of Hyper-G.

Files: COSTOC; ED-MEDIA 95; HM-card (PC Hypermedia Authoring Tool); Hyper-G (software and docs); JUCS (Journal for Universal Computer Science); mm; movies; panmail; photos; prospekt; sa94

Site: ils.nwu.edu

Country: USA

GMT: −6

Organization: Northwestern University; Evanston, Illinois

System: UNIX (SunOS 4.1)

Files: CoVis; c25; Mush; neves; nlp; papers; sourdough

Site: infant2.sphs.indiana.edu

Country: USA

GMT: −5

Administrative Address: barry@noc.unt.edu (Barry Bloom, Doom archive)

Organization: University of Indiana; Bloomington, Indiana

System: UNIX

Comment: Official Doom archive.

Files: Doom; Netrek

Site: info.cern.ch

Country: Switzerland

GMT: +1

Organization: European Laboratory for Particle Physics (CERN); Geneva, Switzerland

Other Access: www.info.cern.ch

System: UNIX (System V Release 4.0)

Comment: This is *the* archive for WWW materials.

Files: IETF; RPC; WWW (Mosaic etc.)

Site: info.er.usgs.gov

Country: USA

Organization: U.S. Geographical Survey; Reston, Virginia

System: UNIX (SunOS 4.1)

Files: contracts; dcw; gils; GIV; GS-MATERIAL; npr; sdts; small-talk; X.500

Site: `info.mcs.anl.gov`

Country: USA

GMT: −6

Organization: Argonne National Laboratory, Mathematics and Computer Science Division

System: UNIX

Comment: Software available is part of ongoing research projects. We may occasionally send you updates on software you download from the /pub/systems directory.

Files: Ada; adirfor (autodiff); ADOLC; `automated.reasoning`; BlockSolve; chammp; Crescendo; Dataphile; DELTA; Dore; fdb; formed; fortran-m; Gels; GenoGraphics; HIPPI_RS6000; Highlights; ibm_sp1; MINPACK-2; mpi; nanotech; news; NeXT; nexus; Otter; p4; pcn; pcrc-ip3; pdetools; PORTAL; qed; RDP; RNAdb; SCIMMS; security; splash_p4; SWE; tech-reports; upshot; volren; whitepapers; xbibtex

Site: `info.rutgers.edu`

Country: USA

GMT: −5

Organization: Rutgers University; New Brunswick, New Jersey

System: UNIX

Files: caipworks; forms (bicycle, camden1, citadel, corporate, Eisenhower, eisenreg); gopher; Info; International Connectivity; Internet; maps; Mosaic; MS-DOS (mirror of `wuarchive:/mirror/ msdos`); Performance; RFCs; Rutgers Press; soc.religion.christian; sounds; WWII; x-files

Site: `info.tva.gov`

Country: USA

GMT: −6

Administrative Address: `gopher-admin@info.tva.gov`

Organization: Tennessee Valley Authority; Chattanooga, Tennessee

System: UNIX (SunOS 4.1)

Comment: Gopher via `info.tva.gov`; if you can't reach the name, try `152.85.3.3`.

Files: comp: galaxy, GNU; docs; p_e_g (Plain English Guide to the Internet); river info; surplus equipment; technology transfer info

Site: `is.internic.net`

Country: USA

GMT: -8

Administrative Address: `admin@internic.net`, `info@internic.net`

Organization: Internet NIC—InfoSource Archive by General Atomics, San Diego, California

System: UNIX

Comment: Major disclaimer.

Files: *The* source of information about the Internet.

Site: `isdres.er.usgs.gov`

GMT: -5

Country: USA

Organization: U.S. Geographical Survey (USGS); Reston, Virginia

System: VAX/VMS running Multinet

Comment: default directory: DUA2:[NETDIST.PUB]

Files: USGS Maps

Site: `israel.nysernet.org`

Country: USA

GMT: –5

Administrative Address: consult@nysernet.org

Organization: NYSERNET; Liverpool, New York

Comment: Try get README|more to read README page by page; idiosyncratic OS, so be sure to read the docs.

Files: CoSN; current business; e-mail; festival; files of Jewish interest (in /israel); folk music; Government info (US & World); literacy; learner; mutlu; ncesgnrl; newspaper; news & services; NYSERNET

Site: iubio.bio.indiana.edu

Country: USA

GMT: –5

Organization: Indiana University Biology Dept.; Bloomington, Indiana

Files: biology archive; molecular bio

Site: jhunix.hcf.jhu.edu

Country: USA

GMT: –5

Organization: John Hopkins University; Baltimore, Maryland

System: UNIX

Files: Internet Talk Radio (ITR); JHU network info; JHU press releases; Mac; mailing lists; MS-DOS; security papers; sendmail configuration files; Tolkien mailing list archive (faqs, images, etc.); weather

Site: kalikka.jyu.fi

Country: Finland

GMT: +2

System: UNIX (System V Release 4.0)

Files: Conquer; Xconquer (Roguelike game)

Site: `kermit.columbia.edu`

Country: USA

GMT: −5

Administrative Address: `ftp-bugs@columbia.edu`, `kermit@columbia.edu` (Frank da Cruz)

Organization: Columbia University Academic Information Systems; New York, New York

System: UNIX

Comment: User ID `ftp` can be used instead of anonymous.

Files: Kermit (home); IBM TCP/IP mods; Packet drivers; PC fonts; RFC1395 bootp server; MM Mail manager; C-Command parsing package; new VMS make; deejay backup system; VMS software

Site: `kum.kaist.ac.kr`

Country: South-Korea

GMT: +10

Organization: KAIST

System: UNIX (SunOS 4.1)

Files: archie; ked; netinfo; SDN info; Sun patches

Site: `kurosawa.unice.fr`

Country: France

GMT: +1

Administrative Address: `marc@kurosawa.unice.fr`

Organization: Universite de Nice (University of Nice), —Institut Non Lineaire de Nice (Nice Non-Linear Institute)

System: UNIX

Files: fractal compression work of Yuval Fisher (INLS University of California, San Diego); fractals (images and software)

Site: labrea.stanford.edu

Country: USA

GMT: −8

Administrative Address: action@labrea.stanford.edu

Organization: Stanford University Computer Science Dept.; Stanford, California

System: UNIX

Files: avg2; bgc; cap; cmm; coda; Concrete Math errata; cs; csd-info; ctwill; cweb; dict; emlp; EmTeX; fax; GNU; hunt; husbands; japan; lookup; lp; mdw; news; p2c.shar; patch; rio; sbprolog; sgb; shap; siam; stinfo; Sun; TeX sources (official); VMS; WWW; X11; X11R5

Site: lib.stat.cmu.edu

Country: USA

GMT: −5

Organization: Carnegie-Mellon University Statistics Dept.; Pittsburgh, Pennsylvania

System: UNIX

Comment: STAT LIB master site

Files: apstat; asacert; asascs; blss; cm; cmlib; crab; datasets; designs; disease; general; glim; griffiths-hill; ims Bulletin; jasadata; jcgs; jqt; maps; master; meetings; minitab; multi; s-news; sapaclisp; xlispstat

Site: linus.mi.uib.no

Country: Norway

GMT: +1

Administrative Address: respl@mi.uib.no (Peder Langlo)

Organization: University of Bergen Math Dept.; Bergen

System: UNIX (HP9000/375, HP-UX)

Comment: Strong appropriate use policies.

Files: calvin (graphics); movfiles; movie; schubert; skaug; XV

Site: lyu.fi

Country: Finland

GMT: +2

Files: Abermud; Amiga; Atari; Conquer; Etherprint; Knight; Larn; Mac; Moria (Mac bins only); Nethack; ULarn; UNIX

Site: m2c.m2c.org

Country: USA

Organization: Massachusetts Microelectronics Center; Westboro Massachusetts

GMT: –5

Files: Archives for cavers mailing list

Site: mammoth.cs.unr.edu

Country: USA

GMT: –7

Organization: University of Nevada at Reno; Reno, Nevada

System: UNIX (SunOS 4.1)

Files: STTNG program guide

Site: marvel.loc.gov

Country: USA

GMT: –5

Organization: Library of Congress; Washington, DC

System: UNIX

Files: client software; collections services; exhibit images; flicc; folklife; general info; iug; LC: access, classification, online; proceedings; reference guides; utilities; viewers; z3950

Site: mary.iia.org

Country: USA

GMT: -5

Organization: International Internet Association; Hackensack, New Jersey

System: UNIX

Comment: The Patriot's archive (/pub/users/patriot), see descript.ion for file info; some other users public directories.

Files: Mush (elenium, help, tools); RSHL (sports archive); The Patriot's Archive: lots of documents on various subjects: case cites, world history, freedom of information act, RKBA, New World order, law, Clinton, FEMA, 1984 or lack of privacy disk, HCI Nazis, Bill of Rights, list of Patriot/Freedom oriented BBS systems, FBI surveillance, Nazi propaganda techniques, how to run a secure computer, world largest permanent downline, FAXified database; uninet

Site: mcafee.com

Country: USA

GMT: −8

Administrative Address: support@mcafee.com, aryeh@mcafee.com (Aryeh Goretsky), mrs@mcafee.com (Morgan Schweers)

Organization: McAfee Associates, Santa Clara, California

System: UNIX

Comment: Directories: pub/antivirus, pub/utility, pub/vsum; this site is mirrored around the world.

Files: McAfee antivirus utilities; Patricia Hoffmann's VSUM

Site: `media-lab.media.mit.edu`

Country: USA

GMT: −5

Administrative Address: `ftp@media.mit.edu`

Organization: Massachusetts Institute of Technology Media Lab; Cambridge, Massachusetts

System: UNIX

Comment: transactions are logged

Files: access; audio; books; DEC; EDS; elwin; Foner; framer; galatea; holography; interface-agents; jill; k-arith-code; mc; MediaMOO; monkeyBrains; mrconsole; music; ne-raves; NeXT; noname; nuno; physics; point_icon; Pro Audio Spectrum (PAS); saus; sci.vw.a; SGI; stoneRave; sysadmin; thinking-about-thinking; VietNet; WaveWorld

Site: `meta.stanford.edu`

Country: USA

GMT: −8

Organization: Stanford University; Stanford, California

System: UNIX (SunOS 4.1)

Files: dtp; funny; ginsberg; hypertext; jujitsu; papers; quotes

Site: `microlib.cc.utexas.edu`

Country: USA

GMT: −6

Organization: University of Texas at Austin Computer Center; Austin, Texas,

System: UNIX

Comment: Access allowed all day, but preferably outside the hours of 06:00 'til 18:00 Central time; transfers are logged.

Files: abroad; AI attic; alec; amadeus; anime; ansa; arch; bsa; Computer Center; cmes; coop; cyperpunks; databaselib; delta-clipper; doc; english; genetic-programming; german; GIF; graphx-fer; hba; lbj; lips; map; mathlib; microlib; natsci; npasswd; nursing; plant-resources-center; realtime; ref-services; registrar; review; sky-watch; snakes; sourdough; statgopher; statlib; tatp; tcc; TeXsis; TXunion; UT; vplab; ytalk; zippy

Site: `milton.u.washington.edu`

Country: USA

GMT: –8

Organization: University of Washington; Seattle, Washington

System: UNIX (Ultrix 4.2)

Files: Commodore; Star Trek info; distribution point for Mentifex AI; Go

Site: `mindseye.berkeley.edu`

Country: USA

GMT: –8

Organization: University of California at Berkeley; Berkeley, California

System: UNIX (SunOS 4.1)

Files: Kanji

Site: `moers2.edu.tw`

Country: Taiwan

GMT: +8

Administrative Address: `yimin@moers2.edu.tw` (Yi-Min Hu)

Organization: Ministry of Education Computer Center, Taiwan

System: UNIX (AIX 3.2, IBM RS6000)

Files: /chinese-pub: chinese applications

Site: mrcnext.cso.uiuc.edu

Country: USA

GMT: –6

Administrative Address: postmaster@mrcnext.cso.uiuc.edu

Organization: University of Illinois at Urbana/Champaign; Urbana, Illinois

System: UNIX

Comment: Transfers are logged.

Files: Amiga; compucom; doom; E-Text archives (Project Gutenberg); hart; kites; Linux; lists; Mac; Nethack; PC; PC Sig2; Simtel-20; UNIX; usage stats; video; WP; zip93

Site: munnari.oz.au

Country: Australia

GMT: +10

Organization: The Australian Gateway

System: UNIX

Files: AARnet; av; big-internet; BSD: fixes, net, sources; comp.sources.unix; FYI; GNU; graphics; idea; ien; iesg; ietf; internet-drafts; Mac; mailers; mg; mh; mtools; MU-CompSci; Multigate; net; netinfo; news; PC; RFCs; SGI; Shake; SNMP; Sun; Sun-fixes; Sun III; tz; UUCP maps

Site: naic.nasa.gov

Country: USA

GMT: –8

Administrative Address: naic@nasa.gov

Organization: NASA Network Applications and Information Center (NAIC) NASA Ames Research Center, California

Other Access: gopher: `naic.nasa.gov`, port 70; WWW: `http://naic.nasa.gov/naic/naic-home.html`

System: UNIX

Files: april drafts; DECnet; DMS; FBI; images; Internet Resource Guide; maps; NASA Resource Guide; NSI Russia Mgt Plan; OSS tables; packet video; RFCs; UNABOM info (/files/fbi); WWW framework

Site: `ncbi.nlm.nih.gov`

Country: USA

GMT: –5

Organization: U.S. National Institute of Health, National Library of Medicine, Bethesda, Maryland

System: UNIX

Files: aimb-db; apc; authorin; blast; cavanaugh; dab; dfa; feature-table; flatfile; genbank: NCBI, repository, toolbox; ghosh; gibbs; gish; jmc; koonin; lisptrans; macaw; MC SYM; mmdb; ncbi; nrdb; nrl3d; pichler; pkb; regexp; repset; searchfmt; security; seg; seq-ambig

Site: `ncifcrf.gov`

Country: USA

System: UNIX

Files: molecular biology archive

Site: `nctamslant.navy.mil`

Country: USA

GMT: –5

Organization: U.S. Navy, NCTAMSLANT

System: VAX/VMS

Comment: Default directory: USER4:[GUEST].

Files: chips; internet; navy public affairs; navy news; npbinfo; sharing

Site: `net-dist.mit.edu`

Country: USA

GMT: –5

Administrative Address: `postmaster@bitsy.mit.edu`, `ftp-bugs@bitsy.mit.edu`

Organization: Massachusetts Institute of Technology; Cambridge, Massachusetts

System: UNIX

Files: MIT worm paper; PGP 2.6

Site: `netmarket.com`

Country: USA

Organization: The NetMarket Company; Cambridge, Massachusetts

Other Access: `www.netmarket.com`

System: UNIX

Comment: NoteWorthy Music's CD catalog

Files: fortune; hal; PGP

Site: `nicosia.ccs.ucy.cy`

Country: Cyprus

GMT: +2

Administrative Address: `postmaster@nicosia.ccs.ucy.cy`

Organization: University of Cyprus CCS; Nicosia

System: UNIX

Files: dactl; RISC 6000; UCY

Site: nova.pvv.unit.no

Country: Norway

GMT: +1

Organization: University of Trondheim; Trondheim

System: UNIX

Files: Apollo; Atari; dikumud; languages; Linux; MUD; numerous UNIX material in /pub/Store/nova; XFree86 (mirror from ftp.xfree86.org)

Site: novell.macc.wisc.edu

Country: USA

GMT: −6

Organization: University of Wisconsin at Madison Academic Computing Center (MACC); Madison, Wisconsin

System: Novell NetWare 3.11 (PC fileserver)

Comment: Directory set to /user1/guest.

Files: archie; charon; cutcp; drivers; ees; fdc14; KA9Q; lwp; macstuff; MOKE (kanji/kana editor for msdos); NCSA; netnotes; netware; nupop; pcip; pmail; spa audit; trumpet; utils; virus; windows; wiscwrld

Site: ns3.hq.eso.org

Country: Germany

GMT: +1

Administrative Address: rhook@eso.org (Richard Hook); fmurtagh@eso.org (Fionn Murtagh) for the swlib archive; postmaster@eso.org for questions about FTP at ESO

Organization: European Southern Observatory (ESO), Garching, ST-ECF

System: UNIX

Comment: Open 24 hours; transfers are logged.

Files: cycle4; cycle5; doc; email; images; ISO; ISU; Mac; Newsletter; obs-proposals; QQQ; security; Shoemaker-Levy 9 (SL9) bulletins, images; standards; star-formation; swlib; texts; texts; UN; WAIS; wref; WWW

Site: nssdca.gsfc.nasa.gov

Country: USA

GMT: –5

Organization: NASA—Goddard Space Flight Center; Greenbelt, Maryland

System: VAX/VMS running Multinet

Comment: Default directory: ANON_DIR:[000000].

Files: active; asm; cdf; cdrom; cobe; coho; data_dist; fits; graphics software; GSFC PID; HQ NRAS; Hubble space telescope images; MD_DOC; models; multidis; ncds; operations; sfdu; space physics; spds; tools

Site: oak.oakland.edu

Country: USA

GMT: –5

Administrative Address: admin@vela.acs.oakland.edu, w8sdz@Simtel.Coast.NET, w8sdz@vela.acs.oakland.edu (Keith Petersen)

Organization: Oakland University; Rochester, Michigan

System: UNIX

Comment: Primary Simtel Software Repository mirror (of Simtel.Coast.NET, which is NOT reachable from the Internet); max. 400 users; Gopher via gopher.oakland.edu, WWW via www.acs.oakland.edu, exceptionally clean software.

Files: BBS lists; ham radio; ka9q TCP/IP; Mac; modem protocol info; MS-DOS; MS-Windows; PC Blue; PostScript; Simtel-20; UNIX

Site: `ocf.berkeley.edu`

Country: USA

GMT: –8

Administrative Address: `ftp@ocf.berkeley.edu, general-man-ager@ocf.berkeley.edu`

Organization: University of California at Berkeley Open Computing Facility; Berkeley, California

System: UNIX (Apollo)

Comment: Directory: /pub/Library/Network.

Files: Amiga; Apollo; Cal Band History; Cal graphics; comics; crossfire; FTP sites; games; gobears; Hello World archive; Help Sessions; Library; Network Info; netrek; NFL draft; OCF; purity; RFCs; Space; Traveller; Usenet Olympics

Site: `orlith.bates.edu`

Country: USA

GMT: -5

Organization: Bates College; Lewiston, Maine

System: UNIX (4.3BSD)

Comment: All files are in /pub/mud.

Files: Mud related

Site: `pcdos.bocaraton.ibm.com`

Country: USA

GMT: –5

Organization: IBM—Boca Raton PCDOS 6.1 to 6.3 stepup service; Boca Raton, Florida

System: UNIX

Comment: no anonymous, use `ftp`; no `dir`, `ls-l`, use `ls`; directories: PCDOS613 contains several language-specific versions.

Files: PC DOS 6.1 to 6.3 stepup

Site: `phil.utmb.edu`

Country: USA

GMT: −6

Organization: University of Texas at Galveston Medical Branch; Galveston, Texas

System: UNIX

Files: c-advisories; clippings; cops; info; network tools; Virus-L; (anti)virus-software

Site: `pitt.edu`

Country: USA

GMT: −5

Organization: University of Pittsburgh; Pittsburgh, Pennsylvania

System: UNIX

Files: local nameserver source; local decnet database; National Institute of Health Guide Online; RFCs; local network docs

Site: `plains.nodak.edu`

Country: USA

GMT: −5

Organization: North Dakota State University; Fargo, North Dakota

Files: K-12 information, Apple; MSDOS; Mac; Amiga; ASCII pics; `comp.sys.handhelds`; list archives

Site: `pomona.claremont.edu`

Country: USA

GMT: –8

Organization: Claremont College, Claremont, California

System: VAX/VMS running Multinet

Files: Astro; bikes; Disney; games; graphics; HPGL2PS; planes; Pomona College Today; utils; VMS; xloadimage; Yale Bright Star catalogue

Site: prep.ai.mit.edu

Country: USA

GMT: –5

Administrative Address: gnu@prep.ai.mit.edu, root@aeneas.mit.edu

Organization: Massachusetts Institute of Technology AI Lab; Cambridge, Massachusetts

System: UNIX

Comment: Limit of 60 users, site is extremely congested, use one of the mirrors.

Files: ACS; Athena; GNU (primary site: this material is mirrored around the world i.e. at wuarchive.wustl.edu, ftp.uu.net, gatekeeper.dec.com, ftp.funet.fi); kerberos; lpf; palladium; palladium2; virus; XNeXT

Site: princeton.edu

Country: USA

GMT: –5

Administrative Address: ftp@princeton.edu

Organization: Princeton University; Princeton, New Jersey

System: UNIX

Comment: If you're on an IBM mainframe and are having problems connecting try executing term chardel off and reconnecting to princeton.edu; loose files in /pub directory, including Maastricht.Treaty.tar.Z.

Files: aabd; amr; Apogee; ASD; Atlas1; BBS; benchmarks; Bicycles; Bitnet; bpw; BT; cwisp; diku; diver; draine; fort; fusion; Graphics; hk; hosts (info on Internet and Princeton Hosts); iams; IRC; katak; lcc; libmast; Maastricht Treaty; ml; morph; Mosaic; mp-render; MS-DOS; MUMBLE; music; netchat; Networking Tools; ntalk; Oberon; PC anti-virus; PC ann; PC gopher; pnn; rec.music.a-cappella; sendmail; sendmail.satellite; SGI fixes; srk; standard ML; Sun; Sun-fixes; t2demo; trees; uw; vfs; Video; virus; Web; Whitney-Graustein; wolf; zsh

Site: pubinfo.jpl.nasa.gov

Country: USA

GMT: –8

Administrative Address: newsdesk@jplpost.jpl.nasa.gov (JPL Public Information Office)

Organization: NASA—Jet Propulsion Laboratory; Pasadena, California

System: NetWare (PC fileserver)

Comment: directories: /educator, /images, /missions, /news, /software, /universe; directory set to /jplpao/public/jplinfo

Files: archive; educator; hires; html; Images and text files from JPL's robotic space missions for NASA; missions; news; sircxsar; topex; universe

Site: qiclab.scn.rain.com

Country: USA

GMT: –8

Administrative Address: root@qiclab.scn.rain.com

Organization: Research & Info Network; Pacific Systems Group; Tigard, Oregon

System: UNIX

Comment: Index file: ls-LR.Z.

Files: astronomy; bench; calculators; cdrom; cisco; cygnus; database; docs; games; graphics; mail; math; misc (huge); multimedia; music; network; NeWS; pas-lovers; phantasia; PostScript; programming; RFC; security; shells; simulation; Solaris; Sun; SunOS-patches; sysadmin; text; ucb; xview

Site: quartz.rutgers.edu

Country: USA

GMT: −5

Administrative Address: bbs@quartz.rutgers.edu

Organization: Rutgers University; Piscataway, New Jersey

Comment: transfers are logged; uploads to /incoming; server can (de)compress, g(un)zip

Files: Humor archive in pub/humor (Monty Python scripts, blonde jokes and the like).

Site: ra.nrl.navy.mil

Country: USA

Organization: US Navy

System: UNIX (SunOS 4.1)

Files: ai; astro; bibliography; biology; chem; comm; comp.sys.mac.scitech; dataAcq; demos; dsp; ElecEng; engAnalysis; geology; graphing; help; imaging; info; Internet; MacSciTech; materialsSci; math; NRLWHOIS; optics; physics; programming; psychology; SEAM92; SEAM93; seam93input; SGI; Sun; virus; visualization

Site: rhino.microsoft.com

Country: USA

GMT: −8

Administrative Address: ftpadmin@microsoft.com

Organization: Microsoft Corp.

System: MS-Windows NT (PC)

Files: prune; TCP/IP; Winsock; wsat; wsatold

Site: rincewind.mech.virgina.edu

Country: USA

GMT: –5

Administrative Address: ftp@rincewind.mech.virginia.edu

Organization: University of Virginia Mechanical & Aerospace Engineering; Charlottesville, Virgina

System: UNIX

Comment: One of the official Terry Pratchett archives (mirrors ftp.cp.tn.tudelft.nl); also through Gopher and the WWW.

Files: NeXT; Pratchett; recipes (wais-sources); sci.physics.research

Site: rinfo.urz.tu-dresden.de

Country: Germany

GMT: +1

Organization: Technische Universitaet Dresden (Dresden Institute of Technology) Computer Center; Dresden, Germany

System: UNIX (SunOS 4.1)

Files: doc; fractals; FTAM networking; ftp-list (general and .de); GNU; graphic; ham-radio; Linux; network; neuron; programming; security; Sun; TeX; X11

Site: risc.ua.edu

Country: USA

GMT: –6

Administrative Address: jford@ua1vm.ua.edu (J. Ford)

Organization: University of Alabama; Tuscaloosa, Alabama

System: UNIX

Comment: Also available through Gopher.

Files: IBM Anti-viral files; Pegasus Mail; Novell-related files; misc MS-DOS TCP/IP files; a games-solution (text only) directory

Site: `rtfm.mit.edu`

Country: USA

GMT: –5

Administrative Address: `ftp-bugs@rtfm.mit.edu`, `rtfm-maintainers@mit.edu`

Organization: Massachusetts Institute of Technology SIPB; Cambridge, Massachusetts

Other Access: `mail-server@rtfm.mit.edu`, send a message with `help` in the body for instructions.

System: UNIX (DECstation 500/25, 24 Mb RAM)

Comment: Primary periodical postings archive site; note that this machine is severely overloaded and you should try local mirrors as shown in the intro docs; max. 50 users.

Files: FAQ posting software; firearms discussion (RKBA articles); humor; news.answers archives; stories (Alice's PDP-10, Mel and the drum memory); Perl; Usenet archives; Usenet/Internet documents; and more

Site: `s.u-tokyo.ac.jp`

Country: Japan

GMT: +9

Organization: University of Tokyo; Tokyo

System: UNIX

Files: docs; fj; ftpsync; GNU; Japanese/Kanji software; kcl; languages; Mac (mirror of `sumex-aim.stanford.edu`); misc; MS-DOS; net; netinfo; OSF/1; tcode; Tron; TeX; UNIX; VMS; X; X11R5

Site: s2k-ftp.cs.berkeley.edu

Country: USA

GMT: –8

Administrative Address: claire@postgres.berkeley.edu (Claire Mosher), aoki@postgres.berkeley.edu (Paul M. Aoki)

Organization: University of California at Berkeley Computer Science Dept.; Berkeley, California

System: UNIX

Comment: Successor of postgres.berkeley.edu for non-tech reports; Epoch file system, there might be delays when files are copied in from optical disks; also available through the WWW.

Files: Ingres (University Ingres DataBaseManagementSystem); multimedia (MPEG software and lots of MPEG movies); Picasso (GUI development system); Postgres (Postgres DBMS); RCS; scan (incoming scanned tech-reports); Sequoia 2000 (Global Change Project); teaching (Computer Science lecture notes); tech-reports (outgoing Computer Science tech-reports); WWW

Site: satftp.soest.hawaii.edu

Country: USA

GMT: –10

Organization: University of Hawaii Satellite Oceanography Laboratory; Honolulu, Hawaii

Other Access: WWW: satftp.soest.hawaii.edu

System: UNIX

Files: avhrr; catalogs; docs; earth images; gms; ocean; papers; seawife; shuttle radar; spectacular; tiwe2; tools

Site: scilibx.ucsc.edu

Country: USA

GMT: –8

Organization: University of California at Santa Cruz; Santa Cruz, California

System: UNIX (Ultrix 4.1)

Files: CA legal info; webmail

Site: scott.cogsci.ed.ac.uk

Country: UK

GMT: 0

Administrative Address: help@cogsci.ed.ac.uk

Organization: University of Edinburgh Cognitive Sciences Dept.; Edinburgh, Scotland

System: UNIX

Files: adger; ai2scheme; alpha; awb; cavedon; docs; elsnet; et; fracas; ginzburg; graphics; HCRC papers; htl htk; Mac; maptask; phonology; SISTA; statling; tagger; time-constraints; tvtwm; vogel; xerion; xxyx; yeats

Site: seagull.rtd.com

Country: USA

GMT: −7

Administrative Address: support@rtd.com

Organization: RTD Systems & Networking Inc.; Tucson, Arizona

System: UNIX

Files: articles; BSDI; citadel; DOS; Dell; ESIX; GIFs; hardware; humor; InterMOO; lyrics; MLBB; MUD; orange-book; sblib; sex; slip; TCP/IP

Site: sepftp.stanford.edu

Country: USA

GMT: −8

Administrative Address: `martin@sep.stanford.edu`, `joe@monte-bello.soest.hawaii.edu`; technical: `mihai@sep.stanford.edu`, `dimitri@sep.stanford.edu`

Organization: Stanford University Stanford Exploration Project; Stanford, California

System: UNIX

Comment: `hanauma` is now aliased to `sepftp`, use `sepftp.stan-ford.edu` now; files of interests to Earth Scientists.

Files: astronomy; CLOP; Cerveny-92; Dmo3D; ERUUG; Earth_Images; Earth_Topography; geology; lowercrust; SCCM240; SEGTeX; sep-dist; SPP; Worldmap; X; Xtpanel

Site: `sjf-lwp.sjf.novell.com`

Country: USA

GMT: -7

Organization: Novell, Inc.; Provo, Utah

System: Netware 3.11 (PC fileserver)

Comment: Default directory: /sys/ftpguest.

Files: BS94; Buyers Guide; dataclub; dev docs; DR-DOS: LAN Workplace for DOS, Mac, OS/2; netman; NW 3.11; NW IP; NW NFS; NW shell; ODI; RFCs; share_w; virusaid; Unixware

Site: `soaf1.ssa.gov`

Country: USA

GMT: –5

Administrative Address: `tkevans@ssa.gov` (Tim Evans)

Organization: U.S. Social Security Administration; Baltimore, Maryland

Other Access: `info@ssa.gov`; put `send index` in body of e-mail message.

System: UNIX

Comment: Limited link—generally available 0700–1800 weekdays.

Files: SSA materials & stats (read README and access.txt for access info).

Site: soda.berkeley.edu

Country: USA

GMT: –8

Organization: University of California at Berkeley; Berkeley, California

System: UNIX

Files: archie; ars-magica; btech; cd-rom; cerebus; chaosium; classes; corewar; crossfire; culture; Cypherpunk archive; dikued; enscriptor; frua; frudge; hiking-club; ikiru; lpf; Mach; mcb130; Netrek; NNTPscan; novel; palladium; quayletool; rec.gambling; rpgindex; runequest; scheme_class; sequent; sfraves; sockets; story-teller; sugar; the4thnation; typing injury FAQ; X11R5; xbattlefront

Site: softlib.cs.rice.edu

Country: USA

GMT: –6

Organization: Rice University; Houston, Texas

System: UNIX

Files: CRPC-TRs; down_n_out; events; fastlink; Fortran-M; HPF; info; irg; Kennedy; miplib; NonEuclid; pcn; pds; renewal; softlib_docs; spib; tsplib; utilities

Site: spdcc.com

Organization: SPDCC; Cambridge, Massachusetts

System: UNIX

Comment: The largest source of gay-related information on the Net.

Files: gaynet; hiv; motss; pihkal; gueercard; sci.med FAQ; SOS; trb

Site: `speech.cse.ogi.edu`

Country: USA

GMT: –8

Organization: Oregon Graduate Institute of Science and Technology Computer Science and Engineering (CSE) Dept.; beaverton, Oregon

System: UNIX

Files: bib; census; conversion; cse523; dec; docs; findphone; landh; lyre; members; mitre; multilang; multi_lang; neural; NIST_multilang; nn_pitch_tracker; opt; osu; phonetic; pitch_data; pitch_tracker; rasta; releases; tools; uswest; vowel_data

Site: `sri.com`

Country: USA

GMT: –8

Organization: SRI International; Menlo Park, California

System: VAX/VMS running Multinet

Comment: Default directory: SYS$USER:[ANONYMOUS].

Files: INFO-VAX; netinfo from `ftp.nisc.sri.com`: Internet Tour, lots of frequent informational postings, stats etc.; RISKS Digest archive; SAXON

Site: `stat.lib.cmu.edu`

Country: USA

GMT: –5

Organization: Carnegie-Mellon University; Pittsburgh, Pennsylvania

Comment: Log in as user `statlib`

Files: Statistical Library (mirrored at `dmssyd.syd.dms.csiro.au`)

Site: stis.nsf.gov

Country: USA

GMT: –5

Organization: National Science Foundation; Arlington, Virginia

System: UNIX

Files: awards; BFA; bulletins; BIO; CISE; EHR; ENG; forms; GEO; grants; MPS; NSB; NSF; OD; OID; SBE; SRS; STIS; STISINFO

Site: sumex-aim.stanford.edu

Country: USA

GMT: –8

Organization: Stanford University; Stanford, California

Comment: Extremely busy host; main Macintosh archives here.

Files: Mac archives; Mycin (Sun4); NeXt; tmycin; several UNIX (Sun) utils

Site: sun.soe.clarkson.edu

Country: USA

GMT: –5

Organization: Clarkson University; Potsdam, New York

System: UNIX (SunOS 4.1)

Files: aaa; Annotated C++; archivers; aviator; C++; ChemSep; comp.graphics; cutcp; dac; docs; encoders; freemacs; galahad; hamimed; hpgl; ISETL; KA9Q; lj2ps; mail.archives; masm6502; Matlab; MS-DOS; NCSA 2.2 TN; Netcon 92/93; Novell; nwsl; Packet Drivers; PostScript; scheme; src; submit; TeX; transfig; UUPC; vectrex; xdm; z88 Turbo-C++; Usenet; VMS software

Site: suna.osc.edu

Country: USA

GMT: –5

Organization: Ohio Supercomputer Center; Columbus, Ohio

Comment: All file operations are logged.

Files: APE (animation production environment); Trollius (portable OS for MIND machines) docs and related papers

Site: sunee.uwaterloo.ca

Country: Canada

GMT: –5

Organization: University of Waterloo; Waterloo, Ontario

System: UNIX

Comment: Directory: pub/jpeg.

Files: Amiga; bicycle; emr; enorgy; fractint; glove; jpeg; mfs; misc; netgame; NNTP; polyblit; radio; raytracers; rend386; shadows; sound; vgif; vr; wattcp; waves

Site: sunny.stat-usa.gov

Country: USA

GMT: –5

Organization: Department of Commerce, Economics and Statistics Administration, Stat-U.S.A. FTP Server; Washington, D.C.

System: UNIX

Comment: Connections and downloads are logged.

Files: budget; defense; export; NII; press

Site: sunsite.unc.edu

Country: USA

GMT: –5

Administrative Address: ftpkeeper@sunsite.unc.edu

Organization: University of North Carolina Office for Information Technology (OIT); Chapel Hill, North Carolina

Other Access: Mail to `ftpmail@sunsite.unc.edu`

System: UNIX (Sun)

Comment: sponsored by Sun Microsystems; directory: /pub/WAIS/UNC; disclaimer applies; see how.to.submit for uploads; Gopher/WAIS: Telnet to `sunsite.unc.edu` and log in as `gopher` or `swais` respectively; server can (un)compress, g(un)zip, tar directories and files.

Files: academic; docs; electronic-publications; GNU; humor; IAFA; Internet Talk Radio; languages; Linux archive; micro; mirror of byrd.mu.wvnet.edu; multimedia; packages; Politics; SAS; Sun related Usenet newsgroups & announcements; UNC; UNIX; WAIS client (nov-cli-visual.zip); X11; XFree86 (mirror from `ftp.xfree86.org`); Z39.50

Site: `swedishchef.lerc.nasa.gov`

Country: USA

GMT: −6

Administrative Address: `jhanson@lerc.nasa.gov`

Organization: NASA—Lewis Research Center; Cleveland, Ohio

System: UNIX

Comment: Strict appropriate use policies; uploads to /anyone; very nice descriptive directory listing.

Files: `alt.education.disabled` archive; describe (descriptive ls); Digital Review Labs benchmark; editors (configured for SGI); GPC (Graphics Performance Characterization) results/samples; GPC_PLB (Picture Level Benchmark); graphics software configured for Silicon Graphics workstations; Image manipulation tools; Information relating to Lewis Mass Storage activities; IRIS Explorer SIGGRAPH92 cd-rom contents; mirror of `ftp.epcc.ed.ac.uk` (/explorer); NASA meatball insignias; PC NFS (binaries and source for IRIX 5)

Site: `sylva.for.ulaval.ca`

Country: Canada

GMT: −5

Administrative Address: `jrthibault@for.ulaval.ca`

Organization: University of Laval Faculty of Forestry and Geo-math; Laval, Quebec

System: Mac

Comment: Introductory text in French & English; site closes periodically for maintenance; Mac to Mac site; use "" when there are spaces in the name of a file or directory: e.g. get "`Internet Archivist`"; internet address will change [probably the IP address].

Files: Home brew; Internet Archivist; `Sumex-aim.stanford.edu` material; Space Archivist; vegetation oriented material: educational material, plantinfo, images, mailing lists

Site: `tecfa.unige.ch`

Country: Switzerland

GMT: +1

Organization: University of Geneva; Geneva, Switzerland

System: UNIX (SunOS 4.1)

Files: docs; MPEG; multimedia-seminar; pictures; software; sounds; TECFA; WWW

Site: `terminator.cc.umich.edu`

Country: USA

GMT: −5

Organization: University of Michigan Information Technology Division; Ann Arbor, Michigan

System: UNIX (SunOS 4.1)

Files: dns; ietf-remail; shakespeare; UNIX; Usenet; X500

Site: thumper.bellcore.com

Country: USA

Organization: BellCore; Morristown, New Jersey

System: UNIX

Comment: Some files are mirrored on ftp.sterling.com.

Files: afa; alg; anish; bcr-ca; bellcore; bier; BSD; C4; crypt; midi; nctu; orator; radio; skey; sounds; TP++; whs70

Site: tlg.org

Country: USA

GMT: −8

Organization: The Little Garden; San Francisco, California

Other Access: WWW at tlg.org

System: UNIX

Comment: TLG provides T1 etc. Internet connections

Files: AUPs; brochure; FAQs (network-related); howto (network related); NACR; Portmaster

Site: tyr.let.rug.nl

Country: Netherlands

GMT: +1

Organization: Rijks Universiteit Groningen (RUG, University of Groningen) Arts and Sciences Faculty; Groningen, Netherlands

System: UNIX

Files: charon; gheta; HP-UX; jrbutils; murkworks; Pmail (program and utilities); Prolog applications; Trumpet

Site: ubvms.cc.buffalo.edu

Country: USA

GMT: −5/-4

Organization: State University of New York at Buffalo; Buffalo, New York

Other Access: E-mail server accepts interactive messages & commands in body of letter; valid commands: help, send, dir, index; `vmsserv@ucbvms` (BITNET) and `vmsserv@ubvms.cc.buffalo.edu`

System: VAX/VMS running Multinet

Comment: Default directory: DISK$ACSDISK2:[VMSSERV].

Files: VAX/VMS; BITNET & Internet info; electronic newsletters

Site: `ucs_wcc.ucs.indiana.edu`

Country: USA

GMT: –5

Organization: Indiana University; Bloomington, Indiana

System: Novell NetWare 3.11 (PC fileserver)

Comment: Directory set to /general/ftp.

Files: MS Windows packet drivers

Site: `ucsbuxa.ucsb.edu`

Country: USA

GMT: –8

Organization: University of California at Santa Barbara; Santa Barbara, California

System: UNIX (SunOS 4.1)

Files: Hungarian material in /hcf

Site: `ucsd.edu`

Country: USA

GMT: –8

Organization: University of California at San Diego; San Diego, California

System: UNIX

Comment: Several loose files in /pub: computer liberty foundation, HHGttI, makemoney, netlib, rzsz, tinymud, z80mu, zoo.

Files: Amiga; cause; CBnet; csl; graphics programs and images; ham radio (mirrored on ftp.tu-chemnitz.de); hosts; HP fixes; INN; Mac; mail; news211; NeXT; nomad; MIDI: apps, data; PPP; security; sendmail UCSD; SGI; sound bites for Sparcstations; Sun fixes; u3b2; Usenet sources; xntp

Site: umnstat.stat.umn.edu

Country: USA

GMT: –6

Organization: University of Minnesota; Minnesota, Minneapolis

System: UNIX (Ultrix 4.1)

Files: bivsurv; docs; fsa; macanova; sbayes; schoolinfo; WWii; XlispStat

Site: una.hh.lib.umich.edu

Country: USA

GMT: –5

Organization: University of Michigan, Harlan Hatcher Library; Ann Arbor, Michigan

System: UNIX (Ultrix 4.1)

Comment: Also available through Gopher, exceptionally good site for social and humanities materials.

Files: census; diss; ebb; genref; gophers; gsp; humanities; inetdirs; news; orms; science; socsci; toc; yalelibs

Site: urvax.urich.edu

Country: USA

GMT: –5

Administrative Address: `hayes@urvax.urich.edu` (Claude Bersano-Hayes)

Organization: University of Richmond; Richmond, Virginia

System: VAX/VMS running Multinet

Comment: Default directory: SYS$USER4:[ANONYMOUS].

Files: MS-DOS: anti-virus utilities; archivers; comm; generic utilities; Rainbow; VMS

Site: `vax.cs.pitt.edu`

Country: USA

GMT: –5

Organization: University of Pittsburgh; Pittsburgh, Pennsylvania

System: UNIX (Ultrix 4.1)

Files: KA9Q

Site: `venice.mps.ohio-state.edu`

Country: USA

GMT: –5

Administrative Address: `kimagure@venice.mps.ohio-state.edu`

Organization: Ohio State University; Columbus, Ohio

Comment: Temporarily new uploads will be made available in directory: /anime-manga/upload/TEMP_NEW.

Files: Anime-Manga archive

Site: `vm.ktu.lt`

Country: Lithuania

GMT: +2

Organization: Kaunas Technical University; Kaunas, Lithuania

System: VM/CMS

Comment: No password needed; Default directory: SCSERV:ANONYMOU (ReadOnly); files are stored on mini-disks (arcdks.100,102,200,304) but I have no idea how to access them (how does VM/CMS work??) [P.R.]

Files: games for PC (Doom, Spear, Ultima); graphics (BMP, GIF, JPG); sounds for PC (AU, MOD, STD, VOC, WAV); VM-UTIL (from `ubvm.cc.buffalo.edu`)

Site: `wgrest.bk.tudelft.nl`

Country: Netherlands

GMT: +1

Administrative Address: `A.deRuijter@bk.tudelft.nl`

Organization: Technische Universiteit Delft (Delft University of Techology) Management Science Dept.; Delft, Netherlands

System: Netware (PC fileserver)

Files: Linux (Slackware); MS-DOS (4dos, animat, archive, auto-cad, batutil, dbase, diskutil, editor, electric, emulator, games, gene-alog, graphics, keyboard, library, memutil, Microsoft, modem, network, printer, sysinfo, tape, turbopas, vga, virus, Uitbuiter, wordproc, xwindows); MS-Windows 3 (archiver, desktop, disk, drivers, editor, font, games, graphics, Microsoft, modem, network, plotter, tape, sysinfo, util); Novell (novfiles, pegasus, TCP/IP, util)

Site: `wilbur.stanford.edu`

Country: USA

GMT: −8

Administrative Address: `lma@foghorn.stanford.edu` (weather), `vera@foghorn.stanford.edu` (YACC)

Organization: Stanford University; Stanford, California

Files: weather gifs; emulators (Apple II, TRS80, Commodore 64); YACC grammars (ADA, C++, SQL); National Association of Graduate and Professional Students (NAGPS) archive; Program Analysis and Verification Group (PAVG)

Site: `wilma.cs.brown.edu`

Country: USA

GMT: –5

Administrative Address: `redsoft@cs.brown.edu`

Organization: Brown University; Providence, Rhode Island

System: UNIX

Comment: Read COPYING_POLICY; server supports on-line (de)compress and tar.

Files: `alt.quotations`; Brown CS Field and Thread packages; ccel; `comp.lang.postscript`; `comp.robotics`; `comp.sources.post-script`; eim; fnord; graphics; graphtext; hyperbole; iclp94; optbook; postscript; ppcp93; splitup; tech-reports; XMX

Site: `wiretap.spies.com`

Country: USA

GMT: –8

Administrative Address: `archive@wiretap.spies.com`

Organization: Spies in the Wire; Cupertino, California

System: UNIX

Comment: Gopher access by Gopher to `wiretap.spies.com`, port 70; tar and compressed tar output is enabled; transfers are logged; anyone uploading pictures to this machine will have their kneecaps broken; look at .files for description of files per directory, .cap is for gopher and generally meaniningless to FTP users.

Files: A lot of documents on several subjects including: US government decisions (Clinton, Economic Plan, GOV, NAFTA), `alt.etext`, E-texts, networking info; `ba.internet`; game-archive; Waffle.

Site: `wuarchive.wustl.edu`

Country: USA

GMT: –6

Administrative Address: chris@wugate.wustl.edu (Chris Myers), husch@wuarchive.wustl.edu (Larry Husch: Mathematics archives)

Organization: Washington University; St. Louis, Missouri

System: UNIX (DEC Alpha AXP 3000, Model 400)

Comment: One of the major US archive sites; open 24 hours; limit of 225 users; transfers are logged; see the arrangement file in /info for info on the contents.

Files: 4.3BSD-Tahoe; comp.binaries: amiga, apple2, atari.st, ibm.pc; comp.sources: amiga, games, misc, sun, unix, x; Elm; GIF; GNU; IEN; MS-DOS (/pub/MSDOS_UPLOADS); Mathematics archives in /edu/math; Mirrors: Simtel20 (/mirrors/msdos or /systems/ibmpc/msdos), CICA (as systems/msdos/win3), Interactive Fiction (IF), sumex-aim.stanford.edu (Info-Mac), Garbo (in systems/msdos/garbo.uwasa.fi), ftp.uml.edu (MS-DOS games and demos in /systems/msdos/msdos-games); sounds; RFCs; TeX; X11

Site: www.ericsson.nl

Country: Netherlands

GMT: +1

System: UNIX

Comment: Also available through the WWW, probably preferred.

Files: datacom; GNU (some utils); Movies (some .mpeg files); Networking; PC (cshow and xwin); Pictures (a couple of .gif files); Pine material; Sounds (loose files, Simpsons, Startrek); Utils; WWW-Utils; X11R5 (seyon, mpeg-player, xplaygizmo)

Site: xmission.com

Country: USA

GMT: −7

Administrative Address: support@xmission.com

Organization: Xmission: Internet Access for Utah, Salt Lake City

Other Access: FSP

System: UNIX

Comment: Anime archive; Salt Lake City, Utah; major Internet provider. Max. 70 users; transfers are logged; user public directories.

Files: altatech; angst; animbear; astech; chipware; geomorph; graphcon; janet; lists; medicode; mindgate; mindshar; snowhare; solution; starnet; Xmission info

Site: york.cpmc.columbia.edu

Country: USA

GMT: –5

Organization: Columbia University; New York, New York

Files: human genetics

Site: zephyr.grace.cri.nz

Country: New Zealand

GMT: +10

System: UNIX

Files: Oberon; cdrom; Cnews; docs; Fnews; genbank; gle; GNU; Linux; networking; news-archive; PH; QI; recreation; silicon; TeX; Ultrix; VMS gle; wairakei

What's on the Disks

▶ ▶ This book's accompanying disks offer two of the most popular pieces of Internet software available today.

- Disk 1 contains NetCruiser, a Windows-based view of the major Internet applications (discussed in Part I of this book).

- Disk 2 contains NetManage's Chameleon Sampler dialup Internet connectivity software, for people using any service provider that offers a SLIP/PPP connection. (Chapter 4 discusses different types of connections, and Chapter 5 offers tips on working with SLIP/PPP connections.)

These two packages were selected to offer all the readers of this book a choice that meets their needs as Internet users. Note that they don't work together; you'll need to work with one or the other. But whether you choose NetCruiser's ease of use or the Chameleon Sampler's flexibility, you'll be able to explore the incredible range of resources and information available online.

▶ ▶ *Installing and Using NetCruiser*

Welcome to Netcom's NetCruiser, the software on this book's Companion Disk 1. If you've got a modem and a PC running Windows 3.1 or greater, this program is the only other thing you'll need to get up and running on the Internet. NetCruiser provides access to e-mail, Gopher, the World Wide Web, Telnet, and more; in short, it provides you with complete Internet access.

In the following pages, we'll show you everything you need to do to get NetCruiser running on your computer and then show you how to use each of NetCruiser's features. We'll provide illustrations and step-by-step instructions. Beginning users will find it most profitable to work through all the steps given. More advanced users can use this appendix more as a reference if they so choose. No matter which category you fall into, you will find that NetCruiser makes navigating the Internet quite easy.

▶ *System Requirements*

Before you do anything, you need to make sure that you will be able to run NetCruiser on your computer. To do so, you must have:

- An IBM-compatible computer with a 386 or better CPU capable of running Windows
- DOS 5.0 or any version more recent than that
- Microsoft Windows version 3.1 or higher
- At least 4 megabytes of RAM
- A modem that runs at 9600 bits per second (bps) or faster

If you've got all five of these things, you are ready to go.

▶ *Installation and Registration*

You need to do two things before you start cruising the Internet: install NetCruiser on your computer, and set up an Internet account with Netcom. NetCruiser does both for you in a single procedure, which should take you about fifteen minutes to complete if you have the following information ready before you start:

- Your modem brand and model
- Your modem's baud rate (speed)
- The port your modem is on (COM1, COM2, etc.)
- Your area code and telephone number
- Your name and address
- A user name for your e-mail address (make it up)
- A password
- A credit card number and expiration date

Installation

Ready?

1. Make sure Windows 3.1 (or higher) is running on your computer.

2. Put the NetCruiser disk that came with this book into your a: drive (or your b: drive if that's your only 3.5″ drive).

3. Start NetCruiser's setup program. Pull down the File menu on the Windows Program Manager and select the Run option. Then, where you are prompted for a command line, type a:\setup (or b:\setup) and click OK.

4. Click on Continue to have the setup program copy NetCruiser into a directory called "netcom" on your c: drive; you may change both the drive and directory if you want to put NetCruiser in another location. Copying takes only a few minutes and the setup program displays its progress as it goes. When the copying is finished, NetCruiser is on your hard disk waiting to be configured, which you will do in the next two steps.

5. In the Modem Settings window shown in Figure H.1, specify what kind of modem you have, its speed, and where it can be found. Select your modem brand and model from the Modem Type pull-down list. If you can't find yours, select "Generic"—the first entry on the list. Next, click on the baud rate or speed at which your modem runs. Note that there is no choice for 14400, nor for 28800. If you have a 14,400-baud modem, select 19200. If you have a 28,800-baud modem, select 38400. Finally, in the Connector box, click on the "com" port to which your modem is attached, and then click OK.

FIGURE H.1 ▶

The Modem Settings window.

Modem Settings

Modem Type   Practical Peripherals PM9600SA V.32

Baud Rate
○ 300   ○ 600   ○ 1200   ○ 2400
○ 4800   ○ 9600   ◉ 19200   ○ 38400

Connector
◉ COM1   ○ COM2
○ COM3   ○ COM4

OK   Cancel

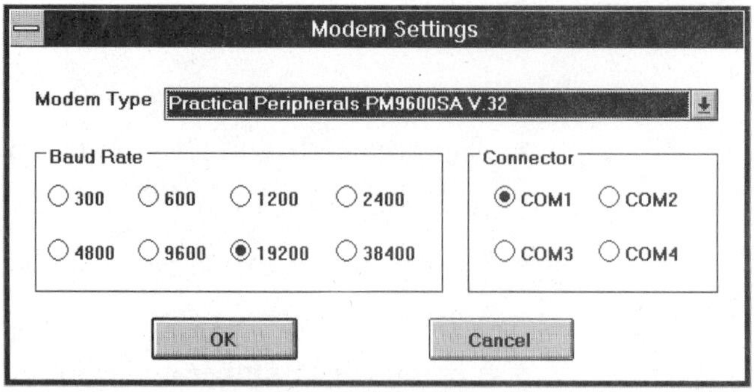

N O T E

> Be careful when entering the modem settings
> information. If you do not do this correctly, you will
> not be able to register the software.

6. In the last step before you set up an Internet account, you must select the telephone number that NetCruiser dials to access Netcom
and get you on the Internet. Since you don't know the proper
number, and the default number should be blank the first time
you install NetCruiser, click on "Directory" and select a number
from the window shown in Figure H.2.

M A S T E R   W O R D S

> To get the most current list of Netcom's local numbers
> (called *points of presence*) for Internet access via
> Netcom, call Netcom at 1-800-488-2558.

Scroll down the list of phone numbers given until you find one for your
area code. If there is more than one number in your area code, pick the
number for the city closest to where you live.

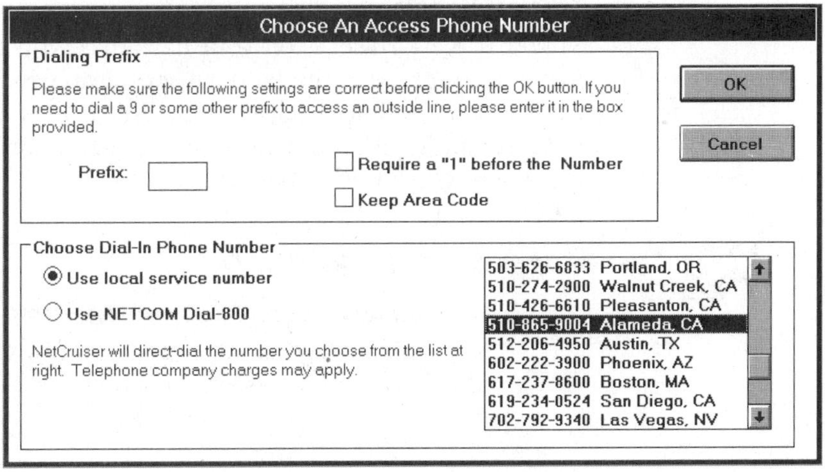

The Companion Disks

ap.
H

FIGURE H.2

*Choosing an access
phone number.*

Choose An Access Phone Number		
Dialing Prefix		
Please make sure the following settings are correct before clicking the OK button. If you need to dial a 9 or some other prefix to access an outside line, please enter it in the box provided.		OK
Prefix: [ ] ☐ Require a "1" before the Number ☐ Keep Area Code		Cancel

Choose Dial-In Phone Number

◉ Use local service number

○ Use NETCOM Dial-800

NetCruiser will direct-dial the number you choose from the list at
right. Telephone company charges may apply.

503-626-6833	Portland, OR
510-274-2900	Walnut Creek, CA
510-426-6610	Pleasanton, CA
510-865-9004	**Alameda, CA**
512-206-4950	Austin, TX
602-222-3900	Phoenix, AZ
617-237-8600	Boston, MA
619-234-0524	San Diego, CA
702-792-9340	Las Vegas, NV

▶ ▶**N O T E**

Not all calls within an area code are local, but some calls to other area codes *are* local.

If your area code does not appear on the list you'll probably have to call Netcom long distance. Netcom provides a toll-free 800 number for just this situation, which you can use by clicking on "Use NETCOM Dial-800."

▶ ▶**N O T E**

Netcom imposes a surcharge of $4.90/hour for using its 800 number. This is cheaper than long distance but not as inexpensive as local access; use a local-access number if one is available.

Finally, if you choose the 800 number or a number outside of your area code, you will need to click on the Require a '1' before the Number and Keep Area Code boxes. When you're done, click OK to return to the Phone Number window. The number you chose will appear there now, so click on OK to have the setup program create NetCruiser's icon and complete the installation.

Registration

Now that NetCruiser is on your hard disk, you need to set up your Internet account, so in the NetCruiser Setup window now on your screen, click on Start Registration. This brings up a welcome message and a reminder about needing your name, address, credit card number, and so on. Click OK to begin.

▶ ▶**M A S T E R   W O R D S**

You can also register at another time by running the NetCruiser Registration program in the Netcom group.

1. First, type in your first and last name, your address, your home phone number, the user name you want and your password (twice). Note that when you have typed in your user name, Net-Cruiser will show you your full e-mail address. It will look something like yourname@ix.netcom.com. When you have entered all the information, check it to make sure it is correct, and then click on Continue.

 ▶ ▶ **N O T E**

> **Your user name can be no longer than eight characters. Your password can be no shorter than six characters. Upper- and lowercase characters are different, so the password *AXY36Z*, for example, is not the same as *axy36z*.**

2. Type in a secret word. This is just in case you forget your password and have to call up Netcom for help. Use any word or name you're sure to remember, but try to pick one that is not easy to guess. In general, words and names that appear in the dictionary are not good passwords. Click on OK once you've typed your secret word; then click on Continue.

 ▶ ▶ **N O T E**

> **If you have questions about installing or running NetCruiser, call Netcom technical support at 1-408-983-5970. If you have any questions about Netcom's billing, call 1-800-353-6600.**

3. NetCruiser now tells you that your first month is free. Click on Continue.

4. NetCruiser is now ready to call in and create your Internet account. Click on Continue and then OK.

5. When prompted, enter your credit card information and click on OK. You are done with installation and registration. You may have to click on OK or Continue in a few more information windows,

but when NetCruiser signs off, you've successfully set up your Internet account.

▶ *Logging into NetCruiser*

NetCruiser makes logging in automatic; start the program, type in your password and user name, and click on Start Login. When you see NetCruiser's main screen, pictured in Figure H.3, you're logged in and on the Internet.

Before you proceed, a few words about NetCruiser's main screen. Throughout this appendix, instructions for each of NetCruiser's features begin from the main screen, usually from the toolbar—the row of icons below NetCruiser's pull-down menus containing all of the main

FIGURE H.3 ▶

The NetCruiser main screen.

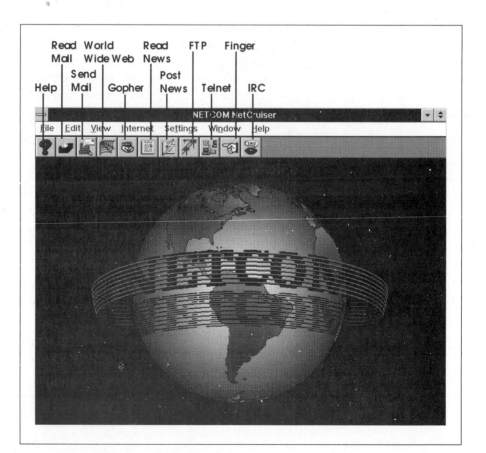

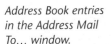

FIGURE H.7 ▶

Address Book entries in the Address Mail To... window.

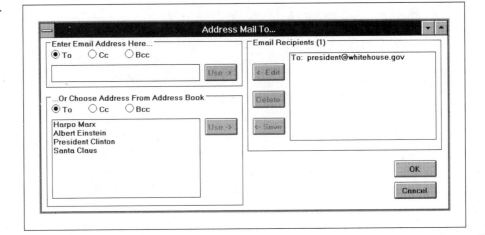

2. From the list of addresses, click on the intended recipient's name and then click on Use->.

3. The recipient's address now appears in the Email Recipients box, also shown in Figure H.7. Click on OK and the Send Mail window appears.

4. Enter a one- or two-word description of your message on the subject line and then type your message in the text area below the ruler.

5. After you've checked your message for mistakes and are ready to send it, click on Send. This procedure is little different from that of sending a message *sans* address book, but without the risk that the message will come back to you undelivered because of a typo in the address.

Sending One Message to Many People

Sometimes you'll find that you need to send the same message to a group of people. There is no reason to type your message over for each person; NetCruiser can send one message to an entire list of addresses and save you a lot of work.

The Companion Disks

▶▶

ap.

H

▶ ▶**M A S T E R   W O R D S**

> For more formal e-mail communications, you can spe-
> cify each address as To, Cc, or Bcc. Use the To button
> for the person to whom the message is directed. Cc, or
> carbon copy, is for someone whom you want to receive
> a copy of the message even though it is not directed to
> this person. Use Bcc when you want someone to receive
> a copy of the message without the knowledge of the
> To recipient.

To send a message to multiple recipients, use the same procedure that
you use to send a message to one person, but repeat the second step.
Either type multiple addresses or select them from your address book.
Figure H.8 shows three intended recipients.

FIGURE H.8 ▶

*Multiple recipients of
one message.*

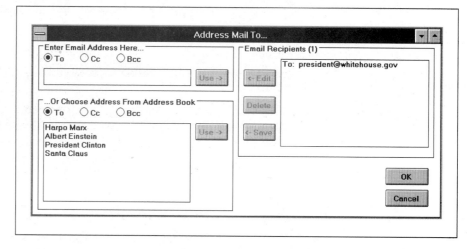

Reading New E-Mail Messages

Once you begin to send e-mail, you will, of course, get some in return.
This section shows you how to use NetCruiser to read the mail you get
and then dispose of it in some way, such as deleting it, replying to the
sender, forwarding it to someone else, or saving it to deal with later.

Reading new e-mail is very easy. To see how, work through the following steps.

1. Click on the Read Mail icon on the NetCruiser toolbar (it's the icon next to the question mark—the one that looks like an envelope popping out of a tissue box).

2. In the window that appears, click on Inbox and then click OK. This tells NetCruiser to check for new mail. NetCruiser then lists the header for each message you received, as in Figure H.9.

N O T E

If you have no new mail, NetCruiser tells you so in a message at the bottom of the window.

The message header gives you some idea of what to expect in the message itself. The header shows you the name or e-mail address of the person who sent the message and the subject of the message.

FIGURE H.9

A list of new mail messages.

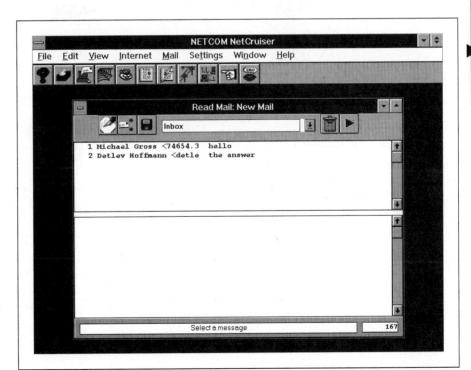

3. Click on the header of the message you want to read and then click on the Read button (a large triangle pointing to the right, like the icon for the "play" button on your VCR). NetCruiser then displays the text of the message, as in Figure H.10.

4. If you're done reading your messages, close the New Mail window. That's all there is to it.

FIGURE H.10 ▶

Reading a new e-mail message.

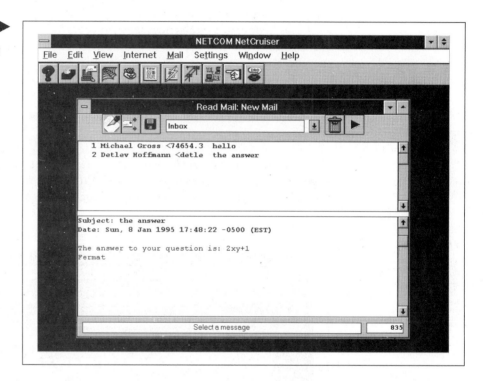

Dealing with Messages Once You've Read Them

If you've closed the New Mail window, please reopen it now (follow the first two steps in the previous section) so you can learn to reply to, forward, save, and delete messages once you have read them.

Replying to a Message Often you will want to write back to a person who has written an e-mail message to you. To do this, you could follow the steps we discussed earlier and write a message from scratch. If, however, you use NetCruiser's Reply feature, you'll save yourself some work because NetCruiser automatically puts the address and subject into your message; all you have to do is type the message text.

To reply to a message, you must have the contents of the message displayed in the message window.

1. Double-click on the header and then click on the Reply button. It's the button all the way to the left with the fountain pen on it.

2. NetCruiser will ask you if you want to put the text of the message you just got into your reply. Click on Yes if you do and No if you don't.

3. Now you are in the familiar Send Mail window; just type your message and send it.

Forwarding a Message Sometimes you will want to send another person a message you've received. You could retype the whole thing, but that would be a waste of time. Instead, NetCruiser allows you to "forward" a message by automatically putting the entire thing into a new message that you address and send.

To forward a message, you must have the contents of the message displayed in the message window.

1. Click on the header of the message and then click on the Forward button. It's the second button on the left—the one showing the half-envelope next to two small arrows.

2. Now address and send the message as you've done before. Either type in an e-mail address or get one from your address book, put in the subject, add some more text to the body of the message explaining what you are forwarding, and send it on its way.

Deleting Messages Most e-mail messages are not worth keeping once you've read them. To delete a message, click on the header of the message you want to delete and click on the Delete button—that's right, the one with the garbage can. Then click on Yes to confirm the deletion.

Saving Messages Sometimes you do want to keep your messages for a while. One way to keep a message is to do nothing after you've read it. The message will just stay in your Inbox for you to read (or forward, reply to, or delete) next time you read your mail. If you take this

The Companion Disks

ap.
H

approach, you will soon find messages piling up in your Inbox and you won't be able to find new messages among all the old ones.

A better way of managing your messages is to save them. To save a message, click on the header of the message you want to save, then click on the Save button—the one with the floppy disk on it.

Saving a message puts a copy of the message into a different mailbox called the Saved Mailbox. You can then delete the message from your Inbox and prevent clutter. To see how to work with messages you've put into your Saved Mailbox, go on to the next section.

Working with Saved Messages

Working with old messages in your Saved Mailbox is exactly like working with new messages in your Inbox, except that NetCruiser doesn't check for new mail when you open the Saved Mail box. You can read messages in the Saved Mail box, delete them, forward them, and reply to them in exactly the same way you do these things in the Inbox. The Saved Mail window looks the same, acts the same, and has the same buttons as the New Mail window discussed above.

You can open the Saved Mail box in two ways. If your Inbox is open, pull down the list in the top center of the New Mail window and select Saved Mail. Alternatively, click on NetCruiser's Read Mail icon and select Saved Mail from the list that appears. Using either method, you can now work with all of your saved messages.

Now you know how to use all of NetCruiser's e-mail tools. Close any windows that are open and let's go on to the World Wide Web.

▶ World Wide Web

The World Wide Web (WWW), discussed in Chapter 11, is perhaps the most spectacular feature of the Internet. Like other features of the Internet such as Gopher (also discussed in Chapter 11), it provides access to very large quantities of information. What is so special about the Web is the way this information is organized; information is displayed on graphical "pages," which contain not only text, but also graphic images. What's more, pages are linked to one another through hypertext links, which allow you to move effortlessly from one page to another related one somewhere (anywhere) else on the Web.

Because the Web is graphical, special software called a Web *browser* is necessary to use it. The most popular browsers are those based on a program called Mosaic, originally developed by NCSA and distributed free of charge over the Internet itself. In late 1994, NCSA sold the rights to commercially distribute enhanced forms of Mosaic to various companies (Spry, Spyglass, etc.); some other browsers available commercially (including Netscape) are not based on NCSA Mosaic but have the same basic features.

The "Mosaic-like" Web browser included in NetCruiser has the same basic features as the various forms of Mosaic; it is good for most general purposes. Note that you cannot currently use any of the other Mosaics or Mosaic-like browsers with NetCruiser.

Connecting to the WWW

Connecting to the Web with NetCruiser is automatic. On the Net-Cruiser toolbar, click the WWW icon—the one displaying a spider web. This connects you to the Web, and brings you to the Netcom "home page" shown in Figure H.11. A home page is usually the first page you see when you connect to a Web site; sites generally use their home pages to identify themselves and to provide an overview of what is available at the site.

Navigating the WWW

Now that you're on the Web, the simplest way to get around is to use the hypertext "links" found on every Web page (NetCruiser, somewhat counter-intuitively, calls these "anchors"). Navigating by links is necessarily nonlinear; there is no one path or route to take. Every page on the Web has multiple links, each of which leads you to another page with multiple links, so you can go wherever you please.

In NetCruiser, links are words that appear underlined and in green by default. They describe generally and briefly the content of the page to which they link. To move from one page to a linked page, click once on the link you want.

Also notice at the top center of NetCruiser's Web viewer that each page has its own address, called a URL, or "Uniform Resource Locator." Rather than using a series of links to get to a specific page, you can go there directly by entering the URL for the page, if you happen to know it.

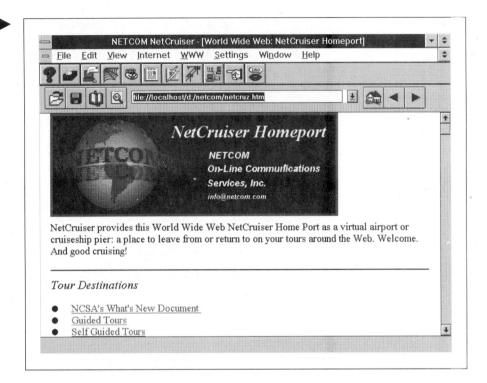

NetCruiser provides you with a few other navigational tools that give you some control over where you're going and where you've been, allowing you to retrace some or all of your steps. For example, Net-Cruiser keeps track of the URLs for all of the pages you visit in a session. Pull down the URL list at the top center of the viewer between the buttons and you will see the URLs for the pages you've visited. To revisit a page, click on its URL.

The buttons to the right of the URL list are also useful. The buttons with the left and right arrows take you one page backward or forward, respectively. The button with the house on it takes you back to the first page you visit in each session— the Netcom home page. Finally, the Interrupt button appears only when data is being sent to your computer to fill the page for display. Use this button, which has a stop sign on it, to stop transmission when it is taking too long. This is most useful if a page has many graphics on it.

WWW Bookmarks

There are always going to be pages you wish to revisit. If you had to manually reenter a URL each time you wanted to revisit a page, that would be more than inconvenient—URLs are quite long and typos are common. NetCruiser's bookmark feature takes care of this problem by allowing you to jump to a page from anywhere on the Web. To create and use bookmarks, work through the following steps.

1. When you are viewing a page you would like to bookmark, click on the bookmark button—the one near the left side of the toolbar with an open book and bookmark on it. This brings up the Book Mark window, as in Figure H.12.

2. Notice that NetCruiser fills in the name and URL of the page you are viewing. You may want to change the name to something more descriptive or something easier to remember. Click on Add to save the bookmark; the bookmark's name will appear on the list in the Book Mark window.

3. Click on Done.

FIGURE H.12 ▶

The WWW Book Mark window.

The WWW Book Mark window showing:
- Book Mark (title bar)
- Name: Labyrinth WWW Home Page
- URL: http://www.georgetown.edu/labyrinth/
- Labyrinth WWW Home Page (list)
- Buttons: Jump, Done, Add, Remove

The Companion Disks

ap.
H

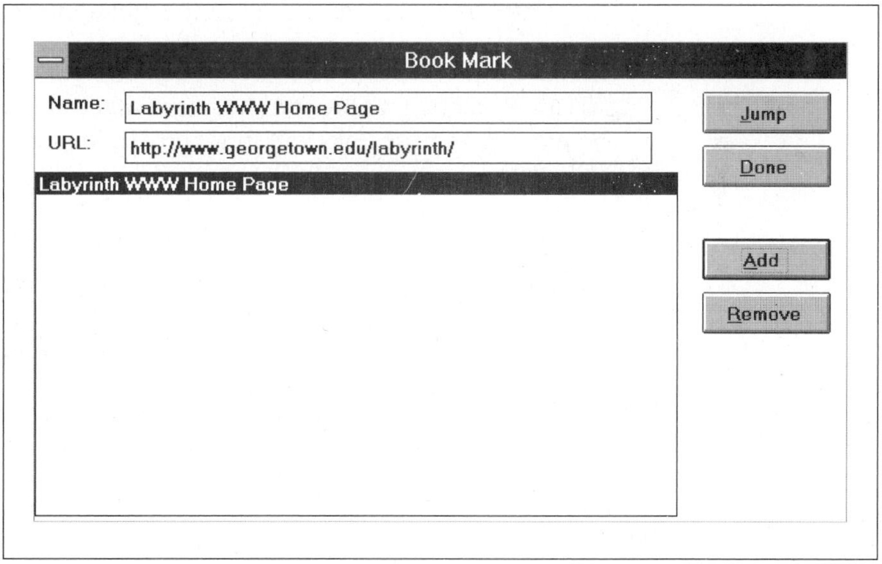

Using a bookmark is no more difficult than creating one. When you wish to jump to a page on the Web that you have bookmarked, do the following.

1. Click on the Book Mark button.

2. From the list of bookmark names on the Book Mark window, click on the name of the bookmark you want to use.

3. Click on Jump and you're there.

Saving a WWW Page

Sometimes in your wanderings on the Web, you'll find a page you'd like to copy and keep. NetCruiser allows you to do this, with the limitation that it cannot save the graphics on a page; it can only save text. To save a page, do the following.

1. While viewing the page you wish to save, click on the Save button—the one with the floppy disk on it.

2. On the Save As window that appears, give the page a filename and click on OK. Note that the default extension for saved pages is .htm and pages are saved in the \netcom directory.

If you wish, you can load a saved page into your current WWW session. Although many graphics on the page will be missing, all of the text will be present and the links will function. To load a saved page, do the following.

1. Click on the Open button, which displays an opening folder.

2. In the Open window that appears, click once on the filename of the page you wish to open and click on OK. Note that you may have to change directories to \netcom to find the correct file.

With these tools and features, you're able to go out and enjoy the WWW.

▶ Gopher

Like the World Wide Web, Gopher gives you access to huge quantities of information located on computers all over the world. These computers are called "Gopher servers" or "Gopher sites." The amount of information available is truly mind-boggling. It includes, among many other things, information from governments, universities, and libraries all over the world. Most of this information is text, but programs and picture files are also available.

Unlike the Web, Gopher is not graphical. Instead of graphical pages, Gopher is structured around text-based menus. Gopher isn't as good-looking as the Web, but it is a lot faster to use.

Getting to Gopherspace

NetCruiser makes it easy to connect to a Gopher server and get into gopherspace. To do so, follow these steps.

1. On the NetCruiser toolbar, click on the Gopher icon. This brings up the Site Chooser, basically a map of the United States, shown in Figure H.13.

2. Specify the Gopher server to which you want to connect. If you know the server's name, type it into the Site Chooser at the Site: prompt and click on OK. Alternatively, you can use the Site

FIGURE H.13

The Gopher Site Chooser.

The Companion Disks

ap.
H

Chooser itself to select a server—it contains a list of Gopher sites in each state. To specify a server in this way, click on the state containing the server to which you want to connect, pull down the Site list, which now contains servers located in the state you selected, click on the server you want, and click on OK.

Once you have followed these two steps, you have entered gopherspace; and the top-level menu of the server you selected appears. From here, you can navigate as you please.

Navigating Gopherspace

At its simplest, navigating gopherspace involves nothing more than double-clicking on a menu entry. NetCruiser helps you along by marking each menu entry with one of five different icons, according to the entry's content or function:

Icon	Entry
A folder	A submenu
A white document with blue "text"	An ASCII text file
A green document with 1s and 0s	A binary file
A tree on an island	A .GIF picture file
A magnifying glass	A *search entry* (an entry that allows you to search gopherspace for a particular word or words).

Thus, double-clicking on a folder takes you to a submenu; double-clicking on a white document displays a text file, and so on.

In addition to these markers, NetCruiser's Gopher window provides some navigation functions. These are the two buttons in the upper-right part of the window. The button with the arrow pointing to the left moves you back one menu level. The Home button moves you to the Gopher server's top-level menu—the one you saw when you first connected. A third button displaying a stop sign appears only in the middle of an operation. This is the interrupt button, which cancels any operation. Use it when Gopher is taking too long to make a connection or to view a file, for example.

These are the basic tools for getting around in gopherspace. The next section will discuss bookmarks, an essential tool if you are going to do any amount of work with Gopher.

Gopher Bookmarks

No doubt you have some sense by now of the vastness of gopherspace and just how difficult it can be to get back to one particular menu that you like after you've gone to a handful of other places.

NetCruiser's bookmark feature is the solution to this very problem. A bookmark allows you to jump to a particular Gopher menu from *anywhere* in gopherspace. To create a bookmark, work through the following steps.

1. First, you must be at the Gopher menu where you want to place a bookmark.

2. Click on the Bookmark button, which pictures an open book with a bookmark in it. This brings up the Book Mark window shown in Figure H.14.

3. NetCruiser automatically fills in the name and address of your current location. You may wish to change the name NetCruiser supplies to something more descriptive or something easier to

The Companion Disks

ap.
H

FIGURE H.14 ▶

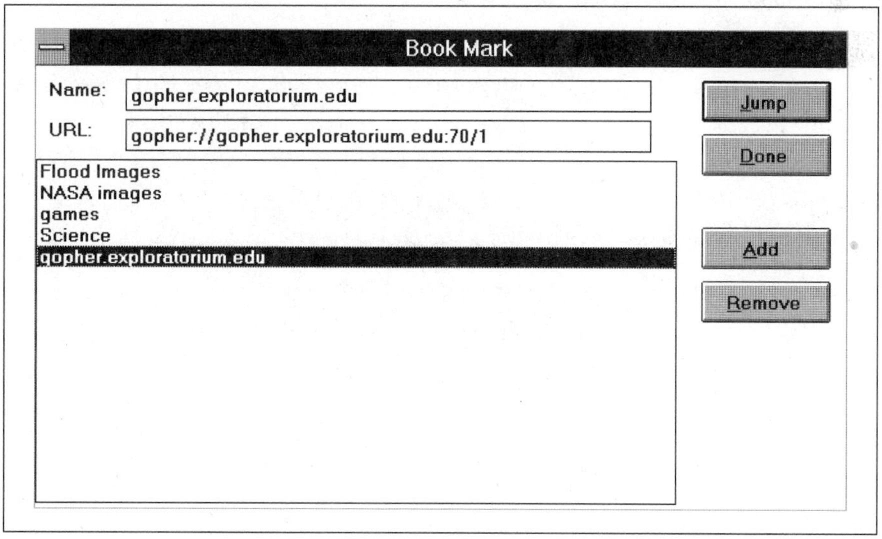

The Gopher Book Mark window.

Book Mark	
Name: gopher.exploratorium.edu	Jump
URL: gopher://gopher.exploratorium.edu:70/1	Done
Flood Images	
NASA images	
games	
Science	
gopher.exploratorium.edu	Add
	Remove

remember. To create the bookmark, click on Add. As in Figure H.14, NetCruiser keeps a list of the bookmarks you create. Now click on Done to close the Book Mark window.

Once you've created a bookmark, you can use it to jump to the marked location from anywhere in gopherspace. This is a two-step operation:

1. Click on the Book Mark button to open the Book Mark window.

2. Click on the bookmark you wish to use and then click on Jump.

Bookmarks, in combination with NetCruiser's other navigating tools, make gopherspace manageable.

Saving Files from Gopher

Finally, NetCruiser not only provides the tools you need to locate information in gopherspace, it also provides a means for saving what you find.

Saving Graphics and Binary Files Saving a graphics or binary file involves little more than double-clicking on it. When you double-click on a graphics or binary file, NetCruiser prompts you for a filename. When you enter one, NetCruiser saves a copy of the file on your hard disk.

▶ ▶**N O T E**

> **By default NetCruiser will save the file in the \netcom directory. If you wish, you can specify a different directory when you enter the filename.**

Saving Text Files Saving a copy of a text file is not quite so automatic, but easy nonetheless.

1. With the text file displayed, click on the Save button.

2. NetCruiser prompts you for a filename. Enter a name and click OK. NetCruiser then saves the file in the \netcom directory on your hard disk.

▶ *FTP*

FTP (File Transfer Protocol), discussed in Chapter 9, allows you to copy files from another computer on the Internet to your own. There are dedicated FTP sites all over the world that maintain collections of software and information of every conceivable kind; Appendix G lists a few hundred of them.

▶ ▶ **M A S T E R   W O R D S**

An important word about etiquette (or netiquette) here. Because FTP sites are located on computers used in business and universities, don't FTP to a site until after 6 PM local time for the site. Many FTP sites have been shut down because of too much public use during business hours.

NetCruiser is a particularly good FTP tool because it automates all of the commands you would otherwise need to navigate between directories on the FTP site and download files. To download a file using FTP, work through the following steps.

1. Click on NetCruiser's FTP icon—the one with the telephone poles and telephone wires. This brings up the FTP Site Chooser, which looks and acts just like the Gopher Site Chooser.

2. Specify the FTP site to which you want to connect. If you know the name, type it into the Site Chooser and click on OK. Alternatively, you can select a site from the Site Chooser. Click on the state containing the site you want, pull down the Site list, click on the site you want, and then click on OK.

3. Click on OK to have NetCruiser log you onto the site as "Anonymous." As discussed in Chapter 9, this is the standard practice. When logging onto an FTP site, you log on as the user "Anonymous" and provide your complete e-mail address as a password. NetCruiser automatically takes care of this for you here.

4. When you first connect, you'll get an introductory message. It's a good idea to read it, since an FTP site often states its policies here. Once you've read the message, you can close the message window.

The Companion Disks

▶ ▶
ap.
H

5. You should now have NetCruiser's FTP window on your screen showing you the root directory of the FTP site, as in Figure H.15. The display between the buttons at the top of the window shows you the name of the current directory. The top window displays the directories contained in the current directory. The bottom window displays the files contained in the current directory.

FIGURE H.15 ▶

NetCruiser's FTP window.

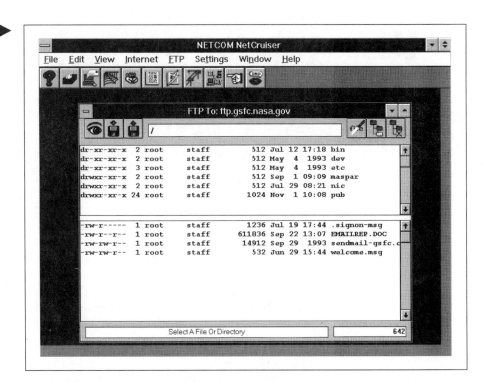

▶▶ **N O T E**

FTP sites typically store available files under the \pub (for "public") directory.

6. Move between directories until you find a file you want to download.

MASTER WORDS

> Many of the better FTP sites index the files in each directory. Look for a file named something like *00index.txt*.

7. When you find a file you want, highlight it and then click on the Download button, which has a disk and a down-arrow on it, to copy the file to your computer.

8. Select the Binary File option to tell both NetCruiser and the FTP site that you are downloading a binary file.

NOTE

> It's a good idea to select a binary transfer even if you are downloading an ASCII text file, as binary transfers are more reliable and error-free.

9. In the Save As window that appears, click on OK. You are telling your computer the name to give the file when it arrives. If you don't like the name the FTP site has given the file, you can rename it here.

Once you have done all this, the file is downloaded to your computer.

▶ *Telnet*

Telnet allows you to log into another computer and operate it from your own. It is most useful for accessing library catalogs and other public information sources. To log into another computer using Telnet, follow these steps.

1. Click on the Telnet icon on NetCruiser's toolbar (it says "TEL-NET" on it). This brings up the Site Chooser, which you've seen before with Gopher and FTP.

2. Specify the Telnet site to which you want to connect. If you know the address, type it into the Site Chooser and click on OK. Alternatively, select a site with the Site Chooser. Click on the state containing the site you want, pull down the Site list, click on the site you want, then click on OK.

3. When you connect, the site will, if it is a public machine, display a welcome and information window. This window will state the site policy and tell you the user name and password you must use to log in. (Most of the machines are not public and do not display a welcome message when you connect.) When you've finished reading, log in as instructed.

From this point on, every site will be arranged differently, and thus must be navigated differently. Some sites will have a straightforward menu structure and will closely resemble Gopher, which you already know how to navigate. Other sites, such as libraries and those that allow data searches, are idiosyncratic but will provide instructions and online help.

▶ Usenet Newsgroups

A Usenet newsgroup (as discussed in Chapter 12) is a conference dedicated to a single subject. Anyone who is interested can participate. Messages (or "articles," as NetCruiser calls them) posted on a newsgroup can be read by anyone who subscribes to the group. There are literally thousands of newsgroups out there. The next few sections will show you how to join a newsgroup, read the messages posted on a newsgroup, and post your own messages.

Joining a Newsgroup

To join a newsgroup, work through the following steps:

1. On NetCruiser's main screen, pull down the Internet menu and select the Choose USENET Newsgroups option. This brings up the Select USENET Newsgroups window shown in Figure H.16.

2. Because there are so many newsgroups, NetCruiser groups them into categories, making any particular one easy to find. Click on a category icon to see the list of newsgroups in that category. The list appears in the lower-left part of the Select USENET Newsgroups window.

3. Scroll down the list until you find a group to which you would like to subscribe. A group's name is descriptive of its content. Click

FIGURE H.16 ▶

The Select USENET Newsgroups window.

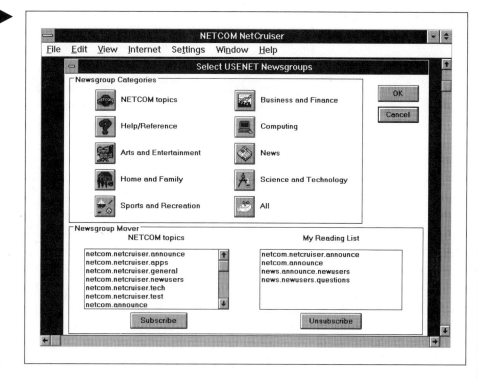

once on the group name and then click on Subscribe. The group is added to your reading list, which is what NetCruiser calls the list of newsgroups you subscribe to.

4. Repeat the second and third steps as necessary. When you are finished subscribing, click on OK.

Reading a Newsgroup Message

Now that you know how to join newsgroups, work through the following steps to learn how to read newsgroup messages.

1. On NetCruiser's toolbar, click on the Read News icon—the one with the newspaper on it. This brings up the list of newsgroups to which you subscribe.

2. Click on the newsgroup you wish to read and then click on OK. This brings up the Retrieve Headers window, shown in Figure H.17, which you use to tell NetCruiser which messages you want to read.

ap.
H

*The Retrieve Article
Headers window.*

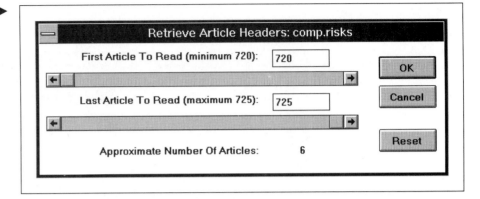

3. All newsgroup messages are numbered, and you specify the ones you want to read by their numbers. The second number shown in the Retrieve Article Headers window is the last message posted to the group. The first number shown is the last message you've read. NetCruiser automatically sets the numbers this way, allowing you to read all messages posted since the last one you read. The first time you read a newsgroup, however, you haven't read any messages yet, so NetCruiser arbitrarily picks the last 100 messages. You may read as many as 400 messages or as few as one (now or at any time) by adjusting the top and bottom message numbers. When you have selected the messages you want to read, click on OK.

4. NetCruiser grabs the headers for the messages you specified and displays them in the Read USENET window, as in Figure H.18. Newsgroup message headers contain the number of the message, its size, the e-mail address of the author, and the subject of the message. Scroll down the list of headers and click on one you want to read, then click on the Read button, which has a single arrow on it. The message appears for you to read. Continue on to the next section to learn how to read more than one message at a time.

Reading Selected Messages

Most of the time you are going to want to read more than one message, but not necessarily all of the new messages posted. NetCruiser makes it

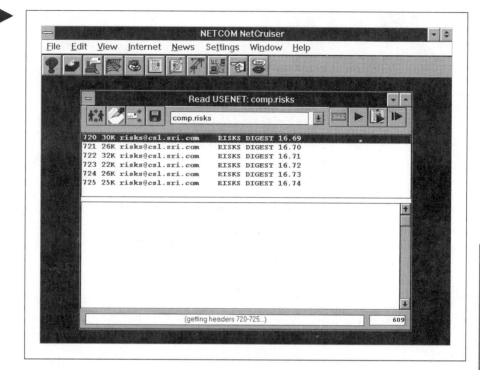

easy to be selective:

1. Select only those messages you want to read (do this by clicking on the message header while holding down the Ctrl key).

2. Click on the Read Next Selected button—the one with a single arrow superimposed over a newspaper. Click this button again to read each message you selected.

Reading the Next Newsgroup

If you subscribe to multiple newsgroups, you can read all of them at a sitting. When you have finished reading the messages from one group, click on the Next Newsgroup button—the one with a double arrow on it. This will retrieve the message headers for the next newsgroup on your reading list. As above, you must specify the numbers of the messages you wish to read.

▶ ▶**N O T E**

> **Newsgroups appear on your reading list in the order you subscribed to them.**

Other Read USENET Functions

NetCruiser provides some other useful message functions located on the Read USENET window. Here is a summary; for more information, turn to *Access the Internet!* (SYBEX, 1995).

- **Reply by e-mail to a message.** Instead of posting a message for everyone to read, you can reply by e-mail message directly to the writer. Click on the Reply by Message button, which has a fountain pen on it. The procedure is exactly like that of replying to an e-mail message.

- **Forward a message.** Click on the Forward button (an envelope and two red arrows) to forward a newsgroup message by e-mail to another person. This is exactly like forwarding an e-mail message.

- **Save a message.** Click on the Save button to save a newsgroup message on your hard disk. Messages are saved to the \netcom\news directory on your hard disk. The first message you save is called 00000001.msg, the second 00000002.msg, and so on.

- **Desubscribe.** Click on the Desubscribe button (it looks vaguely like a ticket) if you don't want to participate in a newsgroup anymore.

Posting a Reply Message

Half the fun of newsgroups is the interaction—posting messages as well as reading them. Work through the following steps to learn how to post a message in response to a message you read.

1. Make sure the message to which you want to reply is displayed in the Read USENET window.

2. Click on the Follow-Up button, which has two arrows between two silhouetted figures. This brings up the Post To USENET window, displayed in Figure H.19. Notice that NetCruiser has

FIGURE H.19

The Post To USENET window.

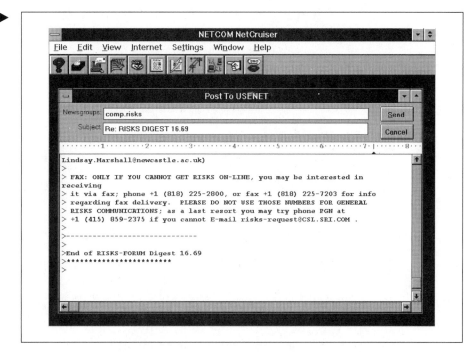

automatically filled in the newsgroup you're posting to and the subject of your message. Notice also that since you are posting a reply, the text of the original message is automatically included. Since so many messages are posted to each newsgroup, it is a good idea to include the text to which you are responding so others know what it is you are writing about.

3. Type your message and click on Send to post it. Then click on Yes to confirm. Keep in mind that your message can be read all over the world. Make sure what you write is really what you want to say.

Posting a New Message

Sometimes, of course, you will want to post a brand new message, not a reply to someone else's. This is also very simple; the procedure is nearly identical to posting a reply. Work through the following steps to learn how.

1. First, on NetCruiser's main screen, click on the Post News icon, which shows a newspaper under a lightning bolt. This brings up the Post To USENET window.

2. When you are replying to a post, NetCruiser automatically fills in the newsgroup to post to and the subject of the message. Here, you must fill them in yourself.

3. Type in your message in the area below the ruler, click on Send and then on Yes to confirm.

 ▶ ▶**N O T E**

You can post practice messages to the group
`netcom.test`.

▶ *IRC*

IRC (Internet Relay Chat, discussed in Chapter 14) allows you to "chat" with other Internet users connected to the same IRC "channel" at the same time. It is, in effect, a live newsgroup. If you want to talk to particular people, however, e-mail and newsgroups are more reliable means of communication; with IRC, you can never be sure if the person you want to talk to is online. IRC essentially allows two kinds of chats, a general public chat, where anyone and everyone on the channel participates, and a private chat with a single user. To participate in a general chat, work through the following steps.

1. Click on the IRC button on the NetCruiser toolbar (the mouth saying IRC). This brings up the IRC Connection window.

2. Choose the network or host on which you are going to chat. The default EFnet is sufficient.

3. Enter the nickname by which you will be known when chatting. The default is your Netcom user name. You should also enter your real name in the Your Name text box.

4. Click on Connect. This brings up the IRC Control Panel, shown in Figure H.20.

5. Click on the Join button, which is the button on the far left that displays a figure entering an open door. This brings up the Join window.

6. Type the channel on which you want to chat and click on OK. Channel names begin with a number sign (#) and each channel is devoted to a particular subject. This drops you in the middle of

FIGURE H.20

The IRC Control Panel.

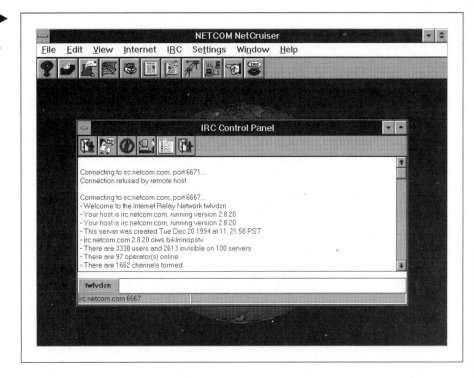

the conversation, as in Figure H.21. The subject of the conversation is displayed on the title bar of the window, the other participants' nicknames are displayed in a column on the right, and the conversation itself appears in the main part of the window.

7. When you are finished chatting and wish to leave, click on the Disconnect button, which is the button on the far right showing a figure leaving an open door, and then click on Yes to confirm.

A private chat resembles a general chat, but there are only two participants, and the subject is entirely up to you. To see how to have a private chat with another Netcom user, work through the following steps.

1. Click on the IRC icon on the NetCruiser toolbar.

2. In the IRC Connection window, make sure NETCOM IRC Hosts is selected at the top of the window, then pull down the list just below and select NETCOM Private as the host.

3. Click on Connect. This brings up the IRC Control Panel again.

ap.
H

The Companion Disks

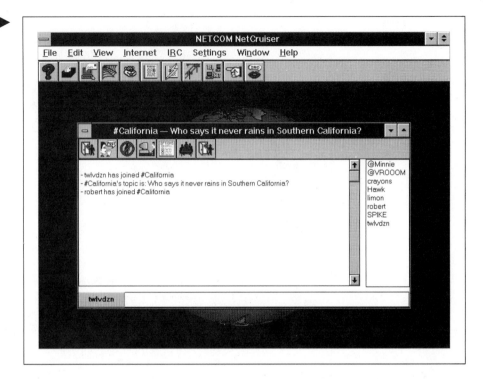

4. Click on the Query button; it shows a head in profile saying "Psst." Now type in the nickname of the person to whom you want to talk.

5. When you are done chatting, click on the Disconnect button and then Yes to confirm.

For more information on chatting, check out the alt.irc newsgroup or get a good beginning tutorial by FTP from cs.bu.edu. The filename is IRCprimer1.1.txt in the /irc/support directory.

▸ *Finger*

Finger (discussed in Chapter 10) is a utility that gives you information about users on systems across the Internet. It gives you a person's real name, whether they've logged in recently, and even whether they have mail waiting for them.

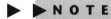

NOTE

Not all systems give out Finger information.

Finger is most useful to you if you can remember what system someone is on but can't quite remember her user name. To learn how to do
this with NetCruiser's Finger utility, work through the following steps.

1. Click on NetCruiser's Finger icon—the one with the pointing finger. This brings up the Site Chooser yet again. This time you can
ignore it, so click on OK.

2. At the User prompt in the Finger window, type the last name of
the person whose address you are looking for.

3. At the Host prompt, type the address of the system where this
person has her account, which is the same as the part of an e-mail
address after the @ sign. For example, if you're looking for a Netcom address, type `netcom.com`. (Note that this address works for
Netcom shell accounts only; you cannot Finger to a NetCruiser
account.) Now click on OK.

4. If you score a hit, NetCruiser will display information about the
person you fingered. Keep in mind that a lot of systems routinely
have Finger capability turned off, so NetCruiser may come back
at you with an error message.

5. Repeat the second and third steps as necessary. When you're
done, click on Cancel.

▶ Getting Help

NOTE

**For technical assistance with NetCruiser, call Netcom
technical support at 1-408-983-5970.**

The Companion Disks

▶▶

ap.
H

As simple and straightforward as NetCruiser is, you may sometimes need additional help. When you get stuck, try the following (in order):

1. Reread the relevant section and try again. Sometimes a little experimentation is all you need.

2. Use NetCruiser's built-in help system. Click on the Help icon on the NetCruiser toolbar—the one with the large red question mark on it.

3. Send a message to Netcom's technical support at support@ix.net-com.com. Be specific. Explain what you are trying to do, how you have tried to do it, and what didn't go right.

4. Call Netcom technical support at 1-408-983-5970.

Good luck, and enjoy!

 ▶ ▶**N O T E**

> **Sybex publishes a book called *Access the Internet!*, written by David Peal, that talks about NetCruiser in greater detail. You can find this book in your local bookstore or, to order it, call Sybex at 1-800-277-2346.**

▶▶ *Installing and Using NetManage's Chameleon Sampler*

Disk 2 contains NetManage's Chameleon Sampler dialup Internet connectivity software. In the following pages we will discuss how to configure and use Chameleon Sampler to connect to the Internet, and how to use the network applications in the Chameleon Sampler to access Internet services.

✎ ▶ ▶ N O T E

> **The following pages describe the installation, configuration, and use of the Chameleon Sampler software in detail. If you need further technical information, or if you experience any problems using the software, please consult NetManage's technical support at 1-408-973-7171 or call your Internet service provider.**

▶ An Introduction to Chameleon Sampler

The Chameleon Sampler included with this book is excerpted from a prior version of NetManage, Inc.'s popular Chameleon TCP/IP for Windows application suite, which supports both LAN and dialup TCP/IP. The Sampler is a dialup-only version, which supports SLIP and PPP connections. Please see the special offer in the back of this book for information on upgrading to the most recent full commercial versions of Chameleon or Internet Chameleon.

SLIP and PPP are protocols that allow TCP/IP data to be transmitted over phone lines using modems. TCP/IP is the language of the Internet. Once you have established a connection using Chameleon Sampler, your comuter becomes a node on the Internet, with its own unique IP address. (Both the PPP and SLIP protocols are discussed in considerable detail in Chapter 5.)

▶ Requirements for Running Chameleon Sampler

Let's take a second to make sure you have all the pieces you'll need to use this software. Chameleon Sampler requires the following:

- An IBM-compatible computer with a 386, 486, or Pentium microprocessor
- Microsoft Windows 3.1 or Windows for Workgroups
- A minimum of 4 megabytes of RAM
- About 1.5 megabytes of disk space

- A high-speed modem; the faster the better but consider 9600 bits per second (bps) a minimum

- A SLIP or PPP account with an Internet service provider (ISP)

As you can see, the requirements for running Chameleon Sampler are not steep. Just about any Windows-compatible machine with a modem will suffice, and Internet interaction is not a very CPU-intensive activity. The real speed bottleneck is the modem's data transfer rate. While there is no fundamental reason you couldn't use a 2400 bps modem to connect to the Internet via SLIP or PPP, we don't recommend the exercise. You'll find it painfully slow—and expensive. If you are paying for your account, you would do well to invest in a fast modem.

One quick note about modems. This version of the Chameleon Sampler supports a maximum computer-to-modem transfer rate of 19.2 Kbps. This might be a little disappointing if you have one of the new V.Fast or V.34 modems that have a connection speed of 28.8 kbps. The full commercial versions of Internet Chameleon and Chameleon support dialup speeds of 115.2 Kbps and high-speed ISDN connections. The upgrade offer in the back of this book has more information about how you can upgrade at a special discount.

Please note: the Chameleon Sampler will only work using SLIP or PPP. It cannot be used with a shell account. (However, you can emulate a SLIP account using a program called The Internet Adapter, discussed at the end of this appendix.) Again, see Chapter 5 for a thorough discussion of SLIP/PPP and shell connections. You will also find a list of Internet service providers in Chapter 4. If you don't already have a SLIP or PPP account, look there for information about providers in your telephone area.

▶ Brief Anatomy Lesson

The Chameleon Sampler is actually a suite of networking software, controlling all aspects of your dialup network connection. Let's take a brief look at the software that makes up the Sampler, and its functionality.

Custom Dialer

The Chameleon Sampler consists of three main parts. The first is the dialer, called "Custom." The dialer application is used to establish and configure the dialup link between your computer and your Internet service provider. Once the connection has been negotiated, the dialer manages the flow of data traffic across your link.

The dialer is where you'll enter all the information describing your modem, as well as all the configuration information required for a TCP/IP connection. Fortunately, you only have to get this working once, and then you can leave it alone. In truth it's really not very difficult. Later in this appendix, we will cover configuration of the dialer in detail.

The TCP/IP Protocol Stack

The second part of Chameleon Sampler is the TCP/IP protocol "stack." This is the part of the software that you don't really see. It's also the most important, because it's the set of software that implements the protocols used for transmitting data on the Internet. Computers on the Internet can communicate with each other precisely because they all follow the TCP/IP model. The dialer might connect you to the Internet, but it's not going to do you any good if you can't receive and transmit data other computers can understand.

The implementation of this protocol stack created by NetManage is compatible with Winsock, the Windows–TCP/IP application standard, which means you can use Chameleon Sampler to run any application program that's also Winsock-compatible. This becomes important when you go looking for other Windows applications to use over your dialup Internet connection.

Network protocol stacks are essentially transparent when they work, but when they don't work neither does anything else. Chameleon Sampler has an excellent reputation as a very robust TCP/IP implementation. Although configuration can be a little more difficult than with integrated packages like NetCruiser, the tradeoff is a much more flexible, powerful network connection.

Network Applications

The third part of Chameleon Sampler is the network applications themselves. The Sampler package provides four applications that allow you to access various Internet services: Telnet, FTP, Mail and Ping.

Telnet and FTP are discussed in Chapter 9; e-mail is the subject of Chapter 8; and Ping is discussed in Chapter 5. Here we will look at the

The Companion Disks

ap.
H

particular incarnations of them offered by Chameleon Sampler. The graphical nature of these traditionally text-based applications is particularly noteworthy.

► *Installation*

Installing Chameleon Sampler is quite simple. Configuring it and getting your IP link working is a little trickier. Let's start with installation.

Chameleon Sampler installs just like any "well-behaved" Windows software—it makes no modifications to your system.ini, and it adds a single short section to your win.ini file under the heading '[TCPIP]'. Here's how to install.

1. Insert the Chameleon Sampler diskette in your disk drive and choose File ➤ Run from the Program Manager menu.

2. Type a:setup in the Command Line text box in the Run window; where a: is the letter of the disk drive containing the Chameleon Sampler diskette.

3. After starting up, Chameleon Sampler will display a short warning about running the software on a computer already connected to a network. If you are already connected to a network, take heed. Loading multiple protocol stacks can be a tricky business; and loading multiple stacks of the same protocol (e.g. TCP/IP) is essentially impossible. Chameleon Sampler is only capable of running over a dialup link. Click Continue to proceed.

4. The Setup program now prompts you to select a directory in which to install. If you would like to install into a directory other than the one suggested, type the directory path into the text box. Click on Continue.

5. Setup will copy the Chameleon Sampler files from the floppy to the installation directory and will then create a program group called "Chameleon Sampler," containing icons for the Sampler applications. You are finished installing. Figure H.22 shows the Chameleon Sampler program group window.

The Chameleon Sampler program group window.

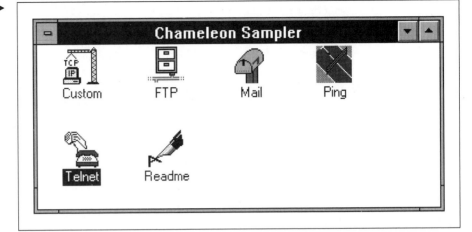

▶ Configuration

The configuration of Chameleon Sampler takes place in three parts—IP configuration, modem configuration, and the chat script. IP configuration sets up the TCP/IP protocol stack so that your computer can receive and transmit Internet data. Modem configuration tells Chameleon Sampler about the type of modem you are using and what port it is on. The chat script is a series of prompts and expected responses that will be used to log in to your Internet service provider's PPP/SLIP server. The Mail application requires some additional configuration, but there's no point in doing it before you get online, so we'll save it for later.

Chameleon Sampler comes with configuration files already written for many popular service providers. Using one of these configurations will make things a little easier; specifically, the chat script has been created for you. But if there is no file for your ISP, don't worry, it's not a big deal.

A Note on IP Configuration

In order to configure Chameleon Sampler you are going to need some information from your Internet service provider. This information will be used to initialize your TCP/IP protocol stack and give your computer a working address as a full Internet node. Since you can't use your SLIP or PPP account without it, all of this information will almost certainly have been given to you when you first signed up with your service provider.

Here is a list of the information you need for configuring the IP portion of Chameleon Sampler:

- Your IP address
- Your host name
- Your domain name
- Your domain name server address
- Your interface type

Your IP address is the numerical address of your computer on the Internet. IP addresses are discussed in depth in Chapter 3, but briefly, this unique address is used by other computers on the Internet to route data to your computer. IP addresses look like this: 198.68.136.109. Each consists of four numbers between 0 and 255, separated by periods. Note: some Internet service providers automatically assign an IP address to you when you log on. If the information from your ISP says something like "Dynamically allocated IP address," you may be able to get away with not configuring this item.

Your host name is the name of your computer—that is, it's the part of your "fully qualified domain name" (FQDN) that identifies the computer making the connection. (Chapter 3 discusses the domain name system.) In the FQDN somebody.something.com, for example, somebody is the host name. Host names must be translated into IP addresses before computers can transmit data to them. Host names can be just about anything, and they don't have to be unique, except within your subdomain.

Your domain name is essentially the name of the network your computer is connecting to. In the example above, something.com is the domain name. When combined with a valid host name, the domain name provides a host address that can be translated into an IP address for sending and receiving data.

The domain name server address is the numerical (IP) address of the computer that translates an FQDN into an IP address. Without a working domain name server you will only be able to use numerical IP addresses to contact other computers, which is much harder. Obviously you have to supply the Setup program with a numerical address before Chameleon Sampler can reach your name server; again, your service provider should have given you this information.

The interface type is the protocol that your computer will be using to send TCP/IP data over your modem. Chameleon Sampler supports PPP, SLIP, and CSLIP. (The differences between the first two protocols are discussed in Chapter 5. CSLIP is Compressed SLIP. Because there are no routing decisions to be made when dealing with a fixed end-to-end link like a dialup connection—there is only one place packets can be going—the CSLIP protocol removes routing information from the stream of data. This increases data throughput.) You are probably tied to a single protocol that your provider is using. If you have a choice, try PPP first.

Configuring the Custom Dialer

Let's start configuring the Custom application to get your Internet connection up and running. Begin by double-clicking on the Custom icon in the Chameleon Sampler program window. You'll see the screen shown in Figure H.23.

When the Custom application first starts up, it loads a default configuration file called tcpip.cfg, as shown in the illustration. If a configuration file has already been created for your service provider, now is the time to load it.

FIGURE H.23 ▶

The Custom dialer application.

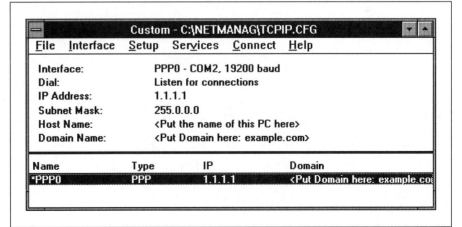

Choose File ➤ Open from the menu bar. Scroll through the list of .cfg files and see if there is one with the name of your ISP. If there is, choose it. If there isn't but you will be using PPP to connect to your ISP, then choose tcpip.cfg. If not, don't worry about it; choose Cancel and we will start from scratch.

The *.cfg files may help to configure some of the aspects of Custom, but you will still need to add information by hand. What the *.cfg files really do is supply certain default information and a reference to a chat script that works. As we will see later, chat scripts are really quite simple.

Adding an Interface If you chose a premade script corresponding to your ISP, the interface will already be set. The interface entry holds the protocol that you will be using to communicate with your service providers computers. There are three possible choices: PPP, SLIP, and CSLIP.

1. Choose Interface ➤ Add from the Custom command menu. You'll see the dialog box shown in Figure H.24.

FIGURE H.24 ▶

The Add Interface window.

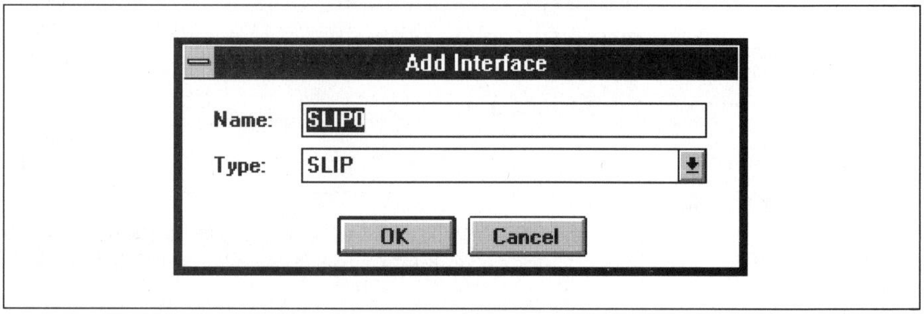

2. In the Name text box you can type a name for the interface. This interface name becomes important later, when we configure the chat script.

3. From the Type drop-down list box, select the connection protocol that your service provider is using, either PPP, SLIP, or CSLIP.

4. Click on OK. Your Custom screen should now look like Figure H.25.

FIGURE H.25 ▶

The Custom window with an Interface added.

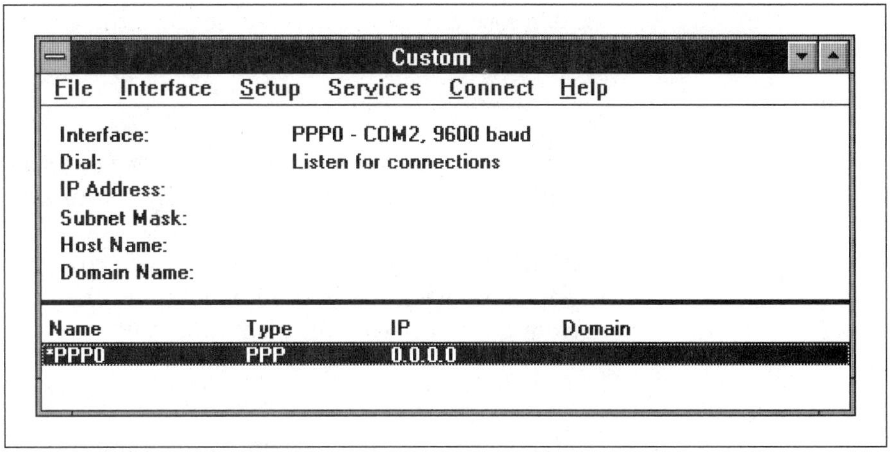

```
┌─────────────────────────────────────────────────────────┐
│ ─                      Custom                      ▼ ▲   │
│  File  Interface  Setup  Services  Connect  Help         │
│                                                          │
│  Interface:          PPP0 - COM2, 9600 baud              │
│  Dial:               Listen for connections              │
│  IP Address:                                             │
│  Subnet Mask:                                            │
│  Host Name:                                              │
│  Domain Name:                                            │
│                                                          │
│  Name            Type        IP           Domain         │
│  *PPP0           PPP         0.0.0.0                      │
│                                                          │
└─────────────────────────────────────────────────────────┘
```

Adding IP Configuration Information Now we enter the information we gathered from our ISP. Some of these entries may already be configured if you chose an existing .cfg file. Let's start with the IP address and work from there.

1. Choose Setup ➤ IP.

2. In the Internet Address window that appears, type in the four numbers that comprise your IP address. The button to the left of the text boxes will zero out your IP address.

▶ ▶ **M A S T E R   W O R D S**

> **Notice how the text under your IP address changes based on the address you enter. You can ignore this completely, but if you are interested you can refer to the discussion of address classes in Chapter 3.**

3. Once you have entered your IP address, click the OK button.

Remember that some service providers will give you an IP address automatically when you connect. Entering your IP address here won't hurt if this is the case. (If your provider uses dynamic IP assignment with PPP, you will need to enter a dummy IP address value of 1_1_1_1.) Let's enter your host name next.

The Companion Disks

ap.
H

1. Choose Setup ➤ Host Name from the Custom menu.

2. In the Host Name text box that appears, type in the host name of your computer and click OK.

Your host name has to be registered with your service provider. You can't change it without telling them first. Your service provider needs to update the name server database so that your host name can be translated into your IP address. Some service providers assign host names dynamically instead of issuing one with each account; if you have such an account, you can leave this item blank.

Next, the domain name:

1. Choose Setup ➤ Domain Name from the Custom menu.

2. In the Domain Name text box that appears, type in the domain name of your computer (usually the domain name of your service provider's network) and click OK.

Finally, we can configure the addresses of your domain servers. The Domain Servers option is found in the Services menu.

1. Choose Services ➤ Domain Servers from the Custom menu.

2. In the Domain Servers window, type in the IP addresses of your domain servers. You can enter up to three separate Domain Servers. If the first Domain Server fails to respond to a request, Chameleon Sampler will try the next, in order. You don't have to enter more than one, though. Be careful to enter this information accurately.

3. Click on OK.

The last IP configuration item you can change (although it is not mandatory) is the host table, a list of the host/domain names and corresponding IP addresses of computers you frequently connect with. When a computer is in your own host table, Chameleon Sampler doesn't need to make a request to your domain server to match a host name to an IP address. Domain servers can become bogged down with requests, or they can crash; so this extra step may save you a little time. Here is how to add a computer to your host table.

1. Choose Services ➤ Host Table from the menu bar.

2. In the Host Table dialog box type the complete name (the FQDN) of the computer you want to add. The Add button will then become undimmed.

3. Click on the Add button.

4. The window that appears will be titled with the host address of the computer you are adding (in the example shown in Figure H.26, a computer called penguin.hip.berkeley.edu). In the provided text boxes type in the four numbers of the computer's numerical IP address.

5. In the Aliases text box you can type an alias for this computer. The alias is usually a simplified name (like penguin). Once an alias has been established, you can refer to that host simply by its alias, without typing its entire host address. Click on the Add button to add your alias.

6. Click the OK button to return to the Host Table window. From here you can add more hosts, or you can click on Save to return to Custom.

FIGURE H.26 ▶

The Add Host window.

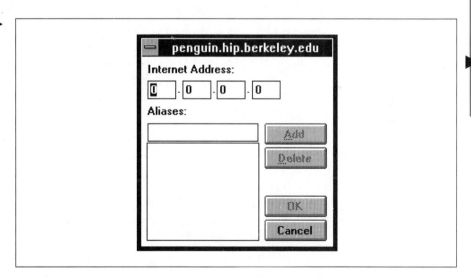

Modem Configuration

Your next task is configuring your modem and your login parameters to match those of your service provider. In this section we'll be configuring the following:

- Modem Port and Speed
- Modem Type
- ISP dialup telephone number

We will start at the top with your modem's port settings.

1. Choose Setup ➤ Port from Custom's menu bar to display the window shown in Figure H.27.

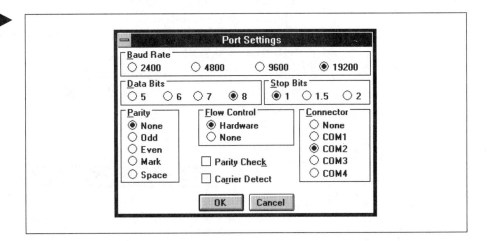

2. The options in the Port Settings window should be pretty straightforward for anyone who has configured a modem in another application. Baud Rate, Flow Control, and Connector settings need to be made according to the type of modem you are using and how it is connected to your computer. If you have a V.32bis (14.4 Kbps) modem or faster, start by selecting a baud rate of 19200, and use hardware flow control.

3. For Parity, Data Bits, and Stop Bits, if you don't have any specific information from your ISP about line settings, start with None, 8, and 1.

4. The Connector setting tells Chameleon Sampler which serial port your modem is connected to. Modems are normally configured for COM1 or COM2, so if you have no idea, try those first. Consult the manuals that came with your computer and/or modem if you don't know the answer.

5. Click on OK when you are done.

Let's take a very brief look at the Modem Settings windows, shown in Figure H.28, where you can set the initialization strings for your modem.

FIGURE H.28 ▶

The Modem Settings window.

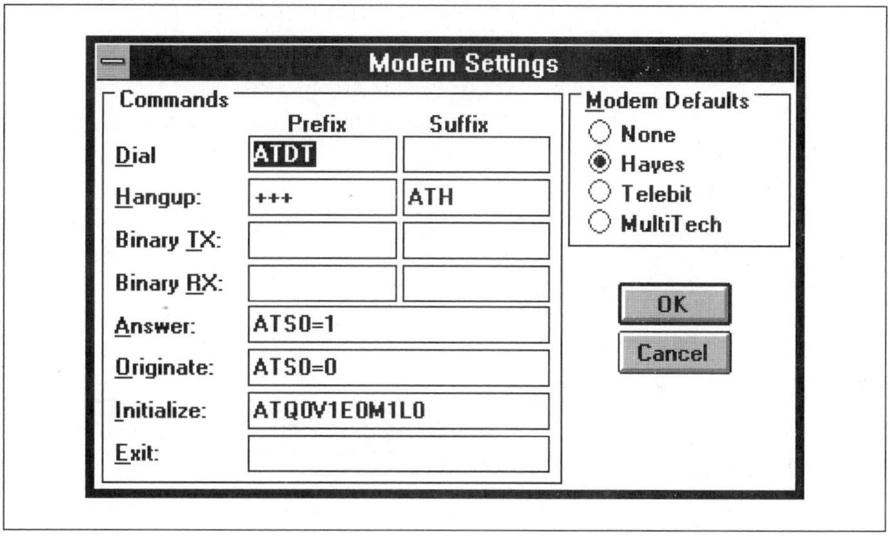

1. Choose Setup ➤ Modem Settings from the Menu bar.

2. From the Modem Defaults section, choose the modem type that most closely matches your own modem. Unless you own a Telebit or MultiTech modem, choose Hayes. Some variation of the Hayes command set is used by just about every modem available today, and this default will work for almost everyone.

3. The default settings in the Modem Settings window are designed to work with the vast majority of modern modems. It is very unlikely that you will need to change anything here. Click on OK.

▶ ▶ **N O T E**

If you get an ERROR response from your modem when trying to dial out to your ISP, it is possible that your initialization string is set incorrectly. It's best to consult your modem's documentation, but here are a couple of hints that may help. The initialization string that is supplied by default is very simple. Chameleon Sampler requires first that your modem return result codes (normally set with Q0 in the init string), second that it display result codes in verbose form as opposed to numeric form (set by V1, and third that it does not echo the commands that are sent to it (set by E0).

Now let's move on to the Dial Settings window, shown in Figure H.29, where you enter the phone number you need to dial to connect to your ISP.

FIGURE H.29 ▶

The Dial Settings window.

Dial Settings
Dial:
Timeout If Not Connected In   30   Seconds
☐ Redial After Timing Out   ☐ Signal When Connected
OK   Cancel

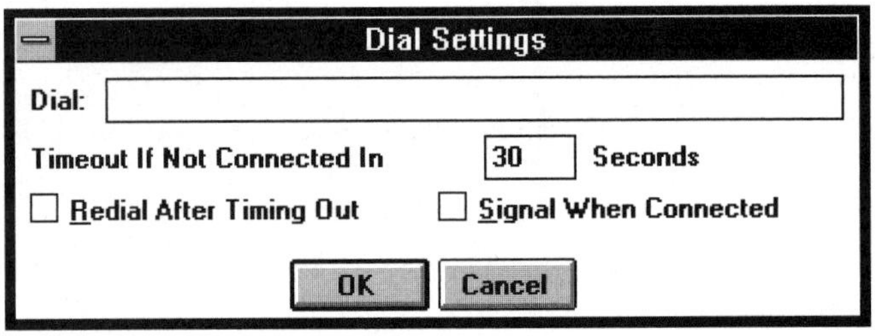

1. Choose Setup ➤ Dial Settings.

2. In the Dial text box, type in the phone number you will dial to access your Internet service provider.

3. The rest of the settings are pretty self-explanatory.

   • In the Timeout If Not Connected In box, type the delay, in seconds, you would like Chameleon Sampler's dialer to wait after dialing and before giving up on the call.

- If you want to redial when a call times out, click the Redial After Timing Out check box.
- If you want to receive notification when you connect to your service, click the Signal When Connected check box.

4. Select OK to return to Custom.

Let's save your configuration now and move on to the script configuration.

5. Choose File ➤ Save. If you created a new .cfg file you will be prompted to name it, and click on OK.

The Chat Script

If the Chameleon Sampler came with a .cfg file that corresponds to the Internet service provider you are using, you are almost done, because a script has already been provided for you. If not, you have to create your own script.

There are three entries in Custom that you need to configure before any chat script will work:

- User Name
- User Password
- Startup Command

The values you submit for these entries are used by the script while initially setting up your connection with your service provider. These items should probably be among the information you received from your service provider when you got your account. Certainly the login name and password must be supplied to you. The startup command may or may not be needed, depending on your ISP's configuration.

1. Choose Setup ➤ Login from Custom's menu bar.

2. In the Login Settings window (Figure H.30), fill in the three text boxes with your user name, your password, and the startup command.

3. Click OK to continue.

On many systems, your user name is the same as your computer's host name. The password is a pretty obvious item; you don't want other

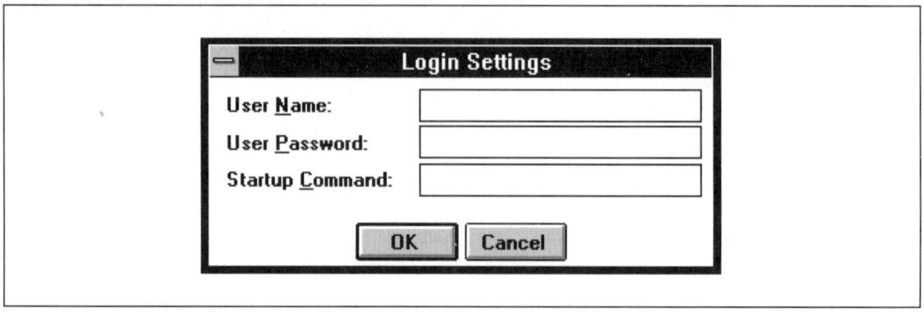

FIGURE H.30 ▶

The Login Settings window.

```
┌─────────────────────────────────────────┐
│  ┌───────────────────────────────────┐  │
│  │ ─      Login Settings             │  │
│  ├───────────────────────────────────┤  │
│  │  User Name:      [             ]   │  │
│  │                                    │  │
│  │  User Password:  [             ]   │  │
│  │                                    │  │
│  │  Startup Command:[             ]   │  │
│  │                                    │  │
│  │        [  OK  ]  [ Cancel ]        │  │
│  └───────────────────────────────────┘  │
└─────────────────────────────────────────┘
```

people to be able to connect and pretend to be you, so you need a password to log on to your service provider's network. The startup command is often the name of the protocol you are using to communicate, like PPP or CSLIP or sometimes slattach if you're connecting to a UNIX host with SLIP.

If you are using a preconfigured cfg file, you are finished. You can proceed to log on. If you aren't, it's time to make a chat script.

The chat scripts reside in a file called slip.ini in your Chameleon Sampler installation directory (c:\netmanag\ if you used the default). For each .cfg file that the Sampler came with, there is a script in the slip.ini file. Under this heading are two lines. One is the SCRIPT line, and the other is the TYPE line. If you created your own .cfg file, Chameleon Sampler will create a new section in the slip.ini file with the Interface name you set in TCP/IP configuration as the heading. It is this section that you must edit.

You can use the Windows Notepad editor (or any other text editor) to edit the slip.ini file. You must save the slip.ini file in straight ASCII when you are done, so be careful if you are using a word processor to edit this file.

The SCRIPT line holds the chat script. The chat script is a very simple series of prompts and expected responses that Chameleon Sampler uses to start your service. Script lines have the following format:

```
SCRIPT=<expect1> <send1> <expect2> <send2> ...
```

and so on—a series of text strings separated by spaces. When your modem connects to your service provider's modem, Chameleon Sampler waits to receive the first entry in the SCRIPT line. When it receives the string <expect1> it transmits the string <send1> and then waits for <expect2>. Using this series of expected prompts and responses,

Chameleon Sampler automates the login procedure for your ISP. Special characters are used in the SCRIPT line to send carriage returns, new lines, pauses, and also to send your user name, password, and startup command, as you entered them in the previous section.

Here is a list of the special characters you can use in a <send> string:

$r	send a carriage-return
$u	send your user name
$p	send your user password
$c	send the startup command
$n	send a new line
$s	send a space
$b	cause a "break"
$t	send a tab
$1–$9	pause the indicated number of seconds
$xxx	send the character whose Hex code is *xx*
$d	send the dialup phone number
$$	send a "$" character
$f	define a prompt

There are also some special characters you can use in <expect> strings:

--	expect a "-" character
-n	skip an expect
-I	expect IP address (to replace your own)
$-	find the string following this symbol

As daunting as this may look, in practice SCRIPT lines are pretty simple. Let's consider an example from the predefined scripts.

```
[PSINet]
SCRIPT=name: $u$r word: $p$r -n $6$c$r -i
TYPE=SLIP
```

This is the script for PSINet, and it works as follows. When Chameleon Sampler firsts connects to PSINet, it waits for the string `name:`. Although the real prompt is probably Username:, you only need four characters to make up an <expect> string. When Chameleon Sampler receives the string name:, it send the user name (sent with $u) and then a carriage return ($r). It then waits for word:, which is the last part of password:, and in response sends the user password and a carriage return (pr). The -n symbol in place of the next <expect> string makes Chameleon Sampler continue to the next <send> string without being prompted. 6c$r makes it wait 6 seconds and then send the startup command and a carriage return. The last command on the line is -I. This makes Chameleon Sampler wait for a numeric IP address, and use it as the numeric IP address of the local computer. PSINet configures IP addresses automatically.

Let's make our own chat script. The first thing you need to do is find out the exact sequence of prompts and responses needed to start up SLIP/PPP service with your service provider. The easiest way to find this information is to connect to your ISP with a standard terminal program and record the login process. Here is an example.

```
Annex Command Line Interpreter * Copyright 1991 xylogics, Inc.

UC Berkeley Terminal Server - Shared High Speed Service
annex-64-3 port 28 ===> PPP

Username: azure
Password:
Switching to PPP.
```

After a short login banner there is a prompt in the form of ===>. Here we entered PPP. Next we were prompted for our user name; We responded with our user name, which also happens to be our host name. We were then prompted for our password. We typed in our password, which was not echoed on the screen, and we were in. That was all there was to it.

So let's write the script to automate this connection. First we find the entry in the slip.ini file that corresponds to the interface name we chose when configuring the dialer, in this case PPP0. We will do all our editing using a standard DOS text editor.

```
[PPP0]
SCRIPT=
TYPE=PPP
```

The first thing we want out script to do is wait for the ===> prompt, and then we want to respond with PPP. Because in our own configuration we entered PPP as our startup command under Setup ➤ Login, we will call that entry directly using the $c special character. We need to end all our send stings with a carriage return special character, $r. Don't be confused by the multiple = characters. One is needed following "SCRIPT"; the others make up our <expect1> string.

```
SCRIPT====> $c$r
```

Next we wait for the "Username:" prompt, but we'll truncate the expect string to name:. We will respond with our user name as configured in Setup ➤ Login, followed by a carriage return; that's ur.

```
SCRIPT====> $c$r name: $u$r
```

Then we do the same for the "Password:"; we wait for "word:" and return our password, along with a carriage return.

```
SCRIPT====> $c$r name: $u$r word: $p$r
```

That's all; we are done with our script. Now it's time to try it out.

 ▶ ▶**N O T E**

> **We could have just typed** PPP, azure, **and our password directly into the <send> fields of the SCRIPT line instead of using the special characters to insert our previous configuration entries. For more information on the scripting syntax, see the README file in the Sampler program group.**

The Companion Disks

▶ ▶
ap.
H

Connecting and Troubleshooting

The first time you try to connect, particularly if you are using a chat script of your own device, things might not work quite right. You can use the Log function to watch your connection as it progresses, and get an idea of what might be going on.

- Choose Setup ➤ Log from the Custom dialer menu bar.

In the resulting Log window, you'll be able to watch the interaction between the Chameleon Sampler and the service provider you're connecting to.

► *Making the Connection*

Okay, it's time to connect to the Internet. Click on the Connect option in the Custom dialer menu bar. Watch in your Log window to follow the modem initialization and the connection to your Internet service provider. If something goes wrong during the modem initialization, check back under Setup ➤ Port and Setup ➤ Modem. If a problem occurs after you have connected with the remote modem, check over your SCRIPT entry again.

If you are having a lot of difficulty resolving connection problems, try calling your service provider. Chameleon SLIP/PPP software is very popular, and your ISP probably can explain how to configure Chameleon Sampler for their specific system.

In order to check that your new connection is configured correctly, you can use the Ping application included in the sampler package.

► *The Chameleon Sampler Applications*

The Chameleon Sampler comes with four applications that allow you to make use of your newly established Internet connection: Ping, Telnet, FTP, and Mail. Since we just got through installing Chameleon Sampler, Ping seems like a good application to discuss, as it is very useful in verifying the configuration of you IP connection.

Ping

Ping, introduced in Chapter 5, is the simplest of the applications supplied with the Chameleon Sampler, but it serves a very useful function. Ping is used to probe a remote computer and see if it is active and responding. It is also useful in checking to see whether your dialup IP link is working successfully.

To start the program, double-click on the Ping icon in the Chameleon Sampler program group. You'll see the window shown in Figure H.31.

Let's try Pinging a computer to see if our connection is working.

1. Choose Start from the Ping menu bar.

The Ping application window.

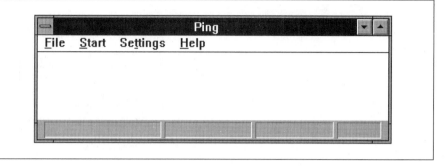

2. In the Host field of the resulting Host windows, type in the name of a computer to ping. Try `ds1.internic.net` if you can't think of one that you're confident is working.

3. Press Enter, or click on the OK button.

After a while, if the computer you Pinged is working (`ds1.internic.net` should be) and your link is working, you should get a response from Ping, like that illustrated in Figure H.32.

Ping's response tells you that your Ping was returned. It also tells you the travel time of your Ping. At the bottom of the Ping screen the status bar changes to reflect the new information.

Ping response.

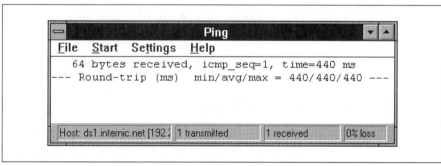

Ping Settings

There are a few settings you can change in Ping. You will find them under the Settings ➤ Preferences menu. (Figure H.33 shows the Preferences window for Ping.) The Iteration count is the number of Pings you want to send out when you Ping a host. You can click on the

Continuous box if you want to send a stream of Pings. The data length setting controls the size of the Ping data itself. The interval setting controls the time between multiple Pings, and the Timeout setting is the amount of time to wait before reporting a Ping as failed.

None of these settings are significant if all you want to do is see whether a remote machine is running or confirm that your link works. But you can, by raising the iteration count, get some idea of the data transfer rate you can achieve to a particular host.

▶ ▶ **N O T E**

Please use Ping with care. It is considered bad form to waste Internet bandwidth with a lot of spurious Pinging.

The Telnet Application

The Telnet program is used to connect to other computers and run an interactive shell on them. Chapter 9 describes the use of Telnet applications in general, so let's take a look at the specifics of Chameleon Sampler's Telnet program.

Double-click on the Telnet icon in the Chameleon Sampler program group to start the application. Figure H.34 shows the Telnet window as it first appears.

The Telnet application window.

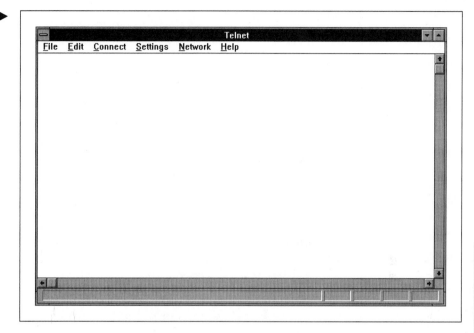

To start a Telnet session, select Connect from the Telnet menu bar. The Connect To window will appear, as shown in Figure H.35.

1. Type the name of the host you wish to connect to in the Host Name text box.

2. Normally you can leave the port setting at 23, the standard Telnet port, but occasionally you might need to change it, particularly if you are MUDding (see Chapter 15).

The Connect To window.

The Companion Disks

ap.
H

3. The Emulate drop-down list is used to choose the terminal emulation to use when accessing the remote computer. For most UNIX machines the default VT100 emulation is the best choice.

4. Click on OK to start your connection.

Once you have logged in to the remote machine, Chameleon Sampler's Telnet behaves in standard Telnet fashion, as described in Chapter 9.

Telnet Configuration

Under the Settings menu you will find a number of options for customizing the behavior of Chameleon Sampler's Telnet.

Under Settings ➤ Preferences you will find the Terminal Preferences window (Figure H.36). Here you can change the following options:

- **Terminal Modes** controls some of the aspects of your terminal emulation.

  Local Echo causes Telnet to echo every character you type. This would work great, except that the remote machine almost always echoes your typing as well. Under most circumstances you can leave this unchecked.

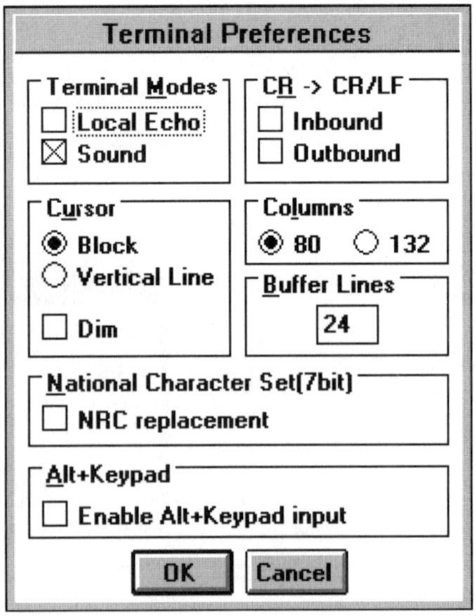

FIGURE H.36 ▶

The Terminal Preferences window.

Terminal Preferences

Terminal Modes
- ☐ Local Echo
- ☒ Sound

CR -> CR/LF
- ☐ Inbound
- ☐ Outbound

Cursor
- ◉ Block
- ○ Vertical Line
- ☐ Dim

Columns
- ◉ 80   ○ 132

Buffer Lines
- 24

National Character Set(7bit)
- ☐ NRC replacement

Alt+Keypad
- ☐ Enable Alt+Keypad input

[OK]   [Cancel]

> **Sound** toggles the terminal bell on and off.

- The **CR -> CR/LF** settings control the translation of carriage return characters into carriage return + linefeeds:

    > **Inbound** translates incoming carriage returns, adding a linefeed before they are displayed on your Telnet screen.

    > **Outbound** translates outgoing carriage returns, before they are sent to the remote system.

- **Cursor** settings control the way the cursor is displayed; as a block or a vertical line, and dimmed or undimmed.

- **Columns** allows you to toggle between a Telnet window with 80 columns or 132 columns.

- **Buffer Lines** is where you set the number of lines that the Telnet program should keep in its scrollback buffer. You can access the scrollback buffer simply by moving the control box in the right hand slider bar. By default this value is set to 24, which is the exact height of the Telnet window itself. This means that there is effectively no scrollback buffer.

- The **National Character Set** selection allows you to transmit special characters of the language you have configured Microsoft Windows to use. When it's selected, your outgoing characters will be replaced by their National Character Set equivalents, so they can be read in their original form on another computer.

- The **Enable Alt+Keypad** option lets you transmit extended ASCII characters, using the standard PC method of holding down the Alt key and typing the ASCII decimal value of the character you want to transmit.

Under the Fonts and Colors menus, you can control the colors used to display characters on screen, and the character font that is used.

Finally, under the Keyboard menu, you will find the Keyboard Mapper. Similar to a keyboard macro, this tool allows you to assign arbitrary character values to keystrokes.

There is one other item you might find interesting in Chameleon Sampler's Telnet menu bar—the Network ➤ Are You There selection. When you select this option while you have an active Telnet session, the Telnet program polls the remote computer to make sure it is active. If the remote computer is functioning correctly, it should send a "yes" response in the Telnet window.

The FTP Application

Chameleon Sampler's FTP application differs considerably from the standard text-based FTP application (described in Chapter 9). It allows you to browse through remote and local directories and perform all the standard FTP functions, using a graphical interface. It also includes an FTP server, so that you can allow other people on the Internet to connect to your computer and retrieve files. (Chapter 19 discusses setting up your own FTP site.) To start the FTP application, double-click on the FTP icon in the Chameleon Sampler window in Program Manager. You'll see the window shown in Figure H.37.

Chameleon Sampler's FTP window is divided into two parts. The left side shows files and directories on your local computer; the right side shows the files and directories of the remote computer that you have connected to. In between the panels that show the files and directories

FIGURE H.37 ▶

The Chameleon Sampler FTP window.

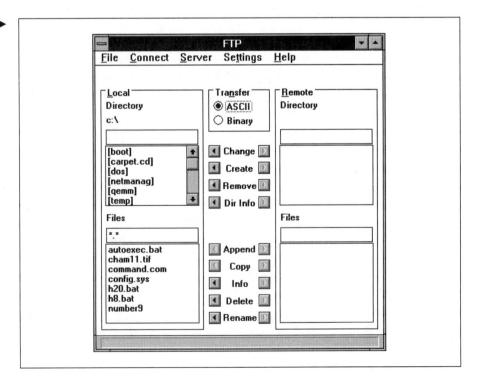

are two columns of buttons corresponding to various actions you can take.

Let's start by logging in to a remote FTP server. Choose Connect from the menu bar. The Connect window (Figure H.38) will appear.

1. Type the name of the host you want to connect to in the Host text box. Clicking on the list box arrow next to this text box displays the list of any hosts that you entered in your host table (back in the Custom application).

2. Enter the user name you will use to connect in the User text box.

3. Enter the password you will use in the Password text box.

4. Click on OK to connect.

There are a couple of other things going on in this window. The System list box allows you to define the type of host you will be connecting to. Normally you can leave this set on Auto. The Description box can show a description of the system you are about to connect to, but you must configure it first. We will get to this in a bit. For now let's just connect to a remote site. We'll try the oak.oakland.edu archive site, and use FTP as our login name to connect anonymously.

FIGURE H.38 ▶

The Connect window.

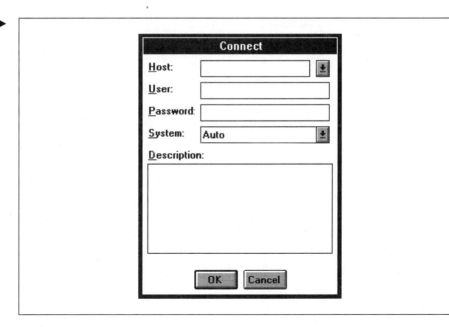

Once we have connected, our FTP window will change, and the list boxes on the right hand side of the window will be filled with the directories and files on the remote machine.

The top half of each window contains a list of subdirectories, and the bottom half displays a list of the files in the current directory. In order to switch directories, you can simply double-click on a subdirectory name in either side of the FTP window, local or remote. Once you switch directories, Chameleon Sampler FTP updates the relevant file list.

At the top of the window, between the two directory windows, is the Transfer setting area. Two selections are available here, ASCII and Binary. You can specify the type of transfer you want to make based on the type of information you are receiving—ASCII for text files, binary for binary data. Because transferring binary data using ASCII corrupts the binary file, you should leave this on Binary.

Now take a look at the command buttons in the middle of the window. There are two rows of buttons; each row corresponds to one half of the screen. If you hit the left Remove button, you remove the highlighted directory on your local machine. If you click on the right Remove button, you will be attempting to remove the highlighted directory on the remote machine. Let's go over the various buttons and what they do.

The directory buttons are Change, Create, Remove, and Dir Info. If you need to get to a directory way down in the tree, you can type its name in the directory list box and then click Change to switch directly to it. To create a new directory, first type the name of the directory you want to create in the text box above the directory list and then click Create. The Remove button removes the currently highlighted directory; don't worry, you'll be asked to confirm first. Dir Info lists information about all the directories currently shown, including creation date, permissions, and so on.

Under the directory buttons are the file buttons. Append take a file from one system and appends it to the other. The Copy button is the one you will probably use most often. This command transfers a file from one system to the other, which is, after all, what FTP is all about. The Copy buttons work in reverse; that is, you click the button on the side of the screen that you want to transfer *to*, not *from*. So to download a file, you click on the left button, not the right.

The Info button retrieves file information for all the files listed. The Delete button deletes the selected file, and the Rename button renames the selected file.

> **N O T E**
>
> **Your ability to manipulate files and directories on remote machines depends on the file permissions that have been set for the remote files. You obviously can't delete a file to which you don't have permission to write. When using FTP anonymously, you will almost never be able to move, rename, or delete files, but there is often a single directory where you can upload files.**

The FTP Server

Chameleon Sampler's FTP program can act as both an FTP client and an FTP server. To start the server portion of the software, choose Server ➤ Settings from the menu bar.

In the Server Settings window (Figure H.39) you must set the Public Directory. This is the directory that will be accessible to people FTPing into your machine. Keep in mind that this directory's contents, and all

FIGURE H.39 ▶

The Server Settings window.

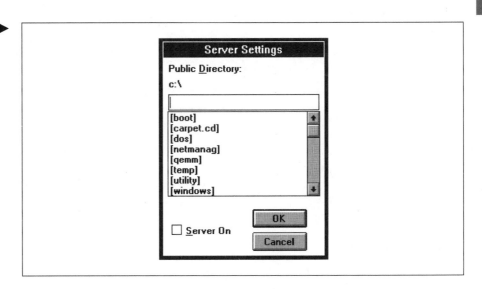

The Companion Disks

▶▶

ap.

H

the subdirectories in this directory are open to anyone who can log in. It is a good idea to create a new, empty directory to use as a public FTP directory.

Once you have selected an appropriate directory, all you need to do to start the server is click on the Server On check box.

Even though you have turned your server on, you still need to create a user name, to allow people to log in. Choose Server ➤ Users to open the Users window (Figure H.40).

To add an FTP account:

1. Enter a user name in the User Name text box.

2. Enter a password in the Password text box.

3. Click on the Save button.

4. Click on Cancel to leave the User dialog box.

That's all there is. If you want to create an anonymous account, just use anonymous as the user name, and leave the password field blank. This will allow anyone to FTP to your computer, so be careful. If you want to see whether anyone is currently logged in to your FTP server, choose Server ➤ Connections from the menu bar. Here you will find a list of all the active FTP connections.

FIGURE H.40 ▶

The Users window.

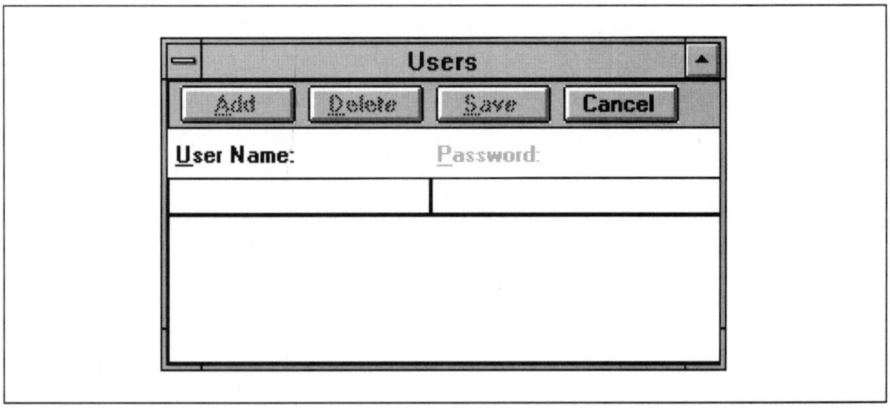

Configuring the FTP Application

Under the Settings menu bar you will find FTP's configuration options. The Preferences menu controls prompting on file manipulations, and whether the FTP program automatically translates filenames when the original filename won't work on the receiving system. Colors controls the colors of the FTP main display windows. Log opens a window that lets you observe FTP events.

The Settings ➤ Connection Profile menu selection brings up a window that allows you to enter and save information for FTP sites that you commonly access. Once you have set this information, the recorded host will show up in the Host list box, in the Connect window. This allows you to access those FTP sites you use often without having to type user name and password information.

The Mail Application

E-mail is the subject of Chapter 8. Chameleon Sampler's Mail application allows you to send and receive Internet e-mail from your local computer. It communicates with the mail server of your Internet service provider using standard Internet mail protocols, SMTP and POP3. As installed, the SMTP portion of the Mail application will accept incoming mail connections from other Internet hosts and drop your incoming mail into your inbox. A problem arises though, when mail for you arrives, but you are not connected to the Internet. Since the sending computer can't reach you, the mail will simply bounce.

This is why your service provider almost certainly provides a place where incoming mail for you is stored for you to retrieve later. Some service providers have mail machines that simply spool your mail and then try to transmit it to your computer every so often. If your ISP offers this service, then you don't really have to do anything to receive mail. Just create a mail account for yourself, and the rest happens automatically.

Other ISPs store your mail on one of their own computers and wait for you to connect and retrieve it. This is the role filled by a POP3 server. In order to connect to a POP3 server, you need some more information from your ISP, namely:

- Your mailbox name
- Your mailbox password

• Your mail server host name

We will use this information in the next section to configure the Mail program, and get it running.

Configuring Mail

The first step in configuring the Mail application is running the program and setting up your mailbox. As installed, Postmaster is the only account set up in Mail. You will use the Postmaster name to log in to the Mail application the first time you use it. Once you log in, you can create a real account for yourself, with your own user name.

1. Double-click on the Mail icon in the Chameleon Sampler group window in Program Manager.

2. The User Login window will appear. Postmaster will already appear in the Username text box. By default, there is no password for Postmaster. Click on OK to continue.

3. The main Mail window (Figure H.41) now appears.

4. Choose Services ➤ Mailboxes from the Mail menu bar. This menu selection appears only when you are logged in as Postmaster, and is the only way you can add new users to the mail system. Most people will only want to define one user for the Chameleon Sampler mail system, but you can add more if you want.

5. In the User text field type the user name you want to use to send and receive mail; then click on the ADD button.

6. The User Configuration window will appear. Give your new mail account a password if you want to restrict access on your local PC

FIGURE H.41 ▶

The Mail application window.

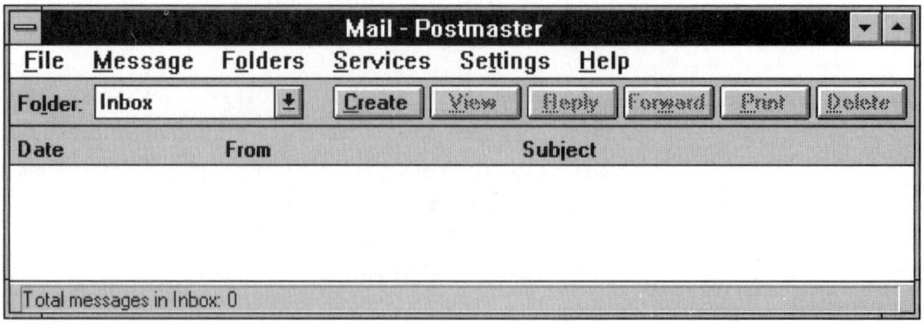

Mail - Postmaster
File   Message   Folders   Services   Settings   Help
Folder: Inbox ⤓   Create   View   Reply   Forward   Print   Delete
Date   From   Subject
Total messages in Inbox: 0

to your mailbox, and put your full name in the In Real Life text box. This name will be included with your e-mail messages, but is not part of your mail address. You also need to set the mail directory for the new account. Chameleon Sampler will, by default, create new mail directories in a subdirectory called EMAIL\ off the NETMANAG\ directory.

7. Click on the OK button to accept your new account.

8. When you return to the Mailboxes window, click on SAVE to save your new account.

9. Choose File ➤ Exit to exit the Mail program.

It's now time to configure your new mail account—the one you will use to send and receive mail. Double-click on the Mail icon, and log in with your new user name. Since most service providers spool incoming mail in a POP3 server, in order to get your incoming mail, you have to configure the Mail application to go and get it for you.

1. Choose Settings ➤ Network from the Mail menu bar. In the resulting submenu you will see two choices: Mail Gateway and Mail Server. A mail gateway is a machine to which you forward all mail; it then sends the mail to its final destination. Simply choose Mail Gateway from the submenu and enter the host address or IP address of the gateway in the resulting window.

2. Choose Mail Server from the submenu, and the Mail Server window will appear. Here is where you input the information you got from your service provider.

3. In the Host text box enter the host address or IP address of your POP3 server.

4. In the User field enter the user name you need to use when logging in to the server.

5. In the Password field enter the password you must use to access the POP3 server.

6. Leave the Mail Dir field blank.

7. Click on OK to save your changes.

Note the check box at the bottom of the Mail Server configuration window. When it's checked, mail will be deleted from the directory on the POP3 server when it is retrieved by Chameleon Sampler's Mail program. This is reasonable default behavior, and you should check this box.

Your Mail application should now be set up correctly and you should be able to receive and send mail. Once again, if you have problems it might be a good idea to consult with your Internet service provider. They can certainly tell you all the information you need about their own mail system, and how you should interface with it.

Sending Mail

Chameleon Sampler's Mail application is pretty comprehensive. In this section we will explore some of its capability. Let's start with the basic task of sending a message.

1. Choose Message ➤ Create from the Mail menu bar. The New Mail window (Figure H.42) will appear.

2. The From line is automatically filled out with your e-mail address.

3. In the Subject field, type in the subject of the message you wish to send.

FIGURE H.42 ▶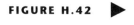

The New Mail window.

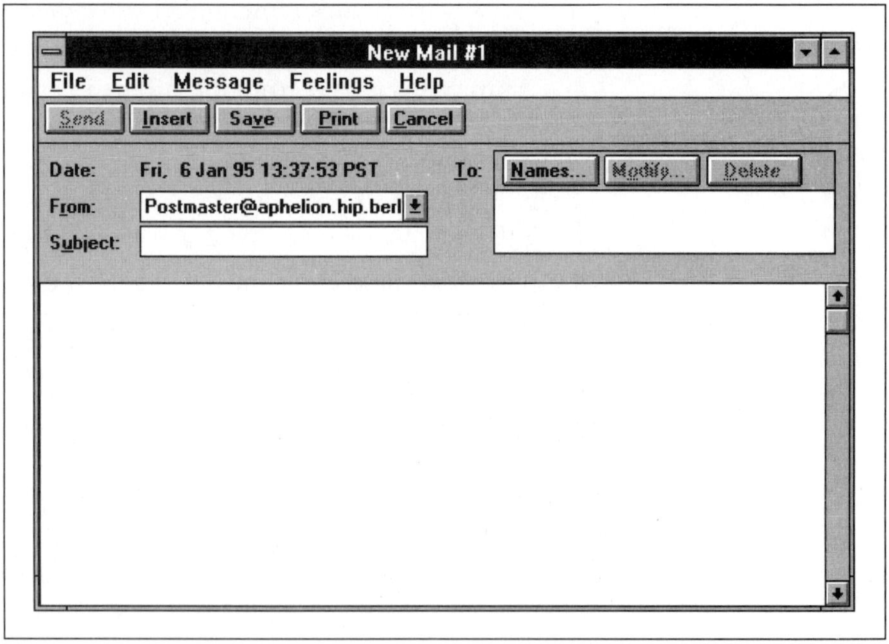

	New Mail #1		
File **Edit** **Message** **Feelings** **Help**			

Send	Insert	Save	Print	Cancel

Date: Fri, 6 Jan 95 13:37:53 PST   **To:** [Names...] [Modify...] [Delete]

From: Postmaster@aphelion.hip.berl ▼

Subject: [   ]

4. To address the message, click on the Names button in the To field. The Names window will appear.

5. In this window, type the address of the message's intended recipient in the Address field.

6. Click on the To button to insert the name in the message's To field. At this point you could instead choose CC to send a message to someone as a copy or BC to send a "blind" copy to someone.

7. Click the OK button to return to the Message window.

8. Type in the body of the message in the large text area provided.

9. Click Send to send the message.

It is possible to compose messages while you are offline, and then save them to be sent automatically when you connect. Mail sent while you are not connected is placed in your Outbox. You can see a list of messages in your Outbox by choosing Services ➤ Outbox from the menu bar. The Mail application will try to send your outgoing mail whenever you start the application, and then repeatedly in fixed intervals controlled by the Retry Timer.

The New Mail window offers you many other options when sending mail. The Insert button will insert the contents of an already existing file into your message. The Save and Print buttons need no explanation. The Edit ➤ Signature menu choice will insert your signature into the current message; and the Feelings menu will insert premade emoticons into your text.

The Address Book

The Mail application comes with an address book where you can store the addresses of people you commonly correspond with. Choose Services ➤ Address Book to bring up the address book window.

In the Address text near the top of the Address Book window, enter a name you wish to keep for future use. Click on the Add button to save the name. If you wish to declare a group instead of an individual, click on the Group check box before clicking Add. When you save the group name a subwindow will appear, quite similar in function to the Address book window. In here type in the names of the people you wish to place in the group, clicking Add after each one. When you send mail to a group, a copy goes to every member.

Folders

When you initially start the mail application, the only folder that you have is your inbox, and the contents of this folder are shown in the main Mail window. To help organize the mail you receive, you can create separate folders and move mail into them. To create a folder choose Folder ➤ Create from the menu bar, and type the name of the folder you want to create in the resulting window. Click on OK.

To move messages into your newly created folder, select the message from the Main window, and choose Message ➤ Move to Folder. Select the folder you want the messages to be placed in from the resulting Move To window. To display different folders in the main Mail window, select the folder you would like to view from the Folder drop-down list in Mail's toolbar.

Rules

A very useful function available in Chameleon Sampler's Mail program is the use of rules. Rules allow you to place incoming mail in specific folders based on information in the message's header. For instance, if you wanted to put all the messages from a particular person into a folder with his or her name, Rules would do it automatically upon receipt of the message.

This is particularly useful if you subscribe to large mailing lists (Chapter 8). The volume of traffic generated by these lists can be daunting, but if all the incoming messages from different mailing lists are placed in different folders, it is much easier to handle.

1. To create a rule choose Services ➤ Rules from the main menu bar. The Mail Rules window (Figure H.43) will appear.

2. In the Rule Name text box type a name for the rule you are going to create.

3. You can choose to match text in the From, To, or Subject sections of incoming messages. Type in the string you want to match (like the address of a mailing list) in the String to Match field, and choose the Field you want to search in by clicking on the appropriate check box in the Field section of the window. You can also

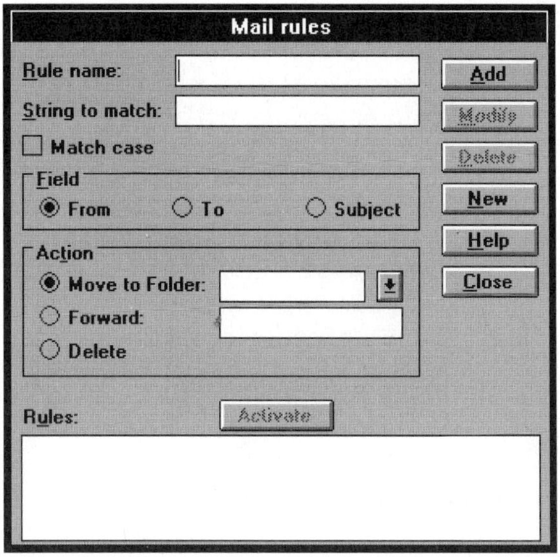

FIGURE H.43 ▶

The Mail Rules window.

select Match Case if you want your search to consider upper and lower case when applying your rule.

4. In the Action part of the window you can choose to do one of three things to an incoming message that matches the rule criteria: move the message to a folder, forward the message to another address, or delete the message. If you choose either Move to Folder or Forward, you will also have to enter a folder name or a forwarding address.

5. Click the Add button to create the rule. The rule's name will appear in the Rules list at the bottom of the window, and to the left of the name will be an asterisk. Rules preceded by an asterisk are active. The Activate/Deactivate button above the rules list toggles rules on and off.

6. Click on the Close button to exit the Mail Rules window.

What's Left?

We haven't tried to cover the Mail application exhaustively in this section, but we've hit the high points. Under the Message menu you'll find options for viewing, forwarding, replying to, and deleting

The Companion Disks

▶ ▶

ap.
H

messages. All these options are very straightforward. Also in the Message menu is the Retrieve Mail command, which causes the Mail application to connect to your POP3 servers and check for new mail. Ordinarily, Mail checks for incoming messages at regular intervals defined in Settings ► Timers.

Under the Settings menu are a number of options for further configuring Mail to suit your tastes. The Preferences window contains many options to tweak the behavior of Mail's various parts. Colors and Fonts are pretty self-explanatory, as is the Log. Signature is where you can define your ASCII signature for inclusion in outgoing messages. And the Timers selection controls how often Mail attempts to deliver outgoing messages, how long Mail will keep trying to deliver a message before giving up, and how often Mail will scan for new messages.

► *In Conclusion*

There are a few things to mention before we end our discussion of NetManage's Chameleon Sampler. We mentioned earlier that the protocol stack used by this software is WinSock-compatible. This means you are not limited to using just the applications that came with the Sampler. Any application that is WinSock-compatible will run on top of Chameleon.

One program you'll almost certainly want to add is a World Wide Web browser. For one of your first uses of Chameleon Sampler, use the FTP client to connect to `ftp.mcom.com` and download the file /netscape/windows/ns100-16.exe. This self-extracting archive contains an evaluation copy of the Netscape WWW browser for Windows. *De rigueur* for well-equipped Net surfers.

You don't have to stop there. There is a lot of WinSock-compatible software out there that you can use—newsreaders, MUD clients, whatever.

One other note. If you don't have a SLIP or PPP account, but do have a shell account, there is a program that will emulate a SLIP connection over a shell account. The program is called the Internet Adapter, TIA. It's available in a 30-day trial version.

To use TIA, you log in to your shell account normally, and then run the TIA software on the remote machine. Once TIA is running, you start up your normal SLIP software, like Chameleon Sampler. TIA looks just like a SLIP server to your own software, and you can then run any of the network applications that work over a SLIP connection, with a few restrictions: You don't get a host name when you connect using TIA, so you can't get mail sent directly to your computer via SMTP. (You can still retrieve mail via a POP3 mailer.) Also, people cannot access an FTP server running on your computer. You cannot use TIA to emulate PPP or CSLIP connections.

If you've downloaded a WWW browser, you can get more information on TIA at `http://marketplace.com`. There you will find information about getting a TIA evaluation license, and FTPing the software itself.

NetManage Chameleon Sampler is one of the most robust TCP/IP stacks we have ever used. After you finish the configuration, it just works. Combined with the large assortment of WinSock-compatible applications now available, it's a superb choice for dialup IP connectivity.

The Companion Disks

▶ ▶

ap.

H

▶▶ Index

Note: Page numbers in **boldface** are a major source of information on a topic; page numbers in *italics* refer to figures.

▶ F

► **I**

▶ *P*

▶ X

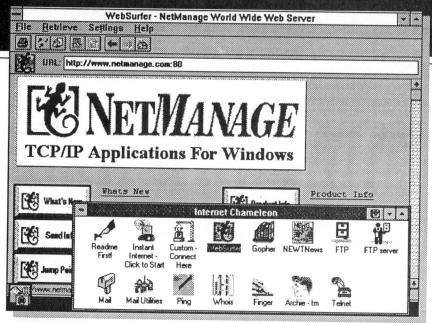

[1645] Mastering the Internet

GET A FREE CATALOG JUST FOR EXPRESSING YOUR OPINION.

Help us improve our books and get a **FREE** full-color catalog in the bargain. Please complete this form, pull out this page and send it in today. The address is on the reverse side.

Name _____ Company _____

Address _____ City _____ State ___ Zip _____

Phone (___) _____

1. How would you rate the overall quality of this book?

❑ Excellent
❑ Very Good
❑ Good
❑ Fair
❑ Below Average
❑ Poor

2. What were the things you liked most about the book? (Check all that apply)

❑ Pace
❑ Format
❑ Writing Style
❑ Examples
❑ Table of Contents
❑ Index
❑ Price
❑ Illustrations
❑ Type Style
❑ Cover
❑ Depth of Coverage
❑ Fast Track Notes

3. What were the things you liked *least* about the book? (Check all that apply)

❑ Pace
❑ Format
❑ Writing Style
❑ Examples
❑ Table of Contents
❑ Index
❑ Price
❑ Illustrations
❑ Type Style
❑ Cover
❑ Depth of Coverage
❑ Fast Track Notes

4. Where did you buy this book?

❑ Bookstore chain
❑ Small independent bookstore
❑ Computer store
❑ Wholesale club
❑ College bookstore
❑ Technical bookstore
❑ Other _____

5. How did you decide to buy this particular book?

❑ Recommended by friend
❑ Recommended by store personnel
❑ Author's reputation
❑ Sybex's reputation
❑ Read book review in _____
❑ Other _____

6. How did you pay for this book?

❑ Used own funds
❑ Reimbursed by company
❑ Received book as a gift

7. What is your level of experience with the subject covered in this book?

❑ Beginner
❑ Intermediate
❑ Advanced

8. How long have you been using a computer?

years _____
months _____

9. Where do you most often use your computer?

❑ Home
❑ Work

❑ Both
❑ Other _____

10. What kind of computer equipment do you have? (Check all that apply)

❑ PC Compatible Desktop Computer
❑ PC Compatible Laptop Computer
❑ Apple/Mac Computer
❑ Apple/Mac Laptop Computer
❑ CD ROM
❑ Fax Modem
❑ Data Modem
❑ Scanner
❑ Sound Card
❑ Other _____

11. What other kinds of software packages do you ordinarily use?

❑ Accounting
❑ Databases
❑ Networks
❑ Apple/Mac
❑ Desktop Publishing
❑ Spreadsheets
❑ CAD
❑ Games
❑ Word Processing
❑ Communications
❑ Money Management
❑ Other _____

12. What operating systems do you ordinarily use?

❑ DOS
❑ OS/2
❑ Windows
❑ Apple/Mac
❑ Windows NT
❑ Other _____

13. On what computer-related subject(s) would you like to see more books?

_____

_____

_____

_____

14. Do you have any other comments about this book? (Please feel free to use a separate piece of paper if you need more room)

_____

_____

_____

_____

- - - - - - - - - - - - PLEASE FOLD, SEAL, AND MAIL TO SYBEX - - - - - - - - - - - - -

SYBEX INC.
Department M
2021 Challenger Drive
Alameda, CA
94501

WHAT'S ON THE DISKS?

*With the help of these disks, you can begin to enjoy the Internet **immediately!***

▶ *The NetCruiser Disk*

On Disk 1, you'll find NetCruiser, a program that connects any Windows 3.1 or better PC equipped with a 9600 bps or faster modem directly to the Internet over an ordinary telephone line. You'll find complete installation instructions in Appendix H.

NetCruiser gives you:

- A friendly Windows interface
- A versatile and easy-to-use e-mail system
- A Usenet newsreader
- Two information-browsing programs (for Gopher and the World Wide Web)
- The Internet's File Transfer Protocol (FTP)
- Telnet
- Internet Relay Chat (IRC)

What's it cost? Netcom, a leading Internet service provider, offers these services at a remarkable savings. You'll get:

- Your own personal e-mail address and mailbox on the Internet
- 40 hours per month of Internet access during prime time, between 9 AM and midnight, at *no charge*
- Unlimited free access to the Internet on weekends and between midnight and 9 AM

You'll get all this for just $19.95 a month, with additional hours during prime time charged at only $2.00 per hour. **Special offer:** with the purchase of this book, Netcom is waiving its $25.00 registration fee.

▶ *The Chameleon Sampler Disk*

NetManage's Chameleon Sampler software, on Disk 2, provides you with a set of tools you can use if you already have an account with an Internet service provider (other than Netcom). You'll receive a fully functional SLIP or PPP connection to the Internet, allowing you to establish a high-speed connection that lets you download and use popular software like Mosaic.

Chameleon Sampler also includes:

- TCP/IP software
- WinSock capability
- Four of the most useful Internet applications: e-mail, Telnet, FTP, and Ping

See Appendix H for instructions on installing and configuring Chameleon Sampler.